Child, Family, and Community

Family-Centered Early Care and Education

Seventh Edition

Janet Gonzalez-Mena

PEARSON

Boston Columbus Indianapolis New York San Francisco Upper Saddle River
Amsterdam Cape Town Dubai London Madrid Milan Munich Paris Montreal Toronto
Delhi Mexico City Sao Paulo Sydney Hong Kong Seoul Singapore Taipei Tokyo

Vice President and Editorial Director: Jeffery W. Johnston
Executive Editor: Julie Peters
Editorial Assistant: Pamela DiBerardino
Developmnet Editor: Jon Theiss
Executive Product Marketing Manager: Chris Barry
Executive Field Marketing Manager: Krista Clark

Program Manager: Megan Moffo
Production Project Manager: Janet Domingo
Full-Service Project Management: Lumina Datamatics
Composition: Lumina Datamatics

Credits and acknowledgments for material borrowed from other sources and reproduced, with permission, in this textbook appear on the appropriate page within the text.

Every effort has been made to provide accurate and current Internet information in this book. However, the Internet and information posted on it are constantly changing, so it is inevitable that some of the Internet addresses listed in this textbook will change.

Library of Congress Cataloging-in-Publication Data
Gonzalez-Mena, Janet, author.
    Child, family, and community : family-centered early care and education / Janet Gonzalez-Mena. — Seventh edition.
        pages cm
Includes bibliographical references and index.
ISBN 978-0-13-404227-5 (alk. paper)
1. Socialization.   2. Child rearing.   3. Families.   I. Title.
HQ783.G59 2017
649'.1—dc23
                                                                                2015030163

5   18

ISBN 10:   0-13-404227-1
ISBN 13: 978-0-13-404227-5

To **Shaquam Kimberly Edwards**, *contributor to this edition. Shaquam took on what I consider the hardest part of this revision— making it into an e-book. She stepped in willingly and capably to meet the creative challenges of bringing the book to life digitally. I'm forever grateful for her contributions! I wrote the first edition of this book on a typewriter. Putting later editions on the computer was a big step forward for me. Shaquam took me into the e-book era, gracefully and enthusiastically, for which I'm thankful.*

Preface

A seminal report published by the National Association for the Education of Young Children (NAEYC) was released just as this revision was about to go to press, titled "Transforming the Workforce for Children Birth Through Age 8: A Unifying Foundation." One of the themes of the report relates to making higher education programs for professionals more effective with a goal of supporting consistent quality. This report couldn't be more timely coming out as it did at the same time as the 7th revision of *Child, Family, and Community*. We are ready for change as a nation. We are ready to be sure that those who work with young children get an excellent education to prepare them for further study, for being a contributing part of the community, and for all-round mature development. Right in line with transforming the workforce comes the transformation of this *Child, Family, and Community* textbook. The 7th edition, now in an e-text format, is startlingly different from the many revisions that preceded it.

This revision, as others in the past, focuses on *contexts*—the contexts in which children are reared and educated. It's not about "the child" or even "children" because those words have no meaning by themselves. Each child is born and raised in multiple social contexts. This text is about the influences of all those contexts. Nurturing and protection of each child must be viewed in terms, not only of the family, but also of the community—its neighborhoods, people, cultures, and institutions—both local and national. Care-and-education institutions are part of this context.

As in earlier editions, the major theories around which this book is based involve the community being the context in which child rearing takes place, no matter what shape or form the families take. This book still focuses on families, but also on the people and agencies outside the family. Some of those people who are using this text are now, or will become, those professionals who work with families and their children.

NEW TO THIS EDITION

E-Text Format

Anyone used to the black and white paperback book will see a world of difference when they take their first look at the new e-text format. There is no comparison. Not that both the e-text and the paper book aren't greatly updated with the latest information and research, but the new format as an e-text has a number of engaging new features. *Note that the Pearson e-text format contains the following digital components: video links, interactive section quizzes called "Check Your Understanding," and end-of-chapter quizzes; other e-text formats do not currently contain these interactive digital elements.*

Videos

Links to video in every chapter of the e-text augment the written word. As students read from the screen, they know that with one click, video appears with further information that comes in a variety of ways. Sometimes the information comes from the mouths of the researchers whose work is mentioned in the chapter. Certainly when students hear from academics who have contributed so much to the field of child development and early childhood education, everything becomes more personal and meaningful. Sometimes students see video clips that demonstrate what the researchers talk about. We look into live classrooms to see examples of various approaches of working with groups of children—or with individuals—or with family members. Footage of actual teachers in classroom scenes show examples of what is discussed in writing. Child development information is portrayed by children themselves in families and in classrooms and more. Community resources come alive as users talk about their experiences. Sometimes the focus is on the environment, which offers inspiration for those students who work in programs that lack rich, or even adequate, developmentally appropriate settings. Often we see and hear people who represent the community resources found in neighborhoods. We also have a chance to see examples of children's behaviors at different developmental levels.

The many videos, three to four in each chapter, bring information beyond the words in the text and bring it in living color with sound and movement. Further, the videos have reflection questions in the text to promote thought or classroom discussion. What could be more meaningful for the generations that are media savvy and know how to use it to their advantage!

A New Interactive Assessment Feature Called "Check Your Understanding."

This new feature, which has been added at the end of each major section in each chapter, is a multiple-choice assessment that aligns with, and asks questions about, each Learning Outcome. The correct answer is noted and feedback is provided. Students can then see what they have learned from reading each section. This makes good sense and is quite effective. They can immediately determine what they forgot or misunderstood, which allows them to go back and reread so they retain the information.

Interactive End-of-Chapter Quizzes

At the end of each chapter there are short-answer format quizzes, with feedback, to assess student understanding—and reinforce learning—of chapter content.

Color Photos

Of course there are also still photographs as always—pictures that give visual emphasis to the concepts written about. In the e-text the photographs are in living color—quite a contrast to black and white photos with "yesteryear" invisibly stamped on them.

OTHER CHANGES AND ADDITIONS

Reorganization of Each Chapter

Helping students grasp and retain what they read is important in any textbook. To that end, every chapter has been more clearly organized with an average of three major Learning Outcomes, with corresponding headings, followed by three to five topic headings that relate to the subject(s) in each major heading. This organization makes it easier for students to follow and remember the information.

Examples of New Topics and Expanded Previous Ones

- **Gender roles.** Discussion and research about young children developing gender roles has been greatly updated and expanded.
- **Mindset.** Carol Dweck's theory on how to help children move beyond a "fixed mindset" that leads them to give up in the face of even a minor failure. Information and examples are included of how to encourage an open mindset. Children with an "open mindset" keep going even when failure occurs or seems inevitable. An open mindset leads to exploration and growth.
- **Grit.** Angela Duckworthy and others explore how what they call "grit" helps people stick to challenges, persist, and achieve success.
- **Self-esteem.** Not a new subject but an important one. The topic of self-esteem has been reworked and expanded in this edition.

A Change in the Order of the Chapters

Chapter 2, "The Societal Influences on Families" (including racism), was too emotionally laden to come so early in the term according to users. That chapter is now Chapter 6, which works better after students have gotten to know each other.

Updated "Further Readings"

Twenty to thirty percent of the list at the end of each chapter under "Further Readings" has been replaced with updated resources.

Highlighted Major Points

A new marginal feature of key brief points from the author are added for interest and emphasis.

FOUNDATIONAL IDEAS SUPPORTING THIS BOOK

- **Theory is presented in easy to understand language.** The book rests on a base of solid academics, constructivist theory, developmental research, anthropological studies, and the personal experience of the author.
- **The chapters place an emphasis on the ecological theory of human development.** Every chapter shows how professionals and families can partner to

support healthy growth and development so that the child functions fully as a competent community member.

- **The book emphasizes cultural contexts.** Valuing diversity, plus acknowledging and understanding cultural contexts, has always been an important foundation of this book. The new edition puts even more emphasis on perceiving and appreciating cultural differences in order to embrace them. The attitude of acceptance that develops challenges the students to expand their definitions of "developmentally appropriate practice."

- **Reflection on personal experience is encouraged.** Readers are asked to bring their own ideas, experiences, and insights to their reading—in accordance with Jean Piaget's ideas about learners attaching new knowledge to existing knowledge. In other words, readers are encouraged to reach into their own experiences to make sense of new information in terms of what they already know. They are encouraged to see how that same approach works equally well when relating to families and conveying information to them. Whether a student, a teacher, or a parent, respect for one's own background, experiences, knowledge, ideas, and insights is important. Because whatever we read always filters through our own subjective experiences, this text acknowledges that fact and capitalizes on it. Thus students can feel at home and find their own voices. They are asked to do the same for the children and families they work with.

- **Anecdotes and examples are provided throughout.** Each chapter contains stories and examples designed to take the subject out of the realm of theory and into the real world of practice. Examples are designed to appeal to both traditional and non-traditional students, reflecting the changing demographics of the United States.

- **Advocacy is emphasized.** The "Advocacy in Action" feature appeals to those students who want to "do something!" about improving the lives of children, families, the education systems, and society in general. This feature gives students ideas about ways of being public and personal advocates.

INSTRUCTOR SUPPLEMENTS TO THIS TEXT

All ancillary resources for instructors are available for download by adopting professors via pearsonhighered.com in the Instructor Resource Center.

Instructor's Resource Manual: This manual contains chapter overviews, activity ideas for both in and out of class, and ways to integrate the digital content into your course.

Online Test Bank: The test bank includes a variety of test items in various formats.

Pearson TestGen: This test-generation software is available in various learning management system formats. Download and use as is or create your own exams with provided items and your own items. Test items included are the same items in the Online Test Bank.

Online PowerPoint Slides: PowerPoint slides highlight key concepts and strategies in each chapter. They can be used to enhance lectures and discussions, or can be posted on your learning management system as an additional study resource for your students.

ACKNOWLEDGMENTS

Special thanks to the reviewers of this edition: Vernell D. Larkin, Hopkinsville Community College; Tonia Padrick, Cape Fear Community College; Tasha Smith, Solano Community College; and Shaquam Urquhart Edwards, College of Marin.

Brief Contents

Contents

**CHAPTER 10   Working with Families to Support
Self-Esteem   218**

**CHAPTER 11   Working with Families around Gender
Issues   242**

The Child in Context of Family and Community

GVictoria/Fotolia

Learning Outcomes

In this chapter you will learn to...

- Explain how to look at context through the lens of bioecological theory.
- Describe the implications of family-centered approaches, including the benefits to children, teachers, and parents.
- Explain the history of family-centered care and education.
- Define multiple lenses through which to look at family-centered approaches, including family systems theory, whole child perspective, Maslow's hierarchy of needs, and culture as a lens.

Why is the title of this book *Child, Family, and Community*? Here's why. Many people go into the profession of teaching in general and into early care and education specifically because they love children. They find they relate well to children, and they enjoy being with them. When these individuals start taking classes, they find that their studies focus on the development and education of children. The course for which this book is designed also focuses on the child, but with a difference. This book takes the position that children must be looked at in context—meaning that each child must be viewed in the context of his or her family, and each family must be viewed in the context of the community/communities/society to which it belongs. Taking this larger view of each child will help readers remember to always keep the context in mind, no matter what aspect of child development and/or education they study.

What are the various contexts that families come in? Culture is certainly one overarching context which relates to ethnicity, and is affected by socioeconomic level, family structure, sexual orientation and all the other variables that make this particular family what it is. Immigrant status, if any, is also a context. With immigrant numbers increasing, language and cultural diversity are becoming more obvious, though ours has always been a diverse country. In one sense we are all immigrants except for people who were on this continent first, those who can be considered indigenous. Their descendants are still here. The rest of the population is made up of immigrants, whether willing or unwilling (Ogbu, 1987). This list of influences on families represents just the tip of the iceberg. It's a sample of all the ways in which families differ from each other by their contexts. For more information about America's children and families, see the website for the Kids Count Data Center.

Another huge influence on children is the community. The child and family are always placed in a community context. What community a family is in makes a big difference. My husband's family moved from Puebla, Mexico, to the San Francisco Bay area in California many years ago—when my husband was 21 years old. They left behind countless relatives. When we visit those relatives and their descendants, we can see the different courses their lives took from those who moved to the United States. Just a few of the influences that have affected the U.S. family and the Mexican family in different ways are the changing international, national, and local political situations; the economies of the two countries and the local economies; and the changes that occur when one culture bumps up against another one, as is happening in both countries.

Education, development, learning, and socialization always occur in a context, and any specific context is embedded in a web of ever-changing other contexts. There is no such thing as a decontextualized child. To study "the child" without understanding the context is like studying a statue of a cat in

Each child must be viewed in the context of his or her family

order to understand its life. This whole book is about the education and socialization of the child in context. Simply put, the book examines the child in the context of developmental theory, which comes in the context of family, which lies in the context of community. All of these contexts can be thought of as environments or settings that hold people, which influence each other and are influenced by culture.

Understanding the bigger picture of how the child becomes a social being in context has been the theme of this book along with a further area of focus and that is on working with the family. Rather than making parent education and involvement just one component and dedicating a chapter to them, this book is about family-centered care and education. To understand both the child and the family in context, we need an encompassing theory.

LOOKING AT CONTEXT THROUGH BIOECOLOGICAL THEORY

The history and foundations of family-centered care and education go way back. Something I learned as a student in an early childhood class in 1967 stuck in my mind. "Your client is not the child, but the *family*." The teacher of that class, Lilian Katz, University of Illinois professor and a pioneer in the field, made that statement. I've never forgotten what she said, but it has taken many years for the field as a whole to begin to understand and embrace that concept. This book is dedicated not only to expanding the understanding, but also to giving specific strategies to the reader about how to take that concept out of the theoretical realm and into the early childhood classroom, child care center, or family child care home.

Bronfenbrenner's Bioecological Model

This particular slant and organization falls in line with the model that Urie Bronfenbrenner first laid out for us in 1979. When he wrote that there are layers of context, he referred to a set of Russian dolls that are nested inside each other, the smallest one at the core. The organization of the book relates to Bronfenbrenner's layers. Simply put, what Bronfenbrenner called a bioecological model of human development means that every child is at the center of what can be visualized as concentric circles of context set in an overarching system of time, which affects all the contexts and changes them continuously (see Figure 1.1). The National Institute for Early Education Research (NIEER) published a document that referred to Bronfenbrenner as "the man who changed how we see human development." The document can be found on the NIEER website.

The microsystems layer, the smallest of the contexts in which the child is embedded, is made up of the environment where the child lives and moves. The people and institutions the child interacts with in that environment make up the microsystems. Examples are immediate family, child care (teachers and peers), and perhaps neighborhood play area, depending on the age of the child; school and religious institutions or spiritual groups may also be part of the system. The younger the child, the smaller the number of microsystems.

The microsystems are set in the mesosystems layer, which relates to the interactions the people in the microsystems have with each other—as parents interact with teachers or, in the case of infants, child care providers or early interventionists, for example. The child is not directly involved with all the components of the mesosystems but nevertheless is affected by them.

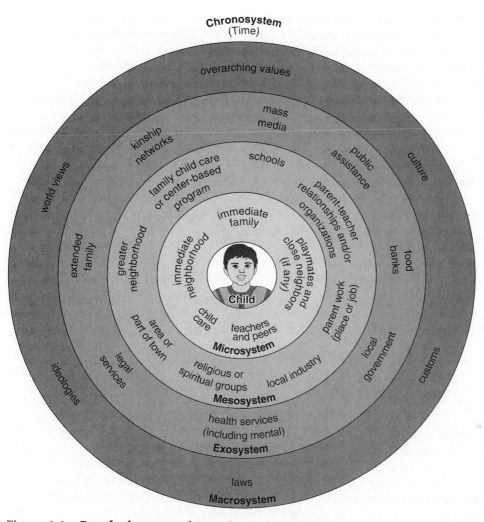

Figure 1.1   Bronfenbrenner's bioecological model
Source: Based on Bronfenbrenner, U. (1979). *The ecology of human development*. Cambridge, MA: Harvard University Press

The exosystems layer is a wider context—and though the child may not have direct contact with it, the systems affect the child's development and socialization—as do all the systems. Because the people in the child's life are affected by the exosystems and mesosystems, the child is also. The exosystems can be thought of as the broader community, including people, services, and environments. Examples of what is in the exosystems layer are extended family, family networks, mass media, workplaces, neighbors, family friends, community health systems, legal services, and social welfare services. An example of how the exosystems affect the child shows up when a parent goes to work or gets laid off from work. The changes in the parent's life have an impact on the child's life. Another example of an exosystem affecting the microsystems is when a family has to move because their apartment building is scheduled to be torn down to make room for urban renewal.

The outer layer, called the macrosystems, contains the attitudes and ideologies, values, laws, and customs of a particular culture or subculture. The chronosystem comprises the largest and the most outward layer of the embedded circles. Brofenbrenner used the chronosystem to hold events that occur over a span of time. It could include family transitions such as divorce or relocations as well as sociohistorical events such as the terrorist attack on the United States that happened on September 11, 2001.

The point of the bioecological model is that each component interacts with other components, creating a highly complex context in which the child grows up. Another point is that the child isn't just a passive recipient of what goes on in his or her life. The child at the center of Bronfenbrenner's bioecological model interacts directly with the people in the microsystems and some in the mesosystems, and the effects of the interaction go both ways. As people affect the child, so the child has an influence on them. Another point is that nothing ever remains static. As a result, the child, systems, and environments are ever changing. Milestones and life events occur as time passes, the child grows, and the contexts change.

Check Your Understanding 1.1

Click here to check your understanding of bioecological theory.

FAMILY-CENTERED APPROACHES

So understanding the child in context, as per Bronfenbrenner's theory, brings up some important questions. One such question is this one that relates to the human service sector: How can early interventionists, social workers, teachers, or child care providers work to support a child without working with the family and the community? Obviously they can't, especially when the family is one that has multiple issues going on, all of which affect the children in the family. One program in California works with children in low-income families in a poverty community to ensure their health and well-being (Bernard & Quiett, 2003). Of course, there is no way to focus on a child, even one in crisis, without addressing the bigger picture. This particular program used home visitors who were qualified social workers and also had to work with the services in the community—a two-pronged approach. Not only did the program focus on the child, but it also involved the family, plus the human service agencies the family need to interface with.

Another more widely known program, one that is much larger and hugely funded, is Geoffrey Canada's Harlem Children's Zone in New York City. Canada's goal has been not only to have every child finish his or her education by graduating from college but also to improve the community in which children are growing up. The Harlem Children's Zone has a comprehensive website that highlights their national model for breaking the cycle of poverty: education, family and community programs, and health. Paul Tough (2009)

Social workers may conduct home visits and connect families with community agencies

Monkey Business/Fotolia

writes the story of what was involved, including parent support, starting with prenatal parenting classes. It became quickly evident that no matter how supportive the program was, there was a good deal of work to be done in the child care and education system and other community services if the children were to succeed in school and in society.

A third example of a family-centered approach is Head Start, which uses a Parent, Family, Community Engagement Framework to work with young children from low-income families. Head Start has long been a leader in the early childhood field by introducing a major parent, family component from the very beginning. To learn more about the Head Start Community Engagement Framework, the PDF document can be downloaded from the Head Start website.

That brings us to educational services. Here's a big question: Why is it that so many education systems don't do what the three examples just described do? Instead many programs expect families to send their children off to child care, preschool, or school and leave the families themselves out of the picture except for enrollment, parent night, and parent/teacher conferences. Since the first edition of this book, that situation has begun to change from programs that called themselves *child centered* to those that take a *family-centered* approach. Part of the reason for this movement is increasing regard for the greater context the family is in, which includes culture, ethnicity, and economics, among others, all of which influence the family's physical and social location in the neighborhood, community, and greater society (Bloom, Eisenberg, & Eisenberg, 2003; Epstein, 2001; Fitzgerald, 2004; Gonzalez-Mena, 2009; Keyser, 2006; Lee, 2006; Lee & Seiderman, 1998; McGee-Banks, 2003). Leaders in the movement see the importance of including the families in all aspects of their children's schooling, care, and education.

> Watch this video to see Geoffrey Canada speak about the Harlem Children's Zone. What do you think about the impact of what he refers to as the pipeline that starts at birth?
>
> www.youtube.com/watch?v=1H0k2TDZF7o

> Watch this video about the comprehensive nature of the Head Start program. What do you think of the teacher preparation requirements that are described?

Family-Centered Defined

What is a family-centered approach? A family-centered approach takes the individual child and the group of children out of the spotlight and instead focuses on the children within their families. In the case of educational programs, that means that parent involvement isn't something the teacher does in addition to the program for children, but that the program includes the family as an integral, inseparable part of the child's education and socialization. Families, along with their children, *are* the program.

What does a family-centered program look like? Family-centered programs offer a variety of services, services in tune with what the parents as individuals and as a group need and want. But more than just services, they offer partnerships between professionals and families. Collaboration is a key word. The point is for professionals to become allies with families and share power. In a partnership, each partner brings a special set of strengths and skills that enhance the group. Through building relationships and ongoing communication the partnership results in mutual learning as both sides share resources and information with each other. Everyone benefits: the early educators, the families, and the children!

The Benefits of Family-Centered Programs for Children

When parents and teachers work together they enhance children's emotional security, which facilitates development and makes it easier for them to develop and learn. The children also benefit when their strengths and needs as individuals are

Early care and education professionals become allies with families and share power

understood in their family context. Continuity between home and program can be another benefit as teachers and parents understand each other better. There's a better chance for cultural consistency as a result of the parent-professional partnership or at least an understanding of and respect for cultural differences. Children's identity formation is enhanced when children don't have to experience uncomfortable feelings around the differences between what they learn at school and what they learn at home.

When children see adults modeling healthy, equitable relations in their interactions with each other, they receive a huge benefit. They learn that adults aren't just polite to each other, but have rich, authentic exchanges and even disagreements. Children gain by seeing how those adults solve their disagreements without harming their relationships with each other. If those adults deal with their own biases and increase their ability to communicate across differences, children are watching equity in action, which goes beyond trying to teach children to be fair by using an antibias approach (Derman-Sparks & Edwards, 2010).

Because positive relationships are important to development, security, and getting along with others, "relationships" is the first item listed in the accreditation standards of the National Association for the Education of Young Children (NAEYC). (For complete information on the NAEYC Accreditation Standards and Criteria, visit their website.) What better way to encourage relationships than to model them every day as professionals and adults interact and collaborate?

The Benefits of Family-Centered Education Programs for Teachers

Teachers and early educators who understand the child within his or her family context can do a better job of supporting development and teaching that child as well as working with the group of children. It makes the job more satisfying as teachers watch children gain in trust and self-confidence. Teachers can learn new and effective teaching and guidance strategies as they observe parents and exchange information with them. There is always a lot to learn about cultural differences, in particular (Cervantes & Hernandez, 2011; Espinosa, 2010).

Since the majority of teachers are European Americans (Ray, Bowman, & Robbins, 2006), most have a good deal to learn about cultures other than their own. As professionals learn more about other cultures they can enlarge their views and gain knowledge and insights on child development, education, desired outcomes, and approaches related to these views. Families add richness to a program and provide resources to professionals.

As parents learn from teachers, they too can gain insights about their children. Sometimes the close contact with families brings teachers attention, acknowledgment, and appreciation that they might not receive otherwise. Partnership-type relationships can be very rewarding! Through relationships with families teachers can become more a part of the local community, if they aren't part of it already.

The Benefits of Family-Centered Programs for Families

Families today often feel isolated. Gone are the days for many of the old extended family where somebody was home or close by to give support or lend a hand to family members who needed it. A family-centered program can become like an extended family to those who desire such a thing.

When families are not part of their children's education, they have to just hope that what the program provides for their children is the same as what they want. That can be a big problem. Barbara Rogoff, author of *The Cultural Nature of Human Development*, said, "The goals of human development—what is regarded as mature or desirable— vary considerably" (2003, p. 18). So if children are to spend big chunks of their lives throughout their childhood in educational programs, it makes sense that the goals of the program match the goals of the families, or at least don't contradict them. With pressures to conform to outcomes and desired results by policy makers and funding sources, it becomes even more important for parents to be knowledgeable and vocal.

Just as teachers can learn from parents, so can parents learn from teachers who look through a child development framework as they observe the children in the school environment with their peers (Copple & Bredekamp, 2009). This gives parents a broader view than just knowing that child in the context of home and family. Families can gain greater knowledge of resources from the professionals in their children's program.

Mutual Benefits

Family-centered programs can expand everybody's horizons. One benefit for both teachers and parents is that of self-knowledge about their own culture—the beliefs and values that come from their roots and group membership. This benefit occurs whenever teachers and parents run into practices that seem wrong, or at least uncomfortable, and are able to talk to each other nonjudgmentally about their differences so they can come to understand not only their own but the other person's views (Im, Parlakian, & Sanchez, 2007). Barbara Rogoff, in her book *The Cultural Nature of Human Development*, has advice about how to expand awareness of one's own culture as well as understand the patterns behind the thought and behavior of other cultures. She suggests that when you run into something you don't understand, it's best to put aside value judgments at first. Once you can see your own cultural patterns you are in a better position to understand others and determine whether a value judgment is necessary or not.

Families, including their children, and professionals gain from the collaborative relationship in several other ways, including:

- Enhanced communication as the groups relate to each other around shared power and decision making
- Supportive relationships leading to networks of mutual support

The community also gains when families and ECE programs work together. These partnerships increase the chances of a better-educated population and a more pluralistic society, one that values the richness diversity brings. As families and professionals work together, another ultimate outcome can be equity and social justice growing from mutual understanding and acceptance.

If you look back on what you've just read, you can see how it fits in with Bronfenbrenner's bioecological model. The child, in his or her microsystem, is influenced by family, teachers, and peers who are also influenced by the mesosystems, exosystems, and also macrosystems, which are where cultural differences, values, customs, and ideologies come in. Laws are part of that outward system as well and are influenced by the culture, values, and ideologies of the people who make them. The chronosystem, the outside layer, in turn affects all the other systems.

Check Your Understanding 1.2
Click here to check your understanding of family-centered approaches.

HISTORY OF FAMILY-CENTERED CARE AND EDUCATION

The roots of family-centered care and education go way back. As professionals we've always known that families are important to children, whether those children are at home or in early care and education programs. We have research to back us up, some of it from a pioneer, John Bowlby (1969, 1973), a researcher noted for his attachment theory and his study of the harm resulting in separating children in hospitals from their parents. We know now about attachment and hospitalization; we are still learning about attachment and education.

Head Start, mentioned earlier, was born in the Mississippi Freedom Schools and is still going strong today. During the War on Poverty of the mid-1960s it became a federally funded comprehensive preschool and social services program with not only a mandate for parent involvement and education but also built-in devices for parents to have some say in the education of their young children in the preschool years. Several generations now have been through Head Start. Today Head Start teachers are sometimes grown-up Head Start children, as are some of the directors.

Urie Bronfenbrenner, mentioned earlier, was co-founder of Head Start. His *Ecology of Human Development* had a big influence on creating family-centered programs. He emphasized that the abstract concept of "the child" doesn't exist (Bronfenbrenner, 1979, 1994). His ideas not only caught hold in Head Start, but expanded the program downward to include infants and toddlers, the idea being not so much to educate the babies but to work with the families because they are the ones that have the greatest influence on their children's lives.

Pioneer parent educator Ira J. Gordon (1968, 1976) created a program in Florida back in the 1960s involving parents of infants with the goal of improving child outcomes. He studied parent education and involvement and eventually came up with a hierarchy of types of involvement (Olmsted et al., 1980), moving from parents being recipients of information, to learning new skills, to teaching their own children, and becoming classroom volunteers. The two top kinds of involvement are becoming a paid paraprofessional and, finally, taking on the role of decision maker and policy advisor.

Today you can find elements of these various levels of involvement in many kinds of programs, including Head Start, other kinds of preschools, kindergartens, and grade schools. Some programs involve parents more than other programs.

The special education law PL 94–142, called the Education of All Handicapped Children Act of 1975, mandated parent involvement in planning for the education of the child. Each child identified with a disability or special need must have an Individual Educational Plan (IEP), or if an infant or toddler, an Individualized Family Service Plan (IFSP). A group of professionals along with the parents create these plans. According to the law and the re-authorized Individuals with Disabilities Education Act (IDEA) in 1990 and 1997, parents must be involved in all aspects of their children's education. PL 108–446 aligned special education with the No Child Left Behind (NCLB) legislation in 2004 and continued the mandate for parent involvement and power so that families disagreeing with a diagnosis or placement can call a hearing.

The "parent as the child's first teacher" is a motto now and a widespread notion throughout early care and education. Parent education materials, classes, and videos are available for new parents to see how important they are to their babies. Preschools involve parents in a variety of ways including volunteering in the classroom. One first-grade teacher has parents

Preschools involve parents in a variety of ways including volunteering in the classroom

come in to the classroom twice a week first thing in the morning to read to their children. Most kindergarten and primary teachers encourage parents to help children with their homework. Also those same teachers usually encourage parents to help their children by finding a quiet place to do their homework and take an interest in school and what their children are learning.

That motto of "parents as the child's first teacher" can also be interpreted in another way in family-centered programs, which emphasize a broad range of parent-support services. Of course parents are welcome to come into the classroom, but they are not mandated to do so. The focus of the support is to help parents with whatever they need rather than telling them how to be involved in their child's education or that they have to take the role of teacher. Some families find that through the kind of support they gain from the program staff and other families in the program, they are better able to organize their lives so they can support their children emotionally and meet their basic physical needs for nutrition, rest, and exercise. Children whose physical and emotional needs are met have the focus and energy for learning. These are real basics.

Douglas Powell wrote about the family-centered program movement way back in 1986. He talked about how many programs at that time were making a shift toward family-orientation (1986, p. 50). Powell used Head Start as an example when he wrote about the shift from child-focused programs to family-centered ones. Head Start today, in its many forms, still makes the family the client. In 1998, Powell acknowledged that the movement toward family-centered programs wasn't as widespread as it should be. He illustrated this using a metaphor of programs as a piece of fabric made of three colors of thread—one color each for children, staff, and parents. He described the most common pattern as a weaving of the child and staff together; the parents end up in a separate section. Many programs still show this same pattern. The family-centered program would make a different fabric, with the parent threads woven throughout the pattern so that all three colors of thread are integrated. In a family-centered program there is no separate section of the pattern just for parents (Powell, 1998, p. 60).

The Epstein Model, based on Gordon's roles for parent involvement, was created by Joyce Epstein (2009), who wrote a handbook called *School, Family, and Community*

Partnerships. The handbook lists the six types of partnerships that reflect Gordon's hierarchy using a little different language and going one step further to include "collaborating with the community."

Here is Epstein's list:

- Parenting
- Communicating school-to-home and home-to-school
- Volunteering
- Helping students learn at home
- Decision making (including families as participants in school decisions, governance, and advocacy through PTA/PTO, school councils, committees, and other parent organizations)
- Collaborating with the community

As parents move up the "involvement ladder," they move beyond thinking about just their own children and becoming an advocate for them to looking at advocating for all children, including ways to improve the program, the school, or the system (see Figure 1.2).

Family-centered care and education is a giant step forward from parent involvement hierarchies. It involves a much larger vision of families being vital parts of their children's care and education.

The NAEYC supports family-centered programs saying, "Young children's learning and development are integrally connected to their families. Consequently, to support and promote children's optimal learning and development, programs need to recognize the primacy of children's families, establish relationships with families based on mutual trust and respect, support and involve families in their children's educational growth, and invite families to fully participate in the program" (NAEYC, 2005, p. 11). The NAEYC also came out with a book, *From Parents to Partners: Building a Family-Centered Early Childhood Program* (Keyser, 2006), and instituted a project in 2007 called Strengthening Family-Teacher Partnerships, which started with several "training the trainer" institutes.

The Harvard Family Research Project (HFRP) has been and is still aggressively working on linking families to their children's educational programs. When parent involvement takes the form of family support, there is evidence that it can lower

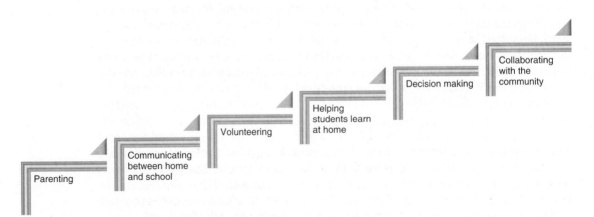

Figure 1.2   Six types of parent partnerships that lead parents to move up the involvement ladder, based on the Epstein model

stress levels in parents and make their lives easier. The HFRP website has links to areas of research and resources.

The Parent Services Project (PSP) was started in the 1980s by Ethel Seiderman in California as a mission to strengthen families by having them take leadership in assuring the well-being of children, families, and communities (Lee, 2006; Lee & Seiderman, 1998). PSP now provides training, technical assistance, and consultation nationally to help programs and schools engage families. Instead of merely involving families, the approach they take is to provide a wide variety of services that reflect the interests and needs of the families enrolled. Instead of predetermining what will be offered, the programs are designed to involve families in deciding, planning, and organizing the activities. As a result, programs trained in the PSP approach find increased parent involvement, leadership, and participation, which strengthens community ties and leads to effective community building (Pope & Seiderman, 2001; Seiderman, 2003). The Parent Services Project website highlights the organization's mission, values, programs, and events.

> ▶ Watch this video about the Patrick O'Hearn School in Boston, Massachusetts, and how school communities change when families become involved. Does the idea of parent involvement bring up feelings of excitement or apprehension for you?

One of the goals of many programs working with parents is child abuse prevention. An approach to preventing child abuse is to focus on what are called "protective factors." Examples of protective factors are: parental resilience, social connections, parenting skills, and child development knowledge. When professionals identify a family at risk for child abuse, they can help most by considering, supporting, and augmenting protective factors. Professional support and help in times of need can go a long way toward lowering child abuse incidents. Early care and education professionals are a logical group for working with parents to gain positive results and lower the risk of child abuse. The delivery system comes from early care and education professionals who learn how to support parents, provide resources, and teach coping strategies that will then reduce stress and prevent child abuse.

One of the premises of all these family-centered early care and education programs is that they work better when professionals understand families and involve them in respectful ways. Instead of the teacher just sharing information with families, there is two-way information sharing. This is true for general early care and education programs and also for special education. There is some evidence that parent involvement is a critical factor in early intervention programs. The rationale is that parents spend more time with their children than early interventionists and should take an active role in the interventions, not just turn their children over to the specialists. Parents have many more opportunities to influence their children's learning and development, and involvement in their children's programs expands their knowledge of and skills in specific ways for their individual child (Mahoney & Wiggers, 2007; Turnbull, Turbiville, & Turnbull, 2000).

Challenges to Creating Partnerships with Families

Responsiveness to families is a theme of this book. It's hard sometimes to be responsive when you think you know more than the family does. Obviously professionals have funds of knowledge from their training, professional education, and experience that most families don't have. Families also have funds of knowledge that professionals don't have (Gonzalez, Greenberg, & Velez, n.d.). It's the professionals' job to acknowledge that fact and to learn from parents as well as teach them. It's more of a sharing of knowledge than it is imparting. It also requires suspending judgments when the professional thinks families are wrong or misguided, even if research backs up the professional. Consider this quote from Asa Hilliard III (2007):

> The great error in behavioral research, now acknowledged by prestigious scholars, is that in most cases there has been a failure to take context into account. Research tends to proceed as if constructs, methods, instruments, and interpretations in culturally embedded studies are universal. Nothing could be further from the truth. Most researchers are ill prepared to do research in a culturally plural environment or to deal with hegemony as it relates to culture.

Rogoff sees that the theories of development studied by teachers and human development specialists have particular ways of regarding development and goals to aim for that reflect the values of the culture of those who create the theories. Not coincidentally, those values usually relate to the developmental theorists own life. (2003, p. 18). Most human development theorists come from a strong literacy background and therefore have held literacy as the hallmark of a successful outcome of development. Piaget, a scientist and thinker, saw the development of reason as the ultimate outcome of development. From these theorists' points of view, it's easy to see societies as primitive when they don't hold these same values or visions.

Hilliard (2004) also has a concern about how the lens of culture is often left out of what he calls mainstream psychology. Though he's looking at the field of psychology rather than human development, the two fields overlap in many places. Hilliard observed that mainstream psychology rarely shows any academic or scientific expertise in culture. In fact, according to Hilliard, many scholars seem to believe that cultural diversity matters are "more political than scientific." He went on to say that there is real resistance among many traditional psychologists to engage in the required scientific study and dialogue about these cultural matters. "Their cultural naiveté is almost legendary." When one looks through a cultural lens, one sees sets of realities that are different from what has been analyzed and studied in the name of psychology and human development.

Check Your Understanding 1.3

Click here to check your understanding of the history of family-centered care and education.

MULTIPLE LENSES THROUGH WHICH TO LOOK AT FAMILY-CENTERED APPROACHES

Context is important. This book emphasizes going deeper to understand children and families in the context of their environment and their community. Context can be viewed from a number of lenses. One of them is Bronfenbrenner's bioecological theory, which includes culture as one aspect of context. Scholars who create and study developmental theories should always use a cross-cultural lens. Anthropologists can help here. Both Rogoff and Hilliard say cultural contexts should be considered when trying to understand individuals and groups—their development, perspectives, and lifestyles. That particular lens, the cultural lens, was viewed as a challenge in the preceding section. Here I want to look at three more lenses through which to look at children in families and communities.

The Family Systems Theory Lens

Another way to understand context and use your understanding to work with families is family systems theory. I first encountered this theory when I read Virginia Satir's *Peoplemaking* and heard her speak, back in the 1980s. To explain the universality of her theory, she used an analogy of the human body—that any surgeon who studies medicine can operate on any human in the world because the organs are the same. The theory behind family systems theory is that families may be very different in many ways, but they all have some things in common and that is that they are governed by systems. One such system is communication, and another is rules. All families communicate with each other. How and to what extent differs, but communication is a given. All families have rules—what they are and how they are carried out is different for each family.

The lens of family systems theory puts the focus on the way the family works rather than on the behavior of any individual in it (Parke & Buriel, 2006). That makes the focus of the family therapist different from that of traditional therapists who work only with individuals. Family members are connected to each other; each one influences the others, and all are influenced by the family system. Understanding those influences and the shifts that take place when changes occur in the family is what guides family therapists. Educators aren't therapists and shouldn't be doing therapy. Their job isn't to diagnose family problems and fix them. Still, educators can find family systems theory useful to further their understandings of how the systems work in each family. Think of the theory as a framework for understanding in a deeper way.

Even though the systems themselves may be the same, they can vary greatly from one family to another in the way they operate. It's also useful to realize that changes, even small ones, can affect the system and the individuals in it. When educators look at a child through a family system lens, they realize that they can't work on behavior changes in children all by themselves, because those children are part of family systems. I think back to times I've been in teacher meetings where a child's challenging behavior is being discussed. A missing ingredient of these discussions was the family's involvement.

Linda Garris Christian (2006) in her article about family systems and their relevance to early educators lists six systems that are useful to understand when working with families. The systems are: boundaries, roles, rules, hierarchy, climate, and equilibrium (see Figure 1.3). She says that all families have these systems, but they look very different from one family to another.

Take *boundaries*, for example, which relate to limits, togetherness, and separateness—what or who is in or out of the family. I remember an exercise from a workshop I attended where the group was asked by the facilitator to think about the family they grew up in. She asked how many grew up in a large family. When participants raised their hands, she then questioned them about how they defined a large family and who was in it. Their answers reflected differences in boundaries. One person counted 50 people in her family. She included blood relatives and close others. Her family might have been called a kinship network by some. Another had an even

| Boundaries |
| Roles |
| Rules |
| Hierarchy |
| Climate |
| Equilibrium |

Figure 1.3 **Based on Christian's view of family systems, there are six systems that are useful to understand when working with families**

larger family, and she included people who were no longer alive. Another person who came from a large family numbered six in her family—herself, her parents, and her three siblings. The boundaries in the families of the first two participants were much looser than those of the third participant as determined by the definition of family members—who was included and who was not.

How emotionally and psychologically close family members are to each other is another part of boundaries. In families where the priority is raising children to be more independent than interdependent, the boundaries are different from those families where interdependence is a top priority. Christian uses the term *enmeshed* to label families who are extremely interdependent. I bristled at that word. It seemed judgmental to me. My experience with people I have known who come from families a therapist labeled *enmeshed* is that they emerged from therapy convinced they had "boundary issues" because they weren't closer to the middle of the boundaries continuum. D*isengaged* is the term Christian used for the families on the other end of the continuum. Just thinking about the cross-cultural views of boundaries in my own family gives me pause. If my mother and mother-in-law had studied to be family systems therapists, I'm pretty sure that my mother would have labeled my mother-in-law's family as "enmeshed" and my mother-in-law would have called my mother "disengaged." Having been part of both those families now for a number of years, I think both labels are too harsh. Certainly, putting on a cross-cultural lens makes a difference in how one views family boundaries that don't fit one's own ideas and experiences.

A danger of using the family systems theory is the temptation to play therapist. Another danger is judging other people's family systems without regard to your own. Obviously early educators are the product of some kind of family systems, and just as we have to understand our own cultures, we have to understand our own family systems so we can stop just looking outward. "Know thyself," said Shakespeare. That's the lesson here.

Understanding and working with family systems theory is a much bigger and more complex job than just focusing on caring for and educating the developing child. But taking a family-centered approach is more complicated, too. The challenges are great, but the rewards are as well.

All of these mandates to deal with the huge complexity in the program; the child, the family, and the community may seem overwhelming! I have warned more than once to be cautious. Perhaps my warnings are too strong and early educators will put aside who they are and what they know so they can just focus on opening up their minds to what the families they work with know. So at this point, it needs to be said that early childhood educators also have the responsibility to share their professional knowledge and personal beliefs with the families. This may be harder in a cross-cultural context and may take more sensitivity than when working with one's "own people." Nevertheless, information sharing has to be a two-way street.

The Whole Child Lens

Educators learn from families, and families learn from educators. This issue becomes important when you realize that this book focuses heavily on the social-emotional aspects of development, even though school readiness and cognitive development are in the spotlight at present as more and more children are failing in school—even middle-class ones (Hernandez, 2011). School readiness is, of course, a concern for everybody, but professionals with a child development background often come at it from a different angle than some other professionals and families by recognizing that social-emotional development is vitally tied to cognitive development.

Way back when I started in this field, I remember the families who came into the program where I taught wanting their children to learn to read. The same is true today. Family members sometimes arrive in programs much more focused on their children's intellect than on their feelings and social abilities. Yet research indicates that matters of the heart are the very foundation of mental growth. A book called *Toward a General Theory of Love* (Lewis, Amini, & Lannon, 2000) gives eloquent scientific explanations for how emotional ties that link children to others create actual changes in the brain structure leading to stability, health, and the ability to think.

Children need to move in order to think

Early care and educational professionals study what has been called "the whole child." The child is made of mind, body, and feelings, and one system is vitally tied into the others. Though child development books may tease out the parts and put them in separate chapters, in reality, the child is always a whole. No matter how much you want to promote school readiness, you can't separate the intellect from the emotions.

What part does the body play in school readiness? How often does a parent look into the preschool play yard, see the children having a good time, and think, "How can they learn if all they do is play here?" Carla Hannaford (2005) answers that question in her book *Smart Moves: Why Learning Is Not All in Your Head*. She is clear that children need to move in order to think. The book brings compelling information from the neurosciences about the relationship of body movement to learning. This is the kind of professional information that early educators can share with parents so that families come to understand that care and education in the early years may be different from their own experience in their childhood or their concepts of what school should be like.

Maslow's Hierarchy of Needs

Another lens through which to look comes from a theorist whose model relates to the whole child concept. Abraham Maslow (1954) studied successful people instead of those with psychological problems coming up with what he called a hierarchy of needs. His model provides important information for anyone concerned with working with young children and their families. His theory rests on the idea that basic needs must be met for growth to occur. The most basic needs of all are physiological and include air, food, water, and rest. A hungry child is motivated to get food and uses all available energy for that end, energy that well-fed children use for going on to meet higher needs. On the next level up is the need for safety. One way that the safety need can be met in young children is by making their lives predictable. Some children especially find their security in the routines of the day. Change the routine, and feelings of safety disappear. Children crying at separation is another expression of safety needs. The next step up is the need for love and belonging, though with the latest information about the importance of relationships to a child's brain development, perhaps this need for relationship is as strong as the need for food, water, air, and rest. Esteem is the next step up in the hierarchy of needs. Self-esteem is part of this level as well as recognition from others. This step has to do with a feeling of self-worth. At the top of the pyramid (see Figure 1.4) is self-actualization, which reflects the need to live up to one's potential—be all that one can be. Although originally Maslow worked to define the self-actualized person, later he decided that it's an ongoing process that lasts a lifetime. So he changed the term to the self-*actualizing* person. Meeting all these needs is behind the ability to seek knowledge, learn, and develop. When children consistently come to school, child care, or early care and education programs hungry, they have less intellectual curiosity and motivation to learn than those whose nutritional needs are met on a regular basis. Head Start figured that out a long time ago and took the responsibility to meet the children's daily nutritional needs. Subsidized school breakfast and lunch programs are based on the same idea for low-income children. This is an example of how the community can meet a child's need when the family cannot. Another example of meeting a different kind of need is when teachers in a full inclusion program gain the skills needed to integrate children with special needs into the group of their typically developing peers so everyone has a sense of belonging.

To truly meet children's needs in education and care programs, the focus must be the family, not just the child. When you relate to families in ways that make them feel understood and valued, you are doing a service to the child. The first goal is to help families feel supported by the program. But the educator's job goes beyond

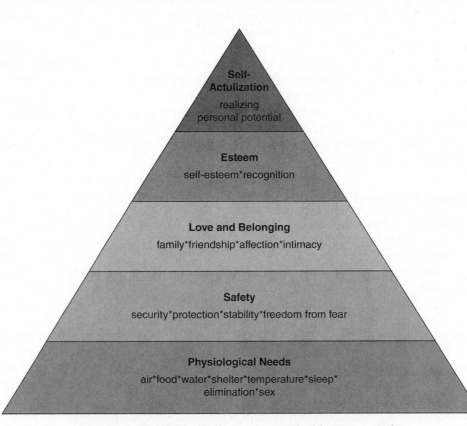

Figure 1.4   **Based on Abraham Maslow's pyramid of human needs**

understanding, valuing, and supporting—most important of all is for families to have the voice to say what they need. That makes each program a little different, rather than some kind of standardized curriculum for parent involvement. It's also very different to find out what families need than it is to just ask them to support the program's goals. The idea is to take a collaborative approach (Gonzalez-Mena & Stonehouse, 2008). A collaborative approach means that change not only occurs within the families, but also within the program as it begins to reflect those enrolled rather than just predetermined policies and practices (Powell, 1998). The movement for family-centered programs isn't just about improving child outcomes, though that may be the focus of some of the leaders in the movement. Other leaders are most concerned about empowering parents through making programs more collaborative. These leaders come from the perspective of parental rights; some also come from wanting to respect diversity and promote equity. Certainly, understanding how social support can lower stress factors and improve parental functioning gives advocates good reason to push for programs that address parents' needs and create family-centered programs.

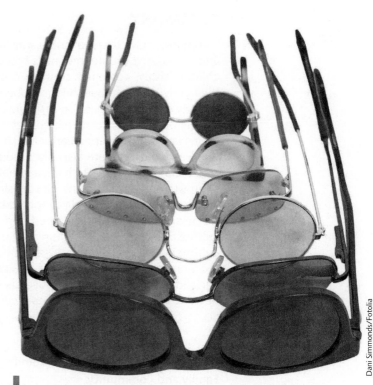

We view the world through the lenses of our family culture

Dani Simmonds/Fotolia

Culture as a Lens

Culture found its way into each of the major sections of this chapter and also ended up in each of the subsections even when it wasn't emphasized. Here at the end of chapter it gets its own heading. Culture is ever present though often unacknowledged. Culture always affects us, even though often it is invisible except when it bumps up against a different culture. Culture affects what we do, what we think, how we perceive, how we behave, and how we interact. It can even affect how we hold our bodies and how close we stand to someone we meet. Cultural differences are an ongoing theme throughout this book.

Another theorist featured prominently in this book is Erik Erikson. His classic *Childhood and Society* (1963) explains how he studied the process of growing up in a variety of cultural and social settings. Erikson was fascinated by cultural differences as well as what has come to be seen as his eight stages of social development which he regarded as psycho-social crises. He explains each of the stages as a challenge, which a person must successfully negotiate before moving on to the next stage. When the challenge isn't met, the person will find issues related to it arising in subsequent stages until he or she finally masters what was missed earlier. These stages as they relate to childhood will be looked at further in the chapters focused on families and children.

Watch this video, in which Sue Bredekamp discusses how some children attend schools where the culture is different from their home culture. Was that true for you? What do you think of her comment about always needing to know more about culture?

Check Your Understanding 1.4

Click here to check your understanding of the different ways to view family-centered approaches.

SUMMARY

The chapter started with a look at why this book is called the *Child, Family, and Community* and considered Bronfenbrenner's bioecological model as part of the reason: because children always come in a context. You can't ever consider a child without thinking of the family in which that child is embedded, which is why family-centered approaches to early care and education programs are so important. The chapter also looked at the history of family-centered education, which included some of the challenges programs face when creating partnerships with families. More ways to look at family-centered approaches were also discussed and included family systems theory and the whole-child concept, which means that though you can tease out particular domains of growth and development, like physical or mental, everything is always intertwined. That led to a discussion of school readiness and Marlow's hierarchy of needs. Though discussions of culture appeared regularly in each section labeled "lens," the term culture didn't get a subheading until the end of this chapter. That's typical of the way culture exists—all the time, every day, but when you are embedded in it, you don't recognize that it's there. To end, the chapter introduced Erikson's theory of psychosocial development which will use his stages as well as themes of culture though the next five chapters, when once again culture shows up in the chapter title.

✓ QUIZ

Click here to check your understanding of Chapter 1, "The Child in Context of Family and Community."

FOR DISCUSSION

1. What do you think about working in a family-centered program? Do you have any experience with that approach?
2. What do you see as the benefits and challenges of a family-centered approach?
3. Thinking about your own life using Bronfenbrenner's bioecological model, can you draw a picture of the various layers of context in which you grew up? Label each layer and provide three influences in each layer.
4. What are your memories of your early care and education? Consider that the term covers programs serving children and families from birth to third grade. To what extent was your family involved in your out-of-home care and education?
5. What is your understanding of Maslow's hierarchy of needs? Do you know someone who you would consider has reached the highest levels?

WEBSITES

Harlem Children's Zone
The Harlem Children's Zone provides comprehensive support to children, from early childhood through college prep, by focusing on issues of education, family, and community and health.

Kids Count Data Center
The Kids Count Data Center is a source for data on child and family well-being in the United States.

National Association for the Education of Young Children (NAEYC)
The National Association for the Education of Young Children (NAEYC) is often considered the nation's leading voice for high-quality education for children from birth through age eight. They provide many resources for professionals about family-centered care and education.

Head Start
Head Start is a national organization that supports the social and emotional development and school readiness of children from birth to age five. The agency is funded by grants from the U.S. Department of Health and Human Services to support low income families with education and social services.

The Harvard Family Research Project
The Harvard Family Research Project (HFRP) is a large, ongoing research program with the goal of evaluating strategies to promote the well being of children, youth, families and their communities. Click on the *Family Involvement* link for a large number of resources on this topic.

Parent Services Project
The Parent Services Project (PSP) focuses on parent leadership training, staff capacity building, family literacy, child development supports, community outreach, and organizing and access to service. This program trains early childhood professionals on how to partner with families in ways that develop and strengthen their leadership qualities and roles in educational programs for their children.

The Ecological Model of Human Development
A National Institute for Early Education Research (NIEER) write-up explains how Urie Bronfenbrenner, one of the founders of Head Start, came up with his bioecological systems theory, which helps teachers and others understand how to see children in context in order to better serve the child and family.

FURTHER READING

Derman-Sparks, L., & Edwards, J. O. (2010). *Anti-bias education for young children and ourselves*. Washington, DC: National Association for the Education of Young Children.

Espinosa, L. (2010). *Getting it right for young children from diverse backgrounds: Applying research to improve practice.* Upper Saddle River, NJ: Pearson.

Im, J., Parlakian, R., & Sanchez, S. (2007). Rocking and rolling: Supporting infants, toddlers, and their families: Understanding the influence of culture on caregiving practices…from the inside out. *Young Children, 62*(5), 65–66.

Tough, P. (2009). *Whatever it takes: Geoffrey Canada's quest to change Harlem and America.* Boston, MA: Mariner Books.

Photographee.eu/Fotolia

Supporting Families Around Issues of Attachment and Trust

Learning Outcomes

In this chapter you will learn to...

- Explain how attachment and trust are related.
- Describe the development of attachment and trust.
- Identify obstacles to attachment.
- Recognize varying attachment patterns.
- Explain the effects of child care on attachment.

HOW ATTACHMENT AND TRUST ARE RELATED

This chapter focuses on supporting families of very young children during their first year of life. Children in this age group are at the beginning of their socialization. What do attachment and trust have to do with socialization? The answer to that question is *everything*. Attachment is important to relationships and social development. It also relates to trust. Further, it impacts cognitive development and even physical development. For example, babies who have a secure attachment tend to explore more. When they explore in a safe, rich, and developmentally appropriate environment they advance their physical skills while developing their intellectual ones.

Think of attachment as a lasting emotional relationship that begins to develop in infancy and serves to tie the infant to one or more people in his or her life. It is a two-way process—adults (first, usually parents or other family members and second, infant caregivers) attach to infants, and infants attach to adults. This two-way process results in a significant relationship. Attachment is a lifelong process that starts in the first year of life and carries throughout the life span. The first early attachment sets the tone for a child's development and defines some of the issues that he or she will carry into adulthood. This chapter focuses on attachment in infancy and the issues and implications for early care and education professionals, teachers, and other professionals working with families.

Everyone who is involved with children and their families—teachers, early educators, and professionals of all sorts—should be concerned about attachment. Long ago we learned about the terrible effects of orphanages that neglected to provide for attachment. It took a wise and innovative pediatrician in Hungary, Dr. Emmi Pikler, to come up with solutions for healthy development in group care. Her theories, research, and practical approaches toward creating attachment in out-of-home care were developed in the 1930s. Due to World War II and the Iron Curtain following the war, much of the Western world was denied this insight for the next several decades. Magda Gerber, an infant expert also from Hungary, arrived in the U.S. in 1956 during the Hungarian revolution. She introduced some new ideas about parenting and attachment starting in the 1970s. Both Gerber and Pikler are being studied today in the U.S. and to some extent around the world. The ideas, theories, and research of both innovators are now starting to be applied to child care as well as orphanages (Gonzalez-Mena & Briley, 2011; Greenwald & Weaver, 2013).

Erik Erikson (1963) is the person better known for bringing attention to attachment long ago as the first stage of his psycho-social theory, in which he named the *eight stages of man* (1963). The first stage is Trust versus Mistrust. Erikson focused on mother-infant attachment, which he saw growing out of the babies' physical and emotional needs being met satisfactorily in the first year. His theory corresponds with the basic three of Maslow's hierarchy of needs (see Chapter 1). Attachment is also important to see in the context of Bronfenbrenner's ecological systems theory (1979), because it happens in the microsystems but is impacted by the other systems as well. One way to look at this chapter is that family involvement in programs for young children has plenty of research behind it showing what an influence attachment has on positive outcomes for children. "To give children a healthy start, early childhood educators should consider themselves working for the healthy development of two generations, children and their parents or caregivers" (Weissbourd, Weissbourd, & O'Carroll, 2010, p. 115).

Bryan Creely/Fotolia

The positive nurturing experiences associated with attachment produce neurotransmitters that give the infant a sense of well-being

Anthropological research that looks cross-culturally (Rogoff, 2003) shows variations on the theme of mother-infant attachment depending on the cultural community. For example, in some cultures the ideal attachment of an infant is to the group and is not exclusive to the mother. Others who have studied attachment cross-culturally are Carol Brunson Day, Alison Wishard Guerra, and Sarah Garrity (Virmani & Mangione, 2013).

Although attachment is an emotional process that we associate with "the heart," other processes engaging the brain are also involved. Healthy attachment provides the foundation for later intellectual development, according to research being done on the brain (Hammond, 2013). The positive nurturing experiences associated with attachment produce hormones called *neurotransmitters* that give the infant a sense of well-being. This sense of well-being reinforces certain pathways in the brain, which leads to mental growth. On the other hand, children who have attachment issues or, worse, no attachment figure(s) lack a sense of security and experience stress, which has a detrimental effect on the brain's development. Bruce Perry (2002, 2006; Perry & Dobson, 2010) in his writings and lectures talks about the chemicals that wash over the brain when babies experience some of the results of lack of attachment, like abuse or neglect.

With school readiness receiving so much widespread attention in the early care and education field, some people think the main message from brain research is that academic teaching should start early. On the contrary, the real message is the important role that social-emotional development plays in intellectual development. In a journal published by the International Mind, Brain, and Education Society, Immordino-Yang and Damasio (2007) make an excellent case for emotional processes profoundly affecting learning, attention, and memory. Although they focus on neuroscience and education, and not on infants, attachment is the foundation of the emotional processes they write about. They say that feelings provide an "emotional rudder" to guide judgment and action. That's one of the reasons that this book focuses on social-emotional development throughout and starts right off with attachment as the basis for early social-emotional development. It's important for early childhood educators and the families they work with to recognize the role that social-emotional development plays in the lives, education, and development of children.

A short article in *Time* brings this point home further (Park, 2007). In 2006 parents spent $200 million on *Baby Einstein* videos to help their babies get ahead intellectually. Yet in a study done at the University of Washington, researchers found that for every hour babies spent watching the videos, they understood an average of seven fewer words than the babies who had no exposure to the videos. The parents of the video-free babies apparently followed the advice of the American

Academy of Pediatrics, which recommends that parents keep babies under age two away from screens and just interact with them instead. Those interactions are likely to result in stronger, healthier attachment. Further, parents and caregivers should regard interaction as a two-way street. Their responsiveness to the baby is vital. It's not just talking to the baby but, even more importantly, responding to what the baby initiates. For more information on the effects of screen time and young children, go to the website for the American Academy of Pediatrics.

Here's another example of how attachment and trust contribute to cognitive development in infants. As mentioned earlier, when children feel secure, they are freer to explore the environment around them. Watch a group of babies in a playroom. You're bound to see some exploration as the ones who are mobile go looking to see what's there. If these babies get too far from their infant care teacher or become startled, they head back to touch base, get a little hug, and gather up their courage to move out again. The greatest explorers are usually the ones who are securely attached. According to Ainsworth's research (1977, 1978), secure attachment can be easily seen in the behavior of infants who are separated from their parents and then reunited with them. Attachment is a matter of trust, which is the subject of the next section.

> ✔ **Check Your Understanding 2.1**
>
> Click here to check your understanding of how attachment and trust are related.

THE DEVELOPMENT OF ATTACHMENT AND TRUST

The basis of healthy care and education is social-emotional development and the basis of that is attachment, which comes from a synchronous relationship, which grows from a number of synchronous interactions. Here's what a synchronous interaction looks like, whether the adult in the scene is the baby's parent, a center-based infant care teacher, or a family child care provider.

The adult is bent over a three-month-old baby who is lying on her back in a play area. The adult is expressionless. The baby rounds her mouth and lets out a breathy sound while reaching out her arms. The adult responds by widening her eyes, rounding her own mouth, and imitating the sound. She reaches for the baby's hands and holds them in her own. The baby pulls her hands away, kicks her feet, and widens her own eyes in imitation of the adult. The adult smiles. The baby smiles back. The adult keeps smiling, makes clucking noises, and claps her hands. The baby turns away. "Oh, that was too much for you," responds the adult, quieting her activity. The baby looks back. The adult smiles. The baby smiles, then arches and reaches. "You want up?" the adult asks, reaching out her arms to the child.

These two are "in sync" with each other. The adult is sensitive to the baby's signals and reads the turning away as a need to tune out, not a personal rejection of her. The baby knows how to "light up" the adult's face. The adult knows how to "turn on" the baby. The two are good together. If they are not already attached, they are becoming attached.

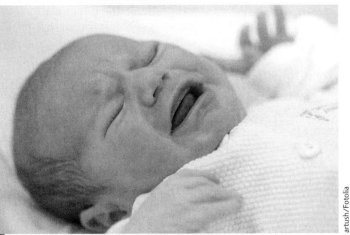

artush/Fotolia

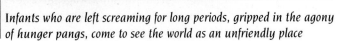
Infants who are left screaming for long periods, gripped in the agony of hunger pangs, come to see the world as an unfriendly place

Babies become attached when people in their lives are sensitive and responsive. That means that they pay attention to the baby's signals and read them accurately, responding readily and appropriately. Adults practice being responsive when they play with babies, as in this scene. They also meet needs by reading babies' cues and responding in a timely fashion with feeding, for example. Both play and meeting needs contribute to the development of attachment.

Imagine yourself a very young baby, lying asleep in a crib. You open your eyes—suddenly you're wide awake. You see nothing except a blur of light—there are no objects, no movement within your visual range. You feel a very uncomfortable sensation in your midsection. You squirm around. Changing position doesn't help. Suddenly you feel desperate. The sensation in your midsection takes over your whole body. You squeeze your eyes shut tight and open your mouth wide. Into your ears comes a piercing sound. You don't know that it's your own cry. You only know that something is terribly wrong, and your whole being reacts to it. Your heart pounds, your face burns, and you scream in agony, then gasp for breath, only to start screaming again once you get your lungs full. You're like this for what seems an eternity but is actually less than two minutes. You feel something touch you. You open your eyes and find something very distinctive and vaguely familiar in front of the blur of light that was all that was there before. The something moves in a way that makes you feel comfortable. As you pause for breath, you hear another sound—not the high, agonized one of before, but a soft, soothing one. You feel a blanket of pleasure surround you, providing immeasurable relief, and, true to your most cherished hope, you find yourself lifted in the air out of the loneliness—the isolation—and snuggled into a pair of warm arms. You're basking in the glow of the feelings of this, when—wonder of wonders—something familiar touches your cheek. You jerk toward the something, manage to get your mouth around it, and begin sucking. A warm, sweet sensation floods your mouth and you're in heaven.

Imagine now a different scene where the hungry baby wakes up and doesn't have to signal her needs because the adult is right there with her and feeding occurs immediately, before the baby even cries.

These two scenes illustrate how, as mentioned earlier, needs, attachment, and trust all come in a bundle in the beginning of life. The scenes are slightly different. In the first one, the infant wakes up alone and must let the adult know about the need for food and comfort. In the second scene, the infant wakes up in physical contact with the adult, who anticipates the needs before crying occurs.

You may prefer one scene over the other—you may actually feel critical of one of the scenes. However, both of these patterns of relating to the needs of the very young infant lead to a healthy attachment, one that serves both the individual and the culture. It's important to remember that attachment patterns are related to parental values and goals (Chang, 1993; Gonzalez-Mena, 1997, 2004, 2008; Virmani & Mangione, 2013). Parents rear their children to fit the world as they perceive it. Attachment is vital. It is a means of ensuring survival of the child and also of the species (Bowlby, 2000). It creates the caring (the feeling) that motivates the *action* of giving care. It ensures that nurturing and protection will be provided to the relatively helpless infant. But beyond physical survival, the first attachments provide the basis for all future relationships.

If the infant finds that when needs arise they are met with reasonable promptness, as in the two prior scenes, he or she comes to see the world as a welcoming place. A sense of trust grows from fulfillment and satisfaction in the first year

of life. Infants who are left screaming for long periods, gripped in the
agony of hunger pangs, come to see
the world as an unfriendly place. They
find that they can't trust anyone to
take care of them. If they give signals
and no one responds, they see themselves as powerless and the world as
cold and hostile. When these children
grow out of infancy, they continue
to view the world with distrust.
Erikson (1963) wrote about this psycho-
social dilemma a long time ago (see
Figure 2.1).

Trust is a lifelong issue for all of
us. However, children who develop a
sense of distrust in infancy grapple
with the issue more intensely than others. Some of these children are left with
unresolved trust issues; others success-

These two are "in sync" with each other

fully deal with the problem if the situation changes and those around them become
more responsive and meet their needs more promptly. Children with unresolved trust
issues often reach adulthood still seeking the early caregiver who left their needs
unmet. Because it is never too late to resolve trust issues, some adults seem continually to choose to connect to people who treat them much as their early caregiver(s)
did. They put themselves back into their infant situation, to perhaps give themselves
another chance to relive the situation and manage a different outcome. The human
being is very resilient! Continually seeking their early caregiver later in life may not
be necessary for those children who find a warm, nurturing person to whom to attach
in their early care and education program. According to Perry, a firm, healthy attachment is one way to get children through hard times in their lives with less damage to
their brain development and therefore to their social-emotional and cognitive development (2006).

Attachment is a powerful process—and it seems that even a little goes a long
way. Look at studies of survivor types—children who manage to cope and live a
productive life in spite of factors in their early years that work against that. The
one thing that all these survivor children have in common is a person they could

Child's Stage	Approximate Age	Task		
Infancy	0 – 1	Basic trust	versus	Basic mistrust
Toddlerhood	1 – 3	Autonomy	versus	Shame and doubt
The preschool years	3 – 6	Initiative	versus	Guilt
School age	6 – 10	Industry	versus	Inferiority

Figure 2.1 **Erikson's psycho-social stages of development**
Source: Based on Erikson (1963)

Watch this video to hear Dr. Bruce Perry and others talks about attachment, trauma, and resiliency. How does high quality caregiving impact brain development?

www.youtube.com /watch?v=RYj7YYHmbQs

attach to sometime in their first year—even though it might not have been an ideal attachment or a long-lasting one. Emmy Werner, a developmental psychologist, did classic research on resiliency over the past 40 years. Her findings show that attachment in the early years with a caregiver who had predominantly positive interactions with the child acts as a protective factor (Werner, 1984, 1995, 2000; Werner & Smith, 1992). These findings are important for early care and education practitioners to know about because they focus on the protective factors that can make a difference in children's lives. In fact, you could be the person who makes the difference in a child's life.

The Strengthening Families Through Early Care and Education research project has identified exemplary family-support programs that show that staff in child care centers and other early education programs can make a difference. Using a "protective factors" framework, the project documents how exemplary programs reduce abuse and neglect. The idea is that programs can intentionally strengthen families while serving their children. One of the protective factors occurs when staff works to build trusting relationships with parents and offers support to them when they are going through difficult periods. That kind of relationship, which can be a type of attachment, is different from what staff provides to children. The website for the Center for the Study of Social Policy has more information on the protective factors framework.

How Secondary Attachments Occur

There are many different ways of getting attached to infants and older children, depending on the individual, the culture, and the situation. Attachment in families is a basic kind of attachment. It is important for those professionals working with children and families to support attachment of child to family and vice versa. When infants started coming into child care in large numbers, great concern for attachment arose. What happens to the attachment of babies who spend more of their waking hours outside the home with people other than their family? One of those concerned is J. R. Lally (1995, 2013). He has been advocating for a number of years for policies, such as small groups, primary caregivers, and continuity of care, to help infants and toddlers gain a sense of trust while not with their families. When those policies are in place and caregivers are well trained, the attachment to family remains strong and attachment to caregivers grows. Attachment doesn't switch from family to caregiver, but rather the attachment to caregiver becomes a secondary kind of attachment (Lally, 1995, 2013). Lally and Peter Mangione's Program for Infant-Toddler Caregivers (PITC) has been training infant-toddler program administrators and staff since 1990 about the importance of secondary attachments in out-of-home care. Further, the PITC training focuses on just how to create those attachments. The worries about attachment issues in babies when both parents work outside the home have lessened today as evidenced by the growing numbers of families successfully using infant-toddler care.

One of the pioneers in attachment in group care was Emmi Pikler, the Hungarian pediatrician mentioned earlier who did many years of attachment research on children zero to three years of age in what is now called The Pikler Institute, directed today by Pikler's daughter, Anna Tardos. Anyone who works with infants and toddlers in groups and individually can learn much from Pikler's research. One of Pikler's findings was how important it is to train the staff very carefully in exactly how and to what extent to promote attachment. Pikler's ideas about attachment are useful today to infant care teachers as well. She stressed in her training that this was a special kind of attachment—one that gave children enough security to develop well and function optimally, but was not so strong an attachment that moving into an adoptive family—or back to their own—would devastate the children when the ties with the caregiver in the Institute were cut (David & Appell, 2001). The Pikler website has information about training that promotes respectful care of infants and toddlers. Today in child care we look at secondary attachment to caregivers as similar to, but not exactly like, what Pikler advocated. However, the means to both are similar.

Attachment, according to Pikler, grew during the one-on-one times when the primary caregiver was able to be intimate and uninterrupted with her primary children. Those times come about during the essential activities of daily living, such as feeding, diapering, dressing, bathing, and grooming.

Becoming attached to someone else's baby is delicate business. Earlier I said that as a professional you may be the protective factor in a child's life. You may be the one that makes a difference. That's a heady thought and needs some serious consideration. Some people who go into social work or early care and education, teaching, or other related professions have a tendency to want to rescue children from their parents. This is a stage many pass through. It is important to recognize those tendencies in yourself and set them aside. If you look down on parents, you can't support them, and it's your job to be supportive. Watch out that you don't find yourself in competition with the family for the child's affection. Be professional at all times, but realize that *professional* in this profession means warm and caring. Be close and attentive, but also be aware of keeping an optimum distance in your attachment to a child. Optimal closeness should be the parents' goal, not yours. The child's attachment to the family is and should be a lot closer than your attachment to the child. The child's past, present, and future are with the family, not with you. Your attachment is important, but it's also temporary. If it is too strong, both you and the child will suffer when you separate, as you are bound to do eventually.

> Be professional at all times, but realize that *professional* in this profession means warm and caring.

Attachment Behaviors

Attachment can be observed in adults and babies alike. There are certain sets of behaviors that indicate attachment is forming or is already fully established. We'll look first at parent behaviors and second at infant behaviors. Some parents show signs of attachment right away. They're smitten with their babies. They feel close to their offspring. They find parenting pleasurable—even the hard and frustrating parts. One mother recalls how her whole life changed when her first baby was born. Suddenly she became important to someone. Her baby depended on her. She had a new interest in world news because it seemed important to make the world a safe place for her baby to grow up in (Gonzalez-Mena, 1995). Not all parents go through such a transformative process, but some do.

Some cultural rituals are related to attachment. Giving a name to the baby and calling him or her by that name are ways of acknowledging the child as an individual. Buying possessions for the new baby is also a way of recognizing individuality and personhood. These are so expected that they don't seem to relate to attachment, but when they don't occur, it can be a sign that something is wrong with the attachment. Be careful, though, about judging across cultures. Attachment behaviors may look quite different.

Signs of Attachment in Infants

When considering signs of attachment in infants, it's important to understand that babies take longer to show signs that they are becoming attached, although careful research shows that signs exist from birth. Research discovered a long time ago that babies just a few hours old can distinguish their mother's smell and her voice, for example (DeCasper & Fifer, 1980). Before long, babies begin to act differently around their primary caregiver (who may or may not be the mother). They may be more animated, less fussy, or more interested and alert.

Eventually some babies begin to show distress when someone they don't know arrives in their field of vision. The distress may accelerate if the stranger approaches. This stranger anxiety shows that the baby can distinguish between the person(s) he or she is attached to and others.

However, some babies never show stranger anxiety, not because they are not attached but because they have had a secure and trusting life with multiple caregivers (either at home or in child care). If babies skip this milestone, some parents and even some experts become distressed because they think it shows lack of attachment. That's not necessarily true.

For some babies, the next milestone is *separation anxiety*, as the baby protests at being away from the caregiver. (More about this subject appears in the next chapter.)

Attachment behaviors can be seen in situations involving both stranger anxiety and separation anxiety—as the baby looks or moves toward the primary caregiver for comfort and reassurance. Clinging, crying, fussing, whining, and following are all attachment behaviors that can show the emotional bond between the child and someone else. Although they are indicators of attachment, an absence of these behaviors does not necessarily signal a lack of attachment in children with multiple caregivers.

Check Your Understanding 2.2

Click here to check your understanding of the development of attachment and trust.

OBSTACLES TO ATTACHMENT

You need to know about these obstacles to attachment so you won't judge parents who don't seem as attached as other parents do. Here are some ways to support parents who need help to increase attachment: Make parents aware of their child's qualities and uniqueness. Encourage them to observe and to ask about what they see. Delicately point out any positive qualities that they may miss. This may be especially important if the baby's temperament and the parent's temperament aren't a good match. There will be more about temperament in the next section.

As mentioned before, stay out of any sort of competition with parents. Don't set yourself up as the expert who's good at working with children—especially their child. When a child is acting out in front of the parent, avoid saying things like, "He only acts like that when you're here. He's fine with me."

Optimum attachment often starts before the baby is born, continues after delivery when the baby and family "bond," and then follows a continuous progression from there (Lieberman & Zeanah, 1995). Many families don't start with optimum attachment. What can get in the way? The following are some reasons parents may not feel an emotional connection to their baby before he or she is born:

- They may be unhappy about the pregnancy or with each other, and those feelings may influence their feelings for the baby.
- The father may not be in a relationship with the mother—so any feeling for the unborn baby on his part will necessarily be "long distance."
- Even for the mother, the reality of the unborn baby may be fuzzy. It's hard to love someone you can't see or touch or interact with.

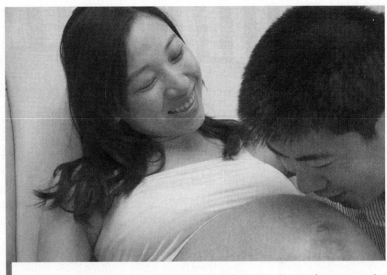

Attachment may begin prenatally, as parents begin to relate to their visions of the growing fetus

Then, at birth, the time may still not be right. The birth itself may not be a pleasant experience, and that unpleasantness can carry over into the period after. Or the birth may be complicated. If the baby or the mother is in any kind of physical distress, medical procedures may take precedence over time alone to "bond" together. For one reason or another, baby and parents often miss out on the initial bonding period. Even if it is arranged so that parents and baby can spend the first hour or so together, there may be worries or disappointments that cast an emotional overlay over the bonding process and prevent the magical happy moment from occurring.

Adoption can present another obstacle to bonding at birth and early attachment. The adoptive parents may not have been a part of the birth or may not have had a period together immediately afterward.

Attachment can proceed very well in spite of all these obstacles, as long as the relationship grows and flourishes, preferably in the first year—the earlier the better. Attachment, the process of creating a close and lasting relationship, may be delayed for many reasons. If the infant is very sick, parents may unconsciously protect themselves from getting attached by putting an emotional distance between themselves and the baby. Sometimes the difficulty is that, for whatever reason, the baby remains unresponsive to the caregiver's initiations. Some infants are born with disabilities, a circumstance that can cut down on their ability to respond. Others simply don't have the kinds of behaviors that draw adults to them. They're not cute or cuddly or smiley. They don't make eye contact. These infants, who don't reward the adults around them, need adults who make a conscious effort to attach. If babies experience early lengthy separation, the attachment process can be disrupted. Babies in foster care may be moved around; changing caregivers can disrupt attachment. These delays or disruptions in attachment can influence future life in drastic ways if a sense of basic trust is not established. The child may put up barriers so that no one can get close. The hurt from loss is too great to chance again.

Temperament and Attachment

Temperament can affect attachment in either a negative or positive way, depending on the temperamental match between the infant and adult, whether parent or infant care teacher. Temperament is built in and can be detected early in a child's life. Genetically determined, temperament becomes obvious as infants show differing levels of activity, emotionality, and sociability that tend to remain the same over time. Thomas, Chess, and Birch (1963), the pioneers in temperament research, categorize babies as "easy," "slow to warm," and "difficult." Their work helps today's parents and caregivers understand how temperament affects behavior and shapes personality. Lally and his colleagues in the WestEd Program for Infant–Toddler Caregivers renamed the categories "fearful," "flexible," and "feisty," which puts them in a more objective light. A good match between parent temperament and child temperament promotes attachment; a mismatch may hinder it. If the two aren't a natural fit, the adult must adjust to the baby rather than expecting the reverse. This is important for you to understand—both when considering your own attachment process with the children you work with and also when working with parents. You can be the one to help a parent understand temperament if a mismatch is getting in the way of attachment between parent and child.

What would a mismatch look like? If an active and intense mother with a high energy level finds herself with a slow, calm, mild baby, she may be disappointed. She may even wonder whether something is wrong with her baby, even though the baby is perfectly fine. If this high-energy mother is not aware of what she is doing, she may overstimulate her baby. She has to learn to read the signs that the baby has had enough. You can help her do that. Some parents keep on after the baby turns away or closes his or her eyes. A serious mismatch occurs when the mother interprets this behavior as boredom and continues to try to "wake the baby up and make her more lively."

Or imagine a calm, relaxed father who loves things done on schedule and appreciates predictability in his life. He'll find a mismatch with a highly active, intense baby who never seems able to regulate his rhythms or body needs. Some babies don't keep any sort of routine; they may get hungry at a different time every day. Napping is as unpredictable as appetite and never follows a schedule. If the father of such a baby doesn't accept that his son is different from himself, he may have trouble being sensitive to the child's needs.

Parents who have children whose temperaments don't match their own have to adjust their expectations, accept their babies as is, and learn to understand them. They have to be flexible about how and when they respond. They have to be supersensitive so that they can meet their babies' needs. All that may be hard for a parent whose temperament isn't flexible or sensitive. This is where professionals can come in to help parents understand their babies and respond to them in ways that make connections. It's important to help parents realize that nothing is "wrong"; it's just that there's a mismatch and it's up to the parent to understand and respond rather than trying to change the baby.

Developmental Differences

Babies who are born with developmental differences may not have the attachment behaviors that draw adults to them. For example, neurological issues can cause babies not to be cuddly. Some stiffen when held. Some even cry out in pain when held or touched. Others who can't control their facial muscles may not smile or look interested in the same way typically developing babies do. Or eye contact may be missing. A child with a visual impairment, for example, may not use eye contact to establish a relationship. A child with a hearing impairment may not respond to soft talking. In these cases it is important for adults to look for the attachment behaviors the children do exhibit. Adults must be constantly aware of the importance of establishing connections even if the baby's behaviors tend to get in the way. Sometimes outside help is needed to support parents, infant care teachers, early educators, or family child care providers when attachment isn't occurring in spite of efforts to encourage a close connection. As you gain experience, you may be the one who provides help to the parents.

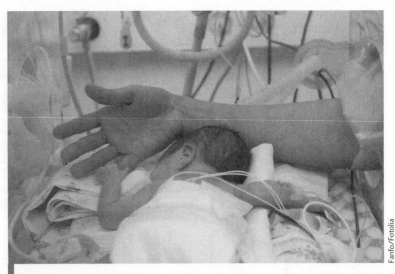

If a baby is very sick and separated from family, attachment may be delayed

Learning to Cope with Feelings of Loss

Babies who are attached experience feelings when separation occurs. Separation is the other side of attachment. Each human has the lifelong task of coming to grips with separations and coping with the feelings that occur as people come into and go out of his or her life. Each broken relationship, physical departure, or death brings into play all the coping skills learned earlier. The skills for dealing with separation begin to develop in infancy.

You can perhaps get in touch with the power of the feelings surrounding separation by thinking back to a time in your own life when you were apart from someone you cared about. Perhaps it was the first day of school, or a trip to the hospital, or even the first time you were left with a babysitter. It may be a less significant event—but one that sticks in your memory—like the time you took the wrong turn in the grocery store and were "lost" for a minute or two. It might be an even more significant event like the day one of your parents walked out, never to return, or the day one of them died. All of us have experience with separation, and those experiences start earlier for some than for others.

If you can remember your feelings surrounding these experiences, you can probably get in touch with one or more of the following: panic, fear, anxiety, misgivings, apprehension, qualms, terror, horror, bewilderment, confusion, annoyance, irritation, anger, outrage, fury, wrath, frenzy, desperation, indignity, sadness, loneliness, desertion, and abandonment. The feelings come from the need for security as well as a sense of loss of control over the situation.

The memory of your pain may be intense, or it may have muted over time. Or perhaps you have a fuzziness around the feelings or even an absence of feeling. You may even dredge up a sense of depression when you get in touch with this early separation experience.

There are all kinds of separation experiences in infancy—some that help the child grow to independence, others that leave scars and long-lasting aftereffects. One common separation infants experience comes when they are put into cribs to sleep by themselves. In cultures that place a high priority on independence, this physical separation from the beginning is regarded as important. Learning to sleep alone

Suzanne Clouzeau/Pearson Education, Inc.

Separation is the other side of attachment; we all have experience with separation, and those experiences start earlier for some than for others

Watch this video, which describes SIDS (sudden infant death syndrome), including risk factors and prevention. What are the preventative measures that were discussed in the video?

as an infant is a skill that is valued by many in this country. It's an important step for children coming to see themselves as separate individuals. Some parenting experts are adamant about babies sleeping alone. Some experts, including Ferber (2006), who wrote *Solve Your Child's Sleep Problems*, say that babies can't get a good night's sleep if they have to "interact" all night with someone else.

Ironically, information on sudden infant death syndrome (SIDS, or crib death) indicated that an undisturbed night's sleep may put infants at risk. In cultures where infants are held, jostled, and put to bed with an adult or another child, the rate of SIDS is dramatically lower than in cultures where infants sleep apart from the hustle and bustle of family life in cribs in their own rooms (Grether, Shulman, & Croen, 1990; McKenna, 2014). Of course, that doesn't mean babies should be in bed with someone. Statistics show that placing babies on their backs to sleep makes sleeping alone in a crib safer. The "back-to-sleep" campaign also lists other risk factors such as cigarette smoke, soft mattresses, overheating, and things in the crib such as pillows and loose covers. Overall, the campaign is designed to lower the risk factor of sleeping alone; it has worked to lower the number of SIDS deaths. The American SIDS Institute has a website with information about risk factors and the latest research.

Where babies sleep can be a cultural issue. Some cultures value sleeping alone and others don't, even if they have the space and means to do so. Some cultures aren't as interested in their children becoming independent individuals as they are in creating a spirit of interdependence and connectedness to others (Rogoff, 2003). In many families both in the United States and around the world, infants and toddlers sleep with the mother or both parents until the next baby comes, then move into the bed of siblings or grandparents. Some European Americans have made an attempt to change the way they were raised by instituting what is called the "family bed" (Thevenin, 1987). More recently, the trend of "co-sleeping" with the baby is finding support and even products to promote it. Sears and Sears (2013) encouraged bed sharing in their book *The Attachment Parenting Book* (2001), and more recently in their revised *Baby Book* 2013, though they also say families should decide if it's right for them and their baby. Of course, it's not safe for postpartum mothers who are exhausted or using sedatives to sleep with their babies. A pamphlet on the Internet provides cautions for keeping co-sleeping safe, many of which are the same for preventing SIDS in cribs. In addition, it warns against the co-sleeping adults going to sleep with the baby on a couch or cushions and advises against adults going to bed with alcohol, drugs, and certain medication in their systems. Healthy Child Care America has a website that outlines the Safe Sleep Campaign and includes downloadable PDF guides for parents and child care providers.

A number of articles and books have been written about getting babies to sleep by themselves because it isn't as easy to accomplish as it might seem. Many babies comfort themselves while alone in the crib by developing an attachment to a particular object. This process fits right in with being part of an object-oriented culture. Most parents and caregivers are delighted when a child attaches to a favorite blanket or a stuffed animal. Experts see this particular way of self-comforting as a sign that the child has coping skills.

Learning to put oneself to sleep and stay by oneself is a step toward independence and is a valued behavior in many families. It's a healthy sign that infants are able to handle separation.

Ethan

Ethan's mother took drugs when she was pregnant. No one was aware of this problem until the day Ethan was born. He arrived in the world full of the harmful substances his mother had ingested, and his first days of life were spent in withdrawal. He suffered and so did the hospital staff who tended him.

"Poor little guy!" said a nurse, as she tried to make him more comfortable.

Getting the drugs out of his system didn't end his problems. Ethan was a difficult baby from the beginning. He cried incessantly—it seemed sometimes as if he would never stop. He'd scream and scream until he finally wore himself out; he'd sleep restlessly for a period and then start again. It was hard to be around Ethan.

His foster mother, a patient woman, understood how hard life was for Ethan. Although she had other babies to care for, she spent special time with him, trying to give him the message that he was cared about—that he was loved. It wasn't easy. When an adoptive family came along that knew Ethan's history and his problems, she was relieved because she felt he deserved a permanent home and parents—a family of his own who could give him a good deal of time and energy—the time and energy she had were stretched so thin!

Ethan's new parents were special people. They didn't go into the adoption expecting to rescue a child and have him be forever grateful to them. They knew something about the kinds of problems that Ethan had at the time and the kinds he was likely to have in the future. They were prepared to deal with these problems.

They started out right away to establish an attachment with Ethan. It wasn't easy— he wasn't an appealing baby. When his new parents picked him up, he stiffened and shook. He didn't cuddle like lots of babies. He seldom seemed relaxed; in fact, his movements were jerky and uncontrolled. He twitched, jiggled, and shook as he lay in his crib.

Ethan didn't like to be touched; often he screamed louder when he was touched than when he wasn't. It was tempting to leave him alone, since picking him up seemed agonizing to him. But his parents knew that leaving him in his crib wasn't the answer, so they did some observing and brainstorming to discover what ways they could pick him up that would cause him the least discomfort. They felt proud when they were able to discover some. It became more rewarding to pick him up.

Ethan didn't look at anyone very often. Even when his parents tried to get his attention, he tended to look away. It's hard to develop a relationship with someone who doesn't make eye contact, but they managed. They just kept on trying until the day came that Ethan looked his mother right in the eye. What a moment that was for her—worth waiting for. That was the beginning of the development of a series of positive behaviors

Check Your Understanding 2.3

Click here to check your understanding of the obstacles to attachment.

that made Ethan easy to love. On the big day when Ethan smiled for the first time, his father grinned back as if his face would split in two. "You're going to be okay, Ethan," he said, patting his son.

Since happily-ever-after stories only occur as fairy tales, I have to tell you that Ethan did continue to feel the influence of his early drug exposure into his preschool years. But with the help of his parents and their love for him, he was able to cope with the cards that life had dealt him.

VARYING ATTACHMENT PATTERNS

The classic research has been done on attachment between mothers and babies. Although attachment patterns can vary significantly from that one pattern, the early research is still worth understanding.

Bowlby and Ainsworth's Research

John Bowlby was the first to apply to humans the idea that attachment behaviors evolved because they promote survival. He took a psychoanalytic view that attachment of infant to caregiver affects an infant's sense of security and ability to trust.

Mary Ainsworth was a student of Bowlby's, and her research is used widely in assessing attachment of infants and toddlers. She set out to study how securely attached babies are to their mothers (Ainsworth & Bell, 1977; Ainsworth et al., 1978).

She used something she called "the Strange Situation," in which a baby is observed in an experimental room with toys designed to entice. The situation involves the mother and a stranger in a series of comings and goings. How the baby reacts to the separation, the stranger, and the reunion is used to judge the type of attachment.

Watch this video, which highlights the research of the Strange Situation. It is set in a laboratory. Have you observed similar behavior outside of a lab setting?

www.youtube.com /watch?v=QTsewNrHUHU

From her research, Ainsworth came up with different types of attachment. If the baby is what Ainsworth called securely attached, he or she uses the mother as a base to move out from and explore the interesting toys in the room. You can see this happening in any setting where there are toys and a baby with enough mobility to get to them. Babies move away from their mothers, checking back periodically to see where they are and crawling back to get a snuggle, hug, or bit of comfort when needed. If the mother leaves, securely attached babies usually show some distress, but not always. They show they are delighted to see her when she returns.

Not so with insecurely attached infants. They may show what's called avoidant attachment, resistant attachment, or disorganized/disoriented attachment. Avoidant attachment shows when babies act the same around the stranger as they do around the mother. They seem not to care when the mother leaves the room. When reunited, they are slow to greet the mother and either ignore or avoid her.

Babies who show resistant attachment stay close to the mother before she leaves and do little exploration in a strange place. They get upset when she leaves, but when she comes back they show anger and sometimes behave in a push-pull fashion—for example, alternating between clinging and pushing her away. Sometimes even picking them up fails to comfort them.

Disorganized/disoriented attachment was the product of more recent research (Howe, 2011; Main & Solomon, 1990; Solomon & George, 1999). This type of insecure attachment shows up as a pattern of confused, contradictory behaviors when reunited with the mother. Sometimes infants look frozen, dazed, and disoriented. Some rock or engage in other repetitive behaviors. Some cry after the mother has managed to get them settled down.

Ainsworth's research provides interesting information, but be careful about judging attachments in families you work with. You're not a researcher, and you can't understand everything about a family based on what you see when they leave their children. One criticism of Ainsworth's way of judging attachment is the unnatural setting. Do babies and mothers behave the same in a laboratory as they do at home or somewhere else?

Another criticism of the Strange Situation as a way of assessing attachment is that it is based on a particular model of mother-child attachment. There are a lot of variations on that model. What if the baby has been in child care and is used to multiple caregivers? Is he really showing insecure attachment if he avoids the mother when she returns, or is he accustomed to having an interesting environment and being separated from his mother? Or what if the baby comes from a large family in which the mother isn't the only caregiver? What if the mother isn't the person the baby is most attached to? What if the baby has two mothers? Or two fathers?

 Watch this video on attachment that shows children struggling with the "reunion." What are some possible causes for a child to behave this way?

www.youtube.com/
watch?v=DH1m_ZMO7GU

Questions About Classic Attachment Research

Ainsworth and other researchers focused on attachment as it relates to the insular or nuclear family. Today we know better. We can see with our own eyes that, even in the nuclear or insular family, caregiving may be shared between mother and father or between one parent and another relative or child care provider. Under these circumstances, attachment is not just between mother and baby, although often the mother remains the primary attachment.

As mentioned earlier, much of the focus on attachment has been related to the insular or nuclear family with mother, father, and child. This, of course, isn't the only kind of family. Another type of family is the single-parent family. Sometimes the parent(s) and baby are not a unit by themselves but are part of a larger extended family. Stack (1991) describes *kinship networks* as clusters of people who are related through children, marriage, and friendship and who come together to provide domestic functions. This domestic network may spread over several households, and changes in individual household composition do not significantly affect cooperative arrangements. The single-parent family that finds itself in this type of network may be thought of as "embedded" rather than alone.

A woman once told me a story about how she had changed her perspective on her family. This person was a single parent with two children who lived with her parents in their house. She thought of her situation as two families living in one house until she decided to have a family portrait taken. She included all five family members, deciding for herself that this was one family rather than two. This story of her family portrait started me thinking about my own family situation as I grew up. My mother, my sister, and I lived most of my childhood in the house of my grandparents. We never had a family portrait taken. We didn't see ourselves as a unit; rather, we were two families—an intact one (my grandparents) and a "broken" one (my mother and her two children). Nowadays, of course, we would call ourselves a single-parent family rather than a broken one, but many would still see us as deprived without a father in the household, rather than enriched because of grandparents and the uncles who lived there for periods during my growing up. I now prefer to think of myself as growing up embedded in my extended family.

The concept of an embedded family is a more positive and realistic one. In an embedded family the attachment might be quite different because of shared caregiving. Certainly that was my experience. My attachment to my grandmothers was as strong as my attachment to my mother. Although we may think of the mother-child dyad as the way "it should be," that's not necessarily so. The child can become attached to several caregivers or to a group rather than to just one or two individuals. When you are used to looking at attachment as an exclusive relationship, you may be concerned about the infant who is attached to multiple caregivers (Zimmerman & McDonald, 1995). However, cultures all over the world raise their children this way. Shared care has advantages over one or even two parents carrying total responsibility for a child's well-being. What a burden that much responsibility can be, especially for a new parent who may have had little previous experience with babies!

Some child care programs function as an extended family, a kinship network, or a family-support system, rather than as just a place to leave children during the day. These programs are able to provide families with the kind of connections they would find in embedded families if they had them. One such family support system is the Parent Services Project, which a visionary child care director, Ethel Seiderman, started in California and which has now spread across the nation. The purpose of this project is to help programs recognize that the well-being and sense of significance of parents are of central importance to the child's development. Furthermore, it emphasizes that support is important to all families, and that social-support networks reduce isolation and promote the well-being of the child, the family, and the community. Parent Services Project has a website full of ideas for engaging and strengthening families.

Judging Attachment in a Cross-Cultural Situation

When a mother doesn't seem sensitive to the baby's emotional signals, seldom speaks to the baby, and/or never holds the baby in a face-to-face position so adult and baby can make eye contact, it is not clear whether these are functional or dysfunctional behaviors. Do they fit customs and expectations and make sense if viewed in cultural context? Or are they left over from a time when survival was the main issue and many babies died before their first birthday? Or do they have another explanation? For example, in a situation in which the baby is never called by the given name, you may not immediately understand what is going on, unless you are of the same culture and social class as the family you're observing. If you don't thoroughly understand the culture and perhaps even the individual family, you can't make judgments about the way people are raising their children and whether they have a healthy attachment.

Language is another area in which an outsider may misjudge what is happening. European American middle-class families are very vocal, and all this vocalization is part of the attachment process. Watch most middle-class European American parents and you'll see that they talk face-to-face with their babies—chattering away as if the baby understands. They even wait for a response, creating a turn-taking situation that imitates real conversations in which both participants talk. Research (done by European Americans on European Americans for European Americans) shows the value of this kind of behavior, not only for attachment but also for future development. For example, this early emphasis on verbalization makes a difference later in school performance; children with good verbal skills do better academically.

In contrast, some families rarely speak to their infants. What may not be clear to the outsider is how much the family is using *nonverbal* communication that the observer isn't aware of. Because a family doesn't behave the same as a European American middle-class family toward babies doesn't necessarily mean that there is an attachment problem—it may be more a matter of cultural difference.

> ✓ **Check Your Understanding 2.4**
> Click here to check your understanding of varying attachment patterns.

EFFECTS OF CHILD CARE ON ATTACHMENT

A question to ask when looking at the effects of child care on attachment to family is: What is the situation of the child's family? Obviously if a family is overwhelmed by stress and the members are not functioning well, and a baby is born into the family at this point, some protective factors may be crucial. The early care and education program can provide these factors. In some situations, as when an overburdened single parent is able to get the support and referral to services needed, the child care program can literally be a lifesaver.

Such programs exist. Some child care and early education programs in the United States today not only give services to children but also give families the support they need to get on their feet so they themselves can provide for their children's needs. These kinds of programs are cost-effective because they deal with attachment and other needs at the beginning rather than trying to fix problems that arise later, which is much more expensive (Pawl, 1995; Raikes, 1996). We could use many more of these kinds of programs! *Prevention* is a key word when looking at early deprivation and attachment problems. Look at the Advocacy in Action feature, "How a Child Care Director Found Financial Support for a New Infant Center," for a story about what one group did to get funding for a badly needed infant program.

ADVOCACY IN ACTION ▶ **HOW A CHILD CARE DIRECTOR FOUND FINANCIAL SUPPORT FOR A NEW INFANT CENTER**

Christina Lopez Morgan, Professor Emeritus

Many years ago, I was director of the children's center at Family Student Housing at a major state-funded university when we realized we needed to open an infant center to respond to students' needs. We badly needed money to finance the operation of the program. I came up with the idea of trying to get students to vote on having a portion of their registration fees go to support the children center's infant program. This was a new use for collecting student fees and no other university had ever proposed such a thing before. (Since then many universities and colleges in our state have done this.) I tried to get permission from the chancellor to proceed with getting this initiative on the student ballot, but he delayed and delayed in responding to the request. About a month and a half before the election he gave us the go-ahead to place our proposal for the fee on the student ballot. I suspect he may have waited deliberately because he thought it would be impossible to get a campaign up and running in such a short time. But we mobilized every resource we had

and started a major ad campaign. We took babies to lunch in strollers and backpacks at the popular eating places on campus. We printed up brochures describing how critical our program was to students who had children. We made buttons that we passed out to everyone that said, "For a slice of pizza you can support quality care for an infant." Or "For the cost of one beer you can support a future UC student." We asked parents to get permission from their professors to make a short plea in all of their classes asking for support of our initiative. We made banners with children and posted them around campus. We had a children's art show on the main quad of campus. We had the older school-age children on the day of the election standing in front of the banner at the entrance to the college wearing "Vote for us" buttons. Even with all of this I doubted that we would win because we represented a very small need for the majority of the students. But we gave it our best shot and to everyone's amazement we got the initiative passed. It was one of the proudest moments of my career.

Unfortunately, these kinds of comprehensive programs are too few in number. If the baby in the above example is placed in a child care program in which he never gets to know any of his caregivers and his mother gets little or no support, it's a different story. Attachment may be delayed because caregivers come and go too fast. Not one of the adults gets to know him well enough to read his signals, understand his uniqueness, or become fond of him. Child care may save his life yet still not provide for his attachment and trust needs. Because of underfunding, that's tragically the state of many child care programs in the United States today. The turnover rate of caregivers and teachers in underfunded programs is shocking.

You can't know exactly how child care affects attachment without considering countless variables that have to do with the quality of the care and the way the family works. One important aspect of quality care is the partnership between the parents and the program. When child care staff and providers develop a collaborative relationship with the parents that includes more than just parent education and involvement, everybody stands to gain—including the child!

Some parents don't have much choice about using child care for their babies and won't until parental leave becomes a societal policy. It may reassure these parents to know that most studies have shown that babies become attached to their own parents even when child care is begun quite early.

How Caregiver and Parent Roles Differ

Good infant care teachers have many of the qualities of good parents, and those qualities promote attachment. Lilian Katz (1980) wrote about these qualities long ago. One vital quality is responsiveness. Another quality is sensitivity. When the infant care teacher learns to read each infant's signals, he or she can respond appropriately and in a timely fashion, that is, if the staff–child ratio is good. Infants learn that they can give messages. They can influence the people in their world. They have personal power. They become attached. The attachment grows out of the sensitivity and the ability of the infant care teacher to read babies' communication and to communicate, and also promotes further communication. Infants become better at sending signals when someone is trying to read theirs. The infant care teacher gets better and better at reading signals as he or she grows to know the baby as an individual. A synchronous relationship results.

Good infant care teachers and good parents have many similar behaviors and goals, but they also have some differences. Katz, professor emerita at the University of Illinois and a longtime leader in the field of early childhood education, wrote about these issues as early as 1980 and has been explaining them to early childhood professionals ever since in her speeches and workshops. Katz (1980) said that the infant care teacher's attachment is necessarily short-term, and it's important for him or her to remember that fact. This

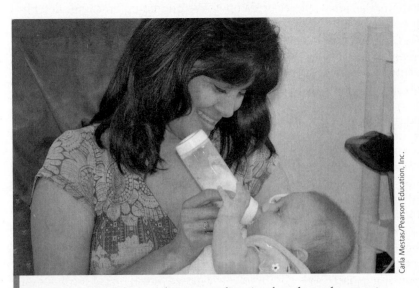

The infant care teacher gets better at reading signals as he or she grows to know the baby as an individual

Carla Mestas/Pearson Education, Inc.

child care arrangement isn't forever; the infant care teacher has little control over the future. It's the parents' job to have a vision for the child's future, just as they have the knowledge of the past. It's the parents—the family—who connect the child in time, giving a sense of continuity. The child has a life beyond child care; that's a fact that the infant care teacher must keep in mind. Though Katz wrote that long ago, her words are as meaningful today as they were when she wrote them.

Parents and infant care teachers differ in the degree of closeness that's appropriate. The goal of *parental* attachment is to establish *optimum closeness* with the child; the *infant care teacher's* goal is *optimum distance*. The child benefits from attachment to both, but it's a different kind of attachment. The infant care teacher must put limits on the degree of attachment; after all, the family may move out of town tomorrow. In addition, infant care teachers usually have other children to consider; they can't allow themselves to get completely wrapped up in just one to the neglect of the others. Figure 2.2 includes a summary of ideas for professionals in general and early educators in particular when working with parents' issues of attachment.

Fairness is another category in which parents and infant care teachers differ. Parents can be advocates for and focus on their own children. They don't have to be fair and consider all the children in the program. Infant care teachers can't afford to favor one child over another. Take note though, that doesn't mean that they must treat all the children in their care alike. Similar treatment in the face of differing needs doesn't create fairness.

Attachment in Full-Inclusion Programs

Full-inclusion programs are those where children with developmental differences, disabilities, and particular challenges are placed in child care with their typically developing peers rather than being separated into special programs. Every adult involved in such programs must aim to help all children feel they belong. That means that the children with exceptional needs must be integrated into the group. Unless the adults in the program have the time and skill to facilitate this integration, some children may feel left out. Although this attention to integration is slightly different from the kind of attachment this chapter has focused on so far, it brings up the issue of attachment not just to an adult or two, but also to the group (California Department of Education, 2009).

Strategies for Working with Families Around Attachment Issues

- Recognize that the well-being and sense of significance of parents are of central importance to the child's development.
- Work to build a trusting relationship with each family.
- See yourself as a support for families instead of merely being there for their children.
- If policies are in place in an infant center that allow attachment between infant care teachers and a small number of children, do what you can to promote that attachment. If there are no such policies, discuss with the people in power the need for them.
- Keep in mind that if you are the child's caregiver, your attachment is secondary to that of the parents. Examine the degree of closeness with each child with a professional eye. Be close enough to help the child feel secure, but not so close that the child turns from family to you.
- Avoid competition with family for the child's affection.

Figure 2.2   **The positive nurturing experiences associated with attachment produce neurotransmitters that give the infant a sense of well-being**

The work of Lev Vygotsky, at the Institute of Psychology in Moscow, has implications for integration. Vygotsky (1978) created what's called sociocultural theory, which emphasizes social interaction as an influence on development and learning. His *zone of proximal development*, or moving children forward from where they are to where they can be, involves peer interaction (Berk, 2001).

SUMMARY

The chapter started with a discussion of the relationship of attachment to trust. It went on to describe how attachment occurs. Certain behaviors show that babies are attached to their parents. The chapter also discussed how sometimes there are obstacles to attachment. It went on to explain how part of attachment is learning to cope with feelings of loss. Attachment shows up in varying patterns; therefore, it is best not to judge attachment in cross-cultural situations. The chapter ended with a look at the various factors that relate to child care and attachment.

✓ QUIZ

Click here to check your understanding of Chapter 2, "Supporting Families Around Issues of Attachment and Trust."

FOR DISCUSSION

1. Have you been aware of attachment occurring? Describe the kinds of interactions that encourage attachment that were part of this experience. Was synchrony involved? How did the attachment serve the people who were becoming attached? Tell about that experience.

2. What are your experiences with obstacles to the bonding or attachment process? Did the people involved get over or around these obstacles? How?

3. Discuss separation anxiety. What behaviors indicate the child is trying to keep the attached person from leaving? What emotions might a child display? How can an adult help the child to separate from the person he or she is attached to?

4. Have you had any experience with how child care might affect attachment? What are your ideas or thoughts about this subject?

5. What are your ideas, thoughts, or feelings about working with families around issues of attachment? What experience do you have in supporting parents' attachment to their infant?

WEBSITES

American Academy of Pediatrics
This pediatric website is dedicated to the health of all children. It is a resource for physical and emotional well-being, including suggestions for appropriate screen time for children.

American SIDS Institute
The American SIDS Institute has a website with information about risk factors and the latest research to prevent sudden infant death syndrome.

Institute for Attachment and Child Development
This website identifies issues that transform the lives of families and children with attachment, behavioral, and emotional disorders and promotes healthy family relationships.

Parent Services Project
Parent Services Project has a website full of ideas for engaging and strengthening families.

Pikler Institute
The Pikler website gives information on the approach used at the Pikler Institute, a residential nursery in Budapest, Hungary. The approach focuses heavily on attachment. The website also has information on trainings in America.

Program for Infant/Toddler Caregivers (PITC)
The Program for Infant/Toddler Caregivers supports and promotes attachment through quality care for infants and toddlers using resources, information, and training. The site includes information on brain research and implications for infant development.

Resources for Infant Educarers™
Resources for Infant Educarers™ is a nonprofit organization that uses the teachings of Magda Gerber to promote a unique philosophy and methodology in working with infants in ways that respect them as individuals.

Zero to Three
Zero to Three: National Center for Infants, Toddlers, and Families is designed for parents and professionals. A leading resource on the first three years of life, the group's mission is to strengthen and support families, practitioners, and communities to promote the healthy development of babies and toddlers.

FURTHER READING

Chen, D. (2013). Inclusion of children with special needs in diverse early care settings. In E. Virmani & P. Mangione (Eds.). *A guide to culturally sensive care*, 2nd ed., pp. 25–40.

Copple, C., Bredekamp, S., & Gonzalez-Mena, J. (2011). *Basics of developmentally appropriate practice for infants and toddlers*. Washington, DC: National Association for the Education of Young Children.

Gonzalez-Mena, J. & Eyer, D. W. (2014). *Infants, toddlers, and caregivers*. New York, NY: McGraw-Hill.

Greenwald, D. & J. Weaver (2013). *The RIE manual for parents and professionals*. Los Angeles, CA: Resources for Infant Educarers.

Hammond, R. A. (2009). *Respecting babies: A new look at Magda Gerber's RIE approach*. Washington, DC: Zero to Three.

Lally, R. R. (2013). *For our babies: Ending the invisible neglect of America's infants*. San Francisco: WestEd and New York: Teachers College Press.

Tardos, A. (Ed). (2007). *Bringing up and providing care for infants and toddlers in an institution*. Budapest, Hungary: Pikler-Loczy Tarsasag.

Weissbourd, B., Weissbourd, R., & O'Carroll, K. (2010). *Family engagement*. In V. Washington & J. D. Andrews (Eds.), *Children of 2020: Creating a better tomorrow* (pp. 114–118). Washington, DC: Council for Professional Recognition and National Association for the Education of Young Children.

Supporting Families with Autonomy- Seeking Youngsters

Learning Outcomes

In this chapter you will learn to...

- Identify the signs of developing autonomy.
- List strategies for dealing with issues of power and control.
- Describe methods for coping with loss and separation.
- Explain the role of partnering with families of toddlers.

ometime around their first birthday, many babies pull themselves to their feet and stagger forward. That first shaky baby step represents a huge developmental leap. The baby is now a toddler, and the central task of his or her life is to become a separate independent being. Erik Erikson (1963) calls this the *stage of autonomy* (see Figure 3.1). Of course, not all babies get up and take steps. Some children with disabilities go through the stage of autonomy without becoming mobile. The term *toddler* doesn't apply to all children, but most of the material in this chapter applies to both typically and atypically developing children after the first year and sometime before the fourth year of life.

The professional's job is not only to appreciate this special stage of life, but to help families also appreciate it. That may be harder than it seems because the behaviors described in this chapter come from particular cultural perspectives and are not universally regarded in the same way. For example, the push behind this stage is for children to recognize their power as individuals and learn to assert this power in acceptable ways. That isn't the goal of all families (more about that later in the chapter).

You may discover that the toddler stage is the hardest one for you to find ways to support families whose perception of and goals for the child are different from those advocated in this chapter. But those kinds of challenges are always present when working with families, even if you're not working across cultures. It's important to keep your professional perspective and also be aware of your personal/cultural perspective while still allowing yourself to open up to each family's perspective. Not an easy job, but nobody ever said working with children and their families is easy!

Many adults find the way that toddlers carry out this thrust for autonomy to be a headache, and your job may be to help support families in ways that reduce the headache. Families sometimes see the behaviors that come along with this push for independence as difficult to manage. The theorists (who generally see things from a perspective that rates independence as a higher priority than interdependence) explain the meaning behind the behaviors and expect adults to understand and put up with the difficulties. The labels put on this stage by some parents (*the terrible twos*) and by some experts (*the terrific twos*) reflect the various ways to look at the behaviors of this stage. The words the theorists use to label the process are *seeking autonomy, separating,* and *individuating.* Experts are willing to concede that the behaviors associated with this stage are sometimes "difficult." The words parents

Child's Stage	Approximate Age	Task		
Infancy	0 – 1	Basic trust	versus	Basic mistrust
Toddlerhood	1 – 3	Autonomy	versus	Shame and doubt
The preschool years	3 – 6	Initiative	versus	Guilt
School age	6 – 10	Industry	versus	Inferiority

Figure 3.1   Erikson's psycho-social stages of development
Source: Based on Erikson (1963).

The labels put on this stage by some parents (*the terrible twos*) and by some experts (*the terrific twos*) reflect the various ways to look at the behaviors of this stage.

commonly use are *stubborn*, *obstinate*, and sometimes even such loaded terms as *willful*, *contrary*, and *spoiled*.

SIGNS OF DEVELOPING AUTONOMY

What are the behaviors that indicate a child who will one day become a member of society is becoming an autonomous individual who is self-sufficient and self-reliant? Remember that the goal is a healthy, successful, productive member of the community. The most notable toddler behaviors are exploration, self-help skills, and a sense of possession. The toddler behavior that can be the most worrisome but important is negativity as the toddler finds his power and defines himself or herself as an individual. Even this behavior also leads to the goal of being a successful member of society who is also a strong individual.

Important as this behavior may be, it is also the one that can trigger child abuse. See the Advocacy in Action feature, "Addressing Child Abuse Prevention: One Person Can Make a Difference," to discover what one town led by one individual did to prevent child abuse.

Negativity

The first sign of developing autonomy is when the darling baby who happily opened his mouth for each bite of cereal or strained vegetables suddenly one day clamps his

---

ADVOCACY IN ACTION ▶ **ADDRESSING CHILD ABUSE PREVENTION: ONE PERSON CAN MAKE A DIFFERENCE**

Here is a story about what one town did to respond to child abuse in the community. When a toddler died as the result of abuse, a group of residents, led by one individual, decided to do something. This was in the time when child abuse was just beginning to be recognized as widespread and a threat to children's mental and physical health. Though laws were in place, they were not yet enough for this particular group of citizens who wanted to prevent abuse in their community, not just punish it. This motivation on their part coincided with some funding set aside for prevention, intervention, and treatment of child abuse. The group went to work.

First they established a hotline for parents to call, just to talk, when they felt as though they might not be able to control themselves. Then they began to educate the community about child abuse and about using the hotline. This group soon discovered that what parents needed was a variety of support services. Some needed parenting information and skills, some needed

relief child care, some needed a job, some needed a place to live, and some just needed relief from the many stresses in their lives that led them to take out their frustrations on their children. The picture was much bigger than anyone had ever suspected.

Today many of these services are in place, including parent support and education groups, relief child care, an emergency aid fund, part-time temporary home service with a helper coming into the home to help with household and child management, and other services. In addition they offer an innovative service they call "phone friend" for children who come home from school to an empty house. All of this because one person cared and figured out how to involve others in advocacy.

For more information about child abuse signs and prevention, visit the Child Welfare Information Gateway and Zero to Three websites. Zero to Three also has a program called Preventing Child Abuse and Neglect (PCAN).

lips shut and turns aside. His meaning is clear. Without a word spoken, this is the beginning of "No!"

The theory says that the child can now begin to see himself as an individual separate from his mother or other object of attachment. He finds power in his difference—he's not the same person as this adult in his life. He finds power, and he uses it.

This is only the beginning. By two years of age, this child is likely to be contrary about everything. If his mother likes peas, he hates them. If his father wants to take him for a ride, he balks. He refuses to get into the bathtub, and when he is finally coaxed in, he refuses to get out again. Life becomes a struggle because he is so busy asserting his individuality.

Sometimes toddlers say "no" so much because they hear the word all the time. If adults use the word *no* as the primary means of managing behavior, the first *no*'s of their children may be imitations of adults. However, even if adults use a variety of means of guiding behavior and minimize the number of *no*'s in their child's life, toddlers still learn to say that magic word. It's important to realize that learning to say no is a vital skill. What would your life be like if you never said no to anything? Do you remember the temptations of your teen years? Do you wish you had learned to say a good strong "No!" earlier? What are your temptations now? Do you find saying no a useful skill in your life today? How much do you remember about your own toddler years? Did the adults who were in your life regard your *no*'s as skill building or as defiance of their authority? Their perception of you then may influence *your* perception of children in the toddler stage now.

Exploration

Exploration starts in infancy, grows out of attachment and a sense of trust, and increases as children move toward autonomy. It may seem ironic that a child who is firmly attached explores more than one who is not. But it makes sense if you think of the attachment as providing a secure base to move out from. In fact, you can even see this phenomenon in action by watching a parent and a young child who are in a strange environment. The child will move out from the parent but will check back regularly. Sometimes it's just a glance; other times she runs back to the parent and clings for a moment before venturing out again.

The other factor in exploration is the freedom to move that the child is given in infancy. The research of Dr. Emmi Pikler (2007) indicates that babies who

Babies who develop their movement skills independent of adults learn that they are capable individuals and become remarkable explorers

develop their movement skills independent of adults learn that they are capable individuals. Their trust in their own skills makes them remarkable explorers (David & Appell, 2001; Gonzalez-Mena, 2004; Pikler, 1971, 1973; Pikler & Tardos, 1968; Tardos, 2007). Babies in the Pikler Institute, a residential nursery in Budapest, are put on their backs where they have the most freedom to use their bodies. They are free of restrictive devices like infant seats, swings, even high chairs. No one puts the babies into positions they can't get into by themselves. Adults don't sit them up, stand them up, or walk them around. As they grow, these babies show an amazing sense of physical security (Tardos 2007). This same approach is also used by the staff at the Resources for Infant Educarers in Los Angeles, California. Founded by Magda Gerber and known as RIE, the program follows the teachings of Emmi Pikler, who was a teacher, mentor, and friend of Gerber (Gerber, 1979; Hammond, 2009; Soloman, 2013).

Infants who learn to use their bodies well and who experience adult appreciation of their exploration urges become toddlers who move around a lot when they feel secure. Toddlers, without urging, spontaneously explore the space around them. In my classes I've asked students to observe a toddler in child care and to map the territory the child moves through. The maps that come out of these observations are amazing. A toddler can cover miles in a single day just by exploring what's in a room or a play yard.

Toddlers explore with their hands—and use their other senses as well. Given something new, they'll bang it, smell it, try to pull it apart, maybe throw it, and quite often taste it. They are little scientists. They want to know what everything can do—how it works.

Toddlers are "doers" but not "producers." They explore, experiment, and try things out to see what will happen. That means if you give them a toy or an activity that is designed to be used in a certain way, they're sure to try a dozen other ways to use it. They are not interested in outcomes or products. They enjoy the process of exploring and experimenting for its own sake, and they don't need anything to show for it. It helps if parents have this information and can appreciate this stage of development. Communities who understand toddlers can also make spaces in neighborhoods for them to play that are safe and developmentally appropriate. This is especially important in low-income urban areas where indoor exploration space may be limited.

Lsantilli/Fotolia

If you give toddlers an activity that is designed to be used in a certain way, they are sure to try a dozen other ways to use it; they are not interested in outcomes or products

Independence and Interdependence

Newborn babies are faced with two major tasks: (1) to become independent individuals, and (2) to establish connections with others. The parents' job is to help their children with these tasks. Most parents focus more on one task than the other. Some even ignore one and leave its accomplishment almost to chance (Rogoff, 2003).

European American parents, developmentalists, and researchers focus on *independence* and individuality, which is also the focus of this chapter (Copple & Bredekamp, 2009; Copple, Bredekamp, & Gonzalez-Mena, 2009). Parents from other cultures are more concerned about their children's ability to create and maintain strong connections. These parents have a different view of practically everything because of their focus on *interdependence,* or mutual dependence, instead of independence.

Parents whose primary goal is to establish and keep connections may have more concern about their children's identity as a family member and little concern about teaching their children self-help skills (Brunson Day, 2010). For example, self-feeding may be postponed because feeding is a time in which connections are nourished. They may continue spoon-feeding long past infancy, into toddlerhood and beyond. This practice can get them in trouble if their child enters child care or other types of toddler- or parent-education programs. Teachers may be shocked when an almost-three-year-old sits down at breakfast the first day and waits to be fed. Parents can be quite surprised and disappointed when they learn of a program's policy on self-help skills.

Although parents who stress independence look down on the idea of "coddling" children, to the parent focused on making connections there's nothing negative about doing things for children, even things they are capable of doing for themselves. These parents see no reason to keep from prolonging babyhood and continuing the closeness. Their attitude makes sense if you understand their goal. They worry about too much independence, so they try to discourage it. Independent-minded parents have the opposite worry. They fear that if they don't encourage independence, their children will remain dependent on them, maybe forever!

Parents who stress connectedness expect their children to be independent as well, but they believe it will happen naturally. In fact, they worry that the drive for independence is too strong; that's why they have to work so hard to maintain connections. See Figure 3.2 for more information on these two approaches.

Self-Help Skills

Another behavior that indicates growing autonomy is the push for self-help skills. How the adults respond to this and to the exploring behavior will determine to

Goals for Families That Value Independence	Goals for Families That Value Interdependence (mutual dependence)
Child is an individual	Child is part of a group
Child is unique and special	Child learns to establish and keep connections
Child develops self-determination	Child learns to accept help graciously
Child becomes self-reliant	Child learns to help others

Figure 3.2   **Goals for families that value independence or interdependence; some families may be a blend of the two**

some extent the child's adult behavior. Children who aren't allowed to touch or to try things on their own get a message about their own capabilities. When restricted to an extreme, they can lose their curiosity, their willingness to take risks, and their drive to be independent of others and do things for themselves.

Consider the difference between these two scenes:

Hannah has unbuckled herself from her car seat and is demanding that she be allowed to climb out of the car by herself. "Hannah do it!" she proclaims loudly.

She has never done this before and nobody knows if she can do it safely or not. Her father, annoyed by her demands, steps back out of reach and says in a sarcastic tone, "Go ahead, little girl, show me how grown up you are!" True to her father's expectations she falls. Crying, she reaches for her father: He picks her up and comforts her. Brushing away her tears, he tells her that she's too little to do things by herself. He makes it clear that she needs him. Later he tells the story, and the whole family laughs at the little girl who is "too big for her britches." It becomes a family joke—the "Let Hannah do it" joke.

Now let's replay that scene:

Here's Hannah, unbuckled from her car seat, demanding, "Hannah do it!" Her father, instead of trying to prove to her that she is too young, decides to help her find out what she can do, but he will protect her while she's making the discovery. Instead of being sarcastic and stepping back, he says, "I'm here if you need my help." He stands far enough away that Hannah can maneuver but close enough to help her if she needs it. She does fine until the slick sole of her shoe slips on the door frame. She starts to fall and reaches out a hand. Her father grabs it and restores her balance. She lets go of his hand, holds on to the armrest, and climbs the rest of the way out safely. They both rejoice at her accomplishment. Later her father tells the family proudly, "Hannah climbed out of the car by herself today!"

Consider the difference in the messages of the two scenes. In scene 1: "You're too uppity and you need a good lesson. When you learn it, you'll know that you're too young to try things on your own." In scene 2, the father encouraged self-help but provided the protection needed for Hannah to be successful. The Hannah of scene 2 sees her father as a facilitator of her independence; the Hannah of scene 1 does not.

When independence is a strong cultural priority, the first stirrings of it prompt adults to begin to encourage and facilitate it. However, in some cultures, *interdependence* is the priority, and signs of independence may trigger a push on the part of the adult to work harder to promote the cultural goal. For example, in Japan some parents find their children too independent from the start, so they begin right away giving lessons in dependence. Teachers of toddlers are concerned about children feeling part of the group more than those children seeing themselves as independent individuals. Examples in Tobin's research show the teachers stepping back and letting the group solve a problem with an individual child instead of intervening. The teachers' behavior relates to their priority of individual children gaining a sense of belonging to the group (Tobin, Hsueh, & Karasawa, 2009). They want to help children see themselves as connected, not separate.

Promoting interdependence isn't the same in all cultures. Tobin's work shows a difference between Japan and China, for example. And, of course, every family in either of those countries isn't the same. This is a matter of themes and variations on the themes. When interdependence is a goal and adults see children begin to assert themselves by pushing aside adult help, it's possible that the lessons in

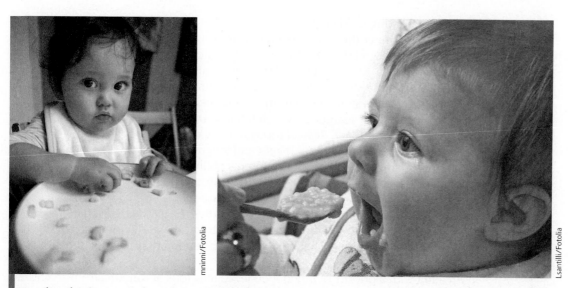

Families that focus on independence might encourage their children to feed themselves; families that focus on interdependence might spoon-feed their children

interdependence will intensify, especially if the specific objective is to teach children to accept help graciously.

Self-Feeding.   Some adults have different priorities for toddlers. Self-feeding, in particular, is not a priority for everybody. For some, the goal for children is learning to help others rather than helping oneself. Therefore, they may model helping skills by spoon-feeding children into the preschool years or beyond. They may justify their actions in a number of ways, including their desire to keep things neat and clean and not waste food, for example. When a professional and a parent see something like self-feeding from very different perspectives, arguments and angry feelings can result.

It's important as a family-support person that you not get into arguments about your different perspectives, but work on your relationship with the family and practice good communication skills so you can work out differences together. See Strategy Box 3.1 for some ideas about how to work through conflicts.

When Conflicts Arise: Strategies for Working with Families

- In the face of differing ideas about care practices, seek to establish common ground with individual families without simply imposing regulations, rules, and restrictions.
- The first step in looking for common ground is to suspend judgment. Make your goal to talk about the differences and see the family's point of view.
- Develop appreciation for contrasting patterns of care and understand that they need not be mutually exclusive.
- Aim for consensus in the face of conflicts and differences in perception.
- If you are feeling highly emotional about a particular issue, do some self-reflection to understand why this is a particular "hot button" for you. Gaining insights into your personal issues may help you better understand the family's perspective.

Toileting.   Toileting toddlers is another area where values of independence and interdependence can collide. Just as no culture produces adults who are unable to feed themselves, no matter how late they start, no culture produces adults unable to toilet themselves. But the approach and the timing can be quite different.

When most child development specialists and early childhood professionals discuss toileting, they consider it from the independence perspective. Their advice is to watch for signs of readiness, which fall into three general categories: physical, intellectual, and emotional. *Physical readiness* means the ability to hold on and let go. A first sign is when children go for longer and longer periods with a dry diaper. Physical readiness also is determined by children's ability to handle their own clothing—pulling down pants, for example. A sign of *intellectual readiness* is when children tell the adult *after* eliminating or indicate in other ways that they are aware and can communicate what is happening with their own bodies. *Emotional readiness* comes when children show a willingness to use a potty or a toilet instead of diapers. The timing for these signs varies with each individual, but in general they seldom appear before the second birthday.

An adult with a priority of interdependence may look at toileting from an entirely different point of view (Gonzalez-Mena, 2013). This person won't wait for a child to reach the age of two but may start when the child is as young as a few months; some may even start at birth, as they try to "catch" the baby and hold him or her over a potty. Readiness takes on a whole different meaning when the goal is interdependence. The KidsHealth website gives information about how the toileting process works, which can be enlightening to those who worry that this approach can have harmful side effects.

Just a few years ago this idea of considering using a potty before two or three years of age was not considered appropriate by most European-Americans and their pediatricians. Times are changing! A new trend toward early toileting shows the idea of moving toward eliminating diapers in infancy is growing. Instead of being considered "old fashioned" or "foreign," it's becoming the latest thing for some European-American parents. An article in *Twins* magazine by Kahwaty (2006) explains not only how to toilet-train a baby, but how to train two of them at once. The article points out that the United States is a "diaper culture" so babies using potties is a "foreign idea." The trend even has a name—infant potty training (IPT) or elimination communication (EC)—and at least one website that is referred to as DiaperFreeBaby. Of course, the research starting way back with Freud and his psychosexual theory indicates that toilet training using the approach described by these articles and websites is harmful. But one has only to look at the context of Freud's time, the society, the culture, attitudes toward sex and children, and so forth to see the kinds of influences that brought Freud to his conclusions. Another consideration to examine is the fact that his patients needed therapy. No one studied the people who didn't need therapy.

Professionals in the United States frown on training children during the first year, partly because in the past this approach has sometimes been associated with using harsh methods. It is important to recognize that toilet training differences can be cultural—or not—and that harshness is not necessarily a part of the process. The *Twins* article warns against using either rewards or punishment or even showing disappointment if the methods aren't successful. The article stresses that the adult should be relaxed and not have an opinion about whether the child goes or not.

Here's how toilet training using a conditioning method works. Timing is crucial. Sometimes the adult can predict based on the baby's regularity. "Time to hold her over the potty," says the adult periodically. Also, the adult learns to read subtle body messages that indicate the baby is about to wet or defecate. The baby learns to let the adult know, and the adult trains the baby to let go at a signal—usually a shoosh or a whistling sound. It's truly amazing to a teacher whose only experience is with toddlers to see how young babies with the help of an adult can manage dry diapers most of the time.

"It's the adult who's trained, not the baby!" is a common reaction to this interdependence approach. Teachers who use the "readiness"-approach rather than the "catch them" approach are sometimes critical of those who wait—and vice versa. Yet each method can work well for the adults and children who are using it. Both approaches eventually result in children who are able to handle all of their own toileting.

Toileting can become difficult when the child perceives that his or her autonomy is being usurped and who then fights back. Some children even feel that the adult is depriving them of something that is rightfully theirs—their body products! The resulting power struggle can be ugly and its effects long-lasting. Some children with an unfortunate toileting history may be left with big control issues that pop up in a variety of arenas. But don't assume that every family who believes in toileting before the first year uses harshness or force.

When a difference between toileting approaches becomes apparent, it is important for the professional to set aside assumptions and judgments and talk about the differences until each party understands the other.

Working with parents around differences in ideas about toileting can be difficult and cause conflicts. Review Strategy Box 3.1 for ideas on approaching a conflict with a family. And always keep the relationship in mind when you enter a conversation about differences. Your first priority should be to keep the relationship intact, if you already have one, or to build a relationship if this family is new. Listen to them!

> ▶ Watch this video to see an early childhood teacher having a conference with a parent about her child using the toilet. Do you think this scenario is focused on toilet training or toilet learning?

A Sense of Possession

It is important to note that not all cultures are object-oriented to the same extent and that not all regard personal possessions as important (Rogoff, 2003). In a culture that does prize personal possessions, a sense of ownership and its counterpart—a willingness to share those possessions—become important developmental steps. What many adults of this culture don't realize is that the one must come before the other. Without a firm sense of possession, children can't truly understand the concept of sharing.

There's quite a difference between the infant who doesn't

Without a firm sense of possession, children can't truly understand the concept of sharing

Alexey Losevich/Shutterstock

have a sense of possession and the toddler who does. Most of us have seen babies receiving gifts that they have no feeling for or interest in. The adults have the concept of ownership—the baby doesn't. That picture is a contrast to a young toddler holding a toy as far out of reach as possible and screaming "Me! Mine!" at an advancing playmate. At that age, the phrase "possession is nine-tenths of the law" applies. It isn't usually about ownership with young toddlers. In other words, the child who has the toy in hand is defending the right to hold it (or play with it) rather than thinking about who it really belongs to. Most of us early care and education teachers have seen a child make a big fuss about preventing someone from taking a toy only to walk away and discard it in a very short time. It's about having momentary control of the toy and resisting giving up control.

The immediate adult inclination in this situation is to rush in with a lesson on sharing. However, it's a little too soon for the lesson to be truly effective. At this point the conflict between the two children over a toy is more a momentary power issue than anything else, and there are feelings on both sides. An effective way to intervene in this situation is to reflect the feelings of both parties rather than to discuss issues of sharing or fairness. If you get good at handling these kinds of conflicts, you provide a model for parents who might get more heavy handed about resolving the situation.

For example, here's a scene of an adult helping two-year-olds who want the same doll. Notice the emphasis on feelings:

Olivia is triumphantly holding a rag doll in her arms. Jacob is standing near her, crying his eyes out. An adult is squatting beside them.

"You both want the doll. Olivia has it," says the adult in a calm matter-of-fact voice.

Jacob sits down on the floor and screams in response to the adult's words.

"I see how unhappy you are, Jacob," says the adult.

Olivia flaunts the doll in front of Jacob's face, saying again, firmly, "Mine!"

Jacob grabs for the doll, connects, and takes it away out of reach. Olivia is the one screaming now.

"Jacob has the doll now," says the adult, announcing the action rather than making any judgment about it. Then the adult reflects the feelings. "You don't like it when he grabs things from you. You can tell him 'No!'"

Olivia screams "No!" at Jacob's departing back. A moment later Jacob drops the doll to pick up a cloth book that is lying at his feet. Olivia starts for the dropped doll, then changes her mind and grabs a page of the book, yelling, "Mine!" Jacob starts to cry.

The adult says, "You don't like that, Jacob! You don't like it when she grabs things. Tell her 'No!'"

A little older toddler may be just beginning to get the concept of ownership. She may be starting to see herself as a person with possessions. She needs to grasp that idea fully before she can understand the idea of sharing. She'll just harbor a grudge if you take the toy away and insist that she share it. Anger and grudges are not involved in the true spirit of sharing, which is the lesson most adults want to get across when they teach the behavior.

The lessons about ownership are a little different and adults can handle them differently. If a toddler comes in to the program with a beloved teddy bear that gives her a sense of security, ownership then may become an issue. Some discussion with parents at the beginning can help caregivers figure out

> She'll just harbor a grudge if you take the toy away and insist that she share it. Anger and grudges are not involved in the true spirit of sharing, which is the lesson most adults want to get across when they teach the behavior.

what to do. Partly it depends on the ages and stages of the group plus the teachers' ability to explain the situation to the other children. If that doesn't work, there is a challenge to protect the child's possession somehow—maybe on a shelf where the child can see it but others can't reach it. None of this is easy, but there are important lessons to be learned by children who grow up in a society where personal possessions are important. They begin learning them in toddlerhood.

In the meantime, learning to share what belongs to the program and is to be used by everybody is very important. That's one advantage in toddlers spending time in early care and education programs. Look at Olivia and Jacob who are now old enough to discuss sharing and ownership with each other.

> They are painting side by side at an easel. Olivia reaches for the brush that Jacob has in his hand—the one that goes in the green paint. "That's mine," says Jacob firmly.
> "No, it's not, it's the school's," says Olivia, "and I need it."
> "I'm using it," says Jacob.
> Olivia continues to reach for the brush and grabs hold of it so Jacob can't paint. "Stop that!" says Jacob.
> "I need the brush!" insists Olivia.
> "Can't you wait until I'm through?" asks Jacob.
> "No," says Olivia.
> "I have an idea," says Jacob. "There's another green brush on the other side of the easel. Let's get that one."
> Olivia lets go long enough for him to reach to the other side and retrieve the brush and the paint container. "Here," he says, handing it to her.
> "Thanks," she replies.
> Later in the same year, at the same easel, Olivia asks Jacob for the brush he is using. He says to her, "I'm almost finished. You can have it in a minute." She waits until he is finished, uses it, and then gives it back to him.

These two have learned the behaviors of sharing and also the spirit. They have experienced the benefits. They understand the concept of possession and ownership. In cultures where private ownership is not an issue and personal possessions do not play a large part in people's lives, this sequence might be very different.

 Check Your Understanding 3.1

Click here to check your understanding of the Signs of Developing Autonomy.

DEALING WITH ISSUES OF POWER AND CONTROL

The behaviors discussed—saying no, exploring the world, learning self-help skills, and gaining a sense of possession—all have to do with issues of power and control. Just as the *infant* came to experience a sense of power through signaling his needs and satisfying them by means of the adults around him, so does the *toddler* need to experience a sense of power through these typical toddler behaviors. Both are on their way to eventually becoming what Maslow called *self-actualized* (Maslow, 1954).

An adult can do much to facilitate this empowerment and the controls that need to go with it to keep the toddler and others safe and secure.

Set Up a Developmentally Appropriate Environment

Not all families have the kind of living conditions that allow them to set up a developmentally appropriate environment, but when they see the one in the early care

Outdoor environments set up for autonomous children provide freedom for exploration with few prohibitions

Pavla Zakova/Fotolia

and education program, they may get ideas about how to make their living situation a bit more developmentally appropriate. Not all communities have outdoor spaces set up for children that are developmentally appropriate, either, though it seems that progress has been made from years past. Such environments provide freedom for exploration with few prohibitions. Think of the difference between a toddler in a playroom set up for her versus spending an afternoon in shopping carts at a grocery store and a mall or an hour in her great aunt's living room, trying to keep her hands off all the precious and fragile treasures sitting around on display. Yes, toddlers need to learn that sometimes they have to sit still and also that there are some things they can't touch. When adults understand toddlers' need to explore and manipulate objects, they can limit these lessons to a few times when it's important and spend the rest of the time teaching them that it's good to move about and that there are many things in the world that they *can* touch.

Let's look at some of the components of effective environments for a group of toddlers. Defining the particular spaces are important. Let's say there is a fairly large area, which is appropriate for the number of toddlers in the group. In that space, the play area should be defined and set off from kitchen facilities (if any), sleeping area, and diapering and toileting area. The eating area can be part of the play space if the toddlers eat at low tables, rather than highchairs. Those tables can serve double duty—be used for table toys between eating times. The play areas should contain low shelves with just the right number of play materials within reach. The right number can be decided by the staff—enough for each child to have a choice, but not so many that picking up becomes a dreaded chore. Eliminating as much chaos as possible is a good goal when thinking about arranging environments for toddlers.

During the day, the children should have a balance of soft and hard materials and spaces. They should also have a chance for some seclusion when they need it—places to crawl into and be alone or with one other child. They also need some open space to move around. Ideally the environment includes an outdoor area that the children can have access to during free play times. That may be the area where they have the most space to move about in. Play objects, those indoors and those outdoors, should provide for both fine motor exploration and manipulation. There should also be some play objects that encourage large motor experiences—moving around. Any toddlers who have special needs should be accommodated when thinking of how to arrange the environment and what to put into it. For example, a child lacking visual capabilities will only feel safe to move around if the furniture stays in the same place, once he learns where everything is.

When toddlers spend their time in an environment that is appropriate for their age and encourages exploration, they won't be faced with so many *no*'s. If they don't have to hear the word *no*, they may decrease their own usage of the word. It is worth encouraging parents to think about what kind of environment says "Yes!" to toddlers and then arrange things so that where toddlers spend their time affirms their developmental needs. At this stage they touch, explore, try things out, and use their bodies to learn about the world. Their natural inclination is to climb, push, poke, prod, and perform a huge variety of other movements (Copple & Bredekamp, 2009; Copple, Bredekamp, & Gonzalez-Mena, 2011; Gonzalez-Mena, 2013). They need a safe place to do all this—a place where they feel empowered rather than prohibited. Often parents can see the advantages of a developmentally appropriate environment without your needing to point it out to them. For more information about creating environments for children, visit the website of Let the Children Play. It includes photographs of beautiful learning spaces in Reggio Emilia–inspired preschools.

▶ Watch this video to see some of the ways that infants and toddlers are supported in their environment. What do you see that supports literacy development?

Appreciate Play

Children gain power through playing. They play with themselves, other people, and objects. Playing is a primary way that toddlers learn and what they learn grows more and more impressive as the research gets increasingly sophisticated (Gopnik, 2009; Hannford, 2005; Jones & Cooper, 2006; Kallo & Balog, 2005; Reifel & Sutterby, 2009; Walker & Gopnik 2014). A baby who discovers her hand in the first year of life (called *hand regard*) is playing with herself. She stares at her hand, wiggles her fingers, and turns the hand around to get a different perspective on it. Some children find their own bodies endlessly fascinating. Later this same child will take a crayon in her hand and enjoy the feeling of circling her arm round and round. She doesn't care if the marks are on paper or on the wall, which is where they'll be if no one is monitoring her. The marks aren't the point of interest—the body movement is. Eventually the marks themselves become fascinating as she watches herself create them. By toddlerhood children who have a chance to explore objects show greater perception and knowledge of those objects and what they can do. In the past, child development research concluded that toddlers' perceptual and mental abilities were less developed than the recent research shows. For example, according to Gopnik, very young children have much greater understanding of cause and effect than most people realize (Gopnik 2009, Walker & Gopnik 2014).

Children explore and play with objects; they also play with people. They play with adults and with each other, though the classic research by Parten (1932) labeled toddlers as mainly playing *parallel* to each other rather than *with* each other. An example of parallel play as described and named by Parten is in the sandbox when two 2-year-olds sit side by side, each shoveling sand and talking, but not paying obvious attention to each other. It may seem as though each is living in his own world, but when you listen, you see that they are influenced by each other's play. They may not interact, but one picks up on what the other is saying or doing and incorporates it into his own play. A short period of observation in a child care program shows that parallel play is not so common today among toddlers who have been in group care and are used to interacting with each other. It definitely wasn't so at the Pikler Institute in Budapest, where groups of children spent their first three years together in residential care. Those children played

Watch this video to see two toddlers interact with each other and with toys. Notice how hard they are working on language to express their ideas.

interactively as young toddlers and even as babies (Gonzalez-Mena, 2004). Children who are in stable group situations where they have peers in their daily lives go way beyond parallel play into true interaction. They talk to each other, carrying on a back-and-forth conversation (Wittmer, 2012).

Toddlers play with things. Anything within reach becomes a toy, as children reach out to learn about their world and the objects in it. They use all their senses. It may not seem important to adults to know how things taste and to discover textures with their tongues. For babies and young toddlers, however, mouthing is a natural way to learn about any object they can get their lips around. That's why it is so important that young children be in a safe environment where they won't get hurt in their explorations. As they grow, their exploration of objects becomes more sophisticated, and they learn how things work and what they can do with them. In a consumer-oriented culture, many adults place a high priority on toys and see them as educational. Even newborns are given toys and encouraged to touch, look at, and hold them.

The typical child care program today relies on toys and other objects as part of its curriculum, and many programs have an abundance of things in their environments. These things may be recognizable, commercially manufactured toys, or they may be "found objects" such as margarine tubs, egg cartons, and lids from frozen orange juice containers. Art supplies and materials include such items as wood scraps from a carpenter shop and homemade play dough consisting of flour, water, and salt (for toddlers old enough to play with it and not eat it). Construction materials made for children are also usually present in early childhood programs and other toddler settings, including those used for therapy and for parent education, ranging from wooden blocks to plastic pieces that link together. Although not literally objects, sand and water are considered educational materials in most programs. You might want to consider the messages you give with your choice of toys. The temptation for many families is to shower their young children with toys. The marketing of toys often emphasizes their educational value, but almost none of those claims have research behind them. Consider that found items and simple substances (such as sand and water—just mentioned) give children more opportunities to explore and interact with the play materials. If you work in a toddler setting, parents can learn from you, just by observing.

Play has roots in imitation. From birth babies imitate what they see. If someone sticks his tongue out, even a newborn baby is likely to do the same. The adult is usually delighted at the baby's response to almost anything he does, and so begins a give-and-take sequence of playful interaction. The socialization aspects of this kind of play are obvious. The child is learning to take turns, which will become useful later when the baby has enough language to take part in real conversations. At the beginning the "conversations" are nonverbal and playful.

At first babies only imitate when they can see what they are imitating. By about age two, the typically developing child has moved from imitating only things he sees to playing pretend in creative and imaginative ways. Jean Piaget (1954, 1962), a pioneer in explaining cognitive development, had an explanation for the growing ability to pretend. The Swiss theorist and researcher explained that the shift occurs when children are able to make "internal representations" of things, actions, behaviors, and patterns. Piaget's stages of cognitive development have guided several generations of early childhood educators to understand more about how the intellect unfolds. The term *internal representations* means the child can hold images in her mind, and it is this ability that allows her to pretend. Using imagination, a block becomes a telephone and the child calls Daddy at work. Imaginary coffee comes out of toy coffee pots, and play dough rolled and molded becomes food. Although none of this may look *intellectual*, it is indeed an aspect of cognitive development. It is also vitally connected to self-development and socialization. This may not be information that is important to pass on to parents, but it is good for early educators to have a grasp of the unfolding of play and an appreciation of the benefits.

In his book *The Power of Play* (2007), David Elkind, child development expert, makes a strong case for spontaneous, imaginative activities rather than passive electronic entertainment and "educational" toys, games, and activities. He worries that free time and lazy periods of unstructured play are endangered species.

Encourage Self-Help Skills

Encourage children to do for themselves what they are capable of; don't do for them what they can do for themselves. This bit of advice comes from an author with a cultural priority on independence and may not apply to those from cultures who see early independence as a threat to interdependence. When independence is a priority, teaching self-help skills as a way of empowerment starts in infancy as the adult includes the child as a full partner in caregiving routines. For instance, diapering is a teamwork affair, and the baby is treated as a whole person worthy of respect, not just as a bottom that must be tended to while the top half is being entertained with something else (Gerber, 1979).

This attitude of teamwork makes the toddler feel a little less rebellious because the adult is sometimes seen as a partner rather than as an adversary. It isn't a cure-all for rebellion, of course, because the struggle to defy the adult is a mark of the toddler stage.

When children are old enough to eat solid foods, giving finger food allows them to practice getting food to their mouths, even if they still need to be spoon-fed. And before long they will want to take over completely. That means the adults have to put up with messy eating for a while until children develop the skills to eat neatly. Children can learn to dress themselves at an early age if encouraged to do so. The learning process starts with undressing. Even a baby can pull off a sock that is sticking out from her toe. Setting it up so it is easy for her is encouraging self-help skills. Putting up with a less-than-perfect performance is also encouraging. Perfectionism on the part of the adult tends to discourage young children's self-help skills. It may be hard to explain that to parents with perfectionist tendencies, but you can demonstrate it without making it a huge issue. Remember that modeling is a powerful teaching tool, with adults as well as with children.

Give Choices

Help toddlers feel powerful by laying out options instead of giving a single directive. Instead of saying, "Get in that bathtub now!" offer an alternative such as, "Do you want to take a bath before supper or after?" When after supper comes and the child still balks, you can say, "After you get in, you can choose between the boats or the blocks to play with." And if the child still balks and it's time for a showdown, you can still give a choice: "Do you want to climb in by yourself, or should I put you in?" This way the child still feels empowered, and you are able to do what you perceive he needs to do. You're not being wishy-washy. The child *will* take a bath, but he has some choices about when, with what, and how he will enter the bathtub.

This is a culturally specific approach based on the concept of life as a series of choices. When you regard learning to make choices as important, you give children practice when they are young so that as they grow up they have had experience with making choices and living with the consequences. In cultures that don't see life in this same way and don't regard learning to make choices as important, giving toddlers choices doesn't make as much sense.

Speaking of choices, a family-centered program also gives choices to families—what kind of support they need, what kinds of activities they want to engage in, and how they want to be involved are just some examples. Giving families choices is an important part of the Parent Services Project. Lee (2006) discusses the approach of family-centered care, which finds out what the families want rather than giving them what the program perceives they need. When teachers try to help by putting on programs that are poorly attended by families, that's a clue that those families were not included in the decision-making process. When parents decide for themselves what parent involvement means, the program has much more success. Parents can even run their own activities rather than having staff put them on for them. Some activities can be a joint effort of staff and parents. One way to increase parent involvement is to offer a menu of services based on what families say they want and need. The Parent Services Project website is a good resource for ways to support families.

Provide Control

Provide the control toddlers need. Here are two scenes that illustrate that principle. Let's go back to Olivia and Jacob, the two-year-olds. In this first scene the adult doesn't provide control for Olivia. Watch what happens. Let's call this adult A.

> They are playing happily and the phone rings. The adult, A., turns her back to answer it, and Jacob grabs the toy Olivia has in her hand. Olivia, who hasn't learned to express her feelings in words yet (though the adults have been working on that) expresses her anger and frustration by sinking her sharp little baby teeth into Jacob's arm. Jacob lets out a yell, and A. comes running. She scolds Olivia, telling her it isn't nice to bite, then puts her in a time-out chair. Olivia keeps getting up, so A. continually puts her back, scolding her each time. Finally she hugs her, lets her up, and warns her not to bite again.
>
> Later that afternoon, when Olivia is tired and a little lonely for her mother and A. is busy with another child, Olivia walks up to Jacob and bites his arm again. She remembers the stir it caused this morning, and she enjoys a repeat performance this afternoon. However, she feels vaguely uncomfortable because she knows that she should control that urge.

> Contrast that scene with this one. This provider is called B.

> Olivia and Jacob are playing together when the doorbell rings. B. knows that Olivia has the urge to bite when she gets frustrated, so rather than taking the chance of leaving her alone with Jacob for even a minute, she takes Olivia with her to open the door.
>
> Later that morning, when Olivia and Jacob are playing together, Olivia gets frustrated. She makes a move toward Jacob's arm; before she can connect, B.'s hand covers her mouth gently. "I know you are unhappy, but I won't let you bite Jacob," she says in a clear tone that doesn't imply judgment—just fact. "You can bite this teething ring," she adds, "or this plastic toy." She offers the choice. Olivia grabs the teething ring and bites down hard. "You really are upset," affirms B.

Adult B. wisely provides the control that Olivia lacks at this age. She prevents the biting from occurring instead of dealing with it afterward in a way that rewards Olivia with extra attention. She also redirects the energy so Olivia can still get her teeth into something, but it's a teething ring instead of an arm.

Of course, it isn't realistic to assume that an adult will be there 100 percent of the time. Even with careful vigilance, Olivia might get her teeth into Jacob sometime. If that were to happen, B. would then deal with the situation as a failure to control on her part—not as badness on Olivia's part. After all, Olivia is using her mouth to express her feelings in the only way she knows how. She lacks control—the control that it's up to the adult to provide.

If the bite occurs, B. responds in much the same way she responded over the toy-grabbing incident earlier in this chapter. She approaches both children, modeling gentleness by touching them both lightly and lovingly. She says, "That really hurts, Jacob." To Olivia she says, "Jacob is unhappy because you hurt him." As she says the words, she touches gently the red place on Jacob's arm. Then she touches the same place on Olivia's arm. After the demonstration of gentleness and the words indicating the feelings, she deals with any first aid needed. She is careful not to give either child a great deal of the kind of extra attention that hooks children on either the victim or the aggressor role. She doesn't turn her back on Olivia and say, "Oh, poor little Jacob, let's put some ice on that bite—poor baby," because she knows that ignoring Olivia may make Jacob feel it's worth it to get bitten in order to enjoy this lavish sympathy. And Olivia is not left with the uncomfortable feeling of being ignored while realizing that she doesn't have the control she needs to keep from hurting someone. Being out of control is as scary for the child experiencing it as it is for the victim.

The adult B. approach provides excellent modeling for parents. It may require some explanation for parents to really understand what B. is doing and why. Of course, there isn't always time to explain everything one does, but squeezing time in to talk to parents is an important part of the job.

Set Limits

Think about how all the adult behaviors described in this section are aimed at socializing very young children to get along with others, learn to live in a group, and eventually become part of a larger community. Setting limits and enforcing them is part of this long-term process with the goal of good community members and productive citizens. Setting limits and enforcing them empowers children by giving them freedom within those limits. You can think of limits as a fence around a pasture. The horse is free to graze within the fence. Without the fence his freedom would have to be limited by a rope, by vigilance, or by training—none of which gives the freedom of the fence.

Limits for toddlers work the same way. The limits may be environmental boundaries, such as a barricade across the stairs, a lock on the toilet lid, or a gate on the driveway. Or they may be human boundaries, such as consistently taking a child off a counter he insists on climbing up on, stopping a child from throwing toys, or holding a kicking child who threatens to hurt others.

Children will test limits until they find that they hold. The child locked out of the bathroom pounds on the door, jiggles the doorknob, and tries to poke something into the keyhole. He gives up when the physical barrier holds. Human boundaries are the same way. The child may continue to climb on the counter, and if the adult gives up and quits stopping him, he gets the message that this isn't a real limit—it doesn't hold if he's persistent enough. If the child is allowed to throw toys sometimes, he doesn't know there's a limit. His test shows that it doesn't hold up. It's hard to have the patience to watch a child continually test the limits. It's tempting to just give in—but that makes it worse the next time. It's good for parents to watch how a toddler teacher handles setting limits. It is quite possible that, as children, many parents got a spanking when they pushed a limit; they may think that this is the only way to handle limit testing. With patience and skill, however, a professional can show them another way that eventually works. Notice that in this section and the previous one, alternatives to time out and spanking were demonstrated. Some family members have a limited repertoire when it comes to guiding behavior. Professionals can open their eyes to a wider variety of approaches to take.

It also helps to understand that to empower a child and provide security at the same time, it is necessary to set limits and hold to them. Because toddlers are persistent and are still discovering things about the world, you can also expect those limits to be tested until the toddler is satisfied that they're firm. The testing makes sense if you understand what's going on. If you don't, it seems as if the child is just trying to make you unhappy with his persistently unacceptable behavior. Don't get unhappy—just outpersist him! Show parents what you are doing and explain if necessary.

Ashley and Emily

Ashley is 17 and has an 18-month-old, Emily, who is driving her crazy. Ashley has just started in a young parent program that allows her to continue her high school education. Emily is taken care of at the school in a portable building that has been set up for infants and toddlers. Although Emily protests at being left in the morning, which really bothers Ashley, she quickly becomes contented while playing with the other toddlers. Ashley misses her, so she pops in briefly between her classes—which almost always results in another crying spell when she has to leave again. That annoys Ashley. Why can't she just come and go without all this fuss!

Whenever she is around Emily, the child clings to her, making it impossible for her to even walk from one place to another. Ashley doesn't like this.

Ashley also doesn't like it when the child care teachers assure her that Emily was fine all day and didn't miss her at all. That doesn't feel good. And she doesn't like the way Emily is beginning to hang around one of the teachers and even hugs her good-bye when they leave at the end of the day. Ashley wonders whether Emily still loves her when she shows affection toward the teacher.

Some of Emily's other behaviors bother Ashley as well. She doesn't like the defiant look Emily gets in her eye when Ashley tells her to do something. That makes Ashley feel angry, and she gets just as stubborn as Emily has become.

Sometimes she feels like hitting Emily, but she talks about that feeling in her parenting class, where she is learning a variety of ways to guide Emily's behavior. Somehow talking about hitting helps her control herself, so she doesn't do it. She's seen another child in the center whose mother got carried away with spanking and ended up abusing her daughter. It was pretty awful, both how the child looked and what happened to her mother. She ended up losing her baby. Ashley couldn't stand to lose Emily, and she cries at the thought that she might ever hurt her. So she is careful to never spank her, no matter what.

Another thing that bothers Ashley is how dirty Emily gets. She insists on doing things for herself—like feeding herself. She isn't very neat! And the child care staff doesn't seem to understand how important it is to Ashley that Emily look like a sweet little doll. They let her feed herself, which means that often her clothes get messed up. Sometimes Ashley comes in and finds Emily in the center's old beat-up clothes, because they ran out of changes for her. Ashley doesn't like seeing her like this.

And the sand! Can't they understand how hard it is for Ashley when Emily gets sand in her hair? It seems that whenever they go out in the yard, Emily ends up with her head full of sand. It's a lot of trouble to wash that out and redo her hair. Besides, Emily *hates* to have her hair washed and puts up quite a fight.

This is all so different from when Emily was younger and she used to just lie around and laugh and look cute. It was a lot easier then. But this is a different stage, and it isn't so easy!

Ashley knew that none of this would be easy when she decided to keep Emily. She had lots of warnings about the life of a teen mother. But with her family's support and the help of the center staff, she's making it. And Emily is an important part of her life!

> ✔ **Check Your Understanding 3.2**
>
> Click here to check your understanding of Dealing with Issues of Power and Control.

COPING WITH LOSS AND SEPARATION

Separation issues start in infancy and continue into toddlerhood and beyond; they are never handled once and for all. The infant who has learned to sleep alone may well become the toddler who, because new fears arise, balks at going to bed and staying there. Even though a toddler copes very well with separation and independence during waking periods, she may resist sleep because she must give up the control she has. Lack of control can be very scary because it means that coping mechanisms don't work in the same way as they do during waking periods. In addition, dreams, which can also create fear, enter in. Parents and child care teachers plus other professionals who recognize this fact will be more understanding when children develop sleeping problems at home or react with difficulty to sleeping away from home.

Saying good-bye can feel like a big loss to a child; with adult support, children learn to cope with separation

Taking Separation in Small Steps

It is easier for children if they first experience separation in small steps. Sleeping alone is one of these steps, though all families don't agree with babies sleeping by themselves. Having a babysitter or being away from the person(s) they are attached to for short periods are other examples of steps of separation. Taking these steps may be questioned by some families who are not anxious for children to learn to separate from them at a young age; however, the reality of child care and other early education programs for very young children is that they will experience separation.

With a succession of periods away from the parent(s), either at home or away from home, children come to trust that the attachment holds and that they will be reunited.

Be aware of the dangers of giving children more to cope with than they can handle. If parents feel a need to take an extended vacation away from their child, they should realize the possible effects of a prolonged separation during the toddler period. Obviously, if the child has someone else he or she is attached to, the effects of such a separation won't be as serious as if the only person or two people in the world the child feels close to suddenly disappear for a few weeks. Such an interruption in attachment can be devastating to the child's sense of trust.

Some sudden and prolonged separations can't be helped, of course. If the child must undergo an extensive hospitalization, he or she will get through it better if parents stay at the hospital with him or her or at least visit frequently. Visiting isn't the perfect solution because of the continual anguish of painful good-byes; it's better if a parent can stay with the child. When this isn't possible, visiting is preferable to nothing, even though parents may be tempted to cut down on their visits because of the pain their departures cause the child. But children who feel deserted can experience depression, according to the research of John Bowlby (2000a, 2000b), who studied the effects of long-term separations in childhood.

A different kind of separation has impacted many families in the past few years—that of military duty overseas in war zones. Separation during war is a major issue with accompanying doubts, fears, and loneliness. The reunion when the missing parent comes back may turn from joy to stress as the returning parent tries to fit in again to the family that has learned to get along with one parent. The child or children may be in a different stage of development from when the returning parent last saw them. The family may be quite distant from relatives or friends due to the frequent relocations military families experience. This is a case when support systems and special intervention may be needed to help families build on their strengths (Williams & Rose, 2007).

Entering Child Care

When a separation such as going into child care is on the horizon, it's best to prepare the child (Balaban, 2006; McCracken, 1986). Imagine being the child of a mother who has been with you day and night for the first two years. Your mother suddenly decides to go back to work, and one day she drives you to a strange place and leaves you there for the entire day. How would you feel?

It's far gentler if families can visit beforehand and can keep the first experiences short so the child gets to know the place and the people. By being left for only an hour or so in the beginning, the child learns that the parent will return after a time. If the day is gradually lengthened, the child gets used to it and it's not such a shock.

Helping Children Adjust.   Some children walk right into child care without batting an eye. They're so intrigued with the new setting that they forget their fears. Other children cling and suffer greatly. In this case, it helps if the parent can let the child make the decision to separate rather than peeling him off and walking out the door, leaving him screaming.

One program has a room for the use of parents whose children hesitate to leave them. The doorway just beyond the "separation room" is open and is filled with the sounds and sights of children playing, which serve to entice the child to leave the parent's side. Parents are asked to be patient about the separation process, and they're given some help and support to make it a healthy coping experience for both parent and child. Of course, everyone doesn't have the option of a slow departure. However, if this approach is proposed and the program promotes it, more families might find ways to ease their children into the new situations and relieve some of the separation upset.

When the good-byes come, it helps to make things predictable. Some parents prefer to sneak out and miss the protests from the child. When they do that—leave the child playing without saying good-bye—trust issues arise. Instead of feeling secure, the child is left with the feeling of never knowing when the parent is there or gone. How can the child feel any power in the world if there's no way to predict what will happen? Saying good-bye may bring tears and protests, but it's the open, honest way of helping the child understand what's happening. It may be hard to explain that to families, but it's worth it.

> Watch this video to see children and families enter preschool and then say good-bye. What strategies do you see the teachers using to support families during the good-bye transition?

Accepting Feelings. When strong feelings are a part of the good-byes, it's important to acknowledge and accept the feelings rather than distracting the child from them. If the early educator has leftover issues of separation and loss from childhood, it may be very hard for him or her to deal with the child's feelings. It's just too painful. If that's your problem, it's important to recognize how your own unresolved issues may be influencing your ability to deal with a child in the throes of a separation. Separation experiences remain with us—especially the unexpressed and unresolved feelings. Bringing these to awareness can help us cope with them in ways that are healthy for us and allow us to be available to the child who needs us.

Many adults who find separation painful because of their own experiences do whatever they can to distract the child and not acknowledge what he or she is feeling. Far better to put the child's feelings into words: "You're upset that your mother left you." It's also important to emit a sense of confidence that the child will be all right and that she will be reunited with the loved one. Don't go overboard, however. If you constantly reassure the child, she'll begin to wonder whether you're reassuring yourself because what you're saying is not true. Better to be empathetic about the feelings and reassuring without discounting them. Your confidence and empathetic acceptance of the child's feelings not only help the child, but give the parent some assurance as well that you know what you are doing and everything will be okay.

> When strong feelings are a part of the good-byes, it's important to acknowledge and accept the feelings rather than distracting the child from them.

It's also important to recognize that parents may have strong feelings about separation. It may hurt to leave their child with someone else. They may feel guilty. Some parents prolong good-byes because of their own feelings of ambiguity. These slow departures can be torture to everyone, especially if the child has shown willingness to be left but has second thoughts because of the way the parent is dragging his or her feet. In these situations, teachers sometimes have to help parents see how the child's feelings are affected by their reluctance to leave. Teachers need to support parents and accept their feelings in the same way they do with children, without supporting detrimental actions such as agonizing, lingering departures.

Helping Children Cope. Some children are comforted and reassured by what's called a *transition object*—some kind of comfort device, such as a stuffed animal or a favorite blanket. Having something from home that they're attached to provides a link between home and child care. Leaving something of the parents at child care can help, too. One child was comforted when his mother left her purse (she carried her wallet with her) because he figured if she forgot to come back for him, she'd at least remember her purse. He knew how important it was to her. Many parents are already aware of the value of transition objects to help separation—though they may not call them that.

Providing something to do that's compelling and interesting is a good technique for helping the child cope with feelings of loss. Often the child will migrate to an interesting activity or a friendly person after the pain of arrival is beginning to pass. Don't hurry this process of moving to an activity or other person, however. Give time for the feelings. There's a fine line between helping children cope with feelings and distracting them from those feelings. It is important that the feelings be accepted and acknowledged. It may also help the parent to know what you are doing and how you are using particular activities or play objects to help the child make the transition. It's always good to explain the problem with distraction, because some families may have never thought about the problem of moving a child away from what he or she is feeling.

In addition, allow the child to play out the feelings. Often you can see children over among the dolls or out in the sandbox, working through what's on their minds. This is a healthy way to deal with feelings that may be hard to express directly in words. You can also point out to parents what's happening—or listen while they point it out to you. The parent may have a greater understanding of the experience the child is playing out than you do. See Figure 3.3 for more tips on helping children cope with separation.

Check Your Understanding 3.3

Click here to check your understanding of Coping with Loss and Separation.

PARTNERING WITH FAMILIES OF TODDLERS

Just as you have been seeing examples of professionals partnering with toddlers, so have you been provided examples of how to partner with parents. Janis Keyser (2007) wrote a popular book on how to partner with parents. See Strategy Box 3.2 for more ideas of how to work with parents in a partnership way.

Working with Families Around Issues of Identity Development

Carol Brunson Day writes about how very young children in child care are developing an identity, which she defines as a "set of organized beliefs about themselves that influences how they behave in social settings." The toddler program is a social setting. Day

• Make the first visits short
• Support parents to be patient with the separation process
• Encourage parents to make time for a slow departure, not a prolonged one, but time enough for the child to settle in and then say good-bye
• Help parents create a predictable good-bye routine, that never includes sneaking out
• Acknowledge and accept feeling, rather than distracting a child from them
• Allow the child to have a transitional object from home to hold on to during good-bye
• Allow children to play out their feelings
• Recognize that children may resist sleep at nap time because it means giving up control

Figure 3.3   Helping children cope with loss and separation in child care

goes on to say that very young children in child care may also be learning that they belong to a particular group. How that group is regarded by others can impact their feelings about themselves. Their feelings are also influenced by how they perceive the other family members regard their own identity (Brunson Day, 2010, p2).

In other words, toddlers are busy figuring out who they are and where they belong. They are developing a sense of self. The goal of the toddler program should be to grow a relationship with families, a relationship in which you can discuss sensitively, with the each one, their ideas about what their toddler needs in

The goal of the toddler program should be to grow a relationship with families

terms of identity development. Part of this discussion may include the practices in your program. It may also include expectations for the toddler's behavior in that setting.

A word of caution here: If you are well-educated in child development and/or early care and education, you may not see how European-American culture is imbedded in what you have learned—in spite of the fact that child development theory is based on research. You may be the authority in your program, but all families may not regard the standard practices of the program as appropriate for their toddler. Of course, some may be very pleased that their child is learning to behave as others do in what is sometimes called "the mainstream culture." But others may have had the experience of children turning their back on the home culture (and language as well) as they enter the mainstream of the society. Most early childhood professionals who have been in the field for a long time know families where the children can no longer communicate with some family members because they have lost their home language. You may have had that experience yourself. To put it simply: Maintaining their children's ethnic identity and home language can be a struggle for some families. It is our job as professionals to recognize that issue and do what we can to understand just what each family in our programs wants for its children.

> Watch this video to hear Karen Nemeth discuss the importance of supporting home language in child care and in schools.
>
> www.youtube.com /watch?v=tBOPY0kCTk8

As you work to form partnerships with parents and other family members, it's important to understand perspectives that may be different from yours. For example, you may be allowing toddlers to express their feelings to you—an accepted practice in early childhood education. Parents may see that behavior as disrespectful to an elder. Here's another example: you may assume that the parent who brings the child is in charge of that child. That may be a wrong assumption. It may not be clear just who is in charge in any particular family. It may be a grandparent or other elder. Respecting varying degrees of status can be very important in the communication involved in developing relationships with family members.

Culture matters! The challenge for professionals in toddler programs is to help each child develop in ways that keep him or her attached to their family and culture. On the other hand, the family may see the program as a way of helping the child fit into the mainstream culture. They may see that it's their responsibility to insure that the child maintains and grows in the home culture. Only by developing a relationship with family members, can the professional understand who they are and what they want for their child.

Broadening Perspectives

While you are broadening your perspective in order to understand each family and its child's behavior, there are also lots of opportunities to help a parent broaden his or her perspective. Take the parent who thinks her child's personality is warped because the child is displaying a good deal of defiance and other kinds of negative behavior. You can offer up the information that you have about the stage of autonomy, which may help the parent see the behaviors in a slightly different light. If this is a first-time parent, she may not realize that children aren't toddlers forever. You can lend perspective the parent may not have. On the other hand, you may wonder why this child crawled under the table and refused to come out when the nurse came to give eye exams. The parent might tell you something you didn't know about the child's medical history and the painful procedures he had to go through for a long time. Maybe you didn't know that he had been hospitalized periodically. With this knowledge the extreme reaction makes more sense. In this case your perspective is broadened.

In conclusion, although you might have entered the early care and education profession because you love children, there is more to it! It's very important that, as a professional, you broaden your focus to embrace the family as well. You don't have to love them, but you do need to respect them as the most important people in their children's lives! For more information about supporting children and families, go to the website for the Early Head Start National Resource Center.

Check Your Understanding 3.4

Click here to check your understanding of Partnering with Families of Toddlers.

Strategy Box 3.2

Creating Partnerships with Families

- Work hard to create and maintain a relationship with each family. Part of it is everyday behavior—greeting family members by name every time you see them. Squeeze in conversations wherever you can.

- Recognize that demonstration is a strong teacher. This chapter offered examples of how early educators and other professionals can model behaviors for families to give them insights and expand their repertory of guidance approaches.

- Recognize that you can also learn from observing. If you encourage the parents to demonstrate for you how they do things, you may also gain insights and expand your knowledge and skills.

- Find ways to share power with the families even though you may have many barriers in the way, such as funding requirements, regulations, and other kinds of mandates.

SUMMARY

This chapter explored the variety of behaviors that toddlers show when they are developing autonomy. It gave signs of developing autonomy and offered ideas of how to work with parents around the issues that arise in this stage of development. Dealing with issues of power and control, what those behaviors look like, and what adults can do to work with the child was also explored. Coping with loss and separation can be a painful part of toddlerhood and again, information about how adults can help was included. An ongoing theme throughout the chapter was partnering with parents to support them and help them see that the toddler behaviors that may be considered difficult are part of an important developmental stage.

✔ QUIZ

Click here to check your understanding of Chapter 3, "Supporting Families with Autonomy-Seeking Youngsters."

FOR DISCUSSION

1. Do you agree that negativity, exploration, self-help skills, and a sense of possession are indeed signs of developing autonomy? What are some examples? Can you think of other signs?

2. Have you ever known a family that valued interdependence over independence? Which parts of this chapter would not pertain to them? Which parts would?

3. How much do you help a child who is struggling to do something on his or her own? What experience do you have in teaching self-help skills? Do you agree that children should be given opportunities to do things on their own, or do you feel better about helping children, especially when they are struggling? Which was stressed more when you were growing up—independence or interdependence?

4. How does typical toddler behavior relate to power issues? Can you give an example of how an adult can empower a toddler? Does everyone agree that toddlers need to feel powerful? How are power and autonomy related?

5. Saying good-bye can be hard for some children. What experience do you have with helping children cope with separation issues? What advice would you have for a parent who is leaving his or her child in child care for the first time? What advice would you have for the teacher/caregiver or family child care provider of that child?

WEBSITES

Child Welfare
Child Welfare is a government organization with the goal of protecting children and strengthening families.

Parent Services Project
The Parent Services Project focuses on parent leadership training, community outreach, and early childhood professional development to support partnering with families.

Let the Children Play
This website is an inspirational resource full of images and ideas for creating beautiful learning environments for children.

Zero to Three
Zero to Three: National Center for Infants, Toddlers, and Families is for parents and professionals. A leading

resource on the first three years of life, the group's mission is to strengthen and support families, practitioners, and communities to promote the healthy development of babies and toddlers.

Early Head Start National Resource Center
The Early Head Start National Resource Center website contains a database of all the Early Head Start Program sites as well as valuable tips and strategies for trainers and many full-text documents on a range of infant- and toddler-related topics.

Pikler Institute
The Pikler website gives information on the approach used at the Pikler Institute, originally a residential nursery in Budapest, Hungary. The approach focuses heavily on attachment. The website also has information on trainings in America.

Program for Infant/Toddler Caregivers (PITC)
The Program for Infant/Toddler Caregivers supports and promotes quality care for infants and toddlers through resources, information, and training. The site includes information on brain research and implications for infant and toddler development.

Resources for Infant Educarers™
Resources for Infant Educarers™ is a nonprofit organization that uses the teachings of Magda Gerber to promote a unique philosophy and methodology in working with infants and toddlers in ways that respect them as individuals.

FURTHER READING

Copple, C., Bredekamp, S., & Gonzalez-Mena, J. (2011). *Basics of developmentally appropriate practice for infants and toddlers*. Washington, DC: National Association for the Education of Young Children.

Gonzalez-Mena, J. (2013). What works? Assessing infant and toddler play environments. *Young Children*, 68(4), pp. 22–24.

Gonzalez-Mena, J., & Eyer, D. W. (2014). *Infants, toddlers, and caregivers*. New York, NY: McGraw-Hill.

Greenwald, D., & J. Weaver (2013). *The RIE manual for parents and professionals*, (2nd ed.) Los Angeles CA: Resources for Infant Educarers.

Guerra, A. W. & S. Garriety (2013). A cultural communities and cultural practices approach to understanding infant and toddler care. In E. Virmani & P. Mangione (Eds.). *A guide to culturally sensitive care* (2nd ed), pp. 41–53. Sacramento CA: California Department of Education.

Gray, H. (2004, September). "You go away and you come back": Supporting separations and reunions in an infant/toddler classroom. *Young Children*, 59(5), pp. 100–107.

Pikler, E. (2007). Give me time: Gross motor development under the conditions at Loczy. In A. Tardos (Ed.), *Bringing up and providing care for infants and toddlers in an institution* (pp. 127–134). Budapest, Hungary: Pikler-Loczy Tarsasag.

Tardos, A. (2007). The child as an active participant in his own development. In A. Tardos (Ed.), *Bringing up and providing care for infants and toddlers in an institution* (pp. 127–134). Budapest, Hungary: Pikler-Loczy Tarsasag.

Van der Zande, I. (2011). 1.2.3.…*The Toddler Years: A Practical Guide for Parents and Caregivers*. Santa Cruz, CA: Santa Cruz Toddler Care Center.

Oleg Mikhaylov/Shutterstock

Sharing Views of Initiative with Families

The United States is built on individual initiative, which has a high value for many in this country. Each community also depends on individuals with initiative. When does initiative begin to develop? What factors facilitate its development? How do adults socialize children to have initiative?

According to Erik Erikson (1963), initiative is the developmental task of the three- to six-year-old. The child of preschool or kindergarten age, whether in a program or at home, is usually bursting with initiative. Here is what Erikson says about initiative: "Initiative adds to autonomy the quality of undertaking, planning and 'attacking' a task for the sake of being active and on the move" (1963, p. 255). Sometimes the behavior behind these urges gets the child into trouble, especially around adults who don't understand developmental ages and stages. Early educators, including kindergarten teachers, can help families appreciate how children learn initiative.

What does initiative look like? Take a look at Briana, a four-year-old who shows initiative.

WHAT INITIATIVE LOOKS LIKE IN A FOUR-YEAR-OLD

Briana runs in the door of her child care center, leaving behind her mother, who is still coming up the steps. She flings a hasty "Hi" at the teacher seated by the door, glances at the interesting "science" display set out to capture the interest of the arriving children, tosses her coat at a hook on the rack by the door, and runs into the classroom with her teacher on her heels.

"Whoa," says her teacher good-naturedly. "Let's go back and do that again." She gently guides Briana back toward her coat on the floor, where her mother waits. Briana kisses her mother good-bye and then starts to take off again. Her teacher grabs her as she goes by. She patiently reminds her again to hang up her coat, which Briana does hastily. Then, released from the teacher's grasp, the lively girl takes off again into the classroom at a fast clip. She heads straight for the art table, which is set up with wood scraps and glue. She elbows her way into a spot at the table, finds an interesting assortment of wood within reach, and begins applying glue to various pieces, which she stacks one on another. She works busily for quite a while, absorbed in what she is doing. After her flighty entrance, the focused attention is quite a contrast. At last she looks up from her project. Turning to a boy sitting next to her, she remarks, "I'm making a house."

He answers, "I'm making a spaceship. See how it launches?" He waves his creation in the air several times. Briana ducks and then turns to the boy on the other side of her. "My mommy's gonna have a baby, and I'm making her a bed," says Briana. The boy ignores her, concentrating on his gluing. Briana goes back to work on her project, concentrating her whole attention on the wood in front of her.

"I need scissors," says Briana to the teacher, who is seated at the end of the table. "I need to put something here," she says, indicating a spot on her wood project. The teacher looks interested and says, "You know where the scissors are."

Briana gets up with her creation in her hand and dances to a nearby table set up with scissors, crayons, various kinds of paper, hole punches, and tape. She sits down at the table and carefully chooses a piece of yellow paper. She painstakingly cuts the paper into an irregular shape, folds it in half, and glues it on a piece of wood sticking out at a right angle from the central core of her work. It takes her about 10 minutes to complete this task. She gets up to leave and then turns back to the table, picks up the paper scraps she left there, and hurriedly glues them on, too. Then she grabs a pencil, writes a B on the paper, then another B, and then a third. She then "flies" her sculpture over to the art table and passes it under the nose of her teacher, saying, "I wrote my name on my art."

She gives her teacher a hug. The teacher hugs her back. "I see" is the response. Then, "If you're finished, put your art in your cubby."

Briana flies her sculpture to a row of lockers by the coat rack, pokes it inside one of them, and takes off running to the dramatic play area. She ignores the children already there and pulls out a frilly smock from a box of clothes, puts it on, pats it down the front, looks in the mirror, and turns away satisfied. She flounces over to the little table, sits down, picks up a small empty teacup, and pretends to drink.

"You can't play," announces a girl already seated at the table. Briana ignores her and continues slurping noisily into the cup. Then she gets up and takes the cup and the pot with her to the sink, where she swishes them around in the soapy water she finds there. She stands there for a long time, relishing the sensory experience. "Let's play house," suggests a boy, thrusting his hands into the soapy water.

"OK," agrees Briana. "I'll be the mom," she says.

"I'm the mom," says the girl who told her she couldn't play.

"Then I'll be the *other* mom," says Briana, squeezing a sponge out and carrying it over to wipe off the table. "You're my baby," she announces to the boy, who immediately falls to the ground and clings to her foot, clawing at her legs and making a whimpering sound.

"Stop being bad!" Briana scolds him in a harsh voice. "Bad baby, bad, bad, bad!" she screams angrily. The boy cries louder. A teacher passing by smiles at them and continues on her way.

"Pretend I have to spank you," Briana tells the boy. He responds by crying even louder.

She gives him a couple of dramatic whacks, which only connect lightly. He screams in agony. Then she gives him a third whack, which accidentally lands hard.

"Hey, stop that! You hurt me." The boy jumps to his feet, and his voice becomes his own. He looks mad.

A quick look of surprise, a touch of fear, then remorse comes across Briana's face. She hastily retreats to where four children are lying on cushions looking at books. She flings herself to the ground and takes a book out of the hand of the only child within reach.

"Don't!" protests the child, reaching to grab it back. Briana holds up a hand as if to slap her, then slowly lowers it. She turns two pages of the book carefully and deliberately, then tosses it back toward the waiting child, gets up, and leaves.

Seeing the door open, she runs toward it, snatching off the smock and dropping it on the floor as she runs. She stops, looking around to see whether a teacher has spotted the smock on the floor. No teacher is around. Briana hesitates. Then she goes back, picks up the smock, and takes it over to the box where she found it. She dumps it in and hurries back to the open door. She pauses in the doorway for a moment, glancing around. Then she shouts "Sarah!" joyfully and runs down the ramp into the play yard.

Analyzing Initiative in a Four-Year-Old

Let's examine that scene in terms of initiative. Can you see it? If you were watching this scene with a parent, could you explain what's good about Briana's behavior? Suppose the parent is comparing what she is watching with her own experience as a child in school. She might be quite critical of what she sees in this scene. Here are some ways to explain that scene in terms of developmental appropriateness. Though Briana and the other children are learning, this is preschool, not school. It is appropriate for four-year-olds. The environment is set up for free choice, and Briana knows how to take advantage of that. She finds lots of things to do—hands-on kinds of activities, sensory experiences, and ways to use her imagination. She is able to move around, socialize, and finally choose to go outdoors and hook up with her friend. The teacher is facilitating learning rather than structuring learning. There will be a group time later in the morning, but even that looks different from either kindergarten or the primary grades.

In a preschool environment, the teacher is facilitating learning, rather than structuring learning

Let's focus on Briana's initiative. Because Briana is four years old, she is able to use her fertile imagination quite effectively, and she can solve problems. She is also becoming increasingly more competent in her physical abilities and communication skills. Her attention span has lengthened, and she can spend long periods in concentrated focus. She's active, curious, and energetic. A phrase that describes Briana is *get-up-and-go*. She's got it!

What does she do with all this energy and newly developed ability? She uses it to make decisions about what she wants to do. She is so interested in everything that you could almost describe her as in an "attack mode." It's not a negative kind of attacking but a thrusting kind of energy that propels her toward activities and materials that draw her. Briana needs no motivation from her teachers to get involved. She has her own inner motivation.

Much of what Briana undertakes is spontaneous, but that doesn't mean that she is incapable of planning and executing a plan. For example, she had something definite in mind when she asked the teacher for scissors at the wood-gluing table. The teacher, seeing creativity as part of initiative, responded in a positive way instead of restricting Briana to what was available on the table for that particular project. Briana also had something definite in mind when she scanned the play yard, found Sarah, and headed over to play with her.

Attention Deficit/Hyperactivity Disorder (ADHD)

It's important to note that some children are as active as Briana but lack her ability to focus attention and concentrate on any one thing. They don't plan out what they want to do but impulsively rush from one thing to another, perhaps destroying things in their path. These children may not yet have learned to channel their energy. Or perhaps they are overstimulated by too many choices or too much going on around them. Because these children are displaying a different kind of high energy, some adults may think of them as hyperactive. Indeed the word *hyper* is now

David Kostelnik/Pearson Education, Inc.

commonly used for children who move a good deal and have trouble being still. There is a condition known as an *attention deficit/hyperactivity disorder* (ADHD for short). There is a lot of information on this disorder on the website of the National Institute of Mental Health. Although this is a diagnosable disorder, there is some controversy over diagnosing and treating children as young as three or four.

Julie and ADHD

Julie is a seven-year-old who has just been diagnosed as having an attention deficit/hyperactivity disorder (ADHD). In a way, her mother, Shannon, is glad to get the diagnosis because it confirms her idea that Julie is not "bad." She has been worried about her for a long time. It seems as though Julie was born kicking. She was an irritable baby who cried a lot. She seemed to sleep very little. She was in constant motion and she hasn't slowed down yet. Once she got on her feet, life got even harder, if that was possible. Julie was into everything. She never sat still for a minute. Shannon compared her with a neighbor child, Hannah, and saw that Julie was very different. By age four, Hannah would sit for periods of time looking at books or drawing with crayons. Julie never did that. When she looked at a book, she flipped through at a rapid rate, threw the book down, grabbed another one, threw it down, and was off to something else in the space of less than a minute. In fact, none of Julie's activities lasted more than a minute. What was wrong?

Shannon decided to send Julie to preschool, but that didn't help much. Although it gave Shannon a few hours of peace each day, the reports from school kept her in a constant state of tension. Every week it was something new. "What can we do about Julie's behavior?" the teachers kept asking. "She's so impulsive that she constantly makes decisions that result in unfortunate consequences. But she doesn't seem to learn from her mistakes. She just keeps jumping into things and making rash decisions." Shannon felt discouraged that they called her in for her ideas and opinions. Why didn't they know how to handle Julie? They were the trained experts!

When the school called a meeting and the teachers and Shannon sat down and did some brainstorming, things improved. They all shared ideas and information about what worked best at home and what worked best at school for Julie. One of the problems was that preschool was so stimulating. There was just so much to do that Julie was overwhelmed with the number of choices. She ended up constantly running around and not doing anything. Also, the room tended to be noisy and sometimes a little chaotic when all the children were inside. Julie reacted to the high energy level of the classroom by losing what little control she had. At home two things captured her attention: television, sometimes, and video games, almost always.

Things didn't improve by kindergarten, and first grade was a nightmare. When the school finally suggested that testing Julie might be in order, Shannon felt relieved. When she got the results, she felt even more relieved. She is now involved with a team of experts who are creating an Individualized Education Plan (IEP) for Julie. (To learn more about IEPs, visit the website for the Center for Parent Information Resources.) Shannon is pleased to see that she is a full member of the team. They listen to what she has to say, so she also listens to what they have to say. One of the decisions Shannon is faced with is whether to medicate Julie. That's where she is right now. She has joined a parent support group and is discussing the pending decision. She has discovered that there are lots of arguments on either side of the decision.

Developmental Conflicts

Let's look at Briana again. With all the energy and activity that this stage of initiative brings with it, Briana is bound to run into trouble—at least occasionally. How she handles adult guidance and corrections has to do with her stage of development.

As a toddler, Briana learned about getting into trouble. In her constant search for autonomy, two-year-old Briana got into trouble all the time. She learned to look for one of her parents or her family child care provider when she did something she knew was wrong. She responded to their reactions by showing shame for what she had done. If they weren't watching, however, and she didn't get caught, she didn't show signs of remorse.

Erikson (1963) defines the major task for toddlerhood as working out the conflict between autonomy and shame or *doubt*. (See Figure 4.1.) Briana has done that and come out with a sense of what she can do that is not greatly overshadowed by a sense of shame. She has managed a positive resolution for this dilemma.

Briana has now, at four, moved into Erikson's next stage, which signifies a new dilemma—that of initiative versus guilt. She's a big girl with a beginning sense of responsibility *and* a budding conscience. She has taken the watchful eye of her parents and teachers inside herself and can now begin to judge her own behavior. She can feel the kind of guilt whose nagging warns her when she's about to violate some behavior standard and gives her a sense of remorse when she carries out the action anyway. Her guilt is useful because it helps keep her in control sometimes. It guides her toward positive and acceptable behavior.

Briana now has an internal government that dictates the ideals and standards of behavior that are requirements of society. Her government is a benevolent one. Her guilt serves as a little warning sign when her parents or teachers aren't present. She needed reminding to hang up her coat, but she knew not to leave the smock lying on the floor. She stopped herself from hitting the child who was trying to grab the book back.

Briana's guilt is not expected to always control her actions. She still needs adults close by to help her control herself when she can't manage. They do this without making too big a fuss, knowing that Briana has the beginning of control within her.

Briana's guilt is only a small sign—a signaling device. It's not a battering ram hitting her over the head or an acid eating away her insides.

Not all children are as fortunate as Briana. Some are governed by an inner tyranny. Daniel Siegel (2011), a pioneer in what is called interpersonal neurobiology, integrates brain research with psychotherapy. He describes in his book *Mindsight* what can happen to adults who judge themselves so harshly to enforce the standards of those around them that they lose their initiative. They're afraid to act. Their

Child's Stage	Approximate Age	Task		
Infancy	0–1	Basic trust	versus	Basic mistrust
Toddlerhood	1–3	Autonomy	versus	Shame and doubt
The preschool years	3–6	Initiative	versus	Guilt
School age	6–10	Industry	versus	Inferiority

Figure 4.1 **Erikson's psycho-social stages of development Erikson (1963)**
Source: Based on Erikson, E. (1963).

> This situation of guilt squashing initiative can happen when adults go overboard and use heavy-handed punishment, accusations, threats, or torments on young children. Children who grow up in this atmosphere may develop an exaggerated sense of guilt, and they torture themselves even for trivial offenses.

energy is sapped by the overkill methods of their inner government. Not all of his patients' struggles stem from Erikson's conflict between initiative and guilt, but some do.

This situation of guilt squashing initiative can happen when adults go overboard and use heavy-handed punishment, accusations, threats, or torments on young children. Children who grow up in this atmosphere may develop an exaggerated sense of guilt, and they torture themselves even for trivial offenses. One of the benefits of being a family-centered program where teachers (or other professionals) and parents get to know each other and spend time together is that parents who use inappropriate discipline can learn gentler, healthier ways of managing their children's behavior. Although it may be tempting to just tell them—and lay a guilt trip on them— there are more effective ways. Modeling has been mentioned throughout this chapter and in the previous ones. When families see strategies working, they may begin to use them themselves. Also, when they begin to understand the stages of development children go through, that can help, too. Some parents learn best by reading—and the program should have a parent lending library. A DVD library is a good idea as well. Some parents learn best by discussion with other parents as well as teachers. Observation is a good learning tool for parents and teachers alike.

Imagination and Fantasy

What's perhaps most notable about the stage of initiative is the way children work their imaginations and how they use fantasy. By the preschool years, pretend play has become far more complex than the simple imitation of infancy (Jones & Cooper, 2006; Jones & Reynolds, 2011; Van Hoorn, Nourot, Scales, & Alward, 2015). The toddler shows the beginnings of the complexity by using objects to stand for other objects (a plastic banana or block for a telephone). By age four, the imagination soars! What was Briana doing when she was playing house? She was doing just what adults do with dreams and daydreams. She was experiencing hopes and fears by dealing with the past symbolically and rehearsing for the future. She tried on roles and feelings in the same way she tried on dress-up clothes. Fantasy play gives Briana practice in interacting with others while in these roles. She also uses fantasy play to express fears and anger and to discover

Monkey Business Images/Shutterstock

What's perhaps most notable about the stage of initiative is the way children work their imaginations and use fantasy

ways to adjust to painful situations. If parents observe fantasy play, you can discuss together what the child is getting out of it. With the parents' knowledge of what goes on in the rest of the child's life, he or she can give you ideas about what you're seeing that you couldn't get otherwise.

✓ Check Your Understanding 4.1

Click here to check your understanding of what initiative looks like in a four-year old.

THE VALUE OF PLAY FOR YOUNG CHILDREN

Play is an arena where children learn new skills and practice old ones, both physical and social. This was discussed in the last chapter on toddlers, but there's always more to say about play—especially when the subject is preschool-age children. It's especially important to keep emphasizing play in light of the endangerment of play when children end up spending their days indoors in front of screens instead of playing indoors and outside. And it isn't just quiet play that counts. Frances Carlson (2011) makes a case for the importance of what she calls 'big body play" and why children should have boisterous, vigorous, physical play. Through play children challenge themselves to new levels of mastery. They gain competence in all areas of development—increasing language, social skills, and physical skills, for example. Briana not only practices such important skills as eye-hand coordination but also at times uses her whole body to improve balance and coordination.

▶ Watch this video to hear more about how active play benefits children's development.

www.youtube.com /watch?v=CKUfraBmjy8

David Elkind, long an advocate for play, says in his book, *The Power of Play*, "One legacy of our Puritan heritage is a lingering ambivalence toward child play" (2007). That ambivalence can show up in preschool and child care classrooms as an emphasis on structured lessons in the name of learning outcomes for "school readiness." Outdoor time may be limited because it's seen as a non-educational recess rather than a chance to learn through playing outside. The parent or program that buys "educational" toys can justify play as educational, but there is little research that shows toys marketed as educational really are. Elkind makes the case that it's of more benefit to children to use their imagination in an environment that lends itself to exploration, initiative, and active engagement with objects, materials, and other children. It's important that teachers don't buy the consumer-oriented mindset that marketers are trying so hard to sell. Teachers can give a different message to parents and counteract some of the hard sell coming from advertising.

Children's initiative is supported in an environment that provides choices, opportunities for exploration, and active engagement with objects, materials, and other children

Erika Landorf-Kelly/Pearson Education, Inc.

Play provides for cognitive development in ways that educational toys don't necessarily address. Cognitive development is tied in with physical and social interactions in the preschool years as children are constructing a view of the world and discovering concepts. So when parents see their children running around, playing outdoors, seemingly doing nothing constructive, a teacher should be there to help the parents look deeper at what's really happening. Teachers can give parents the message that there is nothing passive about play—even if the body is passive for a time, the mind is busy working. Children at play are active explorers of the environment as they create their own experience and grow to understand it. In this way they participate in their own development.

> Teachers can give parents the message that there is nothing passive about play—even if the body is passive for a time, the mind is busy working.

Through play, children work at problem solving, which involves mental, physical, and social skills. While playing, they can try on pretend solutions and experience how those solutions work. If they make mistakes, those mistakes don't hurt them as they would in real life. They can reverse power roles and be the adult for a change, telling other children what to do. They can even tell adults what to do, if the adults are willing to play along.

Play enables children to sort through conflicts and deal with anxieties, fears, and disturbing feelings in an active, powerful way (Frost, Wortham, & Reifel, 2012). Play provides a safety valve for feelings. When they pretend, children can say or do things that they can't do in reality.

 Watch this video to see two children during big body outdoor play. What kind of initiative do you see? What challenges are they creating for themselves?

Play makes children feel powerful and gives them a sense of control as they create worlds and manipulate them. Watch children playing with blocks, or dolls and action figures, or even in the sandbox. Think about how they create the worlds they play in. What power!

Children also get a sense of power by facing something difficult and conquering it—like finding a place for a puzzle piece that just won't fit anywhere or climbing higher on the jungle gym than they've ever climbed before. Think back to your own childhood. Think of a time when you were challenged in play. What was your feeling as you overcame obstacles (including perhaps your own fear) and met the challenge?

Helping families understand the value of play is a big challenge for preschool teachers and for kindergarten teachers who have a play-based curriculum as well as for other professionals who use play therapy. Play may look very unorganized and frivolous to families. It's important to make a good case for play as learning and also for therapeutic goals. See Strategy Box 4.1 for ideas on working with families around issues of play. Figure 4.2 summarizes some benefits of play discussed in this chapter.

Strategy Box 4.1

Helping Families Appreciate Play

- Observe with the family members when their children are playing so that you can see the child through their eyes and give parents input on what you see.
- Help families appreciate the value of play as a way of learning and developing in all the domains of development: mind, body, and feelings.
- Don't just teach families; also learn from them. For example, have families help you understand how to adapt the learning environment so that it is accessible to their culture or the special needs of their particular child.

- Children learn new skills and practice old ones
- Children challenge themselves to new levels of mastery
- Children gain competence in all areas of development
- Children construct a view of their world and discover concepts
- Children are active explorers of the environment as they create their own experiences and participate in their own development
- Children work at problem solving
- Children try new power roles, making sense of their world
- Children develop social and emotional skills by sorting through conflict, playing out fears and feelings
- Children feel powerful as they create imaginary worlds and then manipulate them
- Children feel competent by overcoming obstacles and challenges

Figure 4.2   Play is powerful! What are the benefits of play?

How the Environment Contributes to a Sense of Initiative

The environment reflects whether the adults in charge of it regard developing a sense of initiative to be of value. Individual initiative, like independence, is not a universal priority. In some cultures, individual initiative is less important than going along with the group spirit. Initiative may only count when it obviously serves the group rather than the individual alone. So as you read about how the environment setup relates to the value of initiative, realize that what you are reading reflects the value behind it. When families have a different set of priorities, instead of arguing your side, try creating a dialogue so you can understand more about where they are coming from. Everyone stands to gain when communication comes in the form of a dialogue.

Attention should be given to environments for children in the stage of initiative so that they have choices about what to do. We saw such an indoor environment in the Briana scene. You can imagine that the outdoor environment was also well planned so that children had a variety of choices about what to do in it. Both the indoor and outdoor environment should be set up for active as well as quiet play. Not only should there be choices of developmentally appropriate activities, toys, and materials, but these items will be enticingly arranged to attract attention and draw children to them.

Not all adults see giving children choices as valuable. Some people expect children to adapt to what is and to entertain themselves in the environment of adults, rather than selecting from a number of options that have been provided for them. They disagree with the notion of a child-oriented environment isolated from the real world of adults (Mistry, 1995; Rogoff, 2003). Some adults do not believe in creating learning situations to teach their children; they put their children in adult-oriented environments and expect them to learn by observation, not from playing in an environment specially set up for them. For an example of this different view of what children need and are capable of, see the following "Perspectives on Child Rearing."

Perspectives on Child Rearing

A preschool teacher enjoying a sunny afternoon in San Francisco sat on a bench watching two street musicians playing music from the Andes for a crowd in Ghirardelli Square. She noticed their daughter, who appeared to be about four years old, sitting on a bench next to where the parents were playing. The child sat quietly on the bench until her parents took a break. She had no toys and nothing to do. She seemed to be able to content herself with people-watching and listening to the music. When her parents took a break, she moved over to be with them. She hung around listening to what they were saying and periodically taking short excursions to look in shop windows around the perimeters of the plaza. She was never gone too long but kept coming back to where her parents were. She never demanded their attention while they were talking. When they went back to playing music, she went back to sitting. She never left or distracted them in any way while they were working. She was obviously well trained.

The little girl was a contrast to two little boys, about two and four years old, who were also entertaining themselves as their parents stood watching the performance. They had toys with them that they played with. When they got tired of the toys, they started running around the plaza, with one parent trailing after them. To the preschool teacher the boys' behavior was more to be expected than the girl's behavior, not because of gender but because of age. The teacher marveled at the ability of the girl to sit on the bench. She wondered what would happen if this child went off to child care or to a preschool where active play was considered vital to development. Would the philosophy of the preschool upset the situation the parents had created so they could earn their living? Would the girl get bored with sitting (she never looked bored that afternoon)?

Dimensions of Play Environments

Elizabeth Jones and Elizabeth Prescott (1978) at Pacific Oaks College in Pasadena, California looked at children's play environments in terms of what they call *dimensions*. Their research is as relevant today as it was when they did it. To create an optimum environment for the kind of play that enhances initiative, Jones and Prescott advocate a balance of these dimensions: soft/hard, open/closed, intrusion/exclusion, high mobility/low mobility, and simple/complex.

Balancing the *soft/hard* dimension means that the environment is both responsive and resistant. Softness in play environments comes from things like rugs, stuffed animals, cozy furniture, grass, sand, play dough, water, soft balls, pads, and laps, to name a few. Hardness comes in the form of vinyl floors, plastic and wooden toys and furniture, and concrete.

The *open/closed* dimension has to do with choices. Low, open shelves displaying toys to choose from are an example of openness. Some closed storage is also appropriate, so that the number of choices is manageable. Closed storage also gives a sense of order and avoids a cluttered feeling. Maintaining a balance between open and closed is important.

The open/closed dimension also has to do with whether there is one right way to use a toy or material (e.g., a puzzle, a form board, graduated stacking rings) or whether the toy or material encourages all kinds of exploration. A doll, finger paint, and play dough are open; so is water play. Children need both open and closed toys, materials, and equipment.

The environment should provide for both optimum *intrusion* and optimum *exclusion*, or *seclusion*. Desirable intrusion comes as the children have access to the greater world beyond their play space—for example, through windows that allow them to see what is happening outside but protect them from dangers and noise. Desirable intrusion also occurs as visitors come into the play environment.

The outdoor space is also important to consider when setting up environments to support initiative. Watch this video to see adults create an obstacle course for young children.

www.youtube.com/
watch?v=EUmR3-A8xbg

Seclusion should be provided so children can get away by themselves. Think of the hideaways you had as a young child. Given a little freedom, children will find these kinds of places for themselves; however, in a child care center or home, they sometimes need to be provided. Lofts, large cardboard boxes, and tables covered with sheets provide semi-enclosed private spaces in which children can make "nests" to hide from the world.

A balanced play environment provides for both *high-* and *low-mobility* activities. Children need quiet and still activities as well as opportunities to move around freely and engage in vigorous movement.

Although parents don't necessarily need to be given all of this information about the design of the environment, it is helpful for you to have it in case they have questions. The information in the next paragraph, however, is very relevant to parents and should be communicated.

We all know that young children can be satisfied with the simplest things. A baby can be fascinated with something that an adult wouldn't give more than a glance. This fact relates to the *simple/complex* dimension of the child care environment. As children grow older, they need complexity, which they often provide for themselves by combining simple toys with other materials. Watch a child who finds sand, water, and utensils conveniently close to each other. The park designers may never have thought of how that drinking fountain close to the sandbox would be used, but the four-year-old who finds an empty soda can is almost certain to think of using it to carry water to the sand. Complexity presents increased possibilities for action. Preschool and child care teachers know this, so they put a dripping hose in the sandbox on warm days and give the children scoops, buckets, cups, spoons, and a variety of other implements to use. They know that attention span lengthens when children find or create complexity in the environment. The more complex a material or toy (or combination of materials and toys), the more interesting it is. Blocks are fun. Blocks with small figures and wheel toys are even more fun! Some parents may resist the idea of messy play. You can explain the importance of sensory experiences, but also listen to their ideas about what children do and don't need. And always respect their perspective.

Blend Images/Shutterstock

Sometimes children need to get away by themselves; semi-enclosed private spaces where children can continue to be supervised are an important element to a balanced play environment

✔ **Check Your Understanding 4.2**

Click here to check your understanding of the value of play for young children.

HOW ADULTS CONTRIBUTE TO CHILDREN'S INITIATIVE

Adults contribute to the development of children's sense of initiative in several ways. Adults are responsible for setting up the environments for children's play and making sure it is safe for everybody in it. The Advocacy in Action feature "A Son

Adults are responsible for setting up environments that are safe and inviting

David Kostelnik/Pearson Education, Inc.

Compliments His Mother's Advocacy Work" (in a feature box later in this chapter) tells the story of a mother who enabled her son to take advantage of the environment by advocating for his very special need. This story is told by the son, who is now grown up.

As stated, the kind of environment that adults set up determines to some extent whether initiative is a value. Adults are the ones who must guide and control children's behavior in these environments. How they do that also contributes to a sense of initiative. Guidance methods that encourage children to continue to explore, try things out, and solve problems contribute to their growing initiative. Methods that squelch children's interest, inhibit their behavior, and make them afraid to try things because they might make a mistake take away their confidence in themselves and work against bringing out each child's own initiative. In addition, adults encourage initiative in children by modeling it themselves. As mentioned earlier, all parents may not want to encourage individual initiative. Sometimes they will agree to disagree and

ADVOCACY IN ACTION ▶ A SON COMPLIMENTS HIS MOTHER'S ADVOCACY WORK

Gregory Toy, recent college graduate

Growing up with multiple food allergies has not always been simple. Due to my inability to consume dairy products, nuts, and peanuts, I have been forced to overcome challenges that might appear mundane to the average person: restaurant menus present countless dangers, air travel is often perilous, and birthday parties can be unnerving events. As one of the only children with a restrictive diet, few parents and teachers understood the implications of my allergy, ignoring my medical and dietary needs and consequently excluding me from certain food-related activities. Yet, despite these obstacles, I have had a relatively normal childhood thanks to my mother's relentless efforts to advocate for my inclusion in invaluable experiences.

Though I never gave much thought to my mother's omnipresence, I now recognize her tireless efforts to ensure normalcy, facilitate inclusion, and promote awareness. Indeed, whenever I visited restaurants on class field trips, my mother was there to ensure that I would have the same culinary and cultural experience as other students. When necessary, she would prepare alternative desserts so that I would be able to enjoy myself at friends' birthday parties. Prior to air travel, she would verbally spar with airline representatives in order to ensure that no peanuts would be served en route to our destination. Without a staunch advocate like my mother, I would never have been able to participate in activities that have shaped who I am today.

feel okay about the fact that what goes on in the program is different from what they do at home. Other times you may need to have a deeper discussion about differing perspectives on individual initiative.

Special Considerations for Children with Disabilities

There has been a movement for some years to include children with special needs in environments with their typically developing peers in schools, preschools, and child care centers. It isn't enough to just enroll these children in programs; the programs must be prepared to work with the children and families so that they gain a sense of belonging. A book called *Inclusion Works!* (California Department of Education, 2009) offers many practical strategies to enable the integration of children with disabilities and their families. It's important for adults who have only worked with typically developing children to realize that some children with disabilities arrive in a play environment with less initiative and motivation to play than others. It may be that they have not been encouraged to play and explore. Or children who are medically fragile may have parents who concentrate more on keeping them safe and healthy than on encouraging them to play. Or it may be that the child is interested but has little or no access to the toys, materials, and activities. It's up to the adult to ensure that all children have access, including those with disabilities and other challenges.

Sometimes providing access is as simple as restructuring the environment so that a child in a wheelchair, for example, can move around. Putting toys within reach of a nonambulatory child is another practical strategy. Positioning a child so he feels secure enough to use his hands and arms to explore and manipulate will enable a child who has a disability to more fully experience his environment. Close attention to what interests each child can guide the teacher when selecting toys and materials to make available. Also, being aware of what playthings will build on a child's strengths is important when setting up the environment. Toys and materials that are responsive—that the child can have an effect on—are usually winners. Some toys that are already available can be adapted so they are easier to use. One teacher glued tongue depressors to the pages of a cardboard book to make the pages less difficult to turn for a child with cerebral palsy. One way to figure out how to modify the environment is for teachers to put themselves at the level of the child in question and look around. For example, a child lying on his back may be looking directly into a bright ceiling light.

Jaren Wicklund/Fotolia

Programs must be prepared to work with children with disabilities and their families so that they gain a sense of belonging

Families can be helpful in thinking with you about how to organize or adapt the environment for their child's special needs. They often have access to experts who can be helpful, too. Don't try to figure it out by yourself or with only the help of other early educators. Use the families and their resources. Work together to discover the adaptations that are appropriate for each child.

Children who have attention deficit disorders may be distracted in a play space where there is too much going on. The way their brains are wired seems to give them the urge to seek novelty, and everything attracts their attention. The early childhood educator can simplify the environment, but it isn't enough just to create an appropriate play environment and then expect children with certain challenges to automatically start playing with their typically developing peers. Special strategies are necessary to support interactions with other children and promote skill development (California Department of Education, 2009). One such strategy is to slow down the pace for those who need it and allow plenty of time to react. Some children need the slow pace to help them focus. Others need help to refocus. For example, giving plenty of time for a reaction can be a help to children with Down syndrome, who need the extra time to change the focus of their attention. Asking a question and expecting an immediate response, for example, doesn't work as well as pausing after the question and just waiting quietly for the child to absorb it before expecting a response.

Again, you don't have to discover all this for yourself. Engage the families in helping you understand their children. Share information that you have and listen to what they know. Teamwork is critical for making the environment work for every child in it.

A child with language delays can benefit when the other children see the teacher responding to communication attempts and building on the skills the child has. Modeling has a strong effect, and other children pick up on what the teacher is doing and do it also.

Children with autism benefit from playing with their peers who are more accomplished players. Their ability to play increases with the support of the teacher in an integrated setting where the environment and the learning plan focus on play. Their imagination increases as well (Wolfberg, 2009).

In some cases you may have more information than the parents if they haven't seen their child around other children. Share what you know. Collaborate with the parents to make your programs a good experience for each and every child.

Vygotsky's sociocultural theory has implications for including children with special needs or developmental delays in programs with their typically developing peers. Vygotsky used the term *zone of proximal development* to describe how social interactions increase understanding. Certainly in a play environment there are lots of opportunities for children to help one another move forward in their understanding and skill building (Vygotsky, 1967).

Look at this example. Jayden has taken a puzzle off the shelf. It is harder than any puzzle he ever did before. When he dumps the puzzle upside down the pieces fall all over the place. He looks stunned. He also looks around at the other children. Olivia, his good friend, comes over to Jayden's side and sits down. "That's a hard one, Jason!" she says. He looks distressed, but then notices that Olivia is picking up some pieces and turning them over. He starts doing the same thing. She finds a corner piece and hands it to him. "See where it goes, Jayden?" He does! Right away! He puts the piece where it fits. He looks at the other pieces he dumped. They are all turned over now. Olivia points out that the piece he just put in has a big splotch of yellow on it. Jason gets it! He starts looking for other pieces with yellow on them. He is in his zone of proximal development. He's learning an approach to more complex puzzles—with just a little help from Olivia. The two finish the puzzle and high-five each other.

For more information about inclusive child care, visit the Easter Seals website.

> ▶ Watch this video to hear from a family with a child that has special needs, and the intervention team that supports his development.
>
> www.youtube.com /watch?v=n2MtnUvbh-U

The Shy Child

Some children seem to lack get-up-and-go. Even though they have no developmental differences, challenges, or disabilities, they seem to lack initiative. They may be labeled *shy*, or perhaps they are looked at as withdrawn.

Let's look at one of these children:

> Dakota has always been the quietest child in the preschool she attends. She hangs out on the fringes of things and seldom talks or even smiles. When someone talks to her, she lowers her eyes and stares at her shoes. She follows the routine of the program but never really joins in with anything that is going on. She's so quiet that sometimes she's almost invisible.

What could be going on with Dakota? The place to start answering this question is with the family. What is their take on their daughter? Is she the same way at home as she is at school? Certainly this conversation should be held without indicating that the teachers think something is wrong with Dakota. An exchange of information is what will be helpful. In this situation, what the teachers finally figured out was Dakota fit a particular pattern that they had already discovered in other children.

Here's the pattern: Some children are born extra cautious. This trait may even be in their genes. They don't enjoy putting themselves out in the world, taking risks, trying new things. Sometimes this trait doesn't really hinder them because it's more a matter of timing than a deficiency. Some children are observers; they learn a good deal by watching for long periods before they try something themselves. When they do try something, they make rapid progress because of their careful observations. They may be thought of as being slow to warm up. Other children jump in with both feet without giving a thought to the consequences. If these more impulsive children are successful in their endeavors, they may be valued for their speed and compared with children like Dakota. (B*right* and *quick* are sometimes thought to be synonymous with *intelligent*.) Thus, Dakota's slow, cautious way of doing things may be undervalued in some settings. That wasn't the case in either the family or in the school in this situation with Dakota. The teachers decided along with input from the family that though Dakota may look as though she lacks initiative, it's really a matter of timing more than initiative. An unfamiliar environment slows her down even more. At home with a sibling or a playmate, Dakota is much more secure and outgoing. She doesn't look so shy and cautious. Shyness and caution are situational with Dakota.

The teachers at Dakota's school have discovered that pushing her doesn't do any good. She's very resistant to join an activity until she decides on her own to do so. She has the ability to absorb by watching—far more ability than any of her teachers, who at first worried that she must be bored because they were projecting their own needs onto her. She isn't bored. In fact, they discovered that she was getting much more out of preschool than anyone realized, but she was doing it in her own way. The teachers, with the family's input, decided to be patient with Dakota and to respect her style. They also, when they could, arranged for her to be in smaller groups and play alone with one or two children rather than always urging her to join into large-group activities.

The teachers have discovered that this quiet, cautious child has grown into something of a leader in the class. The other children are drawn to Dakota and are influenced by her. In fact, the day doesn't truly begin until Dakota arrives. The teachers were really surprised when they discovered that Dakota's quiet presence now influences the activities in the classroom. They shared their findings with her parents and invited them to observe their daughter's new-found leadership role.

Factors other than those that influence Dakota may be at work on another child who exhibits similar behavior. Take Brandi, for example:

> Brandi is shy and cautious for entirely different reasons—she has a history of abuse and attachment issues. As a result, she has a great deal of trouble separating from her foster mother, who delivers her to school. She cries loudly and must be peeled off, so that the foster mother, who has other children to deliver to another school, can leave. Once Brandi quits crying, she goes into mourning. She stands by the art table with one finger in her mouth and her eyes staring vacantly. The teachers have decided that she isn't even really "there" most of the time. She stares into space. She sits in circle time silently. She doesn't seem to have learned a single song (compared with Dakota, who never sings at school but at home can go through every word of every verse, complete with hand movements).

Brandi is withdrawn, and it isn't just that she has a slower pace than most children. She has a problem. In fact, this child might well have been born quick, lively, and a willing risk taker, but her life circumstances have beaten her into the child she is now—one who needs more help than her teachers alone can give her. Under ideal circumstances, Brandi's teachers, foster parents, and biological family are working with social workers and therapists to help her adjust to foster care or help her family get back together. She also needs help to resolve her attachment issues and heal the raw scars of her abuse. If all goes well and everyone cooperates, Brandi will get her life back together and her spark will come back. She'll be the child she really is rather than the child she has become.

The vital difference between Dakota and Brandi is that Dakota is the child she is and Brandi is not—she's been wounded.

A Look at Aggression

Let's examine the subject of aggression in the preschool-age child—where it comes from and what to do about it.

We'll start with Cory. He's a four-year-old who attends an all-day preschool in which he is one of a group of 30 children. He gives his teachers a lot of trouble because he seems always to be hurting someone. Someone constantly has to deal with the aftermath of his aggressive behavior. What's going on with Cory?

It's not easy to say what's going on with Cory. There are many possible reasons for his aggressive behavior—some simple and fairly easy to solve and some much more complex. It could be that Cory has just not learned any other way to behave. In that case, he needs to be taught. Or it could be that Cory was rewarded for this behavior in the past and is continuing to be rewarded for it, so he continues his aggressive behavior. It could also be that Cory's behavior is the result of bottled-up emotions. Maybe something is going on at home, and he's feeling very upset by it. He's letting off steam at school. His behavior might even stem from a physical source—either his own body chemistry or influences of the environment interacting with his physical makeup. Or his aggression can come from an extreme defensiveness. The following sections explore these sources of aggression more closely.

Learned Aggression.   Children can learn aggression from watching others get what they want through aggressive means. They may see this on television or in their own homes or neighborhoods. They can even learn it at preschool from watching classmates. They can, of course, also learn it from firsthand experience.

For example, a child wants a toy. She grabs it from another child and pushes him when he fights back. She has the toy—she gets her reward. Or, if adult attention is the reward she's looking for, she gets that attention when the adult marches across the room, grabs the toy out of her hand, and holds her arm tight while squatting down to look her in the eye and give her a good, long scolding. She gets even more attention when she is marched over to apologize. Her final rewards come when she is placed in a time-out chair and brought back every time she gets up. She has the adult's full attention—including eye contact, touch, and a long stream of words. She can get the adult to notice her even from clear across the room simply by her behavior. If she still wants more reward, all she has to do is push one of the adult's buttons. Spitting will probably do it. A "bad word" will usually do it, too.

If this child has learned this way of getting attention, the solution is to give her the attention she needs in other ways and to make her "unlearn" the ingrained behaviors. Behavior modification is the answer. The adult must unlink the behavior and the reward by withdrawing attention rather than pouring it on. This is not easy to do while keeping everyone safe. Sometimes it is a matter of providing physical control while giving the least attention possible. Other times just ignoring the behavior will eventually make it go away. However, if this is a longtime pattern, it will probably get worse before it gets better, until the child learns that the attention she so desperately needs will come but is linked to a different kind of behavior.

The problem is that most adults who have to deal with this kind of aggression in a child are sorely tempted to turn to punishment; they want to hurt the child either physically or emotionally. What they may not realize is that hurting children doesn't work. You don't make a child less aggressive by hurting her—you make her more aggressive. Way back in 1975, Barclay Martin reviewed 27 studies on the effects of harsh punishment and concluded that children were likely to store up frustration from being punished and vent it later, using the violence that was used on them. The message regarding avoiding using aggression to deal with aggression is still valid today.

Power may be behind the child's need for aggression. Power issues are never solved by being overpowered, which is the message behind punishment.

Aggression as the Result of Bottled-Up Feelings.   Some children react to tension with aggression. Their feelings are bottled up inside them, and even a little incident can "uncork" them. What "pours out" is more than the provoking incident calls for. That's a clue to tension as a cause of aggression. Any little frustration can cause "the top to blow off the bottle." When tension is behind the aggression, it is best to work on the source of the tension. However, that may be a job for a social worker and a therapist. If you're Cory's teacher, for example, you don't have the opportunity to work on his home tensions, and you're not a trained therapist. What you *can* do is reduce frustration for him at school. You can also give him outlets for his angry feelings. Some examples of outlets follow:

1. Vigorous physical activity can serve as an outlet—for example, running, jumping, and climbing.
2. Aggressive activities are also beneficial—for example, pounding punching bags, digging in the dirt, hammering nails, and even tearing paper.

3. Soothing sensory activities can help calm the aggressive child—activities like water play, clay work, and finger paint. Cornstarch and water available as a paste to play in is a wonderfully soothing sensory activity.

4. Art and music activities also serve as outlets for emotional expression. Many children paint picture after picture, covering every inch of the easel paper with paint. From the looks on their faces, you can tell that they are finding the activity soothing.

Physical Influences on Aggression.   Teachers *can* work on the problem of physical influences on aggression. For example, Cory's diet may be terrible. Perhaps some family education is in order. Careful observation can determine whether low blood sugar is influencing his behavior. Is he particularly aggressive when he's hungry? Steps can be taken to remedy that situation, both with a change of diet and with increased high-protein snacks. If physical problems are suspected, a visit to the doctor is in order.

It's easy to see how environment can influence behavior. If Cory is part of a group of 30 children and they spend much time together in one classroom, he may well be overstimulated, which can easily result in a lack of control on his part. Crowding is a clear cause of aggression in animals. I think we, as a society, try to ignore this problem in people because crowding is a part of our daily lives and we just expect children to adjust to it.

Other environmental influences can be heat, lighting, and environmental pollution. Even weather can make a difference. If you've ever been with a group of children on a windy day, you know how it can affect their behavior.

Extreme Defensiveness.   According to Selma Fraiberg (1959) in her classic book, *The Magic Years*, some children imagine danger everywhere and interpret every little action of playmates as threatening to themselves. They are defensive to an extreme. Out of their fear, they attack first, rather than waiting to be attacked and then striking back. They need help to change their perspective and come to see the world as a non-threatening place. Their worldview may be due to attachment or abuse issues, in which case those are the areas in which they need help. That help may need to come from a trained therapist rather than a layperson, though teachers may carry out whatever program the therapist suggests. All by themselves, the teachers probably can't solve the problem of Cory's aggression if that problem comes from damage inflicted on him.

No matter what the cause behind the aggression, it's important to be working together with the family to discover what to do about it. Teamwork makes a big difference. Imagine how hard it is on a child to find one approach to

Vigorous physical activity can serve as an outlet for strong feelings

2xSamara/Shutterstock

aggression being taken at home and an entirely different one being used at school. Sometimes just teaming isn't enough—outside expertise is needed. It's also important to recognize when a situation is beyond the ability of the teacher and parents to solve by themselves. In that case they can work together to find the outside resources needed for assistance and support.

Teaching Problem-solving Skills

The roots of violence start in the first years of life as children who don't know how to solve problems turn to aggression. You can spot children in preschool who are at risk for becoming violent teens. They are the four-year-olds who solve all their social problems physically. If they want a truck, they grab it and then sock the little kid who had it first. If accidentally bumped, they shove the offender back harder.

Of course, all children who grab, hit, and shove won't become violent teens. After all, this is normal behavior for young children. Some will outgrow it, but others won't. Instead they will develop deeply ingrained ways of approaching problems, which can lead directly from preschool aggression to teenage violence.

Four weaknesses in problem-solving skills are exhibited by teenage offenders:

1. They make assumptions about a situation and neglect to get further information.
2. They seldom give anyone the benefit of the doubt but see everyone as a potential adversary. They think people are "out to get them."
3. They have a narrow vision of alternative solutions and rely mainly on violence.
4. They fail to consider consequences when they lash out.

Adults can help young children develop problem-solving skills before the weakness becomes ingrained. They can help children clarify situations, consider consequences, and explore alternatives to aggression.

To help, the adult must be on the spot when difficulties arise between children. It's important to intervene before the action gets physical. For example, as the four-year-old grabs for the truck in the other child's hands, the adult can stop him and say, "You really want the truck. I wonder what you can do besides grabbing it." If the child's response shows he can't think of anything but grabbing, the adult can list some other ideas.

This is not a natural approach for most adults, especially when the tendency is to meet child aggression with adult aggression. That's where training comes in. Teachers can learn to take this approach and model it for parents. Aggression can also be the subject of a parent meeting. Certainly most families are interested in both how to keep their children safe from the aggression of other children and managing the aggression they find in their own children. Skillful intervention by adults is a skill well worth learning.

It's important that adults not be critical or judgmental when they intervene. This approach is about talking it through, not giving lectures on being nice. Tone of voice and attitude are all-important as the adult guides the talking. The goal is for the children to begin to see the other's perspective and consider alternative solutions.

Four qualities are important when helping children talk to each other in a conflict situation:

1. Firmness should come through—"I won't let you grab or hurt."
2. Empathy also should come through—"I know how much you want that truck."
3. A problem-solving attitude rather than a power play must be part of the exchange—"He might give it to you if you ask him."
4. Persistence is critical—"Well, asking didn't work. I wonder what else you could try."

The objective is not to solve the problem in a particular way for the child but to help him discover his own alternatives to violence.

Adults often short-circuit this kind of learning by putting children in time-out. Or they solve the problem themselves: "He had it first; give it back to him." "If you're going to fight over that toy, you can't play with it." Those adult actions don't teach the problem-solving skills so necessary for the future.

Skillful intervention makes a difference. We can teach children nonviolence in the preschool years. Of course, teaching alone won't eliminate violence. Other factors come into play. If the child sees violence at home, on the streets, on TV, in video games, and on other electronic devices, the modeling effect comes in. Or if the child is a victim of abuse, the likelihood of his becoming a perpetrator is increased.

Safe Start is a nationwide program designed to deal with the roots of violence through prevention and intervention. Check out the Safe Start Center website for more information. Another organization concerned with young children at risk is The Ounce of Prevention Fund, which also has a website. A public/private partnership based in Chicago and built on decades of research on child development, this program is a promising approach to reducing violence through focusing on children ages birth to five. Brain research points to the impact of early emotional experiences on brain development, altering both structure and brain chemistry. Early experiences set up patterns of response that can last a lifetime. The program stresses prevention approaches that include helping adults understand how to teach children self-control. Adults in the program learn how to set limits, discourage unacceptable behavior, model appropriate behavior, and reduce the risk factors for violence. Early intervention includes quality early childhood education programs for children, including specialized teacher training in violence prevention. These approaches are making a lasting difference.

There is no single simple solution to violence. If we are to create a peaceful world to live in, we must take a many-pronged approach. A good prong to start with is to help children get off to a good start and learn effective nonviolent problem solving in the early years.

Watch this video to see an early childhood professional help children deal with conflict. What strategies did she use to support all of the children?

Empowering the Preschool-Age Child

Adults often believe that to manage children's behavior and set them on the right path, they must dominate them by overpowering them. Trying to *over*power children often leads straight to power struggles, which are the antithesis of *em*powering children. Children miss out whether they win or lose the power struggle. If they win, they discover that they can dominate an adult, which is frightening. Young children know that they need adults, and they want someone to look up to who will protect and support them. It shakes their confidence in the adult to learn that they are stronger than the larger, more experienced adult. If children lose the power struggle, it takes them down a notch or two rather than convincing them of their own power. Power struggles are to be avoided rather than encouraged if you are working on empowerment.

To explore empowerment further, think of a time you felt powerful as a child. Avoid focusing on those times when you were overpowering someone; concentrate instead on personal power that gave you the feeling of being able to be yourself and of having some effect on the world or the people in it. Focus on this feeling. Isn't this a feeling you would like children to have?

When I ask students to give examples of times they felt powerful as a child, they come up with a variety of situations in which they demonstrated effectiveness.

Sometimes the situation has to do with carrying out some responsibility; some remember a time when they were particularly competent at something; others remember a moment of strength or courage—particularly in relationship to being challenged and conquering their fear. Some felt powerful because of their affiliations—the support people in their lives. Some people got a sense of their own power simply from being able to make choices—even when the consequences weren't what they expected.

One way that children in preschool gain a feeling of power is by "dressing up" and trying on powerful roles. They do this by itself or in conjunction with creating their own world and then playing. That puts them in the role of creator—a very powerful position indeed.

Children gain feelings of power by trying on powerful roles

Even something as simple as physically changing perspective makes children feel powerful. One young woman remembered spending time as a child squatting on the top of the refrigerator, looking down from her vantage point at the world and the people beneath her. Another had a secret hideout on the garage roof, under the shelter of a tall spreading tree.

One less than desirable way that children gain power is by misbehaving and making adults angry. Only when you watch a scene of a little child sending an adult into a frenzy do you realize what a feeling of power the child must get from this reaction. It's a little like being the person who pushes the button that sends a rocket into space. Wow! It's also a bit frightening to feel so powerful.

Sometimes a child in a preschool situation will cause a good deal of trouble. This child manages to affect everyone around him. It gets so that everyone breathes a sigh of relief on the days he is absent because things are so different. Children who behave like this are often so needy for power that they get it in the only way they know how—by making a big impact on the environment, including the people in it.

If you recognize power as a legitimate need, it seems reasonable to find ways to empower children so that they won't need to manipulate or disrupt to feel a sense of their own power. The following are some ways that adults can empower children:

• *Teach children effective language and how to use it.* Even very young children can learn to hold up a hand and firmly say "Stop!" to someone threatening them. They won't need to hit or shove once they learn to use the power of words. They can learn to express feelings. They can learn to argue their point. They can become effective language users. Remember, though, that some cultures have a different view of teaching children to express their feelings. The goal is group peace and harmony over individual expression of feelings. It is important to recognize this difference when working with children who come from these cultures.

• *Give children the support they need while they are coming to feel their personal power.* Don't let them continually be victimized until their personal power becomes so trampled that it threatens to disappear from sight all together. Use your personal power *for* them so they can come to use their own eventually. Don't rescue them. Instead, teach them ways to protect themselves—with your support at first; later they can do it without your support.

- *Help children tune in on their uniqueness and appreciate their differences.* Help each child become more fully who he or she really is rather than trying to cast him or her into some preset mold. Do remember, however, that not all cultures see uniqueness and individuality as a value. Some emphasize downplaying any characteristics that make one stand apart from the group.

The idea of empowering children in general, and these suggestions in particular, may be very uncomfortable for some families. That's why you have to use your best communication skills to share these ideas. But don't just talk; also listen. Communication is a two-way street. If you open up to new ideas from the families you work with, you'll expand your view and know more about what to do with each particular child in each particular family. Strategy Box 4.2 gives further ideas about how to work with families around the behaviors of their children in the stage of initiative.

We can empower children and help them experience a sense of their own power. We can empower families as well. Missy Danneberg writes the Advocacy in Action feature "Advocating for Ourselves" on the following pages. Read it to see what a group of directors did to solve a problem created by a situation that was unhealthy and demeaning.

Strategy Box 4.2

Sharing Approaches When Working with Children in the Initiative Stage

- Don't just teach parents; learn from them. They know more about their child than you do. They see the child in different contexts; you mainly see the child in the context of the early care and education program setting.

- Find out parents' views of the theme of this chapter: encouraging children to take initiative. The subject may be something they never thought of before. Or it may be quite a familiar subject. On the other hand, it may not fit their cultural background and will need to be discussed so that you understand where they are coming from.

- Be sure that families know that you are a mandated reporter for abuse. Define the difference between abuse and punishment. Also, help them see the disadvantages of both physical and psychological punishment.

- Demonstrate the many alternatives to punishment explained in this chapter.

- Recognize when you and the parents need outside help for working with their child.

We can't leave the preschool-age child without a discussion of early learning. The scene with Briana showed a developmentally appropriate preschool setting with activities and approaches that encouraged initiative. Unfortunately, everyone doesn't understand the value of such a program. Many well-meaning adults take the position that academics rather than play should be the focus of the preschool curriculum. They base their view on the facts that the early years are important ones and that most young children are equipped with a good memory and a willingness

> ### ADVOCACY IN ACTION ▶ ADVOCATING FOR OURSELVES
>
> **Missy Danneberg, child care director**
>
> Sometimes we get so discouraged or afraid of repercussions that we do not advocate for ourselves. A few years ago at a local early childhood program director's seminar, several directors reported being treated rudely and unfairly by state inspectors. Some of the directors felt embarrassed and questioned what they had done to deserve this treatment. They had filed complaints regarding this treatment and received no response but didn't want to go any further as they felt this would anger the inspectors. The group offered support and advice. When other directors continued to experience this type of treatment, it also was discussed at length at the seminars. The seminar leader felt that though the support and advice were good, some type of action was warranted.
>
> The seminar leader discussed with the group a variety of actions that could be taken, and it was decided to meet with a local state legislative aide and the ombudsman for the state inspector's office to explain the issues. Both meetings went very well, and the directors felt their concerns were heard. Many of the directors found this a powerful experience as it was their first meeting with a legislative aide. Directors also became aware of their rights when dealing with the state agency and procedures to use when they feel those rights are violated.
>
> As a result of these meetings, the state agency held a community meeting to hear all the issues, and changes were made in the procedures for state inspectors. Through this experience these professionals learned about the power of advocating for themselves and where to gain information and support.

to please. A response to this view is: Just because children *can* do something doesn't mean that they *ought* to.

When children are pushed to engage in rote learning or to perform for adults, their initiative can be squashed. Their need to please the powerful others in their lives conflicts with their own inner motivation. The need to please often wins out, and children take to heart the message that adult-directed learning is more valuable than child-directed activity.

> **Check Your Understanding 4.3**
>
> Click here to check your understanding of how adults contribute to children's initiative.

SUMMARY

This chapter focused on the preschool-age child, and started by showing an example of what initiative looks like in a four-year-old. That example was followed by an analysis of the child and her behaviors. The next section looked at the same child in terms of Erik Erikson's theory and gave examples of the development conflict that this child had already come to terms with. She now has the task of developing a sense of initiative without being overwhelmed by feelings of guilt when faced with social restrictions. We examined how adults provide for initiative in children by setting up an appropriate environment and by their own actions. We also looked at shy and aggressive children and explored the roots of these behaviors as well as ways to respond to them. A major part of this chapter concerned how to work with parents in a partnership around the behaviors that come with the stage of initiative. The chapter ended with teaching problem-solving skills and an examination of personal power and how to encourage it in children.

QUIZ

Click here to check your understanding of Chapter 4, "Sharing Views of Initiative with Families."

FOR DISCUSSION

1. The chapter gives the perspective of a culture that values independence, initiative, and individuality. What might be the perspective of a culture that instead puts a priority on interdependence, obedience, and putting the group before one's own needs, urges, wishes, and desires?

2. Consider Briana. Remember how she pretends to spank a boy. If you were the teacher, how would you know that it was just "pretend"? Would you stop that behavior? How would you describe a child who had a high level of initiative but was different from Briana?

3. How do you react to the idea of an "internal government"? Do you believe it is better for children to always have someone in authority watching them and taking charge of their behavior?

4. Analyze the environment you're in right now in terms of the five dimensions named by Elizabeth Jones and Elizabeth Prescott. Is it an appropriate environment for three- to six-year-old children to play in? Why or why not?

5. What is your opinion of the expectations that the street musicians ("Perspectives on Child Rearing") have of their daughter? Are the parents' expectations hampering her development? How much play time do children need? Does it harm them to put the good of the parents over their own urges to play and run around all the time? Remember, these are cultural questions. Different perspectives give different answers. If you talk with someone who disagrees with you, try to create a dialogue instead of a debate or argument.

6. How easy would it be for you to talk to parents about the subjects dealt with in this chapter? To what do you attribute your level of comfort or discomfort?

WEBSITES

Afraid to Ask
This site contains information related to ADHD signs and symptoms, treatment, and common questions, with additional resources listed.

Center for Parent Information Resources
The Center for Parent Information Resources has information and products to train and support families of children with disabilities.

National Association for Family Child Care (NAFCC)
The National Association for Family Child Care is devoted to promoting quality and professionalism in family child care homes. The website has resources for families and accreditation information for providers.

National Institute of Mental Health (NIMH)
Their website provides a great deal of information, including research on health and mental health issues.

National Institute for Early Education Research (NIEER)
The NIEER website has information about research to support high quality, effective early childhood education. The institute offers research-based advice and technical assistance to policymakers, journalists, researchers, and educators.

Ounce of Prevention Fund
The Ounce of Prevention Fund has the goal that all American children, particularly those born into poverty, have quality early childhood experiences in the first five years.

FURTHER READING

Castro, D. C., Anyankoya, B., & Kasprzak, C. (2011). *The new voices/nuevas voces guide to cultural and linguistic diversity in early childhood.* Baltimore, MD: Brookes.

Curtis, D., K. L. Brown, L. Baird, and A. M. Coughlin (2013). Planning environments and materials that respond to young children's lively minds. *Young Children* 68(4), 26–31.

Frost, J., Wortham, S., & Reifel, S. (2012). *Play and child development* (4th ed.). Upper Saddle River, NJ: Pearson.

Jent, J. F., Niec, L. N., & Baker, S. E. (2011). Play and inter-personal processes. In S. W. Russ & L. N. Niec (Eds.), *Play in clinical practice: Evidence-based approaches*. New York, NY: Guilford Press.

Jones, E., & Reynolds, G. (2011). *The play's the thing: Teachers' roles in children's play*. New York, NY: Teachers College Press.

Kersey, K. & M. Masterson. (2013). 101 *Principles for positive guidance with young children: Creating responsive teachers*. Upper Saddle River, NJ: Pearson.

Sandall, S. R. (2003, May). Play modifications for children with disabilities. *Young Children* 58(3), 54–55. Also http://www.extension.org/pages/61358/adapting-the-child-care-environment-for-children-with-special-needs#.VNadUq3TnL8 accessed January 2015.

Van Hoorn, J., Nourot, P., Scales, B., & Alward, K. (2015). *Play at the center of the curriculum* (6th ed.). Upper Saddle River, NJ: Pearson.

Working with Families of School-Age Children

Learning Outcomes

In this chapter you will learn to...

- Explain how elementary school is different from preschool.
- Describe the teaching of prosocial skills and morals.
- Discuss the power of adult attention.

jovanng/Fotolia

It's the first day of kindergarten for Daniel. He's been to preschool and now he is in "real school." He's five years old and he's a little scared. His mother senses his fear—an unsettled feeling that wasn't eased by the orientation the week before. She too is having some qualms. This is nothing like the small, informal setting of the preschool and its cozy play yard with grass, dirt, and a tricycle path circling a little play house. This is school and it's big and hard—in more senses than one. Out beyond the kindergarten room is a playground with crowds of screaming children running around. Mother and son reach the door. A bell rings and the screaming crowd heads toward the building. The mother says good-bye and opens the door. She leans over for a kiss, but Daniel, looking embarrassed, turns away and walks inside, and the door shuts behind him. That closed door makes Daniel's mother want to weep. Her son is growing up. He doesn't need her like he used to. She feels shut out of his life. She turns and walks away.

That's one scenario—here's another.

Mia and her younger sister, Samantha, have never been apart from each other since Samantha was born. Both their parents work so the two of them have been together in child care their whole lives. Today their mother drops Samantha off at the family care home. She and Mia go in to get Samantha settled and then it's time for them to leave. It's Mia's first day at kindergarten. Mia and Samantha were both excited last night, but now that the reality is upon them, it's a different story. Samantha protests loudly and holds onto her mother, trying to keep her from going out the door. She hasn't done that for years! Mia looks worried but walks out bravely. In the car, she looks upset and puts her thumb in her mouth. She hasn't sucked her thumb since she was eight weeks old! Both girls seem to recognize this is a big transition in their lives—not just a one-time event but the beginning of a separation that will be ongoing. School lasts a very long time. Although neither of them fully comprehends that they'll be grown up before they are finished with school and that they will never be in the same classroom together again, they do both sense that beginning today things will not be the same. Imagine their great relief when in the afternoon the child care provider goes to the school to pick up Mia along with the other school-age children in her home. The reunion of the two sisters is something to behold!

SCHOOL IS DIFFERENT FROM PRESCHOOL

Starting school is a major transition in the lives of children and their families, an event full of challenges even when the teachers do a great deal to ease everyone into the new setting and situation. For Mia, the transition was a little easier because she didn't have to change child care arrangements. Family child care programs usually have mixed age groups and provide what is sometimes called "surround care" or before- and after-school care. Children who are leaving home for the first time, as well as those four- and five-year-olds in early care and education programs who have "graduated" into kindergarten, face a whole new program both in kindergarten and in surround care. Those children have a tremendous transition to deal with.

Think about the kinds of ways that teachers and school-age care staff can help parents and their children feel more comfortable. In Daniel's case, the kindergarten teacher had an orientation the week before for new children and their families. They saw the classroom, tried out the desks, learned where things were, and how the schedule worked. The stories of both Daniel and Mia are true; unfortunately,

Starting school is a major transition in the lives of children and their families; it can be quite an adjustment

neither child entered a family-centered school. Let's imagine now that the kindergarten, at least, was family-centered. In a family-centered school, how might the children and their families have been more prepared for this big step forward?

A Family-Centered Approach to Kindergarten

In a family-centered program the teacher sees the importance of creating a relationship with each family, so instead of one big orientation, he or she meets with each family individually or in small groups over a period of time. Some families might even have a home visit before school starts.

In a family-centered program, the relationship starts even earlier than the first meeting before the start of the new school year. Teachers often send out invitations to families, encouraging them to visit the program in action before the end of the last school year. Some families accept the invitation. Some also get to spend time in the school-age child care center at the school.

At first meetings, there are always forms to fill out. But in a family-centered program, completing school forms is not the main purpose of the meeting. Teachers often send out forms ahead, and many families bring the form to the meeting already filled out. The purpose of the first meeting is for teachers and families to make connections with each other. Figure 5.1 illustrates a sample of the kind of form that helps get connections started.

In families where either the child or the parents are worried about separation, the subject is discussed. Parents' feelings about separation are acknowledged, and the teacher, the parents, and the child all brainstorm together about how to ease the separation fears. Teachers know what a big step it is to send children to school for the first time—even for those parents who have had previous experience with early care and education programs.

Family-centered programs try to stagger the entry so all children don't start at the same time. That's not always possible, but when it is, it helps children ease in. Together with the teacher the family decides if a family member should come in and stay with the child until he is comfortable, or if it is best that family members stay out of the classroom until the child gets used to being there on his own.

The School-Age Child and Stages of Development

Starting "real school" comes at a time when children's development is in transition—they are growing out of one stage of development and into another. The change of stages doesn't come at the same age for every child, and it is highly unlikely that this is the first transition phase of a child's life. Children starting kindergarten have already moved through Erikson's first stage, where trust is the major focus. That transition happens during the first year, more or less. Children,

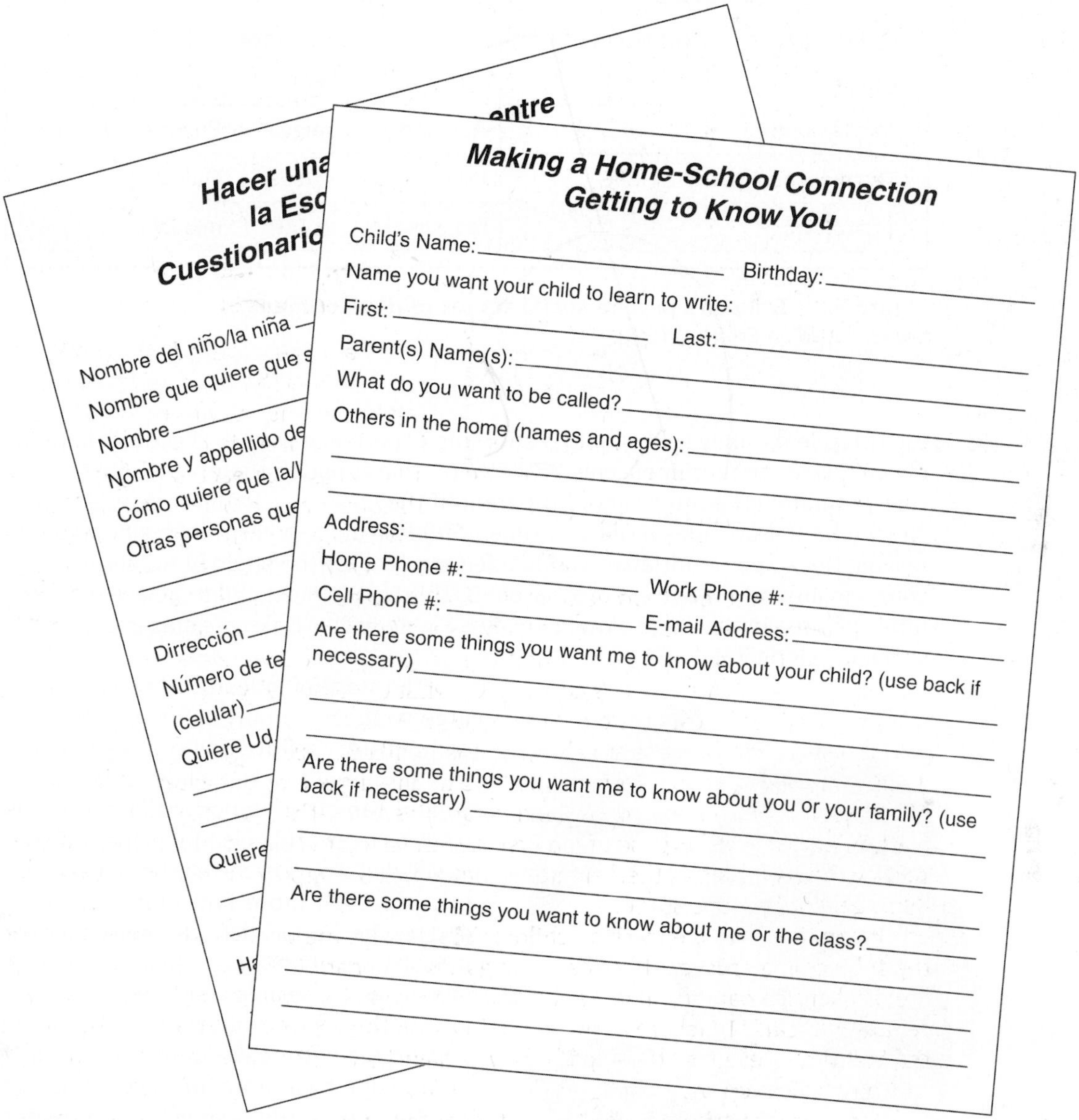

Making a Home-School Connection
Getting to Know You

Child's Name:_____ Birthday:_____

Name you want your child to learn to write:

First:_____ Last:_____

Parent(s) Name(s):_____

What do you want to be called?_____

Others in the home (names and ages):_____

_____

Address:_____

Home Phone #:_____

Cell Phone #:_____ Work Phone #:_____

E-mail Address:_____

Are there some things you want me to know about your child? (use back if necessary)_____

_____

Are there some things you want me to know about you or your family? (use back if necessary)_____

_____

Are there some things you want to know about me or the class?_____

_____

Figure 5.1   Example of one way to start a home-school connection

even those who have satisfactorily developed a basic sense of trust in that first year of life, still have trust issues when they start kindergarten. How much those issues dominate their lives depends on how they resolved what Erikson saw as that first psycho-social conflict all children go through. These children have also moved through Erikson's second stage—that of autonomy, as they have worked on resolving the issues involved with developing an identity that gives them the ability to see themselves as separate people with wants, likes, and the power to say no. Erikson's third stage, the stage of initiative, occurs during what some call the "play years." It usually starts around the age of three and ends around six. That means most children are still in the stage of initiative when they enter kindergarten. Children in

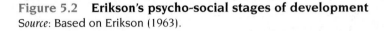

Child's Stage	Approximate Age	Task		
Infancy	0–1	Basic trust	versus	Basic mistrust
Toddlerhood	1–3	Autonomy	versus	Shame and doubt
The preschool years	3–6	Initiative	versus	Guilt
School age	6–10	Industry	versus	Inferiority

Figure 5.2   Erikson's psycho-social stages of development
Source: Based on Erikson (1963).

the "play years" may find school a shocking experience as they discover that play doesn't have the prominence in "real school" that it had in their preschool or child care program. (The after-school program, if they are enrolled in it, may ease the shock a bit if it provides more play time.) Children are in transition in kindergarten, leaving the stage of initiative and headed straight for the stage of industry, which comes in around the age of six or seven. By third grade most children have both feet firmly planted in the stage of industry. See Figure 5.2 for Erikson's stages of psycho-social development.

The stage of industry brings with it the urge to master many skills and become competent

The stage of industry brings with it the urge to master many skills and become competent. Children who have reached this stage want to know how things work. School can be an important factor in this stage as the world of learning opens up beyond what it was in the earlier years. Peers become even more important. Families and teachers appreciate children's urge for industry and mastery and find their role in enhancing these urges rewarding.

At the same time that children are getting ready to leave kindergarten, they are moving to a more advanced stage of intellectual skills, according to Piaget (1952). Up to age two, children are in the sensorimotor stage, where thought is connected to the body and senses. After age two, they move into the stage of pre-operational thought, where they can use symbols and words and have some reasoning skills, but they are still deceived by their senses and go by perceptions instead of reason. When children enter school they are moving toward the concrete operational stage but aren't there yet. They still use some magical thinking and lack organization in their thinking processes. Somewhere between the ages of six and eight children can begin to do operations in their heads. Think of operations as mental actions on the environment. Before this stage, children have to do everything physically, but now they are able to use their heads. The most successful schools are the ones that recognize that children don't all move forward at the same rate in either psycho-social development or cognitive development. Sensitive teachers meet each child where he or she is and help to support each child's progress. It's not easy to respond to individual differences today with the push to get every child up to grade level. Since grade level is an average, that's like saying all children should be of average height rather than recognizing some will be shorter and some taller, which is what makes average height average.

For most children, school comes at just the right time for their psycho-social and cognitive stages. For others the school and the child may not fit each other. Unfortunately most schools expect the child to be ready for them. Another way of looking at children's education, however, is that schools should be ready for each child who comes, even if he or she isn't yet as developed as some of the other children. In schools where developmentally appropriate practice is the foundation for the educational approach, it's more likely that the program is set up to take differences into consideration. The more teachers know about development, the better job they can do. Also, having knowledge about ages and stages lets the teacher add to families' knowledge.

> Unfortunately most schools expect the child to be ready for them. Another way of looking at children's education, however, is that schools should be ready for each child who comes, even if he or she isn't yet as developed as some of the other children.

Children enrolled in surround-care programs may find relief from the stress of trying to keep up with the others. That doesn't mean that school-age care programs don't have to deal with homework. In all settings, sensitive staff who understand developmental issues and children's needs, individually and as a group, can do much to support academic progress in understanding ways. They also can partner with parents in ways that help the child and the family as well as the program.

A collaborative relationship is the kind that family-centered programs aim for—a relationship in which families and teachers are partners. In a partnership both sides can pool their specialized information and skills in order to see the whole picture. For example, families know their own child best, but they may not have a deep grasp of child development. The teacher has experience with more children than the family and has training and education in working with children. So as the family members share what they know about their own child, the teacher can share knowledge of child development and help the parents see how their child is moving through the stages. Parents can also see that these stages apply beyond their own child and are pertinent to all children.

Differences Families Notice Between School and Preschool

There are many educational theories, but from a family's point of view, two approaches in particular may seem at the forefront because they often differ greatly between preschool and elementary school. In preschool the approach may depend on helping children "construct knowledge" through figuring things out by having hands-on experiences. In school it is more likely that the teacher teaches and the children do "seat work" that is related to the teaching.

To explain further, many preschools using what is called a constructivist approach, take developmental stages into consideration and help children at each stage create knowledge through hands-on experiences (Chaille, 2008). The learner is active, and the teacher is more of a facilitator who sets up a rich environment and then helps each child take full advantage of it. It's the opposite from pouring knowledge into the child. "Teaching is not telling" is a motto of the constructivists. Many preschool teachers are constructivists, whether they use that term or not.

A little book by DeVries and Sales (2011) shows how a constructivist can teach physics to young children. Their definition of constructivism comes from Piaget's research: "Children actively create—'construct'—knowledge of the physical world from their experiences when they go beyond what they already know" (p. 11). Children constructing knowledge are looking into their ideas about how things work by testing and refining their assumptions. They come up with hypotheses and keep trying them out.

> ▶ Watch this clip to see children constructing their own knowledge as they learn about worms. What role does the teacher play in this classroom?

School is less likely to be taught by constructivists, for a lot of reasons, which may relate to governmental, community, or parent pressure to teach academics and to use sanctions when children don't perform up to par on the tests designed to measure academic abilities. "Back to the Basics" used to be the term used for this movement toward academics and away from what was sometimes called the "discovery learning" that constructivists promoted.

With children's test scores threatening, teachers may be forced to use more skill drilling and memorization than they would otherwise. Some teachers are complaining that what children learn for the tests is soon forgotten because it goes into their short-term memory instead of long-term memory. But many educators don't see that they have a choice.

Something else that preschool families can't fail to notice when their children enter elementary school is recess, or (in some schools) the lack thereof. In most preschools and child care programs, outdoor play is part of the learning program and involves a lot more than a ten-minute break to go outside and run around or wait for a turn on the swings. The time spent outside is not just a time to exercise because children need a break from learning. Rather, the outdoor program takes place as an extension of the educational environment.

Recess in public schools, however, has become an endangered species. Back in the 1980s children got three recesses a day to play outdoors, plus an hour for lunch. The trend now is to cut back on recess or eliminate it all together and shorten the lunch break. According to Anne Marie Chaker (2006) in "Rethinking Recess," because

Recess is important because play is integral to the academic environment

verkoka /Fotolia

of the pressure for academic accountability and the standardized tests to measure it, schools are cutting back on play time; however, there is no research to indicate that children do better academically without recess than they do with periodic recesses throughout the day. On the contrary, according to the American Academy of Pediatrics (2006), "Play is integral to the academic environment… It has been shown to help children adjust to the school setting and even to enhance children's learning readiness, learning behaviors, and problem-solving skills."

Bringing back recess can offer an opportunity for advocates to go to work. The first step for saving recess is to join forces with others—parents, teachers, and anybody else who wants to keep recess alive in the schools or bring it back if it has already disappeared. Start by researching why children need recess. Spread the word by distributing the information locally. If you don't get results, go higher to the media and/or to state level groups such as the PTA. A lot can be accomplished by a group of advocates wanting the best for children.

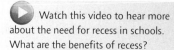

Watch this video to hear more about the need for recess in schools. What are the benefits of recess?

www.youtube.com
/watch?v=M80P01BXkhM

Though public school teachers are under many constraints, joining with families to create family-centered programs gives them some advantages the other programs don't have. For one thing they can better meet the educational and socialization needs of the children if they know what the parents' expectations are. The parents whose children have been in early care and education programs before they reach public school may be used to being included in planning; they may know how to take a supportive role and would be happy to continue the experiences they have had in previous programs. They may be more vocal about their perspectives on learning than parents who have no earlier experience with care and education programs. The Advocacy in Action feature "A Parent Advocates for Her Child Who Has Special Needs" tells a story of a mother who has been advocating for her son throughout his school years. He has never been in a family-centered school. It's a sad story but has a happy ending. Teachers in family-centered programs may find that families have widely diverse expectations. The goal should be to respect all families' perspectives and help them respect each others'. That may be difficult, but it's worthwhile. For more information and resources about children with special needs, go to the websites for the Council for Exceptional Children and Marc Sheehan's Special Education/Exceptionality Page.

Finding Out What Families Want for Their Children

The key to understanding each family is becoming a good communicator and implementing a number of approaches that encourage communication, whether you are a kindergarten teacher, primary teacher, or school-age care staff member.

Finding time to communicate is usually a problem. Teachers and parents have to look for opportunities to have both casual conversations before and after school and planned ones as well. Phone calls and e-mails are one way to keep in touch regularly. Scheduled opportunities such as meetings and conferences are also standard practice. Be sure that meetings are scheduled at times that accommodate all families. Scheduling conferences only in the afternoon eliminates anyone who can't take time off work to attend. Be sure to have interpreters if you don't speak the home language of the families and they don't speak yours. Conferences should be about communicating—not just a one-way report on the part of the teacher. It's important that the teacher listens and isn't the only one who talks. Real communication is two-way—back and forth. There may be some trust issues involved at first until parents understand that the teacher truly does want to listen.

ADVOCACY IN ACTION A PARENT ADVOCATES FOR HER CHILD WHO HAS SPECIAL NEEDS

Ida Wong, *parent*

My son, who is now in eighth grade, has a form of autism called Asperger's. I have spent much of my life advocating for his rights in the school system. I learned to be a difficult parent so school personnel would listen to me and make accommodations for him. Here is an example of the kind of persistent, dedicated work this requires.

Though my son does sometimes struggle with social situations, he has strong academic skills. His Star Test scores placed him at the Advanced level in Algebra I and also in English Language. He was managing all of his schoolwork well until the end of seventh grade, when he began being bullied by another child and mistreated by a teacher who was not sympathetic to his special needs. He was unhappy and had trouble sleeping, and his grades dropped dramatically in the last three months. When the school made his math placement for eighth grade they decided to have him repeat algebra, even though the Star Test results show that he has already mastered algebra concepts and theory. It was clear to my husband and myself that he would not learn anything by repeating the class. We asked that our son be placed in geometry with the understanding that if he was not successful they could put him back in algebra.

School started and he was repeating algebra. So I e-mailed the counselor who forwarded my e-mail to the principal, but I got no response. I sent the principal e-mails every day asking for a meeting but still got no response. I sent three pages of detailed information about my son's history, life and school experience, progress in school, strengths and weaknesses, teachers' comments, a summary of the hospital's autism report, and the results of the Star Testing. I still got no response. I sent the principal another e-mail from my son's autism case manager suggesting we discuss the math placement with the school. No response. I e-mailed him again explaining that my son was moody and not sleeping and had lost his appetite. No response. I visited the school office and asked to see the counselor and the special education teacher, but they would not see me.

As I was leaving a message for them, the secretary told the principal I was there and he invited me into his office! We met for an hour and I showed him all the paperwork I had brought. The principal was stubborn, but finally he listened to me. Today I was told that my son would be moved to the geometry class. He is so happy that he is in his room now studying by himself trying to catch up on all the assignments that he has missed in the class. I fought for his rights. His happy face is my true reward.

Written communication is also important. Of course, make sure any written communication is translated into the languages represented in your classroom. Figure 5.3 shows a sample of a letter from a first-grade teacher to parents (see Figure 5.3). Although this sample letter is a one-way communication designed to inform, it's also an invitation for the parents to communicate with the teacher. This teacher is showing that she is open to listening, and she even gives her home phone number! This kind of letter or announcement is a useful communication from school to home. Some programs also have regular two-way written communication—for example, a journal that goes home and comes back regularly, or a journal that stays in the classroom and whoever wants to write in it can—parents, teachers, children. Interactive bulletin boards are another means of two-way written communication. E-mail or texting are the easiest ways to communicate if it doesn't turn out to be overwhelming to either parents or teachers. Teachers and other staff follow the policy of their center or school when communicating with families.

One area of education that is often minimized in schools is development and learning in the social-emotional domain, including learning to be a moral person with values. The next section looks at how schools, child care, and families can partner to support children's healthy socialization.

Check Your Understanding 5.1

Click here to check your understanding of how school is different from preschool.

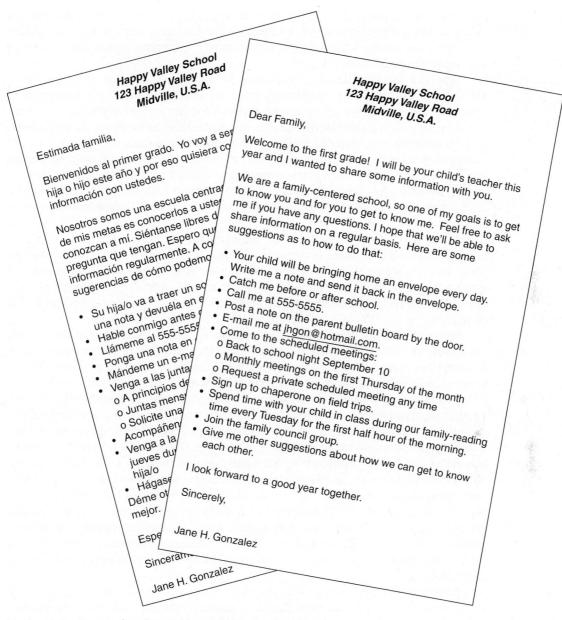

Figure 5.3 **Example of a welcome letter to families**

TEACHING PROSOCIAL SKILLS AND MORALS

Communities depend on their members having prosocial skills. This book looks at the child in context of the family, school, and community as related to Bronfenbrenner's ecological systems theory. It also explores how to help the child grow up to be a productive member of that community. Every chapter has been about how to support healthy growth and development so the child functions as a community member. This section starts with a question. How do children come to know what's important in life and set their goals accordingly? How do children come to know right from wrong? Although the two questions are in many ways the same, the answer to the first question mostly concerns values; the answer to the second mostly concerns morals.

Teachers and families may not agree on including this area of education in the curriculum, and some individuals may find problems with some aspects of it. The question may come up right away: whose morals and whose values? In a diverse society such as the United States there is bound to be some disagreement, but the differing opinions can make for interesting discussions with families as you bring the subject to them. Discussing the subject gives opportunities for all parties to practice respect for each other. One way to frame the discussion is to look for universal values. Another way to frame it is to use the 11 strategies for teaching pro-social development at the end of this chapter to see if there is agreement on some of the ideas.

Where do we get our values? Our values began to come to us in our cribs (or our parents' bed if we slept with them) when we were infants. Values are absorbed along with the breast milk or the formula we drink. They come hand in hand with our culture. They are the *shoulds* and *shouldn'ts* that guide our footsteps through life and the beliefs we feel compelled to stand up for. They tell us what to respect and what to oppose.

Some values are simply absorbed in infancy; others come later in the form of little lessons. "Don't hurt the caterpillar" may reflect a value of life. "Be gentle with your brother" may reflect a value of peace and harmony. "Don't let people push you around" may reflect a value of self-assertion. "Work hard at school" may reflect a value of attaining individual success or of being an asset to your family. As children grow, they continually define, appraise, and, sometimes, modify their values. In cultures that value independence, children are expected to do some deep soul-searching at some point, usually in adolescence. They are expected to examine the set of values they've grown up with and come to their own conclusions about whether to embrace those values or to redefine them and come up with their own set. Upset as parents may be at the possibility that their children will reject their values, these parents aren't entirely surprised because the culture expects people to make up their own minds about values. After all, independence is a value—independence of thought as well as of action. Interestingly enough, even offspring who swung far from their parents' values in the teen years usually come back to them later in life.

Parents from cultures that value interdependence may be far less tolerant if their children threaten to deviate from the set of values the family embraces. The younger generation is not supposed to question the older one. Deciding values is not an individual matter for children—or for adults, either.

Looking at the Decision-Making Process as a Way of Exploring Morals

We—children and grown-ups alike—deal with morals and values with every decision we make. Each time we are forced to choose an action (and each action is a choice, whether we realize it or not), we go through a process of determining whether we're making the right decision. The impulsive person puts less thought into decisions than the more considered one; however, unless the person is reacting from reflexes alone, there is a flash of thought behind each decision.

If you could tune in on the flash, you'd find some of the following questions:

♦ Will I be punished if I decide to do this (either by my own bad feelings or by someone else in a physical or emotional way)?

♦ Will I be rewarded? (Will I gain some benefit, including feeling good about doing this?)

♦ Will this action or decision make someone whom I care about happy—thus making *me* happy (another form of reward)?

♦ Is there a rule (or a law) that requires or forbids it? And if I break the law and get caught, what is the punishment? And if I break the law and don't get caught, how will I feel?

♦ Is this what I would want someone else to do? (This calls into play the Golden Rule: "Do unto others as you would have others do unto you.")

♦ What's the right thing to do? (Using my highest reasoning abilities—is this the best, most right, highest good, or least bad thing to do?)

♦ Who might be hurt by my decision or action?

We don't always ask these questions consciously, but on some level they govern our decisions. We're more aware of that fact when the decision concerns a situation where there is a good deal at stake. The questions above are based on the work of three researchers, Lawrence Kohlberg (1976), Carol Gilligan (1983), and Nel Noddings (2005). Noddings followed Gilligan by focusing on caring, which she saw as transforming schools. She takes the early childhood principles espoused in this book out of preschool, puts them into the K–8 system, and goes even further to include high school and the university.

Lawrence Kohlberg. Kohlberg, the best-known researcher on moral decision making, followed the work of Jean Piaget and saw a pattern of organization of moral thought, which he laid out in progressive stages that linked to Piaget's cognitive stages. Kohlberg described children in the early years as determining what's right and what's wrong by whether they are rewarded or punished. Later they move to being motivated to obey rules in order to uphold a social order. Kohlberg's final stages of development involve a personal commitment to an abstract hierarchy of principles. In Kohlberg's scheme, intellectual development—specifically the ability to reason—is vitally linked to moral development. It is, however, important to note that Kohlberg did his research on men and boys, which sparked Gilligan and Noddings to investigate what some see as feminine approaches to moral decision making, but both these women see their ideas as applying to everybody—not just women.

Children don't worry about research, theory, or stages. Their decision making is usually quick and unconscious. We can help children be more thoughtful about moral dilemmas they face by bringing the questions into the open and examining them. We can also be more thoughtful ourselves about what is motivating children to make the decisions they do. If you look at the questions listed earlier, it is possible to determine, from Kohlberg's view, which ones are most likely to be of importance to younger children. Most children under the age of seven are able to think only in concrete terms, according to Piaget. Although they may feel emotions related to such abstract concepts as love, honesty, and justice, they don't think or reason about them. They do, however, have a sense of what's fair and what's unfair from their point of view. Instead of using sophisticated cognitive processes, young children are more likely to make judgments about right and wrong actions based on their experiences with the

Watch this video to see children presented with a moral dilemma. What do you notice about the difference between the way that the younger children and older children respond?

www.youtube.com/watch?v= riugWInqiaE

Caring relationships are a vital part of teaching

reactions of those around them. They consider the possibility of punishment or reward when trying to decide on the "right thing to do."

Carol Gilligan and Nel Noddings. Gilligan and Noddings' work has focused most on the last of the questions posed in our list: "Who might be hurt by my decision or action?" From their work has come what is called an *ethic of caring*. Gilligan and Noddings see moral decision making as coming from a concern about acting so that the people one cares about will be hurt the least by one's decision. Although their work reflects the moral decision making of women and girls, they assure us that males also use the same types of decision-making processes.

Noddings has written many books and articles about the ethic of caring. Three are *Caring: A Feminine Approach to Ethics and Morals* (2013), *The Challenge to Care in Schools* (2005) and *Educating Moral People* (2002), which presents a caring alternative to character education that deals directly with how to develop morals in children using the ethic of caring. She says that moral development comes from creating conditions and relationships that support moral ways of life rather than teaching children to be virtuous, which is the approach taken by those who use character education. Caring relationships are what count. Caring relationships involve a particular kind of attention from the carer to the cared-for. Noddings calls this attentiveness *engrossment*, which she describes as acutely receptive. Engrossment involves the carer directing motivational energy toward the needs of the cared-for. Another requirement of a caring relationship is that the caring must be detected and received. The response of the cared-for is then received back by the carer in further moments of engrossment.

> **Caring must be genuine and not just a means of coercion or emotional manipulation to get the family or child to behave in ways the teacher deems acceptable.**

This information has implications for teachers and care providers. The National Association for the Education of Young Children (NAEYC) recognizes the importance of relationships—placing "relationships" in the number-one place in its program standards. (For more information about the NAEYC, visit their website.) *Care* is not a word often found in teacher education materials, except in programs for infants and very young children. Yet caring relationships are a vital part of teaching, with implications for the parent-teacher relationship. The more teachers and providers can support parents, the more likely they are to enhance the caring relationships those parents have with their children. Support and care breed more support and care.

Caring must be genuine and not just a means of coercion or emotional manipulation to get the family or child to behave in ways the teacher deems acceptable. Caring relationships have received a good deal of attention from those who train adults to work with babies. Both Magda Gerber (Gerber & Johnson, 1998) and Emmi Pikler (David & Appell, 2001; as well as yours truly, Gonzalez-Mena, 2004) have provided living examples of what Noddings calls *caring relationships*. At the Pikler Institute in Budapest, one can observe caregivers interacting with babies in genuinely caring ways. The caregivers are trained in a practical and effective approach based on an ethic of caring, which makes a huge difference in outcomes of children who spend their first years in an institution. Gerber's work, based on an attitude of respect, also demonstrates caring relationships. Her work can be seen wherever her Resources for Infant Educarers (RIE) associates are at work, in California and elsewhere. Noddings notes how care and trust come together so that positive behavior is more a result of the relationship than of the many manipulative techniques so often used by educators. Following an ethic of care, according to Noddings, is more likely to produce caring, moral people than just teaching them to be good. Diane Carlebach and Beverly Tate (2002) assert that using an approach based on Gerber's work creates *peaceful* people and leads to caring communities.

Besides developing the kind of relationships described by Noddings and others, how can teachers and families together direct children down the path of prosocial behavior? Here's one way, as illustrated by a story I heard once—reported to be a Native American story. A grandfather sharing his wisdom with his grandson told him this: "Everybody has two wolves inside—wolves that battle with each other. One is an evil wolf who is full of anger, envy, jealousy, sorrow, regret, greed, arrogance, self-pity, guilt, resentment, inferiority, lies, false pride, superiority, and ego. The other wolf is good. It is joy, peace, love, hope, serenity, humility, kindness, benevolence, empathy, generosity, truth, compassion, and faith." The grandson listened carefully, then a quizzical look came across his face. "Grandfather," he said, "which one wins the battle?" Grandfather looked at him knowingly and responded with only four words, "The one you feed." A very wise grandfather. He knew the power of attention. What you pay attention to feeds off that attention.

> **Check Your Understanding 5.2**
> Click here to check your understanding of teaching prosocial skills and morals.

THE POWER OF ADULT ATTENTION

When I was getting my teaching credential I observed children in a first-grade classroom. I learned a lot from that experience, but one thing really sticks in my mind—a boy named Ralph. His was the first name I learned in that class of 30 children. I heard the teacher say his name just seconds after I arrived in the classroom, and she continued to say his name at least an average of every five minutes throughout my observation period. "Ralph, please sit down." "Ralph, stop it!" "Ralph, don't push other children." Sometimes she just said "Ralph!" when she saw him doing something he wasn't supposed to. When he was sitting quietly listening, or doing his seat work, or getting along with other children, he never heard his name called. He definitely knew how to get the teacher's attention. He had the teacher's focus on him more than any other child. His behavior was working for him. It wasn't evil behavior, but still, the teacher was feeding the wrong wolf in Ralph.

Paying Attention to the Behavior You Want to Continue

I saw another example of the power of attention while I was observing one of my early-childhood practicum students working in an after-school program. It was snack time and the pitcher of milk on the snack table was empty. One child picked up his empty glass, held it out, and said gruffly to the teacher, "More milk!" Right about the same time another child said, "Please, can I have more milk?" The teacher immediately responded to the second, ignoring the first, who quickly changed his tone and words to sound more like the other child who got such a quick response from the teacher.

Pay attention to children who exhibit the prosocial behaviors you are looking for, such as cooperation and collaboration

Dejan Ristovski/Fotolia

So the message is: pay attention to children who exhibit the prosocial behaviors you're looking for. Notice how gently the big kids help the younger ones. Remark on how nicely Ty is waiting for his turn. You're a good model for parents when you begin to use the power of your attention.

Here's another story about the power of attention. Ana is a family child care provider whose home gets busy after school with the children who come to her. Two of those children have a good deal of trouble getting along with each other. Ugly squabbles constantly break out when they are together. Ana's usual method is to respond to them when they are arguing. She has taught them not to hit each other, but she can't seem to keep them from yelling at each other. She spends a good deal of her time settling their disputes.

Ana talks about these two with her neighbor, Irene, who is a teacher's aide in a nearby elementary school and is enrolled in an early childhood class at the local college. Irene tells her what she learned about the principle that when you pay attention to behavior, it tends to continue; when you ignore the same behavior, it tends to disappear. "What you stroke is what you get," says Irene, quoting from the book she is reading for her class, written by Jean Illsley Clarke (1998), who is an expert on strokes and affirmations. She suggests that Ana start ignoring the arguing. She does. It gets worse.

Ana complains to Irene that the suggestion didn't work. "I ignored them and ignored them and they kept right on fighting."

"Maybe," says Irene, "you took away the attention you were giving them for arguing without replacing it with attention for something else."

"What do you mean?" asks Ana.

"You have to pay attention to them when they *aren't* arguing."

"Oh," says Ana.

She tries that approach. Whenever the two are playing nicely together she remarks about how well they are getting along. It isn't easy to do this because she's not used to it, but she makes a conscious effort. When a squabble breaks out, she leaves the room and starts washing dishes. Sometimes the squabble follows her, but she makes a point of ignoring the angry voices.

Ana doesn't feel entirely comfortable about this approach. It seems dishonest and unnatural to her. Children ought to be good without her making this special effort. After all, cooperative behavior is what's expected. It shouldn't get special notice. It should be the norm. When she was growing up, her mother didn't have to put up with this kind of annoyance. All she had to do was look at her children and the squabbles stopped. She wishes that would work for her, but it doesn't. She begins to notice, however, that the squabbles aren't true disagreements, anyway, but are bids for her attention. She continues to use the approach of paying attention to the positive behavior and ignoring the rest.

It works! Of course, the children still have their disagreements, but not so constantly anymore. Furthermore, Ana has gotten to know the children better and has even grown closer to them since she's not so annoyed at the continual bickering. Ana has learned about the power of attention.

Using Affirmations

Ana also learned about affirmations from Irene. *Affirmations* give messages that validate the person as an individual who has needs and rights. Affirmations are positive messages about expectations. They encourage children to be who they are. They can come in the form of being interested in individuals and expressing appreciation to each one.

Ana knew something about affirmations, though she didn't call them that. Being interested and expressing appreciation was something she did naturally, something she learned from her own parents. She wasn't sure about using affirmations on purpose to help the children feel good about themselves so they wouldn't have such a need to squabble with each other. Ana especially had trouble with the idea that with affirmations she was validating the children as *individuals*. Of course, she recognized that each was a separate person, but what she wanted to emphasize in her family child care home was their *connections* rather than their separateness. She wanted them to focus less on themselves and more on others.

Ana brought up her concern to Irene one evening when the children had gone home. "I don't want them to think about their own needs" was how Ana put it. "That makes them selfish. They should put other people first."

"But until your own needs are met, how can you think of other people?" asked Irene. "Think of this example," she went on. "When you fly, the flight attendant instructs you that in case of a loss of cabin pressure, you must put your own oxygen mask on before you help other people."

"I think that's an extreme example," Ana responded.

"Maybe, but I think it applies. And it points out that your own needs are important *in order for you to help other people*. Isn't that what your goal is—that your children not be selfish?"

"I see what you mean," said Ana.

The two didn't resolve this issue because Irene tended to *always focus on individuals* when she thought about young children and families, and Ana tended to *avoid focusing on the individual*. Irene seemed to emphasize separateness. Ana liked to emphasize relatedness and embeddedness. But they understood that they disagreed on this issue and were friendly about it.

Affirmations can also be used to let children (or adults) know how they *can be* while accepting how they *are* at the present moment. Irene, who understood how this principle worked, used it in the classroom where she was a teacher's aide. One example: she avoided labeling any child as "shy." When one parent talked to her about her son's shyness, Irene shared what she had observed and made it clear that she saw the boy as cautious and careful, putting a little different light on the behavior. Irene used affirmations with this boy, letting him know that he was fine the way he was. If he was slower to accept a new person or situation than other children were, she let him know that was all right, too. She affirmed his need to feel safe. She also affirmed the individuality of his pace. It usually took him a while to warm up and she didn't hurry him. On the other hand, Irene encouraged him to take a few risks, recognizing his potential as a person who could eventually come out of his protective shell and become more able to explore freely. All this was discussed with the teacher and the parents. Everyone agreed with Irene's approaches.

When thinking about strokes and affirmations, it is important to look at both in a cultural context. This chapter, because it is in line with my own cultural background (European-American) and also my training to be a teacher, focuses on independence and individuality to some extent. It's what I know best. The idea is to help children feel good about themselves. In some cultures the focus is on downplaying individuality, keeping the child firmly embedded in the group (Howes, 2010; Rothstein-Fisch & Trumbull, 2008; Rothstein-Fisch, Trumbull, & Garcia, 2009). Along with this focus may come teaching humility instead of pride and putting others before self. As you saw with Ana, strokes and affirmations seemed strange and in opposition to the goals of her family growing up and her situation as a family child care provider.

Also, in some families direct communication is not valued. Subjects may be talked around instead of directly addressed. Indirect communication, in the form of behavior (including body language), is more valued than what is put into words. In fact, in these families, the kinds of statements used in this chapter to illustrate strokes and affirmations may be regarded as uncomfortable or manipulative. When parents want their children to do something, they just tell them to do it, and the children have respect for their parents, so they do it. Those parents don't need to make their children feel good about themselves. The children feel good just being part of the family and fulfilling their role as son or daughter.

These are two very different approaches to child rearing that seem to be oppositional in some ways. The fact that they are different doesn't mean that one way is right and the other is wrong. It means that there are differences, and differences must be acknowledged, accepted, and honored. When people who have diverse perspectives come together, they have opportunities to learn from each other. That is a strong message in this book. We share what we know and believe in with others and remain open to what others have to share with us. So with all that in mind, let's look further at strokes and other forms of positive adult attention.

Children's Response to Positive Adult Attention

Does giving positive adult attention always work? No. There's nothing that *always* works all the time, in every situation, with every child. How children respond to positive affirmations and strokes depends on their previous experience, which relates to their opinions of themselves and their reality about how the world is. Some children feel validated by affirmations; others don't. Some children accept the positive strokes they are given; others ignore or reject them.

Why would that be? These patterns have their roots in early experience. Imagine a baby who is ignored most of the time. He knows at some deep level that he needs attention and, because he is an infant, the strokes he needs are physical as well as social. He needs physical care given in a way that tells him he is cared about. Strokes in one sense of the word relate to physical touch and in another sense mean caring personal attention. The baby needs strokes or he'll die. Because he is an infant, he can't get attention except by crying, and even then his cries are often ignored. He does get fed and changed often enough to keep him alive, but he doesn't receive his full quota of warm caring strokes—either physically or in the form of adults paying attention to him. So when he gets old enough to create a ruckus, he does that. He soon learns that some behaviors bring adults to him. If the behavior is unacceptable enough, they even lavish attention on him—not affection, but attention. It's not positive attention that he receives. He is yelled at, scolded, even punished. But because he is so desperate for strokes—so needing attention of any kind—he accepts these negative responses. He comes to expect them, and when he's old enough to think about such things, he even may regard negative strokes as his due—somehow convincing himself, consciously or unconsciously, that he deserves them.

That attitude, that concept of reality, is what makes it so hard to get through to a child who is used to getting negative strokes. Positive strokes are ignored. Affirmations go in one ear and out the other. They don't relate to the child's reality.

Imagine a child, Michael, who comes from that type of situation early in life and is finally removed from the home, passed through several foster homes, and finally adopted at age four. He now arrives in kindergarten at the age of five. The teacher, aide, and parent volunteers are kind and loving to him, but he doesn't accept that kind of attention. They tell him what a good job he is doing on his art project; he throws it to the ground and stomps on it. He refuses to accept positive strokes. He seems to *need* the negative ones. And he is an expert at getting them. He hurts other children. He destroys their things and laughs about it. He constantly butts heads with the adults. He acts like a general all-round menace.

It is tempting to label this child based on his behavior. He has a knack for making adults very angry. The teacher and aide begin to resent all the time they spend trying to manage his behavior. He spends a lot of time in the principal's office. No one feels like giving him positive strokes anymore. "That just doesn't work," they all agree.

The parents feel equally helpless in the face of Michael's negative behavior. They know what is going on at school; it's much like what goes on at home. They are taking a parenting class and getting some counseling, but they haven't yet been successful at making a difference in Michael's behavior. They remember the first conversation they had with Michael's teacher about his challenging behavior. See Strategy Box 5.1 for the process the teacher used to communicate with the parents about concerns about Michael.

Michael might sound like a child with a disability or mental health issues. Perhaps he is, but nobody yet is willing to take the step forward to get a diagnosis. They may feel helpless, but at the same time they are still hopeful that they can work together to help him improve his feelings about himself and the behavior that goes with them.

There is another child in the class who has been identified as a child with special needs; she has a whole team of professionals, along with the teacher and her parents, who have worked together to create a plan for her education. The plan is called an IEP—an Individualized Education Plan—and was the result of a series of discussions among the team until they came to an agreement about what was needed for this particular child.

Working with Michael's Family to Explore Ways to Support His Development and Learning

- After making some careful observations of specific incidents involving Michael, the teacher recorded what she saw objectively so she could be clear and non-judgmental about Michael's behavior before meeting with the parents.

- She met with the family in a place where they could have privacy and not be overheard or interrupted. She invited any family members the parents thought they should bring along. They came by themselves.

- She let them know that the purpose of the meeting was to find ways to better support their child's development.

- The discussion started with the teacher asking how they, his parents, saw Michael. They shared their views and then the teacher shared her observations. When they compared notes they found there was consistency—what the parents saw at home related to what was happening at school—and they felt they were all on the same page. One difference, however, was notable. The teacher saw Michael with other children and noted that he was something of a bully. The parents didn't see him around other children.

- The teacher shared her perceptions of Michael's strengths and asked his parents to do the same.

- The teacher shared her concerns, using examples from her observations, and the parents shared theirs. They spent the rest of the meeting brainstorming approaches to take with Michael.

An IEP might be in Michael's future but is not part of the discussion at this time. For now, Michael's parents and his teacher are working together to figure out what to do about Michael, but in a less formal system than if he enters the special education system.

Michael is a tough nut to crack, but his behavior makes sense when you understand his history. He is getting his strokes in the only way he knows how. His reality is that he is "bad," and therefore he believes deep down that he deserves the negative attention he gets. The positive strokes he gets from the school and at home are brushed off. They are not part of his reality. They don't belong to him.

The adults in his life frustrate him because he can't get the same intense reaction to his behavior that he used to get from his birth mother and from the people she lived with before he was removed from the home. The teachers don't show their anger as passionately as the people he lived with in his first years. They don't hurt him the way he was used to being hurt. He doesn't understand the reality of the environments he is in now.

What should be done about Michael? The abuse and neglect that still have such a hold on him lie back in his past. Now it is up to the people in his life to help Michael control his unacceptable behavior, learn some prosocial behaviors, and come to feel better about himself.

Here's what they finally come up with as a group—teacher, family, and principal. In spite of the failure of their past efforts, they all continue to focus on the positive aspects of Michael's personality. They search for tiny bits of acceptable behavior. Sometimes they joke that they need a microscope to do this searching, but they discover that when they look hard enough they can find positive behaviors—brief though they may be. Every scrap of positive behavior from Michael brings immediate adult attention—hugs, smiles, words.

They also begin to see Michael in a new light. Instead of a difficult child, they see the behavior for what it is, patterns that he has learned in response to his early environment. The patterns are working against him now, rather than for him, but they can be understood as adaptive behaviors. They discuss how he could be if he overcame his behavior issues and learned to feel good about himself. Once they even took some time at one of their meetings to visualize

> **Instead of a difficult child, they see the behavior for what it is, patterns that he has learned in response to his early environment.**

this new Michael. They closed their eyes and "saw" the potential that lies beneath the difficult behavior.

When the teacher and aide are with Michael, they manage his behavior without rejecting him. It isn't easy. In fact, they really need an extra staff person to do this job properly, but they are able to use the daily parent volunteer to help out so they can do whatever is necessary to focus more fully on Michael.

Little by little they are managing to disconfirm Michael's perception of himself as a "bad person." They're changing his attitude by changing his behavior. They take a prevention approach—physically stopping him before he performs a malicious act.

When they first started this approach, they called in an extra aide so they had plenty of people in the classroom, thus releasing the regular aide to "track" Michael—to keep a constant eye on him. That meant that even when the aide went on a break, someone else was assigned to take over, so that Michael was never un-observed during any part of the first few days of the new approach. He was "tracked" during recess as well as in the classroom. His behavior began to improve—so much so that they were able to reduce the "tracking" to difficult parts of the day. This way they could dispense with the extra aide. The principal agreed to come in sometimes when they needed augmented staffing. Eventually they needed to track Michael only during transition periods, such as arrival and departure times as well as before and after recess, which were always bad times for Michael.

Of course, prevention doesn't always work. Sometimes the adults slip and acci-dentally let Michael do something unacceptable. The other day, for example, while the teacher was tying another child's shoelace, Michael grabbed a shovel from a boy who was digging in the sandbox. When the child protested and tried to get the shovel back, Michael kicked him, and he was continuing to kick when the teacher grabbed him.

The teacher's response was to separate Michael from the other children. He took him inside. The teacher stayed with him—not to scold him and tell him how badly he'd behaved (Michael already knew that) but to let him know that someone will provide the control that he still lacks and that he is supported and cared about.

The idea is to not allow Michael to make others reject him, which is what used to happen regularly. He still hasn't made friends among the children, but he's be-ginning to form an attachment to the regular aide—and that's helping to build trust and to give him a sense of the pleasures of closeness with another person. The Michael who's been locked away inside is starting to emerge.

With Michael, remediation must be done. He must be "reprogrammed." Children usually don't need to be repro-grammed when the adults in their lives pay attention from the beginning to what messages they're giving and strive to emphasize positive ones. Messages, of course, don't come just from words. They come from actions as well—even little actions such as facial expressions, gestures, and body language.

Not all children who come from an unfortunate background like Michael's

altanaka/Fotolia

Adults need to let children know that someone will provide the control that they lack, while also conveying support and care

have his same needs. Take Jay, for example, another five-year-old in the same kindergarten.

Jay is what's called a "resilient child." Jay is like the children Werner (1984, 1995, 2000) and Werner and Smith (2001) described, those who tend to have the ability from infancy on to elicit positive responses from people; who have established a close bond with at least one caregiver during the first year of life; who have a perspective that allows them to use their experiences constructively; who take an active approach toward solving problems; and who have a view of life as meaningful.

Jay was shuffled from relative to relative after his mother left him in the arms of his grandmother the day he was born. His grandmother was able to keep him until he was 15 months old, but then she had a stroke and Jay went to live with his aunt. He's only seen his mother twice in his young life, once last Christmas when she came to visit and once when he was two and a half; and he went to visit her—in prison.

When Jay arrived in kindergarten, he had lived in four different homes and had been removed from the last one because of an abusive situation. You'd never know all this to look at Jay. He's a sunshiny kind of child who beams at anyone who notices him, and he's very good at getting people to notice him. There's something about Jay that attracts people to him, children as well as adults. His special friend in kindergarten is the custodian, and Jay can often be found at recess hanging out with him.

In spite of his difficult home life, Jay seems to have managed to get enough positive strokes when he most needed them—during the first year or so of his life. That period with his grandmother seems to have helped him develop an attitude that he's a person worthy of positive attention. As a five-year-old, he seeks it—*and* he knows how to get it and use it. Notice that in all this discussion of affirmations and positive strokes, the word *praise* was never used. Many teachers, when thinking about helping children develop prosocial skills, tend to zero in on praise. Praise can work, but it has some side effects. It takes some skill to use praise effectively. Let's look a little more closely.

Empty Praise Versus Encouragement

Observe children who have been used to a good deal of praise. Watch them turn to adults after every little accomplishment. "Look at me, Teacher," they say, either verbally or nonverbally. For example, Alexis stands at the easel painting a picture. When she finishes it, she takes it down and carefully carries it over to show the teacher who is busy working with a small group. She waits impatiently for a while, then seeks out the aide and shows it to her. The aide makes a comment, which Alexis barely hears because just then she notices the teacher is getting up from the group. Alexis rushes over and puts the picture in the teacher's face and waits for a response. The teacher looks at it and remarks about the use of color and moves on to something else. Alexis sees the easel is still free, so she lays her picture out to dry and starts on a new picture. She finishes this one in a hurry and goes through the same routine of seeking praise for her accomplishment. Is she really painting for her own pleasure, or is she just producing paint on paper because she's trying to get praise from the adults in the room?

You can see this behavior starting in infancy as a baby puts one block on another and looks immediately for an adult to clap, smile, or say something. One common response is "good boy!" This is the kind of response someone who was just learning about *behavior modification* might give. Behavior mod, as it is called, is a particular approach for changing behavior based on behaviorist theory. The idea is that a verbal reward, called *reinforcement*, will increase the behavior. The baby will be encouraged to try something like this again.

But let's look more closely at that kind of reward. Calling a child a "good boy" when he performs can backfire. What if he tries and tries and doesn't accomplish the feat? Is he a "bad boy"? Or what if he doesn't try at all? Anyone who believes strongly in a positive approach wouldn't tell him that he's a bad boy, but the absence of the label of "good" can easily be interpreted by a child as its opposite. When adults do use both "bad boy" and "good boy" (or "good girl"/"bad girl") to give feedback on behavior, there is a real danger that the children will label themselves in those same terms. As children try to live up to their labels, they limit their options and potential. It's best to avoid global judgments that reflect on the child's worth as a person when using praise to motivate.

These children are working with intrinsic motivation; they are focused on their own process and sense of satisfaction, and are not looking for adult approval to create extrinsic rewards

Alice McBroom/Pearson Education Australia Pty Ltd

The teacher might say "Good job!"—making a nonspecific reference to the behavior (rather than a global judgment of the child). Even better, the teacher might say "Good stacking!" or "Good painting!"—specifically labeling the skill and the outcome. Or the teacher might focus instead on the process—the effort put in: "You worked hard to get that block to stay on top"; "You put a lot of effort into making that picture" (see Gartell, 2007).

Instead of words, the teacher might give a passing smile or a little pat (nonverbal stroke). But let's go a step further and think about how to give encouragement instead of praise. What can you say that will keep a child working on whatever it is—doing it for himself rather than you? The interactions demonstrating praise could be improved if they were designed to move children forward on their own rather than making them dependent on the adult's praise.

All the examples mentioned so far are examples of *extrinsic rewards*—they come from someone else. However, children need to also learn intrinsic rewards—to tune in on their own sense of satisfaction.

One way the teacher and aide can do that for the kindergarten painter is to say, "You must feel good about that picture. It looks like you put a lot of work into it." This statement helps the child tune in on the good feelings of accomplishment. The child learns eventually to stroke herself by bringing this good feeling to her conscious awareness. This approach takes the focus off the outside reward and puts it inside, where it does the most good of all.

Watch a group of children in a classroom or on the playground with adults nearby supervising. Notice that some accomplish great feats and never look to an adult. Others look for attention for each little success, no matter how small. Some adults are that way, too, but it doesn't show the way it shows in children.

Another way to look at motivation is to explore the idea of perseverance, sometimes called stick-to-it-tiveness or more commonly called "grit"

Watch this video of Alfie Kohn talking about the impact of praise. Do you agree? For more information about Alfie Kohn and his work on punishment and rewards, visit his website.

www.youtube.com
/watch?v=QQesSzkZW4s

Watch this clip to see Paul Stoltz describe the acronym GRIT.

www.youtube.com /watch?v=eTbJxLoAtrE

Watch this video to see Sal Khan talk with Carol Dweck about growth mindset.

www.youtube.com /watch?v=wh0OS4MrN3E

(Stoltz, 2014 and Tough, 2012). Angela Lee Duckworth is well known for researching writing, and talking about grit. See her Ted talk on the subject in 2013. Duckworth also credits Carol Dweck for what she calls a "growth mindset," which Dweck developed at Stanford University (Dweck, 2007). Some children may be born with growth mindset or grit, but if they are not, both Duckworth and Dweck have good ideas about how to encourage perseverance in children. Briefly, it has to do with refusing to label children as smart, clever, or intelligent, which then become fixed mindsets. They then have to continue to live up to their label, which they tend to do by avoiding any kind of challenge or experience that might misprove the label they carry around. Ways to encourage a growth mindset is to notice what they are putting effort into and remarking about it. Catch them solving problems and mention what you are seeing. See them struggle and encourage them to keep on.

Teaching Morals by Promoting Prosocial Development

How do teachers, child care staff, other professionals, and parents promote prosocial development in the children they teach, rear, or care for or work with in other ways? It helps to be clear about which prosocial behaviors are important to you. This could be a good exercise for a parent meeting. Start by asking the families to make a list of some behaviors they want to encourage in children. Their lists will probably include such items as sharing, nonviolent conflict resolution, consideration for others, sensitivity to feelings, cooperation, involvement with and responsibility to others, kindness, reverence for life, and respect for self, others, and the earth (nature). Many people will probably have these values on their list regardless of whether they are from a culture emphasizing independence or interdependence. Then ask the families to brainstorm ways to encourage those behaviors that they value in children. What are the ways you can encourage prosocial behavior? Strategy Box 5.2 explains eleven ways to teach morals by promoting prosocial development. These are my ideas. See if you can add some of your own.

Strategy Box 5.2

Teaching Morals by Promoting Prosocial Development

- *Model them yourself.* If you want children to share, they need to see you share. If respect is important, they need to see you being respectful. Modeling is the most powerful way to convey your messages. You'll see your own behaviors reflected in the children around you. If honesty is a value, be honest. If cooperation is important to you, show yourself to be cooperative—don't just expect it from children.

- *Explain why you are setting limits.* Say "I can't let you run in the classroom; you might get hurt or hurt someone," rather than "The rule is no running indoors!" Children need to know the effects of their behaviors. They need to know the reasoning behind your prohibitions.

- *Encourage cooperation by finding ways to get children to work and play together.* Let children do seat work in small groups. Have them do projects that call for cooperation. Every picture doesn't have to be individually drawn—how about painting a mural? Collage can be a group effort.

- *Take a problem-solving approach when dealing with conflicts rather than a power stance.* Help children talk to one another, explain their feelings, and brainstorm solutions. Don't rescue them from the conflict or cut the conflict short by deciding the outcome for them. Let them talk it through. If they don't have the words, provide the words for them.

- *Use guidance approaches. Avoid punishment.* Although punishment may suppress some behaviors, it doesn't eliminate them—they go underground. Benching a child at recess for restlessness in the classroom doesn't make the restlessness go away. It just prevents the child from getting the movement and exercise he needs to settle down and concentrate. Besides, punishment doesn't teach prosocial behaviors—it models antisocial ones.

- *Examine your power relations with children.* Do you *overpower* them rather than *empower* them? Don't rob them of opportunities to develop skills and to experience their own competence by doing things for them or to them. Use your power and your superior size and skills to bring out their own sense of power—their sense of themselves—who they are and what they can do. Empowered people have less need to use force and violent means of solving problems than do people who feel powerless. When you find yourself in power struggles, take a close look at why the parties concerned need to feel power. Take steps to empower them (and yourself, if you are one of the parties).

- *Avoid using competition to motivate.* If you value competition, you probably think that starting early to teach children to compete with each other won't hurt. But it does. Even though we live in a competitive society, we do a disservice to children if we start too young to teach them about competition. Young children are still figuring out who they are. Even though you may see competition as a motivation device, you may be setting up comparisons that damage self-esteem and relationships. Avoid questions such as "Who is the fastest?" or "Who is the neatest?" or "Who got the most right?" or "Who is the best drawer?" Also, don't always play games that have win-lose outcomes. No young child can afford to be stuck with the label "loser." Losers have poor self-images, and they behave according to their labels. Though some children in this age group like competitive games, balance them with noncompetitive ones as well. Many games require cooperation—choose some of those.

- *Help children appreciate the world they live in and the people they share it with.* Adults can do this best by feeling the sense of wonder children feel and encouraging the awe they experience at the beauty and mystery of nature. It's vital to help children perceive their connection to the earth and to all the earth's creatures, including other humans.

- *Give choices.* Only by experiencing the effects of their own actions on the world around them can children understand how things work. When they are faced with choosing from alternatives, they get practice in becoming good decision makers.

- *Teach children to solve conflicts without violence.* Conflict is natural and is to be expected, but violence is never an appropriate response to conflict. Especially never use violence as a last resort because the message then is that when all else fails, you can always fall back on violence. Do allow children their violent *feelings*—it's healthier to feel them than to deny them. Make it clear, however, that children won't be allowed to act on those feelings. Teach a number of ways to express those feelings in ways that do no harm.

- *Teach children to be peacemakers.* Peacemaking is a vital part of moral education. Peace is not an absence of tension or conflict. Creating peace is an active process

Check Your Understanding 5.3

Click here to check your understanding of the power of adult attention.

of balancing opposing forces and dealing with conflicts and tensions. True peace cannot be imposed. Peacemaking requires resourcefulness in using a number of skills, including confrontation, debate, dialogue, and negotiation. The goal of peacemakers is to bring conflicts to the surface and to respect differences while resolving or managing those conflicts in ways that preserve the self-esteem of everyone involved. Children learn both the philosophy and the skills of peacemaking from the adults around them who daily help them settle the numerous disputes that occur in the natural course of life, both at home and in early childhood programs.

SUMMARY

This chapter focused on school-age children. It started with a discussion of a family-centered approach to kindergarten and how such an approach eases the transition from preschool to school; Erikson's stages of development were a focus and included a discussion of how the kindergarten-through-primary-age child is in a transition between Erikson's stages of initiative and industry. Many children reach third grade before they complete the transition. An answer to the question, "What might a family coming from preschool find different in school?" was the next subject in this chapter. The answer to that question was followed by the answer to another question: "How do you find out what families want for their children?" Teaching prosocial skills then led to the subject of moral development. One way of exploring morals is to look at decision-making processes. The rest of the chapter continued to explore behavior, the concept of "grit," prosocial skills, and moral development by discussing the power of adult attention and the use of affirmations. The chapter ended by giving a list of specific ways to create prosocial attitudes in children.

QUIZ

Click here to check your understanding of Chapter 5, "Working with Families of School-Age Children."

FOR DISCUSSION

1. What are your memories of starting school? How do they compare with Daniel's and Mia's? Do you also have memories of after-school child care?

2. What do you remember about being in Erikson's stage of industry? Do you know any children in that stage today? How are they like or different from you?

3. How might the parent-teacher partnerships in the primary grades be like the ones in preschool or child care? How might they be different?

4. What was your reaction to the section about the power of adult attention and the use of affirmations? What are your experiences with using praise to motivate children?

5. What do you know about resilience in children? Have you known a resilient child? What do you think helped that child become resilient?

6. What was your reaction to the list of ways to teach prosocial behaviors? Did some resonate more than others? Were there any that you disagreed with?

WEBSITES

Afterschool Alliance
The Afterschool Alliance works to ensure that all youth have access to affordable, quality afterschool programs. The website includes information about afterschool news, policies, and funding.

Council for Exceptional Children
The Council for Exceptional Children is an international organization dedicated to improving the educational success of people with disabilities and/or gifts and talents. The website includes information about policies, standards, advocacy, and professional development.

Harvard Family Research Project
The Harvard Family Research Project helps stakeholders develop and evaluate strategies to promote the well-being of children, youth, families, and their communities. The website has information about research in early childhood education, out-of-school time, family involvement, and more.

National After School Association
The mission of this agency is to foster development, provide education, and encourage advocacy for the out-of-school-time community.

Resiliency in Action
This is a publishing and training company that focuses on resiliency. Its websites makes available free articles and resources.

FURTHER READING

DeVries, R., & Sales, C. (2011). *Ramps and pathways: A Constructivist approach to physics with young children*. Washington, DC: National Association for the Education of Young Children.

Dweck, C. (2007). *Mindset: The new psychology of success*. New York: Ballantine Books.

Howes, C. (2010). *Culture and child development in early childhood programs: Practices for quality education and care*. New York, NY: Teachers College Press.

Martinez, F. (2005). Early care and education for Hispanic children. *Childhood Education*, 81(3), pp.174–176.

Noddings, N. (2013). *Caring: A feminine approach to ethics and moral education*. Berkeley, CA: University of California Press.

Noonan, M. J., & McCormick, L. (2006). *Young children with disabilities in natural environments*. Baltimore, MD: Brookes.

Pizzolongo, P. J., & Hunter, A. (2011, March). I am safe and secure: Promoting resilience in young children. *Young Children*, 66(2), pp.67–69.

Rothstein-Fisch, C., Trumbull, E., & Garcia, S. G. (2009). Making the implicit explicit: Supporting teachers to bridge cultures. *Early Childhood Research Quarterly*, 24, pp.474–486.

Stoltz, Paul G. (2014). *Grit: The new science of what it takes to persevere, flourish, succeed*. Climb Strong Press.

Tough, Paul. (2012). *How children succeed: Grit, curiosity, and the hidden power of character*. New York: Houghton Mifflin Harcourt.

Andres Rodriguez/Fotolia

Societal Influences on Children and Families

Learning Outcomes

In this chapter you will learn to...

- Describe socialization and the family.
- Understand schools as socializing agents.
- Identify other agents of socialization.

The family is the first and major socializing agent, and as such it has responsibility for early socialization patterns. The family is a microsystem in Bronfenbrenner's ecological model. As the child grows and moves outside his or her home, other agents in the community come into play. They come from beyond the child's immediate sphere (where the mesosystem and exosystem lie). The context called the macrosystem always has an effect on the family and child as they do on all of us. Sometimes the context is not within our awareness except when we bump up against cultures or customs that are different from our own (or break a law). In the past, outside agents in the mesosystem and exosystem were fewer in the child's immediate life. The child may have been influenced by relatives, neighbors, religious institutions, informal community networks, and eventually school, but today the exosystem with its media and technology play a big role in socializing outside the family. Even babies are propped in front of the television and other screens, some of which are interactive. They also are exposed second-hand to violent media and technology for as long as two hours a day when others are watching television and playing DVDs and interactive video games (Rideout & Hamel, 2006; American Academy of Pediatrics, 2011). Toy manufacturers play a role in a baby's media interest by creating toy replicas of what older children and adults have for real. By toddlerhood children are playing with the real thing: iPhones, iPads, computers, video games. As their sophistication and skills grow, so does their variety of media and technology. There are a variety of views of what's appropriate for young children when it comes to media and technology. Studies of language development are clear that babies do not gain by watching videos designed for them as compared to babies who don't watch such videos (Zimmerman & Christakis, 2009; Christakis & Zimmerman, 2009). Worries about children younger than seven years old come from Jane Healy (2011), well known for her work on learning and cognition. She cites research showing that what she calls screens are not good for young children because they need real-world experiences rather than ones that are flat, lacking anything physical or social, and with limited sensory qualities.

Watch this short video to hear Jane Healy talk about what she calls "Brain Cleaning."

www.youtube.com/ watch?v=6ChfQgtkTVA

School, of course is also an important community socializing agent, but just a generation or two ago, most children didn't enter school until kindergarten or first grade. Now children are in out-of-home education and care programs starting in infancy ever since President Clinton signed the Welfare to Work Act back in 1996. As the child grows, the socializing influences expand beyond the microsystem and macrosystem. After-school activities, sports, music lessons, gymnastics, and other activities all are important in many middle-class families who can afford them. Peers, unsurprisingly, become strong socializing forces as the child experiences people outside the family. The point is that the socialization process today is shared by many agents in the community. Other institutions such as hospitals, government agencies, and service industries also come into the picture. These organizations have taken over many of the activities that were once the function of the family, the extended family or kinship network, and neighbors, all of whom used to make up the informal community. Barbara Rogoff's book on life in a Mayan village (2011) is a good example of an anthropological study of how communities (and the lives of the people in them) change over time.

This chapter focuses on four major socializing agents: family, school, peer group, and media/technology. It also focuses on issues of bias and privilege that impact children, families, and communities.

SOCIALIZATION AND THE FAMILY

Because a good deal of this book is devoted to the family, you may be wondering why the family is also included here in this chapter on the community. The family is such an important educational and socializing agent that family-related issues appear and reappear throughout the whole book. In this chapter, we look at the family's place in, and its interface with, society, and we examine the influence of the community on the family and therefore on the child.

Families belong to subcultures and networks that reflect their social class position, ethnic group membership, and, possibly, their kinship. These subcultures and networks influence the ways in which families socialize their children. The language the parents use, and sometimes insist that their children use, influences to some extent their ties to one group or another. "Speak Spanish," demands a mother who sees her children drifting away from their roots to dissolve into mainstream America. "Speak English," demands another, who sees language as a way to carry out her upward-bound goals. "Don't say *ain't*," admonishes another because she feels that's what uneducated people say, knowing that language helps people fit into the "right group." "Gettin' kinda uppity, ain't ya?" asks another mother, who feels alienated by her son's new way of speaking when he comes back from college for a visit at home. She sees language as a divider.

In addition to social class and ethnic group, families are sometimes tied to other families through occupations or interests, which also affect children's socialization. The family that plays music together, for example, influences the socialization of their children differently from, say, a family that plays sports together. The experiences of the children in those two families may be quite different from the children of workaholic parents who are tied to their corporate "family."

Many families have a primary focus of attention; it may be religious activities, or school achievement, or even income opportunities. Some parents actively mold their children to their own interests by constantly involving them in specific activities. The family whose members devote themselves to nature and to ecology issues, for example, may be quite critical of a family that owns the manufacturing plant in town that has been suspected of polluting the environment. Parents also mold perceptions indirectly by the ways in which they evaluate others; children come to see which types of individuals their family prefers to associate with and who should be avoided. They may or may not go along with their parents' evaluations, and indeed may reject them to the point of rebelling. Status—that is, the family's position in society—affects socialization and can in turn affect expectations as well as where children find themselves when they grow.

Children of wealthy families have a different set of experiences and

The family is an important educational and socializing agent

Wong Sze Fei/Fotolia

expectations than, for example, children of poverty-level families. Consider the difference between a child born into a Beverly Hills family with two parents, four cars, and a pile of money compared with a child who was born in jail and who is sent to live with her grandmother in a run-down trailer park near the railroad tracks while her mother serves a term for dealing drugs. Which child is most likely to grow up defining her choices as "the sky's the limit"? Think about Maslow's hierarchy of needs discussed in Chapter 1. Although we don't know more than the bare description of the child in the Beverly Hills family and the child being reared by her grandmother, we could make some assumptions about which child is more likely to have more of those needs met unless the community is able to provide what might be missing. Which is mostly likely to become a self-actualizing individual without professional help? It's important to point out that we don't know the answers to those questions, because wealthy families don't necessarily provide for their children's needs and relatives raising a child with little financial support don't necessarily do a bad job. It's possible that both families will need outside help from their communities. One difference is that the wealthy family can afford to pay for that help, while the other family will most likely have to depend on free services.

The family not only gives the child status but also makes him or her aware of the status of others. Family members teach, whether consciously or not, whom to copy and whom not to copy. The message about the status of outsiders is clear in some families—who is considered "above" and who "below."

Schools also teach—and not just academics. What they teach and how they teach it may be affected by assumptions based on class differences. Adrie Kusserow (2005) reports on some fascinating research she did on subtle differences between social classes. Because she wanted to leave race out of the picture, she focused on two white groups with different income levels, both in New York—one was in Manhattan and the other in Queens. She came up with some big differences in what the term "individualism" means in those two groups. She called what she came up with "hard individualism" and "soft individualism." She also showed how what early childhood teachers value, and therefore teach to, is based on "soft individualism," which was in agreement with what the Manhattan group believed in. Part of the differences centered around the idea of the "self," which the teachers tended to see as delicate and the Queens parents saw as something that needed to be hard and protective. One explanation for the difference came in how the two groups tended to see the world. The Manhattan group saw the world as safe and welcoming, and the Queens families saw it as dangerous and forbidding. Their actions related to their views. The Queens families tended to try to toughen up their children by teasing, criticizing, and disciplining. They avoided using praise and encouragement and frowned on allowing emotional expression in their children. They didn't want to spoil or overindulge their children. The Manhattan families worried about damaging self-esteem, hurting creativity, and blocking self-expression, as did the teachers. The two groups had very different views of what children need. Kusserow gives an example of a teacher conference in a preschool where the parent is totally mystified about the teacher's goals and the kind of open-ended, playful, creative activities used to reach them. The attitudes and ideas of preschool teachers may be very different from those of low-income families. Also, the "goodies" that society has to offer are more available to some children than to others. For some, privilege is a major socializing force; for others, privilege's counterparts—bias and discrimination—play that role.

The Issue of Bias

Kusserow's research pointed to differences in socialization influenced by income level. In looking at "hard" versus "soft" individualism, she pointed out that teachers were more in tune with the families who valued soft individualism. Paul C. Gorski (2007), a teacher aware of the poor performance of children in poverty in school, questions what he calls classist assumptions about why they don't do well. At a workshop in Minnesota, he set out to convince educators that inequities exist. He took the common complaints teachers have, one by one, and pointed out the audience's classist assumptions. For example, one universal complaint was this: Low-income parents don't take an interest in their children's education. The proof: They don't attend meetings at school. In answer to that complaining, Gorski asked how many people in his audience drove to work in a car that day. All of them raised their hands. Then he asked them if they knew how many of their students' families had cars. They didn't know until the school social worker raised her hand with the exact number: 11 percent. Gorski then delineated some of the issues besides transportation problems that keep low-income families from acting like interested middle- and upper-class families. These issues included lack of jobs, holding down several jobs so they could come closer to a living wage, no time off work to come to the school, and no child care to attend meetings. He set out to convince a group of teachers that inequities exist if a child comes from a low-income family.

Bias is everywhere, not just in social class and income level. We've all felt its effects, though some of us are targeted more than others. We feel bias because of our gender, skin color, ethnic background, the way we talk, body type or physical condition, mental capabilities, age, sexual orientation, the amount of money or education our family has, or our family configuration, to name just a few of the factors.

Bias hurts everybody—especially children. It hurts those who are its targets because these children must put energy into struggling against the negative messages that they receive—energy that could be used for development. In addition, bias hurts them because they find their opportunities limited; doors are shut to them (Derman-Sparks & Edwards, 2010; Kaiser & Raminsky, 2012).

Bias also hurts those who are not targets but who believe that they and others like them are superior. This belief not only dehumanizes them but also distorts their reality. Bias is bad for everybody!

We need to become aware of our areas of privilege and how bias works. We need to become sensitized to help ourselves and others think critically and to speak up in the face of bias. The key is empowerment. Members of target groups must be empowered to develop a strong self- and group identity so they can stand up in the face of attack. Some groups have experienced discrimination for generations. Parents in some of those families set about to teach their children early to be proud of their identity and how to stand up against bias. Members of nontarget groups must also teach their children about bias and discrimination, though many do not. For example, Bronson and Merryman, in their book *Nurture Shock* (2009), have a chapter called "Why White Parents Don't Talk about Race" in which they discuss research related to the subject. They answer the question posed by telling stories about white people struggling with how to discuss racial discrimination with their children. It's easier not to talk about it. White people have to work at it as do all members of nontargeted groups. Children in those groups must also develop a strong self-identity, but without a feeling of superiority. Every child must be free, and indeed encouraged, to develop to his or her full and unique potential and have a strong identity.

Classism.   Classism has already been addressed, but let's look more closely at the subject—by examining children from two low-income families who are targets for classism.

The first child is four-year-old Max, whose family is working class and proud of it. His father, Joe, is a seasonal farm worker and in between seasons picks up odd jobs wherever he can, and his mother, Mary, cleans houses for a living. Max lives with his parents and his two sisters, Sonia and Sally, in the apartment of his grandparents located in a working-class neighborhood that is at the bottom of the hill from a new upscale housing development. The school district drew new boundaries when they built the school for this area, and they included Max's neighborhood in the attendance area, so every day Max's sisters walk him to preschool before they go off to their own classrooms in the new elementary school they now attend.

The family is having some problems with what's happening as a result of the contact between their children and the children on the hill. Clothes are one of the problems. The girls feel they need different clothes from what they have always worn. Designer labels have become important to them. They complain that the kids won't like them if they don't dress right. Designer labels aren't an issue for Max. In fact, the rule is that children have to wear old clothes to preschool so they can experience all the sensory activities that the school offers (which tend to be messy).

The issue for Max is T-shirts. The program is doing fund-raising, and they want the families to buy the school T-shirt, which will then be worn on T-shirt Day. All the other kids have them, but the shirts cost a lot. T-shirts aren't the only fund-raising project going on. It seems that papers are always coming home from school announcing something to buy, sell, or donate to. For free public education, there seem to be a lot of expenses, like field trips that require the price of an admission ticket to go to plays or get in the museum. And the parties the children get invited to are expensive, too. Each one requires a present and usually transportation, which presents difficulties. Sometimes specialized equipment is needed, such as roller skates or sleeping bags for slumber parties.

Lately the parties have slowed down for Max and his sisters. That situation is good for the pocketbook but bad for the children's morale. They have begun to feel that they aren't good enough to associate with their classmates; they are starting to believe that that's why they aren't getting invited to parties. At the first open house at school, their parents began to understand their feelings. No one was warm or welcoming to them. When the parents started up a conversation with one couple in the preschool group about the building of the school, the man started complaining about how the school opening had been delayed because of a strike. He made it clear that he thought unions were the root of the economic problems in the United States. Joe told him that he was a union member and that was the end of the conversation. Joe and Mary remembered the old school where everyone was more like them and they felt at home. Here they felt out of place, and they wondered whether the other parents and the teachers were looking down on them.

Is what they are feeling real or just their imagination? It is hard to tell. Maybe some of both. Whether imagination or not, Joe and Mary have vowed to help their children feel good about who they are; they are determined to do what they can to help their children see that money doesn't buy happiness.

Thinking critically about this story, you might ask yourself the following questions:

What exactly do you know about this family? Can you separate your knowledge from your assumptions? If you were working with this family, what else would you need to find out about them? What are the factors that impact the lives of these children and this family? Where would you look for research that relates to the social issues, changes, and transitions this family is going through? Also ask the same questions about the next story.

The other family we will examine has a different story. Peter, who is four years old, was born into a middle-class family. However, soon after Peter's birth, his father left his mother. Daddy came back just long enough to make a baby brother before departing for good, leaving Peter's mother with two boys to raise. The family slipped into poverty practically overnight.

Although Peter's mother was raised with the values, expectations, and behaviors of the middle class, she has begun to change as the effects of poverty mold her. She is unable to keep up with her previous lifestyle. When she was single and after she was first married, she used to enjoy lunch out with her friends; now her lunch hour is full of errands and appointments, and, anyway, she doesn't have the money to squander on a nice lunch. She struggles hard to remain on her former level, but try as she might, she is pulled down. She is beginning to feel strange around people who have so much more money than she does. She also feels strange around the other mothers whose children are in Peter's Head Start class. She doesn't seem to belong anywhere anymore.

She remembers how she and her friends used to criticize poor people who didn't keep their kids clean. "It doesn't cost anything to keep clean," she used to say. But she has discovered that it does. She has to go to the laundromat to do the laundry; that costs plenty—in money, time, and energy. And since her water heater broke, even bathing the boys is harder. She has called the landlord three times already to get it fixed, but she still has had to go without hot water for four days now.

The last straw came when she popped back into the child care center to leave the diaper bag she'd forgotten to drop off and found Peter's little brother being scrubbed down in the sink. She knew then that she'd crossed the line and had become one of the people she used to frown on. She remembers a conversation with a teacher friend about how some kids arrive at school so dirty and smelly that you just want to give them a good scrubbing. Now her own child had become one of them. She was embarrassed to tears—and angry as well. How dare they bathe her baby without her permission? He wasn't that dirty. She'd heated water on the stove and given him a sponge bath that very morning!

We don't know whether this mother is really experiencing a biased attitude. We don't know why the teacher was washing the child or how she felt about it. She perhaps thought she was doing the mother and the child a favor, but the mother perceived the action as an insult, maybe because she had once been on the other side of classism.

Being newly poor, Peter's mother has experienced both sides of the poverty line. Some families have never been on the upside of it. They come from a long tradition of poverty and have never known anything else. They are used to people looking down on them and perhaps even blaming them for their poverty.

For some Americans, social class is hard to see, because we, as a society, deny the existence of such a thing. For a long period, the middle and upper classes were even able to pretend that social class didn't exist because they didn't see poor people before their very eyes. All that is rapidly changing; poverty shows everywhere. Poor people aren't tucked away on the other side of town anymore. They're apt to be downtown in cities and on street corners holding up signs saying "Will work for food."

The National Center for Children in Poverty is a valuable resource with a website containing information on research and public policy.

Social classes exist even though they aren't the permanent, set-in-stone phenomena we see in other countries. We still don't commonly call them *social classes*, though. Sociologists speak of "socioeconomic levels." Whatever you call them, there are differences in the experiences of the children who are raised at each level.

Social class is one factor in socialization, and race is another. There is no biological basis for race, but there is racism, and therefore we have to take race into consideration. Too often race and class are lumped together. Social class may be ignored entirely; for example, when comparing cultural differences of African Americans and European Americans by poverty level, African Americans are compared with middle-class European Americans without acknowledging that there are class differences. It's important to be aware that there are poverty-level people and middle-class people in all cultural groups—and you can't just be blind to social-class differences.

Let's turn now to racism, which is another important factor in the education and socialization of children (Annie E. Casey Foundation, 2011).

> Watch this video to hear teachers speak on how to make classrooms more respectful and welcoming to working-class and poor families. Consider this question: what bias(es) do you have that might impact your work with children and families?
>
> www.youtube.com
> /watch?v=hynRor-MBX4

Racism.   Those who have experienced racism don't have to read about it to understand it. If you haven't experienced it, it's hard to understand to what extent it exists and what it feels like. It's sometimes easier for those who aren't a target of racism to understand it in terms of its counterpart, *privilege* (Wise, 2009, 2011).

Privilege can be thought of as an "invisible package of unearned assets," which it's possible to cash in on whenever it pleases the person carrying the privilege. Most of those who have it are quite unaware of their privilege; they regard it as the way things are. Those who don't have privilege are very aware of its lack. Privilege shows more in its absence than in its presence. It's important to point out here that the other side of any kind of oppression is always privilege. You can't have an oppressed group without also having a privileged group. The teachers in the workshop with Paul Gorski had economic privilege though they probably didn't think of themselves as privileged.

Let's look at the privileges that a four-year-old white, middle-class child, Lindsay, enjoys because of her skin color:

> Lindsay doesn't have to represent "her people," who, in fact, are seldom lumped into one skin color category. If she arrives at preschool dirty, it's an individual family matter or perhaps attributed to her social class, but it doesn't reflect on white people in general. She can wear secondhand clothes. She can pick her nose or even use bad words, and it's her family that's reflected, not the white race. If her family gets her to school late, no one attributes it to either their genes or their culture. If she arrives at school tired, the teachers may blame the parent, but not anyone else. Lindsay's family has the privilege of representing only themselves,

not reflecting or living in the reflection of stereotypes of a group of other people with their same skin color.

Lindsay lives in the best neighborhood her family can afford; though money is, of course, a factor, it is not the major factor. They have the privilege of choosing where they want to live within their price range, and they made that choice assuming that their neighbors would display good or at least neutral feelings toward them. If they have alienated their neighbors, it's more likely because of something they've done rather than because of who they are.

Lindsay will come to see herself and her family as "normal," if she hasn't already. She sees herself and her people represented on television and in books, magazines, and newspapers. She easily finds the food her family eats in the local supermarket. Lindsay's mother can take her anyplace she likes to get her hair cut and feel reassured that someone there will know how to cut it. When Lindsay is older and learns about history, she'll be shown that her people (or at least the males) made this country what it is.

Lindsay's mother doesn't worry about educating her children to detect racism. She doesn't even consider teaching them how to operate when racism is present or how to protect themselves from it.

Angelica and her twin brother, Mario, who go to Lindsay's preschool, have a different experience:

Angelica and Mario's mother is well aware of the possibility of racist attitudes toward her children. One of the antiracist strategies their mother uses is to send them to school fashionably dressed. The teachers sent Angelica home with a parent handbook the first day, with the sentence highlighted that said, "Please send your child in old play clothes." After a week, one teacher stopped the three of them as they were leaving and complained that it was hard for Angelica and Mario to participate in the many and varied messy activities because of their clothing. She asked that they come in old clothes that didn't matter. The mother listened, but the next day Angelica arrived dressed in a new fancy dress and her brother in a starched shirt and a pair of slacks. The teachers never understood why their message didn't get through. If they had been able to have a heart-to-heart talk with this mother they would have discovered that she sees her children's appearances as reflecting on their family. She wants her children to look well cared for. She doesn't want her children to fit into any stereotypes that racists may have of her people. Although racists are everywhere, if Angelica and Mario are well dressed and look well cared for, it will be harder for some people to see them as inferior to other children. She is also well aware that clothes and grooming won't matter to a real racist who will only see skin color.

Thinking about these two stories, can you connect your own life with one of them? Are you a person with racial privilege or are you a person who is a target of discrimination in one or more of the other areas mentioned earlier: gender, social class, skin color, ethnic background, the way you talk, your body type or physical condition, mental capabilities, age, sexual orientation, financial resources, education, or family structure? Feel free to add to this list if you are a target of discrimination in an area not mentioned here. Analyze how your experience with bias and privilege might be affecting your feelings about these stories.

For Janice, the issue is hair:

Janice is the parent education coordinator at a fairly large child care center. One of the parents she has concerns about is Amber, a single parent of a biracial child, Lacy. Amber doesn't know how to take care of her daughter's hair, and it bothers Janice a lot. She sends her in the morning looking uncombed. After nap time, she wakes up looking even worse. Janice has taken to combing Lacy's hair twice a day, on arrival and after nap. Lacy loves it! Janice keeps meaning to ask Amber for a conference to explain to her some of the things she doesn't know about her daughter's hair. She also wants her to understand that a biracial child who looks African American can't afford to look as if nobody cares about her, even if it's not true. People will judge her and her people!

These three stories show some of the factors that affect socialization. The child's race, family income level, and circumstances influence how others respond to him or her on a personal level.

The stories also provide examples of the problems that can arise when teachers and parents aren't partners. For early childhood programs to be positive socializing agents, the partnership model must be in place. Throughout this book the theme of parent-professional partnerships will be stressed. These stories show the sad effects when the teacher operates out of a one-way model in which the teacher is in charge and the parent is the recipient of the teacher's knowledge and expertise. What's lacking in that model is the teacher's awareness and acceptance of the funds of knowledge families already possess when they bring their children to the program (Gonzalez, Greenberg, & Velez, n.d.).

> Watch this video to hear several different people share their ideas about the effects of unconscious bias. Which idea resonates most with you?
>
> www.youtube.com/
> watch?v=F05HaArLV44

While personal racist attitudes affect children's socialization, there's another even more powerful type of racism that affects us all. That is the institutionalized racism that is built into the systems of our country that grew out of its history. If you think back to what you know about the early history of the United States—the preamble to the Constitution, for example—it sounds wonderful: a country where all men are equal. You may be tempted to update that phrase and make it all people are equal, but that wasn't the original intention. The country's government was founded by white men and continues to be dominated by that same group of people. And it wasn't just any white men—it was property owners. They made laws that worked in their own favor. Today when you hear about corporations having "glass ceilings," that's an indication that only some people can rise to the top. The ceiling stops the "others." Only when we refuse to let this happen, only when we examine issues of equity and social justice at the deepest levels of our societal systems, can we eventually get rid of institutionalized racism. Since the beginning of our country, groups of people have worked to dismantle the built-in racism. They have made a difference, but there is still plenty of work to do.

A child's race, family income level, and circumstances can determine the kind of formal education that the child is likely to receive. We've already used examples of children in child care and preschool. Now we turn our focus to the public school system, an important community resource and socializing agent, which lies in Bronfenbrenner's mesosystems layer and, of course, is also influenced by the other systems lying outside of it.

There are websites that can offer teachers support around diversity work, such as the National SEED (Seeking Educational Equity & Diversity) Project on Inclusive Curriculum, which was founded by Peggy McIntosh. Another

> **Check Your Understanding 6.1**
>
> Click here to check your understanding of socialization and the family.

resource is Teaching Tolerance, a project of the Southern Poverty Law Center, which creates newsletters, posts articles and videos, and offers free curriculum ideas.

SCHOOLS AS SOCIALIZING AGENTS

Let's start by looking at public school expectations of behaviors and the mismatches that occur when children arrive with behaviors that work elsewhere but not in school. Antibias education is another aspect of school as a socializing agent that is discussed in this section, as well as the effects of testing on socialization.

A huge issue in early childhood education that has an effect on socialization is school readiness. The readiness approaches become problematic when they are more concerned with the intellect and particularly academic skills without regard to the role that social-emotional development plays in "getting children ready." Socialization is affected when those pushing a narrow aspect of readiness fail to understand the implications of focusing on just one aspect of development and disregarding the others. Some interesting research focuses on this particular issue in one group that consistently has problems in school: African American boys (Zehr, 2011).

School is a socializing agent

Just as the research reported by Zehr shows that the narrow focus on academics and the neglect of socialization skills are ineffective in creating school readiness in that particular group, so others have made it clear that there are better ways to prepare all children for school. Jane Healy (2011) is clear that what children should be doing in their first years is being actively involved and engaged in a variety of multi-sensory experiences including those with intellectually valid content. Intellectually valid content is different from the kind of memorization tasks some programs give young children to do. Lilian Katz, whose writing has had a big influence on our field, was one of my first professors when I was working to become a certified teacher back in the 1960s. She always has maintained that there is a big difference between intellectual matters and academics. Academics are the skills we need to use our intellect, but not the way young children gain knowledge in the first years of life. Young children need the kinds of hands-on experience that such programs as "Tools of the Mind" use to great effect (Bodrova & Leong, 2007).

Some children arrive in kindergarten less ready to grapple with the kindergarten curriculum than other children. That's actually to be expected and isn't necessarily a bad thing. Healy (2011) presents evidence that late bloomers may end up with more intellectual capabilities than earlier ones. Maybe kindergarten ought to be more accepting of differences in developmental timing, although in some cases, the difference in readiness relates to factors other than just individual developmental timing. Some children, for example, enjoy a variety of early experiences that fit nicely into what they need for kindergarten. They gain two important skills for school success: language development and self-regulation. According to Healy, "Self-regulation...turns out to be the strongest predictor not only of school achievement, but also of lifetime success" (2011, p. 20).

Watch this video to hear Jane Healy talk about late blooming kids. Do you remember if you were considered a late bloomer?

www.youtube.com/
watch?v=5Y5FhaH7sp8

Other children's early experiences are different; for them, kindergarten presents an alien world. As a result of these differing experiences, children are sometimes labeled and separated into groups by their "abilities" (this is called *tracking*). If children are tracked and labeled early, their educational course is set, sometimes for life. That means some are given the message that they're learners—winners in the race called school. They tend to take the ball and run with it; they're successful. Others learn early that they're "slow," which they translate to mean "stupid"; they're losers. Once tracking begins, the educational opportunities become limited for some and expanded for others. That's one view of tracking. *Education Week*, an online newsletter for educators, presents both that view and the opposite view—that tracking helps teachers give more attention to the students who need it and helps them learn at their own level rather than being pushed to learn what they aren't ready for.

Getting into Kindergarten

Even getting into kindergarten may be an issue facing families who send their five-year-olds off to public school. Public school administrators and teachers are under a great deal of pressure to provide accountability to government funding sources. Those who pay the bills want to be sure they're getting their money's worth. The way they determine accountability is through test scores, so testing has finally reached clear down to kindergarten and even into preschool. Two examples of accountability through testing are in Head Start and in No Child Left Behind (NCLB). NCLB has been highly controversial since it came into being (Wang, Beckett, & Brown, 2006). Although changes came about when President George W. Bush left office and Barack Obama became president, the push to improve education through testing students and making teachers accountable is still around and still controversial.

As a parent volunteer in my son's elementary school, I have seen the effects of testing on five-year-olds. The day I helped with the standardized achievement tests in kindergarten stands out in my memory. The children were told not to be nervous and that this was nothing to worry about—a contradictory message because everything about the atmosphere that day said, "This is *very important*." In addition, the parents had been sent a notice to be sure that the children got a good night's sleep and a hearty breakfast every day during the week of the testing. So in some cases, the atmosphere both at home and in the classroom conveyed the message that tension existed around these events—that they were different from what the children usually experienced in kindergarten. Even though the children were told not to be nervous (which in itself makes one suspicious enough to be nervous), two cried, one threw up, and one had to go home with a headache the day I was there helping. These events alone were enough to influence the test scores, not only of the afflicted group but also of the group not showing any symptoms.

> Watch this video to hear Sir Ken Robinson speak about standardized tests. What do you think about the role of testing and creativity?
>
> www.youtube.com/watch?v=AqXDfx2q5rw

Ready to Learn

A narrow and simplistic view of what "ready to learn" means focuses on teaching academics to young children. This view ignores the huge societal changes that need to come about to ensure that all children have an equal chance for academic achievement in school. To truly have an equal chance for school success we need to eradicate poverty, give everybody health-care benefits, ensure enough nutritious food, and provide decent

Thomas Perkins/Fotolia

Children develop attention spans by playing for long periods of time and learning how to entertain themselves

housing. Focusing on early academics is a cheaper but far less effective road to school success than what the brain research indicates. Good health and social-emotional stability in the early years of life are the real road to later achievement. Cognitive development is vitally tied to the social-emotional realm of development (Lally, 1998 and 2013; Shore, 1997; Zigler, Finn-Stevenson, & Hall, 2003).

Here are two indicators that early childhood educators agree show that children are prepared to enter kindergarten:

1. *Children who are ready for kindergarten can communicate.* They know how to carry on a conversation. A conversation means not just talking but listening and responding appropriately as well. Adults should start emphasizing communication early (Healy, 2011). Even infants enjoy conversations and taking turns "talking."

2. *Children who are ready for kindergarten can concentrate and focus.* If they can't do that, the problem may be too much television. It might seem as though children develop a long attention span from watching television because they are willing to sit and stare at it for hours. But turn it off and what happens? They don't know how to entertain themselves (Healy, 2011). Overscheduling their time can add to the problem. Children don't develop long attention spans when they are never allowed to just play for long periods, never free to follow their inclinations to get involved in something of their own choice, and never encouraged to work at length on some project they are interested in (Elkind, 2007). Sometimes adults tend to interrupt children and hurry them up to get them going on the next event.

Classroom Behavior

> Expected school behavior may be quite alien to what's needed by some children at home and in the neighborhood where they live. Social skills taught at home may not work in school.

Kindergarten readiness is closely linked to another issue—that of classroom behavior. Most public school classroom teachers depend on parents to send their children to school with ingrained behaviors that allow them to perform according to the rules and enable them to learn in the style the school sees as appropriate to the group size and the ratio of children to teachers. Some parents manage to comply with this expectation. And some children, even in spite of their parents or their home life, are willing and able to conform to what school requires. But other children aren't or can't. Expected school behavior may be quite alien to what's needed by some children at home and in the neighborhood where they live. Social skills taught at home may not work in school.

Consider the streetwise inner-city child who has learned, even by the age of five, to survive by interpersonal skills that allow him to manipulate people and situations. He gets little chance to use those skills in school—except out of the teacher's sight during recess. Interaction during class time is strictly controlled, and certain expectations are enforced according to a set of rules. He comes to school self-reliant and independent, but his manner borders on defiance and that attitude gets him in trouble. He's also aggressive. He knows he can solve problems through physical action, but at school he finds he's expected to use words alone. "Fight back and don't tattle" is the rule at home. School rules are different: "Don't ever touch anybody; tell the teacher if you have a problem." The child who has incorporated the rule from home is going to have problems in school, starting right away in kindergarten.

It may seem reasonable to try to give this family a new set of child-rearing practices to help their child do well in school and eventually rise out of the circumstances the family is in—if not immediately, at least by the next generation. But the truth is that it's not easy to change child-rearing practices. And an outsider taking on such a task is taking on a good deal of responsibility unless he or she clearly understands how the child-rearing practices serve the culture, the family, and the child. In addition, it is quite difficult to get people to change how they are raising their children unless they have a special reason for wanting to change. Changes in child rearing tend to come *after* social and economic changes have come about.

In the meantime, this little streetwise child has a problem. If he conforms to classroom expectations, learns the rules, and takes them home to apply them, they won't work in the same way they do at school. Some children are flexible enough to learn a new set of skills and apply them where they work while keeping the old set for the times when the new set doesn't work. However, other children never adjust to the school environment. Not all children who don't fit valued classroom behavior are physical and aggressive. Take the girl who finds herself in a classroom where self-direction, initiative, independence, and competitiveness are the skills stressed. These skills are the ones seen as functional to the higher-level, higher-paying, middle-class occupations and social positions. But the girl doesn't see the connection and perhaps has no expectations of growing up to work a high-level job anyway. She only knows that while the teacher is urging her to be special, to do well, to stand alone, to stick out, and to be a winner, all she wants is to fit in and be loved. She doesn't want more stars on her star chart than anyone else. She doesn't want to sit isolated and do her own seat work without talking or looking at someone else's paper. She wants hugs and attention from the teacher. She wants to sit on her lap at story time. She wants to socialize with her classmates. She wants the same warm group feelings that she gets at home. She wants to be a part of things, not separate and individual and alone.

This girl won't get in trouble like the little boy in the first example. She'll be thought of as sweet but probably not too bright (though she may, in fact, be quite intelligent). Eventually she will fade into the background and become invisible like the other children who don't give the teacher problems. Feeling that she doesn't fit in, she may give up on education early and find something else to do with her life. Or, less likely, she'll figure out how to learn even under the alien conditions of the classroom and end up going all the way through college as an invisible person, doing very well, but not drawing attention to herself (McKenna & Ortiz, 1988; McWhirter et al, 2007).

Frank Boston/Fotolia

Some children do not want to stand out and be special, they just want to be loved and fit in

Responding to Diversity

When children arrive at school, they may or may not find a cultural environment that reflects themselves or the diversity of the American population. The school environment reflects the attitudes of the people who create it. If the teacher comes from the predominant culture and sees that culture as valuable and therefore worth recognizing, the classroom will likely show white faces in the pictures on the walls, will acknowledge the heroes and holidays of the predominant culture only, and will contain only books written for, by, and about dominant culture people. Perhaps she will make an effort during Black History Month or do something special or celebrate Cinco de Mayo the week of May 5, but that isn't enough response to diversity (Derman-Sparks & Edwards, 2010).

Watch this short clip to hear Dr. Lily Wong Fillmore talk about cultural differences in behavior.

Sometimes teachers who have this attitude don't realize the limitations of what they offer to children. If they are European Americans, they might not understand any culture but their own, which they naturally see as normal and right—the only way. Such culture-blind teachers may claim to be color-blind. In their attempt not to be bigoted, they ignore differences, thinking that noticing them shows prejudices. Even if they are working in all-white classrooms, there is much they can do to bring in diversity (Derman-Sparks & Ramsey, 2006).

Other teachers regard differences as important and take an ethnic studies approach toward acknowledging them. They accept and promote differences in an attempt to increase understanding and acceptance of them. Taking a "multicultural tourist" approach, these teachers may emphasize ethnic holidays, serve ethnic foods, and teach about customs, history, art, or artifacts of assorted cultures. This approach can make some children feel accepted who wouldn't otherwise feel that way, as well as broaden the view and experience of all the children in the classroom. A difficulty is that studying cultures in bits and pieces tends to trivialize or exoticize them. A multicultural tourist approach may also focus more on foreign cultures than on how those cultures have evolved when transplanted to the United States. This approach represents an add-on to the curriculum, rather than a change in it. The classroom reflects the multicultural tourist curriculum by having pictures displayed and books available that show, for example, African tribespeople, Balinese dancers, and Chinese New Year's celebrations. A typical theme for December in a multicultural tourist curriculum is "Christmas Around the World" or the broader "December Holidays," showing celebrations of Hanukkah, Christmas, the Santa Lucia Festival of Lights, and Kwanzaa.

Some teachers approach diversity in the classroom by looking at commonalities in the everyday world rather than just celebrations. "We're all ethnic and cultural beings—same and different at the same time" is the message. This approach may take the theme that we all have needs, but how we meet those needs varies. Teachers may have their children study, for example, ways of carrying babies or kinds of grains eaten by various cultures. Studying breads from around the world as a theme is an example of approaching diversity from the we're-the-same-but-different angle.

Other teachers—more and more since Derman-Sparks's book, *Anti-Bias Curriculum*, came out in 1989—see the importance of changing their whole curriculum to reflect an attitude of respect and dignity toward differences. Her latest book, with co-author Julie Olsen Edwards, *Anti-Bias Education for Young Children and Ourselves* (2010), makes the point that each of us needs to work on ourselves if we are to expand equity to schools, communities, children, and families. An antibias approach aims at true integration and equity, regarding empowerment as an issue. Teachers who use this approach teach their children to be sensitive to realities different from their own as well as to think critically about injustice. Antibias is not just a cognitive approach; it includes feelings and actions, too. A full antibias curriculum includes promoting equity for all aspects of human diversity—culture, race, ethnicity, gender, sexual orientation, ability, and age.

Inequity and Schools

How well children are educated and how good their school experience is for them depends on many factors, not the least of which is how many resources are available at the school they attend. Kozol (1991) wrote an eye-opening book called *Savage Inequalities* about the discrepancies between the funding of inner-city schools in poor districts and schools in richer districts. In a nutshell, his message is that many children are being cheated out of a decent education—they don't have a chance. That was many years ago, but more recent research confirms that large funding differences between wealthy and impoverished communities persist (Baker, et al, 2010; Biddle & Berliner, 2002). Even in districts where public monies are equal for each school, the local community can make a difference. In one rural community the small country school had no multipurpose room. Children ate lunch outside except when it rained and then they ate in their classrooms. There was no indoor meeting space for parents. The next valley over (in the same district) was rezoned and moved from agriculture (which was the economic base of both valleys originally) to putting in housing developments for commuters. The small school in that valley didn't have a multipurpose room, either, but the parents put on fundraisers and were able to cover the construction costs of a new building. Too many schools in cities are in need of repair. Equipment, if there is any, is run-down; materials and books are minimal. Children who live in areas with a wealthier tax base are more likely to attend schools in better conditions, even though now, in these hard times, few schools enjoy an abundance of economic resources. Even so, some of the wealthier districts have twice the funding per child of poorer districts in the same geographic region. We have great discrepancies in our public school system in America today. It's quite likely that the child of wealthy or even middle-class parents will get a much better education than the child of poor parents.

> ✔ **Check Your Understanding 6.2**
> Click here to check your understanding of schools as socializing agents

OTHER AGENTS OF SOCIALIZATION

Of the many other agents of socialization, this chapter will consider first of all the peer group. Very young children are less influenced by their peer group than say, teenagers; however, even in preschool during free play or in kindergarten on the play ground, the observer can see how children affect each other's behavior. Teachers or families may wish that children didn't experience peer pressure; nevertheless, the peer group has some important functions. Other effects on children's perceptions, attitudes, and behavior come from media and technology, both programs and commercial advertising. Much as we all wish for peace in children's lives, the reality is that violence also can have an effect on socialization. We'll start with the peer group.

The Peer Group as an Agent of Socialization

Although the peer group is not as important for younger children as for older ones, it is nevertheless an influence (Eisenberg, et al 2006). Who makes up the peer group for young children? Children in the apartment complex, on the block, and in school or

Peers are a socializing force

Robert Kneschke/Shutterstock

child care become friends and playmates. Sometimes the composition of the peer group is controlled by parents as they arrange to get their children together with other children by making play dates. The formal or informal play group is an example of this kind of peer group. Other times children form their own peer group.

Children don't play in groups at first, though they may interact a good deal with whomever is around. If you watch toddlers in a group situation, such as in an early care and education program, you find that they often play side by side—aware of each other but not interacting very often. One child might influence the content and actions of another's play, but each remains headed in his or her own direction, carrying on a private conversation and individually involved with toys or materials. Then you see that more and more often these pairs of children begin to interact. Soon the pairs become threesomes and the peer group begins to form, eventually becoming a solid group with activities, norms, interests, rules, traditions, expressions, and gestures of its own. The peer group becomes a subculture.

Children's choices of playmates are sometimes affected by gender. Children under age seven may be willing to choose playmates of either gender, but most have a tendency to prefer those of their own gender. By elementary school this influence of gender on choice of playmates becomes notable (Leman & Lam, 2008; Maccoby, 1998).

To see the peer group influence, watch how something called *behavior contagion* works in a preschool classroom. One child starts screaming excitedly over something. In a few minutes the whole room is screaming and racing around after the leader who started it. Or one child starts swinging belly down on the swings, and soon all the swinging children have flipped over to prone positions.

Communication among peers can involve a very sophisticated set of signals. Watch a couple of four-year-olds playing with action figures in a sandbox. Each knows what's pretend and what's not. Adults may not be so sure. When angry noises are heard from a distance, the protective adult may rush over to see what's happening only to discover that the children are just pretending. The children know it's pretend, but the adult wasn't sure—it sounded so real!

Usually adults don't teach children how to play pretend. Children learn informally from each other how to choose and sort out roles and characters, how to determine the direction the action will take, and how to signal when something is pretend and not real. They agree on all this as they go along, usually in a manner that's so smooth it's hard for outside observers to notice. David Elkind is worried that playing pretend is disappearing because of television and video games. Children don't seem to use their imaginations like they used to (Elkind, 2007).

Functions of the Peer Group

The peer group functions so that children learn to give and take as equals. That's a different lesson from relating to parents or teachers. The peer group has its own system of modifying behavior through rewards and punishments, which mostly come in the form of acceptance and rejection: "If you don't play nice, I won't invite you to my birthday party!"

Learning to get along with others who are your age and status is important. Developing relationships of one's own choosing is also important and is different from learning to get along with the people who just happen to be in your life because of the family you were born into.

The peer group also teaches a set of lessons that children don't get from adults; some of these lessons lie in areas that are sensitive and taboo. Much sex education comes from peers—whether parents and teachers like it or not.

The peer group serves as a step in developing independence, as children move out from their parents and family into a new set of circumstances. The group is centered around its own concerns and not necessarily bound by adult norms. It has its own hierarchy.

Another function of the peer group is to place the child in history. We don't recognize ourselves as members of a particular generation until we grow up and look at the generation coming up behind us. It is through the contrast that we identify ourselves as a generation of peers.

Adults can help children get along with their peers. Both teachers and parents can model desirable behavior, reinforce children when they display it, and coach children in social skills. Parents have a big influence on their children's peer relationships (Parke & O'Neil, 2000). A close attachment in infancy helps children develop social competency (Schneider, Atkinson, & Tardif, 2001). When parents interact with their children in ways that promote positive social behavior and take feelings into account, the children tend to do the same with peers. When parents are negative and controlling in their interactions, such behavior can transfer to their children's interactions with peers and can make them less successful socially (Clark & Ladd, 2000).

Television is not an interactive agent, it is a passive form of socialization and children need real interactions with real people

Media and Technology as an Influence on Socialization

Before, technological advances—mass media such as newspapers, magazines, comic books, radio, video games, movies, and especially television—presented a very different form of socialization than any other, because they offered limited opportunities for interaction. Now opportunities for technological interaction abound and the picture is different from that in the past. But let's start with television, which still has a huge socialization effect. It has an influence on children from a very young age and affects their cognitive development as well as their social development (Christakis & Zimmerman, 2006 and 2009; Elkind, 2007; Wright et al., 2001). The very fact that television is not an interactive agent is greatly significant to the development of young children. While watching, children have the feeling that they're interacting, but they're

> While watching, children have the feeling that they're interacting, but they're not. That's one of the disadvantages of television as a socializer—it satisfies social needs to some extent, but doesn't give children the social skills (or the real-life practice in those skills) that allow them to function effectively with people.

not. That's one of the disadvantages of television as a socializer—it satisfies social needs to some extent, but doesn't give children the social skills (or the real-life practice in those skills) that allow them to function effectively with people. Since the average child watches three to four hours of television a day, the time left for playing with others and learning social skills is drastically reduced. Even infants average about an hour and a half of television viewing a day between the time they are born and age two (Wright et al., 2001).

Of course, parents can control the time their children spend watching television, but many don't. They can monitor the selection of programs, but some allow their children to watch whatever happens to be on. Some parents don't consider how they can use television to teach decision making. They don't make children aware that when one program ends they can either weigh the various merits of the next offerings or turn the set off. Some children, especially those with a remote control in hand, flick through the channels periodically, randomly stopping at whatever catches their interest at the moment. That's very different from critically examining options and consciously deciding on one. This is where parent education could be effective. Some parents who grew up with television themselves haven't given much thought to the effects of that medium—and how to decrease these effects. Christakis and Zimmerman (2006) wrote an entire book for parents on how to make television work for their children.

Children learn through watching television. Some of the things they learn are beneficial; others are not. They learn about the world and the ways of the society. They learn something about occupations, for example, getting an idea about what a nurse does, what a doctor does, and how the two relate to each other. They learn about the institutions of the society—what goes on in court, for example. They learn the language to go with these roles and settings—and they learn some language you'd rather they didn't know!

Children also learn about current themes and issues, both from newscasts and dramas—issues such as kidnapping, the homeless, and the spread of AIDS. Most of these issues and themes are not happy ones, and many are very frightening, especially when young children watch programs that are intended for adults.

Children learn more than facts from television; they also get a good daily dose of stereotypes and a lot of misleading information about their world. Most of all, they get a big helping of violence and another of commercial advertising.

Guidelines for Television and Young Children

The following list of television guidelines may seem drastic and unrealistic, but television has a powerful impact on children, so drastic measures to counteract it are called for.

1. *Don't expose infants to television*. Don't use television as entertainment, and don't get in the habit of using it as a babysitter, no matter how tempting it is to do so. Infants are distracted by the disconnected noise and movement of television. They don't need distractions; they need personal interactions with people and objects in the real world. With the 24-hour television channel just for infants, it may seem as if some research says that television is educational for babies. There is no such research!

2. *Examine your own television habits*. If you are addicted to television, the chances are any children around you while you are watching will also become addicted. Deal

with your own addiction and take precautions so that children don't become TV addicts.

3. *One way to avoid the risk of addiction in children is to avoid exposing them to television altogether.* Children grow up just fine with no TV. If you decide you want children exposed, do it with caution and awareness. Don't turn the TV on and flip channels. Using a TV guide, make a conscious decision about what program to watch, turn the set on to watch it, and then turn it off when it is over.

4. *Sit with children while they watch television.* Then you are there to handle feelings, explain what needs explaining, clarify any confusion, and clear up misconceptions. You are also there to turn off the set when the program is over.

5. *Whatever you do, don't let children fill their time with television.* Active play should be the major pastime of the early years, not uninvolved visual entertainment.

The guidelines presented in this box have been used by adults with good success. If you grew up with TV in your life and have never been without it, consider trying two weeks without TV; you'll find it makes a positive difference in your life, once you get over your withdrawal symptoms. Getting loose from the clutches of the television set will also make a positive difference in young children's lives.

Using these guidelines, educators could set up meetings with parents to discuss television and its effects on children. Some of the parents might be interested in trying the two-weeks-without-TV approach. Some parents probably have already made wise decisions about their children's television viewing, and these parents can be im-

Tom Wang/Fotolia

Sit with children while they watch television; it could be fun family time

portant parts of this discussion. From this discussion, an advocacy movement might develop, which is discussed later in this chapter and throughout the book.

Commercial Advertising

In the index of their book for parents, Christakis and Zimmerman (2006) list 33 items under Advertising. What's wrong with commercials on television that advertise? They're compelling, eye-catching, and more interesting than a lot of programming. What's wrong is that they create artificial needs in children (and, indeed, in all of us). They are as manipulative as they can be, coaxing us, practically forcing us, in subtle ways, to go out and buy, buy, buy. They teach consumerism very effectively.

If you want to see how effective television commercials are, stand in the cereal aisle of a grocery store for just ten minutes and watch the interactions between parents and children. None of the child's biological signals related to nutritional needs are in play in the cereal aisle. In fact, even if the shelves were rearranged so the most nutritious cereals with the least additives were

Watch this clip for a visual reminder of how children are targeted for marketing. What thoughts are you left with after viewing such a variety of marketing techniques?

www.youtube.com/watch?v=HKH4 YGKnOSs&list=PL5AA1CB1F810FA7 8D&index=3

at children's eye level, little hands would be reaching and pointing at the familiar sugar-filled cereal boxes they know so well from television. In one study, children indicated that they had successfully influenced their parents' buying decisions (Tinsley, 2002).

Helping parents discuss the effects of advertising on children can give them new views of how consumerism manipulates us all. Some parents have already thought a lot about this and can be resources to other parents who are just beginning to think about it. The editors of Rethinking Schools, a publisher, nonprofit organization, and website, explain the tremendous growth of commercialism aimed at children. Corporate media giants keep figuring out new ways to sell products to children. They go beyond radio and television to the Internet. Movies are advertised in fast-food restaurants as children get movie-related free toys and figures in the meals designed specifically for them. And they are carefully distinguished as toys for girls and toys for boys. Schools aren't immune from advertising brand names. The point made in the chapter called "Moving Beyond Media Literacy" in their book *Rethinking Popular Culture and Media* is that a small number of people with corporate interests control the media and aim them to serve consumption goals rather than information that citizens of a democratic society need.

Violence

Turn on the television set during prime time, and, unless you select your programs carefully, you're likely to see an act of violence within five minutes and several more not too long afterward. Saturday morning is even worse. Eight of ten programs contain violence, with prime-time programs averaging 5 violent acts per hour and Saturday morning cartoons averaging about 20 per hour. The average child in the United States has seen 8,000 murders and 100,000 other violent acts during childhood (Bushman & Anderson, 2001). The American Psychological Association, the American Academy of Pediatrics, and other major associations warn parents to keep their children away from mass media violence. Video programs, television programs, and the nightly news all contain content that's not good for children. Why so much violence and sex? Those things are interesting—and interest sells products—so we get exposed to a good deal of it. The question is: What does it all do to children?

For one thing, research shows that viewing violence influences children in a way that makes them more likely to become violent (Anderson et al., 2003; Singer & Singer, 2005). Watching violence eventually desensitizes us all. If it didn't, how could people sit and eat a meal while watching people in living color be tortured, mutilated, shot, and even blown sky-high before their very eyes? That's enough to turn one's stomach, yet children get used to it by watching television and DVDs and playing video games.

Years of studies show that television watching and aggression go together. Children who watch more television are more aggressive. However, it's hard to tell whether television *causes* the aggression or whether children who are more aggressive just tend to watch more television. However, some experimental studies show that children who are exposed to a violent televised episode are more aggressive when they are put immediately into a real-life anger-provoking situation. These children show more physical aggression than children who watch something nonviolent before being put into the same situation. In a classic study by Bandura and Walters (1963), children modeled the behavior of adults they saw on films punching an inflated "knock-down" figure. Many other studies since have shown similar results.

Christakis and Zimmerman (2006) point out that when violence goes unpunished—has no consequences—kids are more likely to imitate it than when the bad guy gets what's coming to him.

Television viewing of violence and real-life violence are connected. A long-term study followed 300 boys for 30 years. The boys who watched more TV violence at age 8 were involved in more spousal violence and more criminal violence by age 32 (Huesmann & Miller, 1994).

One way to discover the effects of television on children is to study a group of children who have not been exposed to television and then observe them after television comes into their lives. Such a study was done in northern Canada in a remote place where television hadn't yet penetrated. Then, when television was introduced, researchers were able to make comparisons. They found that violent behavior increased in both boys and girls (Hirsch, 1997).

If we want to confront violence in our society, we must pay attention to these kinds of studies. We must regard television as the dangerous device it is and bring it under conscious control. We must not let it continue to influence children in negative ways. The children slouched in front of sets today are the ones who grow up to be tomorrow's citizens. What kinds of citizens will they be?

This is not just a concern for families, but also for the community and for society. Violence affects all of us. There was a time when society took charge of protecting children from the media. The Federal Communications Commission (FCC) put regulations into effect in the 1930s, regulations that were strengthened enough by the 1960s to protect the first of the television generations. These regulations allowed intervention in cases where children were exposed to commercial exploitation or other forms of abuse by the media. The idea was to ensure that television provided for social good, rather than increasing social ills. When the FCC deregulated television, that protection disappeared; the protection is now left up to families, many of whom are not aware of the problems with unmonitored TV watching by children. It's time now to reinstate those regulations. We allow other regulating bodies to protect our children from unhealthy influences. It's time to allow the FCC to continue to do the good work they started. When children watch TV violence they see that violence is acceptable, and some of them begin to use violence themselves as a way to solve problems and deal with conflict (Bushman & Huesmann, 2001). Television is a strong social force. It needs to be used in growth-enhancing ways (Carlsson-Paige & Levin, 1990). Teachers can put together groups of parents who are emotional about the subject of mass media, and maybe they can become advocates (if they aren't already) and help change things. One way to get parents motivated is to share some of the books Diane Levin has written about media messages and their influence on children. See the Advocacy in Action feature, "A Super Advocate: Diane Levin."

Television is a powerful teaching tool because it is in virtually every home across the nation. Whether you're focusing on the negative or the positive effects, or both, it's easy to see that television viewing influences the knowledge, behavior, and attitudes of children. If the lessons are to be beneficial, the positive aspects of the medium must be emphasized and attention must be paid to the negative, because unmonitored watching can teach racial and gender stereotypes, ideas about sexual relationships, and aggressive sexual behavior (Signorelli & Morgan, 2001), as well as general aggression and violence—all while commercially exploiting young children. When adults concern themselves with what children are watching and for how long, TV can be a teaching tool. The tool works best when adults watch with children, explaining to the children what they don't understand and putting a moral light on

ADVOCACY IN ACTION ▶ A SUPER ADVOCATE

Diane Levin

Diane Levin is known internationally for her advocacy. She advocates for things that are important to me personally. For example, I sat at a conference listening to Diane talk about her newest area of advocacy, "So Sexy So Soon." When I heard that Barbie dolls are being marketed to the preschool crowd, I really sat up and took extra notice. My granddaughter is part of that crowd. It seems that Diane is always talking to me, personally. I sat up and took notice when she was talking about war toys—a long time ago. As mother of four boys, that was a big issue with me. I didn't want them to play with war toys and they really *did* want to play with them. I knew the TV was one of the problems and we went a long period with no TV partly because of the violence and partly because of the commercials. Commercial messages are another area of Diane's advocacy. I remember watching an occasional recorded TV program with my youngest son. My purpose in recording the shows was to fast-forward the commercials. He used to beg me, "Just let me see that one, Mommy!" Today he is grown up and is probably the only person I know who has no TV! (He does have

a computer, but now as an adult he shares my attitude about commercials and has a certain invulnerability).

Diane's books have influenced me and many others as well. She wrote:

- Levin, D. E. (2013). *Beyond remote controlled childhood.* Washington, DC: NAEYC.
- Levin, D. E. & Kilbourne, J. (2008). *So sexy so soon: The new sexualized childhood and what parents can do to protect their kids.* New York, NY: Ballantine Books.
- Levin, D. E. & Carlsson-Paige, N. (2006). *The war play dilemma; What every parent and teacher needs to know.* 2nd ed. New York: Teachers College Press.
- Levin, D. E. (2003). *Teaching young children in violent times: Building a peaceable classroom.* Cambridge, MA: Educators for Social Responsibility.

Diane also starts organizations. Here are two: She is a founder of TRUCE (Teachers Resisting Unhealthy Children's Entertainment) and cofounder of the Campaign for a Commercial-Free Childhood (CCFC).

▶ Watch this clip of Diane Levin and Jean Kilbourne discuss their book *So Sexy So Soon*. Were you aware of the push for children to be sexy so young?

www.youtube.com/watch?v=pFK5L_T5KWg&index=1&list=PL5AA1CB1F810FA78D

what children watch. To be an effective early teacher, television must increase developmentally appropriate and growth-enhancing options for children. In addition, parents must become aware of its potential—both good and harmful. A strong campaign of parent education is needed. Imagine the good that could come of a national conference on children's television that provided opportunities for media representatives to talk with children's advocates, educators, parents, and sponsors about television strategies to work for the good of children and society (Boyer, 1991). See Strategy Box 6. 1 for ideas about how to encourage parents to become advocates.

To summarize, television and other media and technology influence the socialization of children in a number of ways. They replace active involvement with the world and the people in it, giving children little chance to learn and practice a variety of social skills. The average young child who watches four hours of television a day misses out on his or her full share of early *active* learning. Television also replaces real needs with artificial ones that are created by product manufacturers and distributors to get children to want, want, want. And it affects children's behavior through the sheer quantity of violence that is portrayed.

Television has benefits, too, especially when adults concern themselves with what children are watching and for how long. It can be a teaching tool when adults watch with children, explaining what they don't understand and putting it into a moral context.

Encouraging Parents in the Role as Advocate

+ Encourage parents to be advocates for their own children. Each child should have his or her own family as a champion!

+ When a parent stands up for his or her own child, appreciate that behavior. Yes, it's a kind of bias, but it's a healthy kind. Support parents in their role as advocate.

+ When a family's advocacy efforts conflict with your perspective or program policy and practice, remember to keep their perspective in mind. Remind yourself that it's good for them to advocate for their child.

+ Be flexible. Acknowledge that there are whole realms of possibilities in addition to what you do or what you believe in.

+ Recognize that advocating for one's own child is a preliminary step to becoming an advocate for the group and from there advocating for all children. Children need advocates. They can't advocate for themselves.

Whether you're focusing on the negative or the positive effects, or both, it's easy to see that television viewing influences the knowledge, behavior, and attitudes of children.

Studies of the effects of television on children have been around a long time and are still going on. But technology is exploding and every year new products come out. We've come so far in such a short time that one wonders what will be next. So how does all this technology affect children? Obviously they have access to far more information through the newer technology, which represents great potential for even greater influence than television. Also the interactive quality is a contrast to television, which is a one-way medium.

It's compelling for people of any age to be able to interact digitally, but those aren't the same as face-to-face interactions with people who are physically present. Just as children can get addicted to television, they can also get addicted to electronic interactions.

Other than addiction is there true harm to children? That's not an easy question to answer. Take cell phones, for instance. Children love them, of course, because they use them to communicate. Obviously doing most of one's communicating electronically makes children miss out on the kinds of personal social interactions of face-to-face contact that lead to a different kind of relationship. Controversy rages over whether cell phones do harm to young brains (or older ones for that matter). There seems to be scientific evidence that they do, but the common conclusion reached by many is that it will take at least ten more years to start seeing the effects and find out if they are harmful.

Besides the social, physical, and neurological damage and theories about causing cancer, what other dangers are connected to children using technology to get online and communicate?

The government of Australia came up with a 600-page report called "High Wire Act: Cyber Safety and the Young" (2011) that lists some of the safety issues of concern, such as abuse of children online (which includes cyberbullying, cyberstalking, and sexual grooming), all of which can have serious repercussions. For example, cyberbullying has ended in suicide for some children. There is, of course, inappropriate content that children can't understand or aren't ready for. "Technology addiction" is a worry as are all the other unhealthy behaviors children can be exposed to such as drinking, smoking, and drug use. Identity theft is always a possibility and breaches of privacy. The old-fashioned behavior of children exploring each other's naked bodies can now be easily photographed by the children themselves. If those photos end up online, they can be involved in sexting and child pornography.

The message is that adults who don't know all that can be going on with "wired" children need to educate themselves and need to monitor children's use of online devices, including cell phones and computers. They need to be aware of the techniques of online predators and how to recognize them and teach their children not to give out personal information. They need to tell children that if something worries, scares, or confuses them while online, talk to a trusted adult. Children need to know about responsible use of the Internet, age-appropriate sexual boundaries, and what it's like to be a victim of bullying. Monitoring is important!

✓ Check Your Understanding 6.3

Click here to check your understanding of other agents of socialization.

SUMMARY

This chapter looked at socializing agents including: the family, the school, the peer group, media/technology, commercial advertising, and violence. The family is the first and major socializing agent and as such has responsibility for early socialization patterns. The chapter also explored how socialization can be related to bias depending on the family the child is in. Schools are important socializing agents, and teachers have a responsibility to recognize bias in their teaching. The peer group grows in importance as socializing agents as the child matures. The chapter ended with a discussion of other agents of socialization, including the many ways the media influences children and a plea for professionals who work with parents to become aware of and monitor media use.

✓ QUIZ

Click here to check your understanding of Chapter 6, "Societal Influences on Children and Families."

FOR DISCUSSION

1. What other socializing agents can you think of besides those discussed in the chapter?

2. Give an example of how the status of the family affects the child's socialization. Give an example of how being the target of bias can affect socialization.

3. How can a family's income level affect the way its children are socialized?

4. Do you know someone who was "tracked" in school? How did that experience affect that person?

5. How are children expected to behave in kindergarten? Do you know a child who doesn't behave that way? Why doesn't he or she? How might that behavior affect that child's kindergarten performance?

6. What would you expect to find on the walls of a kindergarten room where the teacher had an antibias curriculum?

7. What are your feelings, ideas, and experiences in relation to television/media/technology and young children? How do they relate to what the chapter said about television? What do children learn from watching TV?

WEBSITES

The Annie E. Casey Foundation
The foundation is devoted to helping children at risk of educational, economic, social, and health disadvantages. They focus on strengthening families and communities to provide access to opportunity.

Campaign for a Commercial-Free Childhood (CCFC)
CCFC aims to support families in limiting commercial access to children and to end child-targeted marketing.

CLASP (Center for Law and Social Policy)
Part of the organization's work focuses on early care and education; it also promotes policies that support child development and the needs of low-income working parents for expanded availability of resources for child care and early education initiatives.

Common Sense Media
Common sense is a website dedicated to empowering adults and policymakers to help children thrive in a world full of media.

National Center for Children in Poverty (NCCP)
The NCCP is a leading public policy center dedicated to the economic security, health, and well-being of low income children and families. Located at the Columbia School of Public Health, this center offers media resources, publishes a newsletter, does research on child care and early education, and has information on child poverty.

Rethinking Schools
Rethinking schools is an organization started by teachers. They are committed to equity in public education.

Teaching Tolerance
A place for educators to find thought-provoking news, conversation, and support for those who care about diversity, equal opportunity, and respect for differences in schools.

FURTHER READING

Baker, B. D., Sciarra, D., and Farrie D. (2010). *Is school funding fair? A national report card*. Newark, NJ: Education Law Center

Bodrova, E., & Leong, D. J. (2007). *Tools of the mind* (2nd ed.). Upper Saddle River, NJ: Pearson.

Christakis, D. A., & Zimmerman, F. J. (2006). *The elephant in the living room: Make television work for your kids*. New York, NY: Rodale.

Galinsky, E. (2010). *Mind in the making: The seven essential life skills every child needs*. Special National Association for the Education of Young Children Edition. New York: Harper Collins.

Gorski, P. C. (2007, Spring). The question of class. *Teaching Tolerance*, 31, 26–29.

Healy, J. M. (2011, March/April). Impacting readiness: Nature and nurture. *Exchange*, 33(2), 18–21.

Wang, L., Beckett, G., & Brown, L. (2006). Controversies of standardized assessment in school accountability reform: A critical synthesis of multidisciplinary research evidence. *Applied Measurement in Education*, 19(4), 305–328.

Zimmerman, F. J. and Christakis, D. A. (2009). Television viewing in child care settings. *Pediatrics*, 124:6 1627–1632.

Rob/Fotolia

Understanding Families' Goals, Values, and Culture

A worthwhile exercise for all families, teachers, and caregivers is to examine their values, see how they relate to their goals, and decide whether what they are doing with their children is in tune with what they believe in. Take, for example, a family who highly values peace. The family's goal is that each child be raised always to pursue nonviolent solutions to problems. If a parent in this family spanks as a means of controlling behavior, the child-rearing practice is out of tune with the value and the goal.

Anyone who works with families and their children—as a social worker, teacher, aide, director, center-based staff member, or family child care provider—should understand the values and goals the families have for their children. They should examine the policies of their program plus their own behaviors to see whether what they are doing with the children and families is in harmony with what the families want for their children (Gonzalez-Mena, 2010).

Recognizing that cultural learning starts at birth and is mostly nonverbal, it is imperative that those who work with families familiarize themselves with cultural differences. The ideal is that families and the agencies that work with them are involved in a joint process to ensure that each child will remain a full member of his or her own family and culture through a steady developmental progress toward cultural competence. That's not to say that cultures never change, but being part of a changing culture is different from living outside it and lacking the feeling of belonging. Children may well become bicultural eventually through attendance in early care and education programs and through schooling; however, taking on another culture should be adding to what they already have. It's detrimental when children lose the original culture of the family unless it is the family's explicit desire that they do so.

This chapter looks at Bronfenbrenner's ecological systems theory and the way the macrosystem of cultures influences the child's development through the many other systems including family, media, peer groups, schools, and the community. It also takes a particular perspective on that subject and emphasizes the goal of preserving diversity. There is much talk now of diversity, as more and more communities are influenced by immigrants moving in than ever before. But it's important to recognize that this country has always been diverse, even before the first waves of immigrants arrived in what was then thought of as the "new world." Diversity is nothing new. Honoring it is!

This chapter takes the view that Tammy Mann (2010) states nicely in *Children of 2020: Creating a Better Tomorrow*, as she writes about the shifting demographics of the country and about the urgency of working across cultures in positive ways. She says, "Unspoken beliefs that undermine or disrespect the cultural values and beliefs that children and families bring into our programs can impact parental engagement and a child's developing self-concept because adults tend to act on what they believe" (p. 64). That statement is the justification of this chapter.

Preserving diversity is a vital issue for all of us in the United States and the world beyond. It's not just that it's nice to be nice or even that it's good to be fair. Kindness is important and so is equity, especially when one group dominates another. It's not just because of the shifting demographics. Preserving diversity is a way to save us all!

Look at the biological argument. The rain forest that disappears today may well contain a plant that holds the cure for a disease that doesn't yet exist or that we haven't discovered (Rogoff, 2003). As variety in the grain supply is more and more determined by the profit in selling certain seeds and not in others, globalization occurs and diversity disappears. When a devastating disease comes along that wipes out the world's grain supply, there's nothing to replace it. Native grasses with immunities no longer exist and the world goes hungry.

Look at the cultural argument. In the name of unity through uniformity, making everyone in America "American" by putting them in a melting pot moves them away from their culture of origin. Whether intended or not by the society at large, the result is the loss of the original culture. In other words, the process tends to be a subtractive one—one culture replacing another—rather than an additive one resulting in a bicultural person. Cultures disappear frequently in this country, as the last person of that culture who speaks the language dies. When that happens, the survival of all of us becomes riskier. We face an uncertain future, one in which we can't even conceive of the problems that will arise. As cultural diversity diminishes, the solutions to those problems may disappear. For example, Native American wisdom and wisdom from other indigenous peoples has allowed some cultures to continue for countless thousands of years and should not be looked down on as primitive; instead, it should be held in high regard as containing potential solutions we need now and in the future (Brody, 2001; Rogoff, 2011). We have a lot to learn about preserving the environment and alternative approaches to medicine and healing.

We find better, more effective solutions when we have a diverse team working on a problem. Differing worldviews and life experiences bring more opportunities for new and creative ways of looking at things in a new light, which offers a wider range of solutions.

This view of preserving diversity is based on cultural pluralism as a value. *Cultural pluralism* is the label for the idea that groups should be allowed, even encouraged, to hold onto what gives them their unique identities while maintaining their membership in the larger social framework. The old concept of the United States was that of a melting pot, of all cultures blended into one. The new image, for those who believe in cultural pluralism, is of the United States as a salad bowl, where each of the many ingredients retains its own unique identity but the parts combine into a "delicious" whole (see Figure 7.1).

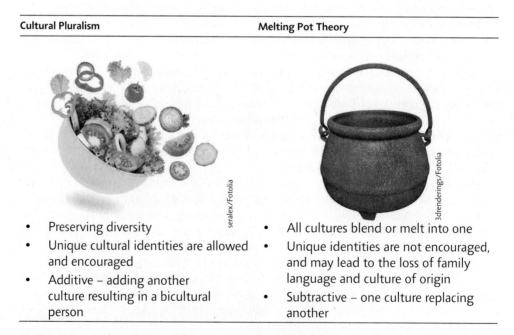

Cultural Pluralism	Melting Pot Theory
• Preserving diversity • Unique cultural identities are allowed and encouraged • Additive – adding another culture resulting in a bicultural person	• All cultures blend or melt into one • Unique identities are not encouraged, and may lead to the loss of family language and culture of origin • Subtractive – one culture replacing another

seralex/Fotolia

3drenderings/Fotolia

Figure 7.1   Cultural pluralism vs. melting pot theory

CULTURAL DIFFERENCES IN GOALS AND VALUES

Our culture affects everything we do, from determining the precise way we move our arms and legs when we walk to deciding the objectives we're moving toward. Culture rules how we position our bodies, how we touch each other, what we regard as mannerly, how we look at the world, how we think, what we see as art, how we sense time and perceive space, what we think is important, and how we set immediate and lifelong goals.

Most people find it hard to talk about their own culture until it bumps up against one that's different. Culture is so much a part of our lives that we don't see it or pay attention to it. Yet it determines our values, which are also so much a part of our lives that they, too, remain invisible most of the time. Values are behind everything we do and every decision we make. They guide us in child rearing and working with children.

Everybody is influenced by his or her culture. Sometimes people describe themselves as a mixture or "a mutt" because their ancestors came to the United States from a number of different countries. They explain that they don't have a culture. What they mean is that they don't have one particular heritage that they can put their finger on—but they do have a culture. It may be influenced by several ethnicities in their background, but nonetheless cultural rules are behind their behavior—whether they keep them or break them. Most of those people who think they don't have a culture are part of the dominant culture of the United States, which is uniquely American but highly influenced by its European roots. It's not that the dominant culture has a blandness about it. There are lots of different flavors within the culture, which can be influenced by the part of town or the area of the country where one grew up. Someone from California has only to spend a short time in New England, the South, or the Midwest to begin to taste those flavor differences, even when among people also of the dominant culture. Many people don't grow up in just one place, as is often the case with military families, for example. Living in several different areas of the country adds its own special flavor.

> Culture is so much a part of our lives that we don't see it or pay attention to it. Yet it determines our values, which are also so much a part of our lives that they, too, remain invisible most of the time.

Most people recognize when they meet up with people of their own culture because they find they have things in common and feel comfortable with each other, unless class differences get in the way. Culture, race, ethnicity, class, gender, religion, and sexual orientation all mix together to make the study of culture difficult and confusing. For this reason instead of continuing to focus on culture alone, I'm going to examine a set of patterns that influence how parents raise their children. This set of patterns has come up in each of the chapters preceding this one, but here the pattern is named and explicitly explained. The pattern has to do with independence and interdependence. Most parents put more emphasis on one or the other, and they set goals for their children based on which one is their top priority

Hemeroskopion/Fotolia

Cultural learning starts at birth, is mostly nonverbal, and influences our values

People who don't grow up in just one place, as is the case with many military families, notice the cultural differences between geographic locations

(Greenfield, Quiroz, & Raeff, 2000; Greenfield, Quiroz, Rothstein-Fisch, & Trumbull, 2001; Rothstein-Fisch & Trumbull, 2008; Rothstein-Fisch, Trumbull, & Garcia, 2009; Zepeda, Gonzalez-Mena, Rothstein-Fisch, & Trumbull, 2006).

How Do the Goals of Independence and Interdependence Differ?

What do families who focus on independence actually do that shows their focus? They encourage early self-help skills, for one thing. They expect toddlers to feed themselves and soon after to dress themselves. They teach their children to sleep alone in their own beds. They may take them into their bed for short periods, but their goal is to get the child back to bed. If they "baby" their children, they feel guilty. Families that emphasize independence can be thought of as pattern 1 individuals.

Families who focus on interdependent relationships are less adamant about babies learning to sleep through the night alone. The idea of "babying" children is viewed in a positive light, not a negative one. Babies and family members tend to have strong connections, so prolonging babyhood makes sense if your goal is *inter*dependence. These families are more worried about maintaining relationships than creating an independent individual, so they see nothing wrong with coddling children. Families that emphasize interdependence can be thought of as pattern 2 individuals.

Pattern 1 and pattern 2 families have completely different ways of meeting their children's needs. Children who grow up in an individualistic home learn that it's each person's job to learn to take care of his or her own needs. But children who grow up in "other"-centered homes learn that the needs of the others are their problem. They still get their needs met because while they are taking care of others, they are being taken care of. In both kinds of homes, basic needs get met, but the process is different in each.

Of course, most people, no matter how they were raised, do become *both* independent individuals and people who create and maintain relationships. Children accomplish both the major tasks even if their families mainly focus on only one. Families expect their children to be both independent and connected, but they work harder on what they believe to be most important. They leave to chance what they are less concerned about or work toward it in random bits and pieces.

Contrasting Cultural Patterns

Because one culture is best seen in contrast to another, I've taken the approach of pointing out cultural patterns that are quite different from each other, rather than listing characteristics of various cultures. These patterns have been introduced earlier but will be expanded on here. It is important to point out that to make a contrast

I've exaggerated differences. Although some families may fit neatly into one category or the other, many defy categorization. As you read about pattern 1 and pattern 2 families, you'll probably find that your family fits somewhere between the two. The point is not to fit families into categories but to show contrasts and differences by highlighting them.

Pattern 1 values people as unique individuals, starting at birth. The emphasis is on independence of both thought and action. Members of this culture regard the individual's feelings highly and encourage expression of those feelings. Individuals in this culture are perceived to have personal power, and they are taught assertiveness from an early age. If you're not a pattern 1 person yourself, you probably know some people who are. You probably also realize that there is diversity even among people who all belong to pattern 1. They aren't all alike.

Pattern 2 sees the group as more important than the individual. Individual uniqueness is valued only as it serves the group. Children are taught to blend in, to fit. They learn to see the group as the basic unit and themselves as a part of it, rather than seeing the individual as the basic unit. In other words, the individual is nothing by him- or herself—the individual counts only as a part of the group. Pattern 2 stresses interdependence (mutual dependence) and obedience. Obedience has to do with the group will, which is often expressed by a hierarchy of authority.

The sense of identity of a pattern 2 person comes from membership in the group rather than from personal competence, power, significance, lovability, or virtue. The behavior of an individual is never just a reflection of him- or herself; instead it reflects on the group and either adds to or detracts from the group identity. Remember, all pattern 2 people are not alike. There is always diversity in any group.

The two patterns differ in their view of the attachment process. The pattern 1 person sees early attachment as important—something that must happen to ensure that the baby will be properly cared for. Attachment and separation cannot be divided and are viewed as two parts of a single process that follows a progression leading to later independence from the family of origin. Indeed, the separation part of the process is as important as the attachment part; occurs in stages throughout childhood and then finally culminates in "leaving home" at some point after adolescence. In the pattern 1 cultures, after an individual leaves home, he or she is expected to take full charge of his or her own life and no longer look for family advice or support more than just occasionally.

The pattern 2 person sees attachment differently. The focus is on keeping the child in the family/group rather than on teaching separation skills. Attachment is not such an issue at the beginning because group expectations ensure that each baby will be taken care of properly—if not by the mother, then by another member of the group. It's not up to the individual to be drawn to the baby and therefore give it the care it needs; instead, it's up to the group member to fulfill an expected role that is unquestioned.

In pattern 1 cultures, an adolescent leaves home and is expected to take charge of his or her own life with only occasional advice or support from family

Check Your Understanding 7.1

Click here to check your understanding of cultural differences in goals and values.

Attachment in pattern 2 cultures is a lifetime process; the child is expected to remain until death a viable member of the family into which he or she is born. Each person in the group is connected to and interdependent on the other members of the group.

How might these themes of individual versus group, attachment versus separation, and independence versus interdependence show up in child-rearing practices? Where might the conflicts lie if a pattern 1 person is the infant care teacher, early educator, family child care provider, kindergarten teacher, or primary teacher of the child in a pattern 2 family?

CONFLICTING GOALS AND VALUES

Consider the differences between an infant program based on pattern 1 and what a baby is used to whose family comes from a pattern 2 culture. The pattern 1 infant care teacher might expect that the parents put their baby daughter to sleep in a crib in a room separate from their bedroom. In fact, if they can afford it, they might give her a room of her own from the beginning. A goal would be to get her to put herself to sleep in her own bed and stay there asleep all night long. Families might vary about when they would expect this to occur—and some would "baby" the child longer than others—but eventually the child is expected to show her ability to manage on her own by sleeping alone.

That's a contrast to pattern 2 parents, who might sleep with their daughter from birth on, never buying her a crib or planning to provide her with a room of her own. They might move her out of the parental bed when another baby comes along, but they most likely would move her into a sibling's bed or perhaps in with her grandmother. Being alone, even when asleep, is not sought after by most members of a pattern 2 culture.

A pattern 1 infant care teacher or early educator may expect to raise each child's self-esteem by emphasizing individuality. The teacher may purposely set out to praise accomplishments—drawing attention to individual behavior. Comments like "You did that all by yourself!" illustrate this emphasis on the individual. Along the same lines, the caregiver or teacher may provide for each child a storage cubby that is decorated with the child's name in bold print and a picture of him or her. The idea is for the child to gain a sense of his or her own personal identity while experiencing private ownership, even in the group situation.

A pattern 2 family may dislike their child being singled out. They would prefer that the early educator point out group accomplishments rather than individual ones. They would like the focus to be on rewarding cooperative efforts instead of individual efforts. A member of a pattern 2 family will likely downplay individual achievement by refusing personal credit when given a compliment. They may be teaching modesty at home to their children and be concerned that at school their child is being taught to "brag" about himself.

Several examples common to preschool and some homes serve to show the difference between a group emphasis and an emphasis on individuals. In one program children use clay to create objects to fire and take home. Another program uses clay to explore and experiment with, and when it is time to clean up, all the clay goes back into the common pot. In one home each of the four children has his or her own small box of crayons. In another home the parent bought a big box of crayons for his six children to share. One program has a finger paint table where children work together to experience the qualities of the material and then wash off the finger paint when they are finished. Another program has separate pieces of paper, and each child does a finger painting, which, when dried, is hung up on the wall and eventually taken home. At home, one mother made play dough and colored each of the wads a different color so the children could tell which one was theirs, while another mother made one big batch all of one color.

These examples are designed not to show right or wrong but to illustrate differences in perceptions of what children need to learn. They also aren't intended to show pure pattern 1 or 2 programs, only in little ways how diversity works. Many programs and parents combine the two styles.

Other differences show up in ordinary daily routine activities. In a pattern 1 culture, the emphasis is on helping oneself; in a pattern 2 culture, the emphasis is on helping others. This difference shows up in the attitude about training for self-help skills. A pattern 1 parent or infant care teacher is in a hurry for the child to learn to feed himself, for example. When the baby first grabs the spoon, many pattern 1 people will get another spoon and let the baby begin to help. If the baby isn't yet capable of using a spoon, finger food is given so the child gets the idea that he or she can feed independently.

A pattern 2 parent is too busy modeling "helping," in keeping with the goal of interdependence, to worry about teaching the baby to "do it himself." Needless to say, pattern 1 children are able to do things for themselves at a surprisingly young age, and pattern 2 children are able to do things for other children at a surprisingly young age. In some cultures around the world with pattern 2 tendencies, preschool-age children take charge of their younger siblings, doing for the baby what was done for them only a short time before.

Toilet training is another area where the two patterns may conflict. The pattern 1 parent or infant care teacher puts the emphasis on self-help, so he or she doesn't see signs of readiness for toilet training until the child is somewhere around two years of age or even much later. To this adult, toilet training starts when children are able to control bladder and bowels, handle clothing, and get to the toilet or potty on their own. Being willing to use the toilet or potty is also a sign of readiness.

A pattern 2 parent has a very different view. With the de-emphasis on self-help and the emphasis on interdependence, the adult is part of the child's elimination processes from the beginning. The adult watches from the early months on for signals preceding bowel and bladder activity. When the signals appear, the adult responds immediately. Eventually the two set up a system of signals that allow the adult to get the child bare-bottomed and to the proper place, and then trigger the elimination response. If you've never seen this, I can assure you, it's impressive!

A pattern 2 parent or infant care teacher may view manners as much more important than self-expression. Learning manners reflects the goal of becoming a good group member. Pattern 2 adults may be horrified as they watch a pattern 1 adult encourage children to speak out, say anything they want to adults, express anger, and eat in less than mannerly ways.

Pattern 2 families emphasize interdependence, and older siblings may take charge of younger siblings

bst2012/Fotolia

To illustrate the difference in the early months, contrast these two approaches. One adult touches a screaming baby lightly on the shoulder and says, "I know you're mad. It's OK to cry!" After reviewing the situation—he's not tired, hungry, or in need of a change—she leaves him alone to express himself, checking in periodically to let him know that he hasn't been deserted. She doesn't try to distract him or lull him with words or touch because she thinks that his expression of emotion is healthy.

Another adult, rocking and lulling, holding the baby tight, says, "There, there, quiet down, it's OK! You're upsetting everyone else. Please don't cry!" She tries to stop the crying, using all the verbal and nonverbal techniques she has. She doesn't regard displays of anger as healthy. She doesn't feel that the baby has the individual right to destroy the peace of the household. She tries to teach him to consider others, even though she understands that he's too young to learn this lesson.

A pattern 1 parent or infant care teacher is understanding when a four-year-old cries when away from home or parents for the first time. But the expectation is that this child needs to learn to cope with separation and that this experience is good for him. The crying may go on for a while, but the adult is confident that the child will gain coping skills and will eventually adjust. The adult sees this period as just one in a long series of separation experiences.

On the other hand, the crying of a pattern 2 child may be considered "bad behavior" because the goal is harmony and equanimity. In their book *Culture and Attachment,* Harwood, Miller, and Irizarry (1995) point out that many Puerto Rican mothers saw crying in this situation as showing a lack of manners. Crying in a pattern 2 child may be devastating to the adults in his life because they don't see that being away from family is in his best interests, even though circumstances have dictated the separa-

Watch this video to hear a teacher speak about the importance of genuinely valuing cultures. What do you think about her statement regarding culture as enrichment?

tion. They may be less willing to look at this situation as good for him. They may have less knowledge about teaching coping strategies or helping with separation because they don't value separation.

A pattern 1 parent or infant care teacher says, "Call me by my first name," in her eagerness to be friendly. She values casualness. The pattern 2 adult, who is more used to respecting titles and lives in a social hierarchy, may be uncomfortable with such informality. She may insist on using the teacher's last name with Mrs., Ms., or Miss in front of it. She may even use the title *Teacher* instead of the name and teach her children to do the same. She doesn't see this first-name business as creating closeness but only showing a lack of respect.

What to Do When Conflicts Arise

Conflicts constantly arise—in families, between parents, and between parents and the professionals who serve them. This subject has been touched on in previous chapters, but here it gets fuller attention. In some cases, but not all, these conflicts have cultural differences at their bases.

In the United States today, the professionals in most areas of expertise, regardless of their home culture, are trained from the perspective of the dominant culture, which has its roots in the immigration of people from Europe who rose to power in government, business, and the professional world. Many of those people don't think of themselves having a culture. When they work with families not of their own culture, they have to figure out how they are different. In the 1960s the term for many people of other cultures, especially if they were people with low incomes, was "culturally deficient." We've mostly moved beyond accepting labels like that, but sometimes the attitude is still there. A strong message in this book, indeed a mandate, is the importance of being sensitive to, understanding of, and respectful of differences—and not just cultural and income differences but also differences in family structure. We must all honor and appreciate diversity if we are to fulfill the dream of a pluralistic society based on equity and social justice.

Though many things have changed since the 1960s, some have not. For example, stereotypes are still with us and affect how we see people from cultures, income levels, and family structures that don't fit the common stereotypes of "good" and "right." In their book *Anti-bias Education for Young Children and Ourselves* (2010), Louise Derman-Sparks and Julie Olsen Edwards give many ideas about how to work with these issues. In the Advocacy in Action feature, "A Three-Step Process for Increasing the Book Selection in a Preschool," Edwards provides a personal story about a program that set about broadening its selection of children's books. Today it isn't too hard to find children's books that represent families from different cultures; however, this story focuses on diversity in family structures. Edwards describes a process this program used for selecting children's books that avoid stereotypes and more accurately represent differences in family structures.

> A strong message in this book, indeed a mandate, is the importance of being sensitive to, understanding of, and respectful of differences—and not just cultural and income differences but also differences in family structure.

▶ Watch this video to hear about how using literature in the classroom is a good way to connect children to home and community culture. Was your family culture acknowledged or discussed when you were a child?

ADVOCACY IN ACTION ▶ **A THREE-STEP PROCESS FOR INCREASING THE BOOK SELECTION IN A PRESCHOOL**

Julie Olsen Edwards, co-author of *Anti-bias Education* (2010)

Several parents and student teachers told the center staff that the children needed books about all kinds of families. We met opposition from a small but vocal group of parents who thought it was a foolish, "politically correct" issue that had no real meaning for children. So the group who wanted change initiated a three-step process.

Step 1: Educate: We pulled together a parent potluck and asked various parents to talk about their family structures. Six types of families were represented by the people who spoke: (1) a two-parent family with mother and father, (2) a two-parent lesbian family, (3) a parents-and-grandparent-combined family, (4) a divorced co-custody family, (5) a single mom whose ex-husband saw their child occasionally, and (6) an adoptive single dad. We asked each person to talk about what was wonderful about his or her family structure, what was hard in the family structure, where and how the child saw positive images of his or her family structure, and how each hoped the center would support the child's identity as a member of his or her family. The panel was very powerful, and at the end, the staff talked about the center's need for more quality children's books that respected and made visible the diversity in family structures.

Step 2: Agitate: But where could we find the books? We contacted bookstores and librarians but got little help. We went to publishers as well as looking online and into the community and talked to representative groups. We gathered titles and created a wish list, which we sent to the head children's librarian in our county and the bookstores and said "Order these!"

Step 3: Organize: Surprisingly, the easiest step was getting the money. We put together a request letter, which families brought to banks, grocery stores, employers, churches, and social groups. They prepared a special letter for grandparents and aunts and uncles. We offered to put the name of the donor into a book when it went onto our shelf. We raised enough money to purchase two copies of every book on our wish list.

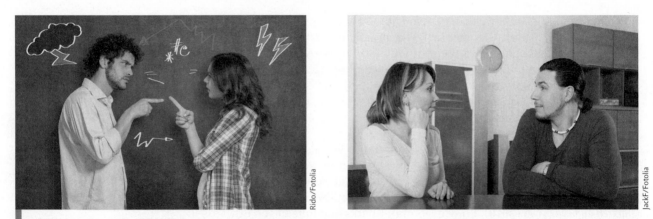

Rido/Fotolia

JackF/Fotolia

People engaged in a dialogue try to understand the other perspective, while people who argue are trying to persuade the other person to their point of view; which photo conveys arguing and which suggests seeking to understand?

So that brings us back to the question: What do you do when you are having a cultural or other kind of conflict with a family? First, become aware that we all tend to look at any situation from our own point of view. It may be very hard to understand another person's frame of reference, which, of course, may be influenced by his or her culture. All of us are ethnocentric—that is, we look out of our own cultural eyes and measure others with our own cultural yardstick. It takes awareness and skill to move from our ethnocentric position.

Dialoguing is an approach to solving a conflict that is effective at helping the disagreeing parties see each other's point of view. Rather than trying to convince another of one's own viewpoint, people engaged in dialogue try to understand the other perspective. The idea is not to win but to find the best solution for all concerned.

The following list summarizes the differences between an argument and a dialogue:

+ The object of an argument is to win; the object of a dialogue is to gather information.
+ The arguer tells; the dialoguer asks.
+ The arguer tries to persuade; the dialoguer seeks to learn.
+ The arguer tries to convince; the dialoguer wants to discover.
+ The arguer sees two opposing views and considers hers the valid or best one; the dialoguer is willing to understand multiple viewpoints.

Most people are better at argument than they are at dialogue. When faced with a conflict or problem, almost nobody considers starting a dialogue. Especially when it is an emotional conflict, many people are likely to jump feet-first into an argument rather than begin a dialogue. When they argue, they are anxious to win, which makes them leap to conclusions.

If you watch people arguing, you can see some types of body language that show each person is trying to convince the other of something. When arguing, many people tend to stand firm and tough when listening—assuming a defensive position. They are anything but open. They seem to be just waiting for their turn. When they talk, they lean forward and make aggressive gestures with their hands. Just by looking at them, even if you can't hear their words, you can tell that they are fighting about something. The body language of someone in a potentially win-lose situation is different from someone who is truly trying to understand another point of view, such as happens when people enter a dialogue. Gestures reflect their attitude—hands, especially. Instead of waving fists or making strong, tense movements, dialoguing people tend to let their hands remain open.

So how does one switch from an argument to a dialogue in the heat of the moment? Start by noticing your body language. Sometimes you can just change your body language, and an energy switch will follow. Then it's a matter of doing one simple thing: listening to the other person. To truly listen, one must suspend judgments and focus on what's being said rather than just gathering ammunition for the next attack. Really hearing someone is extremely simple, but it's not easy.

From then on it's a matter of working through a problem-solving procedure. One procedure for problem solving is called RERUN: the letters stand for reflect, explain, reason, understand, and negotiate.

- *Reflect.* This is the action of acknowledging what you perceive the other person is thinking or feeling. If you understand where the person is coming from, say, "I think you're looking at it this way..." Or if you perceive that the person is full of emotion, acknowledge your perception: "You really sound upset." Those two openers are invitations for the person to talk some more. People who know that their feelings and thoughts are received and accepted by you are likely to be more open to listening—if not right away, eventually. Reflect also includes self-reflection. If you can get in touch with your own feelings you may gain insights about why you have the perspective you have. Strong feelings may indicate something left over from your childhood that is keeping you from being rational about this conflict.

- *Explain.* Remember, we have two ears and only one mouth; that's a reminder that we should listen twice as much as we talk. Only after you have listened, listened, and listened again is it time to explain your point of view.

- *Reason.* Part of the explanation should include the reason you have for your perspective. If you are being entirely honest with yourself, the reason you are in this conflict may not be entirely rational but may be emotional. That's okay, but recognizing that you have hot buttons that put you in conflicts is the first step to doing something about them.

- *Understand.* Next comes the hardest part. Tune in to both thoughts and feelings and try to understand the situation from both points of view. You don't have to say anything out loud at this point; just work to have clarity. You may have to talk inwardly to yourself to get it. And while you're going inward, make sure you understand yourself as well as the other person. Self-reflection is an important part of the process. When you think you understand, you're ready for the next step.

- *Negotiate.* Now is the time for the finale. Try brainstorming together until you can find a mutually satisfying solution. Don't give up. Refuse to take an either-or attitude. ("It's either my way or your way, and it can't be both ways.") If you don't get stuck in a dualistic frame of mind, you can probably find a third or fourth solution that is different from or combines both your stances on the matter. Creative negotiators can open up new avenues of action that no one ever thought of before. Bredekamp and Copple (1997) point out that thinking in terms of either one solution or the other keeps us from communicating across cultures. We need to move into a "both-and" mode. In *Skilled Dialogue* (2012), Barrera and colleagues call the move away from dualistic thinking "third space." They say that third space goes beyond compromise and includes both positions. It's not a meeting in the middle, but finding a different space altogether that is big enough to encompass more perspectives and a larger view of truth.

The finale is seldom final. In only the simplest situations do you negotiate an agreement without communication breaking down. When feelings arise, return to the beginning. Go back through the first four parts (R-E-R-U). You may have to R-E-R-U-N many times before the problem is solved. Be patient.

Strategy Box 7.1 shows how to use the RERUN process with a parent who is concerned that with independence and self-help skills stressed in this program, her child is left to eat on her own. She thinks her child needs more adult help to get the food into her in a neat, clean, non-wasteful manner.

Working with a Family Member Using the RERUN Strategy

* Reflect what you perceive the other person might be thinking or feeling with such words as "It seems like you are uncomfortable with the way we do mealtimes here." Listen carefully to her response. Accept what she says without arguing. See if you can keep the conversation going so you truly understand her perspective.

  The reflect component of this RERUN process also includes self-reflection. Try to become aware of why you have the particular perspective you have and any emotional issues around it.

* Explain. Only when you have a good idea of the other person's perspective and an awareness of what's behind your own is it time to clarify the way your mealtimes work.

* Reason. Give the reason(s) why they are that way. Try hard to both explain and give the reason without being argumentative or defensive. The idea is to create a dialogue so you can continue to discuss your differences without stopping the conversation.

* Understand. When you can see the situation from both points of view and are able to explore it clearly without defensiveness or judgments, then you are ready to see if you and the other person can find common ground. You may have to try looking for different words to use other than the ones you both started out with. This is called reframing. You need to understand in order to reframe.

* Negotiate. Only when you can understand the other person's perspective and you have helped her understand yours can you figure out what to do about your differences. The ultimate negotiation process ends with neither side feeling they had to "give in." Creative negotiators can open up new avenues of action that no one ever thought of before.

Often, instead of taking time to really work through something, we get impatient and reach into the old hip holster to pull out a power play if we have one. It's unfortunate when that happens because one-upmanship destroys relationships rather than strengthening them. It may take a long time to solve a particular problem when the conflict is deep and serious, but a positive outcome in the form of a solution everyone is satisfied with is worth the time and effort it sometimes takes.

Though the RERUN device seems to consist of distinct steps or a sequence to follow, the elements are more holistic than that. They come as a package and may occur in a different order or all mixed up as one. The fact that the acronym spells *rerun* serves as a reminder that you can repeat the process as often as necessary until the problem is solved—you come to an agreement, or you agree to carry on while disagreeing. See Strategy Box 7.2 for more strategies to use in situations where cross-cultural communication is called for.

The suggestions that follow for working on cross-cultural communication are inspired by Derman-Sparks (1989) and her Anti-bias Task Force as well as her latest book with Edwards (2010). These tips are designed to help facilitate communication in a cultural bump involving values, goals, and early childhood child-rearing and educational practices. By the way, I got the term "cultural bump" from Barrera, a friend of mine and professor at the

A cultural bump is a sign that you have to slow down, negotiate, and listen to the perspectives of others

University of New Mexico. A conflict is like a fight. A bump is like something you have to get over—negotiate. Another friend of mine, Marion Cowee, professor at Solano Community College in California, says a speed bump is the perfect image for working across cultures. You have a sign that it's ahead and you see it before you get to it. You slow down and then you can negotiate it. If you hit it at full speed you are likely to damage your car. All that applies to negotiating cultural differences with people who aren't like you.

A Cultural Bump

Helen is a vegetarian. When she put her daughter, Sissy, into child care, she had a talk with the director to explain her dietary beliefs. The director explained to her that the center's food was catered and that the protein was usually a meat dish. She suggested that Sissy be served everything but the meat and that Helen supplement with some kind of protein dish. Helen agreed, and everything went well for a while.

Then the director moved on and a new director was hired. Sissy moved up from the younger group to the older group, and that meant a new teacher. Helen got busy one morning and forgot to send Sissy's protein dish. No one complained, including Sissy, so before long Helen was dropping her daughter off in the morning without the supplemental food. She assumed that her daughter was getting enough to eat without it.

Then one day Helen took the afternoon off and arrived at lunchtime to pick up her daughter. She was horrified to find Sissy sitting at the table with the other children, chewing happily on a chicken drumstick. She looked around to see who was responsible and found a substitute in charge. She complained to the substitute and then thought the matter was settled.

However, a few weeks later Sissy talked about the fish sticks she had had for lunch. Helen stormed into the center, demanding to see the director.

The director pushed herself back from her desk and its huge pile of paperwork and invited Helen to sit down. Angrily, Helen threw herself into a chair, launching into a bitter tirade. When she finally paused for breath, the director said, with concern in her voice and in her facial expression, "I see how upset you are about this!"

That got Helen going again. When she paused, the director said that she wanted Sissy's teacher in on the discussion and went to get her.

When the three of them sat down together, Helen was calmer. "Why did you feed Sissy meat?" she demanded of the teacher.

"I didn't—only fish. I know she doesn't eat red meat," answered the teacher.

"She doesn't eat any kind of meat," Helen shot back.

The teacher looked surprised. "I didn't realize you considered fish meat."

"And chicken!" added Helen.

"Oh!" responded the teacher, biting her lip. "I'm sorry," she went on. "It's just that Sissy always seems so hungry, like she can't really get full on the fruits and vegetables alone. I feel sorry for her."

The conversation went on—give and take—and slowly the facts and feelings on both sides began to emerge. The teacher's misunderstanding about what Helen considered meat gave way to her feelings about Sissy feeling hungry and left out as the other children enjoyed hamburgers and hot dogs and other foods forbidden to Sissy. She was obviously not committed to vegetarianism herself, and it was hard for her to see why Helen felt so strongly about it. She even questioned whether a vegetarian diet was a properly nutritious one for a child.

Helen in turn confessed that she had some resentment that children with food allergies were carefully monitored and given special consideration, yet no one seemed to care what Sissy ate. She felt the program should individualize more.

For a while it looked as if these two might never see eye to eye, yet once the feelings got out in the open, the atmosphere began to change. It became obvious that both were concerned about Sissy, and once they realized that they had that in common, they found it wasn't so hard to sort out the problem and solve it. Respect and communication were the keys, they decided; and when the conversation ended, they both left with good feelings about each other.

 Watch this video to hear a language development coordinator discuss teacher training on culture. What do you think about his comment regarding the need for teacher reflection? How often do you reflect on issues of culture?

Strategy Box 7.2

Strategies for Working on Cross-Cultural Communication

- Build relationships. People who have good relationships are more likely to work on their conflicts in more healthy ways. Relationships sometimes just happen, but more often, they need to be initiated and then nurtured. Commit yourself to working constantly on the total relationship, not just the conflict.

- Know yourself and be clear about what you believe in. Be aware of your own values and goals. Check to see whether your behavior reflects your values and goals. If you are in tune with yourself and are clear about what you believe in, you're less likely to present a strong defensive stance in the face of cultural bump. It is when we feel ambiguous that we come on the strongest.

- Work to bring differences out in the open. Be sensitive to your own discomfort in response to the behavior of others. Tune in on something that bothers you, instead of just ignoring it and hoping it will go away. Work to identify what specific behaviors of others make you uncomfortable. Try to discover exactly what in yourself creates this discomfort. You need to be honest with yourself and do some soul-searching to get your prejudices out in the open. None of us likes to do that, but it's an important part of relationships and clear communication. While you are looking at yourself, look for signs of discomfort in other people in response to your behavior. When you discover discomfort, talk about it!

- Discuss differences. Discussing differences isn't easy to do. Some people shy away from direct discussion of sensitive areas. Many want to cover up differences because they perceive that recognizing them will complicate the relationship. Others avoid discussion of differences in hopes of promoting equality and harmony. Some have never thought about values until they bump up against a set that is different from their own.

- Become an effective cross-cultural communicator. Learn how to open up communication instead of shutting it down. Work to build a relationship with the person or the people with whom you're in conflict. You'll enhance your chances for conflict management or resolution if a relationship exists. Be patient. These things take time.

  Learn about communication styles that are different from yours. Teach your own communication styles. Become aware of body language, voice tone, posture, and position. All of these carry cultural messages that are open to being misinterpreted across cultures. For example, if you're a teacher, and a parent stands too close to you when carrying on a conversation, you may feel that she is pushy or at least strange, whereas she may think she is conveying warmth and friendliness. If a parent is very late to an appointment and then arrives and fails to apologize, you may make assumptions about his priorities or his manners. But he may have a very different time sense from yours and not consider himself late at all. He may have no idea that he has offended you.

  If you tend to talk in a high-pitched voice when you are excited, and others interpret your tone of voice as anger, explain to them what you're really feeling. (Pitches and tones carry emotional messages that are culturally based and not the same across cultures.)

- Problem-solve. Use a problem-solving approach to conflicts rather than a power approach (if you're the one with the power in the situation). Dialogue. Communicate. Be flexible when you can. Negotiate when possible. Notice when you are getting defensive. Defensiveness gets in the way of problem solving. Defensiveness indicates that you have some kind of emotional issue around this conflict. That may be something you need to sort out and understand.

- Commit yourself to education. Learn about other cultures. Become a student of culture if you are in a cross-cultural situation. You don't have to become an anthropologist, but you can use some of the anthropologist's approaches to studying a culture. Read, but don't believe everything you read. Check it out. Observe and listen. Ask, but don't believe everything you are told. Check it out. You'll hear lots of generalizations about particular cultures. Don't get sucked into promoting more stereotypes! Discuss what you are seeing, hearing, reading, and being told with other people of the culture you are learning about. Be a critical thinker. Educate yourself and educate others as well. Check out the Advocacy in Action feature "Speaking Up Against Stereotyping" to see what one concerned citizen did when she discovered her local community center was promoting an unfortunate stereotype as part of what they called a "coloring contest."

ADVOCACY IN ACTION ▶ SPEAKING UP AGAINST STEREOTYPING

A local citizen

Picture this: a mustachioed man with a big sombrero dozing under a tall cactus. This picture was sent to all the elementary students in a school district as part of a community-wide coloring contest promoting a scholarship fundraising fiesta. I couldn't believe the lack of sensitivity and awareness in this choice. I wrote a letter to the community center to let them know how inappropriate it was to advertise a festive, active event with a clearly stereotyped clip art image of Mexican people. They shot back a letter that said they had consulted with two of their Hispanic employees who claimed it wasn't an offensive graphic. The community center stood by their flier and coloring contest.

I decided to keep pursuing the matter. I went to the community's Human Rights Commission and made the case that perpetuating stereotypes legitimizes prejudice. They decided to advise the community center that the flier's graphics were insensitive. The community center sent me a letter that the coloring contest was being called off and that the children were "missing out of a wonderful contest" because of my complaints. I was satisfied. I feel good because my advocacy provided the opportunity for people to reflect on the choices they make. Am I promoting fairness? What do we want our children to be exposed to in terms of images? Sometimes the things that we think are innocuous and not hurtful sneak into our perspectives about others. And sometimes those images we internalize about ourselves.

Watch this video to hear a parent tell her story about an experience with stereotype assumptions and racism. What kind of message might her daughter internalize about herself through the experience?

www.youtube.com
/watch?v=Wf9QBnPK6Yg

> It doesn't do any good to teach children about equity and social justice and then hope they will grow up and make the world a better place. We can't wait. We need to be working on ourselves so we can be models for children about how to do what we hope they will learn.

Helping Children Understand and Value Cultural Pluralism

Just as adults are ethnocentric, so are children. Ethnocentrism relates to the egocentrism that young children struggle with as they slowly learn to see the world from more than one point of view. Adults need to help children work through both their ethnocentrism and their egocentrism. Adults can do that only if they have grappled with their own ethnocentrism. It's a matter of getting children to communicate with each other, accept the reality of another as valid, and learn what it's like to walk in another's shoes.

Some books focus on multicultural or anti-bias education for children. This book has only a small section on that subject because this book focuses more on the effect of the adults in children's lives. It doesn't do any good to teach children about equity and social justice and then hope they will grow up and make the world a better place. We can't wait. We need to be working on ourselves so we can be models for children about how to do what we hope they will learn. Giving lessons to children about getting along across cultures won't work if they look around and see that the adults in their lives aren't treating each other with respect. They won't learn about equity if they learn that some people who are doing the same job as other people have lower status and are getting lower pay. There is a lot to be done to reach a greater level of equity and social justice, and it's not up to children to do it. It's up to us—the adults!

Some children come from a multicultural background and have firsthand experience with cultural pluralism. They may already be good at crossing cultures. This can be a great benefit for them and for those around them who can use them as models. When we see a person who is comfortable operating out of more than one culture, we gain an idea of how it works.

Here is an example of a bicultural child:

David was born in the United States to a Mexican father and a European American mother. The family traveled frequently to Mexico and enjoyed extended visits with the father's family. By the time David entered preschool at the age of four, he was already bilingual and bicultural. He could perform amazing feats, such as making a judgment about which language to speak with someone he met for the first time. He was seldom wrong. He could also switch midstream from English to Spanish when the occasion demanded. For example, if he was playing in the sand with an English-speaking child and a Spanish-speaking child approached, David would speak English with one and Spanish with the other, while playing with both. David fits very well in an all-European American group or an all-Mexican group or a Mexican-American group. He has chameleon-like qualities. He is a truly bicultural person.

Children have the ability to compartmentalize—that is, to understand that one set of behaviors is appropriate at Grandmother's, another at child care, another at school, and still another at home. Although we, as adults, may try hard to make most of the environments children find themselves in consistent, that's not the way the world works. One set of behaviors is expected in the bank, another at the park. Part of socialization is learning how to behave in each of the many environments in which children find themselves. Learning culturally appropriate behavior is one aspect of this same skill.

> **✓ Check Your Understanding 7.2**
>
> Click here to check your understanding of conflicting goals and values.

SUPPORTING HOME LANGUAGE

The example of David brings us to a very important subject. It's the last subject in this chapter, but by far not the least important. The scenario with David is from my own experience as a preschool teacher in a bilingual program for Spanish-speaking children and their parents. In fact, I even wrote an article for *Young Children* back in the 1970s about my experience and what I learned from it. I didn't continue to pursue the subject and eventually became a community college teacher, but I've always remained a strong advocate for supporting home language. I'm not alone. Linda Espinosa also makes a strong case for supporting home language in her 2015 book *Getting It Right for Young Children from Diverse Backgrounds: Applying Research to Improve Practice with a Focus on Dual-Language Learners*, which focuses on the successful education of children from linguistically and culturally diverse backgrounds. Espinosa also sees many advantages in growing up bi- or multilingual. She and other language experts advocate supporting home language and when possible creating bilingual programs.

Language Loss in Immigrant Children

Maria, a first grader comes home from school, throws down her coat and says, "Wow, am I tired!" Her mother responds in Spanish, suggesting she sit down and have a snack. Then she asks what Maria wants to eat. The child answers in English. Her mother tells her to speak Spanish! Maria ignores her.

Maria was in preschool when she started learning English because most of the teachers and some of the children were English speakers. Her parents were pleased that she was learning English and assumed that she would become bilingual. They were surprised and saddened when that didn't happen. She rejected her family's language and embraced the new language whole-heartedly.

Why do so many newcomer families to the United States lose their home language in one generation? Though parents and grandparents may stay fluent in the language they brought with them, it's often the case that their children end up monolingual in English. Some families make a great deal of effort to insure that the next generation retains the home language. Some are successful, but not all. David, mentioned earlier, is an example of a success story.

This situation of English monolingualism makes the United States unique. It also puts us at a disadvantage in the world. Certainly children in the United States can and do learn other languages in school—but usually not until 7th or 8th grade when it is harder to acquire a second language. In other countries foreign languages are introduced early in the education system. Sometimes that also happens in the United States, but not traditionally.

I was in a workshop recently talking about bilingualism when one of the participants mentioned that her family was originally from Germany and no one in her family today spoke a word of German. She was wondering why that was. Her question was, why don't people of European background speak the languages of their original homeland? There is history why immigrants from Europe lost their home language during the last century. The United States fought two wars in Europe in the 20th century. During that period, concerted effort on the part of the government was used to help European immigrants identify themselves clearly as Americans. You can't very well send soldiers overseas to kill their own people. Who knows how many might have kept their European languages and cultural connections if that hadn't happened?

When being bilingual is such an advantage, what are some of the factors working against it? One is a strongly held idea by some that the United States of America is—and should always be—an English-speaking country, *period*! For some people that means exclusively English. A proposition—Proposition 227—on the ballot in California in 1998 known as "English only" became a hot topic among people who highly valued bilingual education. The intent was to make all students in public schools English speaking with no intent related to bilingualism. Perhaps that made sense to all the English speakers, descendants from countries around the world—people who had lost their original language generations ago. To families that valued their home language or wished their children to become (or remain) bilingual, Proposition 227 represented a nightmare. For a time the law was carried out as written, but over the years challenges to it weakened it. Eventually bilingual education came back to California.

Before that proposition hit the ballot box, I was involved in an innovative home-centered preschool program for Spanish-speaking children. I saw that it was possible for children to keep their home language when effort was made to teach them in it. English-speaking children were also enrolled and they learned some Spanish. The idea of the program was to emphasize Spanish to children of Spanish-speaking families during the early years rather than introducing English in ways that made the children turn from their own language to embrace the new one.

Understanding the Advantages of Bilingualism

In my own family I see what an advantage being bilingual is. My husband grew up in Mexico where everybody in his family spoke both Spanish and German (due to his grandfather who immigrated from Germany back in the late 1800s). When my husband first came to the United States, he went into the Navy where he learned English. After he got out he went to college and majored in both his home languages. He eventually became a community college language teacher. Some of the children in his family in the next generations born in the USA managed also to be bilingual (and several are now trilingual), because their parents were absolutely dedicated to the idea of the advantages of bilingualism.

I know from experience how many children come to this country, enter English-only classrooms, and lose their home language. Lily Wong Fillmore (1991, 2000) has written passionately about the loss of home language in English-only classrooms. In an early piece of writing she told her own story as a Chinese immigrant and the pain she suffered when she lost her ability to communicate with her family.

Some recent work in Head Start let me get acquainted with Robert Stechuk, who wrote a book with Susan Burns called *Making a Difference* (2005), which is a framework for supporting first- and second-language development in preschool children of migrant farm workers. They mention the importance of play and active learning experience rather than "language lessons" with flash cards and drills. They make the point that children develop language skills through social interactions—not just with adults, but also with other children. Using accepted preschool practice, teachers put children in environments that let them be active and focus on their interests. Communication comes about naturally in those environments. It's always important to help children continue to develop in their home language, including continuing to build their vocabulary. It's important not to interrupt cognitive development by switching to English and disregarding the cognitive progress they have already made in their home language. English should be an addition to what they have with no subtracting involved. Stechuk and Burns also make the point that saying everything in both languages one right after another doesn't work. Children especially, but even adults, just pay attention to the language they are strongest in. So if they are used to their home language coming last, they don't bother to listen the first time and just wait until they can easily understand what is said.

> It's important not to interrupt cognitive development by switching to English and disregarding the cognitive progress they have already made in their home language. English should be an addition to what they have with no subtracting involved.

As a nation we should be working harder to help all children become bilingual. Bilingual people are different from monolinguals in ways that go beyond language and communication. This is a huge subject that needs much more space than the end of this chapter. My own observations of my husband's family and Mexican friends lead me to believe that they have different personalities depending on what language they are speaking and to whom. In a blog written by Francois Grosjean in *Psychology Today*, titled "How Cultures Combine and Blend in a Person," he explains how dual personalities work.

Watch this video to see Linda Espinosa discuss implications for language teaching and learning. She talks about the importance of what you believe about language learning. What do you believe?

www.youtube.com /watch?v=Ws1jHVNAZR0

Language Relationships

There is an interesting phenomenon called "language relationships" that also happens between and among bilingual people. I have seen evidence of that phenomenon time and again with my husband and his friends. Even in casual conversations, he always spoke Spanish to Pedro, the other Spanish teacher, and German to Gail, the German teacher, though both Pedro and Gail were perfectly fluent in English. He explained to me that it was a matter of what felt more comfortable. I also saw it in the preschool as the Spanish-speaking children in my classes figured out who spoke English and who spoke Spanish. If they were bilingual, they chose which language to speak to which person, just as David did in the scenario.

It has been interesting to watch the language relationships play out in my husband's family. Sometimes it's consciously designed and sometimes it happens at a first meeting—that the two bilingual people decide what language to communicate in. For example, my mother-in-law and father-in-law always spoke Spanish to each other, which I suspect was because that was the language they courted in. When one of their children or grandchildren walked into the room where they were talking to each other, they would immediately switch to German. That was a decision they made, as German was not the official language of Mexico and they wanted the new generations to be fluent (also literate) in German. It was clear to me in the preschool that children who were learning English had a much easier time trying it out with the English-speaking teachers than the Spanish-speaking ones.

This keeping of a family's traditional language and culture is a huge subject and has been since the beginning of this country. This last section has just been a small introduction to some of the issues related to what it means to "become American." It briefly explored how immigrants approach nationality and language in our multicultural, multilingual, and multiracial country.

Check Your Understanding 7.3

Click here to check your understanding of supporting home language.

SUMMARY

This chapter looked at cultural differences in goals and values from a particular framework by contrasting cultural patterns. Called patterns 1 and 2, they represent differing priorities not often discussed but found in families as well as in early care and education programs. The point was that the two patterns can strongly affect child rearing, care, and education practices in both the home and child care center. The chapter then focused on what to do when conflicts arise between the home and program over cultural differences. The chapter ended with helping children value cultural pluralism and how to support home language.

QUIZ

Click here to check your understanding of Chapter 7, "Understanding Families' Goals, Values, and Culture."

FOR DISCUSSION

1. What did you think of the two contrasting patterns in this chapter? Do you or someone you know fit one or the other of these patterns? Which pattern do you think is more likely to emphasize modesty over pride? Why? Which pattern do you think is likely to emphasize manners over honest self-expression? Why?

2. Some people say that to talk about cultural *conflicts* creates a different mindset than if you think of them as cultural bumps or cultural dilemmas. How might different wording change the picture of what is happening when two people or two groups disagree? Can you think of other examples of when a change of vocabulary made a difference?

3. Although the title of one of this chapter's boxes, "A Cultural Bump," indicates that the difference between the parent and the teacher is a cultural one, nothing in the story shows that the two are of different cultures. Does it matter? Is it important to know whether diversity is related to culture, religion, family traditions, or just individual differences? If yes, how might a teacher respond differently after learning what was at the root of the issue?

4. The cultures in this chapter are not labeled. Does that frustrate you? Why do you think the author chose to deal with patterns rather than particular cultural differences? Why do you find no lists in this book of typical characteristics of the most common cultures in the United States and Canada today?

5. What are some of the factors in children's lives that work against their prosocial development?

6. What is your experience with bilingual language development, supporting home language, and learning a new language? What are your feelings about dual-language learning?

WEBSITES

National Association for Bilingual Education (NABE)
The National Association for Bilingual Education advocates for bilingual and English language learners and families. They support and promote policy, pedagogy, research, and professional development to cultivate a multilingual, multicultural society that respects cultural and linguistic diversity.

National Association for Multicultural Education (NAME)
This organization advocates for equity and social justice. Its goals include: respecting and appreciating cultural diversity; promoting the understanding of unique cultural and ethnic heritage; and promoting culturally responsible and responsive curricula, in order to achieve social, political, economic, and educational equity.

World of Cultural Democracy
Webster's World of Cultural Democracy website offers links to resources in the areas of cultural policy, action, issues, and a guide to the cultural landscape.

World Forum Foundation
This organization is a collaborative effort to bring early care and education professionals from around the world together. Started by *Exchange* magazine as an annual conference, the organization now has expanded to working forums and projects.

FURTHER READING

Barrera, I., Kramer, L., & Macpherson, T. D. (2012). *Skilled dialogue*. Baltimore, MD: Brookes.

Delpit, L., & Dowdy, J. K. (2008). *The skin that we speak: Thoughts on language and culture in the classroom*. New York, NY: New Press.

Espinosa, L. (2015). *Getting it right for young children from diverse backgrounds: Applying research to improve practice with a focus on dual-language learners*. Upper Saddle River, NJ: Pearson.

Garcia, E. E. & Frede, E. C. (2010). *Young English language learners: Current research and emerging directions for practice and policy*. NY: Teachers' College Press.

Gillanders, C. & Castro, D.C. (2012). Storybook reading for young dual-language learners. *Young children 66* (1) pp. 91-94..

Gonzalez-Mena, J. (2010). *50 strategies for working and communicating with diverse families, 3rd edition*. Upper Saddle River, NJ: Pearson.

Howes, C., Downer, J. T., & Pianta, R. C. (2012). *Dual-language learners in the early childhood classroom*. Baltimore, MD: Brookes.

Mann, T. (2010). Culturally responsive perspective. In V. Washington & J. D. Andrews (Eds.), *Children of 2020: Creating a better tomorrow* (pp. 61–66). Washington, DC: Council for Professional Recognition and National Association for the Education of Young Children.

Nemeth, K. N. (2014) *Young dual-language learners: A guide for preK-3 leaders*. Philadelphia, PA: Caslon.

Paradis, J., Genesee, F., & Crago, M. B. (2010). *Dual-language development and disorders: A handbook on bilingualism and second language learning (2nd Ed.)*. Baltimore, MD: Brookes Publishing.

iofoto/Fotolia

Working with Families on Guidance Issues

Learning Outcomes

In this chapter you will learn to. . .

- Examine discipline, authority and cultural differences.
- Articulate discussing preventative measures with parents.
- Explain guidance as responding to unacceptable behavior.

H ow do you work with families around the behavior of their children in ways that are comfortable for everybody? Guidance is a hot topic with lots of emotions attached to it. Sometimes those emotions are because of the adults' own childhoods, sometimes because of cultural differences, and sometimes because people haven't thought through their approaches to guidance.

Let's look at what guidance has to do with Bronfenbrenner's ecological model. In this chapter, we're focusing on the close-up world of the child (microsystem), but that world is also influenced by the larger context of the mesosystem, exosystem, and macrosystem. The ultimate goal is to produce well-balanced people who can guide their own behavior, get along with others, and fit productively into society. Effective guidance also relates to the satisfactory resolutions of Erikson's psycho-social conflicts so children emerge from each stage healthy and strong and ready for the next one. Guidance is what gives children the security, protection, and safety of Maslow's hierarchy of needs and allows them to move further toward self-actualization. When adults guide children in loving ways, children perceive the adults' caring motives, which also relates to Maslow's theory. Consider the question of children's rights when thinking about guidance. Everyone might not agree that children have rights, but the United Nations is very clear that they do. See the Advocacy in Action feature "United Nations Rights of Children," and think about the subject of guidance and where it intersects with children's rights.

Take a minute and think about how each one of those rights relates to appropriate and healthy guidance.

It's fairly easy to agree that children need some form of guidance, but does everybody agree about guidance <u>strategies</u>? Definitely not! Individuals and groups have differing ideas about basic human nature, and their ideas influence their approaches to dealing with what they deem as unacceptable behavior in children. I illustrate this in classes and workshops by saying we are going to talk about human nature, focusing on the child. I then create an imaginary line and ask participants to place themselves on it. At one end the child is represented as a flower—at the other end as a tree. I explain the flower end by saying the child is like a seed. When planted in good soil and nurtured, it grows. The potential of a beautiful flower is in the seed and all it that is necessary is for it to have its needs met. On the other end is the tree. It also has its potential built in and must have its needs met to grow; however, to have a tall, straight, shade-giving tree, you must clip and prune. If it just grows wild, it can look very different—crooked or ugly with crowded limbs that encroach on each other. "As the twig is pruned so grows the tree" is an old saying that relates to this end of the continuum.

To make the metaphors more dramatic, I sometimes point to the flower and say that a baby is like an angel—full of good. Inside is a benevolent guiding force, and with love and nurturing, the baby will grow up fine. At the other end is a devil baby—born bad—ready for trouble. The guiding force inside is very different from the angel baby.

When participants place themselves according to their philosophies on the imaginary line of the continuum, most cluster toward the middle, though some are out toward the ends. People toward the flower/angel end are usually those who have taken child development classes and are well trained in early childhood education. They say that the baby *unfolds* in the way he or she was designed to unfold. It's a natural process and a beautiful one, like a rosebud opening. They may have been influenced by the very word *development*, which means unfold. People at the other end

---

ADVOCACY IN ACTION ▸ **UNITED NATIONS RIGHTS OF CHILDREN**

It's easy for some people to think of children as too young to have the full rights that other citizens of a nation have. The United Nations addressed that very issue by creating a Convention on the Rights of the Child under UNICEF, which can be thought of as a huge, multinational advocacy organization. A long, complex document on the rights of the child from the United Nations Children's Fund can be found at UNICEF's website.

Put in a few simple words, the United Nations Convention on the Rights of the Child says, among other things, that no child should be treated unfairly on any basis. The best interests of children must be the primary concern. All children have a right to fair treatment—no matter their race, ability, income level, where they live, what language they speak, and the type of family they come from.

Here are samples of other basic rights: All children have a right to:

- Survival.
- Development to their fullest.
- Health and health services.
- An identity—a name, a nationality, family ties, and an official record of who they are.
- Protection from harmful influences, abuse, and exploitation.
- Full participation in family, cultural, and social life.
- Leisure, play, and culture.

---

of the spectrum have a different view and are usually cynical about the rosy picture painted at the opposite end. They also see a driving force from within, but one that puts temptations and obstacles in the way of positive growth. It, too, is a natural process—but one that needs constant monitoring and intervention if it is to result in a desirable end product. Children are not naturally born pure and good; they cannot be allowed just to unfold according to their human nature. The words vary with the person's philosophical stance or religious background, but what is clear is that the child's sense of direction is not always toward the good. If the child is to turn out okay, he or she needs a good firm adult hand to stay on the right path. Some say that it's more natural to be bad than it is to be good. *Sin* is a word that comes up in this discussion.

Once in a while there's a participant who refuses to stand on the continuum at all and protests that there is no basic human nature, natural unfolding, or driving force. What counts is how the environment shapes a person. This person explains that the way to get the child to behave the way you want is through careful attention to and manipulation of the rewards the child receives. This is a "behaviorist" view, and it is detached from such concepts as "bad" and "good." Behaviors are more likely to be seen as acceptable or unacceptable rather than branded with moral judgments.

All of these views are simplistic, but they make a point about different perceptions of any child or group of children who need guidance. In reality, development is more dynamic and involves a much more complex picture. Children grow and change through a complicated process composed of many interacting elements, some that can be controlled and others that cannot. Keep that in mind as you read through this chapter on guidance. A *dynamic* theoretical view of growth and development makes it clear that behavior is the result of the interplay of the child (and his or her individual genetic makeup) with culture, developmental stage, environmental input, and the natural inclination to imitate or model after others. The perspective on which this chapter is based takes into consideration the dynamic interplay of all these forces. It also urges you to understand that not everybody has the same perspective and to honor differences.

DISCIPLINE, AUTHORITY, AND CULTURAL DIFFERENCES

Discipline is a huge subject and the danger lies in categorizing people or cultures in ways that do everybody a disservice. Discipline is also a loaded word. For years, early childhood experts tried to remove it from the vocabulary of teachers, caregivers, and parents, substituting the word *guidance* instead. But too many parents and educators were uncomfortable with what they considered the lack of discipline being advocated by the experts (*guidance* just didn't do it), so the word has refused to die.

Changing the Word Discipline *to* Guidance

Why did the experts want to change the word *discipline* to *guidance*? It has to do with the associations connected with each word. *Guidance* has a more positive tone to it. To many people, *discipline* means punishment, and punishment means pain or at least humiliation. But it doesn't have to be that way! If you look up the word in the dictionary, you find that discipline and disciple come from the same root word. Think of two people walking along a path—a big person and a little one—a master and a disciple. Discipline might mean punishment to some, but it can also mean guiding and managing behavior, not through punishment but by being attached to a more experienced partner. This partner is someone who is wiser, knows more, and has lived longer than the child. Eventually children internalize the master or the older partner and take charge of themselves. This development of *inner controls*, or self-discipline, is the goal of disciplining children.

Inner Controls versus External Locus of Control

The development of inner controls is one way of looking at what children need in the way of guidance. I and many others in the field of early childhood education come from or have taken on a culture that emphasizes independence and individuality, so it is important to internalize the control. There are other cultural views. For example, in some cultures, as mentioned

When you think of discipline, think of two people walking along a path— a big person and a little one, a master and a disciple; the master is wiser, knows more, has lived longer, and is able to guide the child toward the development of inner controls

Aleksei Potov/Shutterstock

in previous chapters, the emphasis is not on individuality but on being part of the group. Although the partner image may still work, it works in a different way. The idea of "inner controls" at an early age may not be a priority, according to Janice Hale (1986), a longtime advocate for cultural sensitivity to African American children. Hale said that discipline in many African American families depends on what she called an "external locus of control." She described how adults in the black community play a social-control role by creating a network of people who firmly correct behavior and report misbehavior to the parent. Therefore, parents are at the center of this social-control network. For the child, this means that he or she is always under the surveillance of adults. The significant feature of the control system is that it seems to operate externally to the child. Therefore, the child seems to develop an external locus of control.

Hale sees a conflict for children when teachers give children responsibility for their own behavior. She says that in schools where adults often behave as if they expect children to monitor themselves without outside help, the children's behavior may be labeled as problematic. The adults aren't functioning in the ways children expect, so the system the children are used to is not present to guide their behavior.

Lonnie Snowden (1984) also wrote about cultural differences between African American and European American child rearing. Like Hale, Snowden explained how in many African American families responsibility for the control of children's behavior is in the hands of an extensive network of adults. Snowden saw this approach as one of extended parenting, which ensures that children's behavior receives closer monitoring and results in more immediate sanctions than is the norm in the dominant culture. Children feel free to actively explore and take on assertive styles, because they know someone will be there to stop them when they go too far. But most adults in charge of educational programs for children, including school, don't have the same direct and straightforward control over children's behavior. They expect children to be passive and immobile, which many African American children are not. According to Snowden, the cultural conflict is clearly drawn.

Both Snowden and Hale shared their knowledge and insights on African American families many years ago. More recently Adkison-Bradley et al. studied discipline approaches in African American families and concluded that those families studied used an assortment of approaches to managing misconduct. That's a good lesson for all of us—to be aware, when looking for patterns, that we don't stereotype behavior. It's also important to remember that things change over time—including cultures and perhaps ideas about discipline and guidance. Further, we have to think about how children grow up to be adults who become parents. Their own upbringing may or may not have an influence on how they are rearing their children. Some of the approaches to discipline relate to different ideas about authority, about how authority figures should behave, and about how children

Monkey Business Images/shutterstock

In many African American families responsibility for the control of children's behavior is in the hands of an extensive network of adults

should relate to authority (Phillips, 1995). When authority figures behave in ways that aren't familiar to children, the children can feel confused. Some children are used to firm, strict, and sometimes physical guidance, and without it they keep testing the limits. They may even come to the conclusion that the teacher doesn't care what they do. These children can end up labeled as problem children (Gonzalez-Mena & Shareef, 2005; Hale, 1986). Ideas about discipline and guidance get extremely complex when they intersect with culture and oppression. Some groups of people who are targets of racism have to protect their children from the oppressive practices of racist individuals and institutions. Their methods of guidance and discipline may be different from those of groups for whom oppression is just a word. Ideas about what's best for children can vary greatly and be influenced by history and experience, not just by culture alone.

Cynthia Ballenger (1992, 1999) describes her work with Haitian preschool teachers and Haitian children. She sees a system of guidance that does stress inner controls, but not the way this chapter has described them. Children are not encouraged to reason out behavior choices. They aren't expected to learn from consequences of those choices. In the system Ballenger describes, children are taught to be good by appealing to their emotional connections to family and teachers.

Sandoval and De La Roza (1986) discuss the way extended family and interdependent network orientation work to provide external controls in the Latino community. They describe how the mother constantly gives directives to young children, even when they are not misbehaving. It is a way of letting them know that they are constantly being watched and that her "protective eyes" are on them. These constant directives given in public are ways to let others engage in the social control of the children. Anyone who sees children getting into trouble is expected to stop them and treat them as if they were their own.

We can learn from each other, but only if we become aware of what we are doing and begin to discuss our behavior with people who are different from ourselves. Costanza Eggers-Pierola (2005) gives advice about how to have these discussions with Latino families. One of the advantages for children in early childhood education programs is that parents can learn from each other and from early educators.

> Ideas about discipline and guidance get extremely complex when they intersect with culture and oppression. Some groups of people who are targets of racism have to protect their children from the oppressive practices of racist individuals and institutions. Their methods of guidance and discipline may be different from those of groups for whom oppression is just a word.

Teaching Self-Regulation

One way to get out of this either/or dilemma of inner controls or outer locus of controls is to look at some of the newer research on what's called self-regulation (Flore, 2011; Thompson, 2009; Gillespie & Seibel, 2006), which can be defined as the ability to monitor and manage oneself, including directing attention, handling one's feelings, and managing one's thinking and behavior. Though the common term is self-regulation, what really happens is co-regulation, which means at the beginning the child has a partner in getting himself or herself regulated. Let's look at two aspects of self-regulation as it starts in infancy. What happens in infancy affects the type of guidance needed through childhood.

> Watch this video to hear more about self-regulation. How did you feel as you watched the different families helping their children regulate? Was one more familiar to you than another?
>
> www.youtube.com /watch?v=VSCMD0Et9rw

1. *Learning to focus and pay attention.* Ellen Galinsky, in her book *Mind in the Making: Seven Essential Skills Every Child Needs* (2010), lists focus and self-control as the number-one essential skill. Years ago, Magda Gerber, one of my teachers, demonstrated how to teach this skill to a baby. She paid

The beginning of self-regulation starts with babies learning how to focus and pay attention to their own bodies

attention to the baby. She modeled what she was teaching. Gerber advocated the importance of being focused on the baby in sensitive ways, the way a therapist is focused on a client. She also said that no one can take the full attention of another all the time, so this focus was only for periods. The baby learned what it was like to have someone's focus and tended to pay attention back. When there was no need for all that adult attention, the adult let the baby pay attention to himself or herself and what was around in the environment without interrupting the focus.

This idea of non-interruptions is rare in the average adult, especially those who take a "stimulation approach" and keep the baby's senses busy with a succession of talk, movement, or toys that do things such as sparkle, dazzle, and make noises. As soon as the baby's attention leaves, the adult perceives something else is needed to tickle the senses, teaching the baby to continually seek novelty in stimulation. Observing a baby in the care of Magda, or someone who believes in her work, is very different because they see a baby who pays attention to his own body and what it can do. Babies who have learned to focus on their own bodies, hands, feet, and a few simple toys can entertain themselves for long periods without needing outside attention even before they learn to roll over, sit up, or walk.

It's not that the adult ignores the baby and his or her needs! When a basic need arises (hunger, for example), the caregiver, who has been avoiding distracting the baby, then appears and focuses full attention on the baby while meeting the need, once again modeling the behavior she is trying to teach (Gerber, 1998; Hammond, 2009; Tardos, 2007). This is quite a different approach from the average caregiver. Keep in mind that this approach shows how self-regulation comes as the result of co-regulation and represents an early approach to guidance.

▶ Watch this video to see Magda Gerber speak about the inner needs of infants. What do you think about her idea that the adult role is to reduce the stimulation for infants?

www.youtube.com /watch?v=8K9YxI7F_fl

2. *Learning about feelings.* Again the teachings of Gerber (1998) come in here. With her therapist background, she knew the importance of feelings. She taught adults to accept babies' emotional displays and help them recognize and feel their feelings. Crying is communication and self-expression in babies. When they cry they may be communicating a need that can be met by an adult. If the need is met and the baby is still crying, that's when the adult can realize that he is using his main means of expressing a feeling. It may be that all the adult wants is for the crying to go away and will do whatever possible to make that happen. As a result, some people learn from infancy how to do that for themselves. They "stuff" their feelings. Unfelt and unacknowledged feelings can get in the way of healthy self-regulation.

3. *Experiencing consequences*. One approach to guidance that some students learn as they become early childhood educators or when they enter early childhood programs as parents is *consequences*. Often used in early childhood programs, the approach is considered an empowering one. Children are allowed to make choices about their behavior, within limits. Sometimes those choices lead to uncomfortable or undesirable *consequences*. For example, a child who is playing with her food is given the choice of eating it or leaving the table. The choices and the consequences are controlled by the adult so that they don't involve any real risk or harm for the child. But some consequences can still be emotionally painful. It may seem as if using a consequences approach is the same as using punishment, but it is not. Suffering the consequences of your own choices feels different from being punished because someone bigger or more powerful than you decides to punish. Punishment, the time-honored approach to teaching children acceptable behavior, has some side effects that parents, teachers, caregivers, and family child care providers should be aware of.

Problems with Using Punishment to Teach

One problem with punishment is the negativity that accompanies it. Often the adult uses punishment to get even, which triggers a spirit of retaliation on the part of the child. This starts a vicious circle that ends only when one or the other triumphs, sometimes leaving quite a path of destruction in the wake of the conflict. Children who are frequently punished become more devious, not more cooperative. They respond to the hurt, loss, or penalty (the punishment) with anger, resentment, and defiance. Thus, punishment prevents the building of good relationships that are the basis of effective discipline and causes resentment and the urge to strike back.

Children who are punished for trying things out and making mistakes in the process can become inhibited in their development of autonomy and initiative (Erikson, 1963). The urge to explore and experiment is squelched when punishment hangs over a child's head. Learning is reduced. Of course, childhood urges are strong, and many survive in spite of what adults may do to discourage them. However, it is important to understand how punishing young children can affect their later development. Children can come to see new situations as potentially "troublemaking" rather than as opportunities to use their initiative to find out more about the world around them. When those children become adults they may be afraid to try anything new because they were punished for mistakes as children.

When punishments hurt, the teachable moment is lost. Children are most open to learning right after they've done something wrong or made a mistake. That's the time for helping them see what went wrong. If they are wrapped up in pain (physical or psychological), they can't concentrate on the "lesson" the adult has in mind and may instead learn some other lesson that wasn't even intended.

Physical punishment is not an option in an educational setting, but for those adults who still use it at home, it can be especially problematic because it models aggression. Parents who are trying to keep their children from hurting others or using violence to solve problems work against their own goals when they use physical punishment. The message the children get is that it is OK to hurt people if you are bigger and have a good reason.

Worst of all, physical punishment can lead to child abuse when adults go further than they intend to. When a parent first starts using physical punishment, the result of even a little is often resentment. Just as modern germs build up

> When punishments hurt, the teachable moment is lost. Children are most open to learning right after they've done something wrong or made a mistake. That's the time for helping them see what went wrong. If they are wrapped up in pain (physical or psychological), they can't concentrate on the "lesson" the adult has in mind and may instead learn some other lesson that wasn't even intended.

resistance to medicine, so does the resentful child become resistant to punishment. The parent finds it takes more and more punishment to get the same effect. Some children are willing to take a lot, so the parent continues to escalate. It's a vicious cycle. Some parents end up abusing their children when they get caught up in this ugly pattern.

A question someone asked me that has stayed with me for a long time is this: When you are faced with a child's misbehavior, are you more interested in changing the behavior or in winning, controlling, coming out ahead, or making the child suffer? Helping families look at their own motives can be a valuable first step to helping them look at their guidance methods. When we accept people as they are, we give them permission to look deeper and consider changing. When we push people to change, they tend to resist. That's something I've tried always to remember when working with families, children, or anybody else.

General Guidelines for Guiding Young Children

Here are some general guidelines I've found useful in working with young children. They focus on preventing situations where guidance may be needed. If you pass them on to families and are open to discussion, you might learn something more about the family. If you model these behaviors or attitudes, the message is even stronger than the written or spoken word. Maybe families will want to discuss what they see you doing. You might even get into a dialogue with them and expand your view. Everybody stands to gain from discussions about guidance.

• *Learn about developmental stages.* Understanding what's just a stage can help prevent you from having unreasonable expectations for a child. Arranging the environment to fit the age and stage of the children in it is vital. Young children are explorers. They need safe places where they can follow their urges to experience the environment in many ways. Toddlers who are just beginning to climb should be in an environment where climbing is completely safe. Older children also love to climb—if both ages are in the same environment, devise means to prevent the younger ones from getting up on whatever the older ones are climbing. Sometimes fencing off a climbing structure that is unsafe for toddlers works. Other times removing the bottom step of steps or ladders allows both age groups to play safely.

• *Communicate with children what you are doing and why.* Don't reason at length, but provide reasons. If you do this, children will eventually do their own reasoning. Sometimes you have prohibit certain behaviors. You may even have to physically prevent them—like holding a hand that is about to hit. In that case, explain your behavior and go on to say that hitting hurts and you won't let that happen. A younger child may not have the maturity yet to put herself in the shoes of another, but your words may remain and guide the behavior until such time as she can truly understand the other person's feelings. While you are doing that, acknowledge what may be going on in the child. Put that into words also: "You didn't like that she grabbed the ball." If the child is old enough to talk, tell him that he can express his feelings to the child who grabbed. Then do some problem solving out loud with the child. "He really wants the ball and you do, too," states the obvious. "I wonder what we can do about that. . ." offers the idea of problem solving. If the child is old enough to talk, you can ask for ideas. If not, you can continue to do some brainstorming about solutions. Even thinking out loud may work. "I wonder if there is another ball he can play with." You don't have to solve the problem right away—let the child work on it before you come up with a solution.

• *Check communication to see whether it is clear.* If it is not clear you may discover that you have ambiguous feelings about the situation. If you've called the children in for lunch, for example, and they aren't coming in, maybe something is going on. Was breakfast late and nobody is really hungry, but you're trying to keep to the schedule? Maybe the children are picking up on your ambiguity and that's why they aren't responding to you. An example I've dealt with as a parent educator is when children won't go to bed at night. It doesn't take a whole lot of discussion to realize that some parents who have been away all day have very ambiguous feelings about putting the children to bed. Children feel the ambiguity and are less likely to do as they are told than when the parent is very clear and certain. In order to see if your communication is clear, you may have to look inside yourself first. Not that you will always be able to solve the problem of ambiguous feelings that get in the way of clear communication. But recognizing your own ambiguity is a start and it helps you understand why the children aren't doing what you want them to do. Of course, if the issue is safety, it's important to put ambiguity beside and take clear steps toward prevention. "I can't let you swing the bat around like that!" must be said clearly, and must be followed up with immediate steps if the behavior doesn't stop at the first warning. Children need to learn when you say, "I can't let you. . ." that you mean it.

• *Trust children.* Misbehavior often comes as a result of children being thwarted in having their needs met. Look closely at any pattern of misbehavior, and take the attitude that this behavior is trying to communicate something. Trust the child to know what he or she needs, even though on the surface the behavior may look just plain troublesome or contrary. Just because he or she seems to be "out to get you" doesn't mean that there aren't needs behind the behaviors. An example is right before a meal. Children who are very hungry and have to wait may misbehave. This has more to do with needs than anything else. Maybe there is nothing to do right away, but next time, arrange timely snacks as a way of *preventing* misbehavior rather than working hard to figure out how to correct it. Understand children's variety of ways of expressing their needs and, when you figure them out, *help them put those needs into words*. If you aren't good at expressing your needs clearly, you may have to work on yourself first. Remember, you are a model for children. They pick up on what you do more than what you say. But don't go overboard—such as replacing "I want. . ." with "I need. . ." For example, "I need you to look pretty when your grandmother is here" probably can be restated to be clearer.

• *Trust yourself.* You also have needs. You can only make good choices about guiding and disciplining children when your own needs are met. That may not be easy, but it is important. Martyrs don't make good teachers—or parents either. When your needs clash with children's needs, strive to find a balance, so that no one's needs are neglected. Convey the message to children that everyone's needs are important—theirs and yours, too.

You are a model for children. This may be very difficult for you today, depending on how you were raised. Needs may not have been discussed in your family and you may not have had models of people who talked about their needs or yours either. Trusting yourself may also have

Build good relationships; discipline is more effective if it comes from a loving place

Voyagerix/Fotolia

been an issue if you were raised in a household where authority reigned and you learned to do what you were told, regardless of your needs. If that is the case, you may have some work to do to learn to trust yourself and recognize your needs. If you were raised to believe that sacrifice is the most valued behavior in your family, you may have to do some self-examination. Being aware of needs and being able to put them into words are skills to develop and practice!

- *Build good relationships.* Whatever approach you take to discipline will be more effective if it comes from a loving place. Nel Noddings's (2002) approach to creating moral people is to focus on the caring relationship. Her ethic of care involves close, positive, caring relationships. When adults come from a place of genuine caring, guidance and discipline measures work much better than when they are used as mere techniques by an adult without a good relationship with the child. Without any relationship, discipline is a difficult matter.

What follows are 14 concrete examples of ways to guide behavior: seven preventative measures, seven response measures. You may find these useful yourself, or you may want to pass them on to families. You could use them to create workshops for parents on the subject of guidance. Those kinds of workshops are usually well attended.

Check Your Understanding 8.1

Click here to check your understanding of discipline, authority, and cultural differences.

DISCUSSING PREVENTATIVE MEASURES WITH PARENTS

Start with prevention so guidance won't be needed. The following sections present seven things to do *before* the unacceptable behavior occurs. Though they may not seem like guidance techniques, they are effective ways to guide behavior. The first two have to do with the environment, the third with modeling, the fourth and fifth with redirection and control, the sixth with feelings, and the seventh with needs.

Child Abuse: A Story

Carla is dealing with the consequences of abusing her child. Right now she is in a group session with other abusing parents, listening to their stories. She's surprised that some of the themes are the same as hers, though the details are different.

As she listens to the others, she involuntarily goes back to the moment before she threw Cody against the wall, fracturing his skull. She gets a sick feeling in her stomach as the memory floods her.

She had reached the end of her rope that evening—she knew it then and she knows it now. "How much do you think I can take?" she had screamed at Cody, who was standing over a broken plate he had just thrown down from the counter in anger. She remembered the series of incidents that had led up to this confrontation better than she remembered what happened afterward. It had been a bad day!

The problem was that she was so alone. Since Cody's father had left her, she found herself with fewer and fewer social contacts. She knew she needed friends, but it was so hard to make them with two children to support and raise. They took up all her time. And they drove her crazy sometimes. Like that awful rainy Saturday when Cody ended up breaking the plate.

As the other parents in the circle continued talking, it became obvious that being isolated was a theme for most of them. Another problem for Carla was that Cody was so immature. She had told him time and again that now that his father was gone he was the man of the house. But he just didn't live up to any of her expectations. Sure, he was only four, but still. . .

Carla didn't know it yet, but this was another common characteristic of parents who abuse their children. They don't understand developmental stages and often have unrealistic expectations for their children. Carla will learn about this subject from the class she is enrolled in.

She will also learn some techniques for guiding and controlling her children's behavior in positive ways. She knows she needs those techniques. Discipline has always left her feeling helpless. She only knows what she learned from her own parents, who used belittling, sarcasm, and, above all, beating on Carla when she was little.

Carla never thought of herself as an abused child. She figured that all children were punished in the same way she was. She knew that she had more scars than some of her childhood friends, but she accepted that as a fact. She never considered that she could question her parents' methods, and indeed she couldn't—she just would have been beaten harder for talking back.

It's not that her parents didn't love her—Carla knows that they did. In her mind they showed their love by hitting her; in fact, they even told her that. In Carla's experience, love and hurt were linked together.

Carla knows now that she *must stop* abusing Cody. No matter what problems she has, there's no excuse for not controlling herself—she knows that now. She also knows that she's not alone anymore. She's getting help, in the form of education, therapy, and, above all, support. Things will be different now, and eventually Cody and his sister Candace will be back home again.

Carla breathes a sigh of relief as she sits back in her chair, ready to talk. It's her turn now. The group looks at her expectantly.

"I have lots of feelings," she starts out.

Childhelp is an organization that works to help victims of child abuse. Their website includes a national child abuse hotline, definitions of different kinds of abuse, along with information about prevention, intervention, and treatment programs.

---

1. Setting Up an Appropriate Environment. The younger the child, the more he or she needs freedom to move, things to explore, and something to do. For example, you can predict unacceptable behavior when you have a toddler for any length of time in a fancy restaurant, an elegant living room, or a department store. You are more likely to find acceptable behavior when children are in an environment that is age-appropriate as well as suited to their needs and interests.

2. Letting the Environment Provide the Limits. Fence off dangerous areas from young children. Most communities have laws about swimming pools, but they don't expect rules alone to prevent drownings. The same approach could be used in the home or early care and education programs. Put breakables out of reach. Lock doors to rooms that are off limits to children.

This principle works beyond childhood. Freeways and throughways are good examples of how the environment provides the limits. Most are designed so you *can't* go off the on-ramp. Center dividers make it difficult, if not impossible, to cross into oncoming traffic. The safety principles used by highway designers are a good model to keep in mind as you design or help families understand appropriate environments for children.

Sensory experiences such as water play or goop can be very calming to children

Jules Selmes/Pearson Education Ltd

3. Modeling Appropriate Behavior. Model gentleness in the face of aggression. Model courtesy, kindness, sensitivity, sharing, and caring. It works! You may be surprised how much children pick up. If you yell at children to stop yelling, or if you're aggressive in response to aggression, they'll follow your actions instead of your words. Modeling is powerful. It works, either for you or against you. As mentioned throughout this book, modeling also works as a way of working with parents as well. What they see you doing, they may pick up on and start doing themselves—especially when they see it works. Modeling for parents is one of the best ways of expanding their ideas of guidance and discipline.

4. Redirecting Energy. Much unacceptable behavior is just exuberance. It doesn't need to be curtailed; it just needs to be redirected. Find ways to turn potentially unacceptable actions into acceptable ones. Provide time outdoors for a child who wants to run, for example. If exuberance becomes overstimulation, try some calming activities—water play is a good one for the younger child. Playing with "goop" (a mixture of cornstarch and water) will calm almost anyone. Baths are a time-honored calming device.

5. Providing Physical Control when Needed. For the very young child, physical guidance may prevent problems. Stop the hitting hand by gently but firmly taking hold of it, unless you're sure words alone will trigger the control that the child needs to stop his or her own hand. Words may work fine, but don't depend on them by themselves, especially with toddlers. Back up words by providing the physical control that the child may lack. Eventually you can use words alone; perhaps just a look will do it. But children need to know you really mean it—which you show by consistently providing gentle physical control when needed.

To provide this physical kind of guidance, the adult needs to be nearby when trouble threatens. There's a rule of thumb for interaction distance that early childhood teachers have been using for years. You can pass it on to families. Here it is: Speak to a child from the distance of 1 foot for each year. When you ask a two-year-old at 2 feet to control his hitting hand, you're close enough to reach out and control it for him if necessary. Children can hear you shout from across the room, but most won't listen. It takes your close physical presence to be sure that any words they might not want to hear will register.

6. Teaching Appropriate Expression of Feelings. Feelings are important and should be not only allowed and accepted but also appreciated—by yourself and by children. Children need to learn how to express their feelings in ways that don't harm themselves, anyone else, or the things around them. Teach them to say, "I'm angry!" Teach them to accept the feelings even if they don't show them or act on them. Again, it is important to acknowledge that this acceptance of individual feelings comes from a culture that focuses on individuals. People from cultures that do not focus on individuality might not feel comfortable following this advice. In some cultures, group harmony is more important than individual expression of feelings. Jerome Kagan, a researcher concerned with cultural differences, says about the cultures of Java, Japan, and China that respect for the feelings of elders and of authority "demands that each person not only suppress anger but, in addition, be ready to withhold complete honesty about personal feelings in order to avoid hurting another. This pragmatic view of honesty is regarded as a quality characteristic of the most mature adult and is not given the derogatory labels of insincerity or hypocrisy" (Kagan, 1984, pp. 244–245). Reading *Preschool in Three Cultures Revisited* (Tobin, Hsueh, & Karasawa, 2009) provides a view of how cultures change in regards to expression of feelings. The preschool teachers in Japan and China didn't necessarily agree with each other and had quite different ways of working with children's feelings and the resulting behaviors. When two people (such as the parents, the early childhood professional coworkers, or the professional and a parent) with different views about expressing feelings are responsible for the same child, they need to talk about their differences and decide how to work together for the good of the child.

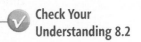 Watch this video to see how an early childhood professional facilitates conflict resolution among a group of children. What strategies did she use?

7. Meeting Needs.   A good deal of undesirable behavior can be prevented when children (and adults, too) are feeling satisfied because their needs are met. Basic needs such as food, rest, and exercise come first; but beyond the basics lie higher needs such as security, protection, love, and closeness. Abraham Maslow, a psychologist, emphasized the importance of recognizing needs in his book *Motivation and Personality* (1970). When any needs are unmet, discipline problems can result.

Check Your Understanding 8.2
Click here to check your understanding of discussing preventative measures with parents.

GUIDANCE AS RESPONDING TO UNACCEPTABLE BEHAVIOR

When unacceptable behavior occurs in spite of your efforts to prevent it, an appropriate and effective response is in order. The responses that follow are all positive approaches. Jane Nelsen (2001), famous for her books on discipline, says not to make children feel bad about themselves in order to motivate them to behave better. In fact, negative approaches usually work at cross-purposes. Children who feel bad about themselves are less likely to behave in acceptable ways unless they are dominated by fear. If you rule by fear, you can damage relationships, an important requirement for positive guidance.

The following sections offer seven effective and healthy ways to respond to unacceptable behavior. They include giving feedback, allowing consequences, using time-out, rewarding some behaviors and ignoring others, teaching desired behaviors, and meeting needs.

1. Giving Feedback.   If the problem belongs to the children involved and you can keep your feelings out of it, the best kind of feedback is "sports announcing." For example, when children are fighting over a toy, you can step in and narrate what you see, express the feelings you pick up, and get the children to talk to one another. This kind of sports announcing leads to problem solving on the part of the children.

If, on the other hand, you have strong feelings because your needs are being trampled on, state them in a sentence that starts with I and contains a feeling word. These "I-messages" were first described by Thomas Gordon (2000), a doctor who has had great influence on parents and early childhood educators and parents with his book *Parent Effectiveness Training* (called PET for short). When using an I-message, the sentence should also encapsulate the behavior in question. For example, if children are screaming their lungs out and it bothers you, say, "I feel nervous [upset, tired] when I hear you scream." Feedback is different from judgmental criticism or blame.

Of course, for families from a culture that does not value individual expression of feelings, an approach such as the one suggested here may feel uncomfortable. Having a discussion about their perspective—if you can listen and not try to persuade—might be profitable to all parties concerned.

2. Allowing Children to Experience the Consequences of Their Actions.   *Natural* consequences don't have to be arranged, according to Rudolf Dreikurs, who co-authored a classic book some years ago called *Children: The Challenge* (Dreikurs & Soltz, 1964). Variations of that book and its offspring have now been read by several generations of parents. Using natural consequences is a matter of stepping back and not rescuing a child from a decision he or she has made. When a child chooses not to wear a sweater when going out to play, the natural consequence is to feel cold. Next time the child will consider the consequences of going outside without a sweater if he is allowed to feel the cold.

Logical consequences (Dreikurs & Grey, 1990) are set up by adults and reflect the reality of the social world. Logical consequences are a direct result of the child's own actions. When children leave their clothes on the floor instead of in the hamper, the clothes don't get washed. If the child can't be trusted not to go into the street, he or she is taken into the house. Children talk during story time and the adult stops reading. The child who spills the milk sponges it up. These are all logical consequences. See Figure 8.1.

As stated earlier, consequences are different from punishment, even though they may cause anguish, because they are related to the child's own actions. They are reasonable, not arbitrary. Adults must be respectful when allowing or applying consequences. If adults are angry or harsh, consequences become punishment.

As a teacher, you can get in difficulties with families for using the consequences approach, partly because it involves letting children make their own decisions—an

Consequences	Natural Consequences	Logical Consequences
are related to childrens actions	do not have to be set up	are created by adults
are reasonable	occur naturally	are a direct result of a child's own actions
are not a arbitrary	Example: Nikko does not wear a coat in the rain, he gets wet	Example: Zina spills a cup of water, she has to clean it up

Figure 8.1   **Consequences**

approach that fits better with an independent/individualistic perspective than with a interdependent, holistic perspective. If you model it while parents are observing, it would be good to ask their opinion. Or discuss the approach beforehand and be sure parents understand. Using consequences to teach may feel cold and uncaring to people from cultures where the adult role is warm and protective and where constant close connections are valued. In her work with Haitian children and teachers, Ballenger (1992, 1999) discovered how uncomfortable they were with the consequences approach. It's hard for some adults to stand back knowing that a child will not like living with a choice he or she is about to make. They feel compelled to protect children from making decisions when the consequences will be unpleasant.

Using Consequences to Guide and Control Behavior

Jean is a mother who decided not to use punishment on her five-year-old, Trevor, anymore. She had learned about using consequences as a discipline method and was ready to try it. She had the perfect opportunity the day she got tired of trying to get Trevor to put his dishes in the dishwasher after eating.

Trevor was very lazy about this—lazy to the point of stubbornness. Up to now Jean would remind him, time after time, but he'd "forget." She began to feel like a nag. She finally got so frustrated that she resorted to threatening him, but that didn't work, either. Nothing worked!

Of course, nothing worked because Trevor knew that if he waited long enough, his mother would put the dishes away for him. Besides, it didn't really matter to him if a few dirty dishes were left lying around. His next meal always arrived right on schedule. The only consequence for leaving dishes on the table was that they magically disappeared eventually anyway. Finally, Jean decided she needed to get more creative about how to handle this problem, which she recognized as *her* problem. She decided that using a "consequences approach" would make it Trevor's problem as well.

She started by asking herself what the ultimate consequence of not putting dirty dishes in the dishwasher would be. She visualized a house full of molding dishes—it looked terrible. Would he mind that? She wasn't sure. Then she visualized an empty cupboard—no dishes for the next meal. That's the ultimate consequence. Even if the dirty house didn't affect him, the empty cupboard would if he didn't find his next meal, all hot and delicious, waiting for him on a clean plate.

So Jean explained to Trevor that she wouldn't remind or nag him anymore about dirty dishes, but she wouldn't put them away, either. She didn't. He didn't, either. By bedtime the first day the place was a dump, but Trevor didn't seem to mind.

Jean was discouraged. She thought she'd see results quicker. How long was this going to take, anyway, she asked herself, looking at the smeared glasses, sticky plates, and crusted forks lying here and there around the kitchen and the family room.

She had a brainstorm. "I'll hurry up the process by adding to the problem," she told her sister, whom she called for moral support. "I'll just quit putting my dishes away, too."

"Do you think it will work?" her sister asked.

"Yes," replied Jean enthusiastically.

That night Jean left a plate on the coffee table, with a dirty glass beside it. The next morning she left her coffee cup on the newspaper by her rocking chair, her cereal bowl and juice glass on the table, and an empty water glass on the television—next to the two empty glasses Trevor had left there the previous day.

It didn't take long. They never got to the point of the bare cupboard. Trevor didn't like the mess once it got really ugly. He picked up his dishes, Jean picked up hers, and that was the end of it.

So how was this different from punishment? For one thing, Jean didn't inflict it on Trevor. She merely quit doing what hadn't worked before and let his own actions show him what the problem was. He learned a lesson about the benefits of household order without being punished. Jean was a bystander—not a moralizer, judge, or jury. She even managed to refrain from saying, "I hope you learned your lesson."

3. Using Time-Out Appropriately.   Time-out (sitting apart, being sent to another room or to a certain place in the same room) was discussed previously as sometimes culturally inappropriate. Here it is looked at as appropriate if done in a certain way with certain children. Time-out can be punishing if done in a punishing way (as can any of the approaches listed here). Time-out used appropriately gives some children who need it a chance to gain control of themselves. This only works when the child is truly "out of control." And it works best with children from families who have a more individualistic orientation. This use of time-out gives adults a chance to become an ally, a helper to the child. The attitude the adult conveys is "I see that you can't control yourself in this situation, so I am going to help you by taking you out of it and getting you into a peaceful, less stimulating situation." This is very different from a punishing attitude, in which the adult is viewed as an adversary rather than as a partner. Time-out should be followed up with a problem-solving session between the child and the caregiver.

Unfortunately, time-out is overused by some adults, who respond to every misbehavior by sending the child off to sit in a chair. It is also abused. Instead of being a positive means of discipline, time-out often takes the place of the stool and dunce cap, an old-fashioned shaming device.

Here again cultural differences come into play. As mentioned earlier, if an adult is from a culture where interconnections are stressed more than individuality, time-out may seem like an extreme punishment. Being cut off from the group is called "shunning" by some and is regarded as a very serious sanction. In some groups, time-out as a way of managing children's misbehavior is avoided because even when done kindly and in the child's best interests, it feels excessive. Children should not be shunned through time-out or any other device.

4. Rewarding Desired Behavior.   Notice when children are "being good." Pay special attention when children are being kind, courteous, sensitive, and helpful. Naturally, these are the times when we are tempted to ignore children because they aren't causing any problems. This is the behavior we expect, so why should we go out of our way to make a fuss over it? Some families feel strongly that expected behavior should not get special attention. That's not the way of behaviorist learning theory, which points out the power of the reward. Adult attention can be considered a reward. Be careful, though, about going overboard. Praise and prizes don't work. In his eye-opening early book *Punished by Rewards*, Alfie Kohn (1999) wrote about how, when we try to manipulate children's behavior through using incentives, side effects arise and our good intentions backfire. In two subsequent books, one for parents and one

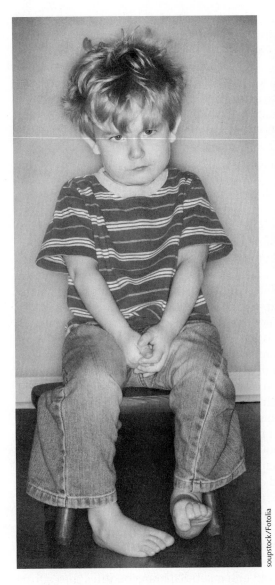

soupstock/Fotolia

Pavla Zakova/Fotolia

Notice the difference in body language between the child that has been isolated and the child who has adult support; which child looks the most open to learning?

for teachers, Kohn (2004, 2006) gives the same message. Citing hundreds of studies, he makes it clear that the more we use rewards to get children to do what we want, the more they lose interest in doing it. Children don't perform as well and they aren't as creative when we entice them to do something by dangling a reward in front of their noses.

It's not manipulative to be honest and sincere. Use your powers of observation to notice behavior that deserves noticing. For example, if you view a child treating a younger child in a gentle manner, you could say, "I see that you're being very careful when you touch Ty." Just regular manners work, too: "I appreciate it when you help me set the table." "Thanks for putting away the tricycle."

5. Ignoring Misbehavior That Is Designed to Attract Attention.

Everyone needs attention—it's like a life-giving substance. When children don't get the attention they need through positive behaviors, they develop negative ones that are hard to ignore. If the message behind these behaviors is "I'm here, notice me," the only way to change the behaviors is to ignore them and then give the needed attention at times when the child is acting acceptably. It's hard to switch, and takes some self control. Instead of reacting to unacceptable behavior unless someone will get hurt, you have to ignore it. For example, walk out of the room when a child is trying on

▶ Watch this video to hear Alfie Kohn talk about moving from rewards and threats to love and reason. Did you hear anything that conflicts with the goals of your family culture?

www.youtube.com
/watch?v=iK3NHA8PZG0

purpose to annoy you. Turn your back on arguing that is designed to get your attention (much arguing among children is for that very purpose). Of course, don't leave children alone if they might hurt each other.

6. Teaching Prosocial Behavior.   Don't just teach what *not to do* through the aforementioned approaches. Take a proactive stance and teach what *to do* as well. Indirect teaching comes about through the already mentioned devices of modeling and paying attention. Direct teaching comes about through talking. Avoid lectures. Instead, use stories and role-plays, and even actually practice prosocial behavior by trying it out in little dramas or puppet shows.

7. Meeting Needs.   Children often behave in unacceptable ways because they are needy. Respond to behaviors from that source by meeting the needs. Don't yell at a boy who is fussing because he's hungry; feed him. Don't give feedback to a tired girl who is out of control; put her to bed. Don't prevent restless children from wiggling; take them someplace where they can get the wiggles out. Of course, you can't always meet each child's needs immediately, and it doesn't hurt them to learn to wait a bit—but not too long! Do what you can to control the truly unacceptable behavior, and put up with behavior that is only expressing feelings about having to wait.

Working with families around guidance and discipline approaches can be rewarding, because it's a subject most families are interested in. See Strategy Box 8.1 for ideas about how to use some of the information in this chapter to expand parents' or other family members' ideas around guidance and discipline. If you give a workshop on discipline, families may come to you as the authority but then may resist what you tell them because it doesn't fit their ideas of what children need. The best approach to take is to have open discussions in which everyone is free to express their ideas. That means the atmosphere must be one of respect and acceptance.

Alan Pence, a noted early childhood expert from the University of Victoria in British Columbia, talked about what happened when educators and First Nations people met to create an early childhood curriculum. The two groups each came with different sets of knowledge and experience. He says, "In the space between these two sets of knowledge was the opportunity to envision and generate something new, something that had not been articulated before" (Pence, 2004, p. 32). Pence and his colleagues have created an early education approach called the "Generative Curriculum," which they first introduced in Canada (Ball & Pence, 1999; Dahlberg, Moss, & Pence, 1999). Training is now being offered in ten sub-Saharan countries through an online course offered by the Early Childhood Development Virtual University (based at the University of Victoria in Canada). One of the exciting parts of the Generative Curriculum is that those who use it are able to make a positive use of the tensions that arise when differing perspectives collide.

Strategy Box 8.1

Working with Families around Ideas of Guidance and Discipline

- Set aside judgments. When two groups or two people have different perspectives on guiding children's behavior, instead of judging right or wrong, early educators must first try to understand those differences and where they come from. Are they cultural, familial, or individual, or do they come from something else?

- At the same time, be clear about your bottom line. Doing harm to children is wrong. But to judge what is truly harmful and not in the best interests of a child, family, or community requires a deep understanding of the perspective of the person or family you are working with and the meanings behind their behaviors. At the same time, you have a legal mandate to report child abuse. Don't be so open minded that you seem to be condoning abuse.

- Try to avoid making families feel defensive. Do what you can to keep yourself from feeling defensive.

- Try to get to a deeper understanding. Try reframing contradictions. Move from dualistic, exclusive perceptions of reality and try integrating the complementary aspects of diverse beliefs into a new whole concept.

- Challenge yourself and your beliefs. Step outside your norms. Open yourself to discovering from families something you weren't aware of.

So my advice is this: When you are in a situation in which differing perspectives are headed toward an argument, try using those tensions in a creative manner. Teach yourself and the families you work with to play what Jones and Cooper (2005) call "the believing game." They suggest that trying to imagine another person's perspective requires suspending reality—playing pretend. They point out that when we encounter people who don't believe what we believe, "we can sneer at them, or fight them, or pretend they're invisible. . . Or we can accept the challenge to 'embrace contraries'" (p. 23). You'll be surprised what you can learn when you embrace contraries!

> **✔ Check Your Understanding 8.3**
> Click here to check your understanding of guidance as responding to unacceptable behavior.

SUMMARY

This chapter discussed replacing the term *discipline* with the word *guidance* to help professionals working with families. The term *discipline* brings up the issue of punishment as a way of guiding behavior. The message was that there are problems with using punishment to teach. A major part of the chapter was devoted to guidelines for preventing unacceptable behavior from happening and guidance for responding to unacceptable behavior that has already occurred. Although working with parents was part of the whole chapter, at the end were some specific approaches to use, such as creating situations where you can discuss with parents different perspectives on guidance.

✔ QUIZ

Click here to check your understanding of Chapter 8, "Working with Families on Guidance Issues."

FOR DISCUSSION

1. How do you feel about using the word *guidance* instead of *discipline*? What associations do you have with each word? Do you prefer one word over the other when talking with parents?

2. Discuss how the environment can be used to curb behavior and restrict a child from doing something dangerous or unacceptable. What is an example of learn-

ing from experiencing a consequence? Is your example a logical or a natural consequence?

3. Can you explain the difference between a consequence and punishment? What are some problems with using punishment to teach? Have you ever experienced any of these problems yourself?

4. Give examples of three prosocial behaviors you would want to teach young children. Have you ever taught these behaviors? If yes, how? Would you use this particular discussion question when working with parents? If yes, why? If no, why not?

WEBSITES

Alfie Kohn
Alfie Kohn is an author who has looked closely at discipline and come up with a good deal of research disputing common parenting and educational practices. His website includes lists of his books as well as articles, a blog, and a schedule of his speaking engagements.

Child Development Institute
You will find child development information on the Child Development Institute's website, including a number of articles on discipline. The institute aims to be a "go to" site for families and professionals.

Positive Discipline
This site features articles relating to disciplining and teaching children appropriate behavior. It includes resources for

parents and teachers, such as online workshops, information, and additional links.

Prevent Child Abuse America
Prevent Child Abuse America has a goal of working to ensure the development of children nationwide. Child protection and abuse prevention information is offered on their website, with additional links.

UNICEF
UNICEF works to promote the rights and well-being of all children. They are an international organization that recognizes the importance of early childhood development and adolescence. Their website has many resources, including a link to a YouTube channel with videos from around the world.

FURTHER READING

Adkison-Bradley, C. Terpstra, J. & Dormitorio, B. (2014). Child discipline in African American families: A study of patterns and context. *Family Journal, 22,* 198–205

Adkison-Bradley, C. (2011). Seeing African Americans as competent parents: Implications for family counselors. *The Family Journal, 19,* 307–313.

Erikson, E. (1963). *Childhood and society.* New York, NY: Norton.

Flore, I. R. (2011). Developing young children's self-regulation through everyday experiences. *Young Children* 66 (4), 46–51.

Galinsky, E. (2010). *Mind in the making: Seven essential skills every child needs.* New York, NY: HarperCollins.

Gonzalez-Mena, J., & Shareef, I. (2005, November). Discussing diverse perspectives on guidance. *Young Children*, 60(6), 34–38.

Kaiser, B., & Rasminsky, J. (2017). *Challenging behavior in young children: Understanding, preventing, and responding effectively* (4th ed.). Upper Saddle River, NJ: Pearson.

Kohn, A. (2006). *Beyond discipline: From compliance to community*. Alexandria, VA: Association for Supervision and Curriculum Development.

Kohn, A. (2014). *The myth of the spoiled child*. Boston, MA: Da Capo.

McLoyd, V. C., Hill, N. E., & Dodge, K. A. (Eds.). (2005). *African American family life*. New York, NY: Guilford.

Tobin, J., Hsueh, Y., & Karasawa, M. (2009). *Preschool in three cultures revisited*. Chicago, IL: University of Chicago Press.

Amble Design/Shutterstock

Working with Families on Addressing Feelings and Problem Solving

Learning Outcomes

In this chapter you will learn to...

- Describe feelings and how adults can manage them when working with children.
- Explain how to teach children to cope with feelings.
- Discuss problem-solving strategies and diverse family approaches to problem solving.

Teachers, early educators, other professionals, and families have to help children cope with their feelings and learn problem-solving skills. This subject is an aspect of self-regulation (Florez, 2011; Thompson, 2009). This chapter is divided into two parts, each representing one of those two subjects and both related to self-regulation. These two subjects may seem unrelated to each other, but consider that emotions carry energy and energy is what is needed for problem solving, especially in difficult situations. When adults and children alike learn to harness the emotional energy that comes with, for instance, anger, they can live much healthier lives. This is a lesson that is hard to learn for most of us because it's not a subject that's taught in school or even in most families. It's also fairly unusual even in a book like this one. But it fits in with Bronfenbrenner's ecological systems theory, again at the microsystems level, but with influences from the total context that the child and family live in. Two very important parts of socialization have to do with handling feelings in positive ways and learning to use problem-solving strategies. I'll start with feelings and then go on to problem solving.

FEELINGS

The perspective this chapter takes is that early educators need to encourage children to feel their feelings, to decide whether and how to express and act on them, and, above all, to decide how to cope with them. In *Mindsight* (2010), Daniel Siegel, a scientist who is an expert in both brain research and psychotherapy, gives examples of people whose brain development was actually damaged as children by their experiences and feelings about them. The good news is that through specific therapeutic techniques, Dr. Siegel is able to create conditions where the patients' brains create the missing neurological connections that were stunted in childhood. It's a complex but eye-opening book that gives an optimistic picture of children who have suffered. The idea that it's never too late is quite hopeful!

Of course, it's better to prevent problems in childhood than it is to wait until adulthood to address them. That's one reason this chapter focuses on feelings and problem solving. Kaiser and Rasminsky (2016) wrote a whole book, now in its fourth edition, on challenging behavior. They have many ideas about how to address such behaviors in the classroom or children's center. They also discuss the importance for professionals who work with children to have knowledge about the resources available for special needs that can't be met without some expert intervention. That doesn't mean that all children with challenging behavior need to be seen as having what are called "special needs" in the education world. But some children do need more help than they can get in an ordinary classroom or children's center. Some of those children arrive with their special needs already identified. The family may be just at the beginning of understanding what "intervention" means and what support is available. Other families may already be experienced in working with professionals around making sure that their child's needs are being met. They may come in to the program well versed in advocating. See the Advocacy in Action feature "Families with Children Who Have Disabilities: Advice for Teachers" to learn more about teaching parents to be advocates for their children.

> ▶ Watch this video to hear Dr. Dan Siegel explain mindsight. What do you think about his comment regarding adults shaping the way that children see their internal world?
>
> www.youtube.com /watch?v=v2pdN7dQIgM

The whole society will benefit as more children grow up whole and healthy because their needs are fulfilled in well-rounded care and education programs

Of course, the point is that the more adults involved with children and families know about development and positive ways of living and working with them, the better off children will be regardless of whether they have identified special needs. In fact, the whole society will profit as more and more children grow up whole and healthy because their needs are fulfilled in well-rounded educational and care programs. Feelings are an important aspect of education and social-emotional development. Children need to accept, sort out, identify, label, integrate, and appropriately express their feelings. Not all families will agree with this way of helping children with their feelings, so handling disagreements about different ways of looking at feelings is also a part of this chapter. When children see adults who are able to take perspectives other than their own, they are learning what Ellen Galinsky (2010) calls the second essential skill every child needs—perspective taking. A powerful way to teach is through modeling the behaviors you want a child to learn. That's why it's a good thing that adults can disagree on socialization practices and talk about their disagreements in ways that show they are working to understand a perspective that's different from their own.

From one perspective (that of this book), the greatest task of all is helping children become socialized while fully experiencing their feelings. Part of the socialization process involves learning to know in each instance whether or not to express feelings; if expressing them is acceptable, then how to express them appropriately becomes the next decision. The ultimate decision is whether to act on the feelings and, if acting is the right thing to do, how to act in socially appropriate ways. These are enormous lessons to learn, and children need adult help to learn them in culturally relevant ways.

Obviously children learn a lot about feelings at home by observing their family members. They also learn from the response they get when they express feelings. Some families have clear ideas about what they want their children to learn about feelings, but not all children grow up with adults who help them with the emotional aspects of development. Some adults demonstrate lopsided emotional development. We all know adults who reached maturity skilled in some areas of feelings but unpracticed and unskilled in others. A person may be good at expressing anger and self-assertion and dealing with power relationships but lack the abilities that lead to intimacy and closeness; this individual is less able to be sensitive, nurturing, loving, tender, and vulnerable. Another person may be skilled in the nurturing mode but lacking in self-assertion and fearful of his or her own power. These people may hold in their anger, fearing it as they would an untamed animal. They keep it all inside by tying it down and locking it in because, in their minds, if this vicious animal gets loose, it will commit unspeakably violent acts as it rages out of control. This perception of anger as a wild, vicious animal hides deep within many tender, nurturing people. Sometimes two people with opposite styles get

There are the adults who see themselves as a mind walking around in a body; they avoid feelings altogether whenever possible. Many of these adults are so afraid of their feelings that they spend years denying them and teach children to do likewise.

ADVOCACY IN ACTION ▶ FAMILIES WITH CHILDREN WHO HAVE DISABILITIES: ADVICE FOR TEACHERS

Donna Sullivan-Patterson, special educator

All families enter our classrooms advocating and wanting the best for their children. For the parents of children with disabilities, "advocacy" may take on a new role in their lives. Many parents (I use the term "parent" and "family" in the broadest sense) of children with disabilities are or will become very skilled in advocating for their child, especially as access for all becomes common practice. It is your task to appreciate, support, and encourage parents on this journey. Family members will demonstrate a variety of skill levels. Those skills are enhanced by the strength and trust of the teacher or other service providers' relationship with them. Open communication is a vital component of this relationship and should include the family and specialists who provide services for the child. Sometimes it is challenging to develop connections between all service providers due to funding issues, time, staffing, and so on, but

it is critical. When all involved have a commitment to best practices, advocacy becomes a driving force that propels equal access and quality programming.

Becoming a strong advocate requires information about what kinds of programs and services are available. Families need to know what questions to ask and of whom. Sometimes they need to know how to ask questions. They also need to know where answers can be found. Resources, both local and national, are critical to advocating for children. Teachers and other service providers need to support families by being a resource and an advocate with them and for them. They need to find time to listen and encourage and to bring providers together. The teacher or child care person may be that family's first experience in general education, and they will carry the tools and your encouragement with them throughout their child's life.

together and parent a child—so the child sees the whole range of emotions but split between two adults.

Then there are the adults who see themselves as a mind walking around in a body; they avoid feelings altogether whenever possible. Many of these adults are so afraid of their feelings that they spend years denying them and teach children to do likewise.

The point of starting this chapter by looking at adult feelings is that children learn about feelings from the adults in their lives. When adults set effective examples and provide modeling of what to do with feelings, children grow up with much more awareness and coping skills than when adults provide restricted models.

It's not up to the early educator, teacher, or other professional to teach parents what to do with their feelings. It is important, though, to understand how much the teaching you do with the children matches what they are learning at home. If there is a serious mismatch, you must talk about it with the family and figure out together what to do about it.

Some people hold anger inside until they are steaming mad and it comes boiling out; do you recognize this pattern in yourself?

Using Anger

Marcie is a 35-year-old stepmother who has recently discovered how to use anger. As a child, she was taught to hide her feelings. She learned early that strong emotion bothered the adults in her life. "Mad is bad" was a motto of her family. She still hears her own mother's voice inside her head telling her "Don't be angry!" and "Oh, just don't think about it!"

And that's just what she learned to do—forget about what was bothering her. But just being willing to forget isn't enough. She had to learn some distraction techniques. Those techniques worked well, and she learned to stuff her feelings deep down inside, hiding them even from herself. One technique she used was "intellectualizing": getting out of her feelings and into her head. But avoiding her feelings caused stewing. Grown-up, Marcie is a master stewer. When she's upset, the simmering is practically audible.

Take the other day when her stepdaughter, Serena, screamed at her, "You can't tell me what to do! You're not my mother!" Marcie felt a surge of anger rising, but as was her practice, she stuffed it down inside herself and calmly responded to the five-year-old in a reasonable voice.

The same thing happened during dinner when Serena complained about the food, only picked at her plate, got up from the table, and 15 minutes later asked for a snack. Marcie handled the situation well, but she was silent and sullen the rest of the evening. When her husband asked her what was wrong, she said, "Oh, nothing. Just tired."

The problem with stewing is that the stuffed anger builds up until it eventually boils over. Then the rage comes pouring out unexpectedly. That happened on the weekend. Marcie was still stewing when she emptied out Serena's dirty clothes basket and at the bottom, all wrinkled and smelling of dirty socks, was the little 100 percent cotton outfit that Marcie had hand-washed and ironed for Serena the week before. Furious that Serena had put it in the dirty clothes without once wearing it, Marcie stomped into the living room where Serena was lying on the floor watching TV. "What's this doing in the dirty clothes?" she screamed at her startled stepdaughter.

"You told me to pick up everything on the floor. And that was on the floor," sassed Serena. Marcie's reason left her. She began to rage. When she finally finished, she was exhausted and heartsick with guilt. She was extra nice to Serena to make up for her own lack of control. This pattern was familiar to both Marcie and Serena: to stuff anger, stew for a long period, suddenly rage, then feel guilty and try to make it up to Serena.

Marcie knows she needs to learn to break that pattern, so at the suggestion of Serena's teacher, she signed up for a parenting class. She's learned that she can recognize anger when it arises and that she can turn off the voices of her parents that tell her to ignore what she's feeling. She can stay with the feeling and fully experience it instead of distracting herself by becoming "intellectual" about it. An important lesson she has learned in the class is that she can still *think* while she's *feeling*, but she must be careful to accept and acknowledge the feelings.

Marcie knows now that whenever she can focus on her anger, she can get a clarity that doesn't come when she's busy distracting and stuffing. The teacher told the class that unfelt feelings can be damaging—physically and psychologically. Felt feelings, and the emotional energy they bring, can be used constructively. Marcie's goal is to use her feelings to improve her relationship with Serena. She knows now that her tension can be released periodically instead of being buried and then exploding. The tension from the anger can be turned into positive energy that would be useful for solving problems.

Marcie is learning to operate out of new patterns. She's learning to feel her anger and use its energy. The bystander might not notice the difference. Marcie still often decides *not* to express her anger directly to Serena. But now she acknowledges the feelings to herself and experiences them fully. She's replaced the models in her life who were so busy avoiding emotions with ones who make good decisions about feelings, those who express and act on their feelings.

Marcie does look happier and more relaxed now that she has learned that anger brings important energy that can be used for problem solving. Serena looks more relaxed, too, since Marcie has begun to move away from the stuffing, stewing, and boiling-over pattern.

This chapter takes the perspective that feelings are important and should be not only allowed and accepted but also appreciated—by yourself and by children. If you are a person for whom the information in this chapter fits and makes sense, it's important that you recognize the families who disagree with this perspective. When two people with different views about expressing feelings are responsible for the same child, they need to talk about their differences and decide how to work together for the good of the child. Remember that at least half of communication is listening, so see what you can understand about the parents' perspective. You are bound to learn something that goes beyond the information in this chapter.

Even if you and families have different perspectives about accepting feelings, it's still useful to consider the benefits of *redirection*. Redirection is one way to handle children's anger as you guide a child from hitting another child to hitting a pillow or pounding clay. Art, music, dance, and physical exercise are classic ways of expressing feelings that should be available to children. You don't have to make a point of the feelings themselves. Also, you don't have to provide anything elaborate. Simple experiences in art, music, movement, and dance work fine. And getting children outdoors to physically use the energy that comes up with anger or frustration can be very helpful. On the other hand, some children can get rid of a lot of anger or frustration simply through tearing paper into very small bits and throwing them into the wastebasket.

What Are Feelings?

Let's look at the word *emotion*, which is what is meant by *feelings*. *Emotion* comes from the Latin word *emovere*, which means "to move out from, stir up, excite." So feelings indicate a stirred-up state of the individual. It is important to remember that the experience of this stirred-up state is subjective. The only way one can know about another's feelings is through communication (verbal and nonverbal), but the communication is not the feeling.

Feelings are complex subjective experiences that are different from but involve the physical and mental aspects of the self. That definition of feelings is derived from Greenspan and Greenspan (1985) in their classic book, *First Feelings: Milestones in the Emotional Development of Your Baby and Child*. Feelings can be felt, expressed, acted on, and thought about, but each of those experiences of feelings is different.

All Feelings Are Useful

If you made a long list of all the feelings you have ever experienced, it would be tempting to divide them into positive and negative feelings. However, all feelings have value and are useful, even the ones we wish would go away. They serve a purpose. Feelings are a reaction to experience; they help us define and organize experience. They give us direction for action. They give us cause for expression. Some of the greatest works of art, music, and dance have come from feelings—and not always pleasant ones.

Learning Feelings

Feelings come naturally. From the beginning, in some cultures, adults teach the labels for those feelings. Children come to understand concepts of emotional states; eventually they can think about feeling.

This labeling starts in infancy, when the adult begins to label the child's emotional state: "That loud noise scared you!" or "I see how unhappy you are that your mommy isn't here to feed you yet." Labeling feelings is part of the socialization process.

The socialization process is also involved in feeding children cultural information about feelings and their expression. There is a fine line between the kind of cultural explaining, shaping, and molding of feelings that adults do to socialize children and manipulating them with value judgments that cut them off from their true experience.

Placing values on feelings—teaching children *what* to feel and *what not* to feel—can do great harm. Rogers (1980) wrote about this subject long ago in his book, *A Way of Being*. He wrote about how infants trust their experience. When they are hungry they want food. They are in touch with their deepest needs, which relate to Maslow's basic needs in his hierarchy of needs model (1954). But if as they grow their parents begin to tell them what to feel or not feel, they come to distrust their own experience. It's even worse if the parents connect love to the issue of feelings, saying things such as, "If you feel that way, I won't love you." Doing so can cut children off from their feelings. Adults have a tremendous responsibility for children's emotional development.

> Placing values on feelings— teaching children *what* to feel and *what not* to feel—can do great harm.

How do adults teach children what to feel? One way is through something quite innocent called *social referencing*.

Social Referencing

Have you ever noticed how a young child who is faced with an uncertain situation will turn to a parent, infant care teacher, preschool teacher, or family child care provider for clues about how to react? This is very helpful; the adult can calm fears. Consider this example: The child is approached by Uncle Mario, a large man with a big beard and glasses. This child has never seen a human who looks like this before. He turns to the trusted adult for cues. The adult smiles, puts an arm around him, and walks confidently toward Uncle Mario, talking to the man as if she trusts him implicitly. Every child won't take the adult's cues, but some will, and what had been a scary situation becomes an ordinary one—the meeting of a new relative. That's social referencing.

Adults use social referencing to calm children's fears, warn them of danger, help them like a new food, even infect them with joy. Children constantly receive unspoken messages about how to react to situations through adult facial expressions, body language, posture, and even muscle tone. They eventually build up what can be thought of as *cultural scripts* about how to respond to specific situations.

Watch this short video to see social referencing in action. What is different about the body language in the beginning and in the end? It goes by so quickly that you may have to watch this twice.

Most children have some tendency toward being influenced in their feelings by important people in their lives. That means adults must be very careful about wielding this influence or they'll put children out of touch with their real feelings. They'll cut them off from their true experience. Here's an example: Anyone who has been around young children very much knows that when a young child falls down, she will often look to her parent or other adult to see how she is supposed to feel. Many adults will automatically put a smile on their faces and say something encouraging like, "You're okay." Magda Gerber taught that in this case, it's best if the adult remains neutral until the child shows some feeling (Greenwald & Weaver, 2013).

Remaining neutral eliminates the possibility of a mistaken response. Consider these two examples of an adult mistake in influencing children's feelings: A toddler falls down. The adult acts as if everything is alright, but the child is hurt. The adult response discounts the child's feeling and makes him question his own reality. Or, conversely, if the adult makes a big fuss over what was only a little hurt, the child learns to ignore reality and exaggerate feelings to get attention.

When children fall down, they often look to an adult to see how they are supposed to feel; it is best for the adult to stay neutral until the child shows some feeling

As a professional, recognize the power of social referencing and use it wisely. When a child looks to you for your reaction to something, decide whether it is beneficial to give it to him in that situation. Know that you can remain neutral and let the child decide for himself how to react. *After* he decides, a supportive verbal or nonverbal response from you is appropriate. Some parents may appreciate observing you when you are using social referencing wisely. They see you remaining neutral at times when you are trying not to influence a child's feelings. That may be a new idea to them.

Social referencing naturally starts in infancy, when babies look to adults to help them understand and interpret the world. The toddler also uses social referencing, but this approach should begin to fade in the preschool years. If it doesn't, its continuing presence may indicate a problem.

The outcome of the overuse of social referencing shows in the joke about the henpecked husband who, when offered a choice of custard for dessert, asks his wife, "Dear, do I like custard?" But it involves more than simple likes and dislikes; it's a matter of a power differential. No one wants children to grow up powerless and unable to express their feelings.

Cultural Scripts

All these warnings aside, it is important to recognize that feelings are influenced by cultural scripts that dictate the proper feelings for each occasion. Scripts can be specific to individual families or cultures, telling their members what they are supposed to feel and how to convey it. These scripts are useful in telling us what someone is likely to feel under certain circumstances. We know what emotion is "called for,"

for example, when someone close dies. Part of the socialization process is to learn these cultural scripts that dictate the correct emotional response to a situation. Even if we don't feel the way the script dictates, it is important to recognize that, in the eyes of others, the definition of *sane* or *normal* depends to some extent on knowing the cultural script.

One advantage of cultural scripts is that we get clues about how another person of our culture feels, even if they don't tell us. But a disadvantage, of course, is that though the unwritten script tells us how someone is *supposed to feel*, there is no guarantee that a person *will feel* as expected. And, of course, our own script may not help us understand a person from another culture unless we know the script of that person's culture as well as our own.

Scripts differ greatly from culture to culture. For example, there is an enormous difference about when it is OK to get angry and express oneself. As has already been mentioned, in cultures such as the European American culture, which stresses individuality, everyone is encouraged to express feelings. The idea is that a person will function better as a group member if he or she enjoys the mental health that comes from expressing feelings. Good early childhood practice and also that of therapists requires that adults accept all feelings as valid and convey that message to children, as well as teaching them appropriate expression of those feelings. The adult's job is to teach the child to recognize and express all feelings appropriately, especially anger.

> Watch this video to hear Dr. Walt Wolfram share examples of nonverbal messages. What do you think about the role that he suggests for teachers?

Anger gets a lot of attention in European American culture. Some therapists, parents, and early childhood practitioners see the importance of allowing a child to express anger thoroughly, even to the point of raging. The idea is for the child to experience the feeling fully, to "work it through." These people see raging (or having a tantrum as it is called in very young children) as a process that should not be interrupted until it is finished; otherwise, the unexpressed feelings may remain unfelt and go underground, popping up again and again as a "leftover" instead of arising as clearly connected to the immediate situation and not to the past. These adults may also assure the child that it is all right to feel whatever it is that he or she is feeling, but it's not all right to hurt someone or oneself. They seek to prove to the child that expression of strong feelings won't result in abandonment. Of course, it is important to recognize when rage is used to manipulate others. If a child is told "no" and then throws a tantrum and it results in his getting what he wanted, that's different from truly expressing rage just to get it out of your system. It's important to become aware of and distinguish those feelings that are designed to manipulate as compared to honest emotional expression. Also, it's important to recognize that not all European Americans deal with anger in the same way. There is great variety in the European American culture.

Some European Americans and also people of other cultures don't have the same view of feelings and their expressions as described in the prior paragraph. They are more concerned about group harmony than about individual expression of feelings, particularly anger. They don't see unexpressed feelings as dangerous to either individual mental health or the group.

Dorothy Lee (1959) said of the Hopi, "It is his duty to be happy, for the sake of the group, and a mind in conflict and full of anxiety brings disruption, ill-being, to the social unit" (p. 21). And Trinh Ngoc Dung (1984) said that in Vietnamese families, "children are taught at an early age to control their emotions" (p. 12).

Although some may feel that the mandate of these cultures is to repress feelings, a situation that is regarded as unhealthy in white, Northern European-derived American culture, others view this approach in a more positive way. For example, in his book *Americans and Chinese*, Hsu (1970) compares the "prominence of emotions in the American way of life . . . with the tendency of the Chinese to underplay all matters of the heart."

He goes on to point out that European American culture focuses on individuals rather than on group membership. His view is that emotions are much stronger when they are concentrated in one person rather than being spread through a group. He compares the individualism of a European American with the Chinese person who is much more embedded in the group. He concludes that shared feelings are much milder than those concentrated in one person (p. 10).

In spite of cultural differences in how you teach children to express feelings, it is important that children be allowed to feel them; children suffer when adults refuse to accept their feelings

The Importance of Accepting Feelings

In spite of cultural differences in how you teach children to express feelings, it is important that children be allowed to *feel* them. The first two years of life are important in socializing a child to feel or not feel. Children suffer when adults refuse to accept their feelings. Feelings are important to spontaneity, to being in touch with one's experience, and to mental health. We *need* our feelings—all of them—to develop in healthy ways (Siegel, 2010).

Letting Go of Responsibility

Julie, mother of four-year-old Alexa, felt shattered when she learned that a friend's teenage son had committed suicide. "I can't believe it," she lamented to another friend, Laura. "She's such a good mother!" All Julie's own hopes and fears about how her parenting skills would ensure her daughter's happiness had come tumbling down around her ears.

"Being a good mother is no guarantee of anything," Laura spouted without thinking. She wanted to comfort Julie, but her words only made matters worse.

A tear rolled down Julie's cheek as she said, "I've always thought if you tried hard and were a good parent, you'd have control over how your children turned out. But this tragedy ruined that theory." She was weeping openly now—tears for her friend and tears for herself.

As the conversation continued, Julie realized she was feeling fiercely protective of her own Alexa. She kept trying to figure out how to keep her happy so that she'd never lose her. What good were parenting skills if they didn't guarantee the happiness and well-being of your child?

Laura wasn't able to comfort her because Julie had learned a cruel lesson about life: Even good parents suffer tragic disappointments and losses because of their children's decisions.

Parents can control (or at least try to control) what *they* do, but they can't control how their children receive, perceive, or react to what they do. They can love their children, but they can't ensure that they feel loved. They can't control their children's personal perspective on things. They can't control the decisions they make about how to act based on those perspectives.

A major task of most parents is to let go. Though the first obvious letting go comes at birth when the cord is cut, letting go continues throughout life, a snip at a time. The most important letting go, and perhaps the hardest, is relinquishing the responsibility for the child's happiness.

Of course, a parent's job is to meet children's needs, and that job logically *should* lead to happiness. It sometimes happens that way, but not always, because life isn't logical and because cause and effect are never simple or clear-cut in human development.

As the child gets older, the parent's ability and responsibility for meeting needs diminish, and the child takes over the job. The parent no longer has the same degree of control of creating well-being or bringing about happiness (assuming he or she was able to do it in the first place). This is a hard realization for parents to swallow. Of course, all parents want their children to be happy, but they can't *make* them happy!

Parents can only do the best they can—improve their parenting skills and take care of themselves and their children. They'll have their expectations and hopes, of course, but they must realize that too many factors are involved for them to take direct responsibility for their children's feelings and the decisions (even life-and-death ones) that result from those feelings.

Even if it were possible to control the feelings and decisions of others, would that be good? Think what loss of freedom that outside control would mean. Imagine feeling the way your parents wanted you to or turning out exactly as they intended!

Healthy Expressions of Feelings

Acceptable expression of feelings is culturally determined. The perspective I am basing this chapter on is what I have learned from being a professional early educator. Some I learned in classes and workshops, some from experience, some from reading. It isn't the way I was raised, but it does fit my middle-class European American culture best. I know from experience and what I've learned from colleagues and families that this typical "early childhood perspective" doesn't fit everyone. So I am trying to be forthright and honest when I say that this chapter is written from one perspective. The strategies for working with parents are designed to make sure that interactions with parents help the early educator who has this perspective expand beyond it.

I will start by stressing the differences among three things: the feelings themselves, the expression of those feelings, and the actions based on those feelings. It is never inappropriate to *feel* whatever one feels. That message should be given to children loud and clear. However, it is sometimes inappropriate to express those feelings, and part of the socialization process is to understand when it is appropriate to express feelings and when it is not. Maturity is in part determined by being able to make good decisions in this area. Deciding when to act on feelings also takes some maturity. Because of all the energy feelings bring forth, the urge is to act each time. However, the young child learns soon enough that getting mad and slugging someone is not a socially acceptable action around most adults. Grabbing what you want has side effects, and taking a bite out of someone because you love them does not get a loving response.

It takes some children a while to learn these lessons. It is wise to be both kind and patient while the child is learning to control the actions brought forth by feelings and to find appropriate ways to express them. Susan Isaacs, a pioneer in early childhood education, gave advice in 1930 to a parent, and that advice is still valid today (Smith, 1985). She assured the parent that determination, obstinacy, and outbursts of temper are very normal and that it takes patience to socialize children. Often adults respond to these behaviors by getting upset. Isaacs explained that it is better to ignore these difficult behaviors than to display adult emotion, because that can make things worse. When adults get upset, the power that gives the child makes it likely that it will happen again. Or the adult getting upset may cause the child to be afraid. It helps to realize that the child has to learn to accept adult ways and desires and also learn to control his or her own behavior. We can't expect perfection, but we can help the child work toward more and more control, reasonableness, and friendly agreement. Isaacs was clear that teaching by spanking doesn't work because the child can't see the difference between the adult behavior and his own violence. Ruling by fear only increases obstinacy. Adults should avoid unnecessary demands and pick only a few issues, making sure they are ones they can follow through on. When the adult gives lots of choices on smaller matters, it is easier to be friendly and understanding.

> **It is wise to be both kind and patient while the child is learning to control the actions brought forth by feelings and to find appropriate ways to express them.**

It may be hard to follow Isaacs's advice in the heat of the moment, but it is worth having patience as a goal. While being patient, you can be teaching words to express the feelings and help the child move toward more acceptable behaviors. When children begin to label feelings, you know they have now conceptualized them, bringing intellectual processes in to help with the emotional ones. Once the mind comes into play, it isn't long until you see the child using "pretend" to help him further understand and cope with feelings. Now the child's mind and body are working in concert with feelings, thus helping the child integrate.

What are some appropriate ways for young children to express their feelings? Many adults encourage direct verbalization and teach children to say, "I'm mad because you took my toy" or "I'm unhappy because my mommy had to go to work." They also teach children to say to each other, "I don't want you to do that" or "I don't like it when you hit me. It hurts."

Many adults agree about this approach—teaching one child to talk to another in a direct way. However, not everyone is comfortable with teaching children to talk so directly to adults. Some feel it is disrespectful for children to tell an adult they are mad at him or her. They are even more uncomfortable if the child translates "I'm mad at you" into "I hate you!" Other adults accept this form of expression, perhaps disregarding the actual words and responding to the feeling behind them. It is common for an adult trained in early childhood education to reflect back the angry feeling by saying something such as, "You're really mad at me right now."

Whatever ways of expressing feelings are acceptable to the adults in the child's

It is common for early childhood professionals to reflect back angry feelings by saying something such as, "You are really mad at me right now"

djedzura/Shutterstock

life, those are the ways that should be taught to the child. Imagine how a parent who is very concerned that his child show a certain kind of respect to adults would feel if he walked into the classroom just in time to hear his child scream "I hate you" at the teacher. Although the teacher may find nothing wrong with this way of expressing anger, it is important to take the parents' perspective into consideration and find some way to accept their feelings and teach another mode of expression.

Examples of ways of expressing feelings that are acceptable to some adults and not to others are:

- Yelling and screaming.
- Stating negative wishes or imagining violent happenings (e.g., "I hope your new toy breaks," "Maybe you'll break your leg," or "I wish my baby brother would die").
- Taking out anger symbolically on toys or other objects (e.g., spanking dolls or pounding pillows).

Most adults agree that name-calling and using obscenities are not appropriate ways for young children to express feelings. It's important, though, to realize that to a young child "bad words" have little meaning except that children know certain words hold power for adults. However, if you listen to young children trying to wield power over *each other*, they don't use adult words. They call each other "baby" or say, "I won't like you anymore." Those expressions have more meaning and carry more weight than all the four-letter words they may have ever learned.

Check Your Understanding 9.1

Click here to check your understanding of feelings.

TEACHING CHILDREN TO COPE WITH FEELINGS

It's good to have some ideas about how to teach coping skills, starting with helping children learn to calm themselves. Of course, just being a calm presence can help—demonstrate to parents how this works. Changing the scene or the situation is another approach that can be used by teachers and parents alike. Help families understand that children practice emotions (including calming themselves) through playing and creating their own worlds. Recognize that feelings may not be pure and simple, but often come in pairs or bunches. Helping children express mixed feelings can be a coping skill. Fear, of course, is a powerful feeling and this section on coping skills gives a variety of ideas about how to help children deal with fears. Anger can be useful. Help parents see that and share the five tips that follow with them.

Developing Self-Calming Skills

One of the greatest skills an adult working or living with young children can have is the ability to calm an upset child. Of course, the optimum is for children to learn to calm themselves, and for that reason adults should respect their attempts to do so. For example, when the crying infant finds a soothing thumb and pops it in, the adult should rejoice and not try to distract or substitute something else. The thumb is an example of a very effective self-soothing device.

If infants are to learn self-calming techniques, the adult must not jump up and respond to each little whimper or tiny demand. Timing is important; it takes skill to create a response gap that is just long enough to allow children to discover ways to meet their own needs. If the adult waits too long, children feel neglected; they may go beyond the place where they can calm themselves. Once the child gets overly excited and chaos sets in, the adult needs to be on hand to stop the momentum and help the child get reorganized. Sometimes

When the crying infant finds a soothing thumb and pops it in, the adult should rejoice and not try to distract or substitute something else. The thumb is an example of a very effective self-soothing device.

this is merely a matter of being present and allowing the child to pick up your calm rhythms. Some adults have the natural instinct of tuning into the child's rhythms, flowing with them until the two are in tune, then slowing the combined rhythm until the child is once more relaxed and calm. Thoman and Browder (1987) wrote a wonderful book that is now out of print giving specifics about how this can be done with a baby. They start by advising the adult to find a quiet, softly lit room and relax completely while holding the baby: "Breathe deeply. Feel all your muscles unwind. . . . Now tune in to your baby. Listen to his breathing. Feel his breathing against your chest. At first, try to match your breathing to your baby's breathing, so you're inhaling and exhaling in unison. Then slowly make your breathing deeper" (pp. 181–182). They say that as the adult changes his or her breathing, the baby's breathing will change to match it.

This approach can be used with some children who are no longer babies. Some children are able to use the adult closeness to bring down their energy level and become calm. Something similar can even be used with a group of children. Some infant care teachers and early educators know how to go with the flow of energy and then bring it down to a less chaotic level. There's usually an ideal time to intervene. Determining this ideal time is a skill adults who live and work with young children can acquire through experience.

Coping by Playing Pretend

Playing pretend is a way that children experience feelings in a manner that they can control. In a sense, they *practice* emotions through playing. They're in charge of the environment and of themselves, which puts them in a very powerful position—often the opposite of their position when they are overcome by a feeling in real life.

Adults who understand how important pretend play is to emotional development encourage children to engage in it. Whether at home, in an early childhood program, or as part of a therapy program, they give children props to get them started. In a center, the props are in what used to be called the "housekeeping corner" and is now called the dramatic play area. When children don't automatically show interest in playing pretend, adults can get them started by playing with them. Adults who see the value of time spent pretending provide opportunities, space, and materials to stimulate imagination. They also provide encouragement.

Two early childhood experts, Susan Isaacs and Vivian Paley, working more than half a century apart, have important ideas about the use of what is called *dramatic play*. Isaacs (Smith, 1985) says that through what she calls "imaginative play, children symbolize and externalize their inner drama and conflicts and work through them to gain relief from pressures." She explains that through creating make-believe situations, children practice predicting or hypothesizing what might happen and play it out. Children free themselves from the here and now of the concrete world by acting as if something were true. They not only revisit the past but project into the future through playing pretend.

Paley (1988) talks about the kind of pretend play she saw daily in her classroom of preschoolers. She says, "Whatever else is going on in this network of melodrama, the themes are vast and wondrous. Images of good and evil, birth and death, parent and child, move in and out of the real and the pretend. There is no small talk. The listener is submerged in philosophical position papers, a virtual recapitulation of life's enigmas" (p. 6).

As children create their own worlds through pretend play, they gain a sense of power. They transform reality and practice mastery over it. No wonder pretend play is appealing. In addition to personal power, children also gain communication skills. Through play with, for example, small figures, they deal with several levels of communication as the figures themselves interact, and the players who control them also interact. Children engaged in this type of play practice negotiation and cooperation in real life and on a pretend level. They can get very sophisticated at expressing feelings through this medium.

Watch this video of girls in dramatic play with the theme of camping. Can you think of any feelings that they may act out in this process?

As an early educator, parent educator, or any other kind of professional working with young children and families, you should thoroughly acquaint yourself with the benefits of play so you can help families and others, including policy makers, appreciate it. It takes some skill to observe with a parent or administrator and point out the benefits without talking down or lecturing. You don't want to flaunt your knowledge, but you do want to expand the families' view of play. Of course, not all families, administrators, funders, or policy makers devalue play as an important activity in children's lives; many, however, have gotten the message that the early years are learning years, and they may not see play as a worthy way of learning.

Coping with Simultaneous Feelings

It would be easier to teach children to accept, express, and cope with their feelings if all feelings came singly. However, almost no feelings come as a single, pure, and simple unit of emotion. Often, two feelings come simultaneously. For example, I feel sad that my dog has died, but I'm greatly relieved that his suffering is over; or I'm delighted about my contract to write a new book, but I'm worried about my ability to do it. Adults recognize mixed feelings. Having simultaneous feelings can be an advantage because we can focus on one to help us cope with the other.

Watch this video to witness Lily's surprise. What simultaneous feelings is she expressing?

www.youtube.com
/watch?v=OOpOhlGiRTM

However, it is a different story for young children, who can only focus on one feeling at a time; they aren't aware of mixed feelings (Harter & Buddin, 1987). We adults can help them begin to experience more than one feeling by verbalizing for them when we perceive they might have mixed feelings (e.g., "You're happy to stay overnight with your friend, but you're scared about being away from home"). Being aware of experiencing simultaneous feelings may take some time, because it only comes as the result of increasing maturity.

Coping with Fear

Uncomfortable as they may feel, fears are useful. They protect and help keep children out of danger. A problem is that sometimes fears get in a child's way of fully experiencing the world. They can limit explorations and discourage healthy risk taking, the things that give children a fuller life and help them expand their experience and knowledge.

Adults can help children deal with fears by doing the following:

• *Taking them seriously.* What may not seem significant to an adult may be terrifying to a young child. It is important for the early educator to be reassuring without discounting the feeling. Children need their feelings validated, even when the adult is convinced that there is no danger present.

• *Modeling.* Children can learn fears from other people. They can also learn not to be afraid by watching others interact with the object of their fear. The child who is afraid of dogs may be reassured when both an adult and another child pet the dog in a friendly, trusting way.

• *Playing out fears.* Sometimes the early educator can find ways for the child to experience something in a safe environment that he or she is afraid of. Sometimes children will do this on their own through pretend play, either in a dramatic play setting or with small figures. Another example of playing out fears is when an adult encourages a toddler to play with a small amount of water in a dishpan or sink to help cope with bathtub fears.

Dowrick (1986), in his classic book *Social Survival for Children*, describes how he trains children in relaxation and helps them visualize themselves feeling brave in situations that scare them. He also talks about alleviating fear in children through helping them perform in graduated small steps following a carefully established hierarchy.

Dowrick gives an example of such a hierarchy: A five-year-old child greatly feared doctors yet needed to go to the dentist. The first step was to help him pretend to be a doctor with another child as patient. That was followed by getting him to play patient with another child as doctor. When he was

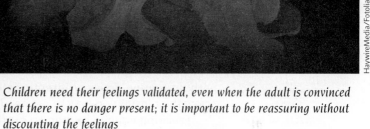

Children need their feelings validated, even when the adult is convinced that there is no danger present; it is important to be reassuring without discounting the feelings

comfortable with that, he was talked into allowing an adult "doctor" to pretend to inspect the inside of his throat. When he was finally able to allow a "pretend" adult doctor to put dental instruments in his mouth, he was ready for his visit to the real dentist. Each step of the play was recorded on videotape and then edited and reviewed by the child. Watching himself in repeated experiences in a benign environment strengthened his coping responses—a kind of self-modeling. In addition, the child was taught relaxation techniques, using positive imagery.

Many early childhood practitioners also use a technique of having children help other children cope with fears. The teacher sends a gentle, outgoing child over to interact with the fearful child who is hanging back from participating in activities. Some early educators have a real talent for linking up one child with another for the good of both. Some go so far as to suggest to parents that so-and-so might be a good friend to invite over. The friendships that result from these linkages sometimes last for years.

Coping with Anger

Sometimes anger carries good, clean, strong energy. Children can learn to use that energy to express themselves, to protect themselves, and, when needs or wants conflict, to work toward problem-solving solutions. The ultimate in problem solving is when the child is able to satisfy the need, thereby eliminating the source of the anger

Adults "Being Put Up Against Themselves"

It is hard for adults who grew up without fully experiencing their feelings to be around children who are able and willing to do so. A crying child can touch sore spots deep within adults who then react from their own pain as much as from the child's. Marjory Keenan (1996), an infant–toddler caregiver, calls this phenomenon "putting one up against oneself" as she tells her story of trying to contend with the lengthy separation agonies of three little girls in her care.

Keenan was professional—warm, caring, and supportive of these girls in their grief. She helped them write daily letters to their mommies telling them they were missed. But nothing worked for long to relieve them of the need to chant pitifully, "I want my mama." It took Keenan two months to finally face her own deep pain of her mother's death when she was just a little younger than these children. She realized what was happening one day in her classroom when the chanting started again. Keenan found herself thinking, "Shut up! You have a mommy, and your mommy always comes and gets you." Keenan's mommy never came back again, and the two-year-old inside of her was reacting. Keenan's feelings finally resurfaced when the three little girls "put her up against herself" with their nearly nonstop lamenting.

"The girls in my class were not consciously trying to upset me," Keenan says. "They were only expressing their true feelings of loss, and these were mirroring my deep pain. The more I listened to the child within me, the less my lamenters irritated me. I began to realize that they were speaking the words that I could only feel internally" (1996, p. 75).

---

without tearing down or intentionally hurting other people. Anger can give extra strength or insight on how to get needs met and to aid this problem-solving process.

Teaching young children to express angry feelings without hurting anyone or anything is a goal for early educators. They help children learn these skills by doing the following:

• *Accepting and labeling the feeling.* "I see how angry you are." "It really makes you mad when she grabs your doll!"

• *Redirecting the energy and helping the child get it out.* "I know you feel like biting your sister, but bite this washcloth instead." "Why don't you go out and run around the play yard three times and see if you still feel so mad."

• *Calming the energy; soothing the chaos.* "I see how upset you are right now. Do you want to sit on my lap and rock a little?" (for the younger child). Or for the older child, a neck massage might help or a suggestion to "try messing around with this goop and see if it makes you feel better." (Time-honored substances for "messing around" are mud and its substitutes—wet clay, cornstarch and water, play dough. Water alone is a great soother in a water-play table, a tub, or a sink.)

• *Avoiding a reward for anger.* Some adults respond to a child's display of anger with so much attention that the behavior is reinforced. If a powerless child can achieve a powerful feeling by displaying anger, she is bound to continue to use the same approach unless someone helps her experience power in a different way.

• *Teaching problem solving.* When children learn to solve problems by communicating in a give-and-take, negotiating way, they feel less frustrated and have less need to try to get their way by using anger.

This last point is a lead-in to the second section of this chapter.

Check Your Understanding 9.2

Click here to check your understanding of teaching children to cope with feelings.

PROBLEM SOLVING

Problems are an important part of life. They are the way children learn, from infancy on. Problem solving is a reasonable way to cope with feelings that arise from problems. The feelings provide energy and motivation to do something. Problems provide challenges that keep life interesting. When teachers and other professionals see problem solving as a skill that children can benefit from knowing, they can help parents and others understand problems, and problem solving, in that way, too.

Using the RERUN *Problem-Solving Process with a Child*

The problem-solving process called RERUN (discussed in Chapter 8) can be used in a dispute between adults as a way to solve cross-cultural disagreements. RERUN can also be used with children. Recall that the elements are *reflect, explain, reason, understand,* and *negotiate*. Here is advice about how to use that same process with a child.

When you encounter a problem to solve, start by checking your own position. Are you clear about the problem? Do you know for sure what you want? Ambiguity on your part will change the whole situation.

I'll use an example from my own life of something I'm very clear about—young children running into the street. Since I have five children and now five grandchildren, I've been through this situation many times. I never take chances. I know there's a problem if my child is close to a street and can't be trusted to stay out of it. Let's say my three-year-old has been playing in the front yard with a toy truck. I have been watching him because he is on the verge of understanding street safety. But just now he rolled the truck down the driveway and has started down after it. I'm not going to take a chance. I move fast and grab him before he goes into the street. Then I go through the RERUN sequence. Here's how it works:

- *Reflect.* As my child squirms and protests, I let him know that his feelings are received and accepted. I reflect them back with such words as, "I see how unhappy you are about being stopped."
- *Explain.* I help my child understand the situation: "I can't let you run in the street."
- *Reason.* I give the reason for my prohibition: "You might get hurt."
- *Understand.* I tune in to feelings—both mine and my child's. I try to understand the situation from both points of view. I don't have to say anything out loud at this point, I just need to be sure I have clarity. I may have to talk to myself to get it.
- *Negotiate.* Since a three-year-old can talk, I can discuss the problem, and together we can look for a mutually satisfying solution. If he had been two, I would have just given two alternatives: "You can stay up here on the porch, or you can play in the backyard." I might do that with a three-year-old, too, if the talk turned into game playing and we weren't working toward a solution.

I try hard not to talk every situation to death. Notice the few words used in this RERUN sequence. The negotiations are the only part that need more than a brief phrase.

With an older child and a less drastic problem, the negotiations can get quite lengthy, but I try to recognize when I'm getting involved in a game. When negotiations are breaking down, I return to the beginning and go through the parts again. I may have to RERUN several times before the problem is solved.

Problem Solving as a Cultural Issue

Cynthia Ballenger (1992, 1999) has been observing the differences between European American culture and Haitian culture for many years. She points out some major differences in child-handling techniques between Haitian and North American preschool teachers. North American teachers focus on the individual child, the feelings, the situation, and the problem. They like to help the child look at consequences and make choices. The teacher remains rather emotionally unattached during the process of problem solving, as I was in the RERUN example just explained. Good or bad behavior is not usually mentioned during a problem-solving process.

Watch this video to observe a teacher facilitate problem solving with a group of children. Would you say that the teacher's approach was more aligned with Haitian or North American approach?

Haitian teachers, on the other hand, clearly distinguish bad behavior. They emphasize group values and the responsibility of the child to the group. Children's feelings are not a focus during this discussion; the discussion is about emotional ties and adult expectation. There's no feeling of detachment as there is when North American teachers are helping a child problem-solve a situation. Haitian teachers don't talk about consequences but rather good and bad behaviors, which relate to respect and obedience. Haitian teachers do not use a detached and individualistic problem-solving technique, like North American teachers, but put emphasis on shared values in a moral community.

In spite of the fact that this chapter is about feelings and problem solving, it's important to realize there are other cultural perspectives on how to handle feelings and problems. You may be more comfortable with the North American way that Ballenger describes. Or the Haitian way may resonate with you even if you aren't Haitian. Don't think of "right" and "wrong" when you compare these two approaches toward managing young children's behavior; think of "different." Much of the material in this chapter may be new to families. Strategy Box 9.1 gives some ideas about how to share it with them.

Strategy Box 9.1

Working with Families around Issues of Feelings and Problem Solving

- Open up conversations with families to discover their perspectives on feelings and problem solving. Be prepared for the fact that feelings are cultural issues and families may have strong ideas about their place in human relationships.

- Create opportunities for conversations when an issue comes up with a particular family. Such opportunities occur in some programs at the beginning and end of the day when families drop off and pick up their children. They can also be scheduled meetings.

- Put on regular meetings to discuss a wide range of subjects, including perspectives on feelings and ideas about problem solving. Try to figure out what prevents some families from attending these meetings and address the problems, whether scheduling, transportation, or child care.

- Create an atmosphere at meetings that feels both welcoming and comfortable. Make sure the families get to know each other. Make each meeting interactive.

- Consider using a "Transformative Education" model instead of a traditional "Parent Education" model for your meetings. Transformative education is defined by a two-way flow of information and knowledge rather than one-way delivery system. In transformative education, two people or two groups come together and interact in such a way that both are transformed by the experience.

Problem Solving and Parenting Styles

How parents respond to seeing teachers working on problem solving with children could be a cross-cultural issue, but it could also be affected by parenting styles, regardless of culture. Three parenting styles were named some time ago by Diana Baumrind (1971, 1986), who did some classic research visiting families in their homes in the late afternoon just before dinner—a time that is stressful in most families with young children. The three parenting styles she named are the *authoritarian approach*, the *permissive approach*, and the *authoritative approach*.

A fourth parenting style was added more recently. It's called uninvolved parenting. See Figure 9.1.

The Authoritarian Approach.   The authoritarian approach is the "do-as-I-say" way of relating to children. Authoritarians see their power as inherent in their position. In conflicts, they see win-lose solutions—and it's important that they win. That's the way they keep their authority.

The strict authoritarian parent demands uncompromising obedience. Rules are established and infractions punished. Parental needs and desires come before child needs and desires. Authoritarian parents may have a good deal of self-respect but may not show respect for the child in ways recognized by adults not of the authoritarian school of thought.

Authoritarian	Authoritative	Permissive	Uninvolved
• "Do-as-I-say" approach to children • Views parent role as one of power • Win-lose approach to conflict, adult wins to maintain authority • Demands uncompromising obedience • Rules are established and punishment occurs if rules are broken • Parent needs come before child needs and desires • Has self-respect, but may not show respect for children • Unlikely to use problem-solving approach if child choice or negotiation is involved	• Firm standards • Provides limits and control • Believes in mutual respect • Guides, protects, and facilitates development • Flexible approach • Listens to children's requests and justifications • Win-win approach to problem solving • Concerned about needs of children and own needs	• Has little control over children • May take the role of guides and friends • Children's needs come first • Win-lose approach to conflict: children win because adult gives all power to child • May resist the structure of problem solving	• Makes few demands on children • Unresponsive • Lacks communication • Neglects to give guidance or set limits • Fails to teach or encourage • Emotionally unavailable • Puts him or herself first, their children last • Detached and dismissive

Figure 9.1   Parenting styles

Authoritarian parenting has a bad reputation with many early educators. To an outsider, one who doesn't believe in an authoritarian approach, authoritarian behaviors may feel very uncomfortable; however, for some families it is the appropriate approach and their children find security in knowing that the adults are in charge. They may take the adults' strictness and demands for obedience as signs of love.

The authoritarian parent is unlikely to embrace the problem-solving approach, if there are negotiations or choices involved.

The Permissive Approach.   Permissive families seek to have little control over their children. These adults may take the role of guides and friends—being warm and involved with their children—or they may be less interested and involved and more lackadaisical. In an extreme permissive approach, it may seem as if parents just lie back and let their children walk all over them. Parental needs take a backseat to child needs. In a win-lose conflict, the children win because the adult doesn't take any power into his own hands. He grants all the power to the children.

From the view of someone who is uncomfortable with permissiveness, it looks as though the permissive parents fail to display self-respect because they let their children win conflicts with them. They find the children dissatisfied and perhaps uncomfortable if they seem to be out of control and have few or no limits set by their parents. They say that it doesn't feel good to treat people like doormats, even when they invite you to do so. The permissive parent may resist the structure of a problem-solving approach, though it is unlikely that even very permissive parents would let their children run in the street. However, Barbara Rogoff, in her book *The Cultural Nature of Human Development* (2003), has many examples of parents from other cultures trusting their young children to do things, like handle machetes and knives, that would be horrifying to most adults in the United States.

The Authoritative Approach.   Neither authoritarian styles nor permissive ones are ideal according to Baumrind's research and those who have followed after her. From Baumrind emerges the "right approach"—the authoritative approach. Authoritative parents listen to children's justifications and requests and make decisions that take into consideration the needs of the child. They provide limits and control when necessary. They believe in mutual respect.

Authoritative parents derive their authority from the fact of their experience, size, and ability. They know that they have lived in the world longer than their children and have expertise their children don't have. They see their role as using reason to guide, protect, and facilitate development.

Authoritative adults have firm standards but employ a flexible approach. They are apt to use what's been called a win-win approach to parenting. They are concerned about their children's needs and also about their own needs. When

Though there is quite a bit of agreement in the field about various approaches to working with children, families don't necessarily fit neatly into the research that guides the field

Frank Fennema/Shutterstock

the two clash, they don't sacrifice one for the other but look for solutions in which both their needs and their children's are met. Resolution leaves both parties satisfied. Children of authoritative parents or parent substitutes are thought to be self-reliant, independent, socially responsible, and explorative. An important device for the win-win parenting used by authoritative adults is the problem-solving process.

Uninvolved Parenting.   Uninvolved parents or parent substitutes demand very little from their children and leave them largely to grow up on their own. They tend to be unresponsive and to lack communication. Uninvolved means they make few demands on their children, fail to teach them, seldom give them encouragement, and neglect to give guidance or set limits. Basically they are emotionally unavailable even when their children need them. Characterized by a lack of love and concern, they put themselves first and their children last. They may manage to meet their children's basic needs but are generally dismissive or detached from their children's life. They fall in a range from being merely detached to being rejecting and even seriously neglectful. Uninvolved parents were themselves usually raised by uninvolved parents.

A Deeper Look at the Four Parenting Styles

The research on the parenting styles above was done on European Americans and applies to European Americans. However, Ruth Chao (1994, 2000) questions the validity for Chinese parenting. She raises a paradox. Authoritarian styles of child rearing predict low achievement in school, yet Chinese children who are raised by authoritarian parents do well in school. Chao proposes that the concept of authority is ethnocentric and does not explain important facets of Chinese child rearing.

Authoritarian child rearing in the United States was handed down from puritanical beginnings, which advocated harsh treatment of children. This view of authoritarianism in child rearing lasted two centuries. It wasn't until World War II that Americans became more permissive. The history of authority in China is very different. Authority in China is not harsh but gentle, coming as it does from a Confucian tradition related not to predestination but to social harmony.

Though authoritarian-style child rearing is equated with distance and harshness in European American tradition, in China it is equated with closeness, both physical and emotional. (The child sleeps with the mother, for example.) The mother is greatly involved in promoting success in the child and is the main caretaker. That situation contrasts with a European American view of independence and individuality.

Training is another concept that differs culturally. To some European American parents, training involves something militaristic, rigid, and strict. The word has negative connotations. Chinese parents regard training as positive—an act of love. The lesson, as always, is to realize that we all look at information through our cultural lenses. Information about such concepts as parenting styles, even those based on research, can be useful but always need to be examined further.

This chapter is bound to give you much to think about when working with families. Though there is quite a bit of agreement in the field about various approaches to working with children, families don't necessarily fit neatly into the research that guides the field. That may leave the professional confused and maybe upset. But that's exactly what this chapter has been about—coping with feelings and using problem-solving approaches to figure out what to do.

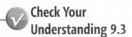

Check Your Understanding 9.3

Click here to check your understanding of problem solving.

SUMMARY

This chapter explored feelings as they relate to children and working with families. It looked at how children learn feelings and some of the ways adults can help children experience, express, think about, and cope with feelings. The chapter also described how to use the RERUN problem-solving process with a child. It then took a look at problem solving as a cultural issue. The chapter ended with an explanation of differing parenting styles.

QUIZ

Click here to check your understanding of Chapter 9, "Working with Families on Addressing Feelings and Problem Solving."

FOR DISCUSSION

1. How does social referencing work? Can you give an example? When is social referencing useful and when is it not? Why would you not want to use social referencing when responding to a toddler who has just taken a spill?

2. Can you give an example of a cultural script? Do you have any cultural scripts? What are they?

3. Which of the three parenting approaches mentioned in the chapter do you prefer and why? How were you raised? How do you think the way you were raised affects you now?

4. Make up a scene involving the RERUN process of problem solving.

WEBSITES

American Psychological Association (APA)
The APA has a page that explains what anger is, how it is expressed, anger management, cognitive restructuring, and more.

Center on the Social and Emotional Foundations for Early Learning (CSEFEL)
The Center is focused on promoting social/emotional development and school readiness for young children from birth to five years. They developed a pyramid model that is highlighted on the website. The Center is a resource for families and professionals, and many of their materials can be downloaded or ordered from the website.

Children Today
Do you know your parenting style? Take a quiz based on Diana Baumrind's research. You will also find other articles and resources on the Children Today website.

Developmental Psychology
This website has a collection of resources about Diana Baumrind's observed parenting styles. It also includes excerpts from her original work on the topic, further information, and a related role-playing activity.

A Place of Our Own
Search "problem-solving skills." Expert and practitioner advice is offered about how preschool-type activities can present situations where children use problem-solving skills, which supports cognitive development.

Royal College of Psychiatrists
The Royal College of Psychiatrists in the United Kingdom has a site that contains a good deal of information, including information that can help adults cope with worries and anxieties in children, such as phobias.

FURTHER READING

Flore, I. R. (2011) Developing young children's self-regulation through everyday experiences. *Young Children* 66 (4), 46–51.

Goleman, D., Boyatzis, R., & McKee, A. (2013). *Primal leadership: Unleashing the power of emotional intelligence*. Boston, MA: Harvard University.

Gonzalez-Mena, J. (2010, May/June). Compassionate roots: Teaching babies compassion. *Exchange*, 46–49.

Guerra, A. W., & Garriety S. (2013). A cultural communities and cultural practices approach to understanding infant and toddler care. In E. Virmani & P. Mangione (Eds.). A *guide to culturally sensitive care* (2nd ed., pp. 41–53). Sacramento CA: California Department of Education.

Matsumoto, D., Yoo, S. H., & Nakagawa, S. (2008). Culture, emotion regulation, and adjustment. *Journal of Personality and Social Psychology*, 94(6), 925.

Okagaki, L., & Diamond, K. E. (2000, May). Responding to cultural and linguistic differences in the beliefs and practices of families with young children. *Young Children*, 55(3), 74–80.

Thompson, R. A. (2009, November). Doing what doesn't come naturally: The development of self-regulation. *Zero to Three*, 30(2), 33–37.

Working with Families to Support Self-Esteem

In this chapter you will learn to. . .

- Discuss the nature and origin of self-esteem.
- Explain ways to support the development of children's self-esteem.
- Discuss how an anti-bias approach to appreciating differences can support children's development of self-esteem.

Much attention now is focused on how to prepare children early for success in school and in life. This chapter looks in depth at a concept called *self-esteem* including how to promote it, because a link is seen among achievement, behavior, positive growth patterns, and high self-esteem. It also briefly leaves the subject of self-esteem per se to look at the concept of mindset and how different mindsets affect paths to success. Throughout, the chapter explores culture differences and issues related to self-esteem including bias and how professionals and families can work together to help children be successful.

EXPLORING SELF-ESTEEM AS A ROAD TO SUCCESS

What does a person with high self-esteem look like? On the surface, this seems like a fairly simple question to answer. Without much thought it's easy to come up with a portrait that's something like this:

> People with high self-esteem have self-confidence that shows in the way they dress, groom themselves, walk, and talk. People with high self-esteem are secure and happy. They're outgoing, energetic, brave, strong, and proud. They're also motivated, successful, independent, and assertive.

That description is a typical one produced by students of mainstream cultural backgrounds. But in a class where the students are diverse and comfortable enough to speak up, the items on the list come into question, as the students discover that the traits listed are not particularly indicative of high self-esteem but rather reflect a cultural ideal.

If you think of a specific person who seems to have high self-esteem, the picture changes, even if that person is of the mainstream culture. The person is not likely to be a walking example of this list of culturally specific ideal traits. Rather, the person is more likely to be himself or herself. And if you compare that person with another who also has high self-esteem, the two may be very different from each other because the second person is also likely to be himself or herself, a unique individual.

High-self-esteem people aren't necessarily happy, though we would like to think that happiness comes from boosting self-esteem. Often people who are themselves and feel good about who they are run into problems when they are in circumstances that challenge their ability to express who they are and have their needs met. A person in a refugee camp may have high self-esteem but probably won't be too happy. More is said about this later in the chapter, but here let me just point out that part of being who you are has to do with feeling your feelings, which means that you'll have a wide range of emotions—not just constant sunshiny happiness.

People with high self-esteem also aren't necessarily talented, good-looking, strong, or financially successful. If they were, ordinary people wouldn't have much of a chance, and people with disabilities would have even less of a chance. Just look around you and you'll discover that a person's looks, abilities, possessions, or wealth aren't necessarily related to self-esteem. Some of the best-looking people in the world feel inferior. They either think they're not *really* good-looking, or they worry that all they have is their looks, which are destined to fade. If they feel significant or powerful based on looks alone, they're in trouble.

Some people have a distorted view of themselves

rubberball/Gettyimages

Actually, if you scratch the surface of people who seem to have high self-esteem, you'll find that some are covering up perceived inadequacies. People are often the opposite of what they seem. The extremely assertive person may be hiding a shy, scared child underneath. The paragon of virtue may have a core of hidden vices. Judging self-esteem in others isn't easy! There's lots of room for error. People just aren't always what they seem.

So instead of trying to judge the degree of self-esteem in adults, let's look at where it comes from in childhood. Let's start with some definitions.

What is self-esteem, anyway? Self-esteem is a valuing process and results from an ongoing self-appraisal in which traits and abilities are acknowledged and evaluated. People with high self-esteem are motivated more from the inside than from rewards given by others. That's the difference between intrinsic and extrinsic motivation. Self-esteem is made up of *self-image*—the pictures we carry of ourselves—and *self-concept*—the ideas we have about ourselves.

High self-esteem comes when, after a realistic appraisal of pluses and minuses, a person decides that she has more positive attributes than negative ones. High self-esteem means that a person feels good about herself—she holds herself in esteem. Overall, she likes herself, warts and all. Low self-esteem means that a person lacks a global sense of self-worth.

Culture and Self-Esteem

This concept of self-esteem or self-worth is entirely tied to culture. For example, in a culture that values independence and individuality, the perception is that infants are born unable to differentiate themselves from the rest of the world. It is the family's job to help the infant learn to draw boundaries and discover her separateness. She must come to see herself as an individual, an independent human being. When she does, she feels successful. Another family from a different culture sees the infant as separate and independent to start with. That family wants to blur the boundaries and de-emphasize the independence. Jerome Kagan, in his classic book *The Nature of the Child* (1984), says, "The Japanese, who prize close interdependence between child and adult . . . believe they must tempt the infant into a dependent role . . . in order to encourage the mutual bonding necessary for adult life" (p. 29). Self-esteem in a family that emphasizes separateness will look different from a family that de-emphasizes separateness.

When a family promotes self-assurance, self-help, competence, and being "special," self-esteem rises if the individual is proud to perceive herself as being in possession of those traits. However, in some cultures, the proud, independent, self-assured individual who stands out in a crowd will be given strong messages about the importance of fitting in, belonging, and putting others first. Culture makes a difference in one's view of what comprises self-esteem. In some cultures, the very notion of holding oneself in esteem is abhorrent, and pride is a no-no. Instead, humility and humbleness are valued (Greenfield, Quiroz, Rothstein-Fisch, & Trumbull, 2001; Rogoff, 2003). People in these cultures find other ways of feeling worthy. Conflicting cultural messages can tear down self-esteem. Although some people can rise above cultural messages and continue to feel good about themselves, others can't. Self-esteem isn't simply deciding that you're great just as you are and giving that message to the world.

Children from any culture can sometimes have an exaggerated sense of their own power, one that doesn't reflect self-esteem at all but rather their stage of cognitive development. Take, for example, the three-year-old who feels angry about having been dethroned by a baby sister. He makes ugly wishes concerning the baby. Then the baby gets sick— or worse, *dies*—and the three-year-old

High self-esteem means that a person feels good about herself—she holds herself in esteem

thinks he caused the tragedy by willing it. The child's misconceptions aren't caused by the degree of his self-esteem but rather by thinking himself capable of willing things to happen. He lacks logic at this age.

Self-perception must relate to reality to create true self-esteem. Exaggerated misperceptions that aren't stage related, as in this example, are delusions. A picture that appeared on the cover of *Newsweek* on February 17, 1992, depicts this problem: An ugly, skinny, weak, flabby, sickly looking man stands in front of the mirror, and the reflection he sees is the opposite of what he is. The mirror shows a strong, well-built, handsome, self-assured man whom we can assume to be talented and intelligent as well. Nothing in the reflection is the same as the man creating it—nothing relates to reality. That's not self-esteem!

Whether trying to change self-esteem or building it carefully from the beginning, the goal is to help the child gain a sense of self that is both culturally valued and true

If, in the name of promoting self-esteem, you try to fool a child by painting him a false picture of himself, it won't work. (If it did, it wouldn't be healthy, anyway.) Take a child who is miserably aware of his lack of ability, feels unloved, has little power to control anything in his life, and is behaving in unacceptable ways. You can't raise this child's self-esteem by telling him that none of what he is experiencing is true. He simply won't believe you. If there is no reality to back up what you're saying, you're wasting your breath. Even if you point out his good traits, if he's focused on what he perceives to be his bad traits, he won't pay attention.

It's harder to change someone's self-esteem than it seems. In fact, only when the person himself decides to change his perceptions will he allow someone else to be effective in helping him. *Changing and building self-esteem in the first place involves a collaboration, not a deception.* The collaboration is not only with individuals, but also with the culture and community. Even media can enter in here and can have positive or negative influence. It's the responsibility of the family to help children with negative media messages, and also the responsibility of the community, though censorship arises as an issue when the community gets involved in shielding children from bad media influences. Again we see the bigger context as Bronfenbrenner's ecological systems theory describes it. Many forces described in this book act on self-esteem. Some have already been mentioned: the child's temperament and match with the temperaments in the family, the family and its parenting styles, peers, schools, neighborhoods, broader community, and society. The goal of the collaboration, whether trying to change self-esteem or building it carefully from the beginning, is to help the child gain a sense of self that is both valued and true.

Dimensions of Self-Esteem

According to Stanley Coopersmith (1967), a pioneer researcher in this area, self-esteem has at least four dimensions: significance, competence, power, and virtue. Your self-esteem depends on what you value, which is likely to be influenced by what your family and culture values for you (which may depend on gender) and where you perceive that you fall in each category (see Figure 10.1).

Significance has to do with a feeling of being loved and cared about, the feeling that you matter to someone. You can't instill this feeling in a child. You can try to influence it with words and deeds, with nurturing and protection, with caring, and with meeting needs, but you can't ensure that the messages you send are the ones the child will receive. A feeling of significance, the feeling that you are important because you are cared about, is a choice the individual makes.

It is vital to understand that children are active participants in the development of their sense of self. No matter what hand fate deals, it's not the events

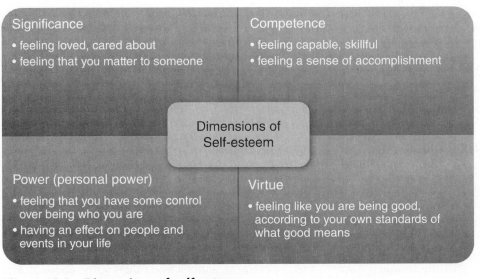

Figure 10.1 Dimensions of self-esteem

themselves that determine self-esteem—it's how the child reacts to those events. Obviously some children are born into more fortunate circumstances than others, yet there are children who have everything going for them who don't feel good about themselves. Other children are just the opposite. They manage to emerge from a series of traumas with self-esteem intact and, indeed, growing. These children seem to be able to use adverse circumstances to their own advantage. They grow and learn from their experiences and come out stronger than ever. They seem to take the negative and twist it around to have a positive effect.

Competence is not something that can be given to the child. You can influence *competence* in a child by helping or allowing him to become increasingly skilled in a number of areas. But whether the child *feels* competent depends on whether he compares himself with someone who is more competent than he is. It's a decision the child makes, not one that you make, though you can help him see that it's better not to make comparisons. You may be tempted to try to influence his decision by making comparisons yourself or demanding perfection—both of which set the child up for failure. If competence is particularly important to him, even without your pushing for perfection, he may experience lower self-esteem even though he is highly competent, simply because he doesn't see himself as competent enough. There's a discrepancy between where he thinks he should be (or wants to be) and where he is. He doesn't meet his own standards (which may or may not have come from his family or his culture).

Power is the third dimension of self-esteem. Feeling that you have some control over being who you are, making things happen in the world, having an effect on the people and events in your life, and living your life satisfactorily gives a sense of power. If power is of major importance to you, having a feeling of it can raise your self-esteem. Notice that power is not defined here as having control over other

> It is vital to understand that children are active participants in the development of their sense of self. No matter what hand fate deals, it's not the events themselves that determine self-esteem—it's how the child reacts to those events.

people—it's not a matter of *overpowering*, but power in the pure sense of the word: personal power, which reflects the root meaning of the word—"to be able." Power has to do with effectiveness.

Virtue is the fourth dimension of self-esteem. Being good is important to some people. Their self-esteem relates to how much of a gap there is between how good they perceive themselves to be and how good they want or need to be. Virtue is not a supreme value to everyone.

The Role of Beliefs and Expectations in Self-Esteem

So suppose that self-esteem depends on two things: the dimensions that are of utmost importance to the individual, and the gap between where this person perceives herself to be and where she wants to (or feels she should) be. Take the housewife who sees herself as good and loved (excels on the scales of virtue and significance) yet values only power and competence, where she sees herself sadly lacking. In this case, her self-esteem may be quite low.

The housewife is a contrast to, for example, a monk who values virtue above all and derives his self-esteem from being obedient to his faith. He doesn't care about power, competence, or significance. These are extreme examples, granted, but they make the point. A discrepancy between where you are and where you want to be on the scale(s) most valuable to you is what counts in self-esteem.

Although self-esteem eventually becomes established and relatively stable over time, it's not forever fixed and static. For one thing, it changes as children develop. If we look at Erikson's (1963) stages of development in view of the dimensions described here, we see that different periods of development have different emphases. For example, power is a particularly strong issue for two-year-olds, who are in Erikson's stage of autonomy. Competence comes into focus in the school-age years when children enter Erikson's stage of industry versus inferiority (see Figure 10.2). Industry, as Erikson uses the term, is about developing areas of competence. Another way to look at self-esteem is to look at Maslow's self-actualizing process. The person who is further along is likely to have higher self-esteem. They go together.

Self-esteem doesn't just change as a child develops, but also changes when circumstances change. It can even change instantly. The child who is competent at many things, active, and talkative at home may become quiet and hide his competence when he enters school for the first time. A severe trauma can also make a difference in the child's feelings about himself. Creating and maintaining self-esteem is a lifelong process—it gets shaped and reshaped.

hirko/Fotolia

Notice that esteem is right below self-actualization on Maslow's hierarchy of needs pyramid

Child's Stage	Approximate Age	Task		
Infancy	0–1	Basic trust	versus	Basic mistrust
Toddlerhood	1–3	Autonomy	versus	Shame and doubt
The preschool years	3–6	Initiative	versus	Guilt
School age	6–10	Industry	versus	Inferiority

Figure 10.2   Erikson's psycho-social stages of development
Source: Based on Erikson (1963).

Self-esteem brings with it self-confidence, which is a vital trait for development. What a child *believes* he can or cannot do sometimes influences what he *can* or *cannot* do. Children who perceive that they lack competence, for instance, may not try something because they've had bad experiences in the past, or simply because they have no confidence in themselves. What we *believe* influences our behavior greatly. Our beliefs create a self-fulfilling prophecy. What we expect is what we get, for no other reason than that we expect it.

Past experience can play a big part in raising or lowering expectations. The research on learned helplessness is eye opening. Dogs who were shocked when they tried to get out of their cages learned to stay in even after the shocks stopped and the cages were left open. They were free to leave, but they didn't perceive it that way. They continued to act on past experience even though the circumstances of the present were different. Their perceptions didn't relate to reality (Seligman, 1975).

Picture this cartoon: A man stands in a cage, gripping bars in both hands with his face pressed up against them. But those two bars are the only ones holding him in the cage—there are no other bars. His perceptions are what are trapping him, not the reality of the situation. Perceptions make up self-esteem, including wrong perceptions.

> Watch this video to hear how teachers' expectations of students affect performance. Did you ever experience a teacher who had negative beliefs about your ability?
>
> www.youtube.com/watch?v=P4wL5t8YH1Q

Where Does Self-Esteem Come From?

Self-esteem, along with self-identity, comes from early experiences and continues up through the school years into adolescence and adulthood. Children define themselves partly by looking at the images that they see reflected in the people and the environment around them (Briggs, 1975; Lally, 1995; Day, 2013). If they develop close attachments with people who love and value them, the reflection they see is positive, and they're likely to have positive feelings about themselves. They decide that they are lovable. If they create an impact on the world—starting as babies when they cry and are responded to in ways that meet their needs—they develop a sense of self-efficacy, which they then include in their self-definition. If they develop a wide variety of competencies that are well received by those around them, they are likely to decide that they are competent. If they learn acceptable ways to behave and are given recognition for their good behavior, they are likely to decide that they are virtuous. Put all together, the child who sees more positive reflections of himself is likely to develop a global sense of self-worth, or self-esteem.

Our beliefs create a self-fulfilling prophecy; children who are labeled and called negative names are likely to internalize those messages, which will affect their behavior and their self-esteem

What if you look at the news, go to the movies, or watch TV shows, and you see people like you either not pictured at all or pictured in negative ways? What will all that do to your self-esteem?

 Check Your Understanding 10.1

Click here to check your understanding of exploring self-esteem as a road to success.

So it seems as though a child who has someone who cares about him and meets his needs and creates positive reflections will likely develop a healthy sense of self-worth. But what if the outside world gives you a different set of messages because of your color, your gender, your ethnicity, or your physical/mental abilities? What if the reflections you see in the eyes of those outside your home depict you as somehow inferior? What if you look at the news, go to the movies, or watch TV shows, and you see people like you either not pictured at all or pictured in negative ways? What will all that do to your self-esteem? These questions are the focus of a book called *Rethinking Popular Culture and Media* (Marshall & Sensoy, 2011) and will be looked at more closely in later chapters.

What if the people and/or institutions you encounter outside your home give you differential treatment and act as if you are inferior? Furthermore, what if those people or institutions create insensitive or even assaultive environments, and you find yourself in those environments?

Under these circumstances, can the positive messages you get from home counteract the negative ones you get from outside? Maybe. Some families provide their children with lessons on how to survive and stand up to racism, sexism, or ableism, which is discrimination or prejudice against individuals with disabilities. Their children go out into the world with a protective shield that can help them maintain their self-esteem even when they are bombarded with negative messages. Surely what children get at home from these aware family members will make them stronger and probably more able to withstand the negative images thrust on them. But what about children who go out into the world with self-esteem already a bit damaged? What happens to them when they enter an insensitive or assaultive environment outside the home? The results can be devastating.

PROMOTING SELF-ESTEEM

This section examines some general ways to support children's development of self-esteem, including some that are specific to changing the negative messages just mentioned above to positive ones.

The first step is to get rid of critical attitudes, labeling, and name calling. Even in the name of socializing a child, *you can't make him feel better about himself by making him feel bad about himself.* That doesn't mean to move right to "La-La Land," where everything is sweetness and light and nothing connects to reality. Of course children misbehave, make adults angry, and act in less than loving ways. They need guidance and protection. They need honest feedback. But the form in which you guide, protect, and give honest feedback matters.

> The first step is to get rid of critical attitudes, labeling, and name calling. Even in the name of socializing a child, *you can't make him feel better about himself by making him feel bad about himself.*

Give More Honest Feedback and Encouragement Than Praise

Some adults, in the name of building self-esteem, vow always to be positive and to praise children at every possible opportunity. They replace honest feedback with constant, overblown praise. Praise is no cure for low self-esteem. All it does is create a need for the child to look to the adult for a judgment of everything he does. He depends on extrinsic rewards rather than intrinsic ones that come from inside himself. Children need coaches, not cheerleaders (Curry & Johnson, 1990; Azria-Evans, 2004). If you overdo praise, your words become meaningless. For example, if you say "Great job!" about every little thing, it becomes an empty phrase. It's more effective and less damaging to use encouragement instead of praise. Call attention to children's legitimate successes, but don't butter them up with heavy judgments. Compare past performances with present ones, but not with those of other children—"You picked up more blocks this time than last time," rather than "You're the best block-picker-upper I've ever seen." Better yet, explain why this behavior is valuable (Hitz & Driscoll, 1988).

Give Children Opportunities to Experience Success

Even more important than just talking is to give children many chances to experience success of all sorts. Challenge them so that when success comes they've worked for it—it didn't just arrive on a platter. Do this by creating a manageable, yet challenging, environment that is appropriate to their age and stage of development. The book *Developmentally Appropriate Practice in Early Childhood Programs Serving Children from Birth Through Age 8*, by Carol Copple and Sue Bredekamp (2009), gives many ideas about how to respond to children appropriately.

When adults give children a helping hand, they also help them experience success. Lev Vygotsky (1978) came up with the term *assisted performance* to describe this helping hand. He suggested that other children can be the ones who provide the helping hand, not just adults. Others now use the term *scaffolding*. Scaffolding is a process that can be viewed as similar to the temporary structure one puts up to paint a

Paul Jenkins/Pearson Education, Inc.

Create an environment for children that gives them opportunities for problem solving and chances to experience success

building. In other words, the adult provides the support the child needs, allowing him to problem-solve at new levels. The scaffolding helps the child experience success, which encourages the child to challenge himself further, thereby meeting with the possibility of new success. Scaffolding, because it is temporary, can be built for a specific need on each occasion and can easily be remodeled to serve changing needs.

Travis

Travis is four years old, and he's big for his age. His size alone commands attention, but his behavior commands even more. He pushes kids around every chance he gets. He walks with a swagger and with a challenge on his face. "Just try to get the better of me," his expression seems to say. He's also loud and sometimes unruly. What he wants, he wants *now*—and he lets everybody know it.

One day at the staff meeting, one of his teachers confessed her discomfort about Travis and his attitude. "I don't like him very much," she said in a quiet voice. "I try, but his behavior just gets in the way of the warm feelings I *want* to have for him. It seems like self-esteem is just oozing out all over him, and I don't like that."

The rest of the staff was silent for a moment, amazed at her confession. Then her coteacher spoke up. "I don't see Travis as a high-self-esteem child," he said cautiously. "Sure, he acts like he's got all the confidence in the world, but I think he's just making up for what he thinks he lacks."

"What do you mean?" asked the first teacher.

"Well, his bullying, for instance. When kids bully, it's not a mark of high self-esteem. Rather, it's a mark of low self-esteem. Kids who feel good about themselves—who they are and their capabilities—don't have to push other kids around."

"What else makes you think that Travis doesn't feel good about himself?" asked the first teacher. "I always thought that he felt *too* good about himself."

"The way he avoids doing anything that would show he's not as capable as the other kids. I think that because of his size people always expect more out of him than he can manage. It must be hard for him. I know I keep forgetting that he's not as old as he looks. So, if it's a problem for me, it's probably a problem for other people, too."

"I've noticed that," acknowledged another teacher. "He puts a lot of energy into avoiding things. But he's so loud about his demands that we pay attention to those and not to the fact that he rarely gets involved in much of anything."

"I wonder if he has picked up my negative feelings," worried the first teacher. "It won't help him much to be around someone who admits she doesn't like him."

"I like him," said her coteacher. "But he probably doesn't know it because I'm always dealing with his negative behavior. That's when he gets attention from me. I think I'll work on changing that situation."

"I wonder how we can help him have more positive experiences in our program," mused the first teacher out loud. "Maybe we can gently move him toward activities that particularly interest him. I saw him trying to fold a paper airplane yesterday. Maybe I can get him to help me set up a project of paper airplanes for all the kids. That might give him some recognition."

"We could focus more on giving him some social skills, so he can quit bullying," was another suggestion.

"I wonder what would happen if we used the video camera and showed him what he looks like when he bullies," another colleague offered. "Or maybe that would be too threatening at this point."

"I think what he needs is a friend," said another. "I've noticed he seems drawn to Paul. Maybe we could encourage that relationship."

"Well," said the first teacher, "I'm glad I brought the subject up. I see Travis differently now, and I'm already beginning to like him better!"

Optimum challenge and risk taking are the secret to development, to learning, and to skill building. Scaffolding supports children so they have experiences with positive results when challenged to take a risk. When children encounter a problem or an obstacle and are about to get stuck in the problem-solving process, instead of rescuing them, adults can provide help—not heaps of help but the smallest amount necessary. In this way adults can facilitate the continuation of the problem-solving process. They provide the missing link in the chain that allows children to move forward toward solutions. Thus, children's success is eventually their own, not the adult's. Experiencing personal success in the face of obstacles gives children messages about their abilities, about their self-worth.

Look at the following scenario, which illustrates scaffolding:

> Dashinique wants to try out for the school play but has to choose a scene, and she can't make up her mind. An adult helps her sort out the possible contenders and then offers to listen to her try the part in each scene to see which works best. The answer becomes obvious to both of them as Dashinique acts out each scene. But then comes the second problem. Dashinique is scared of the tryout. She can speak her lines fine, but the thought of standing up in front of people makes her nervous. Again the adult helps by gathering some people to listen to her say her lines so she can practice in front of them and get used to being watched. It works. By the day of the tryouts, Dashinique has gained self-confidence and does well in spite of a few leftover nerves. Dashinique gets the part, and her success is her own. She only had a small bit of help (but lots of support and encouragement).

> When children encounter a problem or an obstacle and are about to get stuck in the problem-solving process, instead of rescuing them, adults can provide help—not heaps of help but the smallest amount necessary. In this way adults can facilitate the continuation of the problem-solving process.

The next situation shows another example of scaffolding. Look for the difference here between scaffolding and "rescuing," in which adults provide too much help:

> Brandon and Shelby are having an argument over who gets to use the glue gun to finish the craft projects they are both working on. Brandon had it first, but Shelby grabbed it and is holding it out of Brandon's reach when an adult comes up to the table. The adult could rescue Brandon by taking the glue gun from Shelby, but instead he helps the two sort out the situation. He starts by merely saying what he sees: "Brandon wants the glue gun." He waits to see what happens. Shelby answers, "Yeah, but I need it." Brandon cuts in, "I had it first." Shelby responds, "But you were just holding it—you weren't using it." Brandon turns to the adult, "Make her give it to me—I had it first! It isn't fair!" Shelby responds, "I really need it. If I don't hold down this piece the whole thing is going to fall apart." "Well . . .," says Brandon, "I could let you use it for a minute if that's all you want to do. But next time don't grab!" he says emphatically. No longer needed,

the adult walks off, and the two continue to work on their projects. Think about what the children learn and how they feel when they solve a problem themselves rather than depending on adults to fix it.

Most of us are tempted to take care of problems quickly when the solution is something we can deliver. When an adult sees a toddler fall, the urge is to pick him up and set him back on his feet. If the same person saw an adult fall, he would be more likely to come over and ask some questions and see what was needed at the moment. Maybe getting back on his feet isn't the best solution. Even without medical training, most of us know that it is better if the person can get back on his own feet after a fall. It's a test to see whether there is an injury. But with a child we tend to think differently. Why? Does it make us feel powerful? Does it feel good to help someone less capable than we are? Why are we more likely to use a scaffolding approach in a situation involving an adult and just fix the problem for a child? Scaffolding is appropriate for both children and adults. Rescuing doesn't promote self-esteem. It's more important to build real skills and remark about them than it is to try to boost self-esteem through empty words and pretending to be excited about nonexistent successes.

While you're thinking about skill building, consider all skills. Social skills are as important as physical and intellectual ones. When a child doesn't have a clue as to the effect of his or her behaviors on others, help that child come to see what is effective and what is not. Teach the skills the child may lack.

Children Learn from Failure

One of the best feedback devices we have is failure. When we try something and it doesn't work, that's clear feedback. Of course, children need an array of positive experiences every day of their lives. However, in the name of success we sometimes go overboard in protecting children from failure, thus cutting them off from valuable learning experiences.

Watch this video to hear parents and experts share their view about praise and failure. Are there ideas that you agree with?

www.youtube.com /watch?v=z8MM9XB5Li0

The problem with failure is that it often comes accompanied with heavy value judgments, spoken or unspoken. For example, many of us were called "dummy," or something comparable, as children when we made a mistake. It's hard not to pass on that kind of response to children when they make mistakes if that is the way we were treated. However, if children are to learn from mistakes as well as emerge from failure with an intact sense of self-worth, it is important that adults be supportive rather than critical. After all, a mistake is just that. We all make them, and we all stand to learn from them.

Carole Dweck in her book *Mindset* (2007) writes about the value of making mistakes. Some of her studies were about the difference between children who are willing to take on hard tasks even when failure is a real possibility and those who avoid anything they think they won't do well at. Studying preschoolers she discovered when given a choice of a hard puzzle or an easy one, some picked the easy one. It didn't take much to finish the puzzle and though they didn't seem to get much satisfaction, they were clear that their choice was the right one. Observing the children who picked the hard one—even the ones who failed to finish it—she noted that they seemed to like the difficult tasks and obviously got something out of the experience. They were clear that they had made a good choice. Those children seemed to thrive on being challenged no matter the end result. Dweck used the terms *fixed mindset* to describe the first children and *growth mindset* to describe the second group. Children with a fixed mindset were the ones who worried about mistakes and failures and suffered when they occurred. They were continually trying to validate themselves, to prove that they were capable. Those children were a contrast to the students who seemed to see mistakes and failure as paths to learning. They valued learning more than outcomes. "Well, that didn't work" is the attitude of a person with a growth mindset, who then goes on to try something else.

This is a huge subject, but boiled down, if you want to develop a growth mindset in children, avoid praising children for their intelligence, ability, products, or outcomes. Focus instead on their effort. Say, "You tried really hard. I notice you just kept at it and didn't give up." If you say, "You are really smart," you may be leading them toward a fixed mindset. Watch out for complimenting outcomes. For example, "What a beautiful painting!" leads to a fixed mindset and has a different effect from describing what you see without putting value judgments on the end product. "I notice you put these large brush strokes next to the very small ones." Or, for example, you might say, "You used a lot of colors in this painting and I saw how you kept working on it for a long time!" (which leads to a growth mindset).

Helping families understand the value of a growth mindset can make a huge difference in their lives and those of their children. Everyone stands to gain!

> ✓ **Check Your Understanding 10.2**
> Click here to check your understanding ways to encourage children's development of self-esteem.

CELEBRATING DIFFERENCES: AN ANTI-BIAS APPROACH

How adults react to differences in people affects how children react to differences, which influences self-esteem. Louise Derman-Sparks (1989), well-known faculty member at Pacific Oaks College in Pasadena, California, and her anti-bias curriculum task force have brought awareness to issues of bias that were hidden from many until recently. Their latest anti-bias book is called *Anti-bias Education* (Derman-Sparks & Edwards, 2010). Updated and expanded, it now puts more attention on adults working on their own biases instead of just focusing on the children's.

Derman-Sparks says her son's experience was "the initial spark" that got her started. A biracial child, he was already making comments by the age of two that indicated he was aware of skin color and, even more surprising to his mother, asking questions that revealed he was affected by racial prejudice. She says, "I was shocked at how early this began—and then angry when I faced that, as a practicing early childhood educator with a Masters Degree from a highly thought-of university, I knew nothing about the process of identity and attitude development" (personal communication, July 21, 2011). So, her long career of advocacy for anti-bias education began. See the Advocacy in Action feature "Giving an Idea Life" for what Derman-Sparks did besides teaching about anti-bias and writing books and articles on the subject.

The tendency in early childhood education and mainstream cultural child rearing has been to be blind to both privilege and injustice. The motto of many is that "Children are children," by which they mean differences such as skin color and gender don't matter (although the expression "Boys will be boys" dispels the gender-blindness myth). Many people who are "blind" to differences are those who don't carry the bruises and scars left by unfortunate remarks and by the biased behavior of those who promote stereotypes and practice unfair treatment. Conscious and unconscious racism, classism, sexism, and ableism are areas of bias still with us in spite of the fact that many assume that the way to equity is to ignore differences.

> Many people who are "blind" to differences are those who don't carry the bruises and scars left by unfortunate remarks and by the biased behavior of those who promote stereotypes and practice unfair treatment.

ADVOCACY IN ACTION ▶ GIVING AN IDEA LIFE

Louise Derman-Sparks, *author and advocate*

Writing books on anti-bias education isn't enough. I wanted to bring the mission, goals, and ideas of anti-bias education to life. Just as it takes a village to raise a child, it takes a large, committed national village to create specific changes related to equity in early childhood education.

Once I became known for anti-bias work, opportunities opened up for presenting keynotes and workshops at early childhood conferences in most states in the United States. This made it possible to both share my thinking about anti-bias education and also learn from the many thousands of people with whom I have talked over the years. To do that I brought people together in support groups and networks so they could work collaboratively for change in their ECE programs and in the ECE field.

I encouraged and worked with people to build anti-bias education teacher support groups and networks of early childhood educators, so that they could work collaboratively for change in their ECE programs and in the ECE field. The work of committed educators has brought—and is bringing—life to the ideas of anti-bias education and positive change in programs for children and families. This work has grown in scope and depth as people have used and adapted its goals and principles to a wide range of differing historic and cultural contexts throughout the United States and in many countries internationally. Supporters have also built diversity/equity early childhood education networks in many countries.

I hope the day will come when the "anti-bias" part is no longer needed because all children are growing up fully nurtured and able to be fully who they are, with no barriers of prejudice, discrimination, poverty, or war. Then learning about and valuing one another's diversity will be a natural part of growing up. Until that day comes, we must keep on keeping on providing children with strong, culturally appropriate anti-bias education and keeping faith in the possibility of positive change—in ourselves, in others, in our programs, and with other adults to make positive change in our larger society.

Instead of disregarding differences, we should celebrate them. "Celebrate differences"—what does that mean? A loving attempt to do just that occurs regularly, as well-meaning adults bring "culture" into children's lives in order to teach them about people who are different from themselves. I remember a Japanese "tea party" put on in the classroom of one of my children. I attended as a parent guest and happened to sit next to a Japanese parent, who was also a guest. She was aghast at what she saw. "There's nothing Japanese about this!" she whispered to me, insulted by the whole proceeding. What had happened was that the teacher, based on what she had read and on her own ideas, had created a strange conglomeration of stereotypes and fantasy, which she believed was promoting cultural knowledge in the children.

Michael Dorris, in an article titled "Why I'm *Not* Thankful for Thanksgiving" (2011), wrote about this phenomenon as it occurs with Native American children who may know nothing about their own heritage other than the mistaken stereotypes they encounter everywhere. Stereotypes of fighting savages come televised year-round from sports arenas across the country. Thanksgiving arrives every year, and cute little savages come out of the woodwork and get pinned on the bulletin boards, complete with feathers and tomahawks. Throughout the rest of the year, children are told not to act like "wild Indians" (a stereotype) but to sit quietly "Indian-style" (another stereotype) and sing songs that are deeply insulting to Native Americans, such as "Ten Little Indians" (dehumanizing). Those once-common expressions are beginning to change. For example, I hear preschool teachers now saying "Criss-cross, applesauce" instead of "sit Indian style." The question is how much those childhood sayings affected how Native American parents felt about themselves. The other question is, how can anybody's children get a sense of who they are and of their worth if their culture is stereotyped, devalued, and misrepresented?

Many mistakes and insults occur in the name of "celebrating differences." What is largely unrecognized or at least little discussed is that differences are connected with privilege and power. Differences carry values. It shouldn't be that way, but it is; and until that fact is recognized, there is little hope for change. That's where the anti-bias approach comes in. Adults must begin to recognize that value messages, both spoken and unspoken, are constantly sent and received about color, language, gender, and differences in physical abilities. Once adults become aware of the messages, they can begin to intercept them and change things. They can talk about what the media brings into the home. They can point out bias. They can stop teaching children to ignore differences and instead teach them to respond positively and appropriately to differences.

Bias Can Hurt

Although bias is natural, it can be bad for children and bad for adults. It's obviously bad for those who are the target of bias. It not only harms self-esteem but also sucks energy from the developmental process. It hurts to feel inferior. To be disempowered influences your life course.

But bias is also bad for those who are regarded as superior. When you see others as beneath you, you're out of touch with reality. It's dehumanizing to act superior and to enjoy unearned privilege, even when you are not aware of what's happening (Derman-Sparks, 1989; Howard, 1999).

It may seem easier to just pretend we're all alike in the name of equality. It may be easier to say to someone who is a different color than you are, "I don't think of you as different from me." But we're not all alike, and to pretend we are is to ignore the truth. That kind of ignorance can be very insulting. If you are a woman, how would you like it if a man said to you, "I never think of you as female," meaning that remark as a compliment? Personally, I would be shocked if someone looked at me and didn't see me as a female. If you are a man, reverse the situation. Can you imagine yourself without your maleness? What if someone thought it was a compliment to you to remain ignorant of the fact that you are a male? How would you feel?

> It may seem easier to just pretend we're all alike in the name of equality. It may be easier to say to someone who is a different color than you are, "I don't think of you as different from me." But we're not all alike, and to pretend we are is to ignore the truth. That kind of ignorance can be very insulting.

People want others to respond to who they are—not some blind, misguided version of who they should be. They want to be valued for who they are. For example, we would all be very uncomfortable around those who pretend to be "gender-blind," if, indeed, such a thing is even possible. But adults pretend to be "color-blind" all the time in the name of equity. *Discriminating* on the basis of skin color is immoral. *Recognizing differences* in skin color is not, as long as you don't present one color as better than another.

People with disabilities also face these same problems, and any anti-bias approach should include them as well. Children need to learn to appreciate people for who they are and respond respectfully. The push now is for inclusion of children with disabilities into programs of all kinds where their typically developing peers are (California Department of Education, 2009). Inclusion is good for everybody as children have opportunities to get to know people who don't have the same abilities that they have. Inclusion also means that adults have to ensure that all children are treated fairly and with respect. They have to teach all children to get along with each other in the face of what may be big differences in ability. It's good learning for citizenship in a diverse society.

So, how can you teach children to respond positively in the face of differences if they've been taught to be blind to them? How can they respond positively if they've been exposed to biased attitudes and behaviors?

Start by modeling *anti-bias* behaviors. Become aware that the white able-bodied male is a privileged group. That's the group that traditionally has had the power in society. We need to get beyond that societal bias. Acknowledge the existence and experience of others by creating an anti-bias environment; expose children to pictures, books, and experiences of adults and children both like themselves and unlike themselves.

Point out stereotypes in the media when they occur. For example, when a book or a TV program shows weak, helpless women in limited roles, remark about the fact that women can be strong, intelligent people capable of doing many things.

Make it clear that bias is unacceptable. Children understand the concept of fair and unfair. Bias is definitely not fair. It is only fair that people of all races, religions, cultures, and physical abilities be treated with equal respect. It is only fair that both genders be allowed and indeed encouraged to expand beyond the limits of narrow gender roles. It is not fair to exclude someone from playing because of skin color, gender, or ability. Children need to understand that biased behavior is unacceptable.

Watch this video to hear children's ideas of race relations. Are you surprised by any of their comments? Can you think of a way that an anti-bias approach might change some of the children's perspectives?

www.youtube.com
/watch?v=GPVNJgfDwpw

Cultural Differences and Self-Esteem

Who am I? Each of us continues to explore that question throughout our lifetime. The answer we come up with and the value judgment we make about that answer make up our self-esteem.

As children grow, they develop an idea of themselves. This idea influences the behavior of the actual self—the one that operates in the world. The actual self in turn influences the self-concept, which continues to influence behavior. Thus, the actual self and the self-concept are forever tied together, and self-esteem grows from the interaction of the two.

Self-esteem is culturally based and depends on the basic concept of what makes up a person. As stated earlier, one culture looks at each person as a unique, potentially self-sufficient individual; another de-emphasizes individuality and regards each person as an inseparable part of a greater whole. How parents focus their socialization efforts depends on which view they take.

An example that illustrates this point is how two people answer the question "Who are you?" As one talks about herself, she points out her personal characteristics and lists her roles and her accomplishments. She is emphasizing her individuality. The other one answers it by explaining her family lineage. She explains herself by pointing out relationships and ignoring individual accomplishments. A native Hawaiian person explained to me how hard it was to fill out an application for the university that asked her to list her achievements. "That's not who I am," she said. Instead she wanted to explain all the people she was related to in her family, including her ancestors.

Parents whose goal is individualism see their baby arriving in the world connected and dependent. The responsibility of the parent then is to help the baby learn that he or she is separate and apart. So those parents concentrate their efforts on autonomy, stressing self-help skills as the baby is ready. "I can do it all by myself" is music to their ears.

Parents who are more concerned about their children's ability to maintain connections have a different goal. They perceive an independent streak in their baby and see that independence as getting in the way of the close lifelong relationship to family that is their goal. So they focus on showing the baby in every way that dependence is a value and relates to connections—the greatest value. They know that some independence is inevitable, but they want to be sure that the baby is forever connected before he discovers autonomy. These parents focus on interdependence instead of independence. They are more likely to help the baby and young child than to teach self-help skills. They are not eager for the young child to brag, "I can do it all by myself."

How you build self-esteem in the early years is influenced by your view of the individual. However, realize that both views are valid, and they are not mutually exclusive. It isn't an either-or situation. When two people disagree about which is most important—individuality or group embeddedness—it's a matter of *where* they are placing the emphasis and *when* they see independence as an issue. It isn't independence versus interdependence. We all need both to survive. It is a matter of timing. One person may see the importance of *early* independence and its relationship to later getting along in a group. Another may perceive that only through subduing early independent urges can the child be truly part of the group, which will *later* lead to his or her developing or finding the *individual* skills, feelings, dreams, and desires that contribute to furthering group goals.

A valid goal of self-esteem is to enable children to stand on their own two feet as well as to stand together—indeed, lean on each other. It is important to get and give support and to feel good about it.

A True Story from the Author

When I was a new teacher faced with the job of educating parents, I had great enthusiasm for sharing all that I had learned in my teacher training, plus what I knew from experience. My energy was boundless, matched only by my zeal.

I will never forget trying to explain the concept of self-esteem to Teresa, a Mexican immigrant mother. Teresa kept insisting that there was no such concept in Spanish. I didn't give up. I kept trying to explain it to her. She stood there the whole time with a blank look on her face. She wasn't getting it. Finally she said in complete bewilderment, *"Self-esteem* doesn't make any sense at all. You can't esteem yourself; you can only esteem others."

I've been thinking about that exchange for many years. She didn't get what I was saying, but I didn't get what she was saying, either.

I've become less zealous in my parent education efforts as I've gotten older. I am much more willing to accept parents as they are; and if they want to "get better," I'll help—but only when I know what they perceive their weaknesses to be. Mainly I just support them in the good things they are doing. I don't decide where they need to improve; that's their decision. I help parents sort out what isn't working for them rather than tell them what I think and give advice. My motto is: The less advice the better.

But I still try to teach concepts. Although self-esteem is one concept I haven't given up on, I've broadened my view of what I mean when I define self-esteem. I include the fact that though the concept fits European American culture, it probably doesn't fit everybody in the same way.

That's why I am not surprised when my students and I don't agree on what the term *self-esteem* means. For example, a student described a child who thought only of himself, never of others. He had a fierce temper and got out of control when he didn't get his way. He even hit his parents. His parents' efforts to guide his behavior didn't work. This boy didn't get along with anybody and didn't have any friends, either.

The student concluded that the child's problem was his self-esteem; he had too much of it. That isn't the way I see self-esteem. You can't get too much. When you have a good strong sense of self-worth, you are more able to see others as being worthy, too. That's the point. Esteem breeds esteem.

Maybe it was just a translation problem with this student. Like Teresa, this student was a Spanish speaker. However, I suspect that it wasn't a simple language difference. I believe our mismatch went deeper than that.

I decided to start with language as the path to understanding. I looked in my husband's huge Spanish-English dictionary. It had 196 entries under *self* in English and only 13 entries in Spanish. The concept of "self" is different in Spanish, and that difference influences the way people feel about the term *self-esteem*.

My experience with some parents, especially those from cultures where interdependence is more important than independence, is that focusing on "self" is a negative thing to do. To them, any word that has *self* connected to it is suspicious. They don't want to raise "self-ish" children. They want to raise children who put others first and think of themselves last.

I didn't understand that when I was trying to teach Teresa about self-esteem. I did understand it when I read my student's self-esteem paper, and so I put less effort into trying to teach her my way of looking at self-esteem and more into trying to understand her way.

Values show through misunderstandings. Every day I live I discover new ways of conceiving reality. The older I get the less I try to change people in general and parents in particular, and the more I try to tune in on their realities.

This chapter so far has focused a great deal on self-esteem, what it is, and how to build it in children. It also took a good look at some cultural issues around the concept of self-esteem. It took a little side trip into mindsets, which are related in some ways to self-concept and self-esteem. Now it's time to focus on relating to families when it comes to focusing on self-esteem in children. The approach I am taking is to look at *affirmations* as a way of building relationships with families. Affirmations are those positive messages that validate the person or the family. Affirmations encourage people to be who they are. Telling parents you appreciate them says you have positive feelings about their existence. Affirmations focus on strengths and encourage parents to see how they *can be* while accepting how they *are* at the present. Affirmations can create self-fulfilling prophecies that have a positive effect.

An interesting experiment done on children back in the 1960s shows the power of expectations (Rosenthal, 1987). In this study, teachers were shown a list of children who were expected to have a "growth spurt" within the school year. In reality the students were randomly selected. But guess what! Those selected students did show remarkable improvement, while the others didn't. What adults believe about children and what they *expect* from them tends to come true, as they send children messages, both verbal and nonverbal. Those messages, even the ones sent unconsciously, influence children's behavior and performance.

Think about how this study might apply to adults as well. If you regard each parent in a positive light and focus on strengths instead of deficits, you not only strengthen the relationship between the two of you, but you also support that parent in being the best he or she can be.

It has been said that you can't give something that you don't have. Self-esteem falls into that category. There is a direct relationship between the amount of self-esteem adults have and their ability to enhance the self-esteem of the children in their lives, but of course, there are more influences than just parents. Consider once again Bronfenbrenner's ecological systems model. The child lives in a whole context consisting of layers of influences.

It's worth noting that the messages we give as adults are strongly influenced by the ones we've been given as children. Often we are unaware of the connection. We don't even know that messages we carry with us are left over from our childhood. And we, too, of course, like today's children, have been influenced by the whole context we grew up in, including the different era.

In my family when I was growing up in my grandparents' house, we had a joke, but we sort of believed it. My grandmother had a mean stepmother (her perception, I never met the woman; she died long before I was born). We used to speculate that we would all be more psychologically sound if only Grandma's sainted mother had lived to raise her. How much were we influenced by the reality and how much by the wicked stepmother of fairy tales? Though it was only a joke, we were ignoring all the other influences on the three generations of females who lived in that house. Certainly the era and society each generation was born into was a big influence.

So how do we get in touch with the messages we have all been given and still carry with us? One way is to become aware of the voices floating around in your head—the ones that praise, criticize, and tell you how you should act. These voices create what's been called a *life script*. They have influenced you to be who you are. Once you understand the concept of the influence of early messages, you can use this concept to guide you in responding to children and their families in positive ways rather than haphazardly giving out messages that may be negative.

Changing Negative Messages to Positive Ones

If you're walking around with mostly negative messages in your head, it will be hard for you to give out the positive messages

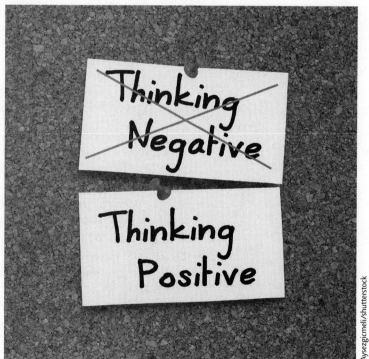

Get rid of those negative message you are carrying around with you

that children need. So I have a suggestion: Get rid of those negative messages you're carrying around with you.

One way to do that is to become aware of the voices and to write down their messages—all of them, the negative ones and the positive ones. If you write each one on a separate slip of paper, eventually you'll have an array of messages. Once you have collected at least 10, sit down and sort them out. Put the negative ones in one pile, the positive ones in another, and any that are a mixture in a third pile. Then take the mixture pile and rewrite those messages so they have a positive effect in your life. Put them in the positive pile. Now take the negative messages and see whether you can rewrite some of those as well. Perhaps you can't. Set aside those you can't rewrite and put the rewritten ones in the positive pile.

Now it's time to deal with the negative messages you're stuck with. Start by spreading them out in front of you. Take fresh slips of paper and write down some positive messages—ones you'd like to hear. Write one for each of the negative messages in front of you.

Once you have replaced those negative messages with some positive ones, pick up each negative piece of paper, tear it up, and throw it away! Make a big deal out of this act of discarding. As you tear up the paper, think about the conscious choice you have made not to listen to that message anymore. Although we can't program other people, we *can* reprogram ourselves!

Imagine yourself as you can be without those negative messages telling you how you are, directing your actions, and creating your personality. Put a picture in your mind of the *new you* acting in accordance with the stack of positive messages you have at your fingertips. Carry that picture with you. Accept it as true. Review the positive messages regularly. Take charge of your life! You can make choices about who you are and how you act. This exercise was inspired by Jean Illsley Clarke in her book *Self-Esteem: A Family Affair* (1998). If you found that it worked for you, consider using it with the parents you work with. See Strategy Box 10.1 for more strategies for working with parents around issues of self-esteem.

Strategy Box 10.1

Working with Families around Issues of Self-Esteem

• Seek to understand each family's view of self-esteem and determine whether your program is giving contradictory messages to children. It's important to be open to differences and to figure out what to do about them in collaboration with families.

• Practice giving affirmations to parents as a means of supporting their strengths and building relationships along those lines. Don't use this as a mere technique, but put your heart into it.

• Be aware of the power of self-fulfilling prophecies for children and for parents. Make sure you take a positive view of everyone in your program, children and adults alike.

• If you have trouble giving positive messages because of your own negative messages from your early years, try the activity suggested on pages 237–238. If it works for you, try it at a parent meeting.

While you are supporting children and parents to be the best they can be, also work on yourself. And while you are doing that, figure out ways to nurture yourself—and encourage parents to do the same. One way is to give nurturing and then leave room for reciprocation. (I'll scratch your back if you scratch mine.) If reciprocation isn't forthcoming, ask for it. This is risky business because if you ask, you might be turned down. However, asking is still a good approach, because unless we tell others our needs, they'll never know about them. When my last son was born 13 weeks early and was hovering between life and death in intensive care, friends said, "What can we do for you?" My first response was, "Oh, nothing." But then I thought about it and said, "Feed us." And they did. Every day when we came home from our lengthy and frustrating visits at the hospital, there was a cardboard box on our doorstep with a full meal inside it. What a blessing! Without our friends we would have lived on fast food and snacks. Not only the nourishment was important to us, but also the message that we were cared about—cared for. We needed that during that period!

We all need affirmations all the time, not just during crisis periods. Let's learn to give them so we can get them, and to get them so we can give them.

> **Check Your Understanding 10.3**
>
> Click here to check your understanding of celebrating differences using an anti-bias approach.

SUMMARY

The chapter started by exploring what the term *self-esteem* means, first by describing a portrait of a person with high self-esteem and then defining self-esteem. Next came a discussion of four dimensions of self-esteem. The chapter then explored the role of beliefs and expectations in self-esteem and where self-esteem comes from. Promoting self-esteem was the next section—with some "how-to" suggestions. A section of how children learn from failure brought up Carol Dweck's research on mindsets. The chapter ended by looking at the role of bias in self-esteem and explained how to celebrate differences by using an anti-bias approach.

QUIZ

Click here to check your understanding of Chapter 10, "Working with Families to Support Self-Esteem."

FOR DISCUSSION

1. How much does self-esteem show? Is it easy to tell who has high self-esteem and who doesn't? The text says that people aren't always what they seem. Do you believe that statement? Has that been your experience? Do you have some examples to back up your opinion?

2. Building self-esteem in a child involves a collaboration, not a deception. What does that sentence mean? What are some ways to collaborate with a child to help build self-esteem? What are some ways to help a child change a bad feeling about herself to a good feeling?

3. No matter what hand fate deals, it's not the events themselves that determine self-esteem; it's how the individual reacts to those events. Explain. Do you

agree? If that is the case, how can adults help children who consistently have reactions that indicate low self-esteem?

4. What effect do bias and stereotyping have on self-esteem? Do you think that children in target groups for bias automatically have low self-esteem? Why or why not?

5. How do labels relate to self-fulfilling prophecy? Can you give examples from your own experience?

6. What are some perspectives that may differ greatly from the information presented in this chapter? Can you explain at least one?

WEBSITES

Cyberparent
Cyberparent is a website with links to a collection of magazines on different subjects. Some of the Cyberparent site's subjects include: listening and self-esteem, the language of self-esteem, and the relationship of discipline to self-esteem.

KidsHealth
The KidsHealth website describes how healthy self-esteem helps children face challenges and conflicts and resist negative pressures. It also discusses how to foster self-esteem in infants and young children.

National Association for the Education of Young Children (NAEYC)
The National Association for the Education of Young Children has a number of resources available for parents and professionals, including books and journals, one of which is called *Young Children*, and regularly has articles on building self-esteem in children.

National Association for Self-Esteem
The National Association for Self-Esteem website outlines the history, aims, and objectives of this organization and gives information about its programs.

Shyness Institute
The Shyness Institute is a nonprofit research corporation. Their website is for people seeking information and services for shyness, social anxiety and related anxiety disorders.

FURTHER READING

Castro, D. C., Ayankoya, B., & Kasprzak, C. (2011). *The New Voices/Nuevas Voces guide to cultural and linguistic diversity in early childhood.* Baltimore, MD: Brookes.

Day, C. B. (2013). Culture and identity development: Getting infants and toddlers off to a great start. In E. Virmani & P. Mangione (Eds.). *A guide to culturally sensitive care* (2nd ed., pp. 2–12). Sacramento CA: California Department of Education.

Derman-Sparks, L., & Edwards, J. O. (2010). *Anti-bias education for young children and ourselves.* Washington, DC: National Association for the Education of Young Children.

Egertson, H. A. (2006, November). Of primary interest. In praise of butterflies: Linking self-esteem and learning. *Young Children, 61*(6), 58–60.

Espinosa, L. (2015). *Getting it right for young children from diverse backgrounds: Applying research to improve practice with a focus on dual-language learners.* Upper Saddle River, NJ: Pearson.

Greenwald, D., & J. Weaver (2013). *The RIE manual for parents and professionals,* (2nd ed.). Los Angeles, CA: Resources for Infant Educarers.

Halvorson, H. (2012). *Nine things successful people do differently.* Boston: Harvard Business School.

Marshall, E., & Sensoy, O. (Eds.). (2011). *Rethinking popular culture and media*. Milwaukee, WI: Rethinking Schools.

Pierce, J., & Johnson, C. L. (2010, November). Problem solving with young children using persona dolls. *Young Children*, 65(6), 106–108.

Tough, P. (2012). *How children succeed*. Boston, MA: Houghton, Mifflin, Harcourt.

Wanerman, T., & Roffman, L. (2011). *Including one, including all: A guide to relationship-based early childhood inclusion*. St. Paul, MN: Redleaf Press.

Ronnie Kaufman/Larry Hirshowitz/Gettyimages

Working with Families around Gender Issues

Learning Outcomes

In this chapter you will learn to...

- Explain why it is important to think about teaching gender roles.
- Discuss gender equity and parenting.
- Discuss differential socialization.

WHY IT IS IMPORTANT TO THINK ABOUT TEACHING GENDER ROLES

What is gender and how is it different from sex? Sex is biological. The sex of a person has to do with body parts, that is, the physical organs that distinguish males from females. Sex is also an activity. The term gender is a social term and differs depending upon culture or an individual or a family's ideas. In most cases the society defines the roles of what it means to be masculine and feminine and includes ideas about appropriate appearance, attitudes, and behaviors. In some societies masculinity and femininity are very strictly defined and regulated, in others they are more fluid and differences are not only accepted but honored. Ideas about sex and gender roles change, and this particular period (as this book is being revised) is a time when the changes are talked about in the USA more than in the past. Further, we as a society are beginning to understand how complex the subjects of sex and gender are even though the definitions in this paragraph seem clear enough.

 Watch this video about human sexuality to hear some rapid-fire definitions of terms.

www.youtube.com /watch?v=xXAoG8vAyzI

Issues around Gender Roles

We live with many misconceptions concerning gender roles. It may seem as though gender roles come automatically when children are born—and to some extent that is true. Shaping a gender role may even start prenatally because parents usually know the sex of their baby *before* birth. Sex and gender roles may be expected to coincide, but that is not always so. For example, in some cases, a child of one sex may be socialized to be the opposite gender (Money & Ehrhardt, 1973). In other cases the child socialized in the gender that matches his or her sex may reject that socialization and feel more like the opposite gender. Today gender is considered more fluid by some (not all) and variations are sometimes accepted by families who feel they understand their child. The society as a whole may not be ready for gender fluidity, but it is becoming more obvious than in the days when it was hidden. There is an organization called Gender Spectrum, in San Francisco, California, that serves as a resource for information about gender and gender fluidity.

Watch this video to hear Dr. Diane Ehrensaft discuss the gender spectrum.

www.youtube.com /watch?v=HpE3d69SiDU

When we look at the socialization of males and females, it may seem as if boys and girls simply learn their respective roles and that's all there is to it. Obviously that's not all there is to it. What are those respective roles? That's a huge question. It's also important to recognize that, while learning is taking place, physiology is also contributing to male/female differences. Exposure to hormones during pregnancy, genetic influences, and other biological factors can influence the development of sexual identity and gender roles. There is a dispute about the degree to which differences are learned and the degree to which physiology influences how children see themselves and what skills they develop. We're still working on answering that question. Science swings back and forth on this issue: Some research seems to show that many of the differences between males and females are biologically determined, while other research emphasizes the role of differential socialization.

A piece of research reported in the Science and Technology section of *The Economist* (2007) comes out on the side of socialization. The article explains a test called "odd man out," which is designed to rate people's ability to spot unusual objects that appear in their field of vision. Men had a 68 percent success rate while women had a 55 percent success rate. It seemed to be a natural difference, so the researchers took it a step further and had one group of volunteers spend 10 hours playing a video game described as "an action-packed, shoot-'em-up" game. The control group played a calm, non-action-packed video game called "Ballance" for 10 hours. When retested on the odd-man-out test, both sexes who played the action-packed game improved their scores but the women's improvement was greater and it brought them up to the same average score as the men. The gains lasted, too—after five months these women scored the same as the men. The Ballance players showed no improvement in their ability to spot unusual objects. So it seems as if this difference isn't biologically determined, but is probably learned.

Research in the 1960s and 1970s also supported socialization. Money and Ehrhardt (1973), who did some rather startling research then, were convinced that they had proven that babies are born gender-neutral and can be assigned one gender or the other without harmful effect. These gender assignments were done to children with ambiguous external genitalia. Sometimes the assignments were wrong. Hormonal corrections were made at puberty when the mistake was discovered, so that the child could continue in the previously assigned gender role to which he or she had been socialized. Other times the assignments were made when something went wrong with a circumcision and a boy would then be castrated and raised as a girl. The research seemed to show that gender roles are more learned than they are natural. In other words, in spite of the fact that genetically the child was a boy, being socialized as a girl made him exhibit typically female behavior.

The case of a person named "Joan" disputed this research. In an article called "A Boy Without a Penis," Gorman (1997) tells the story of Joan, named by researchers Milton Diamond and Keith Sigmundson in a follow-up study that looked at the long-term effects of assigning gender. The baby, a male, was surgically made into a female after a botched circumcision destroyed the penis. The article relates the agonies Joan went through rebelling against the gender assignment she was given. She knew she was a boy, but no one would confirm that. In 1977 at the age of 14, Joan decided she had only two options, to commit suicide or live life as a male. When she confronted her father with her decision, he finally told her the truth, and a sex change operation eventually gave her a body to go with her identity. To what extent are gender roles learned and to what extent are they natural? No one has the final answer to that question yet. That was only the beginning. More cases of babies who were assigned gender at birth have come forth with their distress since Joan suffered with his/her assignment.

Here's a different subject related to gender roles and sexual orientation. How does growing up in a family with same-sex parents affect gender roles and the sexual orientation of the children? Studies suggest that what children learn about gender roles in heterosexual families isn't significantly different from what children learn in gay and lesbian families. Further, there is no evidence to suggest that children reared in same-sex families are more likely to develop a gay or lesbian sexual orientation. Their gender-role behavior and sexual orientation are similar to children reared in heterosexual households.

No matter what is discovered about gender roles and sexual orientation, we still have equity issues to consider. We know that the adults in young children's lives have a great influence over their gender-role socialization and their attitudes about same-sex families. What are some ways that these adults can help children accept each other and honor the family that each comes from? How can adults empower both boys and girls? How can they promote equality of development for both sexes? With stereotypes still such a part of all of our lives, how can adults counteract stereotypes and help boys learn that they can express feelings and be nurturing if they don't already? How can adults help girls learn to be independent, assertive, and capable problem solvers, if they don't already have those traits? What can adults do to enable each child to fulfill his or her own potential rather than grow up bound by restrictive gender roles?

Some History Related to Genderized Clothing

One of the simpler issues relates to clothing. Today boys who desire to take on feminine clothes, styles, and activities are becoming more determined and more visible. Interestingly enough, nobody worries about girls or women wearing pants—that custom started during World War II, perhaps because women were working in factories taking the jobs men left when they got drafted into the military. Maybe that's when looking at a girl as a tomboy wasn't an insult. When a boy is called a sissy—ouch! That nickname is designed to be hurtful. There have always been children who rejected typical gender behaviors, but there are more boys wearing dresses now than in the past (New York Times Magazine, 2012).

Clothing may or may not relate to gender fluidity. I've lived long enough to see

There is no evidence to suggest that children reared in same-sex families are more likely to develop a gay or lesbian sexual orientation; their gender-role behavior and sexual orientation are similar to children reared in heterosexual households

zoomyimages/Fotolia.

huge swings in changes in clothing styles. There was a time in the late 1960s and 1970s when "unisex" was in and boys and girls wore many of the same clothes. Try Googling "unisex fashions in the 1970s" and you can see examples. Sex and gender were not distinguished by colors or styles. It was also a period when many boys wore long hair. It may be hard to realize that there was a time back half a century ago when a boy's haircut started above the ears and was buzzed at the neck. The boy was considered very strange if it didn't. But in the '70s with the unisex clothing styles, long hair for boys was common. One of my sons was in elementary school in that period. He had beautiful curly hair that hung down to his shoulders. One day he came home from school talking about a new boy who was in his class. He had a distressed look on his face as he told the story of playing with the boy at every recess and then found out at the end of the day that the boy thought he was a girl! Yes, he looked like a girl in his unisex clothes and his beautiful hair and sweet face, but his identity was clearly male! He was shocked to be mis-identified because of his appearance and clothing. That was a period of abandoning strict gender roles in children and is quite a contrast to today when so many little girls want nothing more than to dress like and become Disney princesses. Is the idea of boys wanting to wear dresses today different from girls who wear pants, or the unisex clothing trend in the '70s? Maybe...

If there is one important message to come out of this chapter, it's that we must continue to guard against children's lives being shaped by restrictive gender roles, myths about a child's capabilities based on gender, and laws, both written and unwritten, that work against gender equity. We need to move forward and learn lessons from our history. It's important to realize that for a long period at the beginning of our country, only men (white men) had power and privilege. Now that it is written that all of us have power and privilege, let's make sure that's the case! We have the socialization of children in our hands. Let's see how we can make a difference when we work with families and their children around gender issues.

Equity Issues and Gender Roles

There are many hot issues about gender roles. What many people don't think about when they accept traditional gender roles as a given is how narrow and confining these roles can be to children, who grow into adults molded into a role they may not fit at all. Many don't consider how unfair, to both men and women, traditional gender roles can be. The unfairness shows up when we look backward at history to a time when women were clearly considered inferior to men and therefore had few rights as citizens. It's hard to believe that people are still alive today who were born in the days when women in the United States couldn't vote. It may be startling to realize that although the women's rights movement started in 1838, it wasn't until 82 years later that women gained the right to vote. And the right was won only for some women. Others, because of the color of their skin or their lack of education, faced literacy and education taxes, intimidation, and violence at the polls. These women were kept from voting for almost half a century longer, until the passage of the 1964 Voting Rights Act and its 1974 amendments. Even when all citizens gained voting rights, some (both women and men, too) still encountered barriers when trying to register or enter the polls. That situation isn't history—it has happened in every election up to the time this book was revised. Imagine having no say in your government just because you happened to be born female (of any race) instead of male and white. And speaking of discrimination, also imagine, if you can, a woman being considered her husband's property along with his children and cattle. We think those times are long gone in the United States, but remember, each generation is socialized into gender roles, and all the steps toward gender equity could disappear if we don't continue to think carefully about how we socialize boys and girls.

The Women of Today

Every U.S. citizen—male and female—has the right to vote now (even though some still face significant barriers) but life's still no bed of roses for many. Considering women, many African American, Hispanic American, Native American, Asian American, and immigrant women are still undereducated and work in hard jobs for low

The Woman Suffrage photo, taken in 1912, shows how women were fighting for the right to vote, and trying to educate men on why women should vote. Not all women agreed with this idea, as the "Vote No" photo next to it suggests. This is an example of limited and confining gender roles—the idea that a woman could not be "home loving" and also participate in voting.

wages while trying to care for their families (as do numbers of European American women). Women still earn less for equal work than men do (Hegewisch et al., 2014). Barriers still exist for women who are exploring nontraditional jobs and who are struggling to reach higher in the business world. In many arenas, the "glass ceiling" that keeps women at a lower level than men is still in place. Although women have worked their way into most professions, it is still a little surprising when flying to hear a woman's voice from the cockpit say, "This is your captain speaking."

Some of the advances in the cause of equality came about with a lot of effort from the women themselves as well as an organized women's movement with national leaders and lots of publicity. Take, for instance, the issue of domestic violence. In living memory of some of us "older people," there was a time when nobody seemed to care what happened to a woman in her own home. Battered wives who tried to get help had problems making authorities listen—just as originally the only laws protecting battered children were those enacted by the SPCA (American Bar Association, 2008). Believe it or not, animal abuse was illegal more than half a century before child abuse was and spousal abuse laws occurred even later. Times have changed. Now there are not only legal avenues for battered women but also means of protecting them in their own communities. The Advocacy in Action feature "Communicating Concerns" tells a story of a teacher who didn't set out to be an advocate. She only commented on what she observed and was concerned about, but her action may well have saved a child from a life of fear and sorrow. It may even have saved the life of the child's mother. The teacher's concern gave a strong message to a mother who then made an important decision to protect herself and her child.

ADVOCACY IN ACTION ▶ **COMMUNICATING CONCERNS**

Marion Cowee, early childhood educator

I noticed three-year-old Alice was often berated by her friend Evan at preschool. He would yell at her and then sit on her and keep yelling at her and she would do nothing, no crying, no struggling. As teachers, we separated the two and used appropriate guidance for both children. But I was concerned. It is not very often that you see a young child not try to defend herself and not be willing to say that she is being wronged. The next morning after a particularly bad day, I asked Alice's mom to have a little conference with me; I shared that I was concerned that Alice was being mistreated by her friend and that she would do nothing about it. Alice's mom listened but couldn't offer up any insights or solutions. The next day Alice did not come to school; in fact, she didn't come for a week, then two weeks. Later on, I found out that Alice and Alice's mom had moved to a safe house to be away from the husband who was abusing his spouse. Sometimes advocacy is just saying what you observe, and letting that information help adults make their own important decisions to protect themselves and their children.

Note: The National Domestic Violence Hotline has a website with a phone number that can be used to get help 24 hours a day, 7 days a week.

Yes, women did a lot to bring about changes in the kinds of discrimination that limited their lives as well as hurt them. Women's Lib was big when I was a young mother. My first children were born in the 1960s and '70s, a time when many people I knew wanted to downplay femininity in girls—feeling it was limiting their options. For example, as mentioned earlier, clothes and haircuts tended to be unisex, as it was called. Parents bought toys for girls that were sometimes thought of as "boys' toys"—science kits instead of little homemaker ovens. There was a big push for androgynous roles in parenting children. Today, surprisingly, some of these changes are in conspicuous retreat. Toy stores have boys sections and girls sections, which display toys for clearly stereotypical roles in playing.

Still, times have changed and opportunities for women have improved. The first women who managed to work their way into jobs that had traditionally been men's had to be "superwomen." That's less true now, but it's still not easy for women to succeed with so many expectations put on them. It used to be that success came only if women acted like men when they competed in the traditional masculine arena. Now women are exploring new ways to do their jobs, using their feminine perspective, styles, systems, and skills. (Although sometimes they are criticized and punished for their femininity.)

The broadening of roles means, at least, that the old riddle doesn't work anymore—you know the one about the father and son who were in an accident and the father was killed? When they brought the injured boy in for surgery, the brain surgeon took one look, paled, and turned away, saying, "I can't operate on him—that's my son!" It used to be that people wondered how the father could be the brain surgeon if he was dead. (You knew the answer is that the brain surgeon was the boy's *mother*, didn't you?)

Broader roles mean that mothers of young children are less likely to be criticized when they take jobs outside the home. Broader roles mean that some men feel freer to participate more fully in parenting their children; many men are now choosing to be full-time, stay-at-home parents. Men can also now enter more traditional women's fields such as nursing. However, when the average citizen meets a man and a woman dressed in green scrubs in a hospital corridor, the assumption still is that the man is the doctor and the woman the nurse.

Will we continue to move forward to eliminate the institutionalized oppression of women, to broaden gender roles, and to create an increasing range of opportunities for all individuals? This is an unanswered question. Whether women and men are fully able to be who they are and do what they choose depends on how the next generations of children are raised. We can't just sit back and assume that men and women already are or will one day be freed from confining gender roles. Gender roles are learned by every generation. A danger of complacency exists as the younger generations accept as normal what feminists have worked so hard for. How easy it would be to lose the gains isn't clear, but it should be a worry.

Personally I have some big worries. Read on.

Check Your Understanding 11.1

Click here to check your understanding of why it is important to think about teaching gender roles.

GENDER EQUITY AND PARENTING

Just a glance at the book *Cinderella Ate My Daughter* (Orenstein, 2011) relates to the reality of the four-year-old girls I know. What is this princess business anyway!? Business it is—big business. According to Orenstein, Disney in 2009 made $4 billion marketing princess items. A relative reports that at her daughter's preschool in the dress-up corner are mainly Disney princess dresses, which is all the girls go for. The occupational outfits (police, firefighters, construction workers) just sit on the hooks. The boys are too busy running around to put them on, and the girls ignore them. What kinds of messages are girls going for anyway! Except for Mulan, the princesses' role in life is to look pretty and wait for a prince to marry them. And the regular clothes, even when the girls aren't dressed as princesses, are far from unisex outfits! A big surprise came to me one morning recently when I was at a military child care center as the children were being delivered. Military mothers came in fatigues, heavy boots, hair in tight buns under their hats. By the hand they had their daughters dressed in lacy pink dresses with shoes sparkling in sequins. Strange juxtapositions. At least these girls had models of women who don't always dress in pink and lace.

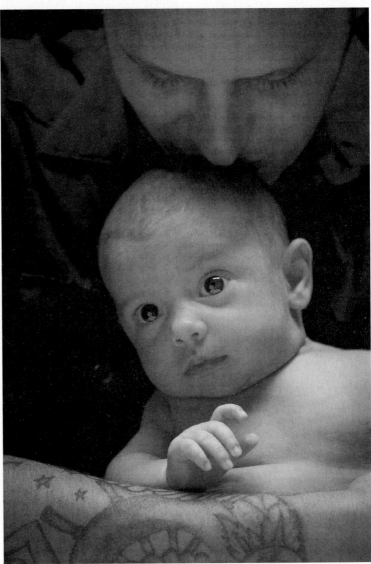

Andy Dean/Fotolia

Broader roles mean that some men feel freer to participate more in parenting their children; a wonderful model of nurturing that can benefit all children

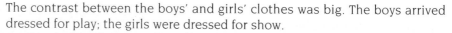

Watch this video to hear Peggy Orenstein talk about hyper-gendered toys. What do you think about marketing companies targeting gender?

www.youtube.com/watch?v=MyStjbB309I

The contrast between the boys' and girls' clothes was big. The boys arrived dressed for play; the girls were dressed for show.

Do clothes shape gender roles? Certainly baby girls in dresses can't crawl the way boys in pants can. Slippery-soled shoes won't run very well. Is that a gender socialization message about being more or less active?

Consider how television pounds out the message that some clothes and toys are for girls and others are for boys and how toy stores are set up in boys' sections and girls' sections. Even a famous fast-food chain that gives away free toys with each child's meal differentiates boys from girls. Apparently the "unisex" toy has become rare or even nonexistent. This situation, including the advertising, works against what nonsexist parents work for. The Family Lifestyles Project, which started in the 1970s, studied the socialization of children in families that emphasized gender-role equality (Eiduson, Kornfein, Zimmerman, & Weisner, 1988; Weisner & Wilson-Mitchell, 1990). In further research, the project assessed children over a three-year period and found them broader in their selection of activities and interests than a comparison group whose parents didn't stress gender-role equality. Without a strong plan beyond just buying trucks for their girls and dolls for their boys, parents run up against their children's opinions once children learn from TV and other forms of advertising which toys are for whom. Is that what is happening today?

Watch this video to hear children talk about their views of gender and toys. Why do you think there is such a difference between the way the girls "act like a girl" and the women portray "acting like a girl"?

www.youtube.com/watch?v=4vU5GGtMhmo

Toys and Gender Roles

Toys play an important part in defining gender roles. If parents buy girls dolls, dollhouses, high-heeled shoes, and makeup, they give one set of messages. If they buy boys chemistry sets, tool kits, doctor's bags, building blocks, and wheel toys, they give another set of messages. Children learn roles and skills from playing; the toys they have to some extent determine which roles and skills they learn.

Visit a child care program and examine the environment, specifically the block area and the dramatic play corner. Vivian Paley (1984) dealt with this subject at length in her informative, easy-to-read book *Boys and Girls: Superheroes in the Doll Corner*. Though the book is not new, the superhero play hasn't changed. Only the names of the heroes, and the few heroines, change regularly. Comic book heroes are now out of the book form and into the movie form. While you are looking into the dramatic play area, notice whether more girls or boys are there. Check out the block area. Is that where you find the boys? If this is the case, examine the factors that might contribute to this situation. Sometimes the adults in the program subtly encourage this kind of gender differentiation. Notice the way the environment is set up. If the dramatic play area

Providing opportunities to play with all kinds of toys will broaden children's interests and skills

Glenda Powers/Fotolia

is a traditional "housekeeping" corner with frilly girls' clothes, shoes, and purses, most boys won't be attracted. If a variety of male or non-gender-specific hats, shoes, ties, and accessories are added, that can help, though it didn't help much in my relative's experience with her daughter's preschool. What helps more is adding a little water to the play sink and maybe some soap suds and sponges.

Because boys tend to dominate block play in many programs, some teachers have tried a variety of approaches to encourage girls to also go into the area. One technique is to arrange the environment so that the blocks are close to the dolls or to put a dollhouse in with the blocks. Another idea is to put up "girls only" signs occasionally to give the message that this is valuable play for both sexes.

Why does it matter if boys never play house and girls never play blocks? It doesn't, if in other areas of their lives they are getting the skills they miss out on by avoiding these two activities. Dramatic play gives boys a chance to be nurturers, to experience domestic relations, and to feel comfortable trying on a variety of emotions. Blocks give girls experience in spatial relations. They learn mathematical concepts as they

Boys AND *girls need block play, as it gives children important experiences in math and science concepts*

David Kostelnik/Pearson Ed Inc

build things. Ordinary wooden "kindergarten" blocks, called by some *unit blocks,* represent multiples of the basic square that is found in the set. Block play contributes a good deal to the concrete experience behind math knowledge and gives the player experiences with principles of physics as well. Frank Lloyd Wright attributed his success as an architect to the set of blocks his mother brought home from a kindergarten conference in Europe back before anyone in the United States had heard of giving children blocks to play with.

It isn't just where children play or what they play with. It's also with whom they play. Young children tend to separate themselves by gender. One kindergarten teacher, Stacey Zeitlin (1997), describes how she purposely matched up boys and girls for a science activity. She made a conscious decision not to let the children select their own partners, as she usually did, but assigned them each a partner of the opposite sex. She was worried how it would work because the children liked to team up with their same-gender best friends during activities like this one. Surprisingly, it worked very well, and she saw how it broke down gender barriers. Children who had never spent time together before spent the rest of the day together. Some continued to seek out their partners as playmates the rest of

> Gender role differentiation and segregation may be something some families value. It's important not to just try to "educate" parents out of their beliefs, but to understand how the beliefs fit into their culture. At the same time it doesn't hurt to put equity issues on the table for discussion.

the year. Zeitlin is now committed to reducing the self- and peer-imposed gender segregation that she sees children practicing.

All of this information has implications for families. Of course, gender role differentiation and segregation may be something some families value. It's important not to just try to "educate" parents out of their beliefs, but to understand how the beliefs fit into their culture. At the same time it doesn't hurt to put equity issues on the table for discussion. Parents who take note of some of the practices you are using may learn from them, come to support those practices, and even take them home. Parent group discussions that are respectful of differences and disagreement can be useful for helping parents examine their practices around arranging play dates, buying toys, setting up a nonsexist environment, and encouraging broader gender roles.

The Power of Language

Language has an influence on gender-role development. Language shapes perceptions. The terms *firemen, policemen,* and *chairmen* give the impression that these jobs are filled by men and that it's an exception when there's a "woman policeman." Better to make these titles non-gender-specific. That can be accomplished by using the terms *firefighter, police officer,* and *chair* or *chairperson.* Children will get the message that either gender may fill these roles.

Kris Timken/Gettyimages

Some titles are already non-gender-specific—for example, *teacher, doctor,* and *president.* However, children may consider them as gender-specific because of their own experiences. There's the story of the English girl who asked her mother, "What are they going to call the new prime minister now that Mrs. Thatcher's gone?"

"By his name, of course," answered the mother.

"But what's his *title*?" persisted the child.

"Prime minister," answered the mother.

"But that's a woman's title!" said the child.

Once when I was talking about language and gender to a group of parents, one of them, a woman from Iran, pointed out to me that my language (English) is more gender-oriented than hers. I was surprised and asked to hear more about that. She then said that, as English speakers, we mention gender every time we talk about a child, since we use either "he or she," or just "he." She then went on to say that in her language the same word encompasses both genders.

Interruption as an Indicator of Power and Importance. Studies of "conversational politics" have found that people use language to show their power, as one person exerts control over another. For example, men tend to interrupt women more than the reverse.

Model gender-neutral language, such as firefighter, so children will broaden their expectations of what is possible

Interruption is an important indicator of relative power and importance. Children learn these interruption patterns early from the people around them. People can become aware of these patterns and can stop using them. It's not easy to do when you're an involved party, but it's possible. It's easier to look for the patterns when they occur between boys and girls and then intervene, insisting that the girls get their say. Empowerment of girls in such ways is important if there is to be gender equity. It's also important to empower boys to be free to be gentle and caring.

> Empowerment of girls . . . is important if there is to be gender equity. It's also important to empower boys to be free to be gentle and caring.

Using Language That Is Direct and Informative.   Teachers can also help empower girls (and boys, too) by teaching them to use assertive language. To do this, teachers need to model such language themselves. Pay attention to how often you end a sentence with a question that dilutes the message. For example, "I want you to sit down in your car seat, OK?" or "It's time for lunch—will you come in now?" Those ways of talking are fine if the child truly has a choice. If not, the statement needs to be clear about what's to be done.

Teachers can model assertive language by cutting down the number of times they hedge with phrases such as *sort of* and I *guess*. They can also quit being ultrapolite. For example, "Your shoes are sort of muddy. It'd be really nice if you took them off before you walk into the classroom. I'd sure appreciate it." That way of talking is very courteous, but it depends on the goodwill of the listener to be effective. When being polite gives the message that the speaker is powerless, it's a good idea to find more assertive ways to speak. It's more powerful for a person to say what she means—to be direct and informative. That's what a lot of men do, and that's why they are more likely to be listened to than women. For example, a direct way to deal with the muddy shoes is this: "Please take off your muddy shoes. They'll dirty the floor." Or: "Muddy shoes belong on the mat by the door." Or, if necessary: "If you walk on the floor, you're going to have to clean up the mud from your shoes."

This whole subject becomes much more complicated when working across language groups. I'm speaking from the point of view of an English-speaking person. Vocabulary, interruptions, and assertive language are different in each language. What I say here may not apply at all to people who speak other languages. It would be interesting to explore this subject further with parent groups. I am well aware that I miss the emotional content of conversations when I'm listening to some languages. I know a German speaker and a Russian speaker who not only sound assertive about everything they say but also a bit angry. It took me a while to realize I was misinterpreting the pitch of their voices, which gave a very different message than the same pitch in English.

Using Modeling to Teach

As the preceding section indicated, modeling is an important method of teaching gender roles. Children imitate the important people in their lives, so when girls see their mother act helpless in the face of a flat tire or their female preschool teachers wait for a man to appear on the scene to unclog toilets or fix the broken handle on the cupboard, they pick up silent messages about women's capabilities. When a boy sees his father hand his mother a needle and thread and a shirt with a missing button, he gets a silent message about men's capabilities; when a boy sees his male teacher turn a child who needs comforting over to a female teacher, the boy gets a message about the role of men in the classroom. Of course, all the people in these examples may have very good reasons for their actions, but the point is that, with enough of these types of genderized examples, children take away a message about their own gender roles.

What makes all this more difficult is that children often see power differential that is determined by gender. In a program where the tasks are shared, children get a broader idea of capabilities as well as appropriateness.

A good deal of modeling comes from television. I tend to notice whenever an old woman is the "bad guy." Powerful elderly females as evil is a stereotype that has been with us for centuries. The witch hunts of the past show how such a negative stereotype can be used to oppress, even kill. Another problem created by the media (and the marketing that goes with it) is the sexualization of girls. *So Sexy So Soon* is Diane Levin's response to the problem (2009). Seeing constant sexy images of women and now even girls is harmful according to the American Psychological Association's 2007 *Report on the Sexualization of Girls*. Sexualization equates attractiveness with sex appeal and leads to a range of physical and mental health problems in girls and women, including low self-esteem, depression, and high-risk sexual behavior. To combat this problem, families and teachers can join advocacy groups and press to make changes. The APA recommends the development of educational media literacy programs in public schools. It also recommends that parents look at media with kids and discuss what they are seeing, while pointing out that becoming sex objects is not a great way to feel valued. Parents should point daughters to better, more positive images of females.

Books can leave strong stereotypical images. In early readers, Dick was always busy fixing something, while Mother, Jane, and Sally stood helplessly looking on. Dick and Father were active in a variety of ways. Mother, Jane, and Sally were passive, except in the kitchen. It seems as though times should have changed by now, but still today it is easy to see that children's books are more often about boys than girls, male animals instead of female ones. You can also easily find females being dependent more often than independent and as poor damsels still needing help. Certainly the many Disney princess books give the message that beauty is important and waiting for a prince is the theme.

Watch this video to see many of the images that children are bombarded with in the media. Which images stood out for you?

www.youtube.com
/watch?v=AWLdSwO_cwo

Help Families Become Aware of Media Messages

Check Your Understanding 11.2

Click here to check your understanding of gender equity and parenting.

In one educational program, whenever the teachers bought new books for the classroom, they made the books available to parents first and asked them to comment on them. They pasted a sheet of paper inside the front cover and had parents write their comments so other parents could see them. That way, families had a broader view of each book than just what they thought or what the teachers thought about the books.

DIFFERENTIAL SOCIALIZATION

Adults socialize girls and boys differently, which results in females ending up in subservient roles. How does this happen? Besides modeling, how else do children learn gender roles and develop a gender identity? Why do many boys gain confidence, competence, mastery, and assertiveness, while many girls come to see themselves as lacking those qualities? Why do many girls fail to identify themselves as strong, responsible, and powerful?

Gender Roles and Cultural Differences

Two parents meet outside the door of the child care center where they have just arrived to pick up their children at the end of the day. They know each other slightly and feel a connection because they are of the same culture, although one was born in the United States and the other in the "old country." Both speak English, but they are more comfortable talking to each other in their own language, which is what they are doing now:

"How did you like the last parent meeting?" inquires Parent A, making conversation.

"Well, to tell the truth, it upset me," answers Parent B.

"Oh?" responds Parent A.

"All that talk about letting boys act like girls and encouraging girls to be powerful bothered me a lot. I just don't think that's appropriate!"

"Yes, I know what you mean," says Parent A.

"I can't stand the thought of my son playing house and wearing dresses. That makes me sick to my stomach. And they let him do that if he wants to."

"Does he want to?"

"How do I know? I'm not there!"

"It does seem kind of strange to me, too, but I don't think it hurts anything." Parent A leans casually against the stair rail.

Parent B stands, nervously rubbing her arms as if she is cold. She looks distressed.

"But the worst thing of all is that the teacher told me to send my daughter in pants and sneakers. She says that she's afraid to get dirty and that it's hard for her to run and climb with a dress and good shoes on. I guess she thinks I want her to look ugly, get dirty, and run around like a wild person!"

Parent A touches her friend's arm. "That really bothers you."

"Yes! That's not proper behavior for a girl! Do you think it is?"

"Well," says Parent A slowly, brushing her hair back from her face, while carefully considering her words, "I don't really like my daughter to get dirty, but I have to admit that what the teacher said is convincing."

"What's convincing? All that garbage about sexism?"

The two parents stop talking in their own language and switch to English as another parent arrives at the bottom of the steps. They greet her and move over to let her go up the steps and into the child care center.

"Yes, sexism and oppression!" continues Parent A, as if there had been no interruption.

Parent B replies passionately, "I don't see that my daughter is restricted in her development. She's going to grow into a woman. She has to know how women act in our culture. She has to fit in. She'll never get a decent husband if she starts acting like the other girls in this country. I don't want her to be like them. I don't want her to lose her culture."

"I know what you mean," says Parent A slowly. "But I've been thinking about whether women's inferior status is something we should just accept because that's the way it's always been."

"Oh, you're as bad as they are!" snorts Parent B angrily, stepping backward on the stair. "I thought you would understand."

When children play with dolls, they act out their own lives, try new roles, and develop language and social skills

elisabetta figus/Fotolia

"I *do* understand," comes the answer, "but at the same time I'm confused. I just don't know what I think."

"Well, I do. And I warn you, if you listen to them, you'll end up like them. You'll be melted right into the melting pot! How would you like that?"

"I don't know," answers Parent A, looking doubtful as she slowly turns and walks to the door of the center. "But I think," she says, pausing and turning around to watch Parent B climb up the rest of the steps, "that ensuring that my daughter grows up with a sense of her self-worth as a person is a good idea. I don't think oppression has to be part of our culture."

"I disagree that women who dress and act the way they are supposed to are oppressed. That's ridiculous. Look at me. Am I oppressed?" Parent B is at the door now, too.

"I'm beginning to understand what you mean about losing our culture. I don't want that to happen. I can be American and still be part of my culture. That's important to me. Let's talk more later," says Parent A, opening the door and stepping back to let her friend walk through first.

Differential Treatment from Parents

Differential treatment starts at birth, when parents perceive their daughters to be more fragile than their sons. Fathers play rough and tumble more with their sons and talk to them in ways that indicate toughness, like "Hi, Tiger!" (Parke, 2002). From early on, many parents encourage their sons to be active, assertive, and strong, and they protect their girls. They do more touching and talking to girls; they stress independence, self-reliance, and achievement-related skills to their boys. What these parents don't know is what Christia Spears-Brown (2014) went to a lot of trouble to find out. She writes about the many studies that show the assumed differences between boy babies and girl babies are just that—assumed. This subject has been well studied and Spears-Brown has a whole chapter on what the research actually shows. Girls aren't more emotional than boys—that's an assumption. Another example is that the difference in activity level of baby boys and baby girls is so small that it doesn't even show. It's the differential treatment based on assumptions that make the difference later on.

When children leave babyhood, if the differential treatment continues into toddlerhood and beyond, eventually, lo and behold, the boys have a tendency to be active, clever, assertive, and aggressive doers, and the girls often turn out to be sweet, dependent, verbal, and social. Whatever natural inclinations children might have been born with can be diminished or magnified by the socialization process.

Differential Treatment in Preschool

This same differential treatment continues when the children leave home for child care or preschool. In 1973, Serbin, O'Leary, Kent, and Tolnick looked at how preschool teachers treated girls and boys. They found that teachers paid attention to boys' disruptive behavior, which reinforced it; the attention acted as a reward and encouraged the behavior to continue. Girls, on the other hand, received attention only when they stood or played near the teacher. Direct reinforcement, even when it is unintended, is a powerful way to influence behavior.

Things haven't changed much from the early 1970s. Observe for yourself how adults in group care spend a lot of time looking over the heads of the girls who hang around them (being dependent and getting attention for it) to notice the boys, who are throwing blocks, hitting each other, or climbing the fence of the play yard. The untrained adult will yell at the boys. The trained one will leave the cluster of girls and go over and handle the problem with the boys in some professional way—often touching them, getting down to their level, and making eye contact while he or she describes the unacceptable behavior and explains why it must stop. Both the yelling and the more professional intervention strategies are rewarding. They say to the boys, "I'm paying attention to you." The attention and the behavior that preceded it become solidly linked. Many boys never learn any other ways of getting the teacher to notice them. And many of the girls never break out of the "be-dependent-to-get-noticed" pattern.

While you are observing, notice how adults make conversation with young children. I'm sure you'll discover that girls are often noticed for their appearance. Child care and preschool staff, plus parents of other children, make remarks such as "Oh, you got your hair cut—it looks very pretty" and "I see you got new

Both boys and girls need space and time for active outdoor play

shoes!" and "What a nice design on your shirt." Those same adults are more likely to notice boys' abilities. They say things like "How strong you are to lift that heavy piece of wood" and "I saw you climb all the way up to the top of the jungle gym!" and "How clever you are. You figured out how to make that work!"

Differential Treatment in Elementary School

Some patterns similar to those that Serbin and her colleagues found in preschool-age children were reported by Thorne (1993), who looked at children in elementary school. Thorne reported that boys controlled much more space on the playground than girls did—up to ten times more. The girls played closer to the building and remained near adult aides who watched over them and protected them. Boys invaded girls' space more often than the reverse. And boys were more likely to define girls as "polluting" or "contaminated" in the old game of "cooties." Thorne also noticed that though boys and girls tend to segregate themselves, when they are mixed together by adults, boys and girls interact in more relaxed ways. When adults are the ones who organize the mix, it legitimizes the togetherness and removes the risk of teasing. Though these studies are now old, observe for yourself! What I see is that things haven't changed too much in school or in preschool in recent years. Granted, some children may be resisting the stereotypical behaviors of their gender reported in these studies, but they tend to be the exception rather than the norms. And maybe those children were always resisting, but they weren't noticed because their behavior was unexpected.

Sexism in Stroking

Jennifer is a single parent, mother of a four-year-old boy, Zach, and a daughter, Jade, who is two and a half. Jennifer knows about the importance of strokes and affirmations, and she gives them regularly. Here are some examples:

She regularly tells her daughter how nice she looks. She is pleased to note that her little girl is already beginning to take an interest in her own appearance. She notices when her daughter plays nicely with her baby doll, when she pets the cat gently. Lately she's been amazed to see that her daughter is trying to help her do things around the house. Small as she is, she works to make the bed, tries to unload the dish drainer, and wants to fold clothes. Jennifer is very happy about these behaviors and, naturally, wants them to continue, so she praises her daughter when she shows a willingness to help. Once when Jennifer was feeling very down about losing her job, Jade caught her with a tear rolling down her cheek. She left the room and came back dragging her own precious "blankey," which she tenderly gave her mother to help her feel better. Jennifer was really touched by this gesture and she told Jade that.

Zach is his mom's "big boy." He feels that he is the "man of the house" and that he needs to be responsible. Of course, he slips now and then, but his mother still loves him greatly—accepting his need to play instead of being grown-up. She thinks his loud manner and his rough play are appropriate, even when they bother her a little. She's proud of the way he figures things out. "You have a good head on your shoulders!" she tells him regularly. She's pleased that he spends so much time playing with the construction toys she's bought him. He creates truly amazing structures and machines. She talks to him about what he'll be when he grows up and how happy she'll be if they can figure out a way to get him into a good college. She has great hopes and aspirations for her son.

When Jade does something well, Jennifer says, "You angel!" When Zach does something well, Jennifer points out what was so good about how he did it. She's more specific with Zach than with Jade.

Anything wrong with this picture? Jennifer is using strokes and affirmations effectively, but she is selective. She is stroking her daughter for some qualities and her son for others. Her children respond accordingly. Her daughter is becoming more and more interested in her appearance and in nurturing others, and her son is coming to see himself as a "doer" and as a capable problem solver who can use his head. Imagine the messages they are receiving about their futures. Will Jade come to see herself as someone beyond an angel who pleases others and makes them happy both by her appearance and by her nurturing actions? Will Zach learn to be a nurturer? How will Zach, the doer, relate to his family when he is grown? Will he go beyond providing the financial support that will come from the brilliant career he's being programmed for?

What Jennifer needs to do is to help her daughter also see herself as a "doer," not just a helper. She needs to catch Jade "thinking." Girls need to know that they are "smart" and capable just as much as boys do. It wouldn't hurt to talk to Jade about college, too, even though the event is far in the future. She could also encourage Jade to play with a wide range of toys, not just those advertised for girls.

Zach needs to see himself as a nurturer as well as a problem solver. His heart should be as big and strong as his head and body. Jennifer can help him do this by finding nurturing men to expose him to, by making it clear that nurturing is appropriate for boys, and by stroking him for any nurturing he might do.

This little family is a reminder of strokes and affirmations and how they should be used wisely.

So how do you work with families around issues of gender equity? Such work can be very touchy. See Strategy Box 11.1 for ideas.

Guidelines for Parents and Educators

Here are some guidelines for teaching young children about gender equity:

◆ *Help children develop awareness of sexist stereotypes.* Point out such stereotypes in pictures, in books, and on TV. Look for stereotypes in commercials as well as in regular programs and movies.

Working with Families around the Subject of Gender Equity

- Probably the place to start is by finding out how each family perceives the gender equity issues around which this chapter is based. This could be a very hot topic. Hone your facilitation skills!

- When you put equity issues on the table for discussion, parents who agree may have already noticed some of the practices and may have taken them home to try themselves. In that case you can pat yourself on the back for doing parent education. But don't try to "educate" parents out of their beliefs if they have some serious disagreements with the material in this chapter. Try instead to see their perspective and understand how it fits into their family culture.

- Help families become aware of media messages. For example, you can create discussions around the gender-role messages that children see on TV. Or ask parents to bring in a children's book and rate it on stereotypical images and messages about gender.

- Share the research in this chapter about gender differentiation in child rearing; discuss the research with families and note their reaction to it. Be sure you and everyone else honor diverse perspectives.

- Try using the guidelines on this page to create discussions with parent groups. Be sure you are open to their perspectives and feelings. Help parents respect each others' differences.

- *Create a nonsexist environment.* Find books and pictures that show all kinds of families, including single-parent families (not just single mothers), gay and lesbian families, and extended families, for starters. These books and pictures should show men and women doing similar activities and include examples of women and men in nontraditional occupations. Invite visitors who are in nontraditional jobs to the home, child care, or preschool to talk about their work. (Or visit these workers at their workplaces.) Expand children's awareness beyond narrow views and stereotypical gender roles.

- *Watch your own behavior.* Do you treat girls differently from boys? What do you notice about each gender? What do you remark about? Do you give both sexes equal physical freedom? Do you allow both to express feelings? Do you encourage both to seek help at times and to be independent as well? Be observant of yourself and catch the ways you may be promoting narrow gender roles. When children ask about the difference between boys and girls, stick to anatomical differences and avoid mentioning dress, behavior, or personality traits.

- *Teach an anti-bias attitude to young children and give them the skills they need to challenge sexism.* Teach children to recognize injustice and to speak out against it. When Brandon says to Lindsay, "You can't come in our fort. Only boys are allowed," help her speak up and say, "That's not fair!" If he tries to exclude her on the basis of her behavior, the situation is different. For example, if he says, "You can't come in because last time you grabbed all the toys," she's getting feedback about something she can change. She can't, however, change the fact of being a girl, so for him to exclude her for that reason is unfair discrimination. Children need to learn to speak up for their own rights. Teach them to do that.

- *Help all children develop empathy.* Notice when children of both genders are sensitive to the feelings of another. Pay attention to behaviors that show caring for another person. Model empathy yourself.

◆ *Help all children become problem solvers, in both the physical and the social worlds.* Teach children to troubleshoot. Help them extend their perspective to include many possibilities. Help them learn to negotiate.

◆ *Broaden children's views of themselves and their capabilities.* Entice them to develop skills they've been avoiding. Find ways to get the girls that need to be out in the yard more into activities that increase their strength, courage, and dexterity. Figure out a way to get the boys who never sit down at tables, given the choice, involved in activities that take eye-hand coordination and require careful manual skills. Some boys who avoid traditional preschool art projects will glue wood scrap sculptures or take apart an old radio.

◆ *Notice how clothes get in the way, especially girls' clothes, and determine activities accordingly.* The crawling baby is hampered if she's in a dress or has lots of ruffles and flounces on her clothes. The slippery shoes of the preschooler keep her from running or climbing. Light-colored pants get stained knees if a girl crawls around on the grass or in the dirt. Will this situation cause problems for her and serve to restrict her activities?

◆ *Last, but definitely not least, check out your own attitudes.* If you see the male of the species as more important, more deserving of power, or worthy of a higher status, you need an attitude adjustment. Until you deal with that attitude problem, you'd better watch yourself carefully when you are around young children. You can't promote equity if down deep you don't believe in it! That's a strong statement, and one that may get me in trouble for including it in a book that claims to be sensitive to cultural differences. But in some cultures gender roles are strictly defined. That may fit the culture and the people in it just fine. The problem for me is when one sex is in power and the other is in a powerless position. I have been told that because I'm judging from outside the culture, I don't really understand the power relationships between the sexes. I have to admit that is a possibility. Still, when oppression exists and I'm told it's cultural, I am in a double bind because I feel it is important to accept and honor differences; *however*, I must also stand up against oppression.

Check Your Understanding 11.3

Click here to check your understanding of differential socialization.

SUMMARY

This chapter started by exploring the question, why think about gender roles? It went on to look at how times have changed and what issues are still present for women of today. An examination of influences on gender equity and child rearing came next, followed by a section on modeling. Modeling is a powerful way to teach children about equity in gender roles. Differential socialization is another factor in inequity issues. Biology is yet another factor that plays a part in creating differences between boys and girls. The chapter ends with a list of guidelines for teaching children about gender equity.

QUIZ

Click here to check your understanding of Chapter 11, "Working with Families around Gender Issues."

FOR DISCUSSION

1. What part do TV and other media and technology play in limiting children's concept of gender roles? Give specific examples. What can be done about any limitations that you perceive?

2. What part does language play in carrying out inequities? How does language influence children's ideas of their capabilities? What can be done to broaden children's views?

3. What if children are exposed to limited models of men's and women's roles? How can children learn about gender equity?

4. Brainstorm some ideas about how to empower both boys and girls.

5. What are some cultural views that are different from the gender equity goals promoted in this chapter?

WEBSITES

American Association of University Women (AAUW)
This organization promotes education and equity for women and girls and includes research on gender issues related to girls. Check out the website.

Gender Spectrum
Gender spectrum provides information, education, resources, training, and support to create a gender sensitive and inclusive environment for children of all ages.

Love Our Children USA
This parenting website is designed to keep children safe and strengthen families. A featured article is titled "Teaching Your Daughters Self-Esteem."

A Mighty Girl
The Mighty Girl website has a collection of books, toys, and movies to promote smart, confident, and courageous girls. They also have a blog and a Facebook page.

The National Domestic Violence Hotline
The National Domestic Violence Hotline has a website with a phone number that can be used to get help 24 hours a day, 7 days a week. They also have information about getting help, getting involved, and staying safe.

Teaching Tolerance
The website of the magazine *Teaching Tolerance* has information about gender-expression and focuses on boys who dress, talk, and act like girls either occasionally or fully.

World Health Organization
The WHO has a website with working definitions about Gender and Reproductive Rights.

FURTHER READING

Brinson, S. A. (2009, January). From *Thunder Rose to When Marian Sang…Behold the power of African American female characters! Reading to encourage self-worth, inform/inspire, and bring pleasure. *Young Children*, 64(2), 26–31.

Brown, C. (2014). *Parenting beyond pink and blue*. Berkeley, CA: Ten Speed Press.

Chang, A., Sandhofer, C. & Brown, C. (2011). Gender biases in early number exposure to preschool-aged children. *Journal of Language and Social Psychology* 30 (4), 440–450.

Christensen, L. (2011). Unlearning the myths that bind us: Critiquing fairy tales and cartoons. In E. Marshall & O. Sensoy (Eds.), *Rethinking popular culture and media* (pp. 189–200). Milwaukee, WI: Rethinking Schools.

Gropper, N., Hinitz, B. F., Spring, B., & Foschl, M. (2011, January). Helping young boys be successful learners in today's early childhood classrooms. *Young Children*, 66(1), 34–41.

Hofmann, S. (2011). Miles of aisles of sexism: Helping students investigate toy stores. In E. Marshall & O. Sensoy (Eds.), *Rethinking popular culture and media* (pp. 207–213). Milwaukee, WI: Rethinking Schools.

Lyman, K. (2011). Girls, worms, and body image: A teacher deals with gender stereotypes among her second and third graders. In E. Marshall & O. Sensoy (Eds.), *Rethinking popular culture and media* (pp. 138–146). Milwaukee, WI: Rethinking Schools.

Soloman, A. (2013). *Far from the tree: Parents, children, and the search for identity*. New York, NY: Scribner.

Steele, C. M. (2011). *Whistling Vivaldi: How stereotypes affect us*. New York, NY: W. W. Norton and Co.

Mat Hayward/Fotolia

Stress and Success in Family Life

Learning Outcomes

In this chapter you will learn to . . .

- Explain the various types of family structure.
- Discuss characteristics of successful families.
- Describe how stress can be a positive force in children's lives.

The family is a microsystem, and as such we will discuss it as a system (Christian 2006; Connors & Caple 2005). So far in this book we have looked at how to work with families around issues related to children's socialization in the context of society and its many influences. We've focused a good deal on education, including school and early education in a variety of settings. This chapter puts the spotlight on the families themselves—their lives outside the times the professional sees them. Obviously children are influenced by much more than the time spent in school and early care and education programs. They live their lives seven days a week, around the clock, whereas they are in the environment of educational systems only a limited number of hours. Although some children spend eight to ten hours a day, five days a week, in out-of-home programs, some preschool-age children are in their educational setting as few as 15 hours a week. Some young children aren't in any education system until kindergarten or first grade. No matter how much time they spend with their families, they are more affected by being part of their families than anything else (unless they have been removed from those families). Professionals, including teachers and early educators, need to take the family setting into consideration if they are truly to understand the child and support the family in a collaborative way. So this chapter looks closely at various families and their stresses and successes.

What is meant by the word *family*? Close your eyes and imagine a family. Does this family fit your *concept* of a family? Look around at symbols of families. Think of the logos of agencies that serve families. What is the image conveyed by most? The images I usually see are a male, a female, and one or two children. Perhaps the balance and symmetry cause this type of family to be chosen as a logo—it's visually attractive. Or perhaps we're still living in the aftermath of the *Leave It to Beaver* tradition. Whatever the reason, many of us carry in our heads an image that doesn't apply to a large number of families in the United States today.

VARIED IMAGES OF FAMILIES

Times are changing. While I was working on this chapter I made a trip to a car dealer, where I had a long wait. As I sat there, a collection of pamphlets caught my eye. I was thinking about images of families and there they were on these pamphlets. What struck me first were two photographs of families—both represented people of color and missed the stereotype of two parents and two children. The pamphlet on vehicle protection had an African American family—mother, father, and one child. The Asian family was represented on the car care pamphlet by a father with a son and a daughter. I had to open up the pamphlet to find the stereotypical family—a white couple male and female with two children, a boy and a girl. This, obviously isn't research, but it struck me that at least maybe some of the people who have something to sell have moved a bit beyond the stereotypical images of families that most of us have seen all our lives. I was glad to see some progress in image expansion. Stereotypical images have an impact on children growing up. It's a subject worth thinking about.

What the photos on pamphlets only hinted at but didn't completely show are the many different ways a family can vary from the mother-father-child(ren) model.

Ways in Which Families Can Vary

Think about the variations. Each family can have more children or fewer. It can involve a marriage or not. The members can all be the same sex or gender. Its members

Andi Berger/Shutterstock

Blended families are adults coming together as a couple who each have children of their own

can vary greatly in age—by more than just two generations. It can include a number of people who are not related but are living under the same roof. It can include people who are related by blood or marriage along with those who are not related and who do not live under the same roof. (This kind of family is called a *kinship network*.) Its members can share the same bloodlines or name, or both, or neither. Its members can share the same history or not. The family can be *blended*—that is, composed of individuals coming together as a couple who each have children of their own. The blended family can live all together or not. The family can be composed of people who have traditional relationships to each other but were not born into them. Children may come into the family from outside—through adoption, fostering, or less formal arrangements.

There are numerous traditional names for these varying kinds of families. They include nuclear, insular, extended, embedded, single-parent, step, blended, adoptive, foster, communal, kinship network, gay, and lesbian.

Families can vary infinitely in their makeup. Each variation has an effect on the socialization of any children in them. Families may originate through interracial or interreligious unions. Families may have members who are differently abled. Families may come about through marriages or affiliations that cross generational lines.

Families and Stress

Though the forms of families may vary greatly, virtually all families experience stress—and always have. Stress is nothing new to family life, though it may seem now with the times changing so rapidly that we are under more stress than in the past. Certainly family structure is changing, and that alone can create stress in those who think back with longing to what they consider the good old days. This chapter looks at the kinds of stresses that affect families today. It also looks at what makes for successful families. The overarching question is: What can early educators do to support families so they have less stress and more success?

It's important to take into account the strengths of families in stress who manage to socialize their children successfully. What enables these families to function effectively under difficult or demanding circumstances? Why do some families remain organized and supportive of each other under extreme pressures? Early childhood educators need to learn how to promote that same kind of togetherness in families that lack it. They need to understand more about the effects of classism, racism, and sexism, as well as cultural and ethnic biases.

You can't take families out of their cultural context. The early childhood profession needs to focus less on universals and more on understanding a variety of cultural patterns of child rearing as they relate to care, education, and socialization. It's important to recognize that the cultural imperatives of families determine which competencies it is appropriate to foster in children. It is vital to understand how educational and socialization techniques, plus child-rearing practices, work to promote the survival of any given culture, even though to a critical eye outside the culture some techniques may look undesirable. Early childhood professionals must avoid equating cultural survival with what may seem to be harmful practices and family breakdown.

There's a lot of talk today about the family breaking down. When a family is not functioning well, raising children is difficult and there's cause to be concerned. However, the definition of *functional family* varies from culture to culture. It's tempting to see a family as dysfunctional when its patterns or structure are different from your image of what they should be, but family structure alone doesn't tell you how well the family functions. It only tells you that it's different from what has been regarded as a traditional family.

For too long society, researchers, and the media have been thinking of the two-parent, middle-class family and their birth children as the standard by which all other families are to be judged. For too long those families that differed were thought not to measure up and were labeled as lacking or deprived. It's time to give legitimacy to cultural differences and alternative lifestyles.

> Watch this video to hear a discussion of the changing American family.
>
> www.youtube.com/watch?v=Ql0Q5uf-AbA

Giving Legitimacy to Cultural Differences and Lifestyles

A good start is to get rid of the term *broken family*, which sounds as if something is wrong, when in reality the so-called broken family may be quite functional. You can't tell by family structure whether a family functions in healthy ways. The single-parent family in apartment A may be quite functional compared with the two-parent, *intact*, but highly dysfunctional family in apartment B next door.

You have to be very careful about making generalizations about family structures. For example, some African American family structures have been portrayed as deficient. Stereotypes of domineering mothers, absent fathers,

Single parent families are fully capable of producing healthy children and providing the support that they need

Andy Dean Photography/Shutterstock

and disorganized families plagued with abuse and neglect sometimes overshadow the reality of families that don't fit what is sometimes thought of as the ideal structure.

It's time to quit looking at differences as deficits and view them instead as legitimate forms in themselves. Families of all types and sizes are fully capable of producing healthy children and providing a support system for all of the people who comprise the family. You can't judge a family's degree of functionality by its structure, patterns, or makeup.

Instead of automatically labeling some family structures as deficient and looking at them as social problems, it's time that we started to see their strengths. We should be supporting diversity in family structure. When we, as a society, come from a point of view that the family is breaking down, rather than changing in form, we put all of our resources into looking at the causes of the breakdown. We already know something about what causes stress in families. We know that you can't separate the way families function from the social, economic, and political realities that influence their lives.

Check Your Understanding 12.1

Click here to check your understanding of varied images of families.

SUCCESSFUL FAMILIES

A successful family is one that functions in healthy ways; it supports and nurtures its members so that everyone's needs are met. Although happiness and satisfaction may come periodically to members of successful families, those aren't the only emotions they experience; they feel a wide range of emotions and are free and able to express them when appropriate. A successful family isn't a perennial sunshine family. It has its ups and downs, just as its individual members do.

There is much talk about dysfunctional families these days. Many people have discovered that some of the ways they were reared weren't good for them—their families were abusive, created codependencies, and taught family members to ignore their own needs. The statistics vary, but it has been said that up to 98 percent of us grew up in dysfunctional families. Yet if 98 percent of us are raised in a particular way, that way must be *normal*—a word often equated with *right* and *good*. So where does that leave us as far as dysfunctional families are concerned?

Because the family prepares its members for society, we'd better look beyond the family to see what this high rate of dysfunction is about. A quick look will show that the so-called dysfunctional family is not so out of tune with the present society, which nurtures a system in which some have power over others and not everyone's needs are met. Power, both in the society and in the family, is often wielded like a sword rather than radiated like light. Privilege and hierarchy, sanctioned by the societal system, often squelch our ability to be who we really are; they take our personal power from us. The dysfunctional family reflects the dysfunctional parts of society.

The theme of the strong dominating the weak is pervasive both in the family and in society. If we take that theme to the extreme, we see that world peace in the past has depended on the strongest nations stockpiling enough weapons to stop each other from making war. That's the ultimate in the power approach to getting along with others. No wonder families have been hard-pressed to help their members grow in healthy, sane ways to become who they really are as unique people—each able to radiate the power inside.

We're beginning to change our approach—but change doesn't happen in an easy, linear way. It is often accompanied by periods of uncomfortable chaos, when things seem to get worse instead of better. Many who desire this change are beginning to create their own scripts instead of living by the old myths of power in which the strong overcome the weak, one race dominates another, and men control the lives of women. Many are altering the themes that have been handed down for generations.

Families are starting to rear their children for the emerging society—one in which it will be possible to raise children without abusing them and to be both connected and autonomous, one in which the dominator model gives way to a true equity model. Parents are learning how to use their power *for* or *with* their children instead of overpowering and dominating them. They are learning to *empower* their children—that is, to allow them to experience personal power, which gives them the feeling of being able to be themselves and of having some effect on the world or the people in it.

Parents are learning how to empower *their children—allowing them to experience personal power—instead of overpowering and dominating them*

People who are empowered don't need to overpower or manipulate others. They are free to experience being who they really are—to fulfill their unique potential; they will resist being cast into some preset mold.

No matter how much things change, all family systems will continue to have some degree of dysfunction, or they wouldn't be of human origin. We'll never live in a perfect world, but we *can* improve it by focusing on what kinds of traits make for successful families—the traits that will allow each member to function effectively within the family and in the society beyond. What are these traits?

Strategy Box 12.1

Working with Families from a Strength-Based Perspective

- The first goal in working with any family is to form a relationship with that family. That means that building the relationship is a top priority any time that you communicate with them.

- Look for every family's strengths and focus on those. When you communicate with the family, remember its members' strengths, which will help you have faith that they can answer many of their own questions and solve a number of their own problems. Don't be the "expert," instead be a supporter and facilitator who helps put them in touch with their own expertise.

- When you have problems finding strengths, examine your own attitudes and look at the stereotypes you hold. Self-awareness on your part is essential if you are to move beyond your biases and stereotypes so you can get to know this particular family and discover its strengths.

- Acknowledge the family's strengths to its members. Notice the skills they use with their children and mention those. Affirmations work with adults just like they do with children by emphasizing positives.

When you focus more on families' successes than on their stresses, you can then work with them from a strength-based perspective. Strategies related to strength-based approaches can be found in Strategy Box 12.1.

Traits of Successful Families

Healthy involvement with each other is one trait of a successful family. Its members feel attachment to each other. They care. They don't just fulfill a social role; they have a deep sense of commitment. They give time and attention to the family. They don't get overinvolved in activities that exclude the family.

People in successful families recognize the signs of unhealthy *codependence*, in which one person encourages and enables another to lean too heavily on him or her, creating bonds that trap both of them. People in successful families understand the importance of independence and healthy *interdependence*. They know how to get their needs met in a relationship that allows the other person to get his or her needs met as well. They know how to take care of others without making them overly dependent on that care. They understand mutual nurturing. One way to look at this trait of successful families is using what Christian (2006), writing about family systems theory, calls boundaries, which relate to togetherness and separateness. A family that values individual decision making, openness to new ideas, and separate identities for each member over close connections and conformity has a different set of boundaries in its system from the one that emphasizes togetherness and sees each member's identity as closely tied to the family. The problem is, if you're from the first family you may see the members of the other family as enmeshed. If you're from the second family you may see the first family as disengaged. It's very hard to determine which families are dysfunctional without understanding how their systems serve them.

Successful families tend to build and maintain self-esteem in their members instead of continually tearing it down. They know how to discipline children and to guide and control behavior in ways that leave self-esteem intact. Virginia Satir, who wrote *Peoplemaking* (1972), found in her practice as a family therapist that developing a feeling of self-worth is one of the primary traits of successful family systems. It is important to recognize cross-cultural perspectives on self-worth. What looks like parental behaviors that tear down self-esteem from one family's perspective may not look the same at all from another family's perspective. It's very hard to judge across cultures. That's why the school, preschool, and child care staff, and other professionals need to reflect the diversity of the society!

Successful families know how to communicate effectively. Communication is another of Satir's family systems. Effective communication means that family members can both give and receive feedback. They have some skill at resolving conflicts in ways that do not neglect anyone's needs. They use problem-solving methods to deal with even small issues when they arise. They know how to cope with problems that can't be solved. They know how to express feelings in healthy ways as is appropriate to their culture. They know how to give and get culturally appropriate strokes or recognition. Communication styles are greatly influenced by culture. Some cultures put much more emphasis on words than others. The ones who use the most words are called *low-context* cultures. They are a contrast to ones that use fewer words, called *high-context cultures*. The mainstream culture of the United States is a low-context culture, while the Chinese culture is a high-context culture because the meaning of communication comes from the context rather than words. Learning the traditions is a task of childhood—so children grow up to share the context and don't need words to communicate (Hall, 1981).

Successful families know how to protect their members, providing a secure environment within the home. Though a safe home is a haven from the outside world, it is also important that family members connect to the greater society. Therefore, two important family functions—protection and connection—seem to be opposites, but in reality they balance one another. Satir says one way of looking at family systems is to understand how every person in the family links to society. The degree of function is determined by how they link and what the results are.

Schools and early care and education programs can provide a helpful link to society—and for some families it's their first experience with societal institutions related to schooling and education. That's another benefit of family-centered schools and early care and education programs. The link can be more than a very loose one, and parents can become vitally involved in their children's education.

Successful families have rules that work for each member and for the family as a whole. "Rules are sets of standards, laws, or traditions that tell us how to live in relation to each other" (Christian, 2006, p. 16). Some families are clear about their rules and put them into words. Other families' rules are buried in the cultural context. When a couple gets married they sometimes discover rules they didn't know they had. They have to work to figure out what to do about contrasting rules. Rules can be about very large things, like how do adults and children talk to elders and who gets served first. When I grew up I wasn't aware of any family rules about who got served first. There may have been some rules, but apparently I never broke them. My husband's family, though, had very strict rules, which I discovered one night after a party. I remember that a decision was made in the kitchen to serve all the children first and get them out of the way before the adults sat down to eat. One elderly grandmother was upset to watch the children eat when the older people should have been served first. She didn't say anything at the time, but the look on her face showed her disapproval. Afterwards she complained about the children being fed before the adults. She had a strong rule in her family about that.

Rules that seem big to some can seem small to others—like taking off shoes when entering a house. If you don't have the rule, it may seem like a foolish and even annoying rule. If you do have the rule, it may be a very important one to you.

Parents and elders in successful families know how to pass on values to the next generation through modeling, discussion, teaching, and problem solving. They also know how to accept differences when value conflicts arise (see Figure 12.1).

Images of Successful Families

So what does a successful family look like? Do its members all have fulfilling jobs, live in nice houses, drive "newish" cars, and live stress-free lives? Of course not. Successful families come in all sizes, shapes, configurations, and financial conditions. Circumstances contribute to success, of course, but they aren't the sole determiners. If they were, rich people in good physical health would automatically be better at creating successful families than sick poor people, but that just isn't the way it works, is it?

> **Healthy Families . . .**
> - Have a healthy involvement
> - Are caring
> - Convey a deep sense of commitment
> - Give time and attention to the family
> - Don't get overinvolved with activities that exclude the family
> - Recognize the signs of unhealthy codependence
> - Understand the importance of both independence and interdependence
> - Know how to get their needs met as well as allowing others to get their needs met as well
> - Know how to take care of others without creating over-dependence
> - Understand mutual nurturing and healthy boundaries
> - Build and maintain self-esteem
> - Use discipline and guidance in ways that leave children's self-esteem intact
> - Develop a feeling of self-worth
> - Know how to communicate effectively (give and receive feedback)
> - Know how to express feelings in healthy ways that reflect their culture
> - Have skills at problem solving and resolving conflict
> - Know how to give and receive recognition
> - Know how to protect their family members and provide a secure environment within the home
> - Maintain connection to society
> - Have rules that work for each member and the family as a whole

Figure 12.1   Traits of successful families

Successful families come in all sizes, shapes, configurations, and financial conditions

Monart Design/Fotolia

No family is 100 percent successful. All families are in process. Think of success as a path—a path where no one gets to the final destination (just as no one reaches human perfection). Some start out on this path farther behind than others.

Compare two families. The first is made up of a couple who both came from stable families where their needs were fairly well met. When they had children, they tended to create the kind of home life they both experienced as children. They have their problems, of course, but they seem to take things in stride. They work at their marriage, at their individual development, and at their parenting.

They had good models in their parents for this work. They are on the path of success.

The second family is composed of a couple who came from less stable homes. They are also working at their marriage, at their individual development, and at their parenting, but they have to work harder because they haven't had the firsthand experience that the first couple had. They've had to come to the realization that their own upbringings were lacking—which means that they've had to *learn* healthy ways of dealing with their children. It didn't just come to them naturally. They are also on the path to success, but it's a rockier road for them, with numerous barricades to climb over and potholes to fall into.

What the two families have in common is that they have a vision of success. They are both on the path, moving toward their vision—and they are determined to make progress.

Six Families

Let's take a look now at six families who, in spite of a number of pressures in their lives, are also struggling along the path to become successful families. Some are much farther along than others, but stress is a theme in all of their lives. Let's see what kind of stresses they are coping with. One thing that these six families have in common is that all are enrolled in the same child care center and two have children in school.

Sara's Family.   Meet Sara. She was a teen parent when she had Ty six years ago; now she is 21. Ty is in school and his two-year-old brother, Kyle, is in the center because Sara is in nursing school at the local community college.

Sara has had a hard time of it since she became a mother at 15. She lived with her mother for the first couple of years, but they argued over how she was raising Ty, and Sara left to join the homeless population of her city. She and Ty lived for a while in her car until the poor old auto quit running, sat in one place too long, and got towed. Then she lived under a bridge between the highway and the river. Pregnant again (as the result of being raped), hungry, and desperate, she finally found a social worker in an agency that hooked her up with some of the services available in her community (more about this in the next chapter).

Now Sara is in nursing school, and life is better, but it still isn't easy. She has financial aid and a place to live, but she's going crazy trying to go to school all day, study all night, and raise her boys at the same time. They reflect her stress and they have stresses of their own. Ty seems to have an attention deficit problem, though the teacher is working with him. He can't seem to sit still and focus, and he becomes frustrated very easily when he can't do something. Then there's Kyle. He appears to be a very sweet child, cuddling up to the teachers whenever he gets a chance. But his brother beats on him, which is starting to make him aggressive toward other children. He has to be watched all the time because he bites. The staff is thinking of putting him in one of the satellite family child care homes available to the center because the stimulation of the center seems to be too much for him to handle.

Sara is learning about communication, discipline, and family relations from a parenting class and from her therapist. She doesn't feel very successful as a family head, but she is moving in the right direction. When she looks at her past, she sees that she has come a long way. She has hopes for the future.

Roberto's Family.   The second family is Roberto's. His four-year-old daughter, Lupe, is in the local Head Start program in the morning, and she comes to the center in the afternoon. Roberto transports her from one program to the other when his old pickup is running and he's not working. Otherwise, his wife, Maria Elena, who takes classes in English as a second language at the adult school, uses the bus to pick up Lupe and deliver her to the center. Maria Elena takes their baby, Paco, with her in the morning to class, where they have child care, but she brings Paco to the center in the afternoon while she cleans houses to support the family. Roberto does odd jobs when he can get them and has been looking for steady work for some time.

Lupe has a hearing loss, and the teachers in the center keep telling Maria Elena and Roberto that they must take her to see a specialist. But they went once and there were so many papers to fill out, none of which they understood, and no one was there to translate for them—so they walked out and haven't gone back. The center staff is working to find them a translator so they can get the help that Lupe needs, but so far they haven't found one. Maria Elena is very worried about Lupe, and so is Roberto, but he is hesitant to put his name on any kind of papers that might bring him to the attention of the government. He just doesn't trust what might happen once the government becomes aware of him and his family. It was bad enough signing up for Head Start and for child care, but at least those papers were in Spanish and he knew what he was signing. He didn't have to depend on someone with limited Spanish trying to explain them to him. His neighbor tells him he's being paranoid about this, but Roberto's family has had some bad experiences with government officials, and he doesn't want to repeat them. Roberto is wary!

Roberto has never even thought of whether his is a "successful" family or not. He's too involved in the daily struggle for survival.

He is anxious that his family live according to the traditions he grew up with, but he sees all of them being changed as the different cultures rub up against each other. He resists that change, but at the same time he appreciates what he and Maria Elena are learning about child rearing from their involvement with Head Start and the child care center. They are beginning to examine some of the "givens" of their own upbringing and thinking about whether they contribute to the goals they have for their children. They are most anxious to retain their culture and be the best parents they can be!

Junior's Family.   The most vocal member of the third family is 12-month-old Junior. He cries all the time. The staff at the child care center tries hard to comfort him, but what works with other children doesn't work with Junior. The whole family—refugees from their homeland—are obviously suffering from having had to flee, but the loudest sufferer is Junior. The center staff has never had a baby in the program who has been so unhappy for so long. He cries all day, every day, except for the periods when he sleeps.

The staff doesn't know too much about Junior's family, except that they live with a number of relatives in a small house that they're pooling their money to buy. Although the house is crowded in the evenings and on weekends, there's no one home during the day to care for little Junior. Everyone's out working. Great-Grandma used to take care of him, but she's sick now and can barely care for herself. Perhaps he misses her, and that's why he cries so much.

Language must be a problem for Junior, too. No one in the center knows more than a word or two of his language, and that must be very scary for him. And he doesn't stop crying long enough to listen to English.

The staff has tried to find out about Junior's diet, but his mother is very vague. She doesn't speak English too well, so she leaves things like food decisions up to them. The center provides the food for the children, but the staff is anxious to respond to any special cultural or family food preferences. They just can't find out from Junior's family what those might be.

Like Roberto's family, Junior's family is also rubbing up against other cultures, but they are so busy surviving in the new country, with its different cultures and different languages, that they are in culture shock. They are still reacting to what is new and strange to them, and they are not yet able to take in any benefits from the broadened experience.

Michael's Family.   The fourth family has one child enrolled in the child care center. Three-year-old Michael is a quiet boy with long dark eyelashes that sweep down on his cheeks when he lowers his eyes, which he does a good deal of the time. He is cautious and slow to warm up to people, but his slightly withdrawn manner has captured the hearts of the staff.

Michael's parents, Margaret and Beth, are a lesbian couple. Although the child comes every day, the staff has barely talked to his parents. They seem to move in and out of the center like shadows. Margaret usually brings Michael. She is friendly to staff but always in a hurry. Because some of the staff members have mixed feelings about this couple, several are rather glad the two women are so unobtrusive and seemingly unwilling to engage in conversation. However, one staff member has strong feelings about the bias this family may be experiencing in the center. She wants to change the atmosphere and be sure that the parents and the child feel comfortable and accepted. She has begun to introduce the subject of anti-bias regularly at staff meetings, and this has brought forth some discomfort among the staff. At the last meeting she pointed out that although the program is committed to "celebrating diversity," there is no physical evidence in the center that lesbian and gay couples are considered normal families. Pictures abound (on the walls and in books) that show all kinds of family configurations, except same-sex parents. No books in the center show gay or lesbian families.

"What can we do to make school more comfortable for and accepting of Michael and his family?" was the teacher's question to the rest of the staff.

"Good question," responded one teacher. "This is something we should talk about. I'm concerned about Michael," she added emphatically.

"I'*m* concerned about his parents as well!" said the first teacher, equally emphatically. "What can we do to raise their comfort level?"

The staff is still working on this question because they are in conflict with each other about what should be done. They can't even agree about the idea of bringing in books and pictures of families like Michael's. Some feel strongly that it's an equity issue they are discussing; others are taking a moral or religious stance. In the meantime, it's easy to see the discomfort level rise in Michael and his parents as they pick up unspoken messages from various staff members.

Although Michael's parents have many traits of the successful family, they are unable to benefit from what the staff might have to offer them to increase their knowledge of child development and family relations because of limited communication.

Courtney's Family.   Courtney's family commands a good deal of staff attention for all sorts of reasons. Courtney, the mother, has been married before, and two of her four children are in the program. Roland, her four-year-old, was abused by his father, and the family lives in fear that one day the father will arrive at school, claim his son, and take off with him. The staff has been warned of the situation and is aware of the restraining order that gives them the authority to refuse to let the father take Roland. Roland, after all his bad experiences, is fearful of men—and he doesn't get along with the other children, either.

Courtney, Roland's mother, a European American, is married to Richard, who is Native American. They have their own child, a two-and-a-half-year-old named Soleil. Roland's half-sister looks more like her father than her mother, and her beauty is remarkable—literally. Adults passing through the center stop to discuss what a lovely child she is.

Soleil is remarkable in other ways, too. She is intellectually mature far beyond her years, but socially she's still a baby. She confuses adults, who don't know what to think of her. They marvel at the way she is teaching herself to read but become distressed by the fact that she kicks, screams, and even bites when a child refuses to give her a toy that she wants to play with.

Courtney is in a drug recovery program and has just decided to continue her education. She wants to become a lawyer. Richard works in construction and is going to college part-time to become a history teacher. He has very strong feelings about his heritage, which the teachers found out about last Thanksgiving when they put up pictures of Pilgrims and Indians on the walls.

One of the teachers was just stapling the last picture up when Richard arrived with Roland and Soleil. He stopped, stared intensely at the picture, then turned abruptly to the teacher and said, "I'm sorry, but it's offensive to me that you're using caricatures of my people as decorations. It feels as if you're making fun of my culture."

The teacher stopped, stapler in hand, shocked by his words. "I don't understand. Thanksgiving stands for friendship and love. That's what these pictures are about—brotherhood—people helping people."

"Maybe that's the way you see it," explained Richard, "but what I see is that you're celebrating a day that marks the beginning of the genocide of my people. I don't want my children to have any part of such a celebration." He left the room abruptly, taking the children with him.

Later, during naptime, the other teachers were shocked to hear such a different version of the happy holiday they had always celebrated. But they took the pictures down and agreed to stress the harvest aspects of Thanksgiving rather than give it a "historical slant."

Richard heard about this through Courtney, who brought the children back later in the day. When he arrived the next morning, children in hand, he remarked about the missing pictures to Roland's teacher and expressed his gratitude about the staff's willingness to see his point of view and make some changes in their celebration. As a cross-cultural family, Courtney and Richard are exploring where their concepts of a successful family coincide and where they collide.

The Jackson Family.   Holidays are a big issue for the sixth family—the Jacksons—as well. They have two children in the child care program and one in school. They are pleased with everything but the celebration of what they consider Christian holidays. At a recent parent meeting, they got caught in the middle of an argument between two groups of parents. It started when Mrs. Jackson asked the staff to downplay religious celebrations. "I don't want my children to learn someone else's religion," she remarked. "We'll teach our religion at home, so please leave religious observances out of the program."

One parent answered her by insisting that Christmas had nothing to do with religion. Two other parents rose to their feet, arguing loudly that it was a terrible shame that Christ had been removed from Christmas and that there ought to be more religion in the center rather than less.

When the director finally got the parents calmed down, Mrs. Jackson spoke up once again, this time about dietary differences. She was concerned that her children were being fed food that violated the dietary restrictions of her religion.

She spoke politely and with great concern. The director asked her to make an appointment for another time to discuss the problem.

Mrs. Jackson arrived the next day at the agreed-on time and found the director in her office waiting for her. The two had met here earlier: Before the family came into the program, they had several discussions about whether the oldest Jackson child, who has spina bifida, could be accommodated in his wheelchair. Several modifications to the environment were required, which Mr. Jackson worked on with the help of Sara and Richard, who both have carpentry skills.

Mrs. Jackson and the director expected to have a good talk this time because they had gotten along well in the past. Mrs. Jackson expressed her feelings that the teachers were not watching what her children ate, and the director promised to do all she could to make sure that the Jackson children were carefully monitored at meal and snack times. She also asked Mrs. Jackson if she would be willing to do a cooking activity with the four-year-old group and teach them how to make one of the special dishes of her culture. She agreed, and that was the beginning of her involvement in the program.

At present Mrs. Jackson is working night and day on a big fund-raiser for a climbing structure for the play yard. She's finding it very satisfying to use her talent, skills, and connections in the community to benefit the program and the children, some of whom, she realizes, are severely financially deprived. She has involved a number of other parents, and they are getting to know and appreciate each other in ways that only come from working together toward a common cause—something they could never have done by just attending parent meetings.

The Jacksons have a lot going for them as a successful family. But, like the rest of the families, they still have a way to go.

Comparing the Six Families.   These six families have varying concepts, images, and dreams of what a successful family is. They all have many stresses in their lives. Their successes include varying degrees of the following:

- Commitment
- Attachment to each other
- Individual independence and group interdependence
- Ability to give and receive nurturing
- Ability to get needs met
- Coping skills
- Methods of building self-esteem
- Effective communication
- Ability to pass on culture, goals, and values

Their stresses include the following:

- Poverty
- Special needs of their children

Most families love their children and want the best for them, though they have different ways of showing their love and different ideas about what "the best" is and how to achieve it

micromonkey/Fotolia

- ◆ Problems with substance abuse
- ◆ Divorce and custody issues
- ◆ Stepfamilies and blended families
- ◆ Lack of support
- ◆ Communication difficulties
- ◆ Inaccessible resources
- ◆ Bias issues

Besides being in the process of building toward success and experiencing stress, what else do all of these families have in common? They're in the same child care program. They love their children and want the best for them, though they have different ways of showing their love and different ideas about what "the best" is and how to achieve it.

How are they different? They represent different cultures and traditions, different family structures (with different degrees of outside acceptance of those family structures), and different degrees of being part of the mainstream culture of the center. They also differ in their ability to handle the stress in their lives.

Real-Life Families: Some Statistics

According to the Children's Defense Fund (2014),

- the majority of children in America under age two were children of color in 2012.
- The majority of all children in ten states were children of color.
- By 2019, the majority of all children nationwide are expected to be children of color.
- One in five children—16.1 million—was poor in 2012.
- Over 40 percent of poor children lived in extreme poverty.
- Over one-third of children of color under two were poor in 2012—during years of rapid brain development.
- Children of color are disproportionately poor. Nearly one in three children of color—11.2 million children—was poor and more than one in three children of color under age five—3.5 million—was poor.
- Black children were the poorest (39.6 percent) followed by American Indian/Native Alaskan children (36.8 percent) and Hispanic children (33.7 percent).
- The largest group of poor children was Hispanic children (5.8 million) followed by White children (5.2 million) and Black children (4.1 million).
- Children in single-parent families were nearly four times more likely to be poor than children in married-couple families.
- More than half of Black children and nearly one in three Hispanic children lived with only one parent compared to one in five White children.
- Nearly 1.2 million public school students were homeless in 2011–2012, 73 percent more than before the recession.

- More than one in nine children lacked access to adequate food in 2012, a rate 23 percent higher than before the recession.

It is interesting that President Lyndon B. Johnson's War on Poverty began nearly 50 years ago, yet children are still the largest group of poor people in the United States. We are the richest nation on earth—first in GDP (gross domestic product) among industrialized nations. We have the greatest number of millionaires and billionaires and are way ahead in health technology, yet we have so many children living in poverty.

If as a nation we are concerned about children not doing well in school, it is important to note (again according to the Children's Defense Fund, 2014) that babies don't get off to an even start. Cognitive disparities between low- and higher-income babies can be perceived by as early as nine months of age. Those increase and by kindergarten are far more noticeable. It's not that we don't know what to do to keep poverty factors from affecting child outcomes. We have found anti-poverty policies that work. Two different projects provide examples of ways to make a difference in outcomes for children. An anti-poverty experiment called the New Hope Project in Milwaukee, Wisconsin showed that a child's outcome can be affected by society's support. The project provided an above-poverty income, health insurance, and child care. As a result children's literacy test scores improved, and children showed more positive social behavior five years later. Another study, by the Minnesota Family Investment Program, also found that supplementing the income of in-poverty families resulted in a measurable difference in outcomes for their children. The results included improvements in children's behavior and school performance (Children's Defense Fund, 2014).

Now think about the six families in this chapter. Imagine yourself—working in the child care program or as a teacher in the school where two of the families have connections or a social worker in the community. What would be your responsibility to support these families to advocate for their children? Check out the Advocacy in Action feature "How to Teach Families to Be Advocates," to get some ideas. Although poverty was a big factor in the majority of the six families, they had other stresses as well. All families have stress. Stress is part of life. When stress eats on people and overwhelms them, it has harmful effects, but stress doesn't have to be bad.

> **✓ Check Your Understanding 12.2**
> Click here to check your understanding of successful families.

ADVOCACY IN ACTION ▶ HOW TO TEACH FAMILIES TO BE ADVOCATES

Strong advocates are greatly needed! Children can't speak for themselves, so adults have to speak for them. When budget cuts come to school districts or child care programs, who can speak for the children? When school districts or state departments of education mandate curriculum that is developmentally inappropriate, culturally inappropriate, or harmful in other ways, who can speak for children? The voices most heard are those of parents—the consumers.

Some families are natural advocates and understand the process. They will protest without urging when their children can't get what they need from the powers that be. Other families have to learn to be advocates. They can learn a good deal from those who teach in or run the school or other programs their children attend. Help families see that when cuts come they don't have to just sit back and watch good things disappear. Help them recognize all the places that advocacy works, such as school boards, other governing bodies, regulatory agencies, and lawmakers at the community level, state level, and even national level.

Early childhood education has benefited greatly in the past from family advocacy efforts. If families don't organize themselves, help them. Recognize potential leaders among families, and nurture their leadership. Help families understand the many courses of advocacy action such as:

- Creating or joining an advocacy group.
- Collecting information about a critical issue.
- Finding and sharing research that relates to the issue, and formulating a position statement.
- Forming or joining a legislative telephone or e-mail tree.
- Keeping up with the issues in the media, and writing letters to the editor.
- Understanding how laws are made.
- Developing a relationship with lawmakers, and keeping in touch with them about the issues that concern children and families.

STRESS AS A POSITIVE FORCE

When the six families and the teachers and staff at the center to which they are all connected think about what to do to help their children, they can start by recognizing that stress isn't necessarily bad. We all need some stress in our lives. Stress can be a growth factor. A physical example of how stress is useful can be seen in the way a baby's bones form to enable the child to walk. The leg bones that connect to the hip socket have a different shape in the newborn than in the child about to walk. What makes the shape change to accommodate walking? Stress—the stress of weight being put on them. A similar example relates to old age. The older woman at risk for osteoporosis babies her bones by never exercising, and creates the very condition she's trying to avoid—her bones grow weak and brittle. Her bones need some stress to help keep them strong.

Of course, too much stress isn't any better than too little. Again, an example from physiology: Look at the sports injuries of children who overuse their pitching arms, for example. Irreparable damage occurs from too much stress.

What is too much stress for one family, or for one person, may be optimum stress for another. Some people are knocked down by seemingly minor setbacks; others manage much harder situations. Still others seem to take on adversity as a challenge and grow from it.

When I was first learning about child development, I took a trip to the high country above the California desert. There I observed a natural phenomenon that I have never forgotten: the bristle-cone pine. I saw this gnarled, ancient tree, bowed by the wind and stunted by lack of water and the thin air and soil of its habitat, as the perfect symbol for the benefits of stress. Instead of weakening under adverse conditions, these trees grow stronger than other plant life in less stressful situations. Using their adversity to the maximum, these trees survive longer than any other living thing on earth. Somehow they take the hardships life has to offer and use them to their own advantage. Some children do that, too.

We know that poverty, abuse, neglect, being shuffled around, lack of attachment, and not getting needs met can adversely affect children's lives. Obviously it is better for children to get what they need, be raised by people who care for them, have a stable home life, and meet loving acceptance inside and outside the home rather than having to live with abuse, neglect, bias, and discrimination. Yet we all know about "resilient children"—those children

Watch this video to hear Dr. Robert Sapolsky speak about positive and negative aspects of stress. Can you relate to what he said about the effect of chronic stress?

www.youtube.com /watch?v=n9mIDshQPcc

who, in spite of much hardship, manage to turn out with healthy personalities and find success and happiness in life.

What We Can Learn from Studies of Resilient Children

Studies by Werner (1984, 1995; Werner & Smith, 1992) and others (Castro & Murray, 2010; Dawes & Donald, 2000; Henderson, 2007; Luthar, Cicchetti, & Becker, 2000; Zautra, Hall, & Murray, 2010) show that there are some protective factors and personality traits that are common to *resilient children*—children who have the psychological strength to recover from misfortune or who emerge intact from a history of severe distress. One vital factor that the children had in common was a sense of connectedness to someone in the early years. These children found

Resilient children have experienced a sense of connectedness at some point in their lives

attachment, usually in the first year (not necessarily to a parent). Many of the children whose parents were not able to meet their needs found or recruited surrogate parents, inside or outside the home. Werner uses the term *recruited* to indicate that attachment wasn't just by chance, that the children had more than a passive role. From this recruited attachment, the resilient children received enough attention and nurturing early on to gain a sense of trust. Their lives may have been marked by abandonment, either physical or emotional or both, but at some period they found someone to believe in them and care about them. Even if they were shuffled from family to family, never belonging anywhere, they found sources of support. They made connections, and those connections seem to have provided enough to keep the children going in positive directions.

One reason these resilient children were able to make connections was that they had the ability to elicit positive responses from others. Even at a very young age, they were somehow able to gain other people's positive attention. These children were problem solvers, taking an active approach toward negotiating, communicating, and grappling with the obstacles that life presented to them. They had not only the willingness but also the skills to take an active rather than a passive role.

Another important commonality these resilient children had was that at some point during their lives they found themselves needed by someone else. They had responsibility thrust on them. They were required to help another person—a younger sibling, for example. Relating to someone else's helplessness gave them a sense of their own power.

Most important of all, perhaps, these children had a tendency to perceive their experiences constructively, and each held a positive vision of a meaningful life. In spite of their hardships, life made sense. In other words, their attitude made all the difference in the world.

Interestingly enough, it wasn't just the resilient children identified by the studies who were able to get over their unfortunate beginnings and move on to lead healthy, fulfilling lives. The other participants in the study—the ones who didn't have the above factors going for them—also were able to work beyond their early childhood problems. It took them longer, but by their 30s and 40s, most were living meaningful lives.

What can adults who live or work with children and have responsibility for their education and socialization learn from this research? How can children from families in stress be helped to be less vulnerable and, indeed, to be resilient? How can children grow up in stressful conditions such as poverty, family strife, instability, disabilities, bias, abuse, and neglect and not be harmed in their development? How can we help them grow in positive ways?

The key is to balance the stressful life events with protective factors. The stress must be decreased or the number of protective factors increased or, when possible, both. The protective factors are those just mentioned—a sense of connection, sources of support, skills for solving problems and for eliciting positive responses from others, and, above all, a positive attitude toward life and a feeling that it will all work out somehow.

> ▶ Watch this video to hear Dr. Sam Goldstein talk about resilience. What do you think about his comments on the connection between the heart and the mind? www.youtube.com/watch?v=isfw8JJ-eWM

Helping All Children Become Resilient Children

How does that information translate into adult behavior? What are some guidelines for parents, teachers, caregivers, family child care providers, and others who work with children and families in stress?

1. *Provide support for the child and for the family.* Encourage connections; help build networks. Children and families need all the support they can get—both formal and informal. The Parent Services Project (PSP) was started in California by Ethel Seiderman and is now nationwide. PSP specifically addresses this need for support for families by child care programs (Lee & Seiderman, 1998; Links, Beggs, & Seiderman, 1997). The idea behind PSP is that by supporting the family you make the family more able to support the child. One of PSP's guiding principles is that support is important to all families and that social-support networks reduce isolation and promote the well-being of the child, the family, and the community.

2. *Teach the skills necessary for making connections and gaining support.* Teach children social skills. Teach them ways to initiate contact and maintain it. This means being there with them while they are playing with peers to guide them toward effective ways to enter play and resolve the issues that come up while playing. Reinforce contacts with peers and adults. They'll learn better if they start early (even in infancy) and have a chance to practice with small numbers of people. Encourage families to focus on positive discipline techniques. Model prosocial behaviors; then pay attention to and reward such behaviors.

3. *Teach problem solving.* Crockenberg (1992) observed 95 mothers using negotiation with their two-year-olds to get them to pick up toys. Crockenberg came up with some interesting conclusions. The effective strategies combined a directive with an explanation, persuasion, or accommodation. That way the mothers gave the message that their wishes were important but also the child's wishes were important. By using this approach, the mothers conveyed information to their children about the way conflicts with others can be resolved. When parents adopt negotiation as an approach to resolving conflicts, they teach their children long-term relationship skills that they can apply to peers.

4. *Give children responsibilities.* Require them to help out. Hook them up with someone who is less capable than they are and needs them. When chores are shared, children gain a sense of being important and belonging. In China, real work is brought into child care centers to be done by the children and then sent back to the factory where it originated. Making real contributions is important. In families with several children, older children often help care for younger ones. In child care centers where children are separated into groups by age, caring for each other can take the place of caring for someone younger. Also plants and animals require care, which can be done by children. In family child care and in other settings where there are mixed age groups, adults can give older children responsibilities for children younger than themselves.

5. *Most of all, provide role models.* Children and families need to see people they can identify with doing all the things just mentioned—finding support, demonstrating social skills and the ability to make connections, using problem-solving skills, and taking responsibility. For early childhood institutions, finding positive role models for children becomes part of the recruitment and hiring process. Training helps, too. In addition, children need role models who have faith that things will work out and that life has meaning. If adults don't have it, they must be seeking it. No one can tell another person just how to do that seeking. Certainly spiritual traditions and religious institutions are a possible path. Therapy can help, too.

I don't mean to downplay the effect that stressful conditions have on children's education and socialization by painting too positive a picture. Neither do I mean to overemphasize resiliency. I just want to point out some obvious changes that could make a difference in some families' lives so that unnecessary stress can be eliminated and children don't need to be "superresilient."

To end on a cheery note, here's what Galinsky (1989) said a long time ago that still applies: "Things can be hard, but they don't have to do us in. It isn't whether good or bad things happen to you; it's how you handle them that matters" (pp. 2–3). She talks about how important it is to teach parents and their children to face problems, practice generating multiple solutions, figure out how to change what can be changed, and learn to cope with what can't. It's a matter of taking a can-do attitude and engaging in continuous problem solving. It's also a matter of getting together as a society to face the conditions that create ever-growing poverty and changing them.

School Success Linked to What Goes on at Home

It's not social class, family structure, parent's marital status, ethnic background, or the amount of money a family has that makes a difference in how well children eventually will do in school. What counts most is what goes on at home.

Parents can be poor, unmarried, and undereducated and still manage to groom their young children for a successful school career. It may be harder if one is poor, unmarried, and undereducated, but it is possible.

How do families manage to create early childhood experiences that result in future school success? They do it in a number of ways—including the way they relate to the children, the kind of home life they provide for them, and what they teach them.

First, children must be protected. Families who groom their children for future success in school know how to protect them, keeping them from physical and psychological harm. They set limits. They monitor whereabouts and behavior.

Check Your Understanding 12.3

Click here to check your understanding of stress as a positive force.

These families see their children as capable and hold a vision of the future that includes the child as an able student. They encourage learning of all sorts by the ways they relate to their children, how they talk to them, and the activities they provide.

They teach their children social skills, defining appropriate behavior for them. They give them feedback to increase their sensitivity to others. They do this in a warm and nurturing way, creating an emotionally supportive environment that emphasizes decision making.

They help their children learn to express themselves. They give them chances to develop a sense of responsibility and learn both leadership and follower skills. They encourage them to concentrate, focus, be attentive, and follow through. Most of all, they respect their children and themselves.

SUMMARY

This chapter started by examining different family constructions and the images we have of what a family means. It then presented characteristics of successful families in general. The chapter also looked at six examples of families and the stresses they face. Though it may not seem obvious that stress can be useful, stress was regarded a possible positive force. The chapter then discussed how studies of resilient children have much to teach anyone working with children and their families, and ended with a section devoted to helping *all* children become resilient children.

QUIZ

Click here to check your understanding of Chapter 12, "Stress and Success in Family Life."

FOR DISCUSSION

1. Give examples of three of the traits of successful families that are present in a family that you know.

2. Have you ever known a family like one of the families in this chapter? How was the family the same as the one in the chapter? How was it different?

3. Have you ever known a resilient child? What do you think made this child resilient? Did this child share the common protective factors and personality traits described in the chapter?

4. Give examples of some things you could do to help all children become resilient.

5. Think of an example of how the following sentence plays out in someone's life: "It isn't whether good or bad things happen to you; it's how you handle them that matters."

WEBSITES

Alcoholics Anonymous (AA)
Information on Alcoholics Anonymous for the general public and professionals appears here. Information is available in English, Spanish, and French.

American Psychological Association (APA)
This website has a Resilience Guide for Parents and Teachers. It also has current articles, with the conclusion that children raised by gay or lesbian parents are as likely to support children's psycho-social growth as children raised by heterosexual parents.

Division for Early Childhood
The Division for Early Childhood (DEC) is one of 17 divisions of the Council for Exceptional Children (CEC), which is dedicated to the educational success of people with disabilities and/or gifts and talents.

Making Lemonade
This is a resource for single parents, with additional sites listed for information on children and parenting, schools, and divorce.

National Center for Children in Poverty (NCCP)
The National Center for Children in Poverty website helps identify and promote strategies that prevent child poverty in the United States and that improve the lives of low-income children and families.

Resilience Research Centre
The centre's Pathways to Resilience Project (PTR) is a research study that examines risk factors and aspects of resilience of youth across different cultures.

FURTHER READING

Castro, F. G., & Murray, K. E. (2010). Cultural adaptation and resilience: Controversies, issues, and emerging models. In J. W. Reich, A. J. Zautra, & J. S. Hall (Eds.), *Handbook of adult resilience* (pp. 375–403). New York, NY: Guilford.

Children's Defense Fund. (2011). *The state of America's children 2011*. Washington, DC: Author.

Dorris, M. (2011). Why I'm not thankful for thanksgiving. In E. Marshall & O. Sensoy (Eds.), *Rethinking popular culture and media* (pp. 100–105). Milwaukee, WI: Rethinking Schools.

Edelman, M. W. (2011). *Child watch column on teen pregnancy.* Retrieved July 2, 2011, from http://cdf.childrensdefense.org/site/MessageViewer?em_id=11381.0

Ginsberg, K. R. (2015) *Raising kids to thrive: Balancing love with expectations and protection with trust.* Elk Grove Village: IL. American Academy of Pediatrics.

Goldberg, A. (2010). *Lesbian and gay parents and their children: Research on the family life cycle.* Washington DC: American Psychological Association.

Kaiser, B., & Rasminsky, J. (2016). *Challenging behavior in young children: Understanding, preventing, and responding effectively* (4th ed.). Upper Saddle River, NJ: Pearson.

Stiffelman, S. (2015). *Parenting with presence: Practices for raising conscious, confident, competent kids.* Novato, CA: New World Library

Zautra, A. J., Hall, J. S., & Murray, K. E. (2010). Resilience: A new definition of health for people and communities. In J. W. Reich, A. J. Zautra, & J. S. Hall (Eds.), *Handbook of adult resilience* (pp. 3–34). New York, NY: Guilford.

Bikeriderlondon/Shutterstock

Early Care and Education Programs as Community Resources

Learning Outcomes

In this chapter you will learn to...

- Define and discuss types of early care and education programs.
- Describe the state of child care in the United States of America today.
- Explain what it means to partner with families.

This chapter focuses on the kinds of programs that serve children in the first eight years of life. Called early childhood education (ECE) programs, the term is defined by the National Association for the Education of Young Children. I use the initials ECE (as do some other people) to mean early *care* and education so that *care* is not looked down as noneducational. Care and education go together in my book. You really shouldn't have one without the other. ECE includes school up to third grade. Traditionally there has been a divide between people who work with children under five years of age and those who work with children older than five. Kindergarten teachers may see themselves in one group or the other or maybe in both. Kindergarten is a transition between what some call "preschool" and "school." This chapter gives an overview of the different kinds of early care and education programs and their benefits to children and families. It also looks at some of the issues around providing full-time child care to working families.

DEFINING TYPES OF ECE PROGRAMS

Early care and education programs are difficult to explain to anyone who hasn't experienced them. They go by different names, serve different age groups, and occur in a variety of settings. The first three years of elementary school, the primary grades 1–3, fall under the category of "early care and education" because developmentally the children are more like their younger peers than they are fourth and fifth graders. Children make a developmental shift around the time they leave third grade into what has been called "the age of reason." By fourth grade most children are cognitively ready for what can be thought of as more traditional schooling. The developmental perspective is that children have different needs in each stage of development.

Exploring the Various Types of ECE Programs

Grades 1–3 are the oldest and perhaps best known of the early childhood programs though they weren't considered *"early childhood programs"* originally. They still aren't thought of in those terms by many families today. Grades 1–3 are school—real school—and they always have been in that category. Certainly the content has changed over the years as have the expectations for children aged 6–9. Back in the 1930s entering first grade was much more like entering preschool than it is now. It was expected that children were leaving home for the first time and perhaps separation from parents might be a problem. Advice was given to parents as to how to prepare for the separation. Part of the advice consisted of instructions to make six-year-olds somewhat responsible for themselves in basic areas such as dressing and toileting. Expectations have changed since then. Now children are expected to have advanced way beyond toilet training and not only have "preacademic skills" but academic ones as well. Schools, along with testing mandates and "grade-level expectations," are less like actual early childhood programs than previously.

Kindergarten is in a category by itself because it isn't quite school, but it isn't preschool, either. Kindergarten was started in the United States because some wise educators saw the need for a transition for children instead of sending them from home directly to school. This was in the days before preschool or child care—the days when mothers were expected to stay home with their children. Of course, mothers without the support of male wage-earners did go to work and had to find care among family members or friends. Then along came kindergarten, which was designed to ease children into the routines and behavior expected of them when they entered first grade. Kindergarten has changed and is more like the first grade of the past; preschool has now become the transition period.

The preschool program is the most well known of the early care and education programs. The term *preschool* is confusing because it brings up different pictures for different people. *Preschool* merely means "before school." Another term for it is prekindergarten, or pre-K. In the past, the preschool program was commonly called *nursery school*, which is the term I prefer because it emphasizes the nurturing part. I was on a campaign for a while to spread the term *nurtury* because nursery school is so old fashioned. But with all the push for readiness and academics, I missed out, so now I just use preschool, even though it annoys me that early care and education programs have to be *pre* anything. It seems to me that they are an institution in their own right—just as children are children—not preadults.

So what does the term *preschool* encompass? It includes half-day programs, some of which focus on parent education and advocate developmentally appropriate practices including free play as a way of learning—not just an activity for recess. Other half-day programs have a named philosophy, such as Waldorf education or Montessori. The largest number of preschools are compensatory programs, Head Start being the best known. States have their own compensatory programs for low-income children. When I first entered the early care and education field in the 1960s, preschools were half-day programs for stay-at-home mothers, who were mostly middle-class housewives. Head Start was begun for a whole different segment of the population. Day care, as full-day programs were called then, was for single mothers who worked or families with two working parents. Some were run by school districts, and some still are. Now the programs are often blended some with half-day programs.

Infant-toddler programs were separate and apart—and to some extent they still are. Back in the '60s when I was a preschool teacher, I worked in a parent involvement program. The children were in preschool, the parents in English as a Second Language classes, and the babies in a "nursery" with a group of untrained volunteers "watching" them. The first programs for infants with trained staff were early intervention programs for children with special needs. Infant care for working families was mainly done by people who took children into their homes for pay. They are called family child care providers.

Carla Mestas/Pearson Education, Inc.

In infant-toddler programs, the practice of early care and education is critical for the well-being of the babies

Now there are infant-toddler programs for working parents—often connected with preschool programs so children can stay in the same location by "moving up" as they mature from infancy, to toddlerhood, to three- and four-year-olds. Some of these programs have a strong parent-education component, while others have parent-involvement, which also may include parent education. When these programs are housed in a school district, the transitions can include kindergarten and elementary school as well. One advantage of this kind of program is that siblings can be together—not necessarily in the same room with the same teacher, but in the same building.

Child care for school-age children can also be in a category by itself and has the unique feature of often including children who are no longer in their "early years." A variety of programs support families who need to have a safe environment and supervision for their school-age children during the hours they work, when their children are not in school. In addition to having educational, developmental, and caring elements, school-age care also has important socialization functions as children learn to get along in groups of their peers in less structured programs than the classroom usually offers.

School-age care often comes in the form of "surround care" where children leave home before school, spend an hour or more in child care in mixed age groups, then go to a classroom where the children are all the same age. After school they go back to the child care program. During school holidays and summer vacations, surround care becomes full-day care to meet the needs of working parents. These programs take place in a variety of settings including homes with family child care providers. If programs are run by schools, they are often in portable buildings on the school grounds or sometimes in a multipurpose room. Some school-age programs are stand-alone programs that serve only children from kindergarten up. They may be privately owned or publicly funded. They may be in their own building or in a rented space. Other school-age programs are part of a comprehensive child care program serving children from birth to 12 years of age. Usually in those programs, the younger children are separated by age, while those in the school-age population are put together in mixed age groups.

Family child care, mentioned above, is another form of early care and education. Those programs were, and still are, conducted in private homes by the people who live there and represent the largest service providers for working parents in the United States. Over the years these programs have become part of the regulatory system. In many states the programs are licensed, and in some, the individuals working in them are trained as well. States vary a great deal in how much attention is paid by government workers, funders, and policy makers to family child care providers.

Though family child care may be looked down on by those early educators who consider themselves more professional, family child care programs have a lot going for them. As a consumer of family child care when my children were little, I've always been aware of the advantages. Usually parents have more choices when it comes to family child care programs. Homes, necessarily (and often by regulation), have smaller groups of children than programs outside the home. Providers can develop personal relationships more easily with children and their families. Continuity of care, an important component of children's early experiences, is more likely to be available in family child care. That means that children can stay in the same home from infancy until the time they don't need the service anymore. Of course that doesn't always happen, but it's possible, whereas in most out-of-home programs children change classrooms, teachers, and sometimes groups every year or even more often.

The picture is necessarily complex when you consider all the programs that fit under the early care and education category. To some extent their purpose may be different as is appropriate for the wide spread of age levels. Certainly the physical facilities are vastly different. The funding may come from a wide variety of sources—including families, local tax money, the state treasury, federal funds, and private funding. The regulations may also come from a wide variety of sources.

Changing Times

In the days when I started in the field, preschool and child care were separate entities, and preschool was considered educational while child care was considered custodial. That doesn't necessarily represent reality, but rather the image many people both inside the field and outside it carried in their heads about the distinction of the two. Some still see the two as separate, but others, such as myself, have been working hard to help everyone see the link between care and education and to quit separating programs by types.

In Australia, where I have traveled quite a bit, a simple descriptive title distinguishes the two. Children go to "sessional programs" or to "long-day programs," and the whole field is called children's services, which connects everything rather nicely. We in the United States are still working at these connections.

The reality is that if staff is well trained, if the groups are appropriate sizes for the ages of the children, and if the environment is set up appropriately to promote development, learning, and caring, any program can provide both care and education—whether the program is part-day in a school following an academic calendar or all day, year round, and whether it is in a separate facility or in someone's home. Good quality care and education don't just happen accidentally—there are lot of people and organizations working hard to make sure that every child has the opportunity to be in a setting that provides both good care and education. We're not there yet, but we're working on it.

Watch this video to hear Nel Noddings and other experts speak on caring and kindness in the classroom. Do you remember having caring and kindness as part of your educational experience as a child?

www.youtube.com/watch?v=g7WbLtc149Y&list=PL4f hRdQDT4Yexd0bUQgN4bq HIkQ3UeS5

Watch this video to hear a transitional kindergarten speak about the benefits of the program.

www.youtube.com/watch?v=MbJFeyesp7E

Making the link between care and education hasn't been easy. What has helped is that Nel Noddings, a Stanford professor, has written several books making a good case for always having a connection between care and education all the way up through the university. She wrote a book called *The Challenge to Care in Schools* (2005) in which she described how public schools from kindergarten up can have a caring curriculum that is educational. She sees a caring curriculum as vital to moral development, a hot topic among families and educators these days. As I read her book, I was anxious to tell her that she was describing what we already do in early care and education programs. So I wrote her a "fan" letter and got a very nice reply! I've never written a fan letter in my life.

Universal pre-K, sometimes called preschool for all (or PFA), is a movement that is gaining momentum. Advocates want to assure that every four-year-old has a chance to attend a free half-day preschool. Though universal pre-K looks different in different states, that's the main push behind it. Some states have already succeeded in instituting the change, while others are still investigating it. According to Morgan and Nadig (2007), there is no standard way to institute universal pre-K. Some states are creating a class before kindergarten in the public school system, while others are considering free education for four-year-olds in a variety of settings. Still others are targeting low-income families for free education for their four-year-olds. There are different ways to look at universal pre-K at this stage of the game (see Figure 13.1).

As the number of child care and education programs continues to increase, many are asking the question: Who is rearing America's children, and how are they being reared? That is an increasingly compelling question. It was a nonquestion just a generation or two ago because America's children were mostly reared by their own families or by specific substitutes whom the families designated. Child rearing belonged to the family. Business, education, and government mostly stayed out of the picture, except for a brief period during World War II and for protective and remedial reasons.

Today the picture has changed. The number of single-parent families in which the parent trains or works outside the home is steadily rising. And in a majority of two-parent families, both parents work outside the home (see Figure 13.2). In some two-parent families, the mother works and the father stays home with the children. Child rearing is now shared, as families use an array of early care and education services. Furthermore, business and government have become part of the picture.

Who is raising America's children? Perhaps you are or will be—either as a parent or as a professional in the education field or other related community services. Some of you may be in the field of early care and education. As the need for services expands and programs struggle to keep up with the need, educators, such as teachers, child care workers, infant care specialists, family child care providers, in-home care providers, and nannies, supplement parent care.

Pro	Con
• Universal pre-K is a good idea. If kindergarten is to become first grade, each child still needs a transitional year. It's good to start children in school early, especially low-income children.	• Universal pre-K is not a good idea. The real need is for full-day programs that have both good care and education. With all the money and attention going into universal pre-K, what are working parents going to do? Universal pre-K requires before and after care. It would be better to use the money to upgrade and expand the existing child care programs
• Universal pre-K is a good idea. All families should enjoy what middle-class families have—access to preschool programs	

Figure 13.1   **Some ways to look at universal pre-K**

Statistics according to a group called "Women Employed" whose mission is to improve the economic status of women and remove barriers to economic equity:

- 64 percent of women work and 54 percent of them work full time.
- 68 million women are in the work force (excluding military). 59 percent have children under 6 and 70 percent have children 6 to 17 years of age.
- 15 million of those women earn less than $25,000 a year at full-time, year-round jobs.
- Females make 77 cents for every dollar earned by males.
- Only one in three workers has paid sick leave to care for their sick children, and 77 percent of the lowest-paid workers have no paid sick leave at all.

Figure 13.2   **Mothers in the workforce**
Source: Retrieved July 21, 2011, from http://www.womenemployed.org/index.php?id=20

Early Care and Education Programs as Child-Rearing Environments

Why does this text keep equating early care and education with child rearing? After all, the United States doesn't have a communal child-rearing system in which children are taken out of the home and socialized into a model consisting of a single set of ideals. We don't believe in social or political indoctrination for our children. Child rearing is an individual matter and always has been. As a society, Americans agree to disagree. Diversity has always been a key theme as well as a strong point of America's people. Families want to rear their children in their own way. However, these days individuals and families must look outside themselves for supplements to what they can provide. They can no longer do all the child rearing themselves.

> You can't park children. Wherever children are, they are growing and learning, being changed by their experiences.

But is child care really child rearing? Yes. You can drive your car to work, park it in a garage, and come back and pick it up in the afternoon, and, except for a new layer of dust, it is almost always in the same condition you left it in. You can even leave your car at home in the garage, take the bus or the train to work, and come back and find it just as you left it.

But you can't park children. Wherever children are, they are growing and learning, being changed by their experiences. They are being reared. *How* they are being reared is a big question. They can be reared in accordance with parental expectations and values, or they can be reared in ways that are quite contradictory.

The challenge for our society in these times is to offer enough choices so that families can find programs in tune with what they want and need for their children. The choices could include both nonparental care solutions such as out-of-home early care and education or in-home care, as well as creative alternatives that allow working parents a greater role in caring for their own children. Flextime, one of these alternatives, allows parents to stagger their work schedules to be with their children, thereby doing the child rearing mostly themselves. Part-time work also allows more parental involvement in child rearing; job sharing is one way to become a part-time worker. In some countries, workers are subsidized to stay home with their children instead of working a full day or a full work-week. Flexible benefits plans and flexible leave and transfer policies can also be creative alternatives that allow parents to spend more time with their children.

Worthy Wages and Quality Care

Kayla is in a quality child care center with a stable staff who knows her well and can provide just the kind of care and education she needs. Staff members are sensitive and well trained, and they have the time and energy to arrange the environment in appropriate ways and to set out a variety of interesting and worthwhile activities that promote growth and development. They are there to guide, protect, and teach Kayla by relating to her on an individual basis and by supporting her development in numerous ways. Kayla is happy in her school, and her mother is happy that she is there. But what about the teachers?

If the teachers are happy, it's because they love teaching and work in a well-funded program in which they are paid what they deserve, have a good benefit package, and have adequate support through staff and other resources. Or perhaps they are happy because they have other sources of income and have figured out how to scrounge up the resources they need. Or they may get so many rewards from teaching that money isn't an issue with them. Many good teachers remain in the field despite the low pay.

However, in most child care programs, the staff is underpaid, and if any of them are the sole support for their families, they have a hard time managing on a child care teacher's wages. Child care teachers' wages reflect their status, which, according to the U.S. Department of Labor Bureau of Labor Statistics, is equated with parking lot attendants. Some refuse to leave the field, even though they are being paid less than prison guards and animal tenders. These dedicated souls are helping to rear the nation's children—rearing these children at the point of their lives when they are very impressionable.

Most early care and education professionals are in the field because they get so many rewards from teaching; they don't always stay in the field because they cannot afford to support themselves on the low wages

Suzanne Clouzeau/Pearson Education, Inc.

What does it mean to children and families that child care teachers are underpaid and undervalued? It means a lot. It means that many people will never even consider going into the field—people who have a lot to offer children. It means that anyone who isn't totally dedicated to the profession and wants to make an adequate living will look elsewhere. It means that few men, especially those who don't have a partner who can supplement their income, will look to child care as a career option. This limits the field drastically.

The problem of low status and salary is reflected in the turnover rate. Many people enter the field only to leave it in a short time when they find the demands of the job too much and the pay too little. One-third to one-half of the people working in child care are new every year according to Marcy Whitebook (2011). That means that children see their teachers constantly changing—continually coming and going. As soon as they get to know and trust someone, that person leaves. Eventually children stop developing relationships with their child care teachers—it's just too painful to keep saying good-bye for good.

That's not good for children.

Quality is tied to status, salaries, and training. Who is going to spend the money for training if the status and salaries are so low?

We are in a crisis situation. We have a great need, as a nation, for early care and education programs. Working in the early childhood education field can lead to a very satisfying career. Yet the money for quality programs just isn't there. Most parents couldn't possibly afford what quality care costs. They need subsidies. A few parents get some subsidies from the government; others get them from employers. But an enormous number receive their subsidies from the teachers who are willing to work for so little pay. That's not the ordinary way to look at subsidizing child care, but it is one way. Don't you think that it is time things changed?

Check Your Understanding 13.1

Click here to check your understanding of defining and understanding ECE programs.

Watch this video to hear ECE professionals share their experiences on advocacy day. What could you do to advocate for ECE?

www.youtube.com/watch?v=vlomSjGfSI0

THE STATE OF CHILD CARE IN THE UNITED STATES TODAY

If we look at child care in European countries, this great nation of ours is way behind. We have been struggling for many years to provide quality care, raise salaries of child care professionals to a living wage, and create a trained workforce. We have struggled to pull ourselves out of the category of "babysitters." We aren't there yet. We have worked to have licensing regulations that provide for health and safety of all, but those vary greatly state by state. We have watched as school teachers have gone through the same processes we are going through. We have seen them do somewhat better than child care providers have managed. It's not just about the professionals who work in child care, but also the families who use child care. Most families can't afford what child care really costs.

As a nation whose future depends on children who spend their early years growing and developing, we need to pay attention to where those children are spending those first years. We also need to know what resources there are to help families who can't afford to be home with their children. It's not like it once was where there was a strong middle class where one person could provide financially for the family, while the other could focus on raising the children. And, of course, many single parents, throughout our history, had to figure out how to raise their children and support them financially. As a nation we should have been paying attention all these years to the question of "Who is raising America's children?"

Today many of the children are being raised in out-of-home care. The future of our country depends on those children being raised well. That means they must have their needs met—not just the basic physical ones, but the social, emotional, and intellectual ones too. That's a big challenge for a country whose citizens often think of how they can take care of themselves and assume they can move forward through personal initiative.

Affordability and Availability

Two A words loom up when we look at requirements for early care and education, especially those for working families: *affordability* and *availability*. When we, as a society, work to create both affordable and widespread early care and education programs that meet families' needs for child care and education, quality often gets lost. We get into a double bind when we deal with both quality and cost: Most parents can't afford to pay what quality programs really cost.

Child care professionals can't afford child care unless it is provided free where they work. Their average salary is far less than other educators and service workers, according to Whitebook, Phillips, and Howes (2014). The families who need care most can't afford it, yet as a society we can't afford not to pay for it, especially for low-income families—and there are more low-income families than before (Austin et al., 2011; Kirp, 2011). We know what works according to Kirp: "providing high-quality early education and child care from crib to kindergarten, a time when children's minds are especially malleable" (2011, p. 2). Quality costs, but it saves in the long run. Studies show that risk factors associated with cognitive delay and other developmental problems can be lessened by early intervention in the form of quality early care and education programs that meet the needs for child care (Illig, 1998; Karoly, 1998). Furthermore, quality early care and education programs can cut the crime rate. Kirp (2011) has a plan that, in addition to improved and accessible early education, also involves starting prenatally to support parents and using community resources better in conjunction with schools. The North Carolina Abecedarian Project showed that early childhood education can make a critical difference in the later success of poor children. This project was a carefully controlled research design project in which children who had an individualized prescription of educational activities and games as a part of their daily routine tested higher in cognitive test scores up to age 21, achieved higher levels in reading and math, completed more years of education, and were more likely to attend college than children not in the program (Campbell et al., 2000).

A study of Head Start called FACES (U.S. Department of Health and Human Services, 2003) showed that the program narrowed the gap between the performances of children from poverty-level families and their higher-income peers. Low-income Head Start children showed significant improvement in social skills, emotional development, and behavior, which were linked to their cognitive development. Parent participation in educational activities with their children was positively correlated with children's behavior and early literacy skills. A different study found that Early Head Start, the program that serves infants and toddlers, also has significant benefits and impacts social-emotional development as well as children's cognitive and language development at age three.

As a society we haven't yet learned the lesson that quality costs but pays off. We aren't willing to pay what child care really costs. We say we can't afford it. As a result, early care and education programs, including child care, in the United States, aren't as good as they could be.

Status and Salaries

According to Whitebook and Sakai (2004), the lower the salary, the higher the turnover rate. The greater the turnover, the lower the quality of services and the more likely for the children to have poor developmental outcomes. In a program with a high turnover rate, it is less likely that children will experience responsive caregiving and sensitive interactions.

Imagine the children in a program with a high turnover rate. They are constantly disrupted by changes in their routines. High turnover means that rules switch as teachers come and go. It means that just as the children get to know a teacher, he or she disappears suddenly and is replaced by a new person. Separation issues don't get resolved. The consistency of the stable environment that children need to flourish is a sought-after vision but seldom a reality.

We need to find ways to solve these problems. It isn't just up to families and early educators to work toward solutions. Indeed, as mentioned earlier, many parents are paying more than they can afford now. A low-income family can pay as much as 26 percent of the family budget for child care. And teachers, by working for poverty wages, are subsidizing child care themselves. No, it's not up to parents and teachers to solve this problem alone. It is in the public interest to help also. Children are the future of America.

Even without platitudes, you can look at the situation from a very personal point of view. When you reach retirement age, you will be dependent on a strong, healthy, productive workforce to keep the society and the economy going. You won't be able to sit back and enjoy the fruits of your own labor if there is no one to carry on.

Even more personally, imagine yourself in a retirement home being cared for by men and women whose own upbringing left much to be desired. If today's society allows its future citizens to be neglected at home or warehoused in an institutional setting, how well will they treat you if and when you need their care in your old age?

The picture of child care is sad. We still have a long way to go. We aren't yet close to creating a system that fills the need and provides quality care. When President Bill Clinton signed away the traditional welfare system in 1996 and changed it to Temporary Aid to Needy Families (TANF), all of a sudden the need for child care increased dramatically, as former welfare recipients became trainees and their children, including babies, needed a place to go. Although infants had been trickling into child care for some time, they now came pouring into the system at a rate programs couldn't keep up with. This situation meant that for TANF to work, child care had to expand, which called for more funding to keep up with the demand and more training dollars to increase the child care workforce. We still haven't met the current need, and a large number of children are in inadequate settings

Our system of child care is notable for its diversity, which is both a strength and a challenge. Creating a seamless system that meets the needs of all children and all families is still a distant dream that we are only just beginning to realize. Unlike some smaller European countries, there is no single policy or program that can address the child care needs of all families and children. No single entity or organization can provide child care for the nation, but rather the responsibility for meeting the nation's child care needs has to be widely shared among individuals, families, voluntary organizations, employers, communities, and government at all levels.

Watch this video to hear the Educare staff discuss the benefits of preschool, and the role of teachers as professionals. What do you think would increase the level of pay and respect for ECE professionals?

www.youtube.com/watch?v=x0o4HgacXA0

Looking at Quality

Defining, measuring, and monitoring the quality of child care are very hard tasks because to some extent the definition of quality is highly subjective and personal. However, the classic study done in the 1970s—the National Day Care Study (Ruopp, Travers, Glantz, & Coelen, 1979)—came up with three variables that influence quality: *group size*, *caregiver-child ratio*, and *caregiver qualifications*. This study helped justify and substantiate the laws and regulations governing child care. It also helped back up the National Association for the Education of Young Children's (NAEYC) accreditation criteria, which are now contained in a major instrument to assess quality across the nation. There are ten NAEYC program standards, which can be found on the NAEYC website, organized into four focus groups. The first group of standards focuses on children and what is needed to support their development and learning. The other three groups focus on what is needed to create and maintain excellence in programs and relate to teachers, family and community partnerships, and leadership and administration (see Table 13.1).

Although we continue to move forward as a profession, in many places in the United States child care remains unregulated—and even where it is regulated, laws and regulations provide only a bottom line (i.e., they define *minimum* standards). Various national and state professional organizations have provided more optimum guidelines, including a book of standards from NAEYC called *Developmentally Appropriate Practice* (Copple & Bredekamp, 2009) and an updated introductory version called *Basics of Developmentally Appropriate Practice: An Introduction for Teachers of Children 3–6* (Copple, 2006). A new "basics" book focuses on infants and toddlers (Copple, Bredekamp, & Gonzalez-Mena, 2011).

Table 13.1   **NAEYC Accreditation Standards**

Focus Area:	Children
Program Standard 1:	Relationships
Program Standard 2:	Curriculum
Program Standard 3:	Teaching
Program Standard 4:	Assessment
Program Standard 5:	Health
Focus Area:	**Teaching Staff**
Program Standard 6:	Teachers
Focus Area:	**Family and Community Partnerships**
Program Standard 7:	Families
Program Standard 8:	Communities
Focus Area:	**Leadership and Administration**
Program Standard 9:	Physical Environment
Program Standard 10:	Leadership and Management

Check Your Understanding 13.2

Click here to check your understanding of the state of child care in America today.

PARTNERING WITH FAMILIES

Meeting the needs of the families enrolled is an important part of any early childhood program; the focus is not just on the children alone. The learning environment can be in schools, centers, or family child care homes. Good care and education, like good child rearing, enhances each child's development as a unique and powerful person who is capable of cooperating with others and living in a group situation. The goal is to partner with parents to establish a sense of being an individual while incorporating a growing sense of community. This happens most easily with a stable, consistent, trained staff, available at least some of the time to interact with children one on one and in small groups. Another contributing factor is plenty of play time during which the child is actively engaged with peers and practices decision making, problem solving, and resolving conflict. These factors include parents as partners.

Adult-Child Interactions in Child Care and Early Education Settings

When looking for high-quality settings, an important question to ask is: What is the quality of adult-child interactions, regardless of the program model? Taking into account that the first program

Partnering with families creates a sense of community

David Kostelnik/Pearson Education, Inc.

Watch this video to hear about the importance of teacher/child interactions, and get an introduction to the three main ideas of the CLASS tool. www.youtube.com/watch?v=2Hw0DbxOmJQ

standard of NAEYC's accreditation model relates to relationships, let's look at adult-child interactions with that in mind.

Most early educators and many parents today would agree that children should spend their days actively involved in exploring and learning about the world and each other. A helpful adult close by is essential for providing resources, input, and guidance. Is that what happens in most child care programs? According to Amanda Wilcox-Herzog (2004), teachers' beliefs and behaviors vary greatly. Teachers' effective interactions with children are vital, but though they have been researched to some extent, more research needs to be done—and training as well. One of the problems is that children outnumber adults in early childhood programs so interactions don't occur as frequently as they should. The quality of the interactions is important as well as optimum frequency. Adult-child ratio and group size affect interactions. Smaller groups and good ratios allow adults to have more sensitive, responsive interactions with children. In programs with less than optimum ratios and group sizes, adults are much more likely to use pressure to seek compliance by issuing demands, giving orders, quoting rules, and even ridiculing and making threats. In homes and in smaller centers, or in large centers where attention is paid to group size and ratios, adult input is more likely to be facilitative—encouraging, helping, and suggesting rather than demanding. Kontos and Wilcox-Herzog in their 1998 research concluded that it is possible to see a connection between sensitive, involved adult interactions with children and enhanced development. The effect of positive relationships shows in cognitive, social-emotional, and language development. From warm, sensitive interactions where adults are nurturing, accepting, and respectful, responsive relationships grow that encourage the development of autonomy and initiative, which, according to Erik Erikson (1963), is vital to healthy development in the early years.

A goal should be to break centers into smaller, self-contained groups. Group size is a vital factor to quality. Way back in 1979, the National Day Care Study (Ruopp et al., 1979) showed that group size has more effect than any other factor on teacher and child behavior and on intellectual development. Yet regulations about group size are still not universal.

Another indicator of quality centers on the question of what place the families have in the program. In extremely child-centered programs, family members may feel unwelcome, especially if they arrive with younger siblings in tow. This book is advocating for family-centered programs where families feel welcome in many ways, including among others:

- Space for them to be comfortable, with provisions for children not enrolled.
- Staff that greets them warmly and finds time to talk to them.
- Communication in many forms coming on a regular basis.
- Opportunities to not only give input to the program, but also become part of decision-making bodies and processes.

To summarize: A quality care and education program provides a safe, healthy, and nurturing learning environment designed to meet the needs—physical, emotional, intellectual—of the individuals and the group. In other words, it combines care and education.

Quality care programs put families at the center of the attention along with their children and do not focus just on children alone. One way to bring families into the picture is to create a sense of community in the program. Strategy Box 13.1 gives

Working with Families to Create a Sense of Community

- Creating a sense of community among the people involved in your program is an important goal when working with families. Start by trying to create a sense of belonging from the beginning by finding out names right away. Check out pronunciation so you get names right.

- Introduce everyone who is part of the program to everyone else.

- Put up a picture board of staff with something written about each person.

- Consider a picture board of families as well.

- Introduce families to each other and help them become resources to each other, such as when families share in carpooling.

- Find out what special interests or skills family members have.

- Make the environment welcoming to everybody.

- Think of meetings as a way to get to know each other better, no matter what the purpose of the meeting is. Get people to interact with each other.

some ideas about how to give families a sense of belonging to the program and to each other.

Creating a sense of community requires not only strategies and skills. Honesty is a part of the picture as well. A preschool director who worked in a highly regarded program housed in a church, but not church related, tells a story about the importance of taking a stand in the name of honesty. See the Advocacy in Action feature "Taking a Stand: Truth and Honesty with the Families You Serve" on page 298 for the story.

Including Everybody: Children with Special Needs

In the past, children with special needs often ended up in special education programs rather than in child care programs designed for everybody's children. Since 1992, when the Americans with Disabilities Act (ADA) was passed, the mandate has been to provide people who have disabilities with access to all community services, including child care. Then, in 1997 came the Individuals with Disabilities Education Act (IDEA) amendments, which state: "To the maximum extent appropriate, children with disabilities…are educated with children who are not disabled." Children with disabilities are to be cared for and educated in a "natural environment," which means an environment where their typically developing peers are to be found. Furthermore, each child must have an individualized education program (IEP), which includes, among other things, a statement of the child's present levels of educational performance, measurable annual goals, short-term objectives, program modifications, or supports.

What is the definition of "a child with special needs"? A child with special needs is one who requires specialized care because of physical, emotional, or health reasons. The kinds of disabilities vary greatly, from physical challenges to developmental differences to illness. They may include communication disabilities, developmental disabilities and delays, emotional and behavioral disabilities, visual and

ADVOCACY IN ACTION ▶ TAKING A STAND: TRUTH AND HONESTY WITH THE FAMILIES YOU SERVE

Preschool Director

As a director of a successful preschool, I loved the respectful and collaborative relationships I had with my students and families of different ethnicities, races, and religions. The school was housed in a church that had a dwindling congregation; the minister wanted to bring the preschool families into the fold. I let the minister know the demographics of our families and that what he was proposing was counter to the mission statement of our school. He said I should not notify the parents that the children would be given Bible instruction once a week by church members; he said our preschool was so good the parents wouldn't even notice. I disagreed and said parents had a right to know and to choose what they wanted for their children, that over the past 20 years parents had chosen our school for its multicultural, non-sectarian, play-based curriculum.

After much negotiation and political wrangling, I finally realized the minister was going to have his way. I let the parents know that when my contract ended in June I would be not returning as director as there were philosophical changes afoot in the coming year. The minister said I had no right to tell them why I was leaving and what changes were going to happen. As an early childhood professional, I have to advocate for the rights of parents to know information critical to their advocacy of their own children. Needless to say, all the Jewish, Hindi, and Buddhist families left the school and many of the Christian families, too.

hearing impairments, exceptional health needs, learning disabilities, and physical challenges. Some children have a combination of several conditions.

How do parents who have children with special needs approach putting their children into child care that is not designated as special education? Some have great hesitation. What if the adults in the program don't pay close enough attention to their child? What if their child gets lost in the crowd? Most parents have this concern, but when the child has special needs, the anxiety may be greatly heightened because of certain risk factors. What if the disability is severe allergic reactions and nobody is paying close enough attention to notice that the child is being served milk or is eating peanuts or is playing around the garden where bees are in abundance? What if the program staff members have informed the family that increasing self-help skills are a major goal of their program, and the family worries that because the child is so physically challenged he will be neglected in the name of making him more independent? Of course, cultural differences enter in here, too. If a family sees dependence as a blessing, not a curse, the parents may not be as eager for their children to learn self-help skills as a family that wants to maximize independence.

Professional early educators recognize that caring for and educating a child with special needs does take extra watchfulness and thoughtfulness. It helps, though, when they remember that a child with special needs is more similar to than different from other children. These children need what all children need: a safe, nurturing environment with adults who respect them and know how to meet their needs. They need chances to explore, to make choices, and to be supported. They benefit from an individualized approach and also from being included in a group.

A book published by the California Department of Education called *Inclusion Works!* (2009) has many practical ideas for how to create child care programs that promote a sense of belonging for children with special needs. It isn't enough just to enroll children with special needs in a program with their typically developing peers; certain steps and procedures for integrating the child with the group need to

Professional early educators recognize that children with special needs benefit from an individualized approach and also from being included in a group

be followed. "The biggest barrier to including a child with a disability or other special need seems to be fear" (California Department of Education, 2009, p. viii). Teachers are afraid that they won't know how to care for a child, won't meet the child's needs, or even may physically hurt the child. Knowledge is power and can take away fears.

How can early educators possibly know all about every condition of every child who might end up in a program that is primarily designed for typically developing children? That is a question often asked by practitioners who are faced with providing care and education for a child with a disability they know little about. How can I meet this child's needs?

One way to find out about a child is to observe that child. "The child is the teacher" is something that Magda Gerber, infant expert and founder of Resources for Infant Educarers (RIE), used to say all the time. Through observations and interactions the early educator can learn a good deal, but not everything. He or she also needs resources. The first and most important resource is the family of the child. When programs take a parents-as-partners approach, they can learn more about all children in their care, including those with special needs. The family knows their child better than anyone else. If the child has been identified as having special needs, the family has already become part of the system of resources and support. The professional early educator can find out from family members what they have been told, what agencies and individuals are working with the child, and who can help the child care program meet the child's special needs. Also, the early educator can share observations with the family and other professionals and ask them what strategies and ideas work at home. Working closely with the family is essential. Connecting with the resources and supports they have is useful, too.

Having Concerns about a Child

Sometimes a child comes into a program without being identified as having special needs, but early childhood professionals have concerns about the child. Professionals with training and experience in development may notice that a particular child isn't following a typical pattern. It may be hard for that professional to put a finger on his or her concerns, but if there is a nagging feeling, it is important for the professional to begin to observe closely. That means writing down what is observed and keeping a record. Writing each observation as objectively as possible and recording the date can show progress or lack of progress as well as provide useful information about the child's developmental differences. Patterns may begin to emerge as the professional notices that the child often seems "stuck," can't remember things, or can't seem to get involved in anything. It may be that the child doesn't get along with other children, has a low energy level, or seems confused often. Perhaps the difficulty has to do with the program, and a change or two makes all the difference. But sometimes what the professional does to help fails to make a difference. After making specific observations and writing down the details, the professional may decide that this child needs more specialized help. Talking to the family about the professional's concern is the next step.

Suggesting to family members that something is going on with their child is a delicate matter and needs to be carefully thought out by the professional before setting up a meeting. Having a positive attitude and approach makes a difference. Having specific information with details about observed behavior gives a clearer, more objective picture than just pointing out problems the child may be having. Using neutral language is a key to keeping things positive, which means avoiding labels and negative judgments but discussing behavior and skills in terms of what has actually been observed. Sharing observations about strengths and areas of weakness to see how well the professional's observations match with the family's observations gives a more complete picture. When early childhood professionals use language families understand, they reduce any possible power differential and open up communication. When they speak in terms of developmental ranges rather than comparing the child to other children, they do the child and the family a service. The point of the meeting should be to share information, gain a clearer picture, and figure out together what has worked, what has not worked, and what is to be done to optimize development for the child in the program. Perhaps further resources are needed. Pooling information about resources is useful.

How do family members feel when called to such a meeting? For some it may be a relief to know that what they have been noticing that has caused them concern is validated by a professional. Others feel a wide range of emotions. Typical reactions are tears, denial, guilt, fear, blame, and anger. Parents may feel they are failures or their child is a failure. If communication has occurred all along, the content of the meeting will be less of a surprise or shock than if this is the first conversation the early childhood educator has had with the parents. Having time to talk and sort things out, including feelings, gives parents the opportunity to cope with what may be painful news. Sometimes it takes a while for the information to sink in, and parents are unable to hear what is said at such a meeting. If the parents have heard and understood, having an idea what to do next can be helpful, too. Perhaps more observations are in order. Or parents may want to contact their pediatrician or local school district about an evaluation and resources.

Questions Concerning Continuity between Child Care and Home

How much should the early care and education program reflect the methods, approaches, and values of the families? If special needs are involved, should there be continuity between what goes on at home and what happens in the program? When what happens at home is different from what happens at the center, the two settings may provide a balance. For example, if the family loves taking care of a child who can do very little for herself, the program can provide more opportunities for the child to try out self-help skills. In such a situation, teaching the self-help skills has to be done skillfully and sensitively if the child is to feel safe and secure away from those who constantly do everything for her.

What about value differences? It is important to consider the following two questions:

• Is *continuity between home and program always valuable*? A look at a cross-cultural example gives one view. In China today, couples are allowed to have only one child. Yet China is very family-oriented, so all the energy that went into the many children of the large families of the past is focused today on a single child. As a result, this child gets a good deal of attention—"spoiling," if you will—from two parents and four grandparents. As many as six adults are all vitally concerned with this one small child. So child care is set up to purposely counteract this effect.

Carla Mestas/Pearson Education, Inc.

In child care settings with multicultural staff, children can learn early to respond in positive ways to diversity and to adapt to people who are different from themselves

Child-adult ratios are large, so that adults cannot focus very much time on any one child. Group expectations are heavy—the child must learn to be a good group member. Although learning to be a good group member happened easily at home in the old days of big families, it might not happen at home as easily now. So the child is learning this lesson at child care. Child care is set up to create a gap between home and program—one is designed to counterbalance the other (Tobin, Wu, & Davidson, 1989). Newer research shows some changes in the 20 years since the first study Tobin and his colleagues did in China, but the group focus is still there (Tobin, Hsueh, & Karasawa, 2009).

• Is *the ideal to aim for racial and cultural similarities between caregivers and children or to aim for diversity*? The advantage in similarity is that when children see adults of the same race as themselves, they identify with these people. When children of color see adults of their race in positions of authority and competence, they have models, which can be valuable for their self-esteem.

When consistency exists between family and program, cultural competence is more likely. All children, no matter what race, culture, or ethnicity, should be in settings that increase their cultural competence. An example of when continuity and consistency are important is when a child is in danger of losing home language and culture. For some children, being in a program where their language is spoken and where they can continue to relate daily on a close basis with people of their culture can make a big difference in helping them to keep their identity intact and to continue to develop in their own language. In infancy such continuity can be especially important because infants aren't born members of their culture but must learn to be culturally competent. If they don't get enough waking hours of exposure to their own people and language, the consequences can be negative.

That's not to say that cultural continuity is vital in every situation. For some children there are advantages of experiencing interracial, multicultural staff and children in their child care settings. They can learn early to respond in positive ways to diversity. Children in America today need to learn to adapt to people who are different from themselves.

Choosing Child Care: Debbie and Walt

Debbie is a physical therapist in her middle 30s. She and her husband, Walt, delayed having children, but now they have 18-month-old Evan. Debbie took a six-month leave when Evan was born, but when it came time to go back to work, she had such strong feelings about leaving him that she and Walt worked out a time-share plan. She went back to work half-time, and he rearranged his work schedule so that he could be home when she wasn't. So far they haven't had to use child care. But now they've decided that their city apartment isn't the right place for Evan to grow up, so they're in the market for a house. In addition, Walt, who has two teenage children from his first marriage, is feeling some pressure because his oldest daughter is applying to expensive colleges. It's time for Debbie to go back to work full-time. She is looking for child care. Here's her story.

Debbie started by calling a friend at work, who recommended the child care center that she uses. Debbie went over right away. She was appalled at what she saw. The place seemed like a madhouse—furniture overturned, paper on the floor, children everywhere yelling and screaming. Debbie couldn't imagine her precious little Evan here! A harried-looking teacher showed her around but was interrupted every ten seconds by some squabble or a child demanding something. After ten minutes the teacher handed Debbie a fistful of papers, told her that all the information she needed was on them, and left her standing wide-eyed by the door. She made a fast exit, depositing the papers in the trash can in the parking lot.

Next Debbie checked the phone book. At random, she picked another place, close to her work. She was astonished to find this center just the opposite of the first one. She arrived to find the children waiting in line to go outside. Although they were talking quietly and wiggling just a bit, they were not unruly. The room was immaculate, a little cold, and on the bare side. Debbie tried to imagine exuberant Evan in this setting. She couldn't. She left without talking to anyone.

The next place Debbie tried was down the street from her apartment. "At last!" she thought as she stepped inside a pleasant, well-lit room alive with healthy child activity. She liked what she saw—clusters of children playing busily, adults on the floor with them. "Good energy here," she concluded. But when she talked to the director, she discovered that this center took only low-income children, and even for them it had a waiting list with 100 names on it. She left, disappointed.

"Your turn," she told Walt when she got home that night. "I'm just too discouraged."

By the end of a week she and Walt had learned a lot about child care. They found a local resource and referral agency that gave them information about centers as well as family child care providers—people who use their own homes for child care.

By the end of two weeks, they had visited a number of centers and family child care homes and found two that suited them that had openings. They sat down to make a decision.

First Walt brought up an earlier discussion about in-home care. "Are you sure you don't want to reconsider looking for someone to come here? If we could find someone, it would be easier."

"Yes, it would be easier, but I want Evan to be with other children. I can't imagine him here all day every day by himself with someone who isn't me or you."

"So what will it be, Mrs. Watson's house or the River Street Center?" asked Walt, ready to settle this question. "They both have pros and cons. The center is more convenient and cheaper. It's warm and homelike. I like the way they plan curriculum around the children's interests. The staff seems stable—I asked each how long he or she had been there and was impressed at the low turnover rate. What do you think?"

"Well," Debbie said slowly, "I liked the center, too, but I wonder how Evan would fit in with those kids. They are so much older than he is."

"Mrs. Watson has a five-year-old and a four-year-old," said Walt.

"Yes, but the group is so small that the older kids are an asset rather than a liability. I don't worry that he will get lost in a crowd of big kids."

"But Mrs. Watson's is twice as far away."

"True, but I really like the fact that he'd be sort of part of a family. He has so many years to be in school, I'd rather he experience family life at this point. And when he's older he could go to the preschool down the block from Mrs. Watson, so he could have a larger group experience before he goes to kindergarten."

"I think you've made up your mind."

"I guess I have. What about you?"

"I think Mrs. Watson's house is great! Let's call her."

An important aspect of child rearing is *care*—the feeling and the function. We can't legislate the feeling, only the function. But we can make it more likely that the feeling will follow if we have well-trained, well-paid, well regarded staff and providers who are not overworked or burned out. This means that, as a society, we have to place a value on child care and on those who provide it.

In April 2015 NAEYC published and released a seminal report, "Transforming the Workforce for Children Birth Through Age 8: A Unifying Foundation." This report looks at the attributes that define the early childhood education profession and acknowledges that many pathways exist for entering into and advancing within the field. The report lays out skills and competencies of early educators. Recommendations are included for aligning competencies with science and research. Examination of how to make higher education programs for professionals more effective is part of the report, as well as supporting consistent quality. This book has emphasized family-centered care and education throughout. In this section we'll look at child care in particular because with this shared care arrangement, a focus on the family is even more vital than in half-day preschools, kindergarten, and the primary grades. Child care is more of a child-rearing environment than school is. Child care workers and parents—who together equal the full picture of child rearing—must be partners. Many parents today can't do it alone. But a child care system can't do it alone, either, no matter how good it is. What parents give is passionate feeling, highly personalized, that comes with a history and a future. Watch a power struggle between a parent and a child, and you'll see emotion seldom seen between two other people. Although providers and teachers are often critical of the passionate exchanges they witness from time to time, it is important to recognize that that's what parenting is about. It's about connectedness, which results in intense interactions. Parenting is passionate business—the anger as well as the love. Parenting is a long-term affair—much longer (excluding certain circumstances) than any child care arrangement. The parents and other family members provide the continuity through the child's life as he or she passes from program to program or from child care to school. Child care and teachers and providers come and go, but children need continuity in their lives, and it's up to the families to provide it.

Parent and caregiver are partners in child rearing: Therefore, it is vital that they appreciate, respect, and support each other.

Acknowledging feelings and building trusting relationships is an important part of mutual appreciation, respect, and support

Carla Mestas/Pearson Education, Inc.

Roadblocks to Mutual Appreciation, Respect, and Support

What gets in the way of this mutual appreciation, respect, and support? One roadblock on the part of some early educators—even those not in full-day care programs—is the "savior complex." I remember my own period of being a savior. I was a beginner, and I thought I knew everything. And besides, I had a great desire to rescue children from their parents—especially the parents I didn't like much or understand very well. I went even further—I saw myself saving the world through the work I was doing with young children. Can you imagine how it must have felt to be a parent trying to communicate with me way up on my high horse?

Another roadblock I've encountered in others I've worked with is anger and resentment. Tune in on the following scene, which takes place in the living room of a modest home:

The sun is still just a hint in the eastern sky as the doorbell rings. A family child care provider in her bathrobe, who has barely managed to get her hair combed at this early hour, rushes to the door, followed by her fussing baby, who keeps raising his arms to be picked up. She is greeted by a mother dressed in a lovely print dress with jacket and jewelry to match. Hiding behind the woman is a sniffling toddler who is wiping her nose on the sleeve of her pajamas. After a rapid exchange of greetings, the mother explains briefly that she will be late tonight because she is taking an important client to dinner. She says a quick good-bye and then turns on her high heels and leaves.

The provider closes the door with a slight slam and leans up against it for a moment before she faces the two needy children who are both fussing at her. Although reminding herself that she made a conscious decision to stay home while her own child is a baby, she is nevertheless resentful of the nice clothes, jewelry, and makeup, as well as the freedom to attend power lunches and client dinners. All of that is totally unrelated to her own day of picking up messes, wiping noses, and changing diapers.

Meanwhile, in the car at the curb, the mother sits for a moment trying to rid herself of the distress she feels at leaving her daughter like this. She wonders whether the sniffles are the beginning of an illness. She wishes she could be there to watch her daughter closely and take care of her. She's resentful that the provider can be in her bathrobe at this hour and not have to worry about makeup or clothes. She starts up her car, thinking about how nice it would be to have all day to play with children instead of dealing with clients and coworkers in a dog-eat-dog world.

Neither woman in this scenario really wants to trade places with the other, but they both harbor resentments. Consider how these resentments might influence communication between the two. Imagine how the provider will feel tonight if the mother arrives later than she promised. Imagine how the mother will feel if the provider calls in the afternoon and says the child has a fever and must go home regardless of the important dinner scheduled. Will either one feel very understanding? Probably not, with all that resentment that was brewing earlier in the day.

A major issue between parents and child care workers is competition—of all kinds but especially competition for the child's affection. Because children are likely to be attached to both their parents and their providers, the competition is often intensified. Although in most cases child care workers remain only secondary attachments for children, parents can feel quite insecure about what they perceive as the threat of being replaced as number one in their child's eyes. It is up to both parents and providers to be aware of the feelings generated by this situation and to learn to respect and relate to each other in supportive ways. Acknowledging the feelings is a first step. Working on the relationship is also a positive approach to take. Setting out purposely to strengthen the relationship is accomplished most easily when all parties involved remind themselves that the child's welfare is at stake.

We have a model for sharing the care of a child: the extended family so prevalent in many cultures. In this model, the child experiences several simultaneous attachments instead of an exclusive one with the parent alone. There may be a single primary attachment, but the child who grows up in an extended family is likely to be parented by more than one person.

Choosing Child Care: Roberto

Roberto is a single parent and a physical therapist who works with Debbie, the mother in our earlier case study. Roberto has custody of his four-year-old daughter, Mercedes. Now he is looking for child care, as Debbie had done previously.

When Mercedes was born, Roberto's mother, Barbara, offered to care for her on a daily basis. The arrangement worked out very well until just recently. Barbara inherited some money, and she's gotten the travel itch. This itch came at a convenient time because Roberto was just thinking that Mercedes needed to expand her horizons a bit. Not that she didn't get what she needed in her grandmother's home, but Roberto wants her in a program with teachers and other children.

Roberto started his child care search about six months after Debbie did. He felt a good deal of pressure from Debbie to check out Mrs. Watson's, where Evan was so comfortably settled, so he did. He liked what he saw, but it wasn't what he wanted for Mercedes. Mrs. Watson was warm and kind and obviously knew how to provide developmentally appropriate activities for the children in her care. She was also motherly to Roberto, but he bristled at that. "I don't need another mother," he told himself.

It was easy to decide against Mrs. Watson's family child care home. What Roberto wanted for Mercedes was a center.

He visited a number of places, including the ones that Debbie had gone to. Roberto wasn't as appalled as Debbie was at the variety of programs he found.

Roberto knew what he wanted. It's just a matter of finding it, he told himself. He wanted a place where Mercedes could experience children and teachers of other cultures—one where teachers were trained to treat four-year-olds as four-year-olds and provide a rich variety of creative activities. It was hard for Barbara to open her house to easel painting, clay and play dough, carpentry, and other messy kinds of projects.

Barbara and Roberto have discussed this subject before. They are in agreement. "Those are the kinds of experiences a child care center should provide—ones it's hard to set up for at home," Roberto told Barbara.

Barbara agreed. "It will be nice for Mercedes to be with other children, too, instead of all by herself with just me."

Roberto found several programs that he liked. The one he liked best was in a church. He worried at first that they might teach religion there but was assured that the program was only renting the Sunday school rooms and wasn't affiliated with the church itself.

What Roberto particularly liked about this program was the racial mix of the staff and the atmosphere. He made a couple of visits and was pleased to see the variety of creative activities, including a sensory table and water play, available for the children. When he brought Mercedes to visit, some children were finger painting. Mercedes dived right in and was soon up to her elbows in oozing reds and yellows. She was having a glorious time smearing paint around. No one got upset that she went beyond the paper a couple of times.

Mercedes loved circle time and was the first to grab some streamers and start dancing to the music. She beamed as the teacher sang her name in a good-morning song. There wasn't anything that Mercedes didn't love.

"This is the place for us," Roberto told the teacher as he walked out the door, Mercedes in tow, protesting.

"Can't I just stay a few more minutes?" his daughter begged.

"You can come back tomorrow and spend all day!" Roberto answered.

Check Your Understanding 13.3

Click here to check your understanding of partnering with families.

SUMMARY

Early care and education programs can be considered child rearing environments, and that's why quality in those programs is so important. Two influences on quality are affordability and availability. Looking at the state of child care in America today, in some ways we have learned a lot, but we haven't yet managed to create high quality child care across the nation. One influence on a program's effectiveness is how well adults and children interact, which can be influenced by such factors as group size and ratios. Because of the many benefits, child care programs should accept and respond effectively to children with special needs. How much should a program strive for continuity between child care and home? The chapter considers this question and sheds some light on the issues involved. The chapter ends with a section on parent-professional partnerships and explores some of the roadblocks to those partnerships.

 QUIZ

Click here to check your understanding of Chapter 13, "Early Care and Education Programs as Community Resources."

FOR DISCUSSION

1. Do you agree that children are actually "reared" in early care and education programs? Can you give the view of someone who agrees? Can you give the view of someone who disagrees?

2. What do you think makes up quality care and education? Explain your answer.

3. What are some ways that families and teachers can come together to create a sense of community in the early care and education program?

4. What do you think about trying to match teachers to children's cultural and language background?

5. What did you think of the scene on page 304, in which both the provider and the parent felt resentment? What solution do you see to this problem? How can the provider and parent communicate better and cope with their feelings?

WEBSITES

Child Care Aware
Child Care Aware is a national network of community-based child care resource and referral agencies that provides a common ground where families, child care providers, and communities can share information about quality child care. The "news" section is up to date and very informative.

Child Care Exchange
This site offers many resources for directors of child care and other early care and education programs, including a daily short e-mail column called ExchangeEveryDay that shares research, gives information, and discusses hot topics of interest to ECE professionals.

Children's Defense Fund (CDF)
The mission of the Children's Defense Fund is to ensure every child a healthy start, a head start, a fair start, a safe start, and a moral start in life.

Division for Early Childhood
Early intervention-related links are on the DEC website, as is information dealing with policy, research, and services.

National Association for the Education of Young Children (NAEYC)
The National Association for the Education of Young Children has a number of resources available for parents and professionals, including books and journals, one of which is called *Young Children*.

National Association for Family Child Care (NAFCC)
The National Association for Family Child Care is devoted to promoting quality and professionalism in family child care homes.

Zero to Three
Zero to Three: National Center for Infants, Toddlers, and Families, for parents and professionals, is a leading resource on the first three years of life to promote diversity and the healthy development of babies and toddlers.

FURTHER READING

Copple, C., Bredekamp, S., & Gonzalez-Mena, J. (2011). *Basics of developmentally appropriate practice: An introduction for teachers of infants and toddlers*. Washington, DC: National Association for the Education of Young Children.

Faber, A. & Mazlish, E. (2012). *How to talk so kids will listen and how to listen so kids will talk*. New York: Scribner.

Kirp, D. L. (2011). *Kids first: Five big ideas for transforming children's lives and America's future*. New York, NY: Public Affairs.

McMullen, M. B., & Apple, P. (2012, September). Babies and their families on board! *Young Children*, 67(5), 42–48.

Modica, S., Ajmera, M., & Dunning, V. (2010, November). Meeting children where they are: Culturally adapted models of early childhood education. *Young Children*, 62(2), 20–127.

Tobin, J., Hsueh, Y., & Karasawa, M. (2009). *Preschool in three cultures revisited*. Chicago, IL: University of Chicago Press.

Whitebook, M., Phillips, D., & Howes, C. (2014). *Worthy work, STILL unlivable wages: The early childhood workforce 25 years after the National Child Care Staffing Study*. Berkeley, CA: Center for the Study of Child Care Employment, University of California, Berkeley.

wavebreakmedia/Shutterstock

Supporting Families Through Community Resources and Networks

Learning Outcomes

In this chapter you will learn to...

- Explain social networks.
- Describe families using community resources.
- Discuss connections to the community.

This chapter explores the contributions the community makes to support families. We'll examine how the community and the institutions and people in it support the family and help it function.

For families to educate and socialize their children in healthy ways, many have needs that exceed their resources. Of course, schools and early care and education programs are important resources, and many families depend on them. But other needs arise, too. Families are never entirely self-sufficient; that's why they live in communities. All depend on their community and the resources in it. Some families are able to seek out those resources more easily than others. It is important for early educators who work with children and families to understand what the resources are and how to access them so they can advise families.

SOCIAL NETWORKS

Some families already see themselves as part of a larger social network, and they know both how to contribute to and how to make use of this network. This is the sign of one aspect of a healthy family system, according to family therapist and author Virginia Satir (1972). Healthy families do not isolate themselves from the outside community if they can help it. They have a broad perspective that includes the world beyond the family, and they use feedback from that world. They are able to give and receive help from the outside social network.

Each family system has its own set of boundaries. For example, some families don't seek help or support from the larger community. They prefer to see themselves as self-sufficient and regard outside support of any kind as a sign of weakness. Of course, no one can be completely isolated and entirely self-sufficient, even those who grow their own food and have their own water source. All families depend on community-built and maintained transportation systems if they wish to go from one place to another that's too far to walk. Even more importantly, they depend on clean air and water, which represent a global interdependence that all of us are becoming more and more aware of. All families depend on a functioning society that keeps enough peace and cooperation so families can live. But beyond the basics, some families don't look for support outside the family. Others find support in kinship or social networks but hesitate to use the formal institutions that have been set up to help them, either because they don't feel comfortable accepting help from an outside source or perhaps because they have just never considered it. Many families have no idea what is available in their communities. Some of these families get along fine; others experience a feeling of isolation.

Isolation has a number of negative effects on families. It limits role models for children. It can lead to a sense of hopelessness. And it can even lead to child abuse. When working with families, teachers, early educators, and other professionals can help families get together with each other. Those families that are engaged in large social networks can be models for those who are more isolated. The school or early care program itself can provide the catalyst for bringing families into a new social network—that of the school, center, or family child care program. See Strategy Box 14.1 for ideas on how to do this.

Box 14.1

Four Ways to Help Families Expand Their Social Networks by Connecting with Other Families in the School or Center

- Make contact information available to each family member, if allowed to do so. Of course, be sure to have permission from every family to be included on the list.

- Make every meeting interactive. Use icebreakers to help people get to know each other.

- For those family members who exclude themselves, make a special effort to introduce them personally to other families in the program.

- Notice which children seem to be connecting with each other. Sometimes families appreciate a little encouragement to get their children together outside of the regular school hours of the program.

Developing a Broad Base of Support

In healthy families each member has a broad base of support and knows how to get strokes from people outside the immediate family. Strokes are ways of giving recognition to someone. They may come through words, such as an acknowledgement. Or they can be physical such as a warm rub on a shoulder. A hug is an intimate stroke. Everybody needs strokes and everybody needs to know how to give them. Sometimes families are under such stress and so involved with each other that stroking is neglected. That's why it helps to learn how to get strokes outside the family. Without a broad base of support, undue pressure falls on those within the family; if those who usually give strokes are unable to do so, the individual is left depleted.

How does one know if his or her support base is broad enough? An exercise called "stroke pie" can tell you. As already mentioned, strokes are behaviors that show recognition, appreciation, and support. Think of the people in your life who give you strokes and provide support for you. Then draw a circle and make a pie-shaped wedge for each person. Make the size of the wedge correspond to the amount of support you receive from that person. Take a look at your stroke pie. Do you have a number of different wedges of varying sizes, or do you have mainly just one or two big wedges? If you are getting more than 25 percent of your support from just one person, you are at risk for stroke deprivation if that person leaves even temporarily, gets angry with you, or for some reason is unable to support you. By the way, did you put your own name on a wedge of your stroke pie? You should be a source of your own strokes. If you have just a limited number of wedges in your pie, you may be overly dependent on a few people for support. That's a sign that you need to broaden your base of support. You can do this exercise

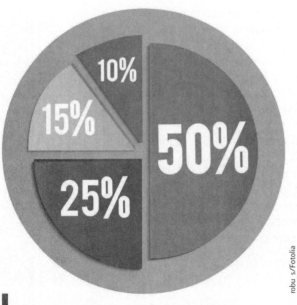

How many people are there in your stroke pie?

at a parent meeting to help make families aware of when they need a larger base of support. You can help families broaden their base by connecting them with other families in the program. Refer to Strategy Box 14.1 for ideas on how to do that.

Here are sample stroke pies of two people, Kim and Jennifer:

Kim assigned three-quarters of the pie to her boyfriend and the remaining quarter slice to her mother. Then came the day that her mother discovered she had cancer, which was about the time the boyfriend found someone else. Kim's strokes disappeared all at once, and she had no one to turn to for support.

Jennifer used to be in that position, too: She was dependent on her husband for most of her strokes, with a few coming from her sister. But when she became a parent and discovered that she needed to give out more strokes than she got back, she knew she'd better broaden her base of support. She purposely developed a close relationship with two mothers she had met in her Lamaze class and another mother she met in the park. She not only started swapping child care with these women but also used them for information and for nurturing, too.

Four years after Jennifer's son was born, her stroke pie looked very different from the way it had looked when she first became a mother. Her pie was now divided into 19 pieces, with friends, relatives, neighbors, her son, parents at her son's school, office mates, members of her parenting support group, and two jogging buddies all represented by slices. Her husband's huge slice was cut down to less than a quarter of the pie, and their relationship was blossoming since she had quit depending on him and her sister so heavily to meet all her emotional needs.

Jennifer created a social network for herself. Each individual and each family has a stroke pie that comprises their social network. Each looks slightly different.

Forms Social Networks May Take

In some families, individual members have their own social networks. In others, the family shares a network that consists of individuals and groups that comprise what can be thought of as a greater family, or an extended family. Again, I'm talking about boundaries in family systems; this is an example of different kinds of boundaries. Some families are attached to a number of people beyond their own relatives in formal and informal ways. In a Mexican family, for example, this attachment may include, besides relatives, *compadres*—the children's godparents. *Compadres* are more than friends; they have a special

Some people find support in extended families

Jack Hollingsworth/Gettyimages

kind of family relationship even though they may not have blood ties. Other families have special friends who are considered "aunts and uncles" to the younger generation. They are like family but are not blood relatives.

For some families, the neighborhood where they live may be the most important part of the social network. Neighbors can become a close-knit group that serves as a mutual aid society—sharing resources, providing guidance for children, and contributing to the social life of its members through periodic gatherings and celebrations of all sorts. Although these kinds of neighborhoods still exist in some places, they are becoming more scarce as the American population increases in mobility and at the same time isolates itself from those who live nearby.

For some families, a religious institution or spiritual practice group serves the same functions as the close-knit neighborhood described earlier, providing friendship, a social life, mutual aid, social services, support, counseling, and education, along with worship services, celebrations, and/or spiritual guidance.

Community Institutions That Serve Families

Other formal and informal groups and institutions with specialized functions make up a part of the social network of the community. Some of them have been around since the country began, such as police and fire departments; others are just now in the process of developing in response to changing needs. Public libraries are long-time institutions that provide a variety of services to families, services that have expanded way beyond books, especially with the development of computer technology, which continues to expand ways of communicating and gaining information and knowledge. The stereotype of the musty old library with little old lady librarians is long gone. It's now full of young and old people at computers and maybe even some geeks. Even that scene is changing with individuals having their own technological devices they can carry in their pockets and access the whole world of knowledge through their apps (applications). But libraries are still valuable, and they themselves suffer funding cuts during periods of financial hardships. See the Advocacy in Action feature "Children Save the Local Libraries" for a story about how a group of children saved their local library. Even children can become advocates!

ADVOCACY IN ACTION ▶ CHILDREN SAVE THE LOCAL LIBRARIES

Julie Olsen Edwards, author, teacher, and director

For several years during the "Week of the Young Child" proclaimed annually by the National Association for the Education of Young Children (NAEYC), the Cabrillo Children's Center in Northern California organized a parade on the Cabrillo College campus to which we invited our families and several other children's programs to participate. It was a pretty simple affair. We met at a designated spot and walked about the campus singing children's songs and carrying child-decorated signs: "Quality child care supports healthy development"; "We care for child care"; "0 to 5 are learning years"; and so on. Then we gathered on the quad and had a community circle time of songs and children's musical instruments. It was always playful and collaborative.

One year we suggested that children come in costumes (more or less) related to favorite children's books, and kids carried signs with the book titles on them. This added to the fun and to the display of children's interests and learning.

The following year our public libraries faced huge cuts. Local branches were to be closed, staff laid off, and hours restricted. Remembering our WOYC parades, a number of families suggested we join the community march to save the libraries. The staff members helped distribute a parent-made flier, and they offered to help families resurrect or re-create costumes based on favorite books. The children and their families were very visible in the march. A reporter asked several of the four-year-olds why they were there and quoted them as saying, "Cuz I love Madeline! I want to read her in the library" and "We need libraries so I can read lots and lots of books." My favorite was Caleb who was quoted as saying, "I don't got truck books, but they do. They got lots and I love trucks."

Along with the children feeling they too could speak up, it was important to our mainly young families to see they could be activists for what they believed in, that they could work together, and that they were an important asset to our community.

Three ongoing trends illustrate the need for formal and informal support for families: the increasing numbers of mothers of infants and young children in the workforce; the growing challenge for low-income families to attain economic self-sufficiency; and the feminization of poverty.

Many families are only one paycheck away from being poor; food banks and homeless shelters can provide food to hungry families

Monkey Business Images/Shutterstock

♦ *Employed mothers.* More mothers than ever before are working. Adding to the trend are the changes in the welfare system, which mean that mothers of children or infants are often found in the labor force. Many of these women are single heads of families and are the only source of financial support for their families. The response to this current trend by the greater society has been to provide outside child care in a number of forms. Government, schools, employers, churches, corporations, and individuals are getting involved in the child care scene.

♦ *Economic challenges.* Growing numbers of families today find themselves in acute economic distress. Because parents are unable to work for a variety of reasons or are working for wages that keep the family mired down in the bog of poverty, children are greatly influenced by lack of money, food, and even shelter. The community response to this problem is lagging far behind the need, as witnessed by the number of homeless in many communities.

♦ *The feminization of poverty.* Someone once said that most women are just one husband away from poverty. Look around you. Who are most in need of financial help? Women. One in five children are in poverty; of those children, nine out of ten live in female-headed households. A generation ago most poor people were old. That has changed now as a result of a local, state, and national response to conditions and problems of the elderly. The composition of the new poverty group is different, and community response has been slow, unfortunately.

Check Your Understanding 14.1

Click here to check your understanding of social networks.

FAMILIES USING COMMUNITY RESOURCES

Let's take a look now at how six families reflect these trends and how they connect with the social networks outside themselves. Notice how each family uses and contributes to the community resources available.

Sara's Family

Sara is a 21-year-old with two sons—Ty and Kyle. She is in nursing school at a community college. Sara went through a very difficult period, being homeless for a while. But by now she's an expert in the resources her community has to offer. She's tied into the financial aid program at her college, which gives her support. She also receives child care in an on-campus subsidized program for low-income students, which is funded by the state. She gives back to these two community resources by serving on the advisory committee of the financial aid program and by contributing volunteer time to the child care center. She was asked to help with fund-raising for the center but made a decision to take care of herself and her sons by declining. She knows that fund-raising can be very time-consuming, and with her studies and her family, time is at a premium right now.

When Sara was pregnant the first time, she received assistance from WIC (Women, Infants, and Children), a federally funded nutrition program designed to help ensure that children get the nourishment they need through the prenatal period and into the first year of life.

Ty was born prematurely, which made life even harder for a time. Going to a support group for a while for "preemie" parents helped Sara get through this period. The group, which was hosted by her local hospital, was led by a social worker and funded by a special foundation grant.

▶ Watch this video to learn about the resources provided by the Woman, Infant, & Children (WIC) program.

www.youtube.com/
watch?v=Wu7oxX0Zfo4

By the time of her second pregnancy (which resulted from being raped while she was homeless), the WIC funding had been cut in half, and she could no longer get into the program, which was unfortunate because she and Ty often didn't have food. She worried about her unborn baby a lot during that period. Kyle was also born prematurely, and by then the funding for the preemie support group had also been cut, so she was on her own. But she did finally get into a teen parent program that enabled her to finish high school. Now she has moved on to college with a plan and hope for her future through the vocational program she is in.

When Sara first went on the Temporary Assistance to Needy Families (TANF) program, she lived in terror that someone would decide that she was neglecting her children and take them away from her. She had seen this happen to several women during her homeless period. She couldn't bear the thought of losing Ty and Kyle, so she was very cautious whenever she discussed anything with her social worker. She felt she had to protect herself. It took her a long time to decide that the worker understood her situation, saw her as a good mother, and wasn't about to report her for neglect to Child Protective Services, which is the government agency in her county that handles child abuse cases.

Recently Sara has discovered a food co-op where, by paying a small amount to join and volunteering a few hours a week, she can get a good deal of food at very reasonable rates. She's also discovered that she can get family counseling services, which the child care center recommended because of Kyle's aggressive behavior. The therapist is also helping her sort out Ty's attention deficit problem. The therapist is talking about referring both boys to a special education program run by the county office of education. Sara is hesitant about taking the next steps for this service because she hates the thought of changing programs. Besides, the hours of the special ed program don't fit her school schedule very well, and she still needs child care. Transportation would be a problem, and she doesn't want her boys shuffled back and forth from one program to another, so she's dragging her feet on following up her investigation of what could be done further for her children. What she doesn't know is that there is a strong movement to include children with special needs in programs with their typically developing peers. It's possible that Sara can get her boys the special services that they may need without moving them to another program.

Because of her low-income status, Sara is entitled to health benefits from the government, though those funds are threatened with cuts. Even with the program she sometimes has a hard time finding a doctor who will see her and the boys.

Sara has been in a lot worse shape in the past than she is now. She remembers eating once a week at a community dinner for the homeless, served in a church by a local women's service group. Sara had very mixed feelings about being there. She couldn't help being grateful, of course, but she felt strangely alienated from everyone there, not only from the other homeless people but also from the good-hearted women who donated their time, energy, and casseroles. She hates being on the receiving end of charity!

> Watch this video to hear a quick overview of the Supplemental Nutrition Assistance Program (SNAP).
>
> www.youtube.com/watch?v=Jw7uT1jOt0o

Christmas has always brought up the same awful feelings, and it still does, even now. It's great that the community rallies once a year to provide gifts for her boys and a turkey for her table, but every year she has those same mixed feelings of gratitude, shame, and anger. She'll be glad when she gets through school and can support herself. Then she'll be the one doing the giving for a change. She can hardly wait.

Roberto's Family

Roberto's family is composed of Roberto, his wife Maria Elena, his four-year-old daughter Lupe, and baby Paco. Roberto at first resisted signing up for any community resources because he was too proud; besides, he was suspicious of anything connected to any government. But one day he found himself persuaded to send his daughter to Head Start, a federally funded preschool program for low-income children. He discovered early on that with Head Start comes a community aide, who helps the family get connected to other services that they need, many of which are provided right at school for the children, such as vision and hearing screening. The hearing screening proved to be a problem because they discovered that Lupe has a hearing deficit, and now the family is expected to do something about it. Roberto is convinced that the hearing problem would have gone away on its own if it hadn't been discovered. Roberto and Maria Elena went to the place the school told them to go, but there were many papers to fill out and no one spoke their language, so they left. Now Roberto feels very uncomfortable every time he gets a notice from school urging him to follow up on the referral they gave him.

While Roberto was still getting used to all the changes in his life that came as the result of enrolling Lupe in Head Start, Maria Elena announced that she wanted to take classes in English as a second language at the adult school. "I won't have time to drive you," Roberto told her firmly, convinced that that would end the matter.

"I can take the bus," said Maria Elena.

"And who will take care of Paco?" asked Roberto.

"They have child care at the school," Maria Elena shot back.

Roberto was stunned. This had all been worked out without him. What would happen to him if his family didn't need him any more? He felt shaken.

He needed to talk to somebody, so he went first to his *compadre*, Juan, godfather of Lupe, and told him how he felt. Just talking about it made him feel better. Then he went to his priest and talked some more. The priest suggested counseling, but Roberto thought that counseling would show the world that something was wrong with him, and that was exactly the problem he wished to avoid. He felt that enough was wrong with him because of what was happening in his family; he certainly didn't want to announce to the world that he was weak and needed help. The priest made another suggestion, however, that Roberto followed up on. He told him about a clinic that might help with Lupe's problem. It was a community effort run by bilingual volunteers, so he would at least be able to talk to someone in his own language—someone who knew something about medicine. Roberto felt much better when he came home from talking to the priest. Maria Elena noticed the difference and gave him a big hug when he came in the door.

Junior's Family

Junior is a 12-month-old who has been crying so hard at the child care center that the teachers are worried about him. His family fled from their homeland and are still trying to settle in. Junior used to be at home with his great-grandma, but now she is sick and he's in child care. This family is still in a survival mode, while experiencing culture shock and language difficulties.

The members of this refugee family are so busy working that they haven't had time to find out about any resources in their community except for child care; and that isn't working out too well, because Junior cries all the time he's there. The family has been relocated several times, and Junior seems to be expressing the suffering all of them feel. Being crowded is nothing new to this family; they've always lived in close quarters with the extended family in one residence. Their house is packed most of the time. They have to eat in shifts, but they work in shifts, too, so that comes out all right.

One thing they're glad of is that Junior doesn't cry at home the way he does at the center. It's not that crying babies haven't always been part of their lives, but now Great-Grandma is sick, and they worry about disturbing her. Oh, yes, they do use a community resource—a home health nurse who comes in to look after Great-Grandma. Although they were suspicious at first of medical care that they didn't understand, they decided it wouldn't be such a bad idea to learn about how things work in this country. The only problem is that language creates terrible barriers, and they don't understand as much as they want to. They often wonder what the nurse is doing and what the various medications are for, but they have to wait until the oldest cousin, who understands English, gets home to find out. Even then things don't always make sense because the approach to health care in this country is so different.

There have been some scary misunderstandings about health matters—like the time Great-Grandma had a reaction to some medication, and they had to take her to the hospital emergency room. That was a horrible experience because they had no idea what was going on. And when they put her in the hospital for two days, it was very frustrating because the medical staff wouldn't let the family take care of her. In fact, they were asked to leave. They didn't understand this at all!

The family is very lonely at times when they think of their native country, but they are learning to make this country home. They know how to support each other, pooling resources and knowledge, which helps a lot. They aren't used to getting outside help, so that's something new to them. They are learning English rapidly and soon will have an expanded view of the community they live in and what is available to them.

Watch this video to hear youth talk about their experience of being immigrants.

Michael's Family

Michael, a three-year-old, is the son of a lesbian couple. Michael and his parents are isolated from many of the social networks that support other families. Michael's parents don't want to be isolated, but they have had bad experiences in the past when they reached out and found themselves rejected. They have their own group of friends, and they find closeness and community there. In some ways they are like Junior's refugee family, who necessarily looks close to home for support.

In other ways they are not like Junior's family because the institutions that they deal with don't recognize them as a family. This became clear and evident the day that Michael fell and needed stitches. Margaret, his birth mother, was at work in another town and couldn't get to the hospital right away. Beth, his other mother, had to hold the crying Michael in the emergency room—no treatment could be started until Margaret arrived to sign permission papers. Beth had no recognized legal connection to Michael.

Having their relationship not regarded as valid or legal by community agencies was nothing new to Michael's parents. They had had previous difficulties not experienced by heterosexual married couples—like not being able to get a loan to buy a house and being refused job-related medical benefits. They also had had countless difficulties living in a neighborhood where some neighbors didn't like them even though they had never gotten to know them. But the incident in the hospital emergency room hurt the most because it involved Michael. After that experience in the emergency room they considered moving to another state to get married but put it off because they both had jobs and ties where they were. But the 2015 Supreme Court ruling on marriage and same sex couples means they can now marry and at least ensure some legal rights where Michael is concerned.

Beth and Margaret aren't without friends. They both have found personal friends and support systems at their places of work. But these systems don't help the family much because, except for a few individuals, the work friends don't know about the rest of the family.

Margaret, especially, feels isolated at work because of the secret she keeps from her friends and associates there. But in her last job she was more open, and she ended up feeling a lot more isolated than she does now. She finally left that job because she couldn't stand it anymore.

Both Margaret and Beth worry about their son and what will happen when he is old enough to understand what outsiders say about the family. They feel very protective of him and of each other and sometimes feel as though they live in a little cocoon separate from the rest of the world. They don't really want to live that way, but they wish they could keep the cocoon for Michael. They know, however, that soon he's going to grow beyond their protection and will be on his own in what feels to them like a cold and cruel outside world.

Margaret is secure about her relationship to Beth, but she suffers from the reaction she gets from so many who find out about it. In the past, she felt angry a lot of the time, and she knew she needed help in coping with the anger. She finally found a therapist to talk to. It took a long time because she looked for someone who would really understand her and could help without judging her family composition. She is surprised that being open and honest with a professional therapist can be so helpful. She's urging Beth, who has the same angry feelings about the way she's treated, to talk with someone, too. However, Beth hesitates, feeling that going into therapy means she's admitting that something is wrong with her.

Things are a little better now because Beth has found a teacher at Michael's center who is accepting and friendly. She feels relieved that at least one outsider isn't cold and cruel.

Courtney's Family

Courtney's family consists of her second husband, Richard; four-year-old Roland, from Courtney's first marriage; and two-and-a-half-year-old Soleil, who is Courtney and Richard's daughter. Roland's two older brothers are also part of this family, but they live with Courtney's parents.

This family has been involved with the legal system for some time; there were issues with both drug abuse and then child abuse during Courtney's first marriage. Now the family lives in fear of the boys' father returning to heap more abuse on previously abused little Roland. There's a restraining order to keep the father from coming near the boys, but Courtney still worries.

Courtney is just about to graduate from a drug rehabilitation program and is very proud of herself for being clean. She has turned her life around and is enrolled in college, the first step toward becoming a lawyer. She has strong feelings about making the legal system work better for everybody.

Richard also has strong feelings about the system. He is a Native American who, though born outside the reservation, has spent periods of his life going back to connect with his roots. He finds the tribal system and the religion of his people appealing, in contrast to impersonal institutions. He knows what real community is—people linked in emotional, social, and spiritual ways, people who provide mutual help and support. Richard's dream is to become a history teacher and to help the next generation see that change is necessary if this country (and, indeed, the planet) is to survive.

Courtney, like Sara, went through a difficult time in the past, which resulted in her being connected with a number of social service institutions—some which seemed to be supportive of her and some that regarded her as "the enemy."

Courtney remembers a very difficult period when she was told that if she didn't leave her boys' father because of the abuse he poured on them, she would lose her children. She felt extremely helpless at that point, and if it hadn't been for a local women's shelter, she never would have been able to take such a big step. When she finally left the shelter and struck out on her own, she was still threatened with the loss of her children because she couldn't provide decent housing for them. The only place she could afford that would rent to her was very run-down. Luckily, there was a new program in her community that was designed to help families overcome obstacles like hers. A social worker from this program, instead of removing her children to foster care, came out with tools to show her how to fix the broken windows, replace the screens, and repair the plumbing, so that she and her children would have a safe place to live. This same social worker gave Courtney some skills for guiding her children's behavior and got her into the rehabilitation program that turned her life around. Courtney is very grateful for the community resources that she sees as saving her life and helping her keep her children.

The Jackson Family

The Jackson family is different from some of the other families because they haven't been through a hard time. They're a stable family, clear about their identity, values, and lifestyle. They're not looking for changes as much as trying to keep things the way they are. Like Margaret and Beth, Michael's parents, the Jacksons' problems arise from being different from, and therefore misunderstood by, the greater community.

Because the Jacksons are not in crisis, they are not looking for the same kind of support as some of the other families examined so far. The community resources they use and enjoy are those of their own group—the religious and cultural groups they belong to—and those of the greater community, resources such as the library, recreation programs and facilities, museums, and other institutions that enhance the quality of their lives and the lives of the other families described in this chapter. The Jacksons appreciate music and plays, and they support the local groups that provide them. This family has no need for general assistance, food programs, housing support, social services, child abuse programs, or legal agencies, at least at present.

It's not that this is a perfect family; they have their problems, too. Their child, who was born with spina bifida, a debilitating condition caused by a birth defect involving the spine, needs specialized services that they get from the school district. Taking care of him used to take up most of Mrs. Jackson's time, but now that he has enrolled in the school, she has more time to herself. Unfortunately, she is feeling isolated at home, and she's thinking of looking for friends outside her religious community. She had hoped to find a friendly group when she moved into the neighborhood she lives in. In her old neighborhood the women got together regularly and talked over coffee. In this one, however, the neighbors don't seem to want to get to know each other. The women are gone during the day and seem to be busy in the evenings and on weekends. Mrs. Jackson invited her next-door neighbors over when she first moved in, but although they were polite and pleasant, they never reciprocated, and now they just talk once in a while across the driveway.

Now, however, Mrs. Jackson has gotten involved with fund-raising at her son's school, and she's beginning to feel connected to a group. She likes the women who are working with her, and she hopes to continue enjoying their company after the fund-raiser is over.

Mrs. Jackson is also involved in a new project. Her father, who has lived by himself since his wife died, is growing more and more feeble, and the Jacksons recently decided that he should move in with them. Mrs. Jackson is busy investigating what kinds of services are available to help them out. She has discovered the senior center near the library, where her father can enjoy company, take part in various classes and activities, and have a hot lunch on the days she works. She's feeling good about how this move will work out. It will be nice to have her father with her—and good for the children to know their grandfather better.

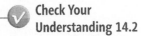 Watch this video to learn about the IMPACT program for children with special needs.

www.youtube.com/watch?v=-NtJozTP97E

✓ Check Your Understanding 14.2

Click here to check your understanding of families using community resources.

CONNECTIONS TO THE COMMUNITY

Each of these families has connections to the community beyond their own doors, yet each perceives that community in a slightly different way. Each uses the services of agencies and informal groups. Some give back as much as they receive; others either aren't in a position to reciprocate or don't yet understand the give-and-take aspects of community living. Many of the families we've examined live with multiple stresses in their lives. Some find the support and services they need; others feel the need for more. Some are denied access to available resources.

Let's look at a summary of the kinds of institutions and programs available in varying degrees to most of these families.

A Summary of Community Resources

Though none of these families has needed police or fire protection lately, they all know that these two community services are available at the touch of the telephone. They also know about the community resources that are available to enhance the quality of their lives—the parks and recreation department, the library, the local museum, and the two-year community college, all of which have regular programs for adults and children.

Some families give back as much as they receive

Child care programs, Head Start and other early education programs, and schools, both public and private, provide education to all members of the family. Local hospitals and the county health department provide preventive care and health maintenance to varying degrees, including some perinatal services and a variety of health education programs. They also, of course, provide services for the sick.

Welfare, a big community resource designed to support people with children, underwent a major change in the 1990s. Welfare in the form of Aid to Families with Dependent Children (AFDC) became Temporary Assistance for Needy Families (TANF) in 1996 and has stricter requirements than the old system. Also, there is a time limitation. Training institutions are full of people getting themselves qualified for the job market. These changes in the system and new challenges to families have created more need for child care than ever before—especially for infant care.

Some other community resources are designed to support families in times of emergency and stress, such as child abuse prevention programs, which offer telephone hotlines, parent education services, and respite child care. Mental health programs that offer therapeutic services and counseling programs are designed as short-term crisis intervention, and some provide long-term help to individuals and families as well. These programs periodically experience reduced funding, which makes them less effective at times. Families who can afford to pay for services continue, of course, to find them available. Substance abuse programs run by both professionals and volunteers also help people get on their feet and live satisfying and productive lives.

Most communities have a variety of support groups. Support groups can be both formal and informal and can respond to any number of needs: general parenting groups, women's and men's support groups, substance abuse, codependency, Overeaters Anonymous—you name it, there's a support group somewhere for it. Mrs. Jackson has even found a spina bifida support group that is attended by parents whose children were born with this condition. She

Community resources are designed to support families in times of need

found it through a local family resource network designed to offer support, information, referral, advocacy, and training to families in her community who have children with special needs.

Finding Community Resources

How do you find out what resources are available in your community? A simple way is to start with the phone book; some have a special section right in front. Or the library may have a listing. In some communities, a local organization such as Head Start or a child care resource and referral agency puts together and updates lists of resources that are available to families.

Of course, anyone who knows how to use a computer or a smart phone can surf the Internet can find countless resources right on the screen. For those without such devices, the local library can provide not only the computer but also some support and technical assistance to use the system.

Word-of-mouth is the way many families find out about the individuals and institutions that can serve them. If a family is connected to a child care center, the chances are someone on staff knows what's available for specific problems. In turn, families can help expand the teachers' knowledge of what's available in the community. Some programs have a rack of brochures from local community resources. Others put together lists of them and keep those lists updated.

Watch this video to see how a school serves as a resource for families.

www.youtube.com/watch?v=sel65jIFRZw

Some families enter "the system" because of a crisis or a problem. That's the way they get introduced to the world of accessible resources in their community. In some cities and towns, a crisis center is available 24 hours a day to serve those who are in serious trauma, for whatever reason. Some communities also have women's shelters where the abused and their children can find refuge. Public health and mental health systems are usually also able to respond to crisis situations.

Rawpixel/Shutterstock

Clergy often serve as counselors and advisers to individuals and families. They can guide their clients to appropriate community resources for their particular problem.

It's not always easy to find just what you need—in fact, it is sometimes downright difficult. However, with persistence, you'll usually locate whatever there might be. Unfortunately, most communities lack the full range of resources that they need, and many families are left to solve their own problems or look for help or support from relatives, friends, and neighbors.

Schools and community agencies can share knowledge about potential resources that might help families

Helping Families Access Services in the Community

+ At least one person in the program or school should become knowledgeable about potential resources that might help families, such as federal earned income tax credit; state income and other tax credits; food stamps; child support income enforcement; child-related resources like health benefits; Medicaid or state child health insurance programs; and child care subsidies.

+ When a program or school includes children with identified disabilities, make sure someone on the staff knows about early intervention of special education services. Parents can help inform the program.

+ Team up with community organizations such as domestic violence, mental health, and substance abuse agencies to address prevention and treatment issues for vulnerable families.

+ Consider expanding the mission of your program to become a human service center in your community.

+ Increase advocacy along with parents and other groups at both state and local levels to improve funding for services that need expanding.

Strategy Box 14.2 gives some ideas of how early educators can help families find the services they might need.

Availability of Community Resources

Although the list of community resources may be lengthy, not all are available in all communities. Even those communities that have a variety may not make them available to all families. What are some of the factors that determine availability of community resources?

Funding is one factor—often there's not enough to go around, or it's stretched so thin that no one program can do a good job of helping and supporting families. Lack of funding results in declining services and increased competition for limited resources.

Some programs serve a specific population, and families must qualify to be eligible to receive services. Furthermore, some families qualify for services but have no access to them because of lack of transportation or language barriers. (Or perhaps they don't even realize that such services exist.)

When families do connect with services available to them, they may find the services inappropriate to their needs—sometimes because of cultural insensitivity on the part of the service providers. Lack of respect may be a factor when there's a mismatch between services and the families they are designed to serve. When clients are looked down on by the people who serve them, it's often because the agency is using a deficit model to define the people who come to them for help. This model may be quite out of tune with the reality of cultural or class differences.

Each of the community resources that families deal with has a spoken or unspoken set of goals and values. When these goals and values are in tune with those of the family, a match is made, and the chances are better that the support or intervention will be effective. Some goals and values are conscious, written into the agency; some are misinterpreted by outsiders; and some are unintended.

For example, one medium-sized town has two agencies serving pregnant women. One is Planned Parenthood, whose purpose is to offer a variety of services as well as counseling that allows women to make decisions that are right for them about family planning. Planned Parenthood is not just for pregnant women; it has a wide range of services for both men and women. It offers abortion as one of several options for pregnant women to consider.

On the other side of town is a group called Birthright, whose goal is to help pregnant women opt against abortion. It provides counseling and support to women who might otherwise find it difficult to have their babies, doing what it can to make it more attractive to continue the pregnancy than to end it. These two agencies, which serve the same population, have contrasting goals and values and are clear about their differences.

Usually an agency's goals are not so clear, and often families don't look beyond the offer of services to understand the agency's goals or value system anyway. Of course, they can find the agency's goals by examining incorporation papers, mission statements, or patterns of board policies. However, families do not usually set out to investigate the goals and value systems of the agency where they seek help or support. They may become aware of a lack of communication, a mismatch, or a lack of respect, which signals a goal or value conflict, but most of us don't even clarify our own goals or values very often, let alone compare them with those of an agency. However, goals and values do make a difference if we are to serve our community and be served by it. Goals and values are themes in the chapter that follows.

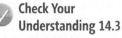

Check Your Understanding 14.3

Click here to check your understanding of connections to the community.

SUMMARY

This chapter discussed the importance of social networks and what isolation can do to a family. It gave ideas about how to help families expand their social networks and use community resources. A major section focused on how six families each use and contribute to community resources. Understanding connections to the community was an important part of this chapter.

✓ QUIZ

Click here to check your understanding of chapter 14, "Supporting Families Through Community Resources and Networks."

FOR DISCUSSION

1. What do you know about the negative effects that isolation can have on families?
2. Name some social networks that you are acquainted with.
3. Give examples of how the families in this chapter might both use and contribute to community resources. Choose examples that haven't been mentioned in the chapter.
4. What would you tell a family about how to find the community resources they might need?
5. Do you know someone who needed a community resource that wasn't available to that person? Why wasn't it available? Do you know someone who used an agency that didn't fit their culture or their needs?

WEBSITES

Campaign for the Civic Mission of Schools
This organization promotes strong community partnership components for K–12 classrooms and includes civic education.

Center on School, Family, and Community Partnerships
This organization, which is part of the National Network of Partnership Schools at John Hopkins University, helps families, educators, and community members work together to improve schools, strengthen families, and enhance student learning and development.

IMPACT
Individualized Movement and Physical Activity for Children Today (IMPACT) is housed in the College of Public Health and Human Science at Oregon State University. It is a program for children with special needs.

The Military Child Initiative (MCI)
This organization aims to improve military educational environments for highly mobile and vulnerable people,

with a special focus on children and families in the military. MCI was initially jointly funded by the U.S. Department of Defense and John Hopkins University. Although the original contract ended, the National Network of Partnership Schools (NNPS) continues to offer technical assistance to districts and schools that serve military families.

Marc Sheehan's Special Education/Exceptionality Page
A helpful site from which to research, this page contains many Internet links to special education-related sites.

National Institute for Early Education Research (NIEER)
The NIEER website has information about research to support high quality, effective early childhood education. The institute offers research-based advice and technical assistance to policymakers, journalists, researchers, and educators.

FURTHER READING

Barnett, W. S. (2011). Effectiveness of early educational intervention. *Science* (333) 6045. 975–978.

Castro, F. G., & Murray, K. E. (2010). Cultural adaptation and resilience: Controversies, issues, and emerging models. In J. W. Reich, A. J. Zautra, & J. S. Hall (Eds.), *Handbook of adult resilience* (pp. 375–403). New York, NY: Guilford.

Curtis, D., & Carter, M. (2015). *Designs for living and learning: Transforming early childhood environments.* 2nd ed. St. Paul, MN: Redleaf Press.

Dombro, A., Jablon, A. R., & Stetson, C. (2011). *Powerful interactions: How to connect with children to extend their learning.* Washington DC: National Association for the Education of Young Children.

Espinosa, L. (2015). *Getting it right for young children from diverse backgrounds: Applying research to improve practice with a focus on dual-language learners* (2nd ed.). Upper Saddle River, NJ: Pearson.

Gonzalez-Mena, J. (2012). Culture and communication in the child care setting. In P. Mangione and D. Greeenwald (Eds.), A *guide to language development and communication.* 2nd ed. pp. 51–60. Sacramento, CA: California Department of Education,

Hirschland, D. (2015). *When young children need help: Understanding and addressing emotional, behavioral, and developmental challenges.* St. Paul, MN: Redleaf Press.

Ispa, J. M., Thornburg, K. R., & Fine, M. A. (2006). *Keepin' on: The everyday struggles of young families in poverty.* Baltimore, MD: Brookes.

Mattern, J. A. (2015). A mixed-methods study of early intervention implementation in the Commonwealth of Pennsylvania: Supports, services, and policies for young children with developmental delays and disabilities. *Early Childhood Education Journal,* (43) 1. 57–67.

Patterson, K., Grenny, J., McMillan, R., & Switzler, A. (2012). *Crucial conversations: How to talk when the stakes are high.* New York, NY: McGraw-Hill.

Social Policy Issues

Learning Outcomes

In this chapter you will learn to...

- Evaluate who is responsible for America's children.
- Describe three or four social policy financial investment needs that benefit children, families, and society.
- Explain how to advocate for children and families.

This book has looked at the ways in which families and their professional partners—teachers, early educators, child care staff, and others—educate, care for, and socialize children within a community context. Along the way we examined various obstacles that interfere with the rights of all children to an effective education and healthy socialization process—obstacles that include poverty, lack of access to quality education and child care, and the media.

What can we do, as a society, to address these issues? What can the community do to ensure that all children get an equal chance to develop high self-esteem and fulfill themselves in this society? How can we help all children "make it"? This chapter examines social policy issues that relate to these questions.

WHO IS RESPONSIBLE FOR AMERICA'S CHILDREN?

An underlying social policy on which this nation was founded is that families are responsible for their own children. However, it is becoming clearer and clearer that, although families must still take primary responsibility for their children, many families are not, at present, able to be completely self-sufficient. It's not that these families care any less about their children than more self-sufficient families do; it's just that they find themselves in circumstances that prevent them from being able to meet all their children's needs. The question is: If families can't meet their own children's needs, how much will the society take over the responsibility for those unmet needs?

The future of our country depends on providing for the needs of America's children—all of our children. If we've reached a place in our economic, political, social, and moral history where masses of children are neglected, it's time for us, as individuals and as a society, to change that situation. What's keeping us from putting forth a giant effort to meet the needs of America's children—of *our* children? One often unspoken theory behind society's reluctance as a whole to put forth monumental effort to improve the lives of all its citizens is the idea that we each get what we deserve. This perspective justifies leaving things as they are. Those who are society's successes, the top of the heap, are given credit for their ability to work hard and be rewarded; the people who fall to the bottom are seen as not having tried hard enough. The view is that the people who live on the crumbs at the bottom of the barrel were born with the same chances of getting the whole contents of the barrel as everyone else. On the surface that may seem to be true. After all, this is America, land of opportunity, home of the free. But let's look at whether all babies are, in fact, born with the same opportunities.

Does Every Child Get an Equal Start?

Let's examine the situations of three pregnant women who live 20 miles apart from each other:

- a 16-year-old who lives with her mother and two sisters in a run-down two-room apartment in a gang-ridden neighborhood at the edge of a decaying industrial section of a large city;
- a 25-year-old who lives with her jobless husband in a small duplex in the older part of a suburban area;
- a 28-year-old who lives with her executive husband in a single-family home, surrounded by grass and flowers on a pleasant tree-lined street in a newer development in the sprawling part of the outer suburbs.

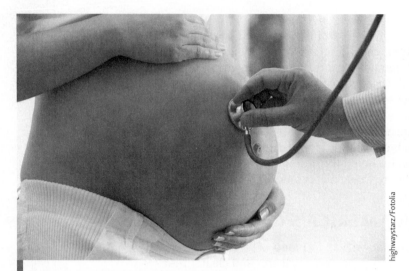

The mother's living conditions, stress levels, and access to healthcare all have an impact on a child's opportunity even before birth

The 16-year-old's baby starts out already behind because of her mother's age, physical condition, and situation, which includes lack of prenatal care, poor diet, the stress of living in poverty, and the industrial pollution of the neighborhood. The second woman's baby also starts out behind because when her husband lost his job, they lost their insurance and medical benefits; so though she's getting prenatal care, she had to go through a hassle to get it and it isn't convenient or close to where she lives either. In addition, she supports the family by working in a child care center for minimum wage, which barely pays the rent, let alone utilities and food. This family is sometimes hungry. The wife receives no benefits from her job, except for sick leave, which she has used up because of frequent illness from being exposed to the numerous childhood illnesses common at the child care center at which she works. She worries constantly about the family's financial condition, about her husband, who is deeply depressed, and most of all about her baby. The third woman's unborn baby gets all she needs before she is born, including good food, plenty of prenatal monitoring, and a relatively healthy and peaceful environment.

We have technology for sick and premature babies. We save lives, especially in dramatic cases. But the poverty factor enters in. Babies born in many families still die before their first birthday. To assess the situation, you have to look more closely at the statistics.

According to a report called "Gone too soon" from Stanford University by Sarah C. P. Williams that is subtitled "What's behind the high U.S. infant mortality rate?" we in the United States should be concerned about our infant mortality rate. It states clearly that the infant mortality rate in the United States of America is higher than most European countries. In the United States, almost one in eight babies is born early, which is double the rate of Finland, Japan, Norway, and Sweden. Though there are a variety of reasons for babies to die at birth or in their first year of life, one factor outweighs all the others—socio-economic differences. Further, the high mortality rate isn't evenly distributed. Babies most likely to die are born prematurely to African Americans, who live in certain states and/or experience high levels of emotional stress during their pregnancy. Changing these statistics will take a huge combined effort to make many changes in the society, including the socio-economic picture and the ability of science to understand the effects of stress and environmental exposures on biology.

Are all children, then, born with equal opportunities in the United States? According to the Children's Defense Fund report *The State of America's Children* (2014), by nine months of age, differences in development are noticeable between low-income babies and higher-income babies.

What about when the babies in these three families reach kindergarten? What are their relative chances of entering public school "ready to learn," as

Watch this video to learn about prenatal care. Are infants whose mothers do not have access to prenatal care born with the same opportunities for wellness as infants whose mothers had prenatal care?

www.youtube.com/
watch?v=qZqGZLwDfdE

the saying goes—or "ready to succeed in public school," which is a better way to put it? Their chances aren't equal if you consider health risks. As a nation, we seem to be going backward as far as health goes. According to the Children's Defense Fund (2011), for the first time in U.S. history, the projected life expectancy for children may be less than that of their parents.

What about early care and education programs? Those can help children succeed when they reach public school. But again, according to the Children's Defense Fund, low-income children are much less likely than their higher-income peers to have access to early childhood programs. Though three of four mothers with children under the age of 18 participate in the labor force (compared with just under half in 1975), only one in seven of the 15 million children eligible for federal child care assistance actually receives it. More than three million children eligible for Head Start and Early Head Start are not served. Which of the babies of the three pregnant women is most likely to arrive at kindergarten prepared? Any guesses?

Ready to Learn: A Goal for All of America's Children

Ready to learn—what does that mean? In the preceding chapter, it was pointed out that readiness is far more than teaching four-year-olds across the nation their ABCs. Readiness means that children must have their basic needs met—food, shelter, health care, security, and peace in the family. They need to know how to make connections with others, cooperate, get along, and feel good about themselves and others. Socialization is an important part of learning, and learning is an important part of socialization. All children need a variety of early experiences that enrich their minds, tickle their curiosity, fill their hearts, and enliven their spirits. They need adults in their lives who understand developmentally appropriate practices and cultural sensitivity and encourage them to embrace learning joyfully.

Let's look again at this issue of "ready to learn." Way back in the early 1990s, President George H. W. Bush and the governors of all 50 states came up with an idea. They stated a goal: By the year 2000, every child in America should start school ready to learn. Did we reach that goal? When George W. Bush took over the White House, his motto was No Child Left Behind. Another worthy goal, but although numerous changes were made in schools across the nation, we haven't even come close to the point that all children start kindergarten on an equal footing and that no children are left behind. Why not?

First, what does "ready to learn" mean, anyway? Anyone who has studied infancy and learning knows that babies are born ready to learn. If we couldn't tell by observation, we now have impressive brain research to back up what a lot of people knew before technology got so advanced. Babies have a lot of learning to do, even in their first year, and in most cases, they come fully equipped to do that learning (Gopnik, 2009). What happens early in life can get in the way. Bruce Perry (2006) studied the effects on the brain of the stress in the lives of children from infancy on. The actual structures of the brain can be changed by unfortunate events during infancy or even by witnessing unfortunate events. The brains of those children may be less able to learn than the brains of children who had no early ongoing trauma in their lives. Daniel Siegel's book *Mindsight* (2011) is hopeful with its many stories of remediation through therapy. Those early traumatic experiences that kept the brains of some children from fully developing can be overcome. That's the good news. The bad news is that it doesn't always just happen—it can take expert therapy.

Pavla Zakova/Fotolia

Children are more ready to learn when they have their basic needs met, such as bellies full of nutritious food

In view of the widespread poverty that continues to grow, how can many families afford to get their children what they need? Food, shelter, safety (Maslow's basic needs) have to come first, and even those very basic needs are out of the reach of some families. According to the Children's Defense Fund (2014) 1.2 million students were homeless, which was 73 percent more than before the recession. It is the responsibility of the educational system to meet children where they are and encourage and support their development from that point. To promote learning for all children, educators must provide a school environment that acknowledges children's diverse backgrounds, helps children transition comfortably into the next instructional level, and provides community supports when necessary. Such provisions support each child's readiness to learn as well as each school's readiness to educate young children.

The concept of school readiness has different meanings to different people. In some cases the difference between ready to learn, which relates to the child's level of development, and the readiness for school may be quite different. Expectations of skills each child brings can vary widely and include social, physical, intellectual, and linguistic skills. Another way to look at readiness is to examine what the school needs in order to be ready for each child who comes. Schools aren't factories. You can't apply exactly the same process to each child and expect them all to come out the same.

It is naïve to think that all it takes to get children up to par is to apply pressure on teachers, who then apply pressure on students. Besides, some education programs designed to ensure that no child is left behind are severely underfunded. Further, one-size-fits-all education policies have the effect of discriminating against poor and minority students and have proven to play a significant role in promoting school failure and an increased drop-out rate (Children's Defense Fund, 2005).

Watch this video to hear about the impact that health has on children's ability to be "ready to learn." Can you see the connection between basic needs and learning?

www.youtube.com/watch?v=p7AyRAMQBkc

Private Citizens Making Changes

Rob Reiner, Hollywood producer and entertainer, is an example of what one person can do if he or she has enough motivation and connections. His story is an illustration of highly successful advocacy! Reiner wasn't thinking "kindergarten" when he put together a huge campaign to bring the results of the brain research to parents and early educators in this country in the late 1990s. An early effort of his was a television special called "I Am Your Child" that showed an array of Hollywood stars telling the nation's parents, early childhood educators, and policy makers that the first years last forever. What happens in those early years makes all the difference. Later that same year, Reiner passed out 7,000 free copies of a videotape with the same theme to participants at the National Association for the Education of Young Children annual conference in Anaheim, California. The campaign has continued and has expanded. For instance, in 1998 Rob Reiner's campaign supported an initiative on the ballot in California (called Prop 10) to place a 50-cent tax on cigarettes and an even bigger tax on other tobacco products. Prop 10 was officially called the Children and Families First Act. Though there was much opposition by tobacco companies and users, the tax, which was designated for promoting child development in the early years, passed. Today councils in every county in the state have what is called First Five programs, which use their share of the tax money to support the healthy development of children five years of age and younger. We don't have to look only to the government to make things happen. It's remarkable what a private citizen can do to make a difference.

Another private citizen who has made a huge difference in the lives of children is Geoffrey Canada. Reiner targeted all children and their parents, Canada focused on a group of black, low-income children in New York City in Harlem. He started a massive effort that included prenatal care, parenting classes, improved infant programs and child care/preschool programs, and excellent elementary schools on through high school. His goal was not getting children ready for kindergarten but getting them ready—from conception on—to go to college. Called Harlem's Children Zone, or HCZ for short, Canada's effort has been highly successful. According to his website, 100 percent of HCZ prekindergarteners have been up to grade level for the past eight years! (Check out Harlem's Children Zone (HCZ) and Paul Tough's book *Whatever It Takes* (2009).)

So the "ready to learn" campaign took avenues beyond what former President Bush and the governors had in mind in the 1990s. And it all started long before anybody was looking at the face of the new millennium and before Bush had the idea. Early childhood educators and others have been working for 100 years to make things better for children and families. Their work came to public attention in the 1960s with the Mississippi Freedom Schools, which the government took over to begin its project of trying to enhance the lives and learning of young children growing up in poverty (Greenberg, 1969).

> **✓ Check Your Understanding 15.1**
> Click here to check your understanding of who is responsible for America's children.

BENEFITTING CHILDREN AND FAMILIES THROUGH FINANCIAL INVESTMENTS

You can't just take the child out of the family and provide education and child care without looking at the factors that influence what the child goes home to. Poverty is a big influence on family life and therefore on children's early development, which affects their ability to learn. The influence of poverty shows up even before they reach kindergarten age.

Money can't buy happiness, so it isn't just poverty that causes problems. But there is a correlation between poverty and stress on families and children. The lack of services and treatment for parents' mental health and substance abuse problems can create family crises. It is estimated that nine percent of the children in the United States live with at least one parent who abuses alcohol or drugs. The nation's homeless population increased by approximately 20,000 people from 2008 to 2009 (3 percent increase). There were also an increased number of people experiencing homelessness in each of the subpopulations examined in this report, which included families (National Alliance to End Homelessness, 2011). Imagine the stress on families to be living on the street!

A key to alleviating poverty is jobs—jobs with benefits that pay enough to live on. Increased employment can be enhanced by community involvement in identifying available jobs, improving access by reducing discrimination and other barriers, improving training, and developing job search and interview skills in underemployed people.

Who is going to do all that? We all must. No single approach will eliminate poverty in America. It will take a massive effort on the part of government at all levels, educational institutions, corporations, foundations, communities, and individuals.

Head Start

Head Start came from the Mississippi Freedom Schools; under the government's watch it was originally conceived as a quick catch-up summer school program that would teach low-income children in a few weeks what they needed to know to start kindergarten. But once it was determined that you can't make up for five years of poverty with a six-week preschool program, Head Start expanded far beyond its original beginnings.

Head Start has been successful in its efforts to meet many of the needs of the population it serves. As an early childhood program that goes beyond educating children, Head Start has had a comprehensive approach designed to provide services that address a variety of family needs. These services have made a difference in the lives of young children and their families. Head Start continued to evolve to do an even better job by expanding and modifying its program to meet even more needs. An original weakness was that Head Start didn't have models that responded to the needs of teen parents and working parents. That changed over the years. Originally conceived as a prekindergarten program for four-year-olds, Head Start has moved downward to serve families of younger-aged children. Early Head Start grants are now being used to provide services to infants and toddlers, pregnant women, expectant fathers, parents, and guardians. The goal is to help families fulfill parental roles and move forward toward economic independence while providing for their children's physical, social, emotional, and intellectual development.

> It is imperative that Head Start retain its family focus because the strength of families directly relates to children's futures. To make a difference, a program like Head Start can't just deal with children; it has to include the whole family.

Head Start's purpose has always been to involve low-income families in the solutions to their own problems by empowering them politically and economically, instead of just offering them services. From the beginning, Head Start was not just a preschool, but a comprehensive program, though every time its funding comes up for renewal, there's a call to cut it back to a narrow preschool focus. It is imperative that Head Start retain its family focus because the strength of families directly relates to children's futures. To make a difference, a program like Head Start can't just deal with children; it has to include the whole family.

Head Start is a national effort, aimed to be locally responsive and locally controlled. If the federal government doesn't provide full Head Start services to each community, the model could be adopted by communities who want to start their own Head Start programs.

▶ Watch this video to hear about the history of the Federal Head Start program. What is your response to President Obama's comment that "early childhood education is one of the best investments we can make, not just in a child's future, but in our country"?

www.youtube.com/
watch?v=StKPrSrWroA

Child Care

With the focus now on preschool for all, as mentioned in Chapter 12, child care gets less attention; resources that could be going to child care programs are now being eyed for preschool programs. A longtime child care director in California, Missy Danneberg, has strong feelings about this situation:

> For as long as I can remember (41 years) there has been confusion about differences or similarities between child care and preschool. Sometimes this confusion seems to only be semantic and other times philosophical. Is child care really different from preschool? The term 'child care' is used for programs providing care for young children usually for the full day while parents work. There may be children who attend all day and other children who attend part of the day depending on the parent's needs. The term 'preschool' is used for programs providing a part-day program for young children, but a lot of these programs also offer a full-day program to meet the needs of working parents. Are you confused yet? If you walk into a 'child care' program, it can look very similar to a 'preschool' program. So why are we wanting to make this distinction, or who is making this distinction? In recent years there has been a lot of advocacy effort put into promoting the educational value of preschool. This has had some very beneficial effects on the funding given to early care and education programs. Also to some it seemed to imply child care was less educational than preschool. Research has shown young children learn through all of their everyday activities including play, so how can child care not be promoting education for young children? (personal communication, June 29, 2011)

As a society we ought to be looking at the needs of all children, whether their parents work or not, instead of focusing on just one segment of the under-five population—the nation's four-year-olds. In fact, if we, as a nation, were looking to put money for young children where it would do the most good, infants would be the place to start. There's plenty of research that shows that what happens in the very first year or two of life sets the stage for the rest of the lifetime. That's when the brain has the most potential for development and also the greatest vulnerability. But, of course, we don't want to start schools for babies. We want to put together a variety of top quality programs for babies whose families work and for babies whose families don't work. Of course, those programs should be family centered, whether the parents are in the labor force or not. Furthermore, all families should have access to all the outside services they need, including health and nutrition services, mental health and social services, special education experts, and respite care for families who need it after hours.

Fotoluminate/Shutterstock

Use your imagination—pretend that every family has full support of all the resources in the community. Imagine what that would look like. Imagine how those children would arrive in kindergarten. If we had such a thing, truly no child would be left behind. Geoffrey Canada had that vision, and he did something about it! What about the rest of us?

Imagine that every family has full support of all the resources in the community; then no child would be left behind and all children would be ready to learn

It is time for this society to consider young children as a national priority. We had a peace movement, a civil rights movement, a women's movement, and an ecology movement. We need a children's movement. The Federal Child Care bill was passed at the beginning of the 1990s. It was reauthorized and signed by President Obama in November of 2014 and represents a big step in the right direction. A demonstration at the nation's capital on June 1, 1996 was another step. The "I Stand for Children" demonstration drew people from across the country to stand in the Capital Mall and show by their presence their concern for the nation's children. The theme has been taken up by local communities since then, and each June 1 different events signal the Stand for Children theme around the country. President Bill Clinton's White House Conference on Children in the mid-1990s was the first of its kind and helped bring further attention to the nation's responsibility to its children. George W. Bush, along with his wife, Laura, held a somewhat similar White House Conference when he first took office, gathering early childhood leaders from around the country to listen to his ideas about the field.

David Kirp, a professor at the University of California in Berkeley, proposes a new movement and lays out the reasons plus some steps to take. In his book *Kids First* (2011), he writes about five big ideas that this movement would encompass. Two of them are strong support for new parents and high-quality early childhood education. He also proposes something that has come up regularly in this book: "community connectedness." He sees linking schools and communities as a way to improve what both offer children.

Culturally Responsive Care

Changing demographics present a challenge to child care programs as diversity increases in some communities. Those who work with children and their families may have difficulties working from a culturally informed perspective because they first have to challenge their own values and beliefs (Mann, 2010). Educators must now more than ever before discover how to deliver *culturally responsive care*. They also have to learn more about children's racial identities (Brunson Day, 2010). A report from California Tomorrow (Chang, Muckelroy, & Pulido-Tobiassen, 1996) proposes five core principles for education and care in a diverse society:

1. Principle 1 involves adults' understanding how racism impacts the development of children's self-identity and their attitudes toward others.
2. Principle 2 advocates building on the culture of families and promoting cross-cultural understanding among children in child care.
3. Principle 3 relates to preserving children's home language and encouraging all children in child care to learn a second language.
4. Principle 4 has to do with child care staff working with families to nurture the well-being of children.
5. Principle 5 involves child care staff engaging in ongoing dialogue with families as well as self-reflection about diversity.

In addition to the five principles, professional development, recruitment and retention of a diverse workforce, ongoing research, and dissemination of research results to parents are all essential to the kind of care that promotes children's healthy development in a diverse society.

This report relates directly to the National Association for the Education of Young Children's (NAEYC) 1996 position statement "Responding to Linguistic and Cultural

Diversity: Recommendations for Effective Early Childhood Education." Both California Tomorrow and NAEYC have as a goal to build support for equal access to high-quality educational programs that recognize and promote all aspects of children's development and learning, enabling all children to become competent, successful, and socially responsible adults.

Diversity is growing in the United States. According to Brunson Day (2010) in the book *Children of 2020*, in the United States just under 41 percent of children are of Latino, Asian, Native American, and African American/African descent. "By 2020, that figure is projected to grow to 47%" (p. 67). If current trends continue, at some point in the 21st century, no single racial or ethnic group will constitute a majority of the U.S. population. That phenomenon already occurred in California in 2003.

In the future, we, as a society, must offer enough choices so that parents can find schools, early care and education, and other community services in tune with what they want and need for their children. Stopping funding cuts and expanding services by providing more programs aren't the only answers. The choices for child care must include programs that allow parents to be with their own children, as well as a wide variety of systems that provide for education and care by others. Creative alternatives in the workplace that allow working parents a greater role in caring for their own children include flextime, which allows parents to stagger work schedules; part-time work; job sharing; parent subsidies, which allow parents to be at home more with their children; flexible benefits plans; and flexible leave policies.

We need more high-quality schools and early care and education programs of all types; we haven't come close to meeting the need. Children from low-income families frequently lack the opportunity to enroll in early care and education programs. We need more child care, but we can't just have *more*—we need to have *better* child care. Cuts to quality initiatives reflect how states are scaling back efforts to improve quality in early care and education programs, including some cuts that involve basic health and safety. We have to upgrade the training, status, and salaries of child care teachers, who are grossly underpaid, putting them in the ranks of the poor. Children suffer from burned-out teachers and high turnover rates. Quality child care makes a difference. We can't promote economic independence for families without also promoting good child care. Child care is a means to family preservation and a key component in school readiness. Indeed, child care is often seen as the answer to problems of the economy, a means of addressing the miseries of poverty, and a strong tool for eradicating bias in the next generation, besides providing general early education for young children.

The problem is that poorly funded child care doesn't live up to all the dreams we have for it. Quality is a major issue. Without quality, child care doesn't do its job. It is hard to have quality when no one wants to pay the cost. Certainly most families can't pay what child care truly costs, if early care and education professionals were paid at the rate of other professionals.

Early childhood programs, such as Head Start, and quality child care can help break the cycle of poverty and disadvantage by serving the parents and by preparing the next generation to take full advantage of educational and training opportunities. Kirp (2011) sees education as the path out of poverty. 70 percent of financially secure post-secondary students graduated from college, compared with 47 percent of low-income students. Students from low-income families drop out of school six times more often than those from wealthy families. Good and widely available early care and education programs can make a difference in these statistics.

The most effective programs do far more than merely deliver early childhood education and care for children. To meet children's needs, they provide comprehensive services to the whole family. They connect the family to the greater community. An example of such a program is the Parent Services Project (PSP) started by Ethel Seiderman (Lee & Seiderman, 1998; Links, Beggs, & Seiderman, 1997). This project serves as a model of how child care can go far beyond just providing care for children by also supporting families.

In inclusion programs, children should be able to make choices and use the materials as independently as they can

Joni Hofmann/Fotolia

Moving toward Full-Inclusion Programs

The U.S. Congress has been passing legislation since 1975 designed to move children with special needs out of isolation and into programs that serve their typically developing peers. The Individuals with Disabilities Education Act (IDEA) of 1990 has supported what's called "inclusion"—that is, integrating children with special needs into early care and education programs of all sorts, including center-based care, family child care, and infant-toddler programs. Inclusion programs encourage children with disabilities to reach higher levels of achievement and develop a broader range of social skills. The programs expose children earlier to the larger world that they will live in as adults. All children benefit when children with special needs are integrated into classrooms with their typically developing peers. They can't just be thrown together, however. Care must be taken to be sure everyone's needs are met and the children with special needs are helped to feel that they belong. That takes training of teachers, caregivers, and family child care providers.

For example, children with disabilities may need support when it comes to making use of a rich environment. Materials should be selected to fit all children's capabilities, including those with special needs. Accessibility is important, too. It doesn't do any good to put children in a rich environment if they can't get to what they're interested in.

Some children need to be taught how to use an environment set up for learning through play. It helps if a teacher is nearby observing and commenting, modeling, and even making suggestions. Judging how a play environment is working depends on observing how children are using it. All children should be using the toys, materials, and activities creatively and to the best of their abilities. They should be able to make choices and use the materials as independently as they can. The degree of engagement can vary widely but should be an indication of how the environment is working.

> **✓ Check Your Understanding 15.2**
>
> Click here to check your understanding of benefitting children and families through financial investments.

ADVOCACY

Anyone who cares about America's future must become an advocate for making the world a better place for children and families. Here are some general ways to do that.

1. *Get involved!*   Start by informing yourself about the status of children and families in your neighborhood, community, state, and nation. Use your own eyes. Visit local programs that serve low-income children and see the effects of poverty. Read.

2. *Do something this week to help children.*   If you're not already involved, volunteer at a Head Start program, a child care program, or a school or another organization in your community. If you are already busy during the day or don't want to work directly with children, offer your services as a fund-raiser. Every program needs more money than it has, and most are involved in varying degrees of fund-raising efforts. If you want to feel good, take a look at a director's face when you arrive in his or her office and offer to help with fund-raising.

3. *Speak out for children!*   Inform others through speaking to religious groups, at candidate forums, and to community groups. Write a letter to the editor of your local newspaper.

4. *Be a role model for your community.*   Don't wait around for someone else to take the reins. If you show you care, others are likely to follow your example.

5. *Register and vote.*   Elect candidates who keep children and families as a priority.

6. *Understand how public policies make a difference.*   Public policies, though they may be conceived of on a national, state, or more local level, influence our lives and those of our children. Policies are decisions about goals and objectives, which become plans of action, translating eventually into programs.

The part of the advocate in helping create policy involves the following steps (adapted from Goffin & Lombardi, 1989):

1. Identify a problem that requires action.
2. Convince someone to accept responsibility for helping to solve the problem. This someone may be the government.
3. Develop and propose acceptable solutions to the problem.
4. Monitor the implementation of the solution.
5. Evaluate the program.

It's important to hold your leaders accountable. One way to do this is to keep track of how lawmakers vote on issues of importance to children and their families. Goffin and Washington (2007) give a lot more information about how to be an advocate for children and families.

Strategy Box 15.1 gives strategies for getting together with families in advocating for all children.

Strategy Box 15.1

Strategies for Involving Yourself and the Families in Advocacy Efforts

+ *Learn about the families in your community*. If you aren't in touch with low-income families, visit a program that serves them. Get a broader view by reading whatever you can find. *The State of America's Children*, published by the Children's Defense Fund, is a good place to start. Share what you learn with families you work with and find out what they already know.

+ *Understand how public policies affect children and families*. Educate yourself about the pros and cons of pending legislation. Educate the families in your program and learn from them as well.

+ *Help create legislation when a need arises*. Join a group that knows how to do this, or find out how to do it and create the group yourself.

+ *Stand up for children—together with their families*. Make your positions known. Contact your legislators. Create letter-writing and e-mail campaigns and petitions. Visit your local lawmaker's office. Go to your state capitol. Go to Washington, DC, if necessary. Make yourselves known. Make yourselves visible and heard.

+ *Join groups that advocate for children*. Many voices are louder than just a few.

+ *Educate yourself about the candidates who make families and children a priority and then cast your vote*. Let them and others know why you are voting for them.

Good health and nutrition in a child's first years are vitally linked to later achievement

szeyuen/Fotolia

Adequate Health Services and Nutrition for All

Let's go back to our discussion of the three pregnant women at the beginning of the chapter. The point of those vignettes is that good health and nutrition are vitally linked to later achievement. To enter kindergarten equally prepared, every child must have a healthy birth, adequate pre- and postnatal care and nutrition, and medical protection and care in the early years.

Adequate nutrition starting before birth is a must for healthy development. WIC (Women, Infants, and Children), a federal nutrition program already in place, can accomplish this goal. Unfortunately, WIC doesn't reach everyone who is eligible for its services.

Health-care delivery has been a patchwork system involving federal, state, and private sectors. Unfortunately, this system hasn't met the need in the past. Under Obamacare, differences in access to affordable healthcare still exist from state to state. But just providing services is not enough. Families must take responsibility to seek out and use the services that are available. Some may need to be educated about how to use medical care services. That's where the early care and education program comes in. Much can be done to help parents seek out what is available to them.

Taking a Preventive Approach

With all of the examples given in this chapter of effective programs and services for families, it sounds as if a lot is being done at this point. However, what is being done is a drop in the bucket compared with the need. Unfortunately, a good many of the services mentioned respond to emergency situations rather than preventing them in the first place. Here's a little parable to illustrate the point:

> Once there was a kindly man walking by a river. He looked out into the strong current and saw a young child struggling in the swirling waters. He threw off his shoes and plunged into the swiftly moving water. It took all the strength he had, but he finally managed to pull the child from the grip of the river, drag him up on the bank, and give him CPR. The child was saved! But lo and behold, the man looked up from the child he had just rescued and saw another child in the water. Again he raced into the river, fought hard, and managed to save this child, too. But the same thing happened. He looked up in time to see yet another child struggling in the swift current. Dead tired, he dragged himself once more to the river and plunged in. He continued in this manner until he collapsed from exhaustion and was no longer able to save any more children. That was the end of his rescue mission. Sadly enough, he had been so busy saving children that he was never able to leave long enough to walk upstream to stop whoever was throwing the children into the river in the first place!

This parable shows how our society operates in regard to children at this point. Instead of taking adequate prevention measures, we allow children to flounder in dangerous waters, and then we try to rescue them. It would be much more economical and energy effective to walk upstream and stop them from being thrown in! It's cheaper and better to prevent damage than to repair it.

A common problem of the rescue approach is that children too often must be rescued from their own parents because they don't get adequate care. That kind of rescuing can be disastrous. Children placed in foster care must deal with the emotional effects of separation and are often left with lifelong scars. Many children could remain at home if there were more programs that focused on strengthening families rather than on removing children. The Doris Duke Foundation is an example of a program that has taken just such an approach.

The costs of taking children from their families are enormous. Besides the emotional costs, there are financial burdens that taxpayers must shoulder. It costs much more to provide foster care than it would to give families what they need to keep their children home. Happily, there has been a recent trend for keeping families together. This trend is reflected in the proposals of the Children's Defense Fund group, which is continually making recommendations for systemic reforms aimed at keeping families intact.

Here are three recommendations that would prevent society from having to rescue floundering children:

1. Create in every community a network of comprehensive services to strengthen families and give them the tools they need to support and nurture their children.

2. Make family preservation services and other specialized community-based treatment available to all families in crisis.
3. Improve the quality of out-of-home placements so that special needs are met and children are returned to families or adopted as appropriate.

Violence and Its Effect on Children and Families

One issue that hasn't been covered yet in this book is the effect of violent conflict in the community on children and families. Some families have come to the United States fleeing from violence in their own countries—from war, blood feuds, oppressive dictators, ethnic cleansing—horror stories none of us like to think about. These refugee families may settle in relatively safe and secure communities but still feel the effects of their previous experiences. And not all families in the United States live in safe communities. Those who are living in communities where rival gangs fight for territory, or where crime and drugs run rampant, also have to deal with violence. At the time of this revision the news is full of horror stories of police shootings of African-American men. Then there is violence in the home that has nothing to do with the neighborhood where the home is situated. Domestic disputes that turn violent can happen anywhere. The aftereffects of violence continue to disrupt the lives of children and their families.

What are some of the specific effects of violence on young children? Some children are direct casualties of violence, but all children suffer physically and emotionally if they are exposed to violence, by witnessing it or even hearing about it. One effect is fear, which is intensified when children hear about violence and see reports in the media. Children need help with their feelings. If they aren't able to explore and express their feelings, those feelings stay hidden inside and eat away at them. The adults in their lives who have also experienced the same violence may be so tender themselves that they may have a hard time allowing children to work through their feelings. With no adult help or support, children can't begin to understand or make any sense out of what is going on. One way they try to work through their fears is through play, but how many early educators allow children to re-enact violent scenes? Most are uncomfortable with even pretend violence, though children are drawn to that kind of play—even those who haven't experienced violence first-hand.

Children who have been exposed to violence can experience post-traumatic stress syndrome, which often goes unrecognized. Without help, or at least guidance and support, children's world views become distorted, setting them up for continuing the conflict and violence in the next generation (Connolly, Hayden, & Levin, 2007; Finkelhor, Turner, Ormrod, & Hamby, 2010; Sternthal, Jun, Earls, & Wright, 2010). Families also feel the effects of violent conflict. Some have to deal with the terrible stress that comes when a family member is killed or injured. Many military families are dealing with these issues at present. Children are caught in the stress and feelings of the adults. Because male members of families are most likely to be directly involved in the violence, some families end up without any adult males, which makes it harder for the family to survive and leads to a lack of role models for male children. Families are sometimes displaced as a result of violent conflict, and that puts additional stress as they end up economically deprived and with physical and mental health issues. Children's lives are disrupted by such moves as they face separation issues as well as a challenge to their sense of cultural identity and feeling of belonging (Connolly et al., 2007).

Communities are also disrupted by violence, especially if there are opposing violent factions in the community whose fights can destroy any sense of togetherness and feelings of trust and safety. Deep divisions can result, and communities can literally disintegrate from within.

So the question is: What can early educators do to support families and children in such situations? One answer is to provide the very best early education programs that we can. We have to provide ongoing support to families and get them together so they can support each other. The environments we create must be places where children can safely explore physically and also explore their feelings with trained adults there to help when needed. The relationships we create with children must be the kinds that facilitate their social and emotional competence. Where possible, getting children in touch with nature can be a great source of healing. A wonderful new movement started recently in British Columbia, Canada called the "nature kindergarten." One of the leaders is Dr. Enid Elliot, who has been involved in early childhood education there for more than 25 years. The idea is to give children the experience of spending every morning outside in a natural setting. The afternoon is set aside for learning through play indoors. The first program was located in a school with access to old growth forests bordering on a lagoon. The goal was for them to develop confidence about being outside while gaining investigation skills and working with others. The children loved it, of course! With the freedom to move, usually only allowed at recess, they spent each morning experiencing weather while enjoying physical activity as they learned about plants, wild life, and each other. The idea of the nature kindergarten is spreading beyond its beginnings. Imagine children who currently spend most of their time indoors—at home or at school—having such experiences. A nature kindergarten could be life changing for them!

Obviously, early educators need skills to do all this—skills that go way beyond their training in getting children ready for academics by promoting early literacy and numeracy. Further, early educators need skills that help them work with adults as well as children. It's a big order, but it's worth it!

The final question is: What can early education do to make local communities and the world a more peaceful place?

There are many ways to work for a more peaceful world. Strategy Box 15.2 has some specific close-up and personal strategies early educators can use in their work with children and families.

Give children the experience of spending lots of time outside in a natural setting

Irina Schmidt/Fotolia

Box 15.2

Strategies for Working with Families and Their Children around Peacemaking

- ♦ Continually explore the idea of moving from a dominator model to an equity one. Another way of putting this idea is always looking for a win-win solution to problems and teaching others to do the same. Peace isn't won; it's made.

- ♦ Create effective partnerships with families in which power and decision making are shared.

- ♦ Become a model for others by solving problems and working through conflicts without using one-upmanship and power plays.

- ♦ Teach children to resolve conflicts and deal with issues without using aggression.

This whole book has been about peacemaking, about coming together—families and professionals. This book has been about healing the split so the fabric is whole—not a fractured fabric with teachers and children in one section and families in another. We must integrate the families into the whole program—not just create a separate part called parent involvement. And when the parts are integrated, there will still be disagreements, conflicts, and issues, but peacemaking includes knowing how to resolve those by using problem-solving methods to figure out what to do when there is disagreement.

Peace isn't won; it is made. Peace never comes once and for all. You have to continually work at it. Whenever there are two people or two groups who interact, there is the potential for conflict. It isn't about just "making nice" but about understanding how to see beyond one's own perspective, how to honor and respect differences, how to find common ground and come to agreements. This is not easy. It takes time and energy. But we have to stop using a dominator model where one person or group uses what's called one-upmanship to gain control over the other. We need to firmly implant an equity model in our minds and hearts and always work toward peaceful settlements of any problems. We teach children to do that. We can do that ourselves as well.

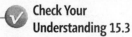

Check Your Understanding 15.3

Click here to check your understanding of advocacy.

SUMMARY

The chapter started by asking the question, who is responsible for America's children? It went on to deal with the issue of "equal starts" and explanations of what "ready to learn" means. Exploration of some of the issues related to the goal of "ready to learn" followed. Making changes was the next subject. Economic development, one of the themes of this chapter, was discussed along with Head Start and child care. The last part of that section looked at full-inclusion programs for children with special needs and why public policy should focus on integrating children with special needs with other children. The subject of how to be an advocate for children, emphasized throughout the book, comes into focus once again in this chapter through a discussion of adequate health services and nutrition. The book ends with an emphasis on peacemaking as an answer to the violence many children experience in their lives and in the media.

✓ QUIZ

Click here to check your understanding of Chapter 15, "Social Policy Issues."

FOR DISCUSSION

1. What are your ideas, feelings, and experiences related to equal opportunity for children? Does Head Start contribute to equality of opportunity? If yes, how? What are your ideas about getting the nation's children "ready to learn"? What are your ideas about "leaving no child behind"?

2. What are your experiences with the health care system, and how do you think it affects young children?

3. If you were to make recommendations to create or improve on our national child care system, what would those recommendations be? What could schools and child care programs do to support parents that they aren't doing now? What would parents need in order to be able to do what you suggest?

4. Have you ever been involved in advocating for children? If yes, what are your experiences? If no, how might you become involved?

5. What are your ideas about and experiences with peacemaking?

WEBSITES

Center for Law and Social Policy
Part of CLASP's work focuses on early care and education and promotes policies that support child development and the needs of low-income working parents on expanding availability of resources for child care and early education initiatives.

Children's Defense Fund (CDF)
The Children's Defense Fund educates the nation about the needs of children and encourages preventive investment before they get sick or into trouble, drop out of school, or suffer family breakdown. Its site contains resources and information about the organization's goals and programs.

Future of Children
The Future of Children seeks to promote effective policies and programs for children by providing policy makers, service providers, and the media with timely, objective information based on the best available research.

Harlem Children's Zone
Using the motto "whatever it takes," Harlem Children's Zone's goal is to involve hundreds of people to change generational poverty by addressing the needs of the whole community.

National Head Start Association (NHSA)
The National Head Start Association provides services for impoverished children from birth to five years of age and their families. Its site contains research and resource information, including the history and goals of the organization.

Stand for Children
The Stand for Children organization is committed to building a voice strong enough to give all children an opportunity to grow up healthy, educated, and safe.

FURTHER READING

Barbour, C. H., Barbour, N. H., Scully, P. (2010). *Families, schools, and communities: Building partnerships for educating children*. St. Paul, MN: Redleaf

Derman-Sparks, L., LeKeenan, D., & Nimmo, J. (2014). *Leading early childhood programs: A guide for change*. New York, NY: Teachers College Press.

Gopnik, A. (2013). Poverty's vicious cycle can affect our genes. Wall Street Journal, September 20, page C2.

Nguyen, K., Subramanian, S., Sorensen, G., Tsang, K., Wright, R. (2012). Influence of experiences of racial discrimination and ethnic identity on prenatal smoking among urban black and Hispanic women. *J. Epidemiological Community Health*, 66. 315–21.

Recchia, S. L. & Lee, Y-J. (2013). *Inclusion in the early childhood classroom: What makes a difference?* New York, NY: Teachers College Press.

Siegel, D. J. (2011). *Mindsight: The new science of personal transformation*. New York, NY: Bantam.

Sykes, M. (2014). *Doing the right things for children*. St. Paul, MN: Redleaf.

Tough, P. (2009). *Whatever it takes: Geoffrey Canada's quest to change Harlem and America*. Boston, MA: Mariner Books.

Washington, V. & Andrews, J. D. (Eds.). (2010). *Children of 2020: Creating a better tomorrow*. Washington, DC: Council for Professional Recognition and the National Association for the Education of Young Children.

Zigler, E. & Styfco, S. J. (2010). *The hidden history of Head Start*. New York, NY: Oxford University Press.

References

PREFACE

Allen, L. & Kelly, B.B. (Eds.). (2015). *Transforming the Workforce for Children Birth through Age 8: A Unifying Foundation.* Washington, DC: The National Academies Press. Retrieved May 29, 2015, from http://iom.nationalacademies.org/Reports/2015/Birth-To-Eight.aspx.

CHAPTER 1

Bernard, B., & Quiett, D. (2003). *Nurturing the nurturers: The importance of sound relationships in early childhood intervention.* San Francisco, CA: WestEd.

Bloom, P. J., Eisenberg, P., & Eisenberg, E. (2003, Spring/Summer). Reshaping early childhood programs to be more family responsive. *America's Family Support Magazine,* 36–38.

Bowlby, J. (1969). *Attachment and loss* (Vol. 1, *Attachment*). New York, NY: Basic Books.

Bowlby, J. (1973). *Attachment and loss* (Vol. 2, *Separation: Anxiety and anger*). London, England: Hogarth.

Bronfenbrenner, U. (1979). *The ecology of human development: Experiments by nature and design.* Cambridge, MA: Harvard University Press.

Bronfenbrenner, U. (1994). Ecological models of human development. In T. Husen & N. Postlethwaite (Eds.), *International encyclopedia of education,* Vol. 3 (2nd ed., New York, NY: Elsevier Science, pp. 1643–1647).

Buck, L., & Wiler, B. (2009). Advocacy for young children. In S. Feeney, A. Galper, & C. Seefeldt (Eds.), *Continuing issues in early childhood education* (3rd ed., pp. 391–407). Upper Saddle River, NJ: Pearson.

Center for the Study of Social Policy (CSSP). (2010). *The protective factors framework.* Washington, DC: Author. Retrieved September 8, 2011, from http://www.cssp.org/reform/strengthening-families/the-basics/protective-factors

Cervantes, W., & Hernandez, D. J. (2011, March 3). *Children in immigrant families: Ensuring opportunity for every child in America.* First Focus. Retrieved June 20, 2011, from http://fcd-us.org/resources/resources/show.htm?doc_id=463599

Christian, L. G. (2006). Understanding families: Applying family systems theory to early childhood practice. *Young Children, 61*(2), 12–20.

Copple, C., & S. Bredekamp, S. (Eds.). (2009). *Developmentally appropriate practice in early childhood programs serving children from birth through age 8* (3rd ed.). Washington, DC: National Association for the Education of Young Children.

Derman-Sparks, L., & Edwards, J. O. (2010). *Anti-bias education for young children and ourselves.* Washington, DC: National Association for the Education of Young Children.

Epstein, J. L. (2001). *School, family and community partnerships: Preparing educators and improving schools.* Boulder, CO: Westview Press.

Epstein, J. L. (2009). *School, family, and community partnerships* (3rd ed.). Washington, DC: Corwin.

Erikson, E. (1963). *Childhood and society.* New York, NY: Norton.

Espinosa, L. (2010). *Getting it right for young children from diverse backgrounds: Applying research to improve practice.* Upper Saddle River, NJ: Pearson.

Fitzgerald, D. (2004). *Parent partnership in the early years.* London, England: Continuum.

Gonzalez-Mena, J. (2009). Family centered care and education. In S. Feeney, A. Galper, & C. Seefeldt (Eds.), *Continuing issues in early childhood education* (3rd ed., pp. 369–386). Upper Saddle River, NJ: Pearson.

Gonzalez-Mena, J., & Stonehouse, A. (2008). *Making links: A collaborative approach to planning and practice in early childhood programs.* New York, NY: Teachers College Press.

Gonzalez, N., Greenberg, J., & Velez, C. (n.d.). *Funds of knowledge: A look at Luis Moll's research into hidden family resources.* Retrieved June 6, 2011, from http://www.usc.edu/dept/education/CMMR/FullText/Luis_Moll_Hidden_Family_Resources.pdf

Gordon, I. J. (1968) *Parent involvement in compensatory education.* Chicago, IL: University of Illinois Press.

Gordon, I. J., & Breivogel, W. F. (1976). *Building effective home-school relationships.* Boston, MA: Allyn & Bacon.

Hannaford, C. (2005). *Smart moves: When learning is not all in your head.* Salt Lake City, UT: Great River Books.

Hernandez, D. J. (2011, January 27). *Middle-class children falling further behind.* Foundation for Child Development. Retrieved June 26, 2011, from http://fcd-us.org/resources/search?topic=0&authors=Donald+J.+Hernandez&keywords=middle+class+children

Hilliard, A. G. (2004). *Assessment equity in a multicultural society.* New Horizons for Learning. Retrieved from http://education.jhu.edu/newhorizons/strategies/topics/multicultural-education/assessmentequityinamulticulturalsociety/

Hilliard, A. G. (2007). What do we need to know now? A speech presented at a conference on Race, Research, and Education, held in Chicago at an African-American symposium sponsored by the Chicago Urban League and the Spencer Foundation.

Im, J., Parlakian, R., & Sanchez, S. (2007). Rocking and rolling: Supporting infants, toddlers, and their families: Understanding the influence of culture on caregiving practices… from the inside out. *Young Children, 62*(5), 65–66.

Keyser, J. (2006). *From parents to partners: Building a family centered early childhood program.* Washington, DC: National Association for the Education of Young Children, and St. Paul, MN: Redleaf Press.

Lee, L. (2006). *Stronger together: Family support and early childhood education.* San Rafael, CA: Parent Services Project.

Lee, L., & Seiderman, E. (1998). *Families matter: The parent services project.* Cambridge, MA: Harvard Family Research Project.

Lewis, T., Amini, F., & Lannon, R. (2000). *A general theory of love.* New York, NY: Vintage Books.

Mahoney, G., & Wiggers, B. (2007). The role of parents in early intervention. *Children and Schools,* 29(1), 7–15.

Maslow, A. (1954). *Motivation and personality.* New York, NY: Harper and Row.

McGee-Banks, C. A. (2003). Families and teachers working together for school improvement. In J. A.Banks & C. A. McGee-Banks (Eds.), *Multicultural education: Issues and perspectives* (4th ed., pp. 402–410). New York, NY: Wiley.

National Association for the Education of Young Children (2005). *Families and community relationships: A guide to the NAEYC early childhood program standards and related accreditation criteria.* Washington, DC: Author.

Ogbu, J. U. (1987). Variability in minority school performance: A problem in search of an explanation. *Anthropology and Education Quarterly,* 18, 313–334.

Olmsted, P. P., Rubin, R. I., True, J. H., & Revicki, D. (1980). *Parent education: The contributions of Ira J. Gordon.* Olney, MD: Association for Childhood Education International.

Parke, R. D., & Buriel, R. (2006). Socialization in the family: Ethnic and ecological perspectives. In W. Damon & R. M. Lerner (Eds.), *Handbook of child psychology,* Vol. 3 (6th ed). Hoboken, NJ: Wiley.

Pope, J., & Seiderman, E. (2001, Winter). The child-care connection. *Family Support,* 19(4), 24–35.

Powell, D. R. (1986). Research in review. Parent education and support programs. *Young Children,* 41(3), 47–53.

Powell, D. R. (1998). Research in review. Reweaving parents into the fabric of early childhood programs. *Young Children,* 53(5), 60–67.

Ray, A., Bowman, B., & Robbins, J. (2006). *Preparing early childhood teachers to successfully educate all children.* Retrieved June 6, 2011, from http://fcd-us.org/resources/search?topic=0&authors=Ray&keywords=successfully+educate

Rogoff, B. (2003). *The cultural nature of human development.* New York, NY: Oxford University Press.

Seiderman, E. (2003). Putting all the players on the same page: Accessing resources for the child and family. In B. Neugebauer & R. Neugebauer (Eds.), *The art of leadership.* Redmond, WA: Exchange Press.

Tough, P. (2009). *Whatever it takes: Geoffrey Canada's quest to change Harlem and America.* Boston, MA: Mariner Books.

Turnbull, A. P., Turbiville, P. V., & Turnbull, H. R. (2000). Evolution of family-professional partnerships: Collective empowerment as the model for early twenty-first century. In P. Shonkoff & S. J. Meisels (Eds.), *Handbook of early childhood intervention* (pp. 630–650). New York, NY: Cambridge University Press.

Zehr, M. A. (2011). Expert's call for early focus on black boy's nonacademic skills. Retrieved June 17, 2011, from http://www.edweek.org/ew/articles/2011/06/15/36ets.h30.html?tkn=UNQFX36g%2FWXRcQX4pRuYiefFUdobegYv10Kp&cmp=ENL-EU-NEWS1

CHAPTER 2

Ainsworth, M. D. S., & Bell, S. (1977). Infant crying and maternal responsiveness. *Child Development,* 48, 1208–1216.

Ainsworth, M. D. S., Blehar, M. C., Waters, E., & Wall, S. (1978). *Patterns of attachment. A psychological study of the Strange Situation.* Hillside, NJ: Erlbaum.

Anderson, C. A., Berkowitz, L., Donnerstein, E., Huesmann, I., Rowell Johnson, F. D., & Linz, D. (2003). The influence of media violence on youth. *Psychological Science in the Public Interest,* 4, 81–110.

Annie E. Casey Foundation. (2011). Retrieved September 19, 2011, from http://www.aecf.org/KnowledgeCenter/SearchResults.aspx?source=topsearchKC

Bandura, A., & Walters, R. H. (1963). *Social learning and personality development.* New York, NY: Holt, Rinehart & Winston.

Berk, L. (2001). *Dialogues with children: Creating learning environments at home and school.* New York, NY: Oxford University Press.

Biddle, B. J., & Berliner, D. C. (2002). *In pursuit of better schools: What research says.* Tempe, AZ: Education Policy Studies Laboratory, College of Education, Educational Leadership & Policy Studies, Arizona State University.

Bodrova, E., & Leong, D. J. (2007). *Tools of the mind* (2nd ed.). Upper Saddle River, NJ: Pearson.

Bowlby, J. (2000) *Attachment and loss: Vol. I. Attachment.* New York, NY: Basic Books.

Boyer, E. L. (1991). *Ready to learn: A mandate for the nation.* Princeton, NJ: Carnegie Foundation for the Advancement of Teaching.

Bronfenbrenner, U. (1979). *The ecology of human development.* Cambridge, MA: Harvard University Press.

Bronfenbrenner, U. (Ed.). (2005) *Making human beings human: Bioecological perspectives on human development.* Thousand Oaks, CA: Sage.

Bronson, P., & Merryman, A. (2009). *Nurture shock.* New York, NY: Twelve.

Bushman, B. J., & Anderson, C. A. (2001). Media violence and the American public: Scientific facts versus media misinformation. *American Psychologist,* 56, 466–489.

Bushman, D., & Huesmann, L. R. (2001). Effects of televised violence on aggression. In D. Singer & J. Singer (Eds.), *Handbook of children and the media.* Thousand Oaks, CA: Sage.

Byrnes, D. A., & Kiger, G. (Eds.). (2005). *Common bonds: Anti-bias teaching in a diverse society* (3rd ed.). Olney, MD: Association for Childhood Education International.

California Department of Education. (2009). *Inclusion works! Creating child care programs that promote belonging for children with special needs.* Sacramento, CA: Author.

Canada, G. (1995). *Fist stick knife gun: A personal history of violence.* Boston, MA: Beacon Press.

Canada, G., & Nicholas, J. (2010). *Fist stick knife gun: A personal history of violence (A true story in black and white).* Boston, MA: Beacon Press.

Carlsson-Paige, N., & Levin, D. E. (1990). *Who's calling the shots: How to respond effectively to children's fascination with war play and war toys.* Philadelphia, PA: New Society.

Cernoch, I. M., & Porter, R. H. (1985). Recognition of maternal axillary odors by infants. *Child Development,* 56. 1593–1598

Chang. H. (1993). *Affirming children's roots. Cultural and linguistic diversity in early care and education.* San Francisco, CA: California Tomorrow.

Christakis, D. A., & Zimmerman, F. J. (2006). *The elephant in the living room: Make television work for your kids.* New York, NY: Rodale.

Clark, K. E., & Ladd, G. W. (2000). Connectedness and autonomy support in parent-child relationships: Links to children's socio-emotional orientation and peer relationships. *Developmental Psychology, 36,* 485–498.

David, M., & Appell, G. (2001) *Loczy: An unusual approach to mothering* . (M. Clark & J. Falk, Trans.). Budapest, Hungary. Pikler-Loczy Tarsasag.

Day, C. B. (2013). Understanding the social context of infant/toddler care. In E. Virmani & P. Mangione (Eds.), *A guide to culturally sensitive care* (2nd ed., pp. 1–10). Sacramento, CA: California Department of Education.

DeCasper, A. J., & Fifer, W. P. (1980). Of human bonding: Newborns prefer their mothers' voices. *Science, 208* 1174–1175.

Derman-Sparks, L., & the ABC Task Force. (1989). *Anti-bias curriculum: Tools for empowering young children.* Washington, DC: National Association for the Education of Young Children.

Derman-Sparks, L., & Edwards, J. O. (2010). *Anti-bias education for young children and ourselves.* Washington, DC: National Association for the Education of Young Children.

Derman-Sparks, L., & Ramsey, P. G. (2006). *What if all the kids are white? Anti-bias/multicultural education withyoung children and families.* New York, NY: Teachers College Press.

Elkind, D. (2007). *The power of play.* Cambridge, MA: Da Capo Press.

Erikson, E. (1963). *Childhood and society.* New York, NY: Norton.

Ferber (2006). *Solve your child's sleep problems.* New York, NY: Fireside.

Gerbner, G., Gross, L., & Signorielli, N. (1986). Living with television: The dynamics of the cultivation process. In J. Bryant & D. Zillman (Eds.), *Perspectives on media effects.* Hillsdale, NJ: Erlbaum.

Gonzalez-Mena, J. (1995). *Dragonmom.* Napa, CA: Rattle Ok Press.

Gonzalez-Mena, J. (1997, September). Understanding the parent's perspective: Independence or Interdependence? *Exchange,* 61–63.

Gonzalez-Mena, J (2004, September). What can an orphanage teach us? Lessons from Budapest. *Young Children,* 26–30.

Gonzalez-Mena, J. (2008) *Diversity in early care and education: Honoring differences.* New York, NY: McGraw-Hill.

Gonzalez-Mena, J. (2013). Cultural sensitivity in caregiving routines: the essential activities of daily living. In E. Virmani & P. Mangione (Eds.), *A guide to culturally sensitive care* (2nd ed., pp. 56–65). Sacramento, CA: California Department of Education.

Gonzalez-Mena, J., & L. Briley (2011). Improving infant mental health in orphanages. *The Signal: Newsletter of the World Association for Infant Mental Health,* 19(4), 14–17.

Gonzalez, N., Greenberg, J., & Velez, C. (n.d.). *Funds of knowledge: A look at Luis Moll's research into hidden family resources.* Retrieved June 6, 2011, from http://www.usc.edu/dept/education/CMMR/FullText/Luis_Moll_Hidden_Family_Resources.pdf

Gorski, P. C. (2007, Spring). The question of class. *Teaching Tolerance, 31,* 26–29.

Greenwald, D., & J. Weaver (2013). *The RIE manual for parents and professionals.* Los Angeles, CA: Resources for Infant Educarers.

Grether, J, Schulman, J., & Croen L. (1990, April) Sudden infant death syndrome among Asians in California. *Journal of Pediatrics,* 116(4), 525–528.

Guerra, A. W., & S. Garriety (2013). A cultural communities and cultural practices approach to understanding infant and toddler care. In E. Virmani & P. Mangione (Eds.), *A guide to culturally sensitive care* (2nd ed., pp. 41–53). Sacramento, CA: California Department of Education.

Hammond, R. A. (2013). Educaring, interpersonal neuroscience, and selective intervention. In D. Greenwald & J. Weaver (Eds.), *The RIE manual for parents and professionals* (2nd ed., pp. 148–160). Los Angeles, CA: Resources for Infant Educarers.

Healy, J. M. (2011, March/April). Impacting readiness: Nature and nurture. *Exchange,* 33(2), 18–21.

High-wire act: Cyber-safety and the young. (2011) Retrieved June 16, 2011, from Parliament of Australia Joint Committee at http://www.aph.gov.au/house/committee/jscc/report.htm

Hirsch, K. W. (1997). Media violence and audience behavior. In A. Wells & E. Hakanen (Eds.), *Mass media and society* (5th ed., pp. 479–505). Greenwich, CT: Ablex.

Howe, D. (2011). *Attachment across the lifecourse.* London: Palgrave.

Howes, C., & Ritchie, S. (2002). *A matter of trust.* New York, NY: Teachers College Press.

Huesmann, L. R., & Miller, L. S. (1994). Long-term effects of repeated exposure to media violence in childhood. In L. R. Huesmann (Ed.), *Aggressive behavior: Current perspectives* (pp. 153–186). New York, NY: Plenum.

Immordino-Yang, M. H., & Damasio, A. (2007). We feel, therefore we learn. The relevance of affective and social neuroscience to education. *International Mind, Brain, and Education Society,* 1(1) 3–10.

Kaiser, B., & Rasminsky, J. (2012). *Challenging behavior in young children: Understanding, preventing, and responding effectively* (3rd ed.). Upper Saddle River, NJ: Pearson.

Katz, L. G. (1980). Mothering and teaching: Some significant distinctions. In L. G. Katz (Ed.), *Current topics in early childhood education* (pp. 3, 47–63). Norwood, NJ: Ablex.

Kozol, J. (1991). *Savage inequalities: Children in America's schools.* New York, NY: Crown.

Kusserow, A. (2005, Fall). The workings of class. *Stanford Social Innovation Review,* 38–47.

Lally, J. R. (1995, November). The impact of child care policies and practices on infant/toddler *identity formation. Young Children,* 58–67.

Lally, J. R. (1998, May). Brain research, infant learning, and child care curriculum. *Child Care Information Exchange,* 121, 46–48.

Lally, J. R. (2013). *For our babies: Ending the invisible neglect of America's infants.* San Francisco, CA: WestEd and New York, NY: Teachers College Press.

Leman, P. J., & Lam, V. L. (2008, September/October). The influence of race and gender on children's conversations and playmate choices. *Child Development,* 79(5), 1329–1343.

Lieberman, A. F., & Zeanah, C. H. (1995, July). Disorders of attachment in infancy. *Infant Psychiatry,* 4(3), 571–585.

Maccoby, E. E. (1998). *The two sexes.* Cambridge, MA: Harvard University Press.

Main, M., & Solomon, J. (1990). Procedures for identifying infants as disorganized/disoriented during the Ainsworth Strange Situation.

In M. Greenberg, D. Cicchetti, & E. M. Cummings (Eds.), *Attachment in the preschool years: Theory, research and interventions* (pp. 121–160). Chicago, IL: University of Chicago Press.

Marshall, E., & Sensoy, O. (2011). *Rethinking popular culture and media.* Milwaukee, WI: Rethinking Schools.

Maslow, A. (1954). *Motivation and personality.* New York, NY: Harper and Row.

McKenna, J. (2014). Night waking among breastfeeding mothers and infants: Conflict, congruence or both? *Evolution, Medicine & Public Health,* 3–17.

McKenna, T., & Ortiz, F. I. (Eds.). (1988). *The broken web: The educational experience of Hispanic American women.* Encino, CA: Floricanto.

National Research Council and Institute of Medicine. (2000). *From neurons to neighborhoods: The science of early childhood development.* Washington, DC: Board on Children, Youth, and Families, Commission on Behavioral and Social Sciences and Education. National Academy Press.

Park, S. (2007, August 27). How not to raise a genius. Is Baby Einstein doing your child more harm than good? *Time,* 170, 46.

Parke, R. D., & O'Neil, R. (2000). The influence of significant others on learning about relationships: From family to friends. In R. S. L. Mills & S. Duck (Eds.), *The developmental psychology of personal relationships* (pp. 15–47). New York, NY: Wiley.

Pawl, J. H. (1995, February-March). The therapeutic relationships as human connectedness. Being held in another's mind. *Zero to Three,* 15(4), 48–49.

Perry, B. (2002). Childhood experience and the expression of genetic potential: What childhood neglect tells us about nature and nurture. *Brain and Mind,* 3(1), 79–100.

Perry, B. (2006). Applying principles of neurodevelopment to clinical work with maltreated and traumatized children. In N. B. Webb (Ed.), *Working with traumatized youth in child welfare.* New York, NY: Guilford Press.

Perry, B. D., & Dobson, C. (2010) The role of healthy relational interactions in buffering the impact of childhood trauma. In E. Gill (Ed.), *Working with Children to Heal Interpersonal Trauma: The Power of Play.* New York, NY: Guilford Press.

Raikes, H. (1996, July). A secure base for babies: Applying attachment concepts to the infant care setting. *Young Children,* 51(5), 59–67.

Rideout, V., & Hamel, E. (2006). The media family: Electronic media in the lives of infants, toddlers, preschoolers and their parents. Retrieved June 6, 2011, from http://www.kff.org/entmedia/upload/7500.pdf

Rogoff, B. (2003). *The cultural nature of human development.* New York, NY: Oxford University Press.

Rogoff, B. (2011). *Developing destinies*: A *Mayan midwife and town.* New York, NY: Oxford University.

Schneider, B. H., Atkinson, L., & Tardif, C. (2001). Child-parent attachment and children's peer relations: A quantitative review. *Developmental Psychology,* 37, 86–100.

Sears, W., & Sears, M. (2001). *The attachment parenting book.* New York, NY: Little, Brown and Company.

Sears, W., & Sears, M. (2013) *The baby book.* New York, NY: Little Brown.

Shonkoff, J. P., & Phillips, D. (2001, April/May). From neurons to neighborhoods: The science of early childhood development—An introduction. *Zero to Three,* 21(5), 4–7.

Shore, R. (1997). *Rethinking the brain: New insights in early development.* New York, NY: Families and Work Institute.

Signorielli, N., & Morgan, M. (2001). Television and the family: The cultivation perspective. In J. Bryant & J. A. Bryant (Eds.), *Television and the American family* (2nd ed., pp. 333–351). Mahwah, NJ: Erlbaum.

Singer, D. G., & Singer, J. L. (2005). *Imagination and play in the electronic age.* Cambridge, MA: Harvard University Press.

Solomon, J., & George, C. (1999). The measurement of attachment security in infancy and childhood. In J. Cassidy & P. Shaver (Eds.), *Handbook of attachment* (pp. 287–318). New York, NY: Guilford.

Stack, C. B. (1991). Sex roles and survival strategies inn an urban black community. In R. Staples (Ed.), *The black family: Essays and studies* (4th ed.). Belmont, CA: Wadsworth.

Szalavitz, M., & Perry, B. (2010). *Born for love: Why empathy is essential and endangered.* New York, NY: Harper.

Thevenin, T. (1987). *The family bed.* Garden City, NY: Avery.

Thomas, A., Chess, S., & Birch, H. G. (1963). *Behavioral individuality in early childhood.* New York, NY: New York University Press.

Tinsley, B. R. (2002). *How children learn to be healthy.* New York, NY: Cambridge University Press.

Virmani, E., & P. Mangione (Eds.). (2013). *A guide to culturally sensitive care* (2nd ed.). Sacramento, CA: California Department of Education.

Vygotsky, L. S. (1978). *Mind in society: The development of higher psychological process.* Cambrindge, MA: Harvard University Press (original works published 1930, 1933, and 1935).

Wang, L., Beckett, G., & Brown, L. (2006). Controversies of standardized assessment in school accountability reform: A critical synthesis of multidisciplinary research evidence. *Applied Measurement in Education,* 19(4), 305–328.

Werner, E. E. (1984), November). Research in review; Resilient children. *Young Children,* 40(1). 68–72.

Werner, E. E. (1995, June). Resilience in development. *Current Directions in Psychological Science,* 4(3), 81–85.

Werner, E. E. (2000, February-March). The power of the protective factors in the early years. *Zero to Three,* 20(4), 3–5.

Werner, E. E., & Smith, R. S. (1992). *Overcoming the odds: High risk children from birth to adulthood.* Ithaca, NY: Cornell University Press.

Weissbourd, B., Weissbourd, R., & O'Carroll, K. (2010). Family engagement. In V. Washington & J. D. Andrews (Eds.),*Children of 2020: Creating a better tomorrow* (pp. 114–118). Washington, DC: Council for Professional Recognition and National Association for the Education on Young Children.

Wise, T. (2005). *White like me: Reflections on race from a privileged son.* Brooklyn, NY: Soft Skull Press.

Wright, J. C., Huston, A. C., Murphy, K. C., St. Peters, M., Pinon, M., Scantlin, R., & Kotler, J. (2001). The relations of early television viewing to school readiness and vocabulary of children from low-income families: The early window project. *Child Development,* 72, 1347–1366.

Zehr, M. A. (2011). Expert's call for early focus on black boy's nonacademic skills. Retrieved June 17, 2011, from http://www.edweek.org/ew/articles/2011/06/15/36ets.h30.html?tkn=UNQFX36g%2FWXRcQX4pRuYiefFUdobegYv10Kp&cmp=ENL-EU-NEWS1

Zigler, E. F., Finn-Stevenson, M., & Hall, N. W. (2003). *The first three years and beyond: Brain development and social policy.* New Haven, CT: Yale University Press.

Zimmerman, L., & McDonald L. (1995). Emotional availability in infants' relationships with multiple caregivers. *American Journal of Orthopsychiatry*, 65(1), 147–152.

CHAPTER 3

Balaban, N. (2006). *Everyday goodbyes: A guide to the separation process.* New York, NY: Teachers College Press.

Bowlby, J. (1969). *Attachment and loss: Vol. 1. Attachment.* London, England: Hogarth.

Bowlby, J. (2000a [1972]). *Attachment and loss: Vol. 2. Separation: Anxiety and anger.* New York, NY: Basic Books.

Bowlby, J. (2000b [1980]). *Attachment and loss: Vol. 3. Loss: Sadness and depression.* New York, NY: Basic Books.

Bronfenbrenner, U. (1979). *The ecology of human development.* Cambridge, MA: Harvard University Press.

Bronfenbrenner, U. (2000). Ecological system theory. In A. Kazdin (Ed.), *Encyclopedia of psychology.* Washington, DC: American Psychological Association and Oxford Press.

Bronfenbrenner, U. (Ed.). (2005) *Making human beings human: Bioecological perspectives on human development.* Thousand Oaks, CA: Sage.

Brunson Day, C. (2010). Racial identity. In V. Washington & J. D. Andrews (Eds.), *Children of 2020: Creating a better tomorrow* (pp. 67–72). Washington, DC: Council for Professional Recognition and the National Association for the Education of Young

Carlebach, D., & Tate, B. (2002). *Creating caring children: The first three years.* Miami, FL: The Peace Education Foundation.

Copple, C., & Bredekamp, S. (2009). *Developmentally appropriate practice in early childhood programs* (3rd ed.). Washington, DC: National Association for the Education of Young Children.

Copple, C., Bredekamp, S., & Gonzalez-Mena, J. (2011). *Basics of developmentally appropriate practice for infants and toddlers.* Washington, DC: National

Association for the Education of Young Children.

David, M., & Appell, G. (2001 [1973, 1996]). *Loczy: An unusual approach to mothering.* Translated from *Loczy ou le maternage insolite*, by Jean Marie Clark; revised translation by Judit Falk. Budapest, Hungary: Pikler-Loczy Tarsasag.

Elkind, D. (2007). *The power of play.* Cambridge, MA: Da Capo.

Erikson, E. (1963). *Childhood and society.* New York, NY: Norton.

Gerber, M. (1979). *The RIE manual.* Los Angeles, CA: Resources for Infant Educarers.

Gonzalez-Mena, J. (2001, September). Making meaning of separation: Contrasting pictures of the first good-bye. *The First Years, Nga TauTuatahi* (New Zealand Journal of Infant and Toddler Education), 3(2), 4–5.

Gonzalez-Mena, J. (2004, September). What can an orphanage teach us? Lessons from Budapest. *Young Children*, 59(5), 26–30.

Gonzalez-Mena, J. (2008). *Diversity in early care and education: Honoring differences.* New York, NY: McGraw-Hill.

Gonzalez-Mena, J. (2013). What works? Assessing infant and toddler play environments. *Young Children*, 68(4), 22–24.

Gopnik, A. (2009). *The philosophical baby.* New York, NY: Farrar, Straus and Giroux.

Gray, H. (2004, September). "You go away and you come back": Supporting separations and reunions in an infant/toddler classroom. *Young Children*, 59(5), 100–107.

Greenfield, P. M., Quiroz, B., Rothstein-Fisch, C., & Trumbull, E. (2001). *Bridging cultures between home and school.* Mahwah, NJ: Erlbaum.

Greenough, W., Emde, R. N., Gunnar, M., Massinga, R., & Shonkoff, J. P. (2001, April–May). The impact of the caregiving environment on young children's development: Different ways of knowing, *Zero to Three*, 21(5), 16–24.

Greenwald, D., & J. Weaver (2013). *The RIE manual for parents and professionals* (2nd ed.) Los Angeles, CA: Resources for Infant Educarers.

Guerra, A. W., & S. Garriety (2013). A cultural communities and cultural practices approach to understanding

infant and toddler care. In E. Virmani & P. Mangione (Eds.), *A guide to culturally sensitive care* (2nd ed., pp. 41–53). Sacramento, CA: Calfironia Department of Education.

Hammond, R. A. (2009). *Respecting babies: A new look at Magda Gerber's RIE approach.* Washington, DC: Zero to Three.

Hannaford, C. (2005). *Smart moves: Why learning is not all in your head.* Salt Lake City, UT: Green River.

Jones, E., & Cooper, R. (2006). *Playing to get smart.* New York, NY: Teachers College Press.

Kahwaty, D. H. (2006, March/April). Toilet-training newborns: Parents grab hold of trend to potty-train infant twins. *Twins*, 20–23.

Kallo E., & Balog, G. (2005). *The origins of free play.* Budapest, Hungary: Pikler Loczy Tarsasag.

Keyser, J. (2007). *From parents to partners: Building a family centered early childhood program.* Washington, DC: National Association for Education of Young Children.

Lee, L. (Ed.). (2006). *Stronger together: Family support and early childhood education.* San Rafael, CA: Parent Services Project.

Maslow, A. (1954). *Motivation and personality.* New York, NY: Harper and Row.

McCracken, J. B. (1986). *So many good-byes: Ways to ease the transition between home and groups for young children.* Washington, DC: National Association for the Education of Young Children.

National Association for the Education of Young Children (1996, January). Linguistic and cultural diversity position paper. *Young Children*, 51(2), 4–12.

Parten, M. B. (1932). Social participation among preschool children. *Journal of Abnormal Psychology*, 27, 756–759.

Piaget, J. (1954). *The construction of reality in the child.* New York, NY: Ballantine.

Piaget, J. (1962). *Play, dreams and imitation in childhood.* New York, NY: Norton.

Pikler, E. (1971). Learning of motor skills on the basis of self-induced movements. In J. Hellmuth (Ed.), *Exceptional infant*, Vol. 2 (pp. 54–89). New York, NY: Brunner/Mazel.

Pikler, E. (1973). Some contributions to the study of gross motor development of children. *Journal of Genetic Psychology*, 113, 27–39.

Pikler, E. (2007). Give me time: Gross motor development under the conditions at Loczy. In A. Tardos (Ed.), *Bringing up and providing care for infants and toddlers in an institution* (pp. 135–150). Budapest, Hungary: Pikler-Loczy Tarsasag.

Pikler, E., & Tardos, A. (1968). Some contributions to the study of infants' gross motor activities. In *Proceedings of the 16th International Congress of Applied Psychology.* Amsterdam, Netherlands: ICAP.

Reifel, S., & Sutterby, J. A. (2009). Play theory and practice incontemporary classrooms. In S. Feeney, A. Galper, & C. Seefeldt (Eds.), *Continuing issues in early childhood education* (2nd ed., pp. 238–254). Upper Saddle River, NJ: Pearson.

Rogoff, B. (2003). *The cultural nature of human development.* New York, NY: Oxford University Press.

Sandovsky, A. (Ed.). *Child and adolescent development* (pp. 52–64). New York, NY: Free Press.

Soloman, A. (2013). *Far from the tree: Parents, children, and the search for identity.* New York, NY: Scribner.

Szanton, E. S. (2001, January). For America's infants and toddlers, are important values threatened by our zeal to "teach"? *Young Children,* 56(1), 15–21.

Tardos, A. (2007). The child as an active participant in his own development. In A. Tardos (Ed.), *Bringing up and providing care for infants and toddlers in an institution* (pp. 127–134). Budapest, Hungary: Pikler-Loczy Tarsasag.

Tobin, J., Hsueh, Y., & Karasawa, M. (2009). *Preschool in three cultures revisited.* Chicago, IL: University of Chicago Press.

Van der Zande, I. (2011). *1.2.3....The Toddler Years: A Practical Guide for Parents and Caregivers.* Santa Cruz, CA: Santa Cruz Toddler Care Center.

Van Hoorn, J., Nourot, P., Scales, B., & Alward, K. (2007). *Play at the center of the curriculum* (4th ed.). Upper Saddle River, NJ: Pearson.

Vinson, B. M. (2001, January). Fishing and Vygotsky's concept of effective education. *Young Children,* 56(1), 88–89.

Walker, C. M., & Gopnik, A. (2014). Toddlers infer higher-order relational principles in causal learning. *Psychological Science,* 25 (1) 161–169.

Williams, D. S., & Rose, T (2007, July). I say hello; You say good-bye: When babies are born while fathers are away. *Zero to Three,* 27(6), 13–19.

Wittmer, D. (2012). The wonder and complexity of infant and toddler peer relationships. *Young Children* 67(4), 16–25.

Wittmer, D. S., & Petersen, S. H. (2006). *Infant and toddler development and responsive program planning: A relationship-based approach.* Upper Saddle River, NJ: Pearson.

Zepeda, M., Gonzalez-Mena, J., Rothstein-Fisch, C., & Trumbull, E. (2006). *Bridging cultures in early care and education.* Mahwah, NJ: Erlbaum.

CHAPTER 4

Barkley, R. A. (1997). *ADHD and the nature of self-control.* New York, NY: Guilford.

Berk, L. E. (1994, November). Vygotsky's theory: The importance of make-believe play. *Young Children,* 50(1), 30–39.

Bodrova, E. (2008). Make-Believe play versus academic skills: A Vygotskian approach to today's dilemma of early childhood education. *European Early Childhood Education Research Journal,* 16, 357–369.

Bronfenbrenner, U. (1979). *The ecology of human development.* Cambridge, MA: Harvard University Press.

Bronfenbrenner, U. (2000). Ecological system theory. In A. Kazdin (Ed.), *Encyclopedia of Psychology.* Washington, DC: American Psychological Association and Oxford Press.

Bronfenbrenner, U. (Ed.). (2005) *Making human beings human: Bioecological perspectives on human development.* Thousand Oaks, CA: Sage.

California Department of Education. (2009). *Inclusion works! Creating child care programs that promote belonging for children with special needs.* Sacramento, CA: Author.

Carlson, F. M. (2011). *Big body play: Why boisterous, vigorous, and very physical play is essential to children's development and learning.* Washington, DC: National Association for the Education of Young Children.

Chandler, L. (1998). Promoting positive interaction between preschool-age children during free play: The pals center. *Young Exceptional Children,* 2(2), 13–19.

Curtis, D., Brown, K. L., Baird, V., & Coughlin, A. M. (2013, September). Planning Environments and Materials that Respond to Young Children's Lively Minds. *Young Children,* 68(4), 26–31.

Duckworth, E. (2001). *"Tell me more": Listening to learners.* New York, NY: Teachers College Press.

Edmiaston, R., Dolezal, V., Doolittle, S., Erickson, C., & Merritt, S. (2000). Developing individualized education programs for children in inclusive settings: A developmental framework. *Young Children,* 55(4), 36–41.

Eggers-Pierola, C. (2005). *Connections & commitments. Reflecting Latino values in early childhood programs.* Portsmouth, NH: Heinemann.

Elkind, D. (2007). *The power of play.* Cambridge, MA: Da Capo.

Elliot, E., & Gonzalez-Mena, J. (2011). Self-regulation: Taking a broader perspective. *Young Children,* 66(1)(16–24).

Erikson, E. (1963). *Childhood and society.* New York, NY: Norton.

Ferguson, C. J., & Dettore, E. (2007). *To play or not to play: Is it really a question?* Olney, MD: Association for Childhood Education International.

Fraiberg, S. H. (1959). *The magic years.* New York, NY: Scribner's.

Fromberg, D. P. (2002). *Play and meaning in early childhood education.* Boston, MA: Allyn & Bacon.

Frost, J., Wortham, S., & Reifel, S. (2012). *Play and child development* (4th ed.). Upper Saddle River, NJ: Pearson.

Gopnik, A. (2012, July-August) Let the children play. It's good for them! *Smithsonian Magazine.*

Greenberg, P. (1990, January). Why not academic preschool? *Young Children,* 45(2), 70–80.

Hirsh-Pasek, K. Golinkoff, R. M., Berk, L.E., & Singer. D.G. (2009). *A mandate for playful learning in preschool: Presenting the evidence.* New York, NY: Oxford University Press.

Hyson, M. (2004). *The emotional development of young children* (2nd ed.). New York, NY: Teachers College Press.

Jacobs, G., & Crowley, K. (2007). *Play, projects and preschool standards: Nurturing children's sense of wonder and joy in learning.* Thousand Oaks, CA: Corwin.

Jensen, E. (1998). *Teaching with the brain in mind.* Alexandria, VA: Association for Supervision and Curriculum Development.

Jent, J. F., Niec, L. N., & Baker, S. E. (2011). Play and interpersonal processes. In S. W. Russ & L. N. Niec

(Eds.), *Play in clinical practice: Evidence-based approaches*. New York, NY: Guilford Press.

Jones, E. (2003, May). Playing to get smart. *Young Children* 58(3), 32–33.

Jones, E., & Cooper, R. (2006). *Playing to get smart*. New York, NY: Teachers College Press.

Jones, E., & Prescott, E. (1978). *Dimensions of teaching-learning environments: Vol. 2. Focus on day care*. Pasadena, CA: Pacific Oaks.

Jones, E., & Reynolds, G. (2011). *The play's the thing: Teachers' roles in children's play* (2nd ed.). New York, NY: Teachers College Press.

Kamii, C. (with L. B. Housman). (2000). *Young children reinvent arithmetic: Implications of Piaget's theory* (2nd ed.). New York, NY: Teachers College Press.

Katch, J. (2001). *Under deadman's skin: Discovering the meaning of children's violent play*. Boston, MA: Beacon.

Katz, L. G., & Chard, S. (2000). *Engaging children's minds: The project approach* (2nd ed.). Stamford, CT: Ablex.

Kelly, J. F., & Booth, C. L. (1999). Child care for children with special needs: Issues and applications. *Infants and Young Children, 12*(1), 26–33.

Kemple, K. M. (2004). *Let's be friends: Peer competence and social inclusion in early childhood programs*. New York, NY: Teachers College Press.

Kern, P., and Wakeford, L. (2007, September). Supporting outdoor play for young children: The zone model of playground supervision. *Young Children 62*(5), 20–25.

Kersey, K., & Marsterson, M. (2013). *101 Principles for Positive Guidance with Young Children: Creating Responsive Teachers*. Upper Saddle River, NJ: Pearson.

Klein, M. D., & Chen, D. (2001). *Working with children from culturally diverse backgrounds*. New York, NY: Delmar.

Kostelnik, M., Onaga, E., Rohde, B., & Whiren, A. (2002). *Children with special needs: Lessons for early childhood professionals*. New York, NY: Teachers College Press.

Levin, D. E. (2002). *Teaching young children in violent times: Building a peaceable classroom* (2nd ed.). Cambridge, MA: Educators for Social Responsibility and Washington, DC: National Association for the Education of Young Children.

Maslow, A. (1954). *Motivation and personality*. New York, NY: Harper and Row.

McCathren, R. B. (2000). Teacher-implemented prelinguistic communication intervention. *Focus on Autism and Other Developmental Disabilities,* 15(1), 21–29.

Mistry, I. (1995). Culture and learning in infancy: Implications for caregiving. In P. L. Mangione (Ed.), *Infant/toddler caregiving: A guide to culturally sensitive care*. Sacramento, CA: California Department of Education and the Far West Laboratory for Educational Research.

Noonan, M. J., & McCormick, L. (2006). *Young children with disabilities in natural environments*. Baltimore, MD: Brookes.

Odom, S. (Ed.). (2002). *Widening the circle: Including children with disabilities in preschool programs*. New York, NY: Teachers College Press.

Okagaki, L., & Diamond, K. E. (2000). Responding to cultural and linguistic differences in the beliefs and practices of families with young children. *Young Children, 55*(3), 74–78.

Olds, A. R. (1998). Places of beauty. In D. Bergen (Ed.), *Play as a medium for learning and development* (pp. 123–127). Olney, MD: Association for Childhood Education International.

Paley, V. G. (1986). *Bad guys don't have birthdays: Fantasy play at four*. Chicago, IL: University of Chicago Press.

Paley, V. G. (1992). *You can't say you can't play*. Cambridge, MA: Harvard University Press.

Paley, V. G. (1999). *The kindness of children*. Cambridge, MA: Harvard University Press.

Pellegrini, A. D., & Smith, P. K. (Eds.). (2005). *The nature of play*. New York, NY: Guilford.

Perry, J. (2001). *Outdoor play: Teaching strategies with young children*. New York, NY: Teachers College Press.

Rogoff, B. (2003). *The cultural nature of human development*. New York, NY: Oxford University Press.

Sandall, S. R. (2003, May). Play modifications for children with disabilities. *Young Children, 58*(3), 54–55.

Shonkoff, J. P., & Phillips, D. (2001, April–May). From neurons to neighborhoods: The science of early childhood development—An introduction. *Zero to Three, 21*(5), 4–7.

Shore, R. (1997). *Rethinking the brain: New insights in early development*. New York, NY: Families and Work Institute.

Siegel, D. J. (2011). *Mindsight: The new science of personal transformation*. New York, NY: Bantam.

Stinger, D. G., Golinkoff, R. M., & Hirsh-Pasek, K. (Eds.). (2006). *Play = Learning: How play motivates and enhances children's cognitive and social-emotional growth*. New York, NY: Oxford University Press.

Thornberg, R. (2006) February). The situated nature of preschool children's conflict strategies. *Educational Psychology, 26*1(1), 109–112.

Tough, P. (2012). How *children succeed: Grit, curiosity, and the hidden power of character*. Boston, MA: Houghton Mifflin Harcourt.

Van Hoorn, J., Nourot, P., Scales, B., & Alward, K. (2010). *Play at the center of the curriculum* (5th ed.). Upper Saddle River, NJ: Pearson.

Vygotsky, L. S. (1967). Play and its role in the mental development of the child. *Soviet Psychology, 12*, 62–76.

Wasserman, S. (2000). *Serious players in the primary classroom: Empowering children through active learningexperiences* (2nd ed.). New York, NY: Teachers College Press.

Wellhousen, K., & Kieff, J. (2001). *A constructivist approach to block play in early childhood*. Albany, NY: Delmar.

Wolfberg, P. J. (2009). *Play and imagination in children with autism* (2nd ed.) New York, NY: Teachers College Press.

CHAPTER 5

American Academy of Pediatrics: The Committee on Communications and Committee on Psychological Aspects of Child and Family Health. (2006, October 9). Clinical report: The importance of play in promoting healthy child development and maintaining strong parent-child bonds. Retrieved May 3, 2007, from http://www.aap.org/pressroom/playFINAL.pdf

Axtmann, A., & Dettwiler, A. (2005). *The visit: Observation, reflection, synthesis for training and relationship building*. Baltimore, MD: Brookes.

Bredekamp, S., & Copple, C. (Eds.). (1997). *Developmentally appropriate practice in early childhood programs serving children from birth through age 8*. Washington, DC: National Association for the Education of Young Children.

Briggs, D. C. (1975). *Your child's self-esteem*. New York, NY: Dolphin.

Bronson, M. (2000). Research in Review: Recognizing and supporting the development of self-regulation in young children. *Young Children*, 55(2), 32–27.

Butterfield, P. M., Martin, C. A., & Prairie, A. P. (2004). *Emotional connections: How relationships guide early learning.* Washington, DC: Zero to Three.

Card, N. A., & Hodges, E. V. (2008). Peer victimization among schoolchildren: Correlations, causes, consequences, and considerations in assessment. *School Psychology Review*, 23, 451–461.

Carlebach, D., & Tate. B. (2002). *Creating caring children: The first three years.* Miami, FL: Peace Education Foundation.

Chaille, C. (2008). *Constructivism across the curriculum in early childhood classrooms: Big ideas as inspiration.* Upper Saddle River, NJ: Pearson.

Chaker, A. M. (2006, October 10). Rethinking recess. *Wall Street Journal.*

Clarke, J. I. (1998). *Self-esteem: A family affair.* Minneapolis, MN: Winston.

Coopersmith, S. (1967). *The antecedents of self-esteem.* San Francisco, CA: Freeman.

Curry, N. E., & Johnson, C. N. (1990). *Beyond self-esteem: Developing a genuine sense of human value.* Washington, DC: National Association for the Education of Young Children.

David, M., & Appell, G. (2001 [1973, 1996]). *Loczy: An unusual approach to mothering.* (J. M. Clark & J. Falk, Trans.). Budapest, Hungary: Pikler-Loczy Tarsasag.

Delpit, L., & Dowdy, J. K. (2002). *The skin that we speak: Thoughts on language and culture in the classroom.* New York, NY: New Press.

Derman-Sparks, L., & the ABC Task Force. (1989). *Anti-bias curriculum: Tools for empowering young children.* Washington, DC: National Association for the Education of Young Children.

Derman-Sparks, L., & Ramsey, P. G. (2006). *What if all the kids are white? Engaging white children and their families in anti-bias/multicultural education.* New York, NY: Teachers College Press.

DeVries, R., & Sales, C. (2011). *Ramps and pathways: A constructivist approach to physics with young children.* Washington, DC: National Association for the Education of Young Children.

Diffily, D., & Sassman, C. (2006) *Positive teacher talk for better classroom management: Grades K–2.* New York, NY: Scholastic.

Dorris, M. (1978). Why I'm not thankful for Thanksgiving. *Interracial Books for Children Bulletin*, 9(7), 6–9.

Dweck, C. (2007). *Mindset: The new psychology of success.* New York, NY: Ballantine Books.

Erikson, E. (1963). *Childhood and society.* New York, NY: Norton.

Gartell, D. (2007 May). You worked really hard on your picture! Guiding with encouragement. *Young Children*, 62(3), 58–59.

Gerber, M., & Johnson, A. (1998). *Your self-confident baby.* New York, NY: Wiley.

Gilligan, C. (1983). *In a different voice.* Cambridge, MA: Harvard University Press.

Gonzalez-Mena, J. (2004 September). What can an orphanage teach us? Lessons from Budapest. *Young Children*, 59(5), 27–30.

Gonzalez-Mena, J. (2008). *Diversity in early care and education.* New York, NY: McGraw-Hill.

Greenfield, P. M., Quiroz, B., Rothstein-Fisch, C., & Trumbull, E. (2001). *Bridging cultures between home and school.* Mahwah, NJ: Erlbaum.

Grieshaber, S., & Cannella, G. S. (2001). *Embracing identities in early childhood education: Diversity and possibilities.* New York, NY: Teachers College Press.

Gross-Loh, C. (2007, March/April). Give me that old-time recess. *Mothering*, 54–63.

Harter, S. (1983). Developmental perspectives on the self-system. In E. M. Heatherton (Ed.) & P. H. Mussen (Series Ed.), *Handbook of child psychology: Vol. 4. Socialization, personality, and social development* (4th ed., pp. 275–386). New York, NY: Wiley.

Hitz, R., & Driscoll, A. (1988). Praise or encouragement? New insights into praise: Implications for early childhood teachers. *Young Children*, 43(5), 6–13.

hooks, b. (2003). *Rock my soul: Black people and self-esteem.* New York, NY: Atria.

Howard, G. (1999). *We can't teach what we don't know: White teachers, multiracial schools.* New York, NY: Teachers College Press.

Howes, C. (2010). *Culture and child development in early childhood programs: Practices for quality education and care.* New York, NY: Teachers College Press.

Kagan, J. (1984). *The nature of the child.* New York, NY: Basic Books.

Kern, P., & Wakeford, L. (2007, September). Supporting outdoor play for young children: The zone model of playground supervision. *Young Children*, 62(5), 20–25.

Kohlberg, L. (1976). Moral stages and moralization. The cognitive-development approach. In T. Lickona (Ed.), *Moral development and behavior.* New York, NY: Holt, Rinehart & Winston.

Kranowitz, C. S. (1998). *The out of sync child: Recognizing and coping with sensory integration dysfunction.* New York, NY: Paragee.

Lally, J. R. (1995, November). The impact of child care policies and practices on infant/toddler identity formation. *Young Children*, 51(1), 58–67.

Landy, S. (2002). *Pathways to competence: Encouraging healthy social and emotional development in young children.* Baltimore, MD: Brookes.

Markus, H. R., Mullally, P. R., & Kitayama, S. (1997). Selfways: Diversity in modes of cultural participation. In U. Neisser & D. Jopling (Eds.), *The conceptual self in context* (pp. 12–61). New York, NY: Cambridge University Press.

Marshall, H. H. (2000, November). Cultural influences on the development of self-concept. *Young Children*, 56(6), 19–22.

Martinez, F. (2005). Early care and education for Hispanic children. *Childhood Education*, 81(3), 174–176.

Maslow, A. (1954). *Motivation and personality.* New York, NY: Harper and Row.

Morrison, J. W. (2001, Spring). Supporting biracial children's identity development. *Childhood Education*, 77(3), 134–138.

Noddings, N. (2002). *Educating moral people: A caring alternative to character education.* New York, NY: Teachers College Press.

Noddings, N. (2005). *The challenge to care in schools.* New York, NY: Teachers College Press.

Noddings, N. (2013). *Caring: A feminine approach to ethics and moral education.* Berkeley, CA: University of California Press.

Noonan, M. J., & McCormick, L. (2006). *Young children with disabilities in natural environments.* Baltimore, MD: Brookes.

Paley, V. G. (1992). *You can't say you can't play*. Cambridge, MA: Harvard University Press.

Piaget, J. (1952). *The origins of intelligence in children*. New York, NY: International Universities Press.

Rhodes, M., Enz, B., & LaCount, M. (2006, January). Leaps and bounds: Preparing parents for kindergarten. *Young Children, 61*(1), 50–51.

Roberts, W. B., Jr. (2006). *Bullying from both sides: Strategic interventions for working with bullies and victims*. Thousand Oaks, CA: Corwin.

Rogoff, B. (2003). *The cultural nature of human development*. New York, NY: Oxford University Press.

Rothstein-Fisch, C., & Trumbull, E. (2008). *Managing diverse classrooms: How to build on students' cultural strengths*. Alexandria, VA: Association for Supervision and Curriculum Development.

Rothstein-Fisch, C., Trumbull, E., & Garcia, S. G. (2009). Making the implicit explicit: Supporting teachers to bridge cultures. *Early Childhood Research Quarterly, 24*, 474–486.

Seligman, M. E. P. (1975). *Helplessness: On depression, development and death*. San Francisco, CA: Freeman.

Stoltz, P. (2014). *Grit: The new science of what it takes to persevere, flourish, succeed*. Climb Strong Press.

Teaching Tolerance Project. (1997). *Starting small: Teaching tolerance in preschool and the early grades*. Montgomery, AL: Southern Poverty Law Center.

Tough, Paul. (2012). *How children succeed: Grit, curiosity, and the hidden power of character*. New York, NY: Houghton Mifflin Harcourt.

Vygotsky, L. S. (1978). *Mind and society: The development of higher psychological process*. Cambridge, MA: Harvard University Press.

Wardel, F. (1993, March). How young children build images of themselves. *Exchange*, 90.

Werner, E. E. (1984, November). Research in review: Resilient children. *Young Children, 40*(1), 68–72.

Werner, E. E. (1995, June). Resilience in development. *Current Directions in Psychological Science, 4*(3). 81–85.

Werner, E. E. (2000, February-March). The power of protective factors in the early years. *Zero to Three. 20*(4), 3–5.

Werner, E., & R. Smith (2001). *Journeys from childhood to midlife: Risk, resilience, and recovery*. Ithaca, NY: Cornell University Press

CHAPTER 6

American Academy of Pediatrics Council on Communications and Media Executive Committee. (2011, November). Media use by children younger than 2 years. *Pediatrics, 128*(5), 1040–1045.

Anderson, C. A., Berkowitz, L., Donnerstein, E., Huesmann, I., Rowell Johnson, F. D., & Linz, D. (2003). The influence of media violence on youth. *Psychological Science in the Public Interest, 4*, 81–110.

Annie E. Casey Foundation. (2011). Retrieved September 19, 2011, from http://www.aecf.org/KnowledgeCenter/SearchResults.aspx?source=topsearchKC

Baker, B. D., Sciarra, D., & Farrie, D. (2010). *Is school funding fair? A national report card*. Newark, NJ: Education Law Center

Bandura, A., & Walters, R. H. (1963). *Social learning and personality development*. New York, NY: Holt, Rinehart & Winston.

Biddle, B. J., & Berliner, D. C. (2002). *In pursuit of better schools: What research says*. Tempe, AZ: Education Policy Studies Laboratory, College of Education, Educational Leadership & Policy Studies, Arizona State University.

Bodrova, E., & Leong, D. J. (2007). *Tools of the mind* (2nd ed.). Upper Saddle River, NJ: Pearson.

Boyer, E. L. (1991). *Ready to learn: A mandate for the nation*. Princeton, NJ: Carnegie Foundation for the Advancement of Teaching.

Bronfenbrenner, U. (1979). *The ecology of human development*. Cambridge, MA: Harvard University Press.

Bronfenbrenner, U. (Ed.). (2005) *Making human beings human: Bioecological perspectives on human development*. Thousand Oaks, CA: Sage.

Bronson, P., & Merryman, A. (2009). *Nurture shock*. New York, NY: Twelve.

Bushman, B. J., & Anderson, C. A. (2001). Media violence and the American public: Scientific facts versus media misinformation. *American Psychologist, 56*, 466–489.

Bushman, D., & Huesmann, L. R. (2001). Effects of televised violence on aggression. In D. Singer & J. Singer (Eds.), *Handbook of children and the media*. Thousand Oaks, CA: Sage.

Byrnes, D. A., & Kiger, G. (Eds.). (2005). *Common bonds: Anti-bias teaching in a diverse society* (3rd ed.). Olney, MD: Association for Childhood Education International.

Canada, G. (1995). *Fist stick knife gun: A personal history of violence*. Boston, MA: Beacon Press.

Canada, G., & Nicholas, J. (2010). *Fist stick knife gun: a personal history of violence (A true story in black and white)*. Boston, MA: Beacon Press.

Carlsson-Paige, N., & Levin, D. E. (1990). *Who's calling the shots: How to respond effectively to children's fascination with war play and war toys*. Philadelphia, PA: New Society.

Christakis, D. A., & Zimmerman, F. J. (2006). *The elephant in the living room: Make television work for your kids*. New York, NY: Rodale.

Christakis, D., & Zimmerman, F. (2009). Young children and media. *American Behavioral Scientist, 52*(8), 1177–1185.

Clark, K. E., & Ladd, G. W. (2000). Connectedness and autonomy support in parent-child relationships: Links to children's socio-emotional orientation and peer relationships. *Developmental Psychology, 36*, 485–498.

Copple, C., Bredekamp, S., and Gonzalez-Mena, J. (2011). *Basics of Developmentally Appropriate Practice: An Introduction for Teachers of Infants and Toddlers*. Washington, DC: National Association for the Education of Young Children.

Curtis, D., Brown, K. L, Baird, L., & Coughlin, A. M. (2013). Planning environments and materials that respond to young children's lively minds. *Young Children, 68*(4), 26–31.

Day, C. B. (2013). Understanding the social context of infant/toddler care. In E. Virmani & P. Mangione (Eds.), *A guide to culturally sensitive care* (2nd ed., pp. 1–10). Sacramento, CA: California Department of Education.

Derman-Sparks, L., & Edwards, J. O. (2010). *Anti-bias education for young children and ourselves*. Washington, DC: National Association for the Education of Young Children.

Derman-Sparks, L., & the ABC Task Force. (1989). *Anti-bias curriculum: Tools for empowering young children*. Washington, DC: National Association for the Education of Young Children.

Derman-Sparks, L., & Ramsey, P. G. (2006). *What if all the kids are white? Anti-bias/multicultural education with young children and families*. New York, NY: Teachers College Press.

Eisenberg, N., Fabes, R. A., and Spinrad, T. L. (2006). Prosocial development. In N. Eisenberg (Vol. Ed.), W. Damon & R. M. Lerner (Series Eds.), *Handbook of child psychology: Social, emotional, and personality development*, Vol. 3 (pp. 646–718). New York, NY: Wiley.

Elkind, D. (2007). *The power of play*. Cambridge, MA: Da Capo Press

Elliot, E, & Gonzalez-Mena, J. (2011, January/February). Self-regulation: Taking a broader perspective. *Young Children* 16–24.

Ferber, R. (2006). *Solve your child's sleep problems*. New York, NY: Fireside.

Galinsky, E. (2010). *Mind in the Making: The Seven Essential Life Skills Every Child Needs*. Special National Association for the Education of Young Children Edition. New York, NY: Harper Collins.

Gerbner, G., Gross, L., & Signorielli, N. (1986). Living with television: The dynamics of the cultivation process. In J. Bryant & D. Zillman (Eds.), *Perspectives on media effects*. Hillsdale, NJ: Erlbaum.

Gonzalez-Mena, J. (2009). Family-centered early care and education. In S. Feeney, A. Galper, & C. Seefeldt (Eds.), *Continuing issues in early childhood education* (pp. 369–387). Upper Saddle River: NJ: Pearson.

Gonzalez-Mena, J. (2012) Culture and communication in the child care setting. In P. Mangione & D. Greenwald (Eds.), *A guide to language development and communication* (2nd ed., pp. 51–60). Sausalito, CA: WestEd and Sacramento, CA: California Department of Education.

Gonzalez-Mena, J. (2013). Cultural sensitivity in caregiving routines: The essential activities of daily living. In E. Virmani & P. Mangione (Eds.), *A guide to culturally sensitive care* (2nd ed., pp. 56–65). Sacramento, CA: California Department of Education.

Gonzalez-Mena, J. (2013). What works? Assessing infant and toddler play environments. *Young Children*, 68(4), 22–24

Gonzalez-Mena, J., & L. Briley (2011). Improving infant mental health in orphanages. *The Signal: Newsletter of the World Association for Infant Mental Health*, 19(4), 14–17.

Gonzalez, N., Greenberg, J., & Velez, C. (n.d.). *Funds of knowledge: A look at Luis Moll's research into hidden family resources*. Retrieved June 6, 2011, from http://www.usc.edu/dept/education/CMMR/FullText/Luis_Moll_Hidden_Family_Resources.pdf

Gopnik, A. (2012, July-August). Let the children play. It's good for them! *Smithsonian Magazine*.

Gorski, P. C. (2007, Spring). The question of class. *Teaching Tolerance*, 31, 26–29.

Greenwald, D., & Weaver, J. (2013). *The RIE manual for parents and professionals*. Los Angeles, CA: Resources for Infant Educarers.

Gross-Loh, C. (2013.) *Parenting without Borders*. New York, NY: Penguin Group.

Guerra, A. W., & Garriety, S. (2013). A cultural communities and cultural practices approach to understanding infant and toddler care. In E. Virmani & P. Mangione (Eds.), *A guide to culturally sensitive care* (2nd ed., pp. 41–53). Sacramento, CA: California Department of Education.

Hammond, R. A. (2013). Educaring, interpersonal neuroscience, and selective intervention. In D. Greenwald and J. Weaver (Eds.), *The RIE manual for parents and professionals* (2nd ed., pp. 148–160). Los Angeles, CA: Resources for Infant Educarers.

Healy, J. M. (2011, March/April). Impacting readiness: Nature and nurture. *Exchange*, 33(2), 18–21.

Hirsch, K. W. (1997). Media violence and audience behavior. In A. Wells & E. Hakanen (Eds.), *Mass media and society* (5th ed., pp. 479–505). Greenwich, CT: Ablex.

Huesmann, L. R., & Miller, L. S. (1994). Long-term effects of repeated exposure to media violence in childhood. In L. R. Huesmann (Ed.), *Aggressive behavior: Current perspectives* (pp. 153–186). New York, NY: Plenum.

Howe, D. (2011). *Attachment across the life course*. New York, NY: Palgrave.

Kaiser, B., & Rasminsky, J. (2012). *Challenging behavior in young children: Understanding, preventing, and responding effectively* (3rd ed.). Upper Saddle River, NJ: Pearson.

Kersey, K., & Masterson, M. (2013). *101 Principles for positive guidance with young children: Creating responsive teachers*. Saddle River, NJ: Pearson.

Kozol, J. (1991). *Savage inequalities: Children in America's schools*. New York, NY: Crown.

Kusserow, A. (2005, Fall). The workings of class. *Stanford Social Innovation Review*, 38–47.

Lally, J. R. (1998, May). Brain research, infant learning, and child care curriculum. *Child Care Information Exchange*, 121, 46–48.

Lally, J. R. (2013). *For our babies: Ending the invisible neglect of America's infants*. San Francisco, CA: WestEd and New York, NY: Teachers College Press.

Lavin, D. (2013). *Beyond remote-controlled childhood*. Washington, DC: National Association for the Education of Young Children

Leman, P. J., & Lam, V. L. (2008, September/October). The influence of race and gender on children's conversations and playmate choices. *Child Development*, 79(5), 1329–1343.

Maccoby, E. E. (1998). *The two sexes*. Cambridge, MA: Harvard University Press.

Marshall, E., & Sensoy, O. (2011). *Rethinking popular culture and media*. Milwaukee, WI: Rethinking Schools.

Maslow, A. (1954). *Motivation and personality*. New York, NY: Harper and Row.

McKenna, T., & Ortiz, F. I. (Eds.). (1988). *The broken web: The educational experience of Hispanic American women*. Encino, CA: Floricanto.

McWhirter, E. H., Torres, D. M., Salgado, S., & Valdez, M. (2007). Perceived barriers and postsecondary plans in Mexican American and European American adolesencts. *Journal of Career Assessment*, 15, 119–138.

National Research Council and Institute of Medicine. (2000). *From neurons to neighborhoods: The science of early childhood development*. Washington, DC: Board on Children, Youth, and Families, Commission on Behavioral and Social Sciences and Education. National Academy Press.

Parke, R. D., & O'Neil, R. (2000). The influence of significant others on learning about relationships: From family to friends. In R. S. L. Mills & S. Duck (Eds.), *The developmental psychology of personal relationships* (pp. 15–47). New York, NY: Wiley.

Rideout, V., & Hamel, E. (2006). The media family: Electronic media in the lives of infants, toddlers, preschoolers and their parents. Retrieved June 6, 2011, from http://www.kff.org/entmedia/upload/7500.pdf

Rogoff, B. (2011). *Developing destinies: A Mayan midwife and town.* New York, NY: Oxford University.

Schneider, B. H., Atkinson, L., & Tardif, C. (2001). Child-parent attachment and children's peer relations: A quantitative review. *Developmental Psychology, 37,* 86–100.

Sears, W., Sears, M., Sears, R., & Sears, J. (2013) *The Baby Book Revised – ebook.* New York, NY: Little Brown and Company.

Shonkoff, J. P., & Phillips, D. (2001, April/May). From neurons to neighborhoods: The science of early childhood development—An introduction. *Zero to Three, 21*(5), 4–7.

Shore, R. (1997). *Rethinking the brain: New insights in early development.* New York, NY: Families and Work Institute.

Signorielli, N., & Morgan, M. (2001). Television and the family: The cultivation perspective. In J. Bryant & J. A. Bryant (Eds.), *Television and the American family* (2nd ed., pp. 333–351). Mahwah, NJ: Erlbaum.

Singer, D. G., & Singer, J. L. (2005). *Imagination and play in the electronic age.* Cambridge, MA: Harvard University Press.

Szalavitz, M., & Perry, B. (2010). *Born for love: Why empathy is essential and endangered.* New York, NY: Harper.

Tinsley, B. R. (2002). *How children learn to be healthy.* New York, NY: Cambridge University Press.

Tough, P. (2012). *How children succeed: Grit, curiosity, and the hidden power of character.* Boston, MA: Houghton Mifflin Harcourt, 2012

Virmani, E., & Mangione, P. (Eds.). (2013). *A guide to culturally sensitive care* (2nd ed.). Sacramento, CA: California Department of Education.

Wachs, T. (2004, March). Temperament and development: The role of context in a biologically based system. *Zero to Three,* 12–21.

Wang, L., Beckett, G., & Brown, L. (2006). Controversies of standardized assessment in school accountability reform: A critical synthesis of multidisciplinary research evidence. *Applied Measurement in Education, 19*(4), 305–328.

Wise, T. (2009). *Between Barack and a hard place: Racism and white denial in the age of Obama.* San Francisco, CA: City Lights.

Wise, T. (2010). *Colorblind: The rise of post-racial politics and retreat from racial equity.* San Francisco, CA: City Lights

Wise, T. (2011). *White like me: Reflections on race from a privileged son.* Brooklyn, NY: Soft Skull Press.

Wright, J. C., Huston, A. C., Murphy, K. C., St. Peters, M., Pinon, M., Scantlin, R., & Kotler, J. (2001). The relations of early television viewing to school readiness and vocabulary of children from low-income families: The early window project. *Child Development, 72,* 1347–1366.

Zehr, M. A. (2011). Expert's call for early focus on black boy's nonacademic skills. Retrieved June 17, 2011, from http://www.edweek.org/ew/articles/2011/06/15/36ets.h30.html?tkn=UNQFX36g%2FWXRcQX4pRuYiefFUdobegYv10Kp&cmp=ENL-EU-NEWS1

Zigler, E. F., Finn-Stevenson, M., & Hall, N. W. (2003). *The first three years and beyond: Brain development and social policy.* New Haven, CT: Yale University Press.

Zimmerman, F. J., & Christakis, D. A. (2009). Television viewing in child care settings. *Pediatrics, 124*:(6), 1627–1632.

CHAPTER 7

Ballenger, C. (1999). *Teaching other people's children.* New York, NY: Teachers College Press.

Bandtec Network for Diversity Training. (2003). *Reaching for answers: A workbook on diversity in early childhood education.* Oakland, CA: Bandtec Network for Diversity Training.

Barrera, I., Kramer, L., Macpherson, T. D. (2012) *Skilled dialogue.* Baltimore, MD: Brookes.

Bredekamp, S., & Copple, C. (Eds.). (1997). *Developmentally appropriate practice in early childhood programs serving children from birth through age eight.* Washington, DC: National Association for the Education of Young Children.

Brody, H. (2001). *The other side of Eden: Hunters, farmers, and the shaping of the world.* New York, NY: North Point Press.

Bronfenbrenner, U. (1979). *The ecology of human development.* Cambridge, MA: Harvard University Press.

Bronfenbrenner, U. (Ed.). (2005). *Making human beings human: Bioecological perspectives on human development.* Thousand Oaks, CA: Sage.

Bruno, H. E. (2003, September–October). Hearing parents in every language: An invitation to ECE professionals. *Child Care Information Exchange, 153,* 58–60.

Butterfield, P. M., Martin, C. A., & Prairie, A. P. (2004). *Emotional connections: How relationships guide early learning.* Washington, DC: Zero to Three.

Carlebach, D., & Tate, B. (2002). *Creating caring children: The first three years.* Miami, FL: Peace Education Foundation.

Charney, R. S. (2002). *Teaching children to care: Classroom management for ethical and academic growth.* Greenfield, MA: Northeast Foundation for Children.

Copple, C. (Ed.). (2003). *A world of difference: Readings on teaching young children in a diverse society.* Washington, DC: National Association for the Education of Young Children.

Cummins, J (2000). *Language, power, and pedagogy: Bilingual children in the cross fire.* Tonawanda, NY: Multilingual Matters.

David, M., & Appell, G. (2001 [1973, 1996]). *Loczy: An unusual approach to mothering.* (J. M. Clark & J. Falk, Trans.). Budapest, Hungary: Pikler-Loczy Tarsasag.

Delpit, L., & Dowdy, J. K. (2008). *The skin that we speak: Thoughts on language and culture in the classroom.* New York, NY: New Press.

Derman-Sparks, L. (1989). *Anti-bias curriculum.* Washington, DC: National Association for the Education of Young Children.

Derman-Sparks, L., & Edwards, J. O. (2010). *Anti-bias education for young children and ourselves.* Washington, DC: National Association for the Education of Young Children.

Eggers-Pierola, C. (2002). *Connections and commitments: A Latino-based framework for early childhood educators.* Newton, MA: Educational Development Center.

Epstein, J. L. (2006, January). Families, schools, and community partnerships. *Young Children, 61*(1), 40.

Erikson, E. (1963). *Childhood and society.* New York, NY: Norton.

Espinosa, L. (2010). *Getting it right for young children from diverse backgrounds: Applying research to improve practice.* Upper Saddle River, NJ: Pearson.

Friend, M., & Cook, L. (2003). *Interactions: Collaboration skills for school professionals* (4th ed.). Boston, MA: Allyn & Bacon.

Gandini, L., & Edwards, C. P. (Eds.). (2000). *Bambini: The Italian approach to infant-toddler care.* New York, NY: Teachers College Press.

Garcia, E. E., & Frede, E. C. (2010). *Young English language learners: Current research and emerging directions for practice and policy.* New York, NY: Teachers College Press

Gerber, M. (1998). *Dear parent: Caring for infants with respect.* Los Angeles, CA: Resources for Infant Educarers.

Gillanders, C., & Castro, D. C. (2012). Storybook reading for young dual-language learners. *Young children, 66* (1) pp. 91–94.

Gilligan, C. (1982). *In a different voice.* Cambridge, MA: Harvard University Press.

Goldenberg, C., Gallimore, R., & Reese, L. (2003). Cause or effect? A longitudinal study of immigrant Latino parents' aspirations and expectations, and their children's school performance. *American Educational Research Journal, 38,* 547–582.

Goldstein, L. (2002). *Reclaiming caring in teaching and teacher education.* New York, NY: Lang.

Gonzalez-Mena, J. (2002, September). Working with cultural differences: Individualism and collectivism. *The First Years: Nga Tautuatahi, 4*(2), 13–15.

Gonzalez-Mena, J. (2007). *50 early strategies for working and communicating with diverse families.* Upper Saddle River, NJ: Pearson.

Gonzalez-Mena, J. (2008) *Diversity in early care and education.* New York, NY: McGraw-Hill.

Gonzalez-Mena, J. (2010). *50 Strategies for working and communicating with diverse families.* Upper Saddle River, NJ: Pearson

Gonzalez-Mena, J., & Peshotan Bhavangri, N. (2001, March). Cultural differences in sleeping practices. *Exchange, 138,* 91–93.

Goodman, J. F., & Lesnick, H. (2001). *The moral stake in education.* New York, NY: Longman.

Greenfield, P. M. (1994). Independence and interdependence as developmental scripts: Implications for theory, research, and practice. In P. M. Greenfield & R. R. Cocking (Eds.), *Cross-cultural roots of minority child development* (pp. 1–37). Mahwah, NJ: Erlbaum.

Greenfield, P. M., Quiroz, B., & Raeff, C. (2000). Cross-cultural conflict and harmony in the social construction of the child. *New Directions for Child and Adolescent Development, 87,* 93–108.

Greenfield, P. M., Quiroz, B., Rothstein-Fisch, C., & Trumbull, E. (2001). *Bridging cultures between home and school.* Mahwah, NJ: Erlbaum.

Grosjean, F. (2008). *Studying bilinguals.* Oxford: Oxford University Press.

Guerra, P., & Garcia, S. (2000). *Understanding the cultural contexts of teaching and learning.* Austin, TX: Southwest Educational Development Laboratory.

Harwood, R. L., Miller, J. G., & Irizarry, N. L. (1995). *Culture and attachment: Perceptions of the child in context.* New York, NY: Guilford.

Hoffman, M. L. (2000). *Empathy and moral development.* Cambridge, MA: Cambridge University Press.

Hofstede, G. (2001). *Culture's consequences: Comparing values, behaviors, institutions, and organizations across nations* (2nd ed.). Thousand Oaks, CA: Sage.

Howes, C., Downer, J.T., Pianta, R. C. (2012). *Dual-language learners in the early childhood* classroom. Baltimore, MD: Brookes.

Kaiser, B., & Rasminsky, J. S. (2003, July). Opening the cultural door. *Young Children, 58*(4), 53–56.

Kohlberg, L. (1976). Moral stages and moralization: The cognitive-developmental approach. In T. Lickona (Ed.), *Moral development and behavior* (pp. 31–53). New York, NY: Holt, Rinehart & Winston.

Lee, L. (2002). *Serving families: A handbook on the principles and strategies of the parent services project approach.* San Rafael, CA: Parent Services Project.

Levin, D. E. (2002). *Teaching young children in violent times: Building a peaceable classroom* (2nd ed.). Cambridge, MA: Educators for Social Responsibility and Washington, DC: National Association for the Education of Young Children.

Lustig, M. W., & Koester, J. (2003). *Interpersonal competence: Interpersonal communication across cultures* (4th ed.). New York, NY: Addison Wesley Longman.

Mann, T. (2010). Culturally responsive perspective. In V. Washington & J. D. Andrews (Eds.), *Children of 2020: Creating a better tomorrow* (pp. 61–66). Washington, DC: Council for Professional Recognition and National Association for the Education of Young Children.

Martini, M. (2002, February–March). How mothers in four American cultural groups shape infant learning during mealtimes. *Zero to Three, 22*(4), 14–20.

Maslow, A. (1954). *Motivation and personality.* New York, NY: Harper and Row.

Nemeth, K. N. (2009). *Many languages, one classroom: Teaching dual and English language learners.* Beltsville, MD: Gryphon House, Inc.

Nemeth, K. N. (2012). *Basics of supporting dual-language learners.* Washington, DC: NAEYC.

Nemeth, K. N. (2014) *Young dual-language learners: A guide for prek-3 leaders.* Philadelphia, PA: Caslon.

Nguyen, A.-M., & Benet-Martinez, V. (2007). Biculturalism unpacked: Components, measurement, individual differences, and outcomes. *Social and Personality Psychology Compass, 1,* 101–114.

Noddings, N. (2002a). *Educating moral people: A caring alternative to character education.* New York, NY: Teachers College Press.

Noddings, N. (2002b). *Starting at home: Care and social policy.* Berkeley, CA: University of California Press.

Noddings, N. (2005). *The challenge to care in schools.* New York, NY: Teachers College Press.

Paradis, J., Genesee, F., and Crago, M. B. (2010). *Dual-language development and disorders: A handbook on bilingualism and second language learning* (2nd ed.). Baltimore, MD: Brookes Publishing.

Patterson, K., Grenny, J., McMillan, R., Switzer, A., & Covey, S. R. (2002). *Crucial conversations: Tools for talking when the stakes are high.* New York, NY: McGraw-Hill.

Poussaint, A. F. (2006, January). Understanding and involving African American parents. *Young Children, 61*(1), 48.

Powers, J. (2006, January). Six fundamentals for creating relationships with families. *Young Children, 61*(1), 28.

Quintero, E. P. (2004, May). Will I lose a tooth? Will I learn to read? Problem posing with multicultural children's literature. *Young Children, 59*(3), 56–62.

Raeff, C., Greenfield, P. M., & Quiroz, B. (2000, Spring). Conceptualizing interpersonal relationships in the cultural contexts of individualism and collectivism. *New Directions for Child and Adolescent Development, 87,* 59–74.

Reese, L. (2002). Parental strategies in contrasting cultural settings: Families in Mexico and El Norte. *Anthropology & Education Quarterly, 33,* 30–59.

Rogoff, B. (2003). *The cultural nature of human development.* New York, NY: Oxford University Press.

Rogoff, B. (2011). *Developing destinies: A Mayan midwife and town.* New York, NY: Oxford University Press.

Rothstein-Fisch, C. (2003). *Readings for bridging cultures: Teacher education module.* Mahwah, NJ: Erlbaum.

Rothstein-Fisch, C., & Trumbull, E. (2008). *Managing diverse classrooms: How to build on students' cultural strengths.* Alexandria, VA: Association for Supervision and Curriculum Development.

Rothstein-Fisch, C., Trumbull, E., & Garcia, S. G. (2009). Making the implicit explicit: Supporting teachers to bridge cultures. *Early Childhood Research Quarterly, 24,* 474–486.

Shweder, R. A., Goodnow, J., Hatano, G., LeVine, R. A., Markus, H., & Miller, P. (1998). The cultural psychology of development: One mind, many mentalities. In W. Damon & R. M. Lerner (Eds.), *Handbook of Child Psychology: Vol. 1. Theoretical models of human development* (5th ed., pp. 865–937). New York, NY: Wiley.

Siraj-Blatchford, I., & Clarke, P. (2000). *Supporting identity, diversity and language in the early years.* Philadelphia, PA: Open University Press.

Some, S. (2000). *The spirit of intimacy: Ancient African teachings in the ways of relationships.* New York, NY: HarperCollins/Quill.

Stechuk, R. A., & Burns, M. S. (2005) *Making a difference: A framework for supporting first and second language development in preschool children of migrant farm workers.* Washington, DC: Academy for Educational Development.

Sue, S., & Moore, T. (Eds.). (1984). *The pluralistic society.* New York, NY: Human Sciences Press.

Trumbull, E., Greenfield, P. M., Rothstein-Fisch, C., & Quiroz, B. (2001). *Bridging cultures between home and school: A guide for teachers.* Mahwah, NJ: Erlbaum.

Trumbull, E., Rothstein-Fisch, C., & Greenfield, P. M. (2000). *Bridging cultures in our schools: New approaches that work.* San Francisco, CA: WestEd.

Trumbull, E., Rothstein-Fisch, C., & Hernandez, E. (2003). Parent involvement—according to whose values? *School Community Journal, 13*(2), 45–72.

U.S. Department of Health and Human Services, Administration on Children, Youth and Families. (2000). *Celebrating cultural and linguistic diversity in Head Start.* Washington, DC: Department of Health and Human Services.

Werker, J. (2012). Perceptual Foundations of Bilingual Acquisition in Infancy. *Annals of the New York Academy of Sciences: The Year in Cognitive Neuroscience, 1251,* 50–61.

Wong Fillmore, L. (1991). When learning a second language means losing the first. *EarlyChildhood Research Quarterly, 6,* 323–346.

Wong Fillmore, L. (2000). Loss of family languages: Should educators be concerned? *Theory Into Practice, 39*(4), 203–210.

Zepeda, M., Gonzalez-Mena, J., Rothstein-Fisch, C., & Trumbull, E. (2006). *Bridging cultures in early care and education.* Mahwah, NJ: Erlbaum.

CHAPTER 8

Adkison-Bradley, C. Terpstra, J., & Dormitorio, B. (2014). Child discipline in African American families: A study of patterns and context. *Family Journal, 22,* 198–205.

Adkison-Bradley, C. (2011). Seeing African Americans as competent parents: Implications for family counselors. *The Family Journal, 19,* 307–313.

Ball, J., & Pence, A. R. (1999). Beyond developmentally appropriate practice: Developing community and culturally appropriate practices. *Young Children, 54*(2), 46–50.

Ballenger, C. (1992, Summer). Because you like us: The language of control. *Harvard Educational Review, 62*(2), 199–208.

Ballenger, C. (1999). *Teaching other people's children.* New York, NY: Teachers College Press.

Berk, L. E., & Winsler, A. (1995). *Scaffolding children's learning: Vygotsky and early childhood education.* Washington, DC: National Association for the Education of Young Children.

Blair, C., & A. Diamond. (2008). Biological processes in prevention and intervention: The promotion of self-regulation as a means of preventing school failure. *Development and Psychopathology, 20,* 899–911.

Bodrova, E., & D.L. Leong. (2007). *Tools of the mind: The Vygotskian approach to early childhood education.* Upper Saddle River, NJ: Pearson

Bradley, C. (2000). The disciplinary practices of African American fathers: A closer look. *Journal of African American Men, 5,* 43–61.

Bradley, C. (1998). Child rearing in African American Families: A study of disciplinary methods used by African American parents. *Journal of Multicultural Counseling and Development, 26,* 273–281.

Brault, L., & Brault, T. (2005). *Children with challenging behavior: Strategies for reflective thinking.* Phoenix, AZ: CPG Publishing.

Brehm, S. S. (1981). Oppositional behavior in children: A reactancy theory approach. In S. S. Brehm, S. M. Kassin, & F. X. Gibbons (Eds.), *Developmental social psychology theory* (pp. 96–121). New York, NY: Oxford University Press.

Bronfenbrenner, U. (1979). *The ecology of human development.* Cambridge, MA: Harvard University Press.

Bronfenbrenner, U. (Ed.). (2005). *Making human beings human: Bioecological perspectives on human development.* Thousand Oaks, CA: Sage.

Bronson, M. (2000). Research in review: Recognizing and supporting the development of self-regulation in young children. *Young Children, 55*(2), 32–36.

Bronson, M. (2000). *Self-regulation in early childhood: Nature and nurture.* New York, NY: Guilford.

Campbell, S. B., Pierce, E. W., March, C. L., Ewing, L. J., & Szumowski, E. K. (1994). Hard to manage preschool boys: Symptomatic behavior across contexts and time. *Child Development, 65,* 836–851.

Dahlberg, G., Moss, P., & Pence, A. (1999). *Beyond quality in early childhood education and care: Postmodern perspectives.* London, England: Falmer.

Diaz, R. M., Neal, C. J., & Amaya-Williams, M. (1996). *The social origins of self-regulation: Vygotsky and Education.* New York, NY: Cambridge University Press.

Dreikurs, R., & Loren, G. (1990). *Logical consequences: A new approach to discipline.* New York, NY: Dutton.

Dreikurs, R., & Soltz, V. (1964). *Children: The challenge.* New York, NY: Duell, Sloan, & Pearce.

Drifte, C. (2004). *Encouraging positive behavior in the early years: A practical guide.* London, England: Paul Chapman Publishing.

Eggers-Pierola, C. (2005). *Connections and commitments: Reflecting Latino values in early childhood programs.* Portsmouth, NH: Heinemann.

Erikson, E. (1963). *Childhood and society.* New York, NY: Norton.

Flore, I. R. (2011). Developing young children's self-regulation through everyday experiences. *Young Children, 66* (4), 46–51.

Galinsky, E. (2010). *Mind in the making: Seven essential skills every child needs.* New York, NY: HarperCollins.

Gerber, M., & Johnson, A. (1998). *Your self-confident baby.* New York, NY: Wiley.

Gil, D. G. (1970). *Violence against children: Physical child abuse in the United States.* Cambridge, MA: Harvard University Press.

Gillespie, L. G., & Seibel, N. (2006). Self-regulation: A cornerstone of early childhood development. *Young Children, 61*(4) 34–39.

Gonzalez-Mena, J. (2008). *Diversity in early care and education: Honoring differences* (5th ed.). New York, NY: McGraw-Hill.

Gonzalez-Mena, J., & Shareef, I. (2005, November). Discussing diverse perspectives on guidance. *Young Children, 60*(6), 34–38.

Goodman, J. F., & Balamore, U. (2003). *Teaching goodness: Engaging the moral and academic promise of young children.* Boston, MA: Allyn & Bacon.

Gordon, T. (2000). *PET: Parent effectiveness training.* New York, NY: Wyden.

Hale, J. E. (1986). *Black children: Their roots, culture, and learning styles.* Baltimore, MD: Johns Hopkins University Press.

Hammond. R. A. (2009). *Respecting babies: A new look at Magda Gerber's RIE approach.* Washington, DC: Zero to Three.

Howes, C., & Ritchie, S. (2002). *A matter of trust.* New York, NY: Teachers College Press.

Hyson, M. (2004). *The emotional development of young children* (2nd ed.). New York, NY: Teachers College Press.

Jones, E., & Cooper, R. (2005). *Playing to get smart.* New York, NY: Teachers College Press.

Kagan, J. (1984). *The nature of the child.* New York, NY: Basic Books.

Kaiser, B., & Rasminsky, J. (2012). *Challenging behavior in young children: Understanding, preventing and responding effectively* (3rd ed.). Upper Saddle River, NJ: Pearson.

Kohn, A. (1999). *Punished by rewards: The trouble with gold stars, incentive plans, A's, praise, and other bribes.* Boston, MA: Houghton Mifflin.

Kohn, A. (2004). *Unconditional parenting: Moving from rewards and punishment to love and reasoning.* New York, NY: Atria.

Kohn, A. (2006). *Beyond discipline: From compliance to community.* Alexandria, VA: Association for Supervision and Curriculum Development.

Kohn, A. (2014). *The myth of the spoiled child.* Boston, MA: Da Capo.

Kranowitz, C. S. (1998). *The out of sync child: Recognizing and coping with sensory integration dysfunction.* New York, NY: Paragee.

Lee, L. (Ed.). (2006). *Stronger together: Family support and early childhood education.* San Rafael, CA: Parent Services Project.

Marion, M. (2015). *Guidance of young children* (9th ed.). Upper Saddle River, NJ: Pearson.

Maslow, A. H. (1954). *Motivation and personality.* New York, NY: Harper & Row.

Maslow, A. H. (1968). *Toward a psychology of being.* New York, NY: Van Nostrand.

Maslow, A. H. (1970). *Motivation and personality.* New York, NY: Harper & Row.

McLoyd, V. C., Hill, N. E., & Dodge, K. A. (Eds.). (2005). *African American family life.* New York, NY: Guilford.

Nelsen, J. (Ed.). (2001). *Positive discipline: A teacher's A–Z guide* (2nd ed.). Rocklin, CA: Prima.

Nelsen, J., & Glenn, H. S. (1996). *Positive discipline.* New York, NY: Ballantine.

Noddings, N. (2002). *Educating moral people: A caring alternative to character education.* New York, NY: Teachers College Press.

Noddings, N. (2003). *Caring.* Berkeley, CA: University of California Press.

Noddings, N. (2005). *The challenge to care in schools.* New York, NY: Teachers College Press

Ostrosky, M., & Sandall, S. (2001). *Teaching strategies: What to do to support young children's development.* Denver, CO: Division for Early Childhood of the Council for Exceptional Children.

Pence, A. (2004). Finding a niche in building ECE capacity. *Interaction, 18*(1), 31–33.

Phillips, C. B. (1995). Culture: A process that empowers. In J. Cortez & C. L. Young-Holt (Eds.), *Infant/toddler caregiving: A guide to culturally sensitive care* (pp. 2–9). Sacramento, CA: California Department of Education.

Rand, M. K. (2000). *Giving it some thought: Cases for early childhood practice.* Washington, DC: National Association for the Education of Young Children.

Reynolds, E. (2001). *Guiding young children: A problem-solving approach.* New York, NY: McGraw-Hill.

Sandall, S., McLean, M. E., & Smith, B. (2000). *DEC recommended practices in early intervention/early childhood special education.* Longmonth, CO: Sopris West.

Sandall, S., & Ostrosky, M. (1999). *Young exceptional children: Practical ideas for addressing challenging behaviors.* Denver, CO: Division for Early Childhood of the Council for Exceptional Children.

Sandoval, M., & De La Roza, M. (1986). A cultural perspective for serving the Hispanic client. In H. Lefley & P. Pedersen (Eds.), *Cross-cultural training for mental health professionals.* Springfield, IL: Thomas.

Segal, M., Masi, W., & Leiderman, R. (2001). *In time and with love: Caring for infants and toddlers with special needs.* New York, NY: New Market Press.

Shapiro, S., & White, C. (2014). *Mindful parenting book.* Oakland, CA: New Harbinger Publications.

Siccone, F., & Lopez, L. (2000). *Educating the heart: Lessons to build respect and responsibility.* Boston, MA: Allyn & Bacon.

Snowden, L. R. (1984). Toward evaluation of black psycho-social competence. In S. Sue & T. Moore (Eds.), *The pluralistic society.* New York, NY: Human Sciences Press.

Tardos, A. (Ed.). (2007). *Bringing up and providing care for infants and toddlers in an institution* (pp. 135–150). Budapest, Hungary: Pikler-Loczy Tarsasag.

Thompson, R. A. (2009, November). Doing what doesn't come naturally: The development of self-regulation. *Zero to Three, 30*(2), 33–37.

Tobin, J., Hsueh, Y., & Karasawa, M. (2009). *Preschool in three cultures revisited.* Chicago, IL: University of Chicago Press.

Trickett, P. K., & Kuczynski, L. (1986). Children's misbehavior and parental discipline strategies in abusive and nonabusive families. *Developmental Psychology*, 8, 240–260.

CHAPTER 9

Ballenger, C. (1992, Summer). Because you like us: The language of control. *Harvard Educational Review*, 62(2), 199–208.

Ballenger, C. (1999). *Teaching other people's children.* New York, NY: Teachers College Press.

Baumrind, D. (1971). Current patterns of parental authority. *Developmental Psychology Monographs*, 4, 99–103.

Baumrind, D. (1986). Socialization and instrumental competence in young children. In W. W. Hartup (Ed.), *The young child: Reviews of research*, Vol. 2 (pp. 202–224). Washington, DC: National Association for the Education of Young Children.

Baumrind D, Larzelere R., & Cowan P. (2002, July). Ordinary physical punishment: Is it harmful? Comment on Gershoff (2002). *Psychological Bulletin*, 128(4), 580–589

Beoglovsky, M., & L. Daly (2015). *Early learning theories made visible.* St. Paul, MN: Redleaf.

Bilmes, J. (2012). *Beyond behavior management: The six life skills children need.* St. Paul, MN: Redleaf Press.

Bronfenbrenner, U. (1979). *The ecology of human development.* Cambridge, MA: Harvard University Press.

Bronfenbrenner, U. (Ed.). (2005). *Making human beings human: Bioecological perspectives on human development.* Thousand Oaks, CA: Sage.

Bruno, H. E. (2007, September). Gossip-free zones: Problem solving to prevent power struggles. *Young Children*, 62(5), 26–32.

Butterfield, P. M., Martin, C. A., & Prairie, A. P. (2004). *Emotional connections: How relationships guide early learning.* Washington, DC: Zero to Three.

Chao, R. K. (1994). Beyond parental control and authoritarian parenting style: Understanding Chinese parenting through the cultural notion of training. *Child Development*, 65, 1111–1119.

Chao, R. (2000). The parenting of immigrant Chinese and European-American mothers: Relationship between parenting styles socialization goals and parental practices. *Journal of Applied Developmental Psychology*, 21(2), 233–248.

David, M., & Appell, G. (2001 [1973, 1996]). *Loczy: An unusual approach to mothering* (J. M. Clark & J. Falk, Trans.). Budapest, Hungary: Pikler-Loczy Tarsasag.

Day, C. B. (2013) Culture and identity development: Getting infants and toddlers off to a great start. In E. Virmani & P. Mangione (Eds.), A *guide to culturally sensitive care* (2nd ed., pp. 2–12). Sacramento, CA: California Department of Education.

Dowrick, P. W. (1986). *Social survival for children: A trainer's resource book.* New York, NY: Brunner/Mazel.

Dowrick, P. W. (2012). Self modeling: Expanding the theories of learning. *Psychology in the Schools*, 49(1), 30–41.

Dung, T. N. (1984, March–April). Understanding Asian families: A Vietnamese perspective. *Children Today*, 13(2), 10–12.

Erikson, E. (1963). *Childhood and society.* New York, NY: Norton.

Galinsky, E. (2010). *Mind in the making: The seven essential life skills every child needs.* New York, NY: HarperCollins.

Gerber, M., & Johnson, A. (1998). *Your self-confident baby.* New York, NY: Wiley.

Goleman, D. (2000). *Working with emotional intelligence.* New York, NY: Bantam.

Goleman, D. (2005) *Emotional intelligence: Why it can matter more than IQ.* New York, NY: Bantam Dell.

Goleman, D., Boyatzis, R, & McKee, A. (2013). *Primal leadership: Unleashing the power of emotional intelligence:* Boston, MA: Harvard University. Gonzalez-Mena, J. (2007). What to do with a fussy baby: A problem-solving approach. *Young Children*, 62(5), 20–25.

Gonzalez-Mena, J. (2010, May/June). Compassionate roots: Teaching babies compassion. *Exchange*, 32(3), 46–49.

Greenspan, S. I. (1999). *Building healthy minds.* Cambridge, MA: Perseus.

Greenspan, S. I., & Greenspan, N. T. (1985). *First feelings: Milestones in the emotional development of your baby and child.* New York, NY: Viking.

Greenspan, S. I., & Wieder, S. (1998). *The child with special needs: Encouraging intellectual and emotional growth.* Reading, MA: Perseus.

Greenwald, D., & Weaver, J. (2013). *The RIE manual for parents and professionals*, (2nd ed.). Los Angeles, CA: Resources for Infant Educarers.

Guerra, A. W., & Garriety, S. (2013). A cultural communities and cultural practices approach to understanding infant and toddler care. In E. Virmani & P. Mangione (Eds.), A *guide to culturally sensitive care* (2nd ed., pp. 41–53). Sacramento, CA: California Department of Education.

Harter, S. (1998). The development of self-representations. In N. Eisenberg (Ed.), *Handbook of child psychology: Vol. 3. Social, emotional, and personality development* (5th ed., pp. 553–618). New York, NY: Wiley.

Harter, S., & Buddin, B. J. (1987). Children's understanding of the simultaneity of two emotions: A five-stage developmental acquisition sequence. *Developmental Psychology*, 22(3), 388–399.

Hsu, F. L. K. (1970). *Americans and Chinese: Purpose and fulfillment in great civilizations.* Garden City, NY: Natural History Press.

Hyson, M. (2004). *The emotional development of young children* (2nd ed.). New York, NY: Teachers College Press.

Kaiser, B., & Rasminsky, J. S. (2012). *Challenging behavior in young children: Understanding, preventing, and responding effectively* (3rd ed.). Upper Saddle River, NJ: Pearson,

Kagan, J. (1985) *The nature of the child.* New York, NY: Basic Books.

Keenan, M. (1996, September). They pushed my buttons: Being put up against myself. *Young Children*, 51(6), 74–75.

Klein, M. D., & Chen, D. (2001). *Working with children from culturally diverse backgrounds.* Albany, NY: Delmar.

Lee, D. (1959). *Freedom and culture.* Upper Saddle River, NJ: Pearson.

Maslow, A. (1954). *Motivation and personality.* New York, NY: Harper & Row.

Matsumoto, D., Yoo, S. H., & Nakagawa, S. (2008). Culture, emotion regulation, and adjustment. *Journal of personality and social psychology*, 94(6), 925.

Paley, V. G. (1988). *Bad guys don't have birthdays: Fantasy play at four.* Chicago, IL: University of Chicago Press.

Parke, R. D., & O'Neil, R. (2000). The influence of significant others on learning about relationships: From family to friends. In R. S. L. Mills & S. Duck (Eds.), *The developmental psychology of personal relationships* (pp. 15–47). New York, NY: Wiley.

Petersen, S., Bair, K., & Sullivan, A. (2004). Emotional well-being and mental health services: Lessons learned by early Head Start Region VIII programs. *Zero to Three, 24*(6), 47–53.

Rogers, C. R. (1980). *A way of being.* Boston, MA: Houghton Mifflin.

Rogoff, B. (2003). *The cultural nature of human development.* Cambridge, MA: Oxford University Press.

Rogoff, B. (2011). *Developing destinies: A Mayan midwife and town.* New York, NY: Oxford University Press.

Russ, S. W. (2013). *Pretend play in childhood: Foundation of adult creativity.* Washington, DC: American Psychological Association.

Siegel, D. (2010). *Mindsight: The new science of personal transformation.* New York, NY: Bantam.

Smith, L. A. H. (1985). *To understand and to help: The life and work of Susan Isaacs.* Cranbury, NJ: Associated University Presses.

Thoman, E. B., & Browder, S. (1987). *Born dancing: How intuitive parents understand the baby's unspoken language and natural rhythms.* New York, NY: Harper & Row.

Thompson, R. A. (2009, November). "Doing what doesn't come naturally: The development of self-regulation. *Zero to Three, 30*(2), 33–37.

Van der Zande, I. (2011). 1, 2, 3… *The Toddler Years: A Practical Guide for Parents and Caregivers.* Santa Cruz, CA: Santa Cruz Toddler Care Center.

Van Hoorn, J., Nourot, P., Scales, B., & Alward, K. (2007). *Play at the center of the curriculum* (4th ed.). Upper Saddle River, NJ: Pearson.

Walker, C. M., & Gopnik, A. (2014). Toddlers infer higher-order relational principles in causal learning. *Psychological Science, 25*(1) 161–169.

Wittmer, D. (2012). The wonder and complexity of infant and toddler peer relationships. *Young Children 67*(4), 16–25.

CHAPTER 10

Azria-Evans, M. (2004). Self-esteem and young children: Guiding principles. *Dimensions of Early Childhood, 32* (1), 21–27.

Bredekamp, S., & Copple, C. (Eds.). (2006). *Developmentally appropriate practice in early childhood programs serving children from birth through age8* (3rd ed.). Washington, DC: National Association for the Education of Young Children.

Briggs, D. C. (1975). *Your child's self-esteem.* New York, NY: Dolphin.

Bronson, M. (2000). Research in Review: Recognizing and supporting the development of self-regulation in young children. *Young Children, 55*(2), 32–27.

Butterfield, P. M., Martin, C. A., & Prairie, A. P. (2004). *Emotional connections: How relationships guide early learning.* Washington, DC: Zero to Three.

California Department of Education. (2009). *Inclusion works! Creating child care programs that promote belonging for children with special needs.* Sacramento, CA: Author.

Castro, D. C., Ayankoya, B., & Kasprzak, C. (2011). *The New Voices/Nuevas Voces guide to cultural and linguistic diversity in early childhood.* Baltimore, MD: Brookes.

Clarke, J. I. (1998). *Self-esteem: A family affair.* Minneapolis, MN: Winston.

Coopersmith, S. (1967). *The antecedents of self-esteem.* San Francisco, CA: Freeman.

Copple, C., & Bredekamp, S. (2009). *Developmentally appropriate practice in early childhood programs serving children from birth through age 8.* Washington, DC: National Association for the Education of Young Children.

Curry, N. E., & Johnson, C. N. (1990). *Beyond self-esteem: Developing a genuine sense of human value.* Washington, DC: National Association for the Education of Young Children.

Delpit, L., & Dowdy, J. K. (2002). *The skin that we speak: Thoughts on language and culture in the classroom.* New York, NY: New Press.

Day, C. B. (2013). Culture and identity development: Getting infants and toddlers off to a great start. . In E. Virmani & P. Mangione (Eds.), *A guide to culturally sensitive care* (2nd ed., pp. 2–12). Sacramento, CA: California Department of Education.

Derman-Sparks, L. (1989). *Anti-bias curriculum: Tools for empowering young children.* Washington, DC: National Association for the Education of Young Children.

Derman-Sparks, L., & Edwards, J. O. (2010). *Anti-bias education for young children and ourselves.* Washington, DC: National Association for the Education of Young Children.

Dorris, M. (2011). Why I'm not thankful for thanksgiving. In E. Marshall & O. Sensoy (Eds.), *Rethinking popular culture and media* (pp. 100–105). Milwaukee, WI: Rethinking Schools.

Dweck, C. (2007). *Mindset: The new psychology of success.* New York, NY: Ballentine.

Egertson, H. A. (2006, November). Of primary interest. In praise of butterflies: Linking self-esteem and learning. *Young Children, 61*(6), 58–60.

Eggers-Pierola, C. (2005). *Connections & commitments: Reflecting Latino values in early childhood programs.* Portsmouth, NH: Heinemann.

Epstein, J. L. (2006, January). Families, schools, and community partnerships. *Young Children, 61*(1), 40.

Erikson, E. (1963). *Childhood and society.* New York, NY: Norton.

Espinosa, L. (2010). *Getting it right for young children from diverse backgrounds: Applying research to improve practice.* Upper Saddle River, NJ: Pearson.

Goldstein, L. (2002). *Reclaiming caring in teaching and teacher education.* New York, NY: Lang.

Gonzalez-Mena, J. (2008). *Diversity in early care and education.* New York, NY: McGraw-Hill.

Greenfield, P. M., Quiroz, B., Rothstein-Fisch, C., & Trumbull, E. (2001). *Bridging cultures between home and school.* Mahwah, NJ: Erlbaum.

Greenwald, D., & J. Weaver (2013). *The RIE manual for parents and professionals* (2nd ed.). Los Angeles, CA: Resources for Infant Educarers

Grieshaber, S., & Cannella, G. S. (2001). *Embracing identities in early childhood education: Diversity and possibilities.* New York, NY: Teachers College Press.

Halvorson, H. (2012). *Nine things successful people do differently.* Boston, MA: Harvard Business School.

Harter, S. (1983). Developmental perspectives on the self-system. In E. M. Heatherton (Ed.) & P. H. Mussen (Series Ed.), *Handbook of child psychology: Vol. 4. Socialization, personality, and social development* (4th ed., pp. 75–386). New York, NY: Wiley.

Hitz, R., & Driscoll, A. (1988). Praise or encouragement? New insights into praise: Implications for early childhood teachers. *Young Children,* 43(5), 6–13.

hooks, b. (2003). *Rock my soul: Black people and self-esteem.* New York, NY: Atria.

Howard, G. (1999). *We can't teach what we don't know: White teachers, multiracial schools.* New York, NY: Teachers College Press.

Kagan, J. (1984). *The nature of the child.* New York, NY: Basic Books.

Kranowitz, C. S. (1998). *The out of sync child: Recognizing and coping with sensory integration dysfunction.* New York, NY: Paragee.

Lally, J. R. (1995, November). The impact of child care policies and practices on infant/toddler identity formation. *Young Children,* 51(1), 58–67.

Landy, S. (2002). *Pathways to competence: Encouraging healthy social and emotional development in young children.* Baltimore, MD: Brookes.

Markus, H. R., Mullally, P. R., & Kitayama, S. (1997). Selfways: Diversity in modes of cultural participation. In U. Neisser & D. Jopling (Eds.), *The conceptual self in context* (pp. 12–61). New York, NY: Cambridge University Press.

Marshall, E., & Sensoy, O. (Eds.). (2011). *Rethinking popular culture and media.* Milwaukee, WI: Rethinking Schools.

Marshall, H. H. (2000, November). Cultural influences on the development of self-concept. *Young Children,* 56(6), 19–22.

McMullen, M. B., Addleman, J. M., Fulford, A. M., Moore, S. L., Mooney, S. J., Sisk, S. S., & Zachariah, J. (2009, July). Learning to be me while coming to understand we: Encouraging prosocial babies in group settings. *Young Children,* 64(4), 20–28.

Morrison, J. W. (2001, Spring). Supporting biracial children's identity development. *Childhood Education,* 77(3), 134–138.

Noddings, N. (2002). *Educating moral people: A caring alternative to character education.* New York, NY: Teachers College Press.

Paley, V. G. (1992). *You can't say you can't play.* Cambridge, MA: Harvard University Press.

Pierce, J., & Johnson, C. L. (2010, November). Problem solving with young children using persona dolls. *Young Children,* 65(6), 106–108.

Roffman, I., & Wanerman, T. (2011). *Including one, including all: A guide to relationship based early childhood education.* St. Paul, MN: Redleaf Press.

Rogoff, B. (2003). *The cultural nature of human development.* New York, NY: Oxford University Press.

Rosenthal, R. (1987) Pygmalion effects: Existence, magnitude, and social importance. *Educational Researcher,* 16(9), 37–41.

Seligman, M. E. P. (1975). *Helplessness: On depression, development and death.* San Francisco, CA: Freeman.

Teaching Tolerance Project. (1997). *Starting small: Teaching tolerance in preschool and the early grades.* Montgomery, AL: Southern Poverty Law Center.

Tesser, A., Wood, J. V., Stapel, D. A. (2005). *On building, defending, and regulating the self: A psychological perspective.* New York, NY: Psychology Press.

Tough, P. (2012). *How children succeed.* Boston, MA: Houghton, Mifflin, Harcourt.

Vygotsky, L. S. (1978). *Mind and society: The development of higher psychological process.* Cambridge, MA: Harvard University Press.

Wardel, F. (1993, March). How young children build images of themselves. *Exchange,* 90.

Youngquist, J., & Martinez-Griego, B. (2009, July). Learning in English, learning in Spanish: A Head Start program changes its approach. *Young Children,* 64(4), 92–98.

CHAPTER 11

American Bar Association (2008, Fall) A short history of child protection in America. *Family Law Quarterly* 42 (3). Retrieved July 22, 2015, from http://www.americanbar.org/content/dam/aba/publishing/insights_law_society/ChildProtectionHistory.authcheckdam.pdf.

American Psychological Association. (2007). *Report of the APA Task Force on the sexualization of girls.* Retrieved July 22, 2015, from http://www.apa.org/pi/women/programs/girls/report-full.pdf.

Bailey, J., Bobrow, D., Wolfe, M., & Mikach, S. (1995). Sexual orientation of adult sons of gay fathers. Special issue: Sexual orientation and human development. *Developmental Psychology,* 31, 124–129.

Chang, A., Sandhofer, C., & Brown, C. (2011). Gender biases in early number exposure to preschool-aged children. *Journal of Language and Social Psychology,* 30(4), 440–450.

Christensen, L. (2011). Unlearning the myths that bind us: Critiquing fairy tales and cartoons. In E. Marshall & O. Sensoy (Eds.), *Rethinking popular culture and media* (pp. 189–200). Milwaukee, WI: Rethinking Schools.

Cox, A. J. (2006). *Boys of few words. Raising our sons to communicate and connect.* New York, NY: Guilford.

Cuddy, A., Crotty, S., Chong, J., and Norton, M. (2010, May). Men as Cultural Ideals: How Culture Shapes Gender Stereotypes. Harvard Business School Working Paper, No. 10–097.

Derman-Sparks, L., & Edwards, J. O. (2010). *Anti-bias education for young children and ourselves.* Washington, DC: National Association for the Education of Young Children.

Eiduson, B. T., Kornfein, M., Zimmerman, I. L., & Weisner, T. S. (1988). Comparative socialization practices in traditional and alternative families. In G. Handel (Ed.), *Childhood socialization* (pp. 73–101). Hawthorne, NY: Aldine.

Else-Quest, N. Hyde, J., & Linn, M. (2010). Cross-national patterns of gender differences in mathematics: A meta-analysis. *Psychological Bulletin,* 136, 103.

Fagot, B. I. (1978). The influence of sex of child on parental reactions to toddler children. *Child Development,* 49, 459–465.

Gurian, M. (1997). *The wonder of boys.* New York, NY: Putnam.

Hofmann, S. (2011). Miles of aisles of sexism: Helping students investigate toy stores. In E. Marshall & O. Sensoy (Eds.), *Rethinking popular culture and media* (pp. 207–213). Milwaukee, WI: Rethinking Schools.

Levin, D. (2009). *So sexy so soon.* New York, NY: Ballantine.

Lucas-Stannard, P. (2012). *Gender neutral parenting.* Pretoria, South Africa: Verity Publishing.

Lyman, K. (2011). Girls, worms, and body image: A teacher deals with gender stereotypes among her second and third graders. In E. Marshall & O. Sensoy (Eds.), *Rethinking popular culture and media* (pp. 138–146). Milwaukee, WI: Rethinking Schools.

Miller, C. C. (2014, June 6). For more fathers who stay at home, it's a choice. *New York Times,* B3.

Money, J., & Ehrhardt, A. A. (1973). *Man and woman, boy and girl.* Baltimore, MD: Johns Hopkins University Press.

New York Times Magazine (2012, December 8). What's so bad about a boy who wants to wear a dress? *New York Times Magazine*, 15.

Paley, V. (1984). *Boys and girls: Superheroes in the doll corner*. Chicago, IL: University of Chicago Press.

Parke, R. D. (2002). Fatherhood. In M. Bornstein (Ed.), *Handbook of parenting* (2nd ed.). Mahwah, NJ: Erlbaum.

Parke, R. D., & Brott, A. (1999). *Throwaway dads*. Boston, MA: Houghton Mifflin.

Patterson, C. J. (2002). Lesbian and gay parenthood. In M. H. Bornstein (Ed.), *Handbook of parenting* (2nd ed.). Mahwah, NJ: Erlbaum.

Pollack, W. (1998). *Real boys*. New York, NY: Random House.

Pomerleau, A., Bolduc, D., Malcuit, G., & Cossette, L. (1990). Pink or blue: Environmental gender stereotypes in the first two years of life. *Sex Roles*, 22, 359–367.

Rheingold, H. L., & Cook, K. V. (1975). The content of boys' and girls' rooms as an index of parent behavior. *Child Development*, 46, 459–463.

Ruble, D. N., & Martin, C. L. (1998). Gender development. In W. Damon (Gen. Ed.) & N. Eisenberg (Vol. Ed.), *Handbook of child psychology*, Vol. 3 (pp. 933–1016). New York, NY: Wiley.

Serbin, L. A., O'Leary, F., Kent, R. N., & Tolnick, I. J. (1973, December). A comparison of teacher response to the preacademic and problem behavior of boys and girls. *Child Development*, 44(4), 776–804.

Soloman, A. (2013). *Far from the tree: Parents, children, and the search for identity*. New York, NY: Scribner.

Steele, C. M. (2011). *Whistling Vivaldi: How stereotypes affect us*. New York, NY: W. W. Norton and Co.

Thorne, B. (1993). *Gender play: Girls and boys in school*. New Brunswick, NJ: Rutgers University Press.

Turner-Bowker, D. M. (1996). Gender stereotyped description in children's picture books: Does "Curious Jane" exist in literature? *Sex Roles*, 35, 461–488.

Tzuriel, D., & Egozi, G. (2010). Gender differences in spatial ability of young children: The effects of training and processing strategies. *Child Development*, 81, 1417–1431.

Weisner, T. S., & Wilson-Mitchell, J. E. (1990). Nonconventional family lifestyles and multischematic sex typing in six-year-olds. *Child Development*, 61, 1915–1933.

Weitzman, L. J. (1979). *Sex role socialization: A focus on women*. Mountain View, CA: Mayfield.

Zeitlin, S. A. (1997, September). Finding fascinating projects that can promote boy/girl partnerships. *Young Children*, 52(6), 29–30.

CHAPTER 12

Akbar, N. (2003). *Akbar papers in African psychology*. Tallahassee, FL: Mind Productions.

Armesto, J. C. (2002). Developmental and contextual factors that influence gay fathers' parental competence: A review of the literature. *Psychology of Men and Masculinity*, 3, 67–78.

Blimes, J. (2004). *Beyond behavior management: The six life skills children need to thrive in today's world*. St. Paul, MN: Redleaf Press.

Breslin, D. (2005). Children's capacity to develop resiliency: How to nurture it. *Young Children*, 60(1), 47–52

Carnegie Task Force on Meeting the Needs of Young Children. (1994, July). Starting points: Executive summary of the report of the Carnegie Corporation of New York Task Force on Meeting the Needs of Young Children. *Young Children*, 47(5), 58–60.

Casper, V. (2003, January). Very young children in lesbian- and gay-headed families: Moving beyond acceptance. *Zero to Three*, 23(3), 18–26.

Castro, F. G., & Murray, K. E. (2010). Cultural adaptation and resilience: Controversies, issues, and emerging models. In J. W. Reich, A. J. Zautra, & J. S. Hall (Eds.), *Handbook of adult resilience* (pp. 375–403). New York, NY: Guilford.

Children's Defense Fund. (2014). *The state of America's children* 2004. Washington, DC: Author.

Children's Defense Fund. (2011). *The state of America's children*. Washington, DC: Author.

Christian, L. G. (2006). Understanding families: Applying family systems theory to early childhood practice. *Young Children*, 61(2), 12–20.

Crockenberg, S. (1992, April). How children learn to resolve conflicts in families. *Zero to Three*, 12(5), 11–13.

Dawes, A., & Donald, D. (2000). Improving children's chances: Developmental theory and effective interventions in community contexts. In D. Donald, A. Dawes & J. Louw (Eds.), *Addressing childhood adversity* (pp. 1–25). Cape Town, South Africa: David Philip.

DeJong, L. (2003, March). Using Erikson to work more effectively with teenage parents. *Young Children*, 58(2), 87–95.

Dorris, M. (2011). Why I'm not thankful for thanksgiving. In E. Marshall & O. Sensoy (Eds.), *Rethinking popular culture and media* (pp. 100–105). Milwaukee, WI: Rethinking Schools.

Edelman, M. W. (2011). *Child watch column on teen pregnancy*. Retrieved July 2, 2011, from http://cdf .childrensdefense.org/site /MessageViewer?em_id=11381.0

Galinsky, E. (1989, May). Problem solving. *Young Children*, 44(4), 2–3.

Galinsky, E. (2010). *Mind in the making: Seven essential skills every child needs*. New York, NY: HarperCollins.

Ginsberg, K. R. (2015) *Raising kids to thrive: Balancing love with expectations and protection with trust*. Elk Grove Village, IL: American Academy of Pediatrics

Goldberg, A (2010). *Lesbian and gay parents and their children: Research on the family life cycle*. Washington, DC: American Psychological Association.

Grotberg, E. (2009). Three Sources of Resilience. *Head Start Bulletin*, 80(33–34), 102.

Hall, E. T. (1981). *Beyond culture*. Garden City, NY: Anchor Press/Doubleday.

Henderson, N. (2007). Hard-wired to bounce back. In N. Henderson (Ed.), *Resiliency in action: Practical ideas for overcoming risks and building strengths in youth, families, and communities*. (pp. 9–15). Ojai, CA.

Kaiser, B., & Rasminsky, J. (2015). *Challenging behavior in young children: Understanding, preventing, and responding effectively* (4th ed.). Upper Saddle River, NJ: Pearson.

Keyser, J. (2006). *From parents to partners: Building a family centered early childhood program*. Washington, DC: National Association for the Education of Young Children and St. Paul, MN: Redleaf Press.

Korfmacher, J., & Marchi, I. (2002, November). The helping relationship in a teen parenting program. *Zero to Three*, 21(2), 21–26.

Lee, L. (Ed.). (2006). *Stronger together. Family support and early childhood education*. San Rafael, CA: Parent Services Project.

Lee, L., & Seiderman, E. (1998). *Families matter: The parent services project.* Cambridge, MA: Harvard Family Research Project.

Links, G., Beggs, M., & Seiderman, E. (1997). *Serving families.* Fairfax, CA: Parent Services Project.

Luthar, S. S., Cicchetti, D., & Becker, B. (2000). The construct of resilience: A critical evaluation and guidelines for future work. *Child Development, 71,* 543–562.

Marshall, E., & Sensoy, O. (2011). *Rethinking popular culture and media.* Milwaukee, WI: Rethinking Schools.

Masten, A.S., & A.H. Gewirtz. (2006). Resilience in development: The importance of early childhood. In R. E. Tremblay, R. DeV. Peters, M. Boivin, & R. G. Barr (Eds.), *Encyclopedia on early childhood development.* Retrieved September 30, 2015, from http://www.child-encyclopedia .com/resilience/according-experts /resilience-development-importance- early-childhood.

McCoy, M. L., & Keen, S. M. (2009). *Child abuse and neglect.* New York, NY: Psychology Press.

Meyer, I. H. (2003). Prejudice, social stress, and mental health in lesbian, gay, and bisexual populations: Conceptual issues and research evidence. *Psychological Bulletin, 129*(5), 674–697

Morrison, J. W. (2001, Spring). Supporting biracial children's identity development. *Childhood Education, 77*(3), 134–138.

National Association for the Education of Young Children. (2005). *Families and community relationships: A guide to the NAEYC early childhood program standards and related accreditation criteria.* Washington, DC: National Association for Education of Young Children.

Odom, S. L., Teferra, T., & Kaul, S. (2004, September). An overview of international approaches to early intervention for young children with special needs and their families. *Young Children, 59*(5), 38–43.

Okagaki, L., & Diamond, K. (2000, May). Responding to cultural and linguistic differences in the beliefs and practices of families with young children. *Young Children, 55*(3), 74–80.

Parke, R. D., & O'Neil, R. (2000). The influence of significant others on learning about relationships: From family to friends. In R. S. L. Mills & S. Duck (Eds.), *The developmental psychology of personal relationships* (pp. 15–47). New York, NY: Wiley.

Patterson, C. J. (2000). Family relationships of lesbians and gay men. *Journal of Marriage and the Family, 62,* 1052–1069.

Payne, R. K. (2003). *A framework for understanding poverty.* Highlands, TX: Aha Process.

Satir, V. (1972). *Peoplemaking.* Palo Alto, CA: Science and Behavior Books.

Seploch, H. (2004, September). Family ties: Partnerships for learning: Conferencing with families. *Young Children, 59*(5), 96–100.

Stiffelman, S. (2015). *Parenting with presence: Practices for raising conscious, confident, competent kids.* Novato, CA: New World Library.

Stonehouse, A., & Gonzalez-Mena, J. (2004). *Making links: A collaborative approach to planning and practice in early childhood services.* Castle Hills, NSW, Australia: Pademelon Press.

Swick, K. (2004). *Empowering parents, families, schools, and communities during the early childhood years.* Champaign, IL: Stipes.

Werner, E. E. (1984, November). Research in review: Resilient children. *Young Children, 40*(1), 68–72.

Werner, E. E. (1995, June). Resilience in development. *Current Directions in Psychological Science, 4*(3), 81–85.

Werner, E. E., & Smith, R. S. (1992). *Overcoming the odds: High risk children from birth to adulthood.* Ithaca, NY: Cornell University Press.

Willis, C. (2009, January). Young children with autism spectrum disorder: Strategies that work. *Young Children, 64*(2), 81–89.

Zautra, A. J., Hall, J. S., & Murray, K. E. (2010). Resilience: A new definition of health for people and communities. In J. W. Reich, A. J. Zautra, & J. S. Hall (Eds.), *Handbook of adult resilience* (pp. 3–34). New York, NY: Guilford.

CHAPTER 13

Aronson, S., & Spahr, P. M. (2002). *Healthy young children: A manual for programs.* Washington, DC: National Association for the Education of Young Children.

Austin, L. J. E., Whitebook, M., Connors, M., & Darrah, R. (2011). *Staff preparation, reward, and support: Are quality rating and improvement systems addressing all of the key ingredients necessary for change? Executive Summary.* Berkeley, CA: Center for the Study of Child Care Employment, University of California at Berkeley.

Axtmann, A., & Dettwiler, A. (2005). *The visit: Observation, reflection, synthesis for training and relationship building.* Baltimore, MD: Brookes.

Balaban, N. (2006, November). Easing the separation process for infants, toddlers, and families. *Young Children, 61*(6), 14–19.

Bredekamp, S. (Ed.). (1984). *The accreditation criteria and procedures of the National Academy of Early Childhood Programs.* Washington, DC: National Association for the Education of Young Children.

Butterfield, P. M. (2002, February–March). Child care is rich in routines. *Zero to Three, 22*(4), 29–32.

California Department of Education. (2009). *Inclusion works! Creating child care programs that promote belonging for children with special needs.* Sacramento, CA: Author.

Campbell, F. A., Pungello, E. P., Miller-Johnson, S., Burchinal, M., & Ramey, C. T. (2000). *Early learning, later success: The Abecedarian study early childhood educational intervention for poor children,* executive summary. Chapel Hill, NC: University of North Carolina, Frank Porter Graham Child Development Center.

Center for Research in Economic and Social Policy, University of Colorado. (1995). *Cost, quality, and outcomes in child care centers: Technical report.* Denver: Author.

Children's Defense Fund. (2000). *The state of America's children yearbook.* Washington, DC: Author.

Cook, R. E., Tessier, A., & Klein, M. D. (2000). *Adapting early childhood curricula for children in inclusive settings* (5th ed.). Upper Saddle River, NJ: Pearson.

Copple, C. (2006) *Basics of developmentally appropriate practice: An introduction for teachers of children.* pp. 3–6 Washington, DC: National Association for the Education of Young Children.

Copple, C., & Bredekamp, S. (Eds.). (2009). *Developmentally appropriate practice in early childhood programs serving children from birth through age 8* (3rd ed.). Washington, DC: National Association for the Education of Young Children.

Copple, C., Bredekamp, S., & Gonzalez-Mena, J. (2011). *Basics of developmentally appropriate practice: An introduction for teachers of infants and toddlers.* Washington, DC: National Association for the Education of Young Children.

Curtis, D., & Carter, M. (2000). *The art of awareness.* St. Paul, MN: Redleaf Press.

Division of Research to Practice, Office of Special Education Programs. (2001). *Synthesis on the use of assistive technology with infants and toddlers.* Washington, DC: U.S. Department of Education.

Dombro, A. L., & Lerner, C. (2006, January). Sharing the care of infants and toddlers. *Young Children, 61*(1), 29–33.

Edmiaston, R., Dolezal, V., Doolittle, S., Erickson, C., & Merritt, S. (2000). Developing individualized education programs for children in inclusive settings: A developmental framework. *Young Children, 55*(4), 36–41.

Erikson, E. H. (1963). *Childhood and society.* New York, NY: Norton.

Fromberg, D. P., & Bergen, D. (Eds.). (2006). *Play from birth to twelve: Contexts, perspectives, and meanings* (2nd ed.). New York, NY: Routledge, Taylor & Francis Group.

Gandini, L., & Edwards, C. P. (Eds.). (2000). *Bambini: The Italian approach to infant-toddler care.* New York, NY: Teachers College Press.

Goh, Esther C.L. (2011). China's one-child policy and multiple caregiving: raising little suns in Xiamen. (PDF). *Journal of International and Global Studies.* New York, NY: Routledge.

Goldstein, L. (2002). *Reclaiming caring in teaching and teacher education.* New York, NY: Lang.

Gonzalez-Mena, J. (2000, July). In the spirit of partnership: High maintenance parent or cultural difference? *Exchange, 134,* 40–42.

Gonzalez-Mena, J. (2002). *Infant/toddler caregiving: A guide to routines* (2nd ed.). Sacramento, CA: California Department of Education with WestEd.

Gonzalez-Mena, J., & Eyer, D. (2007) *Infants, toddlers, and caregivers.* New York, NY: McGraw-Hill.

Gonzalez-Mena, J., & Stonehouse, A. (2000, January). Responding in the spirit of partnership: The high

maintenance parent. *Child Care Information Exchange, 131,* 10–12.

Greenman, J. (2003). Places for childhood include parents, too. In B. & R. Neugebauer (Eds.), *The art of leadership* (pp. 316–319). Redmond, WA: Child Care Information Exchange.

Greenough, W., Emde, R. N., Gunnar, M., Massinga, R., & Shonkoff, J. P. (2001, April–May). The impact of the caregiving environment on young children's development: Different ways of knowing. *Zero to Three, 21*(5), 16–24.

Greenspan, S. I. (1999). *Building healthy minds.* Cambridge, MA: Perseus.

Greenspan, S. I., & Wieder, S. (1998). *The child with special needs: Encouraging intellectual and emotional growth.* Reading, MA: Perseus.

Illig, D. C. (1998). *Birth to kindergarten: The importance of the early years.* Sacramento, CA: California Research Bureau.

Jacobs, G., & Crowley, K. (2007). *Play, projects and preschool standards: Nurturing children's sense of wonder and joy in learning.* Thousand Oaks, CA: Corwin.

Jamblon, J. R., Dombro, A. L., & Dichtelmiller, M. L. (1999). *The power of observation.* Washington, DC: Teaching Strategies.

Karoly, A. (1998). *Investing in our children.* Santa Monica, CA: Rand.

Kids count data book. (2003). Baltimore, MD: Annie E. Casey Foundation.

Kirp, D. L. (2011). *Kids first: Five big ideas for transforming children's lives and America's future.* New York, NY: Public Affairs.

Kontos, S., & Wilcox-Herzog, A. (1997, January). Teachers' interactions with children: Why are they so important? *Young Children, 52*(2), 4–12.

Kostelnik, M., Onaga, E., Rohde, B., & Whiren, A. (2002). *Children with special needs: Lessons for early childhood professionals.* New York, NY: Teachers College Press.

Kranowitz, C. S. (1998). *The out of sync child: Recognizing and coping with sensory integration dysfunction.* New York, NY: Paragee.

Kusserow, A. (2005, Fall). The workings of class. *Stanford Social Innovation Review,* 38–47.

Lee, L. (2002). *Serving families: A handbook on the principles and strategies of the parent services project approach.* San Rafael, CA: Parent Services Project.

Lombardi, J. (2003). *Time to care: Redesigning child care to promote education, support*

families and build communities. Philadelphia, PA: Temple University Press.

Morgan, G., & Nadig, S. (2007). Trends in education and care. Retrieved August 26, 2009, from http://www.ccie.com/resources/view_article.php?article_id=5017112

Noddings, N. (2002a). *Educating moral people: A caring alternative to character education.* New York, NY: Teachers College Press.

Noddings, N. (2002b). *Starting at home: Care and social policy.* Berkeley, CA: University of California Press.

Noddings, N. (2005). *The challenge to care in schools.* New York, NY: Teachers College Press.

Noddings, N, (2005). What does it mean to educate the WHOLE child? *Educational Leadership, 63*(1).

Noddings, N. (2013) *Education and democracy in the 21st century.* New York, NY: Teachers College Press.

O'Brien, M. (1997). *Inclusive child care for infants and toddlers: Meeting individual and special needs.* Baltimore, MD: Brookes.

Peck, L. R., and Bell, S. H. (2014). The role of program quality in determining Head Start's impact on child development. OPRE Report #2014–10, Washington, DC: Office of Planning, Research and Evaluation, Administration for Children and Families, U.S. Department of Health and Human Services.

Phipps, P. A. (2003). Working with angry parents: A customer service approach. In B. & R. Neugebauer (Eds.), *The art of leadership* (pp. 326–329). Redmond, WA: Child Care Information Exchange.

Pinto, C. (2001, Spring). Supporting competence in a child with special needs: One child's story. *Educaring, 22* (2), 1–6.

Ramey, C. T., & Campbell, F. (1991). Poverty, early childhood education, and academic competence: The Abecedarian experiment. In A. Huston (Ed.), *Children in poverty: Child development and public policy.* New York, NY: Cambridge University Press.

Raver, S. A. (1999). *Intervention strategies for infants and toddlers with special needs* (2nd ed.). Upper Saddle River, NJ: Pearson.

Ruopp, R., Travers, J., Glantz, F., & Coelen, C. (1979). *Children at the center: Final results of the National Day Care Study.* Boston, MA: ABT Associates.

Schweinhart, L., Barnes, H., & Weikart, D. (1993). *Significant benefits: The High/Scope Perry preschool study through age 27.* Ypsilanti, MI: High/Scope Press.

Segal, M., Masi, W., & Leiderman, R. (2001). *In time and with love: Caring for infants and toddlers with special needs.* New York, NY: New Market Press.

Shonkoff, J. P., & Phillips, D. (2001, April–May). From neurons to neighborhoods: The science of early childhood development—An introduction. *Zero to Three, 21*(5), 4–7.

Stonehouse, A., & Gonzalez-Mena, J. (2004). *Making links: A collaborative approach to planning and practice in early childhood.* Sydney, Australia: Pademelon Press.

Szanton, E. S. (2001, January). For America's infants and toddlers, are important values threatened by our zeal to "teach"? *Young Children, 56*(1), 15–21.

Tobin, J., Hsueh, Y., & Karasawa, M. (2009). *Preschool in three cultures revisited.* Chicago, IL: University of Chicago Press.

Tobin, J. J., Wu, D. Y. H., & Davidson, D. H. (1989). *Preschool in three cultures: Japan, China, and the United States.* New Haven, CT: Yale University Press.

U.S. Department of Health and Human Services. (2003). *Making a difference in the lives of infants and toddlers and their families: The impacts of early Head Start.* Washington, DC.

U.S. Department of Labor Bureau of Labor Statistics. (1999, December). Table 48, Marital and Family Characteristics of the Labor Force from March 1999. In *Current population survey, December 1999* (p. 293). Washington, DC: U.S. Government Printing Office.

Vinson, B. M. (2001, January). Fishing and Vygotsky's concept of effective education. *Young Children, 56*(1), 88–89.

Whitebook, M., Howes, C., & Phillips, D. (1993). *The National Child Care Staffing study revisited.* Oakland, CA: Child Care Employee Project.

Whitebook, M., & Sakai, L. (2004). *By a thread: How child care centers hold onto teachers, how teachers build lasting careers.* Kalamazoo, MI: Upjohn Institute for Employment Research.

Whitebook, M. (2011, February 28). Workshop given at University of California, Berkeley, on early child care and education workforce called Stability, Trust, and Skill in the ECCE Workforce.

Whitebook, M., Phillips, D., & Howes, C. (2014). *Worthy work, STILL unlivable wages: The early childhood workforce 25 years after the National Child Care Staffing Study.* Berkeley, CA: Center for the Study of Child Care Employment, University of California, Berkeley.

Whitehead, L. C., & Ginsberg, S. I. (1999). Creating a family-like atmosphere in child care settings: All the more difficult in large child care centers. *Young Children, 54*(2), 4–10.

Chapter 13 Page 296. Wilcox-Herzog, A. (2004). How experience and education relate to teachers' beliefs and behaviors. *Journal of Early Childhood Teacher Education, 25,* 11–18.

Zigler, E. F., Finn-Stevenson, M., & Hall, N. W. (2003). *The first three years and beyond: Brain development and social policy.* New Haven, CT: Yale University Press.

Zill, N. (2003, May). *Head Start FACES 2000: A whole-child perspective on program performance, fourth progress report.* Washington, DC: U.S. Department of Health and Human Services.

CHAPTER 14

Barnett, W. S. (2011). Effectiveness of early educational intervention. *Science* (333). 6045. 975–978.

Bennett, R. (2006, January). Future teachers forge family connections. *Young Children, 61*(1), 22–28.

Bushman, B. J., & Anderson, C. A. (2001). Media violence and the American public: Scientific facts versus media misinformation. *American Psychologist, 56,* 466–489.

Children's Defense Fund. (2000). *State of America's children 2000.* Washington, DC.

Children's Defense Fund. (2004). *The state of America's children 2004.* Washington, DC.

Clark, K. E., & Ladd, G. W. (2000). Connectedness and autonomy support in parent-child relationships: Links to children's socio-emotional orientation and peer relationships. *Developmental Psychology, 36,* 485–498.

Curtis, D., & Carter, M. (2015). *Designs for living and learning: Transforming early childhood environments* (2nd ed.). St. Paul, MN: Redleaf Press.

Daly, L., & Beloglovsky, M. (2015). *Loose parts: Inspiring play in young children.* St. Paul, MN: Redleaf Press.

Dombro, A. Jablon, A. R., & Stetson, C. (2011). *Powerful Interactions: How to connect with children to extend their learning.* Washington, DC: National Association for the Education of Young Children.

Duncan, G. O., & Brooks-Gunn, J. (2000). Family parenting, welfare reform, and child development. *Child Development, 71,* 188–195.

Epstein, J. L. (2009). *School, family, and community partnerships* (3rd ed.). Washington, DC: Corwin.

Espinosa, L. (2010). *Getting it right for young children from diverse backgrounds: Applying research to improve practice.* Upper Saddle River, NJ: Pearson.

Golden, O. (2000). The federal response to child abuse and neglect. *American Psychologist, 55,* 1050–1053.

Gonzalez-Mena, J. (2007). *50 early childhood strategies for working and communicating with diverse families.* Upper Saddle River, NJ: Pearson.

Gonzalez-Mena, J. (2009). Family centered care and education. In S. Feeney, A. Galper, & C. Seefeldt (Eds.), *Continuing issues in early childhood education* (3rd ed., pp. 369–386). Upper Saddle River, NJ: Pearson.

Hirschland, D. (2015). *When young children need help: Understanding and addressing emotional, behavioral, and developmental challenges.* St. Paul, MN: Redleaf Press.

Ispa, J. M., Thornburg, K. R., & Fine, M. A. (2006). *Keepin' on: The everyday struggles of young families in poverty.* Baltimore, MD: Brookes.

Joshi, A. 2005. Understanding Asian Indian families: Facilitating meaningful home-school relations. *Young Children, 60*(3), 75–78.

Kilgo, J. L. (Ed.). (2006). *Transdisciplinary teaming in early intervention/early childhood special education: Navigating together with families and children.* Onley, MD: Association for Childhood Education International.

Kirp, D. L. (2011). *Kids first: Five big ideas for transforming children's lives and America's future.* New York, NY: Public Affairs.

Lally, J. R. (2010). *A guide to creating partnerships with families* (2nd ed.). Sacramento, CA: California Department of Education and Wested.

Lally, J. R. (1998, May). Brain research, infant learning, and child care curriculum. *Child Care Information Exchange*, 121, 46–48.

Lee, L. (Ed.). (2006). *Stronger Together. Family support and early childhood education*. San Rafael, CA: Parent Services Project.

Maccoby, E. E. (1998). *The two sexes*. Cambridge, MA: Harvard University Press.

Mattern, J. A. (2015). A mixed-methods study of early intervention implementation in the Commonwealth of Pennsylvania: Supports, services, and policies for young children with developmental delays and disabilities. *Early Childhood Education Journal* (43), 1. 57–67.

McCoy, M. L., & Keen, S. M. (2009). *Child abuse and neglect*. New York, NY: Psychology Press.

McLoyd, V. C., Hill, N. E., & Dodge, K. A. (Eds.). (2005). *African American family life*. New York, NY: Guilford.

National Research Council and Institute of Medicine. (2000). *From neurons to neighborhoods: The science of early childhood development*. Board on Children, Youth, and Families, Commission on Behavioral and Social Sciences and Education. Washington, DC: National Academy Press.

Parke, R. D., & O'Neil, R. (2000). The influence of significant others on learning about relationships: From family to friends. In R. S. L. Mills & S. Duck (Eds.), *The developmental psychology of personal relationships* (pp. 15–47). New York, NY: Wiley.

Patterson, K., Grenny, J., McMillan, R., & Switzler, A. (2012). *Crucial conversations: How to talk when the stakes are high*. New York, NY: McGraw-Hill.

Payne, R. K. (2003). *A framework for understanding poverty*. Highlands, TX: Aha Process.

Poussaint, A. F. (2006, January). Understanding and involving African American parents. *Young Children*, 61(1), 48.

Powers, J. (2006, January). Six fundamentals for creating relationships with families. *Young Children*, 61(1), 28.

Ray, J.A., & Shelton, D. (2004). E-pals: Connecting with families through technology. *Young Children*, 59(3), 30–32.

Ritchie, S., & Willer, B. (2005). *Families and community relationships*. Washington, DC: National Association for the Education of Young Children.

Satir, V. (1972). *Peoplemaking*. Palo Alto, CA: Science and Behavior Books.

Schneider, B. H., Atkinson, L., & Tardif, C. (2001). Child-parent attachment and children's peer relations: A quantitative review. *Developmental Psychology*, 37, 86–100.

Shonkoff, J. P., & Phillips, D. (2001, April–May). From neurons to neighborhoods: The science of early childhood development—An introduction. *Zero to Three*, 21(5), 4–7.

Shore, R. (1997). *Rethinking the brain: New insights in early development*. New York, NY: Families and Work Institute.

Signorielli, N., & Morgan, M. (2001). Television and the family: The cultivation perspective. In J. Bryant & J. A. Bryant (Eds.), *Television and the American family* (2nd ed., pp. 333–351). Mahwah, NJ: Erlbaum.

Tan, A. L. (2004). *Chinese American children and families: A guide for educators and service providers*. Onley, MD: Association for Childhood Education International.

Tinsley, B. R. (2002). *How children learn to be healthy*. New York, NY: Cambridge University Press.

White, E. (Qoyawayma, P.). (1992). *No turning back: A Hopi woman's struggle to live in two worlds*. Albuquerque, NM: University of New Mexico Press.

Wright, J. C., Huston, A. C., Murphy, K. C., St. Peters, M., Pinon, M., Scantlin, R., & Kotler, J. (2001). The relations of early television viewing to school readiness and vocabulary of children from low-income families: The early window project. *Child Development*, 72, 1347–1366.

Zautra, A. J., Hall, J. S., & Murray, K. E. (2010). Resilience: A new definition of health for people and communities. In J. W. Reich, A. J. Zautra, & J. S. Hall (Eds.), *Handbook of adult resilience* (pp. 3–34). New York, NY: Guilford.

Zigler, E. F., Finn-Stevenson, M., & Hall, N. W. (2003). *The first three years and beyond: Brain development and social policy*. New Haven, CT: Yale University Press.

CHAPTER 15

Barbour, C. H., Barbour, N. H., Scully, P. (2010). *Families, schools, and communities: Building partnerships for educating children*. St. Paul, MN: Redleaf

Boyer, E. L. (1991). *Ready to learn: A mandate for the nation*. Princeton, NJ: Carnegie Foundation for the Advancement of Teaching.

Brunson Day, C. (2010). Racial identity. In V. Washington & J. D. Andrews (Eds.), *Children of 2020: Creating a better tomorrow* (pp. 67–72). Washington, DC: Council for Professional Recognition and the National Association for the Education of Young Children.

Buck, L., & Wiler, B. (2009). Advocacy for young children. In S. Feeney, A. Galper, & C. Seefeldt (Eds.), *Continuing issues in early childhood education* (3rd ed., pp. 391–407). Upper Saddle River, NJ:Pearson.

Carnegie Task Force on Meeting the Needs of Young Children. (1994, July). Starting points: Executive summary of the report of the Carnegie Corporation of New York Task Force on Meeting the Needs of Young Children. *Young Children*, 49(5), 58–60.

Chang, H. N. L., Muckelroy, A., & Pulido-Tobiassen, D. (1996). *Looking in, looking out: Redefining child and early education in a diverse society*. San Francisco, CA: California Tomorrow.

ChartsBin. (2011). *Current world infant mortality rate*. Retrieved July 7, 2011, from http://chartsbin.com/view/1353

Children's Defense Fund, The State of America's Children 2005 Report, from http://www.childrensdefense.org /library/archives/state-of-americas-children/state-of-americas-children-2005-report.html

Children's Defense Fund, The State of America's Children 2014 Report, from http://www.childrensdefense.org /library/state-of-americas-children/

Chiu, Y., Coull, B., Cohen, S., Wooley, A., Wright, R. (2012). Pre- and postnatal maternal stress and wheeze in urban children: effect of maternal sensitization. *American Journal of Respiration & Critical Care Medicine*, 186, 147–154.

Chiu, Y., Bellinger, D., Coul, B., Anderson, S., Barber, R., Wright, R., & Wright, R. (2013). Associations between traffic-related black carbon exposure and attention in a prospective birth cohort of urban children. *Environ Health Perspectives*, 20: [Epub ahead of print].

Compton-Lilly, C. (2004). *Confronting racism, poverty, and power: Classroom strategies to change the world*. Portsmouth, NH: Heinemann.

Connolly, P., Hayden, J., & Levin, D. (2007). *From conflict to peace building: The power of early childhood initiatives*. Redmond, WA: World Forum Foundation.

Cook, R. E., Tessier, A., & Klein, M. D. (2000). *Adapting early childhood curricula for children in inclusive settings* (5th ed.). Upper Saddle River, NJ: Pearson.

Dahlberg, G., Moss, P., & Pence, A. (1999). *Beyond quality in early childhood education and care*. London, England: Falmer.

Derman-Sparks, L., LeKeenan, D., & Nimmo, J. (2014). *Leading early childhood programs: A guide for change*. New York, NY: Teachers College Press.

Edmiaston, R., Dolezal, V., Doolittle, S., Erickson, C., & Merritt, S. (2000). Developing individualized education programs for children in inclusive settings: A developmental framework. *Young Children, 55*(4), 36–41.

Enlow, M., Egeland, B., Blood, E., Wright, R., Wright, R. (2012). Interpersonal trauma exposure and cognitive development in children to age 8 years: a longitudinal study. *Journal of Epidemiol Community Health, 66*, 1005–1010.

Family Connection of St. Joseph County, Inc. (1996). *Information about children & families: Black infant mortality*. Retrieved July 7, 2011, from http://community.michiana.org/famconn/blinmort.html

Feerick, M. M., Knutson, J. F., Trickett, P. K., & Flanzer, S. M. (Eds.). (2006). *Child abuse and neglect*. Baltimore, MD: Brookes.

Feerick, M. M., & Silverman, G. B. (Eds.). (2006). *Children exposed to violence*. Baltimore, MD: Brookes.

Fennimore, B. S. (2014). *Standing up for something every day: Ethics and justice in early childhood classrooms*. New York, NY: Teachers College Press.

Finkelhor, D., Turner, H., Ormrod, R., & Hamby, S.L. (2010). Trends in childhood violence and abuse exposure: evidence from 2 national surveys. *Archives of Pediatrics and Adolescent Medicine, 164*(3), 238–242 and references.

Goffin, S. G., & Lombardi, J. (1989). *Speaking out: Early childhood advocacy*. Washington, DC: National Association for the Education of Young Children.

Goffin, S., & Washington, V. (2007) *Ready or not: Leadership choices in early care and education*. Washington, DC: National Association for the Education of Young Children.

Gopnik, A. (2009). *The philosophical baby*. New York, NY: Farrar, Straus and Giroux.

Gopnik, A. (2013). Poverty's vicious cycle can affect our genes. *Wall Street Journal* September, 20, C2.

Greenberg, P. (1969). *The devil has slippery shoes: A biased biography of the Child Development Group of Mississippi*. London, England: Collier-Macmillan.

Hirschland, D. (2015). *When Young Children Need Help*. St. Paul, MN: Redleaf.

Kelly, J. F., & Booth, C. L. (1999). Child care for children with special needs: Issues and applications. *Infants and Yyoung Children, 12*(1), 26–33.

Kirp, D. L. (2011). *Kids first: Five big ideas for transforming children's lives and America's future*. New York, NY: Public Affairs™.

Lakshmanan, A., Chiu, Y. H., Coull, B. A., Just, A. C., Maxwell, S. L., Schwartz, J., Gryparis, A., Kloog, I., Wright, R. J., Wright, R. O. (2015, January). Associations between prenatal traffic-related air pollution exposure and birth weight: Modification by sex and maternal pre-pregnancy body mass index. *Environmental Research, 137C*.

Lee, L. (2002). *Serving families: A handbook on the principles and strategies of the Parent Services Project approach*. San Rafael, CA: Parent Services Project.

Lee, L., & Seiderman, E. (1998). *Families matter: The Parent Services Project*. Cambridge, MA: Harvard Family Research Project.

Links, G., Beggs, M., & Seiderman, E. (1997). *Serving families*. Fairfax, CA: Parent Services Project.

Lombardi, J. (2003). *Time to care: Redesigning child care to promote education, support families, and build communities*. Philadelphia, PA: Temple University Press.

Love, J., Raikes, H., Paulsell, D., & Kisker, E. E. (2000). New directions for studying quality in programs for infants and toddlers. In D. Cryer & T. Harms (Eds.), *Infants and toddlers in out of home care* (pp. 117–162). Baltimore, MD: Brookes.

Mann, T. (2010). Culturally responsive perspective. In V. Washington & J. D. Andrews (Eds.), *Children of 2020: Creating a better tomorrow* (pp. 61–66). Washington, DC: Council for Professional Recognition and the National Association for the Education of Young Children.

McLoyd, V. (1998). Socioeconomic disadvantage and child development. *American Psychologist, 53*(2), 185–204.

National Alliance to End Homelessness. (2011, January 11). *State of homelessness in America 2011*. Retrieved July 6, 2011, from http://www.endhomelessness.org/content/article/detail/3668

National Association for the Education of Young Children. (1996, January). Position statement: Responding to linguistic and cultural diversity: Recommendations for effective early childhood education. *Young Children, 51* (2), 4–12.

Nguyen, K., Subramanian, S., Sorensen, G., Tsang, K., Wright, R. (2012). Influence of experiences of racial discrimination and ethnic identity on prenatal smoking among urbacn black and Hispanic women. *Journal of Epidemiological Community Health, 66*, 315–321.

Nieto, S. (2000). *Affirming diversity: The sociopolitical context of multicultural education* (3rd ed.). New York, NY: Addison Wesley Longman.

Noddings, N. (2002). *Starting at home: Care and social policy*. Berkeley, CA: University of California Press.

O'Brien, M. (1997). *Inclusive child care for infants and toddlers: Meeting individual and special needs*. Baltimore, MD: Brookes.

Odom, S. (Ed.). (2002). *Widening the circle: Including children with disabilities in preschool programs*. New York, NY: Teachers College Press.

Perez, K. (2013). *The new inclusion*. New York, NY: Teachers College Press.

Perry, B. (2006). Applying principles of neurodevelopment to clinical work with maltreated and traumatized children. In N. B. Webb (Ed.), *Working with traumatized youth in child welfare*. New York, NY: Guilford Press.

Putnam, J. W. (Ed.). (1998). *Cooperative learning and strategies for inclusion* (2nd ed.). Baltimore, MD: Brookes.

Recchia, S. L., & Lee, Y-J. (2013). *Inclusion in the early childhood classroom: What makes a difference?* New York, NY: Teachers College Press.

Schreier, H. M., Hsu, H. H., Amarasiri-wardena, C., Coull, B. A., Schnaas, L., Tellez-Rojo, M. M., Tamayo, T., Ortiz, M., Wright, R. J., Wright, R. O. (2015).

Mercury and psychosocial stress exposure interact to predict maternal diurnal cortisol during pregnancy. *Environmental Health: A Global Access Science Source*. Mar, 14(1).

Shames, S. (1991). *Outside the dream: Child poverty in America* (Introduction by J. Kozol; afterword by M. W. Edelman). New York, NY: Aperture.

Shore, R. (2003). *Rethinking the brain: New insights into early development.* New York, NY: Families and Work Institute.

Siegel, D. J. (2011). *Mindsight: The new science of personal transformation.* New York, NY: Bantam.

Stacey, S. (2015). *Pedagogical Documentation in Early Childhood.* St. Paul, MN: Redleaf

Sternthal, M. J., Jun, H.-J., Earls, F., & Wright, R. J. (2010). Community violence and urban childhood asthma: a multilevel analysis. *European Respiratory Journal, 36*(6), 1400–1409.

Sykes, M. (2014). *Doing the Right Things for Children.* St. Paul, MN: Redleaf.

Thaxton, S. M. (2003). Grandparents as parents—Understanding the issues. In B. & R. Neugebauer (Eds.), *The art of leadership* (pp. 323–325). Redmond, WA: Child Care Information Exchange.

Tough, P. (2009). *Whatever it takes: Geoffrey Canada's quest to change Harlem and America.* Boston, MA: Mariner Books.

Washington, V., & Andrews, J. D. (1998) *Children of 2010.* Washington, DC: National Association for the Education of Young Children.

Whitebook, M., Phillips, D., & Howes, C. (1993). *National Child Care Staffing Study revisited: Four years in the life of center-based child care.* Oakland, CA: Child Care Employee Project.

Williams, S., C. P. (2013) Gone too soon: What's behind the high U.S. infant mortality rate? Retrieved April 20, 2015, from http://sm.stanford.edu/archive/stanmed/2013fall/article2.html.

Wright, R., Fischer, K., Chiu, Y., Fein, R., Cohen, S., Coull, B. (2013). Disrupted prenatal maternal cortisol, maternal obesity, and childhood wheeze: Insights into prenatal programming. *American Journal of Respiratory Critical Care Medicine, 187,* 1186–1193.

Zigler, E. F., Finn-Stevenson, M., & Hall, N. W. (2003). *The first three years and beyond: Brain development and social policy.* New Haven, CT: Yale University Press.

Zigler, E., & Styfco, S. J. (2004). *The Head Start debates.* Baltimore, MD: Brookes.

Zigler, E., & Styfco, S. J. (2010). *The hidden history of Head Start.* New York, NY: Oxford University Press.

Index